# NEWCOMER'S ®
# HANDBOOK

## FOR MOVING TO AND LIVING IN THE

# San Francisco Bay Area

Including San Jose, Oakland, Berkeley, and Palo Alto

**5th Edition**

**503-968-6777**
**www.firstbooks.com**

Newcomer's Handbook for Moving to and Living in the San Francisco Bay Area, 5th Edition

Newcomer's Handbook® and First Books® are registered trademarks of First Books.

Author: Daniel King (5th edition); Previous editions: Scott van Velsor, Sabrina Crawford, Ruth Rayle, and Michael Bower
Editors: Andrew Durkin, Linda Franklin, and Linda Chaplik
Cover design and layout: Erin Johnson Design, Masha Shubin, and Emily Coats
Cover images: Erin Johnson Design, Jillian Gregg, and Nicholas Winchester
Interior design: Erin Johnson Design
Interior layout and composition: Masha Shubin and Emily Coats
Interior photos by Scott van Velsor and Shannon Corr
Maps provided by Scott Lockheed and Jim Miller/fennana design
Transit map courtesy of Bay Area Rapid Transit

Paperback:  ISBN-13: 978-1-937090-62-3   ISBN-10: 1-937090-62-0
Kindle:     ISBN-13: 978-1-937090-63-0   ISBN-10: 1-937090-63-9
ePub:       ISBN-13: 978-1-937090-64-7   ISBN-10: 1-937090-64-7

Printed in the USA on recycled paper.

Published by First Books®, 503-968-6777, www.firstbooks.com.

**What readers are saying about *Newcomer's Handbooks*:**

I recently moved to Atlanta from San Francisco, and LOVE the ***Newcomer's Handbook for Atlanta***. It has been an invaluable resource—it's helped me find everything from a neighborhood in which to live to the local hardware store. I look something up in it everyday, and know I will continue to use it to find things long after I'm no longer a newcomer. And if I ever decide to move again, your book will be the first thing I buy for my next destination.

– Courtney R.
Atlanta, Georgia

I recently got a copy of your ***Newcomer's Handbook for Chicago,*** and wanted to let you know how invaluable it was for my move. I must have consulted it a dozen times a day preparing for my move. It helped me find my way around town, find a place to live, and so many other things. Thanks.

– Mike L.
Chicago, Illinois

Excellent reading (***Newcomer's Handbook for the San Francisco Bay Area***) ... balanced and trustworthy. One of the very best guides if you are considering moving/relocation. Way above the usual tourist crap.

– Gunnar E.
Stockholm, Sweden

I was very impressed with the latest edition of the ***Newcomer's Handbook for Los Angeles***. It is well organized, concise and up-to-date. I would recommend this book to anyone considering a move to Los Angeles.

– Jannette L.
Attorney Recruiting Administrator for a large Los Angeles law firm

In looking to move to the Boston area, a potential employer in that area gave me a copy of the ***Newcomer's Handbook for Boston***. It's a great book that's very comprehensive, outlining good and bad points about each neighborhood in the Boston area. Very helpful in helping me decide where to move.

– no name given (online submit form)

# TABLE OF CONTENTS

# CONTENTS

# CONTENTS

THE HILLIEST, CHILLIEST, FOGGIEST CORNER OF CALIFORNIA, THE MOST revolutionary tech inventions in history, and the highest housing costs in the country—these are just a few of the headlines that are shaping San Francisco's reputation as the most coveted destination on the planet. Welcome to this tiny slice of West Coast magic. From the Gold Rush of the 1840s to the dot-com '90s and today's tech rush, the Bay Area has seen more invention and reinvention than any other American region. It has introduced the personal computer, the smartphone, the self-driving car, Internet-ready eyewear, and a parade of other creations from locally based legends Google, Apple, Facebook, Twitter, Tesla Motors, and countless other game-changers. Its fortunes have gone up, down, and up again, like San Francisco's rollercoaster streets. Newcomers are arriving by the thousands, some with high hopes for tech breakthroughs, but most with hopes on a more personal scale: simply to find a home, find work, find a kind of future, and invent something more private: their own identities, and a pathway into the Bay Area.

It all sounds manageable and irresistible—until you see the numbers. San Francisco tops the United States in rent. The median one-bedroom here reached $4,225 recently, blowing Manhattan and everywhere else out of the water. Income inequality is growing faster in San Francisco than any other city. The housing supply is shrinking, tensions are escalating, and protests are mounting, as affordable housing vanishes almost as quickly as it's created. Just 20 percent of all San Franciscans can afford the average home today, which topped $1.225 million recently. This scenic, windswept Bay Area—with a population of 7 million people—is projected to add 2.1 million people by 2040, creating a need for 700,000 new homes. While the Bay Area is the fastest engine of wealth creation anywhere, San Francisco faces an affordable-housing crisis. The city is witnessing the fastest displacement of artists and activists that it has ever seen.

While gentrification is a familiar fact in many cities, it's nowhere more amplified and hotly debated than in San Francisco, a city of just 49 square miles. The Bay Area dream—social progress, invention, community strength, striking gold—is under pressure by hard realities laid bare in today's San Francisco, where the widening gap between accelerating wealth and deepening poverty is hitting like an earthquake. Almost 25 percent of San Francisco residents are below the poverty line—more than at any other time in history, according to the Public Policy Institute of California and the Stanford Center on Poverty and Inequality.

At the same time, San Francisco enjoys countless reasons to celebrate. The city boasts the highest rate of job growth in the country. So long, "recession" of—when was that, 2008, 2009? Cranes of construction fill the sky today. Ask any longtime local, and you're likely to hear a connection drawn between the record-high rents and the tech startups' land grabs and office expansions. Google's and other tech leaders' double-decker buses transport more than 14,000 workers every day between San Francisco and Silicon Valley, making headlines when street protestors blockade them in opposition to gentrification. As the tech crowd grows, anti-tech sentiment grows with it, so in a gesture of reconciliation, Google gave San Francisco almost $7 million so low-income kids can ride public buses for free.

Where would the Bay Area be—where would the world be—without local inventions? This is the birthplace of home sharing (Airbnb and Couchsurfing, headquartered in San Francisco), car sharing (Uber and Lyft, headquartered here), friend sharing (Facebook and Twitter, based here), skills sharing (Craigslist, a San Francisco original), activity sharing (Eventbrite, also based here), reviews sharing (Yelp, based here), and knowledge sharing (Coursera and Khan Academy, headquartered here), as well as countless other websites seeded and grown locally. Today's so-called sharing economy is the Bay Area's newest calling card, a top draw for tech talent.

While Google, Apple, and Facebook are local giants, they're also a bit late to the party. This town long ago became a birthplace of cultural revolution: the free-speech movement, the antiwar protest movement, the voter mobilization movement, the gay and transgender rights movement. This is the birthplace of the first black-studies course taught at a college or university; the first Chinatown in North America; the first Asian-American jazz festival; and the first Mexican-American cultural center. The Bay Area's list of firsts is endless. Even before the US Supreme Court ruled in 2015 that gay marriage is a guaranteed right nationwide, San Francisco had planted the flag, becoming one of the first American cities to issue marriage licenses to same-sex couples. San Francisco doesn't mirror national trends; it sets them.

As a newcomer, you're joining this conversation at an exciting moment in the Bay Area. To many locals, San Francisco is becoming a "playground of convenience" for tech companies that flip neighborhoods and houses so they can set up shop and make billions while underperforming in community outreach. To tech leaders, that's a clichéd caricature of what's happening—a misplaced critique that underestimates the cultural and economic returns that tech giants give the Bay

Area. California, we're reminded by history, is constantly changing. Nothing's ever static here. And displacement is ongoing: thousands of Ohlone Native Americans were ousted in the 1700s by Spanish missionaries, followed by Mexican settlers, who were bulldozed by the United States military. Waves of demographic changes span generations.

Good luck branding this a good thing to the thousands of San Franciscans (80 percent of all locals today) who can't afford to stay here, and who see a link between rising rents and the growing tech presence. It's a familiar struggle to San Francisco's African-American community, whose population has declined 35 percent since the 1990s and today stands at just 6 percent of the city's 840,000 residents. Bay Area filmmakers set out in 2014 to create a timely film titled *The Last Black Man in San Francisco*, which has gained citywide acclaim and stirred national conversation even before its release.

San Francisco's ideals of inclusion are being put to the test after generations of breakthroughs and breakdowns, crashes and comebacks—from Japanese internment, when thousands of Japanese Californians were forcibly removed from their homes, to the Chinese Exclusion Act and other laws that banned Chinese from moving here, marrying across color lines, owning land, and living outside of Chinatown.

Through it all, San Francisco has been a leader of change. It elected the first openly gay public official, Harvey Milk, in 1977. It is San Francisco—not New York—where the United Nations was originally conceived and its charter signed, in 1945. If you've ever set eyes on Craigslist or Airbnb, or held a smartphone, you have the Bay Area to thank (or curse) for it. San Francisco today is asking itself tough questions about its past and present, as construction roars ahead. Seven of the ten highest-rent cities in the nation are Bay Area hotspots, and the highest peak in the contiguous United States is nearby: Mount Whitney (elevation 14,505 feet). The tallest trees in the world are practically at your doorstep, a short drive to Redwood National Park.

Architecturally, the Bay Area is blessed with stately Victorians nestled in dramatic hills with the Pacific Ocean over your shoulder. San Francisco is the only place in the country where you can ride a moving national landmark (cable cars) while taking in head-spinning views of the Golden Gate Bridge, Alcatraz Island, or the city skyline. Today, hopeful homeowners are looking beyond San Francisco to the East Bay and South Bay and North Bay, as the real estate rush expands outward and lights up towns like San Carlos, Foster City, South San Francisco, Daly City, El Cerrito, Hayward, and the newly incorporated city of Oakley.

There's also the blissfully mild weather—clear skies inland, fog near the coast, cooling off in the evening. Temperatures rarely dip below 40° or above 80° Fahrenheit. Rain used to exist, but it's a distant dream today, as the worst local drought in 1,200 years recently entered its fifth year. Water conservation has prompted a state of emergency. (Not even Google has invented rain, but stay tuned.) As a general rule, towns further from the coastline, in the South and East Bay, are prone to drier, warmer, smoggier weather.

This *Newcomer's Handbook®* is intended to help make your arrival as seamless, enjoyable, and informed as possible while guiding you through local conversations already in progress. Within these pages are sights and sounds—and semi-secrets—of Bay Area communities, including lists of neighborhood resources like websites, police stations, post offices, libraries, hospitals, public schools, community groups, and transportation routes. In addition to descriptions of neighborhoods, this guide walks you through the biggest of Bay Area challenges: searching for a new home (**Finding a Place to Live**), moving your belongings (**Moving and Storage**), setting up bank accounts (**Money Matters**) and utilities (**Getting Settled**), finding furniture shops (**Shopping for the Home**), seeking out patches of green and stretches of sand (**Greenspace and Beaches**), and greening your home to improve energy efficiency (**Green Living**). This 5th edition includes previously unreported neighborhoods, with a complete refresh of established hotspots—including a roundup of new mobile apps. Also new to this edition is a fleshed-out **Food** section, and a new chapter, **Media Landscape**, that traces the rise and fall of local newspapers, magazines, journalistic websites, and book publishers transforming the Bay Area. There is no *one* Bay Area perspective. But these pages place you inside a range of Bay Area possibilities. Brace yourself: the hills are steep.

## LOCAL LINGO

For newcomers who hear "BART" and think of a 10-year-old cartoon misfit instead of the Bay Area's train system, or hear "Dogpatch" and picture a scruff of Golden Retriever instead of San Francisco's fast-growing neighborhood, the following list of terms and phrases will be useful:

- **The Avenues**: the numbered streets in the Sunset and Richmond neighborhoods, running out toward the ocean
- **BART**: Bay Area Rapid Transit, the under- and aboveground subway-style train network that connects the East Bay and Peninsula with San Francisco
- **Bay Area**: the nine counties including and surrounding San Francisco: Alameda, Contra Costa, Marin, Napa, San Francisco, San Mateo, Santa Clara, Solano, Sonoma
- **The Chron**: the *San Francisco Chronicle*, the city's major daily newspaper
- **The city**: the way most natives and local newspapers refer to San Francisco; wherever you are in the Bay Area, "the city" always means San Francisco, much to the eye-rolling indignation of proudly local Oakland residents
- **Dogpatch**: south of the Giants' baseball stadium, a district just east of Highway 280, north of Hunters Point, and bordering the Bay; many industrial-chic condos are built here, and it's a growing hub of biotech businesses
- **The dot-com boom**: the 1990s Internet revolution

- **The dot-com bust**: the end of said dot-com boom
- **East Bay**: Alameda and Contra Costa counties, but often just refers to Oakland or Berkeley, though there are many increasingly popular towns near them
- **Ex-dot-comers**: those who were heavily involved in the Internet boom and have since moved on to other, often non-tech-related career pursuits
- **General**: San Francisco General Hospital
- **The Haight**: the Haight-Ashbury neighborhood; also refers to the retail shopping district along the upper section of Haight Street
- **It's-It**: famous locally made ice cream sandwiches
- **Mavericks**: the big-wave daredevil surf competition south of San Francisco; also the name of the actual surfing spot, just off the shore of Pillar Point Harbor in Half Moon Bay
- **Mitchell's**: famous locally made ice cream (arguably better than It's-It, above)
- **MUNI**: San Francisco Municipal Railway, the city's bus and light-rail system
- **NOPA**: North of Panhandle; a district just north of the Haight and south of Geary Boulevard
- **North Bay**: Marin, Sonoma, and Napa counties
- **Oaktown**: Oakland
- **Pink Section**: special weekend arts and entertainment supplement in the *San Francisco Chronicle*
- **See's**: famous locally made chocolates
- **Silicon Valley**: the birthplace of the tech revolution, headquartered an hour south of San Francisco
- **SOMA**: area south of Market Street
- **South Bay**: Santa Clara County
- **Tender-nob**: the slice of overlapping land in San Francisco where the Tenderloin and Nob Hill neighborhoods meet
- **TL**: the Tenderloin neighborhood; typically refers to the rougher sections

## ADDRESS LOCATOR

### SAN FRANCISCO

San Francisco's hills—47 of them, by some counts—prevented city planners from implementing a grand, area-wide roadway grid, so finding any desired street address can be a challenge. If printed maps are undesirable giveaways that you're new to town, open Google Maps on your smartphone instead. Virtually all locals do. Those foldout tourist maps distort proportions and exclude large chunks of geography that will prove important to a resident. Transit maps are useful if you're not relying on your car to get around, but they don't offer enough details to serve as your primary guidance tool.

In case your smartphone's battery dies and you're unable to access Google

Maps, purchase a laminated cardstock map at any bookstore. Members of the American Automobile Association (AAA) can get free maps.

With map in hand, or smartphone in pocket, spend a few moments finding the major streets and highways listed below:

- First there's **Market Street**, San Francisco's main downtown corridor, starting across from the Ferry Building. As with all east-west streets that begin at the eastern edge downtown, address numbers begin there and increase as you head toward the ocean. Market Street serves as the border between the Financial District, Union Square, and Tenderloin neighborhoods to the north, and the South of Market (SOMA) district to the south. For north-south streets, address numbering begins at Market, with the lowest numbers at Market. On streets north of Market, the numbers increase as you go north.
- Another main street is **Van Ness Avenue**, which runs north-south and begins one block west of 10th Street, crossing Market. It serves as part of the Highway 101 connection to the Golden Gate Bridge, along with **Lombard Street**, **Marina Boulevard**, and **Doyle Drive**. Street numbers increase as you travel north on Van Ness.
- **Geary Street** splits off from Market downtown, and runs west all the way to the Pacific Ocean—although once it crosses into "the Avenues," its name changes to **Geary Boulevard**. Numbering begins downtown and increases as you go west.
- "**The Avenues**" is the locally accepted name for the area served by the numbered roadways in the Richmond and Sunset neighborhoods, **3rd Avenue** through **48th Avenue**, and it's important to know because the city also has numbered "streets," **1st Street** through **30th Street**. Don't confuse the streets and the avenues, as they're entirely different neighborhoods. The numbered streets begin in the SOMA neighborhood and run north-south until the Mission District, where they run east-west into the Potrero Hill, Bernal Heights, Castro, and Noe Valley districts after 14th Street. When someone tells you "24th," you'll need to clarify, "24th Street or Avenue?"
- **19th Avenue** is a major connector roadway to become familiar with, along with **Park Presidio Boulevard**, feeding onto Golden Gate Bridge from **Interstate 280** and **Highway 1**. 19th Avenue splits off from Highway 280/1 just inside San Francisco's city limits, and runs out through the Sunset District and into Golden Gate Park. Its name changes to Park Presidio Boulevard on the northern side of the park. If traffic is painfully bad on 19th Avenue, as it often is, **Sunset Boulevard** is just a few blocks to the west and is usually a good alternate route through the Sunset.
- **Highway 101** enters San Francisco from the south; however, it splits off toward the San Francisco–Oakland Bay Bridge, where Interstate 80 begins. I-80 will take you through the northern half of the East Bay, out to Sacramento, the Sierra Nevada, and all the way to New York.

- **Interstate 280** has a relatively new extension near the Highway 101 split, which drops drivers off along the Outer Mission and Dogpatch neighborhoods of San Francisco and directly onto 6th Street at Townsend. This is a helpful option to get to a Giants ballgame or into the beating heart of downtown. This freeway does not reconnect to the San Francisco–Oakland Bay Bridge.
- **Octavia Boulevard/Fell Street:** this connection dramatically altered the way commuters use city streets. Damage from the 1989 earthquake was finally repaired decades later, making this a critical east-west corridor from the bridge and Highway 101. Follow the signs toward Golden Gate Bridge or Highway 101 North and stay toward the left. Octavia crosses Market Street in the depths of the Castro district and continues to Fell Street, which heads west toward Ocean Beach and Golden Gate Park.
- **San Francisco–Oakland Bay Bridge**, also the beginning of Interstate 80, is a double-decker hulk of steel that spans across to Treasure Island and onward to the East Bay. The bridge is under constant repairs, so drivers should be aware of major rerouting and potentially crippling delays.

## BEYOND SAN FRANCISCO

Two major highways, Highway 101 and Interstate 280, running north and south, connect San Francisco with the Peninsula and the South Bay, while numerous highways help you navigate the rest of the Bay Area. For ease and accuracy, use the Google Maps app on your smartphone (hands-free, or you'll be fined, per California law).

- **Highway 101** is notoriously crowded and weaves through the heavily populated cities of the Peninsula and South Bay. Highway 101 goes all the way from Los Angeles through much of the state of Washington.
- A more scenic and less crowded drive is **I-280** (known as Junipero Serra Freeway), which starts near the Bay Bridge on the San Francisco side and goes south past Daly City, continues down the west side of the Bay, and culminates at the I-680 junction.
- Close to the San Francisco Airport, **I-380** links Highway 101 with I-280.
- **Highway 85**, also known as Stevens Creek Freeway, connects 101 with 280 from Mountain View to Cupertino.
- **Interstate 880** is another connector for 101 and 280, slicing through the city of San Jose.
- Farther north, **Highway 92** runs through the Peninsula, around San Mateo, and heads west to the coast, ending in Half Moon Bay.
- Another coastal connector (and motorcyclist's dream) is **Highway 84**, which links Redwood City with Woodside and then, like Highway 92, goes all the way to the coast, ending at Highway 1.

- By far the most scenic, majestic roadway in the Bay Area, and arguably in the country, **Highway 1** twists and turns along the western edge of the coast, going south to LA and north to Washington. Treat yourself.
- Both the San Mateo–Hayward Bridge and the Dumbarton Bridge connect the South Bay with the East Bay.
- The longest bridge in the Bay Area, the 6.8-mile **San Mateo–Hayward Bridge** links Foster City with Hayward via Highway 92.
- The **Dumbarton Bridge** connects Fremont and Newark in the East Bay with Palo Alto and Menlo Park. The southernmost bridge crossing the Bay, the Dumbarton Bridge is part of Highway 84, which can be accessed via the Willow Road off-ramp from Highway 101.

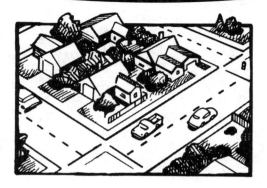

# CITY OF SAN FRANCISCO

O NLY 49 SQUARE MILES, SAN FRANCISCO IS A COMPACT CITY WITH microclimates in weather and wealth. The difference of a few blocks can mean the difference of millions of dollars in home sales, several degrees in temperature, and a few notches in crime rates—as well as degrees of deliciousness in noodle soups, steamed dumplings, and fresh-squeezed juices. On one block, you're in the heart of homelessness (the Tenderloin), and one block over you're in a neighborhood so awash with tech dollars that a $7 cup of coffee hardly makes locals flinch (mid-Market Street). The contrasts are concentrated. As tech wealth soars in San Francisco, poverty deepens, sharpening neighborhood distinctions.

Along with boasting the most farmers' markets and restaurants per capita of all American cities, San Francisco has the highest concentration of tech startups. In postcards, songs, films, and storybooks, this city is a picturesque land of creativity, cool fog, and tempting nightlife. When you look past that sound bite, however, San Francisco is struggling with a crisis of culture and conscience. The city's housing shortage and escalating rents are the toughest in the United States, driving local debates about tech-fueled gentrification. Long-overlooked neighborhoods are newly popular, some of them the fastest-growing districts anywhere. Three of the country's most competitive neighborhoods for homebuyers are in San Francisco—the Sunset, the Castro, and Bernal Heights—the latter named the "hottest" neighborhood nationwide by the real estate site Redfin.

Real estate is like gold in the Bay Area, and as San Francisco's median home price topped $1.2 million heading into 2016, the rank-and-file—including first-time homebuyers—are looking east and south of the city to bid on condos. Hopeful homeowners seeking backyards are treading east to Vallejo, Stockton, Hayward, and El Cerrito. North of San Francisco, in Marin County, you'll find small burgeoning towns with dramatic landscapes, stunning views, and breathtaking hiking trails. The further north you go, the less expensive it gets, but the longer

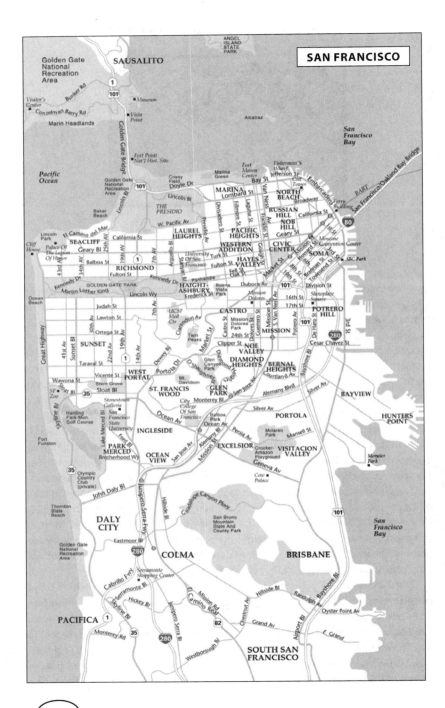

your commute into San Francisco. In the northeast, Sonoma and Napa counties are known for their award-winning vineyards tucked into rolling hills.

Deals can still be found—particularly in the East Bay—but for many newcomers, the dream of homeownership takes a backseat to economic reality. Most residents rent, deferring the responsibility for upkeep, repair, taxes, mortgage, and insurance to landlords. To get a flavor of neighborhoods, read the descriptions below, but also be sure to visit three excellent websites based in San Francisco: www.sf.curbed.com, www.48hills.org, and www.facebook.com/vanishingsf.

San Francisco's most dominant physical feature is its hilltop fog. The Mission, Potrero Hill, Noe Valley, and the Castro neighborhoods are less foggy than the Richmond, Sunset, Stonestown, and Diamond Heights, which awaken to fog so dense you can barely see your hand. Fog burns away by noon, making way for clear skies and temperatures in the 70s. Hours later, the fog tumbles in again from the Pacific Ocean, cooling these neighborhoods to the 40s and 50s.

Irresistible aromas also define the neighborhoods. Fresh-baked focaccia fills the air of North Beach (Little Italy), while steamed crab and sourdough permeate the Fisherman's Wharf area, near the barking sea lions—more than 1,000 of them—that belly-flop onto Pier 39's boat docks. And the lure of dim sum captures your attention in the Richmond. A salty ocean bite awakens the air along the western edge of the Sunset District, and an "interesting" odor of cable-car brakes hits you while descending the steepest slopes on Russian Hill and Nob Hill. Herbal remedies fill Chinatown's air along with hand-pulled noodles, and in San Francisco's parks you'll find the scent of eucalyptus.

The city's diversity stems from waves of immigration since the early Ohlone Native Americans—newcomers from Spain, Mexico, Russia, Italy, Ireland, China, Japan, the Philippines, Korea, India, Latvia, and the American South, each establishing roots in particular neighborhoods before branching out. Many newcomers today are searching beyond San Francisco to East Bay cities further out than Oakland and Berkeley. A one-bedroom in San Francisco can cost more than an entire three-bedroom house in the surrounding areas.

More than 7 million people live in the Bay Area, 840,000 of them in San Francisco. The city's population nearly doubles during weekdays when commuters arrive for work, clogging freeways and jamming steep streets. Some of the nation's worst morning and evening commutes are here, despite the semi-efficient Bay Area Rapid Transit (BART) system. Where the BART trains don't go, dozens of other transit systems do, including buses, trolleys, cable cars, commuter trains, shuttles, light rail, and ferryboats. Be prepared to add hours to your commute when using public transportation.

In 2014, California began construction on a high-speed rail link that's projected to zip you down from San Francisco to Los Angeles in half the time it takes to drive—a voter-approved project that has met fierce opposition by locals, who have filed lawsuits to derail it. The link aims for completion by 2029. Stay tuned.

A note about names: think twice before calling San Francisco "Frisco" or "San

Fran"—easy giveaways that you're neither from here nor familiar with local lingo. Even "SF" is considered a kind of gaffe. Use the full name, and you'll be in good shape.

For tips on how to go about finding a house or apartment, see **Finding a Place to Live** after the **Neighborhoods** section.

# HISTORY AND LOCAL COLOR

San Francisco is no stranger to booms and busts, crashes and comebacks—from the Gold Rush of the 1840s to the tech rush today. Called "the city" by those who live here, San Francisco was originally home to more than 100,000 Native Americans known as Ohlones, who met waves of brutal newcomers exploring the western frontier. Mexico briefly ruled this area after winning independence from Spain, but got bulldozed by the United States military shortly before the Gold Rush. Conscripted labor at gunpoint and spear-point is a central part of the Bay Area's narrative of development—but so are community empowerment, solidarity, and accomplishment. The free-speech movement, the antiwar movement, the labor-rights movement, and the gay-rights movement were all set in motion locally and expanded nationally.

Compared to Los Angeles, San Francisco is very compact—nearly twice the population per square mile. San Francisco has 840,000 residents in 49 square miles, and every inch teems with activity: from biking in Golden Gate Park, to hang gliding at Ocean Beach, to finding the spiciest Szechuan dish in Chinatown and the freshest herb-goat-cheese flatbread at the Ferry Building. And a network of new food trucks has rolled into San Francisco's parks, drawing salivating crowds (www.offthegrid.com). Track the trucks' locations on your smartphone by downloading the mobile app "Off the Grid Markets." Note also that San Francisco recently became the first city in the world to install public parklets—colorful sidewalk extensions for pedestrians. Take a glance at pavementtoparks.sfplanning.org/parklets.html.

Historically, San Francisco got its start in 1776, when a military base (*El Presidio Real de San Francisco*, or the Royal Fortress of Saint Francis) was built in the northern corner of the city by Colonel Juan Bautista de Anza. Later that year Franciscan priests opened Mission Dolores, which still stands in the heart of the Mission District as the city's oldest surviving building. A tiny village known as Yerba Buena ("good herb" in Spanish) sprang up between the Mission and the Presidio. Yerba Buena officially changed its name to San Francisco in 1847, and a year later the territory was ceded to the United States at the end of the Mexican war. At the same time, miners struck gold in the Sierra Nevada Mountains, and prospectors rushed in, growing the city's tiny population from 500 to 25,000 within a year. In 1850, the same year that California became the 31st state in the union, the city of San Francisco was officially incorporated.

By almost any measure, San Francisco has been a proudly liberal city since the 1906 earthquake and fire that flattened much of it and ushered in the twentieth century—from the 1950s poetry spark that ignited the Beat Generation, to the 1960s hippie counterculture of Haight-Ashbury, to the '60s and '70s black power movement, to the political and cultural birth of the gay-rights revolution and sexual liberation in the 1970s through today. The Bay Area is a creative masterpiece of thousands of individual and collective voices—painters, musicians, and writers from Joan Didion to Sonia Sanchez, Dashiell Hammett to Armistead Maupin, Herb Caen to Ralph Gleason, Angela Davis to Daphne Muse. San Francisco's illustrious music scene didn't start with the Grateful Dead and Jefferson Airplane—and it hasn't stopped with them either. There are also the sounds of jazz pioneers Pharoah Sanders, Jon Jang, Mark Izu, and Meklit Hadero—and the images of photographers Ansel Adams, Imogen Cunningham, and Dorothea Lange, as well as the conceptual brilliance of artist Marco Centin. Murals painted by Diego Rivera dot the city—turning up in the most unexpected places. The Mission's richly colorful galleries and the city's top museums are celebrated alongside rock and hip-hop bands in festivals and parades citywide—including the annual Gay Pride festivities.

A few years ago the artist Leo Villareal installed 25,000 LED lights on one side of the Bay Bridge, creating a two-mile-long glittering light show of never-repeating patterns. The installation awed residents, and it was slated to end in 2015, but by popular demand it will resume in 2016 permanently.

Along Market Street stand towering temples of economic power in the Financial District, home to the largest concentration of banks and financial service companies on the West Coast. Also downtown is Union Square, with ultra-chic designer boutiques. The square itself—an elevated open green—is surrounded by the largest cluster of restaurants of any city in the United States.

The neighborhood descriptions below shine a light on the characteristics of each district and provide information about housing, weather, public transit, post office locations, emergency services, hospitals, public safety agencies, and local attractions. We start at the city's northeast corner, with the first-ever neighborhood in San Francisco—Chinatown—as well as neighboring North Beach (Little Italy), then climb the steep slopes of upscale Nob Hill and Russian Hill, through the bustling Tenderloin, then work west to luxurious Pacific Heights, the Marina District, and Cow Hollow—continuing toward the foggy beaches of the Richmond and the breathtaking views of Seacliff. We then drop south across Golden Gate Park to the cool coastal shores of the Sunset District, continuing to Stonestown and Park Merced. Turning east we work our way back to the center of town through the colorful Victorians of Haight-Ashbury and the Western Addition, to Civic Center and the nightclubs and high-rises of SOMA. We then journey south to the Mission District, through the Castro, to Noe Valley, Glen Park, and Diamond Heights, before summiting the peaks of Potrero Hill and Bernal Heights. Then it's out to the Excelsior, Ingleside, Portola, and Visitacion Valley, before arriving at the city's southeastern edge: Bayview/Hunters Point, near the San Mateo County line.

# HOUSING

Finding an apartment or house in the Bay Area is a full-contact sport, with heavy overbidding, crowded open houses, an inventory crunch, all-cash buyers, and the highest rents in the nation. Daunting, yes. The cost of housing has jumped faster than anywhere else in the United States. Come prepared financially and psychologically. There's a reason why San Francisco has the most competitive housing market anywhere. Stories spread of homeowners getting unsolicited offers of $4 million above their homes' values, making properties' "list prices" essentially irrelevant to their ultimate sales prices. Housing today is an auction block. The asking amount is merely a starting point in a bidding war. But take solace in knowing that you're not alone. This city's courts of public and legal opinion are acutely aware of the affordability crisis. Steps are being taken. The Bay Area is required by law to set aside at least 15 percent of large new residential buildings as "affordable" (below-market-rate), and San Francisco has pledged to aim higher, reaching for 33 percent. But below-market-rate housing vanishes almost as quickly as it's created, so the city recently established the Housing Trust Fund to fund below-market-rate housing.

In the Mission District, for example, the median one-bedroom surpassed $4,000 in 2015. That's a staggering jump of more than 150 percent between 2011 and 2015. New luxury condos are coming up fast, creating a state of emergency for affordable housing. City officials and housing activists recently proposed a moratorium on new market-rate housing in the historically Latino neighborhood of the Mission, where displacement grows. The effort was narrowly voted down.

As developers see it, this city desperately needs new housing to cope with growing population and rising demand, while anti-displacement protestors say the new luxury condos exacerbate the affordability crisis. Housing assistance coalitions have formed, including the San Francisco Housing Action Coalition (www.sfhac.org) and the San Francisco Anti-Displacement Coalition (www.antidisplacementcoalitionsf.com). The San Francisco Tenants Union holds a series of excellent tenant "boot camps"—free workshops that empower renters to fight unlawful evictions and prevent displacement.

As a newcomer yourself, you'll have a narrow needle to thread, joining longtime locals in hunts for affordable apartments. There are excellent first-time homebuyer programs funded by the government, and housing lotteries for affordable units. To learn more, visit www.sf-moh.org and www.affordablehousingportal.org.

Even in tech-rich San Francisco, just a slim percentage of people can afford homes. Consider these median home prices from mid-2015:

| | |
|---|---|
| San Francisco | $1.2 million |
| San Mateo County | $952,000 |
| Marin County | $940,000 |
| Santa Clara County | $830,000 |
| Alameda County | $645,000 |

| | |
|---|---|
| Napa County | $550,000 |
| Sonoma County | $493,000 |
| Contra Costa County | $483,000 |
| Solano County | $335,000 |

And consider the trends between 2011 and 2015:

| | |
|---|---|
| Contra Costa County | +90 percent |
| Alameda County | +85 percent (Oakland jumped a whopping 133%) |
| Solano County | +84 percent |
| San Francisco | +76 percent |
| San Mateo County | +73 percent |
| Santa Clara County | +69 percent |
| Napa County | +67 percent |
| Sonoma County | +64 percent |
| Marin County | +47 percent |

(Source: Paragon Real Estate, www.paragon-re.com)

A big factor in the housing hunt is Airbnb, whose website lets private home-owners rent out their homes on a short-term basis. Headquartered in San Francisco, Airbnb has attracted a mountain of press, especially in 2015, when San Franciscans took to the ballot box over a proposal to limit Airbnb rentals to 75 nights per year. Controversy surrounds Airbnb because it removes apartments from the housing market in a city that urgently needs housing for locals. A study commissioned by the city showed that every home converted to a short-term rental costs San Francisco up to $300,000 annually. But Airbnb disputes that claim, saying short-term renters are good for the city, boosting San Francisco's economy by spending a total of $56 million locally, and giving homeowners a crucial source of income.

Does Airbnb speed or slow the exodus of locals? It's a raging debate.

Architecturally, San Francisco is blessed with ornate, historic Victorian homes, known by three distinct types: Italianate (straight rooflines, bold brackets), Stick (flat bay windows, thin wooden corners), and Queen Anne (balconies, round turrets, highly decorative details). Victorians range from simple cottages to elegant gingerbread-style mansions. Built between the 1870s and the 1910s, they feature high ceilings with elaborate fixtures. Rooms tend to be small, but generally have double doors that, when opened, create one spacious room. The grander Victorians have fireplaces and marble fixtures, and front rooms almost all have bay windows. Also common are Edwardians, built in the 1900s and 1910s. These are similar to Victorians but less ornate. Built-in oak cupboards are common in the typical Edwardian dining room. Edwardian apartment buildings, many built in the

1920s, are generally stucco and brown brick, and often feature fire escapes and steam-heating radiators.

Many homes in the Richmond and Sunset neighborhoods were built during the Depression. They are snug and comfortable, with fireplaces, hardwood floors, and built-in book cabinets. Housing from the 1950s, '60s, and '70s, scattered city-wide, tends to be boxy. Rooms are smaller, walls and ceilings plain, and bathrooms and kitchens lack windows. Once you reach South San Francisco and Daly City, you'll find entire neighborhoods composed of this architectural style.

Newer housing skews toward hyper-modern condos with attention to natural lighting and asymmetry. The city's newest condos are the priciest, concentrated in the South of Market area (SOMA), particularly in the Mission Bay neighborhood, which is undergoing wide-scale development, with a colossal new medical center nearby.

For tips on searching for housing, consult the **Finding a Place to Live** chapter.

## GETTING AROUND SAN FRANCISCO

The city is notoriously tricky to navigate by car, owing to rollercoaster hills, an abundance of one-way streets, too many "no left turn" signs on Market Street (the strangely curving main street), and perpetual parking woes. But San Francisco is a pedestrian- and bike-friendly city despite the hills—at least for those able to navigate the steeper inclines. Public transportation, made up of an army of gas and electric buses operated by San Francisco Municipal Railway (MUNI), is relatively easy to use—though getting out of town is another matter entirely. Meticulously restored antique streetcars travel Market Street and the waterfront street of Embarcadero, while historic cable cars climb the city's steepest hills. Bay Area Rapid Transit (BART) has a handful of stops in San Francisco, most of them downtown. Locals lament that that's not nearly enough. MUNI's growing light-rail network is a popular transit option, and a new "Central Subway" metro link is being built—slated for completion in 2019—connecting Market Street to Union Square and Chinatown. For a progress report on the new system, visit www.centralsubwaysf.com.

## CITY RESOURCES

San Francisco is a bit of an anomaly in that it's both a city and a county. The city is run jointly by the mayor and an elected Board of Supervisors.

Neighborhood-by-neighborhood community resources and information are listed beneath each profile below, but here, to get you started, are basic citywide numbers and websites you're likely to need.

**City Website**: www.sfgov.org
**Board of Supervisors**: 415-701-2311, TTY 415-701-2323

**Mayor's Office**: 415-554-6141
**City Hall**: 415-554-4933
**Public Transportation**: MUNI, 415-701-4500, www.sfmta.com; BART, 415-989-2278, www.bart.gov
**Parks, Open Space, and Gardens**: For detailed information, hours, maps, and complete listings, contact the **San Francisco Recreation and Park Department**, 415-831-2700, www.sfrecpark.org

## SAN FRANCISCO NEIGHBORHOODS

## CHINATOWN, NORTH BEACH, TELEGRAPH HILL

**Boundaries:** Chinatown: **North**: Broadway; **East**: Kearny St; **South**: Bush St; **West**: Powell St; North Beach: **North**: Fisherman's Wharf; **East**: The Embarcadero; **South**: Broadway; **West**: Columbus Ave (Telegraph Hill is at the east corner of North Beach, with Stockton St as the border)

The largest and oldest **Chinatown** in North America is a bustling destination with narrow alleys, historic parks, and hilltop cafés featuring the subtle aromas of steamed Shanghai dumplings calling your name from all corners. It's a deeply rooted community, whose Chinese and Chinese-American families began arriving in waves in the 1850s, when Gold Rushers flocked to San Francisco with high hopes for reward. But the opportunities were scarce for newcomers from China, who faced hostility and discrimination that forced them into this neighborhood. Today Chinatown encompasses 24 square blocks of thriving traditions. It's a lively district where you'll find lower-income housing—mostly single-room occupancy hotels (SROs), which make up three-quarters of local apartments. You're bound to find housing bargains, especially if you speak Cantonese, but turnover today is lower than it was a decade ago. Chinatown's population has plateaued statistically in recent years, as more Cantonese speakers head to faster-growing neighborhoods like the Richmond, Sunset, and Excelsior districts, or ditch San Francisco entirely for the East Bay towns of Milpitas, Fremont, and Oakland, each of which is quickly diversifying.

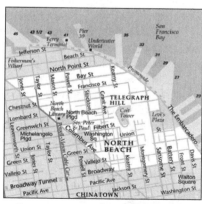

*Chinatown, North Beach, Telegraph Hill*

*Chinatown*

As tech offices sweep the Bay Area, Chinatown is starting to feel the frenzy. The neighborhood's first co-working tech space opened recently, and community leaders are protesting landlords who try to evict longtime tenants to make way for the new growth. Tech offices are slated to replace Chinatown's historic Empress of China landmark, placing this neighborhood's identity at a crossroads. But local leaders welcome some of this change, including the long-awaited City College campus, which opened in a new 14-story building; and the new Chinese Hospital, with 100,000 square feet of upgrades. A gourmet marketplace is also in the works—China Live, a mega-emporium on Broadway Street. It has already broken ground and is one of the neighborhood's largest projects in decades. The market's designers hope to reflect local pride in Chinese heritage while drawing newcomers of all backgrounds to an upscale food court with sleek shops. Whether fixed-income locals will be able to afford China Live is an open question, but the market's front doors will open onto Chinatown, and its back doors onto North Beach (Little Italy), bridging the communities.

As a newcomer, don't mistake these high-profile projects as a social shift—Chinatown is proudly slow to change. It's best known for historic rituals, etiquettes, ceremonies, and dialects—from the Chinese New Year dragon parade to the word-of-mouth get-togethers at the legendary Clarion Music Center (816 Sacramento St, www.clarionmusic.com). The blissful scent of hand-pulled noodles freezes you in your tracks near barrels of dried mushrooms, Szechuan peppercorn, and live frogs for sale under rows of red-tasseled Chinese lanterns dangling over-head. Shuffle past the tourists on Grant Avenue and wander up Stockton Street, where locals crowd the bakeries.

If you have a car here, don't. Parking is a problem, and you won't need one: the city's first-ever Central Subway is coming to Chinatown in 2019. It's a light-rail station under construction at Stockton and Washington streets, making China-town especially viable if you rely on public transit.

Historically, Chinatown is the birthplace of San Francisco. It's a neighborhood built on hardship, heroism, and breakthrough. It was also built on the backs of Chinese labor—the same community that would build the railroads. The Chinese Exclusion Act of the 1880s prohibited all Chinese immigration, and Chinese were banned from owning land, living outside Chinatown, and marrying across racial lines. This neighborhood became a hotspot of opium dens and brothels, many of whose women had been kidnapped or sold into the trade. When Chinatown was flattened in the 1906 earthquake and fire, Chinese merchants rose to the occasion again, rebuilding this neighborhood from scratch.

Portsmouth Square is a living legend: it's the oldest public space in San Francisco, where Chinatown meets the Financial District. The park is undergoing a renovation, but however it appears, the local traditions aren't likely to change. Elder women will still host the tai chi groups, and elder men will still huddle around high-stakes games. And the stampedes of tourists, avalanches of them, will slide down narrow alleyways to find the oldest dim sum restaurant in the nation, the last live-chicken market in the city, and the spot where California first flew the American flag. History is written and told in Chinatown's streets.

Steps away is **North Beach**, the vibrantly active Italian neighborhood and red-light district that actually was a beach until the late 1800s, when it was packed with landfill. Today's North Beach has an old-world charm mixed with cheesy (literally and figuratively) tourist-trap menus at romantic bistros tucked between bakeries with fresh focaccia. Good luck resisting the mouthwatering aroma of crushed garlic and fresh oregano, as well as the city's most heavily promoted nightlife. "Lively" here used to mean jazz clubs—Miles Davis, John Coltrane, Thelonious Monk, Billie Holiday, and other jazz legends all played here—but almost all the clubs are gone. The long-running Enrico's jazz club closed not long ago. The iconic Jazz at Pearl's

*North Beach*

did too, leaving practically nowhere for local jazz in this neighborhood, although the successor to Pearl's hosts a few jazz nights. "Lively" today means high-end strip clubs, one of which, it claims, is the oldest in the United States.

Broadway and Columbus are the main streets, but Grant, Union, and Vallejo streets, especially near Washington Square Park, are also filled with shops. The one-time home of the Beat Generation, North Beach became the gathering spot of ideas and identities for poets, novelists, and intellectual leaders of all genres in the 1950s and '60s—the "beatniks," as they were called by *San Francisco Chronicle* columnist Herb Caen. Adorned in all black, with sandals, berets, and dark glasses, the most famous of the bunch included San Francisco's first poet laureate, Lawrence Ferlinghetti, who opened City Lights Bookstore, which still runs today; as well as Jack Kerouac, Allen Ginsberg, Amiri Baraka (LeRoi Jones), and other literary and political giants.

Homages to the Beat-poet hangouts are colorful attractions in today's North Beach, which visitors know as the neighborhood where Francis Ford Coppola wrote the script for *The Godfather,* and where the first Italian restaurant in the United States opened, in 1886. Broadway still boasts neon signs that flicker and flash all night long, gleaming down on crowded sidewalks. The late-night vibe has reached Columbus and Grant avenues, creating a bustling nightlife. The art-deco Bimbo's 365 (a legendary music venue) on Columbus Avenue features bigger-name rock bands and a velvet interior that fulfills your 1950s movie-star fantasy.

For a classic San Franciscan experience, head to the city's longest-running musical, *Beach Blanket Babylon,* at Club Fugazi, 678 Beach Blanket Boulevard (Green Street). Upper Grant Avenue is also home to trendy clothing shops and vintage jewelry stores. Because of spiraling rents, several merchants are being replaced by costly boutiques—but there are no chain stores, thanks to neighborhood activists who have fought vehemently to keep North Beach's character intact.

At dusk, Italian elders play bocce ball at a small court near Aquatic Park, while nearby at Joe DiMaggio Playground on Lombard and Mason streets, teens gather for pickup basketball games. This is where baseball hall-of-famer Joe DiMaggio got his start with his kid brothers.

True to its name, North Beach used to have a long beach along the area's northern edge, between Telegraph Hill on the east and Russian Hill on the west. Shortly after the 1906 earthquake and fire that devastated the neighborhood, the city dumped debris from the earthquake and built a series of breakwaters and piers to create the tourist haven of Fisherman's Wharf and Pier 39. At the northern end of Embarcadero, you'll find dozens of seafood shacks and tourist shops, including Ghirardelli Square—heaven for chocolate lovers.

Most North Beach residents live in three-story Edwardian apartments, flats, or condos built on the ashes of the fire from the 1906 earthquake. While North Beach is still home to several Italian families, demographics are far more diverse today. Vacancies are not the easiest to come by, and parking your car (why do you have a car here?) is downright impossible. Buses and cable cars are preferable.

Another desirable neighborhood, and not as hectic as North Beach, is nearby **Telegraph Hill**. Formerly called Goat Hill, it became Telegraph Hill in 1853, as the site of the West Coast's first telegraph station. From here, spotters scouted for ships entering the Bay. After sighting a ship, spotters used Morse code to notify port officials. The hill features breathtaking views of the Bay, including Alcatraz Island, the country's first military prison. Telegraph Hill's narrow streets are lined with small cottages and condos, beautiful hidden gardens, and even fewer rental

*Telegraph Hill*

vacancies than the rest of North Beach. Many residents have no choice but to walk up tiny stairways and paths to homes that are compact, due to the neighborhood's 40-foot height limit.

Coit Tower, the area's most prominent icon, rises 210 feet from the top of Telegraph Hill. A monument to the city's firefighters, the tower was built in 1934, and can be reached by climbing the 377 steps along Filbert Street. While you're there, listen carefully for the wild parrots in the trees. Many believe that the local flock—now more than 100 birds—was started when a few domesticated parrots escaped from their cages. A documentary, *The Wild Parrots of Telegraph Hill*, tells the story.

**Websites**: www.sfgov.org, www.sanfranciscochinatown.com
**Area Code**: 415, 628
**Zip Codes**: 94133, 94108, 94104, 94111
**Post Office**: North Beach Station, 1640 Stockton St, 800-275-8777, www.usps.com
**Police Station**: Central Police Station, 766 Vallejo St, 415-315-2400; main non-emergency number, 415-553-0123, TTY 576-1711, www.sf-police.org
**Emergency Hospitals**: California Pacific Medical Center, 2333 Buchanan St, 415-600-6000, www.cpmc.org; Saint Francis Memorial Hospital, 900 Hyde St, 415-353-6000, www.saintfrancismemorial.org
**Library**: North Beach Library, 850 Columbus Ave, 415-355-5626, www.sfpl.org
**Public Schools**: San Francisco Unified School District, 555 Franklin St, 415-241-6000, www.sfusd.edu
**Community Resources**: Telegraph Hill Dwellers, 415-273-1004, www.thd.org; North Beach Neighbors, www.northbeachneighbors.org; Telegraph Hill Neighborhood Center, 660 Lombard St, 415-421-6443, www.tel-hi.org; North Beach Business Association, 415-989-2220, www.northbeachbusinessassociation.com; Chinese Culture Center, 750 Kearny St, 415-986-1822, www.c-c-c.org
**Public Transportation**: MUNI, 415-701-2311, TTY 415-701-2323, www.sfmta.com; *MUNI buses*: 15 Third, 30 Stockton, 10 Townsend, 41 Union, 39 Coit; *Cable*

*Car:* access to Hyde St line at Ghirardelli Square area and to Mason St line at Bay and Taylor sts. MUNI bus and cable car connections to BART and light-rail stations along Market St

# RUSSIAN HILL, NOB HILL

## LOWER NOB HILL

**Boundaries:** Russian Hill: **North**: Aquatic Park; **East**: Columbus Ave; **South**: Broadway; **West**: Van Ness Ave; Nob Hill: **North**: Broadway; **East**: Kearny St; **South**: California St; **West**: Van Ness Ave

The strenuous uphill hike is worth every step—physically and financially, if you can budget for it—when you reach the top of **Russian Hill**, one of the city's most exclusive and elegant neighborhoods. Hidden hilltop gardens, mesmerizing architecture, and startling views of the Bay frame this neighborhood's upscale restaurants and cafés. Despite its name, you won't find Russian bakeries or gravestones of the Russian sailors buried here before the Gold Rush. What you will find is a neighborhood dotted with small parks frequented only by locals. The hilltop is crowded with high-rise condos and stately apartments serviced by brass-buttoned attendants. Victorian mansions and a few converted firehouses sit next to Edwardian flats and more modest "earthquake cottages" built as temporary shelter after the 1906 earthquake. Tucked between them are secluded playgrounds, most impressively Michelangelo Park and Ina Coolbrith Park. Sterling Park's tennis courts offer views of the Bay so surreal that they have been known to take an opponent's eye off the ball.

The streets are rollercoasters. And just when you're tired of asphalt, you find a surprising patch of green. Twisting staircases ensure access to these public spaces, surrounded by leafy sidewalks and iconic cable cars clanging up the hills. Tourists outnumber residents on these nostalgic rides. At their peak, cable cars ran in eight lines, using more than 100 miles of track. Today there are three cars, two of which serve Russian Hill and Nob Hill (the Mason and Hyde lines); the third rumbles through

*Russian Hill, Nob Hill*

Nob Hill and the Financial District along California Street.

If hills don't deter you, you'll enjoy the crookedest (Lombard) and steepest (Filbert between Hyde and Leavenworth) streets in the city, both in Russian Hill. (Actually, the street with the most turns is Vermont Street in Potrero Hill—but don't tell the hordes of tourists.) The zigzagging Lombard Street is on Russian Hill's eastern slope, where each day hundreds of gleeful drivers navigate the eight near-hairpin turns that are squeezed into just one block. Homeowners on this street pay a fortune for the honor—or horror, depending on your perspective—of living here. The constant camera clicks make sense when you see this narrow street first-hand, as it winds along charming houses and lush flowering bushes.

*Russian Hill*

As an indication of Russian Hill's character, consider the controversy that erupted when Target tried to open on Polk Street, known for its small boutiques and cafés. The superstore was met with resounding opposition from neighbors who claimed any big-box retailer would crush independent merchants and make traffic a nightmare. Target backed down and didn't move in. Financially and socially, locals have pull. On the north side of Russian Hill is the San Francisco Art Institute, with a packed calendar of public exhibitions. Although the school attracts many students, Russian Hill is not the artistic enclave it was in the early 1900s, when poets, painters, and photographers such as Ina Coolbrith, Maynard Dixon, and Dorothea Lange lived in the area. Today, tech marketers and investment bankers outnumber artists a trillion to one, as today's Russian Hill has the second-highest prices per square foot in the city.

The neighborhood's commercial core is upper Polk and Hyde streets, where trendy cafés overshadow hole-in-the-wall takeout spots. The first Swensen's ice cream parlor in the country opened here in 1948 and continues to attract first dates with its neon sign at the corner of Union and Hyde streets. Lower Polk Street, once plagued by drug busts and violence, remains rough in patches bordering the Tenderloin, but the area is fast transforming and now hosts an array of lively and safer restaurants and bars. For an up-to-the-minute glimpse of Russian Hill, visit Russian Hill Neighbors at www.rhnsf.org.

Just south of Russian Hill is the more formal, fashionable **Nob Hill**, where looming mansions and lavish apartments attract ultra-wealthy tenants. In the 1800s the city's newly rich were known as *nobs*, or *nabobs*, often said interchangeably with the word *snob*. Ask around today, and you'll find that almost no one here minds the name's unflattering origin. Many locals even pride themselves on being the punch line of "Snob" Hill's reputation for palaces of privilege on top of the world. But as San Francisco faces an affordable-housing crisis of record-high rents, Nob Hill is increasingly synonymous with misplaced glamor. In the past few years, the city's cultural center of gravity has left Nob Hill for other districts; Nob Hill is no longer the "it" spot. Those who chase prestige here are chasing ghosts of nostalgia. But it's still an immaculately beautiful and highly desirable destination, only minutes from downtown.

Huntington Park, at the apex of Nob Hill, is supremely welcoming—an idyllic lawn for lazing away a Sunday afternoon (as long as you don't have to find parking). Neatly framed by colorful flowerbeds, the park neatly complements Grace Cathedral across the street—the West Coast's largest Gothic cathedral. This high-vaulted landmark hosts the city's largest yoga event, a Tuesday night ritual for up to 700 people. (Get there early. It fills up fast.)

Although more modest buildings also exist in Nob Hill, the district is dominated by the city's grandest, priciest hotels: the Fairmont, the Mark Hopkins, the Stanford Court, and the Clift, each with upscale restaurants and bars, several with panoramic views. The sandstone-exterior Flood Mansion, at 1000 California Street, built by James Clair Flood—who made his millions in mining stocks—is the only surviving building from the cluster of grand 1800s buildings.

Closer to theater and shopping, **Lower Nob Hill** lies between California Street to the north, Powell Street to the east, Geary Boulevard to the south, and Polk Street to the west. Sometimes called "Tenderloin Heights" or "The Tendernob," the area shares an unclear border with the Tenderloin, San Francisco's most impoverished neighborhood, where 6,000 homeless people live. It's a telling contrast, never more amplified than today, as Nob Hill towers over the Tenderloin. Lower Nob Hill is home to exclusive restaurants and hotels, and many private clubs. Some apartment buildings are art-deco masterpieces, with Egyptian-style lobbies and sparkling elevators. But there are also inexpensive youth hostels.

Views run the gamut, from brick walls to breathtaking panoramas. Many buildings have hidden gardens, complete with fishponds. But just like the rest of San Francisco, Lower Nob Hill is no longer a moderately priced fallback. Just the opposite. And like your chances of finding a spacious, affordable apartment, parking is nearly impossible. (Monthly parking rentals are available at commercial garages.) Most people who live here walk to work, either to the Financial District or South of Market or Union Square—or to the BART stations on Market Street.

**Websites**: www.sfgov.org, www.nobhillassociation.org

**Area Code**: 415, 628

**Zip Code**: 94109, 94133

**Post Office**: Pine Street Station, 1400 Pine St, 800-275-8777, www.usps.com

**Police Station**: Central Station, 756 Vallejo St, 415-315-2400; main non-emergency number, 415-553-0123, TTY 415-576-1711, www.sf-police.org

**Emergency Hospitals**: California Pacific Medical Center, 2333 Buchanan St, 415-600-6000, www.cpmc.org; Saint Francis Memorial Hospital, 900 Hyde St, 415-353-6000, www.saintfrancismemorial.org

**Library**: North Beach Branch, 2000 Mason St, 415-355-5626; Main Branch, 100 Larkin St, 415-557-4400; Chinatown Branch, 1135 Powell St, 415-355-2888, www.sfpl.org

**Public Schools**: San Francisco Unified School District, 555 Franklin St, 415-241-6000, www.sfusd.edu

**Community Publication**: *Nob Hill Gazette*, 5 3rd St, Suite 222, 415-227-0190, www.nobhillgazette.com

**Community Resources**: Russian Hill Neighbors, 1819 Polk St, #221, 415-267-0575, www.rhnsf.org; Nob Hill Association, 235 Montgomery St, #870, 415-346-8720, www.nobhillassociation.org; Cable Car Museum, 1201 Mason St, 415-474-1887, www.cablecarmuseum.org

**Public Transportation**: MUNI, 415-701-2311, TTY 415-701-2323, www.sfmta.com: *Russian Hill MUNI buses*: 1 California, 27 Bryant, 19 Polk, 31 Balboa, 41 Union, 45 Union-Stockton, 30 Stockton; *Cable Cars*: Hyde, Mason, and California St lines (MUNI bus and cable cars provide access to BART and MUNI Light-Rail stations along Market St); *Nob Hill MUNI buses*: 1 California, 3 Jackson, 4 Sutter; *Cable Cars*: California, Mason, and Hyde lines, all Market St lines

# TENDERLOIN

**Boundaries: North**: California St; **East**: Powell St; **South**: Market St; **West**: Van Ness Ave

Widely acknowledged as San Francisco's most neglected, impoverished neighborhood, this long-struggling downtown district is seeing improvements, but progress is slow, and it still has the city's largest homeless population. In the shadows of soaring tech offices and nearby luxury condos, the Tenderloin exemplifies San Francisco's widening gap between accelerating wealth and chronic poverty. You'll save a bundle here, with easy transportation, walkable everything, and delicious after-hours Indian and Vietnamese restaurants. Just be ready for the reality of people struggling to survive. To live in the Tenderloin today, at the height of this tech boom, is to know firsthand the city's wounded—the San Francisco that the real estate rush skipped, and that city officials, for decades, forgot. Given its

*Tenderloin*

affordability and proximity to shopping and theaters, many newcomers find the Tenderloin a practical landing point for getting their bearings while considering their next steps.

The Tenderloin does have hip new bars and galleries tucked between residential motels, strip clubs, massage parlors, homeless shelters, and soup kitchens. Marketing-spin sites like Yelp try their best to dub this neighborhood the "Trendyloin," but a name change and rebranding aren't what residents are calling for; what's needed, they urge, are improved housing and health services. The dollars are starting to come in: the revamped Boeddeker Park glows after a $9.3 million upgrade, but community leaders question the wisdom of putting millions into a park that kids hardly use, instead of into housing and food resources. Big-name help is also arriving from the San Francisco Giants, as the baseball team joins 150 groups that have funded local cleanup—part of the Tenderloin Health Improvements Partnerships.

For housing, you'll find low-income apartments with serviceable rooms, nearly 80 percent of them rent controlled or permanently "affordable"—more than anywhere else in the city. Despite the area's rough sidewalks, if you search carefully, you might find a nice, clean, sunny little spot in a semi-secure art-deco building, with an elevator and terrific views.

In 2015 a major museum opened—the Tenderloin Museum, with local art shows and walking tours that illuminate the historic roots of this district, where Muhammad Ali, Sugar Ray Robinson, and George Foreman boxed at the Cadillac Hotel; where Miles Davis played his distinctive music at the Black Hawk jazz club; where Dashiell Hammett wrote *The Maltese Falcon* in a local apartment.

To walk the Tenderloin's alleys is to encounter this past—a creative portal that's obscured by today's dingy streets and crowded stoops. But change keeps coming, including author Dave Eggers's announcement that his literary program, 826 Valencia, is opening a storefront in the Tenderloin—a 5,000-square-foot space at the corner of Leavenworth and Golden Gate streets. The shop, slated to open in 2016, will provide bookmaking and storytelling workshops, as well as afterschool education.

Nowhere in San Francisco is the culture clash of gentrification clearer than the border of the Tenderloin, where the neighborhood bumps into upscale Union

Square, Nob Hill, and mid-Market Street. Just a few blocks away, Twitter's lavish art-deco headquarters stands near Yammer, Spotify, Zoosk, Zendesk, and other tech giants whose arrivals are hotly debated. Twitter received a tax break of some $60 million to move to mid-Market Street recently, a major revenue concession by the city—and cause for concern among Tenderloin residents. Before Twitter moved in, Market Street's outlook was grim. The storefront vacancy rate was 30 percent. The mayor embraced Twitter by promising it a free pass from added payroll tax for six years. That saved the company a ton, and the Tenderloin voiced its dissent.

For Twitter's part, the tech leader has launched projects to improve the Tenderloin, including investments through volunteer work. But there are miles to go before fulfilling an earlier mayor's 10-year plan to abolish chronic homelessness in the Tenderloin. Those 10 years are long up, and the Tenderloin is still waiting—with more than 6,000 homeless people. There are some 60 liquor stores here, but no supermarket or bank. There are parts of the Tenderloin where no tourist walks intentionally, and parts where it's the hippest, most fashionable corner of San

*Tenderloin*

Francisco—where high-rollers high-step over 15 homeless people on every sidewalk to enter a password-only speakeasy. That's a familiar story in American cities today, but it's nowhere more vivid than the compact Tenderloin.

The Tenderloin's name came from the cut of meat that, generations ago, police could only afford to buy after patrolling rough streets, for which they were paid more. Not much has changed: the scars of this neighborhood, both physical and psychological, are on display everywhere here. Opportunities, futures, and legacies await newcomers who identify with the Tenderloin's crossroads.

**Websites:** www.sfgov.org, www.tndc.org
**Area Code:** 415, 628
**Zip Code:** 94102, 94103, 94109

**Post Office**: Civic Center, 101 Hyde St; Federal Building Finance Station, 450 Golden Gate Ave, 800-275-8777, www.usps.com

**Police Station**: Tenderloin Station, 301 Eddy St, 415-345-7300, TTY 415-474-5763; main non-emergency number, 415-553-0123, www.sf-police.org

**Emergency Hospitals**: California Pacific Medical Center, 2333 Buchanan St, 415-600-6000, www.cpmc.org; Saint Francis Memorial Hospital, 900 Hyde St, 415-353-6000, www.saintfrancismemorial.org

**Library**: Main Branch, 100 Larkin St, 415-557-4400, www.sfpl.org

**Public Schools**: Tenderloin Elementary, 627 Turk St, 415-749-3567, www.sfusd.edu

**Community Publication:** Street Sheet, 486 Turk St, 415-346-3740, www.streetsheetsf.wordpress.com

**Community Resources**: Bay Area Women's and Children's Center, 318 Leavenworth St, 415-474-2400, www.bawcc.org; George Coates Performance Works, 110 McAllister St, 415-392-4400, www.georgecoates.org; Tenderloin Museum, 398 Eddy St, 415-830-4640, www.tenderloinmuseum.org; Glide Memorial Church, 330 Ellis St, 415-674-6000, www.glide.org; Golden Gate Theatre, 1 Taylor St, 415-551-2000; American Conservatory Theater, 415 Geary St, 415-749-2228, www.act-sf.org; Orpheum Theatre, 1192 Market St, 415-512-7770, www.shnsf.com;Tenderloin Neighborhood Development Corporation, 201 Eddy St, 415-776-2151, TTY 866-427-2151, www.tndc.org

**Public Transportation**: MUNI, 415-701-2311, TTY 415-701-2323, www.sfmta.com; *MUNI buses*: 19 Polk, 27 Bryant, 31 Balboa, 38 Geary, 76 Marin Headlands, all Market St buses. BART, Powell/Fifth and Market sts

# PACIFIC HEIGHTS, MARINA DISTRICT, COW HOLLOW

PRESIDIO
PRESIDIO HEIGHTS
LAUREL HEIGHTS

**Boundaries:** Pacific Heights: **North**: Broadway; **East**: Van Ness Ave; **South**: California St; **West**: Arguello Blvd; Marina: **North**: Marina Blvd; **East**: Van Ness Ave; **South**: Lombard St; **West**: Lyon St; Cow Hollow: **North**: Greenwich St; **East**: Laguna St; **South**: Vallejo St; **West**: Divisadero St

In a city with no shortage of luxurious neighborhoods that are getting more expensive by the minute, it's hard to crown one neighborhood the "most" exclusive and lavish, but **Pacific Heights** is probably it. Ultra-elegant mansions with neatly trimmed gardens and carefully arranged flowerbeds are common in this prestigious community, with dramatic views of the Bay. The pinnacle of privilege for those who live here, and the embodiment of extravagance and excess for those who won't or can't, Pacific Heights set this city's all-time record for condo prices, with a $30 million penthouse sale in 2015. That record won't last long, however, as San Francisco's housing market keeps reaching new heights.

With regal architecture, hidden staircases, eucalyptus groves, and striking views of the Golden Gate Bridge and Alcatraz, Pacific Heights is undeniably spectacular. Some of the mansions were rebuilt in the wake of the 1906 earthquake and fire, while others are glorious survivors. The neighborhood today is home to a handful of celebrities and almost-celebrities who enjoy the relative anonymity that San Francisco affords—the closest equivalents to paparazzi and screaming fans are the adoring, shy pedestrians who, with "proper" Pacific Heights etiquette, are too polite to shout and ask for autographs. It's a quiet enclave, with international consulates, top private schools, and graceful art-deco high-rises creating an atmosphere of protected wealth. While houses have private gardens, there's no gated-community feel or any star maps for sale.

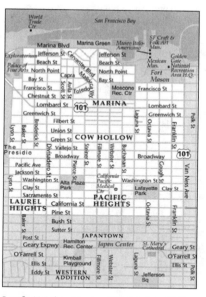

*Pacific Heights, Marina District, Cow Hollow*

Fillmore Street gets the busiest, with gourmet grocers, wine bars, sushi bars, chic fashion designers, and pricey boutiques. Frequently sunny and easily walkable, the street connects with Geary Boulevard, which leads to Japantown and the Fillmore District, with a mix of movie theaters, music clubs, and bars.

The steep Lyon Street stairs are dreamlike, and locals also head to nearby Presidio for running, hiking, and biking. Down the hill is the Bay, with countless sailboats and windsurfers. Buying a home on the quiet residential streets of Pacific Heights is a multimillion-dollar proposition. Further down the hill, toward Cow Hollow to the north, rents decrease slightly, and the supply of apartments increases (also slightly). Larger spaces can be found by heading south to the Western Addition.

In the middle of Pacific Heights, at the corner of Jackson and Steiner streets, is Alta Plaza Park, with postcard views of Alcatraz Island and Marin County to the north, and Mount Davidson to the south. Tennis courts and a playground are popular, and it's dog central in the mornings. Lafayette Park, on Washington Street, just across from the Spreckels Mansion, is another coveted hangout for kids and sunbathers.

Just north of Pacific Heights is **Cow Hollow**, named after the herds of cattle that grazed here in the 1860s. One of the area's prized landmarks is the Octagon House at Gough and Union streets, a nineteenth-century oddity that is described in the book *A Home for All* by Orson Fowler.

*Cow Hollow*

Once the cows were moved out of Cow Hollow, the neighborhood became residential, and it wasn't until the 1950s that ground-floor apartments on Union Street became storefronts and restaurants. Today the street is brimming with trendy boutiques and bars. After the 1906 earthquake and fire, San Franciscans rebuilt the city with astonishing speed. The land around the **Marina District** was created by landfill—mostly from debris caused by the earthquake—which is highly subject to liquefaction during earthquakes. Many Mediterranean-style homes were built here in the 1920s and '30s. The 1989 Loma Prieta earthquake hit the Marina District hard, destroying scores of the most desirable homes and apartment buildings. The homes were rebuilt to higher seismic standards, but the ground underneath remains comparatively unstable, and seismic maps show the neighborhood as a high danger area in the event of another major earthquake.

Historically, the Marina was a quiet spot occupied by longtime locals, many of them older. But in the past few decades it has transformed into the premier playground for the city's wealthiest 20- and 30-somethings. Chestnut Street bustles every day of the week with trendy shops, eateries, and bars. Locals stream every day to Marina Green and the Presidio for outdoor fun. Marina Green is popular for kite flying and informal soccer and football matches. Running and biking are also routine rituals along the waterfront.

The eastern end of the Marina District is home to **Fort Mason**, a former military destination that now houses museums, bookstores, art galleries, public service organizations, and a renowned vegetarian restaurant, Greens (Building A in Fort Mason), with one of the city's most spectacular waterfront views. Home to nonprofit groups as well as a theater and a gallery, the Fort Mason Center (www.fortmason. org) also hosts classes ranging from yoga to photography to driver's education.

At the western end of the Marina District sits the **Presidio**, the former military base, now a spectacular national park, arts and cultural hub, sports magnet, and shorebird lagoon. Crissy Field, packed with joggers, dog walkers, and bird watchers, spans 100 acres of open shoreline. Habitat restoration work is in progress, so steer clear of restricted areas, which are noted by posted signs. The Crissy Field Center runs environmental education programs throughout the year, with a variety of hands-on kids' classes.

The area of **Presidio Heights** sits between the Presidio, Presidio Avenue, Arguello Boulevard, and California Street, and differs little from Pacific Heights except for the view. Many homes overlook cypress and eucalyptus groves, the golf course of the Presidio, or Julius Kahn Park. Sacramento Street, from Divisadero to Walnut, boasts antique stores and chic consignment shops. It's one of San Francisco's most desirable destinations. **Laurel Heights**, which extends from Laurel Village to the southern end of Pacific Heights, is served by the tiny, excellent shopping strip called Laurel Village, highlighted by Bryan's, a locally famous meat market. Prices here, though slightly lower than Pacific Heights, are still among the city's highest.

*Marina District*

**Website**: www.sfgov.org

**Area Code**: 415, 628

**Zip Codes**: 94109, 94115, 94123, 94129, 94118

**Post Offices**: Marina Station, 2055 Lombard St; Presidio Station, 950 Lincoln Blvd; 800-275-8777, www.usps.com

**Police Stations**: Northern Station, 1125 Fillmore St, 415-614-3400, TTY 415-558-2404, main non-emergency number, 415-553-0123, www.sf-police.org

**Emergency Hospitals**: California Pacific Medical Center, 2333 Buchanan St, and 3700 California St, 415-600-6000, www.cpmc.org; Saint Francis Memorial Hospital, 900 Hyde St, 415-353-6000, www.saintfrancismemorial.org

**Libraries**: Presidio Branch, 3150 Sacramento St, 415-355-2880; Golden Gate Valley Branch, 1801 Green St, 415-355-5666; Marina Branch, 1890 Chestnut St, 415-355-2823, www.sfpl.org

**Public Schools**: San Francisco Unified School District, 555 Franklin St, 415-241-6000, www.sfusd.edu

**Community Publication**: *Marina Times*, 3053 Fillmore St, #238, www.marinatimes.com

**Community Resources**: Marina Community Association, 1517 N Point St, #465, www.mca-sf.org; Cow Hollow Association, 415-749-1841, www.cowhollowassociation.org; Marina Merchants Association, www.themarinasf.com; Union St Association, 1686 Union St, 415-441-7055, www.unionstreetsf.com; Presidio Homeowners' Association, www.presidiohoa.com; Pacific Heights Residents Association, 2585 Pacific St, www.phra-sf.org; Fort Mason

Center, 415-345-7500, www.fortmason.org; Presidio National Park, 415-561-4323, TTY 415-561-4314, www.nps.gov/prsf; Crissy Field Center, 415-561-3000, www.parksconservancy.org; Palace of Fine Arts, 3301 Lyon St, 415-567-6642, www.palaceoffinearts.org; Jewish Community Center, 3200 California St, 415-292-1200, www.discoverjcc.com; Friends of the SF Pubic Library, Fort Mason, 415-771-1076, www.friendssfpl.org

**Public Transportation**: MUNI, 415-701-2311, TTY 415-701-2323, www.sfmta. com; *Pacific Heights, Presidio, and Laurel Heights MUNI buses*: 1 California, 24 Divisadero, 41 Union, 45 Union-Stockton; *Marina and Cow Hollow MUNI buses*: 22 Fillmore, 28 19th Ave, 30 Stockton, 41 Union, 43 Masonic, 45 Union-Stockton

# THE RICHMOND, SEACLIFF

INNER RICHMOND
OUTER RICHMOND
WEST CLAY PARK

**Boundaries:** Richmond: **North**: Lincoln Park and the Presidio; **East**: Arguello Blvd; **South**: Fulton St and Golden Gate Park; **West**: The Great Highway/Pacific Ocean; Seacliff: **North**: Seacliff Ave/Pacific Ocean; **East**: 27th Ave; **South**: California St; **West**: Lincoln Park/Legion of Honor

The ocean crashing against the cliffs to your right, and the subtle scent of dim sum and delicate curries luring you from the left, with Golden Gate Park behind you—these are the sensory delights of this quiet neighborhood in San Francisco's northwestern area. Diverse and brimming with delicious Asian eateries, **the Richmond** is an increasingly popular destination. Divided by the park, the Richmond and the Sunset neighborhoods are called "the Avenues," as numbered avenues run through each. The Richmond, like the Sunset, is a non-touristy escape from the

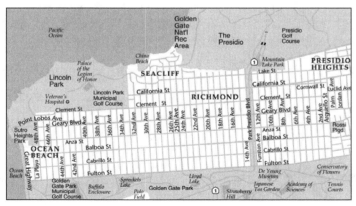

*The Richmond, Seacliff*

*The Richmond*

commotion of trendier districts closer to downtown. To live in the Richmond is to greet the morning fog and breezes from the ocean. There are days when the rest of the city is clear and sunny while the Richmond is encased in a cold blanket of fog. In exchange, you'll have pristine trails, windswept hikes, and easy access to the Golden Gate Bridge, as well as a wider array of houses, in-laws, and apartments. While San Francisco's median home prices recently passed the million-dollar-mark for the first time in history, parts of the Richmond are still temptingly well below it. And rentals are cheaper here than in many similarly safe neighborhoods.

Keep in mind that "the Richmond" is distinct from "Richmond." The former refers to the San Francisco neighborhood; without the article, you're talking about a city outside of San Francisco. What you'll miss by moving to the Richmond is a manageable commute to Silicon Valley, as this neighborhood is tucked in San Francisco's northwest corner, so think again before moving here if you work south of the city. For others, the Richmond is a strong pick, divided into two sub-districts: Inner Richmond and Outer Richmond. **Inner Richmond** is younger, pricier, more accessible to downtown, and harder for parking—it's a restaurant hub. **Outer Richmond** is more restful, non-commercial, and packed with hikes along peaks overlooking waves and wildflowers. Both inner and outer areas are heavily Asian-influenced in the storefronts, demographics, and languages—with thriving Russian and Eastern European communities in Outer Richmond. Surfers and families tend to prefer Outer Richmond, whereas younger, single professionals working downtown often prefer Inner Richmond for proximity.

Memorize this and you're off to a good start: "Geary, Clement, Balboa." Geary Boulevard is the wider commercial street that's more car-oriented than Clement. Clement is walkable and stocked with Vietnamese, Korean, Chinese, Thai, Japanese, and Burmese delights. Balboa is quieter still. Each strip has karaoke bars. The neighborhood's diversity runs from Russian churches and cozy Irish pubs to Chinese cafés and European bakeries whose poppy-seed scents are irresistible.

For housing, you'll find single-family homes, a handful of Edwardians, and 1920s duplexes. The Richmond is also home to one of the most cherished independent bookstores in San Francisco—Green Apple Books, at 506 Clement Street, with an annex at 520 Clement Street. Browsers travel from across the Bay Area just to wander the creaky hardwood floors and look through the impressive collection of used and new books, as well as videos and DVDs. A few blocks away is the city's most well-stocked Asian market, New May Wah, at 707 Clement Street, with fresh galangal, Thai basil, Szechuan chili, jackfruit, and pretty much any ingredient you might want. Clement Street is also home to discount shops—Kamei Housewares & Restaurant Supply is outstanding, and is the best and cheapest option for setting up an apartment (minus big-ticket furniture).

The neighborhood of **Seacliff** is a sharp detour in demographics, design, and prices from the Richmond. Seacliff costs a fortune—it was the second-most expensive neighborhood in San Francisco in 2015, near or at the top of every exclusive list. And it's tiny—a little chunk of coastal land, next to Baker Beach. Picture a bright, unobstructed view of copper-red Golden Gate Bridge and the dreamlike Marin mountains outside your windows. There—you're under the spell of Seacliff. Now just gather several million. The median single-family home here hovers around $3 million—peanuts compared to the $6 million median home price in Pacific Heights.

A little west of Seacliff, beyond the busy pulse of the Richmond and all the way to the lip of the Pacific Ocean, is **Lands End**. Featured in Alfred Hitchcock's classic noir *Vertigo*, Lands End is perched above 32nd Avenue and El Camino Del Mar. Overlooking the Golden Gate Bridge, it offers one of the city's most exhilarating ocean views. The trail winds along the coast and culminates in the concrete ruins of the Sutro Baths. Built in the late 1800s but later destroyed by a fire, the Sutro Baths were once the world's largest public swimming pools. More than 10,000 people swam at a time in seven glass-enclosed pools, with lifeguards paddling in rowboats. Swimmers could rent bathing suits and towels in one of 500

*Seacliff*

heated dressing rooms. It cost a dime to get in and a quarter to swim. Besides the swimming pools, there were carnivals, a Ferris wheel, and arts festivals. The baths were turned into an ice-skating rink in the 1950s—but a fire engulfed the site in 1966, and the ruins have stood ever since. Today it's a hollowed cove with wild brush—the relics of a former pleasure palace where you can catch local rock bands playing word-of-mouth shows in the caves. And in 2015 the National Parks Service started hosting theater here. The party continues.

**Websites**: www.sfgov.org

**Area Code**: 415, 628

**Zip Codes**: 94118, 94121

**Post Office**: Golden Gate Station, 3245 Geary Blvd; Geary Station, 5654 Geary Blvd, 800-275-8777, www.usps.com

**Police Station**: Richmond Station, 461 6th Ave, 415-666-8000; TTY 415-666-8059, main non-emergency number, 415-553-0123, www.sf-police.org

**Public Schools**: San Francisco Unified School District, 555 Franklin St, 415-241-6000, www.sfusd.edu

**Emergency Hospitals**: California Pacific Medical Center, 2333 Buchanan and 3700 California St, 415-600-6000, www.cpmc.org; UCSF Medical Center, 505 Parnassus Ave, 415-476-1000, ucsfhealth.org; St. Mary's Medical Center, 450 Stanyan St, 415-668-1000, www.stmarysmedicalcenter.org

**Library**: Richmond Branch, 351 9th Ave, 415-355-5600, www.sfpl.org

**Community Publication**: *Richmond Review*, 415-831-0461, www.sunsetbeacon. com; and www.richmondsfblog.com

**Community Resources**: Palace of the Legion of Honor, 34th Ave and Clement St, 415-863-3330, www.famsf.org; Lincoln Park Golf Course, 300 34th Ave, 415-221-9911, www.lincolnparkgolfcourse.com; Richmond District Neighborhood Center, 741 30th Ave, 415-751-6600, www.rdnc.org; PAR (Planning Association for the Richmond), www.sfpar.org

**Public Transportation**: MUNI, 415-701-2311, TTY 415-701-2323, www.sfmta. com: *Inner Richmond MUNI buses*: 1 California, 2 Clement, 3 Jackson, 4 Sutter, 5 Fulton, 21 Hayes, 28L-19th Ave Limited (to Daly City BART), 29 Sunset, 31 Balboa, 33 Ashbury-18th, 38 Geary; *Outer Richmond MUNI buses*: 1 California, 2 Clement, 3 Jackson, 4 Sutter, 5 Fulton, 18 46th Ave, 28L-19th Ave Limited (to Daly City BART), 29 Sunset, 31 Balboa, 33 Ashbury-18th, 38 Geary; *Golden Gate Park Free Shuttle*, 415-831-2727, www.goldengateparkconcourse.org

# SUNSET DISTRICT, PARKSIDE

**INNER SUNSET**
**OUTER SUNSET**
**GOLDEN GATE HEIGHTS**
**ST. FRANCIS WOOD**
**FOREST HILL**
**WEST PORTAL**

**Boundaries:** Sunset: **North**: Golden Gate Park and Lincoln Way; **East**: Stanyan St; **South**: Ortega St; **West**: Great Highway/Pacific Ocean; Parkside: **North**: Ortega St; **East**: Dewey and Laguna Honda boulevards; **South**: Sloat Blvd; **West**: Great Highway

If you're searching for a cloudless neighborhood insulated from the fog and breeze and warmed by bright skies, this isn't it. The fog in the **Sunset** is so thick it's almost solid, and the breeze can sting. Rest assured that clear days do come around, but the fog and just-in-case sweaters are badges of honor in this southwest corner of the city. The Sunset is San Francisco's largest neighborhood. And the housing numbers are in: this district just became (brace yourself) the most competitive real estate market in not just California, but the entire United States—based on number of sales above asking price, offers per home, and all-cash sales. That's an abrupt change for the Sunset, partly due to trendier neighborhoods' saturation, and to the Sunset's coastal appeal. Golden Gate Park is an iconic treasure in your backyard. The beach is steps away. Navigation is easy (avenues are numbered, and most streets are alphabetized). Cheap eats are everywhere. Street parking is manageable. And more than half of San Francisco's top-rated schools are here.

The Sunset's biggest appeal is its diversity. Families of Chinese, Vietnamese, Korean, Russian, Italian, and Irish backgrounds welcome newcomers across languages and nationalities in a non-touristy, fuss-free atmosphere. Although far

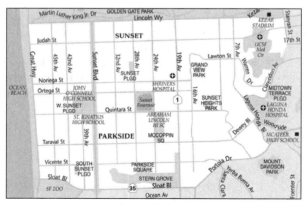

*Sunset, Parkside*

from downtown, the Sunset has reliable transportation—the N-Judah is most locals' best bet, a streetcar so popular that a gossip website tracks its every move (www.njudahchronicles.com). This neighborhood also boasts access to highways that feed directly onto the Golden Gate Bridge northbound and I-280 South.

The Sunset comprises **Inner Sunset** on the east and **Outer Sunset** on the west, and is divided by 19th Avenue. While locals consider the entire area "the Sunset," the homes south of Ortega Street to Sloat Boulevard are technically **Parkside**. And the hilly area around Lomita and 16th avenues is known as **Golden Gate Heights**. To decide between them, keep in mind that Inner Sunset is more expensive—as well as younger and hipper. It is anchored by the University of California at San Francisco (UCSF) Medical Center, a premier teaching hospital. Outer Sunset, closer to the beach, has more senior citizens and kids, and less nightlife; it's the second-safest district in the city. The most burning question locally is whether the National Park Service will ban the beachside bonfires. Bonfires are a crowd-pleaser in Outer Sunset, but cleanup is costly. Authorities are deliberating.

Nightlife throughout the Sunset is primarily word-of-mouth parties and back-

*Sunset*

yard BBQs, but street scenes come alive along Lincoln Way. The second-oldest bar in the city, Little Shamrock, was founded in 1863, on Lincoln at 9th Avenue—a *Cheers*-like pub that captures the neighborhood's welcoming warmth. A newcomer in his 30s, dog in lap, can easily start a barstool conversation with a lifelong local in his 70s, crossword in lap, while a table of jigsaw puzzlers enjoys pitchers. Newer nightlife includes the modern bubble-tea cafés and late-night Korean and Chinese dessert shops, brightly lit and sociable for students.

Outdoor adventures are abundant, with bike and jogging trails, museums, and colorful gardens flanked by sports fields. Daring souls take the plunge into the icy Pacific Ocean with surfboards, while Fort Funston—on the Great Highway—is a hang glider's paradise. Lake Merced, another leisurely enclave, attracts dog-walkers and runners, and the San Francisco Zoo is at your doorstep. The zoo is currently dealing with scandals, however: a baby gorilla was crushed to death recently by a faulty automatic door, prompting investigations and local protests. The zoo's chimpanzee treatment has also jeopardized its accreditation, and café conversations throughout this neighborhood are passionate about the topic.

Happier and healthier conditions are easily found at Stern Grove, the beloved 33-acre park that has held free concerts since 1938. A packed festival comes alive in the summers when 20,000 concertgoers crowd the eucalyptus amphitheater, newly shining after a $15 million makeover. Nearby is a scenic golf course, Harding Park, overlooking the lake—future home to the 2020 PGA Championship.

Before the 1906 earthquake and fire, the Sunset was a lump of forgotten sand dunes, considered too foggy and windy for residential development. The post-1906 real estate boom opened new markets, and today the Sunset is a working-class haven for teachers, health care workers, firefighters, small-business owners, artists, and students.

Two upscale neighborhoods, **St. Francis Wood** and **Forest Hill**, border the Sunset on the east, where you'll find some of the city's best-tended homes, with prices to match. The lots are large, giving these exquisite mansions substantial space. The streets are winding, with elegant fountains.

Down the hill is another hidden treasure, **West Portal**, named the safest neighborhood in the city in 2015—combining the lowest crime rate with the highest smile-per-pedestrian rate. With its friendly 1950s charm, mom-and-pop counters, and an old-time movie house, West Portal has a cozy atmosphere that's just starting to modernize. It's a refreshingly unassuming and overlooked family enclave in the middle of a dense city. West Portal Avenue, the main street, has thriving independent shops. Most residents ride a streetcar downtown through the Twin Peaks tunnel; the trip to Union Square is just 20 minutes.

**Website**: www.sfgov.org
**Area Code**: 415, 628
**Zip Codes**: 94122, 94116, 94132
**Post Offices**: Sunset Station, 1314 22nd Ave; Parkside Station, 1800 Taraval St, 800-275-8777, www.usps.com
**Police Station**: Taraval Station, 2345 24th Ave, 415-759-3100, TTY 415-351-2924, main non-emergency number, 415-553-0123, www.sf-police.org
**Emergency Hospital**: UCSF Medical Center, 505 Parnassus Ave, 415-476-1000, www.ucsfhealth.org
**Libraries**: Sunset Branch, 1305 18th Ave, 415-355-2808, Merced Branch, 155 Winston Dr, 415-355-2825, www.sfpl.org
**Public Schools**: San Francisco Unified School District, 555 Franklin St, 415-241-6000, www.sfusd.edu
**Community Publication**: *Sunset Beacon*, 415-831-0461, www.sunsetbeacon.com

**Community Resources**: Sunset Neighborhood Beacon Center, 3925 Noriega St, 415-759-3690, www.snbc.org; Inner Sunset Merchants Association,www.innersunsetmerchants.org; Golden Gate Park, 415-831-2700, www.sfrecpark.org; Stern Grove Festival, 415-252-6252, www.sterngrove.org

**Public Transportation**: MUNI, 415-701-2311, TTY 415-701-2323, www.sfmta.com; *Sunset MUNI buses*: 6 Haight-Parnassus, 57 Parkmerced, 18 46th Ave, 26 Valencia, 29 Sunset, 66 Quintara, 7/7R Haight-Noriega; *LRV*: N-Judah; *Parkside MUNI buses*: 57 Parkmerced, 18 46th Ave, 23 Monterey, 28 19th Ave, 29 Sunset, 35 Eureka, 48 Quintara-24th St, 52 Excelsior, 66 Quintara, 89 Laguna Honda; *LRV*: L-Taraval, K-Ingleside, M-Oceanview

# STONESTOWN, PARK MERCED

### LAKESHORE

**Boundaries:** Stonestown: **North**: Sloat Blvd; **East**: 19th Ave; **South**: Brotherhood Way; **West**: Lake Merced Blvd; Lakeshore: **North**: Sloat Blvd; **West**: Great Highway/Pacific Ocean; **East**: Lake Merced Blvd; **South**: San Francisco/San Mateo County Line; Park Merced: **North**: Holloway Ave.; **East**: 19th Ave; **South**: Brotherhood Way; **West**: Merced Blvd

As far away from downtown as you can get in San Francisco without slipping into the ocean—while still linked to amenities and activities—the neighborhoods of Stonestown, Park Merced, and Lakeshore meld together around the campus of San Francisco State University (SFSU), which serves 30,000 students. The school recently opened a branch downtown, but this is its hub, framed by the beach and a lake. SFSU recently secured a $17 million grant from the National Institutes of Health to support underrepresented minorities in science—a reflection of the growing diversity of both the university and the neighborhood. The campus has

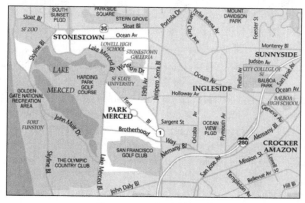

*Stonestown, Park Merced*

long been an engine of progressive change locally and nationally; in the 1960s, it launched the first black-studies courses at any college or university in the United States. Today the neighborhoods around SFSU are celebrated for coalitions of Filipino-American students, Korean-American families, Italian-American seniors, and many newcomers across nationalities and incomes.

The fog-bound **Stonestown** area, near the campus, comes with its own mall, the Stonestown Galleria—an upscale destination with department stores, boutiques, cafés, movie theaters, a medical center, and—*bingo!*—free parking (unlike the Westfield mall downtown). You'll find scores of apartments nearby, many of them home to elder residents and students.

A new Sunday farmers' market is a welcome addition to the neighborhood. It's a year-round outing named "best family-oriented farmers' market" by the *SF Weekly*. There's also big housing news: a multibillion-dollar apartment complex, the largest in San Francisco, is on the way. Called Parkmerced, it is projected to include 8,900 new apartments over 20 years (1,572 in the next few years), 80,000 square feet of office space, and half a million square feet of underground parking. Longtime locals debate the change, with community leaders claiming

*Stonestown*

that the complex will displace existing residents. The California Supreme Court stepped in and sided with the developers, who plan to deliver more than 3,000 rent-controlled homes and 900 below-market-rate apartments. It's the largest below-market-housing investment ever made on the city's west side.

Also in the air are rumors of proposals to create a 19th Avenue subway— the first subway in this coastal neighborhood's history. Locals aren't holding their breaths. The earliest the subway could be completed is 2020, if feasibility studies go forward.

Much of the housing nearby is a haven for SFSU students who want (and can afford) a garden or tower apartment that's a five-minute walk to campus. **Park**

**Merced**, with an array of one-, two-, and three-bedroom townhouses, is a multi-acre development with a new fitness center, movie theater, conference space, and shaded trails. The shores of Lake Merced are just minutes away, as is access to I-280 and 101 South, making this a popular spot with commuters who work on the Peninsula or in the South Bay. Just don't plan to live here if you work in the East Bay, unless you want a marathon commute. But schools are excellent here. The neighborhood boasts the prestigious Lowell High School; in 2015 it was ranked the best in California among large public schools by *U.S. News & World Report.*

Lake Merced is one of the city's main reservoirs, surrounded by a wooded park and the 18-hole Harding Park Golf Course. Paddle boats and rowboats are available for rent. The western edge of Lake Merced is known as **Lakeshore**, where surprisingly few San Franciscans visit, unless they're rent gliding from the cliffs of Fort Funston or fortunate enough to score a luxury apartment or condo lining John Muir Drive. Rents are steep, amenities exceptional, and the atmosphere serene along the drive, but vacancies are rare. If you can afford it, and if living far from downtown is worth it, keep checking for openings.

**Website**: www.sfgov.org

**Area Code**: 415, 628

**Zip Codes**: 94132

**Post Offices**: Lakeshore Plaza, 1543 Sloat Blvd, 800-275-8777, www.usps.com

**Police Stations**: Taraval Station, 2345 24th Ave, 415-759-3100, TTY 415-351-2924; Ingleside Station, 1 Sergeant John V. Young Ln, 415-404-4000, TTY 415-404-4009; main non-emergency number, 415-553-0123, www.sf-police.org

**Emergency Hospital**: UCSF Medical Center, 505 Parnassus Ave, 415-476-1000, www.ucsfhealth.org

**Library**: Merced Branch, 155 Winston Dr, 415-355-2825, www.sfpl.org

**Public Schools**: San Francisco Unified School District, 555 Franklin St, 415-241-6000, www.sfusd.edu

**Community Resources**: San Francisco State University, 1600 Holloway Ave, 415-338-1111, www.sfsu.edu; San Francisco Golf Club, Junipero Serra Blvd and Brotherhood Way, 415-469-4100; Harding Park Golf Course, Harding Dr off of Skyline Dr, 415-664-4690, www.tpc.com; Lake Merced, Lake Merced Blvd, 415-831-2700, www.sfparksalliance.org; Fort Funston, Fort Funston Rd and Skyline Blvd, www.parkconservancy.org; San Francisco Zoo, Sloat Blvd at 47th Ave, 415-753-7080, www.sfzoo.org

**Public Transportation**: MUNI, 415-701-2311, TTY 415-701-2323, www.sfmta.com; *Stonestown MUNI buses*: 57 Parkmerced, 18 46th Ave, 23 Monterey, 26 Valencia, 28 19th Ave, 29 Sunset; *MUNI Metro*: M Oceanview; *MUNI rail*: K-Ingleside, M-Oceanview; *Lake Merced MUNI buses*: 18 46th Ave, 88 BART shuttle (to nearby Daly City BART station)

# HAIGHT-ASHBURY

**COLE VALLEY**
**BUENA VISTA PARK**
**PARNASSUS/ASHBURY HEIGHTS**

**Boundaries:** Haight-Ashbury: **North**: Oak St; **East**: Divisadero St; **South**: Parnassus St; **West**: Stanyan St; Buena Vista Park: **North**: Haight St; **East**: Divisadero; **South**: Roosevelt Way; **West**: Masonic Ave; Parnassus/Ashbury Heights: **North**: Parnassus Ave; **East**: Buena Vista Ave and Roosevelt Way; **South**: Clarendon Ave and Tank Hill Park; **West**: UCSF Medical Center

The psychedelic '60s and flower-power counterculture that made this neighborhood the headquarters of antiwar protests and hippie hangouts have long gone, but don't tell that to the locals. Stand at the corner of Haight and Ashbury streets, and you're at ground zero of the '60s revolution, where the Grateful Dead, Janis Joplin, Joni Mitchell, Jimi Hendrix, Jefferson Airplane, and countless other musicians lived, recorded, and rebelled. Fragments of those glory days are preserved and promoted along Haight Street today. But the scene has changed. Bellbottoms and sideburns have been replaced by selfie-sticks and smartphones. The Haight's hippie legacy has become a Disneyland of its own making: double-decker peace-and-love tour buses, refrigerator magnets of the neighborhood's iconic street signs, and Jerry Garcia's smile enlarged across shop windows.

Living in the Haight today—also called Upper Haight (locals don't call it **Haight-Ashbury** anymore)—is exciting, but there's more to it than just nostalgia. You'll have enviable, front-row access to Golden Gate Park, whose entrance is hard to miss. Bike rentals line the walkways, and encampments of blissed-out artists and stoned skaters include dogs, kittens, and even pigs on leashes—most wearing handkerchiefs. It's a familiar sight in the Haight—so familiar, in fact, that the city recently passed an anti-vagrancy law known as the "sit/lie ordinance," prohibiting sitting and lying on sidewalks here. You'll still encounter friendly backpackers with offers of "kind bud" (look it up). But today's Haight is unlike it was in 1967, when the Summer of Love brought 100,000 hippies to the neighborhood. Today it's filled with fashion boutiques and pricy vintage-clothing stores with fishnet bodysuits, as well as colorful tattoo parlors and incense shops. There's still the city's best and largest record store, Amoeba Music.

A music lover's paradise with a vast used-CD section, Amoeba

*Haight-Ashbury*

*Haight-Ashbury*

recently added a medical marijuana doctor to its store, allowing anyone with a California ID to stop in and apply for a pot permit. Medical marijuana is now legal in San Francisco. Dozens of pot dispensaries have opened citywide, and the Haight is renowned for its smoke scene. The oldest smoke shop in San Francisco is on Haight Street.

The biggest housing change is the popularity of Airbnb (www.airbnb.com), whose short-term private rentals have hit the Haight like an earthquake. Airbnb reportedly takes 30 to 40 percent of apartment rentals off this neighborhood's market, making newcomers' housing options somewhat tricky. But if you choose to make the Haight your home, you're in good company, and you'll find some of the city's most elegant architecture. Century-old Queen Anne houses with sweeping steps and sash windows sit across from stately Edwardians and other ornate houses with neatly painted balconies. Residents liken these homes to colorful cakes slathered with whipped cream, cherries, and bright frosting—the decorative details are classic San Francisco.

The scene has changed since the Beat era. A Whole Foods opened recently in the center of the Haight. Residents are split between applause for the store, and groans about gentrification. A few blocks down, the Red Vic movie house bid farewell recently after a 30-year run as a cherished landmark, where wooden bowls of popcorn exemplified the Haight's welcoming spirit, and barefoot kids in tie-dyed shirts filled the seats.

**Cole Valley**, a small, friendly, less-seedy neighborhood on the southern edge of the Haight, is bounded by Carl and Cole streets. It's quieter than the Haight and is home to several medical professionals and students from nearby UCSF Medical Center. Cole Street is packed with cafés, bakeries, bars, and restaurants, from quick bites to elegant dining. Hardware stores, health-food shops, and dry cleaners are also on offer, and homes here are slightly more expensive than in the Haight. But the commute to downtown is convenient; just hop MUNI's N-Judah and you'll get there in under 10 minutes.

The **Buena Vista Park** neighborhood, surrounding the 36-acre Buena Vista Park, has curvy, hilly streets, magnificent homes, and plenty of wealthy occupants. The lookout from the top of Buena Vista Park offers a stunning panorama of San Bruno Mountain to the south, Mount Diablo to the east, Mount Tamalpais and the Golden Gate Bridge to the north, and, when the fog lifts, the Farallon Islands to the west. Though right in the middle of the city, this park—with eucalyptus groves and stately pines—convinces you that you've left the city entirely.

Even more charming neighborhoods—with older, refurbished homes— include **Parnassus** and **Ashbury Heights**, south of Haight Street. These districts boast ornate Victorians and Edwardians, as well as apartment buildings whose residents claim that the wild parrots of Telegraph Hill come to visit, often in flocks of 20 or more. (To learn more about these notorious parrots, visit www.pelicanmedia.org.)

**Websites**: www.sfgov.org, www.haightashbury.org

**Area Code**: 415, 628

**Zip Code**: 94117

**Post Office**: Clayton St Station, 554 Clayton St, 800-275-8777, www.usps.com

**Police Station**: Park Station, 1899 Waller St, 415-242-3000, TTY 415-681-6487, main non-emergency number, 415-553-0123, www.sf-police.org

**Emergency Hospitals**: St. Mary's Medical Center, 450 Stanyan St, 415-668-1000, www.stmarysmedicalcenter.org; UCSF Medical Center, 505 Parnassus Ave, 415-476-1000, www.ucsfhealth.org

**Library**: Park Branch, 1833 Page St, 415-355-5656, www.sfpl.org

**Public Schools**: San Francisco Unified School District, 555 Franklin St, 415-241-6000, www.sfusd.edu

**Community Publication**: *Haight Ashbury Voice*, www.hanc-sf.org

**Community Resources**: HealthRight 360 Free Medical Clinic, 558 Clayton St, 415-746-1950, www.healthright360.org; Haight Ashbury Neighborhood Council, 415-753-0932, www.hanc-sf.org; Cole Valley Improvement Association, www.cviasf.org; Haight Ashbury Merchants, www.thehaight.org

**Public Transportation**: MUNI, 415-701-2311, TTY 415-701-2323, www.sfmta.com; *MUNI buses*: 5 Fulton, 6 Haight-Parnassus, 7 Haight, 33 Ashbury-18th, 37 Corbett, 43 Masonic, 21 Hayes, 24 Divisadero, 66 Quintara, 7/7R Haight-Noriega: *MUNI rail*: N-Judah

# WESTERN ADDITION, CIVIC CENTER

**THE FILLMORE**
**JAPANTOWN**
**LOWER HAIGHT**
**ALAMO SQUARE**
**HAYES VALLEY**
**LOWER PACIFIC HEIGHTS**
**NORTH OF PANHANDLE (NOPA)**

**Boundaries:** Western Addition: **North**: Pine St and Pacific Heights; **East**: Polk St and the Tenderloin; **South**: Haight St and the Lower Haight; **West**: Masonic and Richmond; Civic Center: **North**: Turk St; **East**: Larkin St; **South**: Market St; **West**: Gough St

Nestled between the upscale neighborhood of Pacific Heights and the hippie hangouts of Haight-Ashbury, the **Western Addition** is one of the most culturally diverse neighborhoods in the city. Boasting rows of restored Victorians, the area's chic restaurants and bed-and-breakfasts stand in stark contrast to its auto-repair shops and thrift stores. Housing choices are varied, including railway flats, colorful mansions, single-family Victorians, public housing, and luxurious new condos that are highly controversial in today's tech-driven San Francisco. As in most of the city, living near public transit and vibrant nightlife is expensive. But a few below-market-rate housing opportunities can still be found in the Western Addition because much of the area had, until now, resisted gentrification. Nearby Hayes Valley, the Fillmore, and Japantown were all tilting in the affordable direction during the recession of the late aughts, but each district has rebounded dramatically.

The center of San Francisco was a wasteland of sand dunes until the 1850s, when the city pushed westward—which is how the Western Addition got its name. The neighborhood survived the 1906 earthquake and fire without much damage, and afterward, many Japanese-Americans sought refuge here. During World War II, African-American soldiers and their families moved into the vacancies left by the interned Japanese population—which had been forcibly removed by the government without cause—and cultivated a pioneering music scene that flourished on Fillmore Street. The **Fillmore District**'s 1940s jazz sounds continue to evolve with the annual Fillmore Jazz Festival today—the largest free, public jazz festival on the West Coast, attracting more than 100,000 fans.

Thousands of locals had lined

*Western Addition, Civic Center*

up for Billie Holiday at the Champagne Supper Club, and John Coltrane, Duke Ellington, and Louis Armstrong at Bop City in the '50s and '60s. The Fillmore had two dozen nightclubs in one square mile, where the music thrived despite city officials who discriminated overtly and boastfully against black residents: the San Francisco Housing Authority had banned black tenants from almost every San Francisco neighborhood. The Fillmore became a de-facto home for the majority of black San Franciscans, whose population had grown by nearly 700 percent during World War II, as migrant laborers moved west for dollar-an-hour shipbuilding jobs.

The Fillmore's jazz landmarks were eventually bulldozed by the city's Redevelopment Agency, decimating the community. Facing backlash and political pressure, the Redevelopment Agency was dissolved in 2012. And the story continued in 2014, when Bay Area filmmakers began making a timely film titled *The Last Black Man in San Francisco*. On the site of the former Bop City jazz club, a legendary bookstore, Marcus Books—the oldest black bookstore in the United States—was an iconic destination that closed in 2015. It's rumored to be reopening in another location soon.

Part of the Lower Fillmore area, **Japantown** is the oldest of only three remaining Japantowns in the United States, all in California. San Francisco's Japantown is home to elegant architecture, exceptional ramen and sushi bars, karaoke clubs, and import-supply stores nestled between larger landmarks like the Kabuki Theater Cinema Complex and the relaxing Kabuki Springs and Spa. Japanese stationery, books, kimonos, and cosmetics are all available here. This is the neighborhood where taiko drumming was popularized in the 1960s, when the San Francisco Taiko Dojo, the first organized taiko group in the United States, was founded. (The group would perform at Carnegie Hall for the Japanese emperor.) Mochitsuki—the delicious mochi-pounding festival—takes place here annually.

Old Victorians, new public housing, and some high-rise condos make up the housing options in this part of the Western Addition. If you're moving to Japantown, note the history you'll be stepping into: this is one of the sites where the government forcibly removed and sent to internment camps thousands of Japanese San Franciscans. Their families later received a presidential apology from Ronald Reagan, but the strain is still felt in the neighborhood.

**Divisadero Street** is the less-gentrified artery of the Western Addition. Divisadero separates the **Lower Haight** from the Upper Haight or Haight-Ashbury. The Lower Haight has a distinctly different feel from its more famous counterpart. In recent decades, students, artists, musicians, and herbalists have lived in the Lower Haight's cavernous railway flats, although prices are rising. Garages and gas stations hinder the cohesiveness of the street's commercial center, but a big car wash on Divisadero will soon be replaced with luxury condos, a trend quickly spreading across the city. Independent businesses maintain influence in the neighborhood: a BBQ restaurant, a video store, a popular record shop, a terrific Middle Eastern deli, a delicious Ethiopian restaurant, many taquerías, and a high-end organic grocery store (Bi-Rite) all testify to the street's diversity.

*Alamo Square*

Housing near Divisadero Street is mostly Victorians split into flats, and Bay-windowed apartment buildings. The sidewalks of the Lower Haight mirror the Upper Haight—packed with cafés, bars, cheap eats, secondhand retail shops, hair salons, and tattoo and piercing parlors. Nearby is picture-perfect Alamo Square Park (between Fulton, Scott, Hayes, and Steiner streets), a hilltop park with wind-swept evergreens, weeping willows, a tennis court, and stunning views of the Bay. From the northern side of the park you can see the Painted Ladies, a row of six exquisitely restored Victorians made famous by every press photograph you've ever seen of San Francisco—and by the opening credits to the TV show *Full House*.

The **Alamo Square** neighborhood, like the rest of the Western Addition, is considerably safer than it was in the 1980s. The area has received an upgrade in the past several decades as large, dilapidated public housing structures have been replaced with clustered, mixed-income townhouse communities. Within walking distance of Haight, Divisadero, and Hayes streets, Alamo Square offers access to the best of all districts, plus easy links to transportation downtown.

**Hayes Valley** is hipper and pricier than it's ever been—and aesthetically sleeker. A $10 cup of fresh-squeezed juice? No problem. The neighborhood is a high-end urban destination with gourmet and upscale everything. Housing includes Victorians, Edwardian flats, hidden-away cottages, several new condos, and townhomes. Locals spend days browsing for the perfect pair of billion-dollar high heels, glancing at contemporary art, and hunting for ultra-modern end tables.

The biggest change is the completion of the Octavia Grand Boulevard, which replaced the much-maligned and never-completed Central Freeway. The four-lane road opened a decade ago and carries commuters from the freeway across Market Street and into the city's heart.

**Lower Pacific Heights**, located roughly between California Street, Presidio Avenue, Van Ness Avenue, and Geary Boulevard, was previously considered part of the Western Addition until real estate agents tagged it with the catchier name of Lower Pacific Heights. The area differs from the bulk of the Western Addition, in

*Civic Center*

that it's hilly, and rents are higher. Sturdy, comfortable apartments from the 1920s with brick fronts and kitchen built-ins abound, side by side with mansions.

The **Civic Center** neighborhood has ultra-chic new condos within blocks of chronic poverty, so it's best to see for yourself which block an apartment is on before making decisions. Centrally located and transit-centered, the area is packed with tourists, thanks to the nearby BART station. It is home to the ballet, opera, symphony, and a new jazz center—but also to federal, state, and city buildings, including the renovated City Hall, glowing with gold-and-marble accents. Also here are Hastings College of Law, the Asian Art Museum, and the Main Library. Some sections of the Civic Center, particularly those in the Tenderloin, are rough, with many homeless. Real estate agents have been known to place listings of available apartments under "Civic Center" for places that are actually in the Tenderloin.

Living here requires some travel for groceries and laundry, and Civic Center's section of Market Street is still packed with strip clubs. But if you look hard, you may find a spacious apartment with a secured entrance on a quiet street.

**North of Panhandle**—or NOPA, one of the city's newest named neighborhoods—stretches from Fell to Turk streets and from Divisadero to Masonic. With a strong sense of community, this area features a dive-like yet spacious music venue, the Independent; a farmers' market from July to December; and Mojo Bicycle Café, a signature San Francisco fusion of bike gear retailer, repair shop, coffee bar, and pub. While not officially recognized as a neighborhood under the city's zoning codes, this area has a buzz that's gaining momentum.

**Website**: www.sfgov.org
**Area Code**: 415, 628
**Zip Codes**: 94115, 94117, 94102, 94109
**Post Offices**: Steiner St Station, 1849 Geary Blvd; Clayton St Station, 554 Clayton St, 800-275-8777, www.usps.com

**Police Stations**: east of Steiner St: Northern Station, 1125 Fillmore St, 415-614-3400, TTY 415-558-2404; west of Steiner St: Park Station, 1899 Waller St, 415-242-3000, TTY 415-681-6487, www.sf-police.org

**Emergency Hospitals**: California Pacific Medical Center, 2351 Clay St. #510, 415-392-3225, www.cpmc.org; California Pacific Medical Center, Davies Campus, Castro and Duboce streets, 415-600-6000, www.cpmc.org; Post Street Surgery Center, 2299 Post St. #108, 415-923-3770, www.poststreetsurgery.com; St. Francis Memorial Hospital, 900 Hyde St, 415-353-6000, www.saintfrancismemorial.org

**Library**: Main Library, 100 Larkin St, 415-557-4400; Western Addition Branch, 1550 Scott St, 415-355-5727, www.sfpl.org

**Public Schools**: San Francisco Unified School District, 555 Franklin St, 415-241-6000, www.sfusd.edu

**Community Resources**: Alliance Française de San Francisco, 1345 Bush St, 415-775-7755, www.afsf.com; The Fillmore, 1805 Geary Blvd, 415-346-6000, www.thefillmore.com; the Museum of Performance & Design, Veterans Building, Fourth Floor, 401 Van Ness Ave, 415-255-4800, www.mpdsf.org; Ella Hill Hutch Community Center, 1050 McAllister St, 415-567-0440, www.sfparksalliance.org; War Memorial Opera House, 301 Van Ness Ave, 415-621-6600, www.sfopera.com; San Francisco Ballet, 301 Van Ness Ave, 415-861-5600, www.sfballet.org; Louise M. Davies Symphony Hall, 201 Van Ness Ave, 415-864-6000, www.sfsymphony.org; Bill Graham Civic Auditorium, 99 Grove St, www.billgrahamcivicauditorium.com; Alamo Square Neighbors Association, 415-248-9356, www.alamosq.org; North of Panhandle Neighborhood Association, 415-267-6113, www.nopna.org; Hayes Valley Neighborhood Association, 1800 Market St, www.hayesvalleysf.org; Hamilton Recreation Center and Pool, 1900 Geary Boulevard, 415-292-2111, www.sfrecparc.org

**Public Transportation**: MUNI, 415-701-2311, TTY 415-701-2323, www.sfmta.com: *MUNI buses*: east-west: 38 Geary, 2 Clement, 3 Jackson, 4 Sutter, 5 Fulton, 21 Hayes, 31 Balboa; north-south: 22 Fillmore, 24 Divisadero, 43 Masonic, 49 Van Ness-Mission, 47 Van Ness; inter-city: 76 Marin/Headlands; *Golden Gate Transit buses* (to and from Marin County), www.goldengatetransit.org: 10, 70, 80, 93

# SOUTH OF MARKET (SOMA)

**SOUTH BEACH**
**MISSION BAY**

**Boundaries: North** and **West**: Market St; **South**: 16th St; **East**: San Francisco Bay

San Francisco's skyline and storyline are changing at warp speed as today's tech rush grows—nowhere more so than the **South of Market area (SOMA)**, where cranes crowd the sky. The tallest building in city history is currently under construction here; scheduled for completion in 2018, it is part of a flurry of condos and office

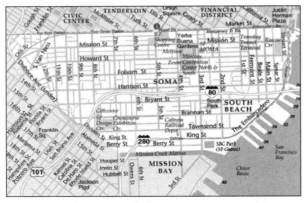

*SOMA*

towers that make this industrial-chic neighborhood a symbol of changing San Francisco. Today's SOMA story goes like this: tech industry booms, salaries jump, rents climb, and high-rise condos multiply, displacing lower-income artist-students while high-paid tech crowds move in. SOMA is Exhibit A. This neighborhood stretches across the city's northeast corner, where tunneling bores plow beneath pedestrian-packed sidewalks to install the massive new Central Subway, aiming for 2019 completion. Meanwhile, the warehouses, hip eateries, hipper galleries, and homeless encampments give this neighborhood its cultural diversity.

The San Francisco Giants' ballpark is at the north end, while SOMA's south end is getting a new sports arena as early as 2018, to house the Golden State Warriors. Yes, San Francisco may have its very own NBA team, as the 2015 champions weigh the possibility of ditching Oakland and moving to SOMA's Mission Bay district, to play in a glassy waterfront arena. If that happens, the team might change its name to the San Francisco Warriors. If you move here, prepare for game-day traffic.

Demographically, SOMA caters to youngish clubgoers, tech marketers, and convention organizers. Between them, homeless families find any stretch of sidewalk to exist on, mostly outside the pawnshops, discount centers, and delis. The contrasts are growing, and the costs—financially and culturally—are adding up. SOMA is a distinctly urban area, with occasional patches of green tucked behind buildings. Grassy lawns are found at Yerba Buena Gardens, on Mission Street between 3rd and 4th streets. But don't expect most condos to include a rooftop garden; it's mostly beautified pavement, though you can score a Bay-view balcony with a swimming pool if you have a few million to your name. Greener pastures are 20 minutes away by train or bus.

A few years ago, SOMA was in an economic rut, singing a sort of recession blues after the dot-com bust and financial meltdown. Tech startups were closing; planned skyscrapers were halted. In the aftermath of the recession, SOMA returned briefly to its art-gallery roots by hosting new studios and small theaters, but today it's humming again with big towers and big business. Salesforce.com, the city's largest tech employer, owns almost 10 office buildings in the neighborhood, with its newest coming soon to the new Transbay Terminal. The Salesforce Tower—the city's tallest building—should open by 2018.

If you live here, you'll likely spend more for housing than any other neighborhood's residents. That's a point of contention across San Francisco, where the housing crunch displaces families facing underhanded eviction efforts. From the perspective of developers, the more housing the better, so they're building faster and higher than ever—so high, in fact, that SOMA's height restrictions have been relaxed to accommodate the building frenzy: the old limit of 400 feet has been "upzoned" with the aim of boosting the housing supply to meet demand. Just how much of the housing will be "affordable," and by whose standards? That's the most pressing question in SOMA today. City voters passed an affordability law requiring new buildings to make a portion of new units affordable to middle- and low-income occupants (to learn more, see the **Finding a Place to Live** chapter).

Renovations are also nearing completion on SOMA's thriving museum scene. The San Francisco Museum of Modern Art (SFMOMA) is set to reopen in 2016 after a multi-year expansion and upgrade. The Museum of the African Diaspora, blocks away, is impressively renovated, beaming with strong programs after a $1.3 million redesign. The new Filipino Cultural Center and the new Mexican Museum, both coming to Mission Street, will contribute to SOMA's arts community, joining the nearby Contemporary Jewish Museum and Yerba Buena Center for the Arts.

But the Cartoon Art Museum, sadly, didn't survive the tech boom, as its rent doubled in 2015, forcing it to pack up and look elsewhere for space. It is the only museum on the West Coast devoted exclusively to cartoons, comics, and animation. If it is able to find funding and relocate, be sure to visit.

While this neighborhood has a growing community of bicyclists, you're more likely to step outside and see decked-out quasi-tank Hummers coasting down Mission Street at a cool 5 MPH—full volume, windows down. That's the atmosphere in SOMA today. The **South Park** section of the neighborhood is similarly

*SOMA*

industrial-chic but changing quickly. South Park originated in the mid-1850s as an upscale area with elegant English-style townhouses. It surrounds an oval European-style park between 2nd and 3rd and Bryant and Brannan streets, and was the first posh neighborhood in San Francisco. Today the park remains, but the mansions do not. Wealthy San Franciscans moved to newer neighborhoods after the 1906 earthquake and fire destroyed their homes, and in the ensuing years this area became more industrial than residential. By the late 1970s, photographers, graphic designers, and artists moved into the neighborhood, attracted by cheaper rents. In the 1980s a couple of restaurants tested the waters. In the 1990s some multimedia startups rented space in warehouses that had been converted into live-work spaces, creating what was known as "Multimedia Gulch." Bordering the park, you'll find excellent cafés and elegant restaurants near top tech startups and architecture and design firms.

Once a weedy wasteland of crumbling buildings and pothole-filled streets, **Mission Bay**—or **China Basin,** as it is called by old timers—is now the city's urban renewal heartland, with construction of condos, apartments, and office buildings, and the recently completed MUNI 3rd Street light-rail project, which connects the southeast neighborhoods (Visitacion Valley, Bayview, Mission Bay) to downtown San Francisco. Long one of the city's last underdeveloped outposts, Mission Bay is undergoing a legally challenged and complex multimillion-dollar upgrade—transforming more than 300 acres of abandoned rail yard to an ultramodern high-density urban hub—that will continue for years.

In the southwest corner of Mission Bay, the transformation is largely complete. A handful of tall condo complexes, luxury apartments, and glassy offices with ground-floor retail have sprung up in the once-vacant area between 3rd and 4th streets along King Street. The upscale restaurants, winding bay-front walkways and bike paths, and neatly manicured parks create an extension of the revitalized Embarcadero. Folks visit to watch the boats in the breeze at South Beach Harbor, walk along the fishing pier, and spot the Bay Bridge or a Giants game at AT&T Park.

Originally part of a larger waterway—a marsh and mudflat system that connected Mission Creek to San Francisco Bay—Mission Bay was crossed by Long Bridge, a wooden causeway (where 3rd Street is now). After the 1906 earthquake, rubble was dumped here, and the Southern Pacific Railroad settled in, using this area for its rail yards.

With its distinctly modern high-density flavor, the development of Mission Bay is a sample of San Francisco's new direction. Touted by its developers as one of San Francisco's "newest neighborhoods," Mission Bay will still take several years to truly come into its own, but those who enjoy an urban waterside setting with easy access to downtown nightclubs should feel at home. Newcomers looking for a neighborhood with a more residential feel will want to head elsewhere.

Buried amid the noise of all the new construction, and tucked under Interstate 280, is an old San Francisco gem, the **Mission Creek Marina**, host to a houseboat community: 20 floating homes and 35 small boats. Less affluent than

Sausalito's floating home communities, the tiny, tight-knit enclave that floats on Mission Creek is one of the city's hidden treasures. Mission Creek Park has been entirely restored and is now a haven for dog-owners living in the upscale condos that line the channel. A variety of birds call this area home, giving it the feel of a tiny island of nature amid new four- and five-story towering structures.

**Website**: www.sfgov.org

**Area Code**: 415, 628

**Zip Codes**: 94103, 94105, 94107

**Post Offices**: Bryant Station, 1600 Bryant St; Brannan St Station, 460 Brannan St, 800-275-8777, www.usps.com

**Police Station**: Southern Station, 850 Bryant St, 415-553-1373; main non-emergency number, 415-553-0123, www.sf-police.org

**Emergency Hospital**: San Francisco General Hospital, 1001 Potrero Ave, 415-206-8000, sfgh.ucsf.edu

**Library**: Mission Bay, 960 4th St, 415-355-2838, www.sfpl.org

**Public Schools**: San Francisco Unified School District, 555 Franklin St, 415-241-6000, www.sfusd.edu

**Community Resources**: Rincon Hill neighborhood blog, www.rinconhillsf.org; San Francisco Museum of Modern Art, 151 3rd St, 415-357-4000, www.sfmoma.org; Yerba Buena Center for the Arts, 701 Mission St, 415-978-2787, www.ybca.org; Cartoon Art Museum (possibly relocating in 2016), 415-227-8666, www.cartoonart.org; CounterPULSE, 1310 Mission St, 415-626-2060, www.counterpulse.org; Gene Friend Recreational Center, 6th and Folsom streets, 415-554-9532, www.sfrecpark.org; SOMArts Cultural Center, 934 Brannan St, 415-863-1414, www.SOMArts.org; California Historical Society, 678 Mission St, 415-357-1848, www.californiahistoricalsociety.org; AT&T Park (San Francisco Giants), 24 Willie Mays Plaza, 415-972-2000, www.sfgiants.com; UCSF Mission Bay Campus, 16th and Owens streets, www.ucsf.edu/mission-bay 415-476-9000; South Beach Harbor, The Embarcadero at Pier 40, 415-495-4911, www.southbeachharbor.com

**Public Transportation**: MUNI, 415-701-2311, TTY 415-701-2323, www.sfmta.com: *MUNI buses*: 9 San Bruno, 12 Folsom, 14 Mission, 15 3rd St, 26 Valencia, 27 Bryant, 30 Stockton, 45; *MUNI rail*: all routes along Market St and the new E-Embarcadero line and T line; *BART*: all trains along Market St; Transbay Bus Terminal for AC Transit, Sam Trans, Golden Gate Transit and Greyhound buses, on Mission St, between 1st and Fremont sts; *Caltrain Station* on 4th and King sts.

# MISSION DISTRICT

## MISSION DOLORES

**Boundaries: North and East:** Highway 101; **South:** Cesar Chavez (formerly Army) St; **West:** Valencia St

San Francisco's most coveted hotspot for sun-filled parks, stylish galleries, pop-up restaurants, and cultural festivals is the **Mission District**, whose pet-friendly coffee bars are tucked between hidden gardens, yoga studios, and hip clothing boutiques—all of which have multiplied in recent years. The cost of living has also multiplied, as have the luxury condos and reasons for moving here (or leaving here). The Mission is an increasingly popular destination for the city's high-paid tech workers, employed by companies like Facebook, Google, eBay, and Yahoo, whose double-decker commuter buses hurtle down narrow streets and stir debate over affordability for lower-income families. Consider, for example, that in 2012, Facebook founder Mark Zuckerberg moved into the neighborhood, buying a hilltop house for $10 million, just blocks from scenic Dolores Park.

Set against a backdrop of stately palm trees and rolling hills, Dolores Park is the city's liveliest hangout, with enough BBQs, bicycles, Frisbees, oversized burritos, and outdoor movies to make it a picnicker's paradise. The park is wrapping up a multiyear renovation to modernize the tennis and basketball courts, swing sets, and irrigation system.

Overlooking the park's grassy slopes is Mission Dolores Church, the city's oldest surviving structure, dating to the late 1700s. Turn two blocks east, and Valencia Street welcomes you with bustling lines outside high-end bakeries and gourmet pizzerias—a scene so popular that even whispering the h-word ("hipster," shhh) is likely to earn you a local's knowing glance.

Another block east, Mission Street, is a dividing line between tech-centered gentrification (on the west side) and, on the east side, the deeply rooted Latino community that's a hub of creative street fairs, neighborhood coalitions for social justice, discount clothing stores, and fruit stands a fraction of the cost of the nearby Whole Foods. The further east you live, the quieter, less expensive, and more Spanish-speaking the experience. With the influx of highly paid tech workers, however, the neighborhood's housing prices have soared, and longtime

*Mission District*

residents are leaving. The Latino population has dropped by somewhere between 20 and 40 percent over the past decade—even though Latino residents were half of the Mission's population 15 years ago. It's a contentious topic in the Mission. This neighborhood is ground zero for housing battles in the Bay Area today, as the Mission has seen just 2 percent net growth of below-market-rate housing, and a tidal wave of new luxury condos. In 2014 the mayor officially designated the Mission the "Latino Cultural District." Still, the Mission's median home prices jumped almost 150 percent from 2011 to 2015, quickening the displacement.

Wherever you live in the Mission, you'll spot almost 500 colorful murals adorning the buildings, adding a backdrop of artistic activism to the land- scape. Many locals see a connection between the rising costs, demographic shift, anti-displacement protests, and targeted violence, much of it gang-re- lated—a rough reality that many newcomers seem to tune out. The eco- nomic and cultural contrasts abound in this compact neighborhood.

The neighborhood is one of the few in San Francisco on the subway line—BART stations are on 16th and 24th streets—making the commute easy in all directions. And the biggest draw is the fashionable food culture,

*Mission District*

which has recently attracted commercial walking tours. The neighborhood's changing personality is summed up by do-it-yourself everything: small-batch chocolatiers, designer ice-cream shops, create-your-own-bicycle studios, and crème brûlée stands.

A new Thursday farmers' market, at Bartlett and 22nd streets, connects farmers to the Mission's "foodies"—another buzzword that's both proudly claimed and disowned by locals. The market pulls in local musicians who supply blues and country music to the outdoor vendors.

One of the liveliest community events is a bimonthly block party called Mis- sion Arts Performance Project (MAPP). Along Folsom between 22nd and 23rd streets, the sprawling get-together attracts diverse groups of musicians, dancers, and painters in living rooms and garages. The festival is a beloved symbol of the Mission's pride in community; it's run by the Red Poppy Art House, a nonprofit that's unfazed by the growing challenges of sustaining an independent arts scene. A few years ago, San Francisco's oldest nonprofit art space, Intersection for the Arts, shut its doors and left the neighborhood. But community centers like the Red Poppy Art House are proving resilient.

Historically, the Mission gets its name from the sixth Alta California mission, which started in the late 1700s as part of an evangelizing effort to spread Chris- tianity among Native Americans. The original building still stands, at 3321 16th Street. It's a monument made famous by Alfred Hitchcock's film *Vertigo*, which sets one of its climactic scenes there.

Today, many signs of local history are obscured: you'd never know that

Dolores Park, pleasant and cheery, used to be a cemetery, or that a zoo and conservatory occupied a two-block stretch of Valencia Street in the nineteenth century. Nor would you know that California's first professional baseball stadium stood at Folsom and 25th streets, now a public park. After the Gold Rush, the Mission became home to working-class immigrants from Ireland, Germany, Italy, Mexico, and the American South. Families struggled to plant roots here in spotty conditions—a far cry from the chic lofts, pricy flats, luxury condos, and elegant Victorians dotting today's neighborhood.

If one theme characterizes the Mission now, it's the coexistence of disparate communities. Flourishing boutiques and designer shops sit side by side with community centers for social justice, including the Women's Building on 18th Street, an iconic landmark. Students with rolled yoga mats ride fixed-gear bicycles past older couples wiring their wages to relatives in Guatemala, El Salvador, and Nicaragua. The tech-company commuter shuttles are constantly in the headlines, and are occasionally met by street protestors demanding that the companies pay higher local taxes.

It's no wonder that the Mission is an enviable, if divided, neighborhood. Conveniences are walkable, the weather is temperate, the parks are well maintained, and the social calendar is packed.

**Websites**: www.sfgov.org, www.sfmission.com, www.missionlocal.org
**Area Code**: 415, 628
**Zip Code**: 94110, 94103
**Post Office**: Mission Station, 1198 S Van Ness Ave; Potrero Center, 1655 Bryant St, 800-275-8777, www.usps.com
**Police**: Mission Station, 630 Valencia St, 415-558-5400, TTY 415-431-6241, main non-emergency number, 415-553-0123, www.sf-police.org
**Emergency Hospital**: San Francisco General Hospital, 1001 Potrero Ave, 415-206-8000, www.sfghf.org
**Library**: 300 Bartlett St, 415-355-2800, www.sfpl.org
**Public Schools**: San Francisco Unified School District, 555 Franklin St, 415-241-6000, www.sfusd.edu
**Community Resources**: Red Poppy Art House, 2698 Folsom St, 415-826-2402, www.redpoppyarthouse.org; Mission Community Market, Bartlett at 22nd sts, www.missioncommunitymarket.org; Mission Neighborhood Centers, 362 Capp St, 415-206-7752, Mission Cultural Center, 2868 Mission St, 415-643-5001 (offers classes in dance, art, and more), www.missionculturalcenter.org; Women's Building, 3543 18th St , 415-431-1180, www.womensbuilding.org; Inner Mission Neighbors, 2922 Mission St, www.innermissionsf.com; Precita Eyes Mural Arts and Visitor Center, 2981 24th St, 415-285-2287, www.precitaeyes.org; Mission Merchants Association, www.sfmission.com; Mission Economic Development Association (MEDA, offering free financial guidance to low-income families), 3505 20th St, 415-282-3334, www.medasf.org; Roxie

Theater, 3117 16th St, 415-863-1087, www.roxie.com; Dolores Park, www.doloresparkworks.org

**Public Transportation**: MUNI, 415-701-2311, TTY 415-701-2323, www.sfmta.com: *MUNI buses*: 55 16th St, 9 San Bruno, 12 Folsom, 14 Mission, 22 Fillmore, 26 Valencia, 27 Bryant, 33 Ashbury-18th, 48 Quintara, 49 Mission, 53 Southern Heights, 67 Bernal Heights; *BART*: 16th St Station and 24th St Station

# THE CASTRO

**CORONA HEIGHTS**
**DUBOCE TRIANGLE**

**Boundaries: North and West:** Market St; **East**: Dolores St; **South**: 22nd St

Like the rainbow flag soaring above this historically hip neighborhood, **the Castro**'s identity is instantly recognizable, colorful, and welcoming. As the birthplace of the national gay rights and transgender rights movements, the Castro is so influential that to live here is to step inside a consciousness-raising revolution. This is where Harvey Milk, in 1977, became the country's first openly gay elected politician; where gay bar-goers forged a climate of pride, acceptance, and visibility; where the first museum of gay and transgender history opened a few years ago; where the city showed up to get down on party night when same-sex marriage was ruled legal by the US Supreme Court in 2015. But the Castro isn't just where parades are held and victories won. This is also where defeats have been suffered, lives lost, and blood shed in traumatic clashes with police over the decades. For newcomers of all gender and sexual identities, the Castro is San Francisco's most cohesive, bustling community.

It's also a judgment-free zone. This is party central, where *oontz-oontz* nightclubs attract locals and tourists alike. Bars are so packed that people spill onto the sidewalks, recently prompting the city to widen the sidewalks. Other landscape changes include new rainbow-painted crosswalks for pedestrian safety, as well as walk-of-fame plaques honoring gay-rights leaders. The sidewalks also boast new etchings of gay-rights breakthroughs, including same-sex marriage victories. No patch of pavement is more important than the southeast corner of 18th and Castro streets, where photo collages memorialize beloved community figures.

Wander along Castro Street today

*The Castro*

from 18th to Market streets, and you're at the center of designer boutiques, stylish sex-video shops, trendy eateries, lively coffeehouses, and the new offices of the San Francisco AIDS Foundation, next to the 24-hour Walgreens pharmacy. Store names skew toward the obvious: the Sausage Factory, Hand Job Nail and Spa, Moby Dick, Rock Hard. There's no denying the Castro's empowering openness, which can be traced to the 1970s, when gay men (not as many women at the time) moved into this neighborhood. Many of them were sailors who'd been kicked out of the Navy because of their sexual orientation. Many moved here, encountering struggle and setback before—and after—Harvey Milk's rise into public office. Milk was dubbed "the unofficial Mayor of Castro Street." The Castro has seen historic clashes with police, most famously when they orchestrated a violent baton-swinging raid on a gay bar where the popular Harvey's now is. The assassination of Harvey Milk, one year after his election, hit the Castro like an earthquake. More than 70,000 people showed up in silent mourning at City Hall on the night of Milk's slaying.

Today, there is an ongoing question about whether the Castro is becoming "less gay." A recent survey showed that more heterosexual newcomers come to the Castro than ever before—a sign that gay newcomers feel increasingly safe in neighborhoods throughout the city, not just the Castro. It's also a sign that heterosexual newcomers feel at home in the nation's most famous "gayborhood" (as it is nicknamed locally).

Housing prices, however, are less welcoming. The Castro was the second-most competitive neighborhood for homebuyers in the United States in 2015, according to real estate website Redfin. Each house for sale attracts at least three offers, and more than 25 percent are sold in all cash. Airbnb has taken a chunk of rentals off the local market, so finding that perfect place can be a challenge. Newcomers tend to stay for the long haul, leaving few vacancies. If you don't mind sharing, consider pooling with a few housemates to rent a medium-size Victorian, or find a room in an established household. The Castro boasts some of the city's most beautifully maintained homes, including dozens of Victorian cottages, rows of two- and three-story Edwardians, and a handful of 1920s stucco flats.

Recently, Jane Warner Plaza, along Market Street, was permanently barricaded from cars and transformed into a plaza with patio seating. It has been redesigned with new lighting, chairs, art, and entertainment, including flowerbeds in the barrier protecting the parklet from cars. There's a new Whole Foods nearby, and a new senior center for gay and transgender elders needing housing assistance. The beloved health center Magnet—a resource for gay and trans men—is moving around the corner from 18th to Market streets. Lyric, a revered resource for at-risk LGBT youth, is at 127 Collingwood St (415-701-6150, www.lyric.org).

More than half of the Castro's merchants also live here—so the neighborhood is a close-knit community. The Castro Theatre is a stunning landmark, an ornate movie palace showing new and vintage films—built in 1922, it still has the Wurlitzer organ that is played before shows.

In 2011, after the economic collapse, this neighborhood was still struggling commercially. A Different Light Bookstore, which specialized in lesbian and gay literature for 26 years, closed. So did several other businesses. The recovery was slow at first, but the Castro has bounced back. Still in business, roaring along, is Cliff's Variety hardware store, a beloved family-run institution.

*The Castro*

Walk across Market Street, the northern boundary of the Castro, and you're stepping into the **Corona Heights** area. A kind of bedroom community for the Castro, Corona Heights has elegant Victorian homes along steep and narrow streets. A selection of contemporary apartments can be found in this area, many of them with sweeping views of the southeastern section of the city and the Bay. Rentals are rare in this upscale section. Turnover is slower here than in some areas of the city, as people who put down roots tend to stay.

Twin Peaks shelters Upper Market and the Castro, keeping the fog away, and many of these homes have sun decks. Kids come from all over the city to visit the Randall Museum, on Museum Way in Corona Heights, which features an earthquake exhibit, live animals, art and science programs, films, lectures, concerts, and plays.

Also to the north, the three-way intersection of Market, Duboce, and Castro streets forms **Duboce Triangle**, a small, busy, and increasingly popular neighborhood. Duboce Triangle lets you break away from the Castro's nightlife commotion while still being (or feeling like you are) in the Castro. In 2015 this tiny neighborhood witnessed the most expensive condo sale in its history—$2.63 million—almost a million more than the asking price. Rents have gone up more in Duboce Triangle than any other neighborhood in San Francisco, rising 52 percent in one year recently. The tech boom continues.

**Website**: www.sfgov.org
**Area Code**: 415, 628
**Zip Code**: 94114, 94110
**Post Office**: 18th St Station, 4304 18th St, 800-275-8777, www.usps.com
**Police Station**: Mission Station, 630 Valencia St, 415-558-5400, TTY 415-431-6241,
    main non-emergency number, 415-553-0123, www.sf-police.org

**Emergency Hospitals**: San Francisco General Hospital, 1001 Potrero Ave, 415-206-8000, www.sfghf.org; California Pacific Medical Center, Davies Campus, Castro and Duboce sts, 415-600-6000, www.cpmc.org

**Library**: Noe Valley Branch, 451 Jersey St, 415-355-5707, www.sfpl.org

**Public Schools**: San Francisco Unified School District, 555 Franklin St, 415-241-6000, www.sfusd.edu

**Community Resources**: Castro Theatre, 429 Castro St, 415-621-6120, www.castrotheatre.com; Eureka Valley Recreation Center, 19th and Collingwood sts, 415-831-6810, www.sfparksalliance.org; Randall Museum, 199 Museum Way, 415-554-9600, www.randallmuseum.org; Castro/Eureka Valley Neighborhood Association, www.evpa.org

**Community Publications**: *Bay Area Reporter*, www.ebar.com; San Francisco Bay Times, www.sfbaytimes.com; *Mister SF*, www.mistersf.com

**Public Transportation**: MUNI, 415-701-2311, TTY 415-701-2323, www.sfmta.com: *MUNI buses*: 24 Divisadero, 33 Ashbury-18th, 35 Eureka, 48 Quintara-24th; *MUNI rail*: F-Market, J-Church, K-Ingleside, M-Oceanview; Shuttle: S-Castro to downtown; *BART*: 24th St Station

## NOE VALLEY

**Boundaries: North**: 22nd St; **East**: Dolores St; **South**: 30th St; **West**: Diamond Heights Blvd

Surrounded by hills, filled with sun, and envied by almost every other San Francisco neighborhood, this picturesque oasis of upscale shops and stroller-friendly sidewalks is a family haven—so pleasant that it is many newcomers' top choice for raising kids, if you can afford to move here. Odds are you can't. **Noe Valley** recently became one of the city's most competitive areas, with almost 90 percent of homes selling above asking price. The neighborhood's growing popularity can be traced to its cozy gardens, walkable conveniences, cheerful smiles, fogless parks, and easy access to downtown and the South Bay.

*Noe Valley*

The nickname for Noe Valley—"Stroller Valley"—is so commonly heard that it's an eye-roller to locals, but it fits: the daily parade of parents with strollers moves up and down 24th Street, patronizing the designer toy stores, dessert counters, and home-décor boutiques. It's a breeze for newcomers to stock up and settle in

*Noe Valley*

without leaving the neighborhood. The community is proud of its self-contained atmosphere, which feels removed from the city, even though it's a short walk to Mission nightlife. Amenities, seclusion, safety, and tranquility give Noe Valley its banner appeal—and its soaring prices.

Not long ago, Noe Valley was runner-up in San Francisco's word-of-mouth contest between family-friendly neighborhoods—trailing its crosstown rival, Pacific Heights. Today Noe Valley's unassuming charm is preferred over Pacific Heights' formal elegance. Noe Valley's biggest change—and the cause of cost jumps—is summed up by this line in housing ads: "Proximity to tech shuttles—right this way."

Is that a turn-on or turnoff? It's appealing to the tech newcomers commuting to Silicon Valley, but it's a sore point for locals wary of the rising tech wealth inching their way. Community leaders are skeptical of tech dollars flooding this tight-knit neighborhood and displacing favorite local businesses. Case in point: recently, a profitable shoe-repair shop and cherished Noe Valley landmark, in business for more than 70 years, was squeezed out—as were a hardware store, music-instrument store, record store, and two bookstores (a third remains). More commercial development is underway.

Consider this recent headline from the *Noe Valley Voice* newspaper: "Is Noe Valley at Risk of Losing Its Charm?" Local opinion is split, but local charm is abundant. Recent proposals for retail expansion include a 3,345-square-foot four-unit project, a five-unit commercial conversion of a residential home, and a five-story mixed-use development.

Many of Noe Valley's popular landmarks haven't changed. There's the tranquil scene at Noe Children's Playground, shaded by pine trees and nestled under Twin Peaks, with a swing set, tennis court, basketball court, and dog run. Unlike other parks, this one is quiet, rarely home to competitive pickup games, and never a large crowd. It's a true respite.

The recent arrival of Whole Foods on 24th Street got mixed reviews when it replaced a less-famous market, but Whole Foods has since won local acceptance.

It's a convenient pairing to the farmers' market across the street on Saturdays, with live bluegrass music. Other perks include health-and-beauty spas, bagel stores, Irish pubs, and a British-style tearoom. The less-fashionable commercial strip, with mom-and-pop shops, is Church Street from 24th to 30th streets. It is famous for Drewes Brothers Meats, which has been here since 1889. And the Noe Valley Ministry is a Presbyterian Church that hosts classes and concerts, with themes that run from religious to jazz to classical.

**Websites**: www.sfgov.org, www.noevalley.com
**Area Code**: 415, 628
**Zip Codes**: 94114, 94131
**Post Office**: Noe Valley Station, 4083 24th St, 800-275-8777, www.usps.com
**Police Station**: Mission Station, 630 Valencia St, 415-558-5400, TTY 415-431-6241, main non-emergency number, 415-553-0123, www.sf-police.org
**Emergency Hospitals**: San Francisco General Hospital, 1001 Potrero Ave, 415-206-8000, www.sfghf.org; California Pacific Medical Center, Davies Campus, Castro and Duboce sts, 415-600-6000, www.cpmc.org
**Library**: Noe Valley Branch, 451 Jersey St, 415-355-5707, www.sfpl.org
**Public Schools**: San Francisco Unified School District, 555 Franklin St, 415-241-6000, www.sfusd.edu
**Community Publication**: *Noe Valley Voice*, 415-821-3324, www.noevalleyvoice.com
**Community Resources**: Noe Valley Ministry, 1021 Sanchez St, 415-282-2317, www.noevalleyministry.org; Friends of Noe Valley, www.friendsofnoevalley.com; Natural Resources, 816 Diamond St, 415-550-2611, www.naturalresources-sf.com
**Public Transportation**: MUNI, 415-701-2311, TTY 415-701-2323, www.sfmta.com: *MUNI buses*: 24 Divisadero, 33 Ashbury-18th, 35 Eureka, 48 Quintara 24th; *MUNI rail*: J-Church, K-Ingleside, M-Oceanview; *BART*: 24th St Station

## GLEN PARK, DIAMOND HEIGHTS

**Boundaries: North**: Clipper St; **East**: Dolores St/San Jose Ave; **South:** Bosworth St; **West**: O'Shaughnessy Blvd

Long overlooked but quickly rising in popularity, **Glen Park** is a neighborhood to watch—worth considering for its wooded roads and steep, curved hills that frame a windswept canyon high above the city. It's nestled between the more upscale Noe Valley to the north (which is more competitive for housing) and the more artistically eclectic Bernal Heights to the east. Glen Park is quieter than both—and more affordable by far, despite early signs of "Glentrification," as the locals call it. As San Francisco's housing crisis escalates, it's surprising that this rustic neighborhood has escaped newcomers' radars for so long, but that's starting to change. Today this neighborhood is an underrated "sleeper" that's just woken up: couples run their dogs and toss balls in the hilltop parks, while slow-paced storefronts retain a fuss-free warmth. If hidden cottages and mountainside hikes with 360-degree views are what you're after—with none of the showmanship and fashion of Noe Valley—Glen Park is worth exploring.

A car is definitely helpful with the hills, but it's not essential, as the BART station is steps away. An annual festival comes to life on the hilltop. So far, the city's high-paid tech crowd seems to consider Glen Park a runner-up to the more fashionable neighborhoods, so the wheels of wealth haven't yet turned in Glen Park's direction. But they're starting to. A telling sign of the neighborhood's impending transformation is the flashy housing that's popped up next to older cottages. The new look: green modernism, with floor-to-ceiling windows, an electric charging station in two-car garages, drought-tolerant landscaping, and energy-friendly features. But that's not the norm in rustic Glen Park, and most residents are content with keeping the neighborhood less trendy and more laid back.

The shopping strip around Chenery and Diamond streets is more of a pleasant blip than a full-service selection. It's a sleepy, small stretch (blink, and you'll miss it), with cafés, a bar, and an independent market, where diverse groups prepare to trek uphill. Café conversations range from which jazz trio played the bookstore a block away, to chatter about the recent neighborhood proposal to convert garages into residential housing. (If passed, that proposal would add hundreds of in-law units to Glen Park.)

What sets this neighborhood apart is topography—jagged, sprawling, and wild. When people think of Glen Park, they tend to think Glen *Canyon* Park, which is in the neighborhood, and is the second-largest park in San Francisco—a rare treat for a city not known for untouched frontiers. With 70 acres, the canyon began as a eucalyptus grove in the 1850s, but was replaced by the nation's first dynamite factory (the factory exploded in the 1860s). It then became an amusement park—with a bowling alley, hot-air balloon rides, a tightrope walker, and a zoo.

Today the park doesn't need to try so hard, as its natural, sweeping beauty lures sunbathers and bird-watchers, with hawks soaring above the canyon and the creek.

Before the 1906 earthquake, Glen Park was a faraway patch of dirt roads, wetlands, and ranches inhabited by dairy farmers. After, as fires blazed downtown, residents ran for the hills. When the first streetcar reached the area, Glen Park finally became a viable choice for the working class. Highway 280 was built in 1957, cementing Glen

*Glen Park, Diamond Heights*

*Diamond Heights*

Park's reputation as the convenient retreat that it still is. Though growing quickly, it's off the beaten path.

The hilltop residential neighborhood of **Diamond Heights**, adjacent to Glen Park, is similarly up-and-coming—it was named the safest neighborhood in the city in 2015, according to citywide statistics. This sound bite is sure to drive costs up a bit. Below-market-rate rent can still be found here, despite the rule of thumb that says the higher the elevation the higher the price. Overlooking Noe Valley, Diamond Heights contains rows of apartment complexes, a no-frills Safeway shopping center, and dizzying views of city lights and the Bay. Parking is not a problem. And if you like fog and wind, you'll have no shortage of both. Although BART is not accessible, buses are an option; still, a car is best. Streets are named after precious stones—Turquoise, Jade, Topaz, Quartz, Amber, and others, a reflection of the rugged, rural landscape framing this hilly neighborhood. Across Market Street, to the north, sit the looming Twin Peaks. Climb up on clear days to view the snow-capped Sierra Nevada mountain range, 200 miles to the east. Nearby Sutro Tower is used by television and radio stations to beam their signals—at 981 feet, it is the tallest structure in the city.

**Website**: www.sfgov.org

**Area Code**: 415

**Zip Code**: 94131

**Post Office**: Diamond Heights Station, 5262 Diamond Heights Blvd, 800-275-8777, www.usps.com

**Police Station**: Ingleside Station, 1 Sergeant John V. Young Lane, 415-404-4000, TTY 415-404-4009; main non-emergency number, 415-553-0123

**Emergency Hospitals**: San Francisco General Hospital, 1001 Potrero Ave, 415-206-8000, www.sfghf.org; St. Luke's Hospital, 3555 Cesar Chavez St, 415-647-8600, www.stlukes-sf.org

**Library**: Glen Park Branch, 2825 Diamond St, 415-355-2858, www.sfpl.org

**Public Schools**: San Francisco Unified School District, 555 Franklin St, 415-241-6000, www.sfusd.edu

**Community Resources**: Glen Park Association, P.O. Box 31292, 94131, 415-908-6728; Glen Park Recreation Center, 70 Elk St, 415-337-4705; Diamond Heights Community Association, P.O. Box 31529, 94131; Friends of Glen Canyon Park, 140 Turquoise Way, 94131, 415-648-0862; Glen Canyon Park, O'Shaughnessy Blvd and Bosworth St, 415-831-2700

**Public Transportation**: MUNI, 415-701-2311, TTY 415-701-2323, www.sfmta. com; *MUNI buses*: 23 Monterey, 26 Valencia, 35 Eureka, 44 O'Shaughnessy, 52 Excelsior; *MUNI rail*: J-Church line; *BART*: Glen Park Station

# POTRERO HILL

### DOGPATCH

**Boundaries: North**: 15th St; **East**: San Francisco Bay; **South**: Cesar Chavez St; **West**: Highway 101

Perched atop this hillside neighborhood and surrounded by wooded walkways are century-old homes with startling views of the downtown skyline from almost every corner. Much like the Mission, its neighbor to the west, **Potrero Hill** is one of the sunniest districts in the city, as the fog rarely makes its way this far south and east. It's also one of the safest during earthquakes. The hill barely budged during the 1906 quake that rocked much of the city. Today this hip district is a popular oasis for high-paid professionals and families taken in by the sleek condos converted from industrial warehouses. And no neighborhood in San Francisco offers easier commutes than Potrero Hill, as two major freeways and a Caltrain station are steps away, and three pedestrian-and-car bridges are being rebuilt and fitted with enhanced lighting and safety features.

If you decide to live here, be ready to climb. Potrero, which means "pasture" in Spanish, boasts steep streets, including the crookedest street in San Francisco (Vermont Street—not to be confused with Lombard Street, the tourist magnet across town). While the hill's terrain has kept shape, the community's character is rapidly changing. This change is marked by a frenzy of new offices and condos that have displaced hundreds of artists and students over the past few years. Once considered an affordable industrial district, the area

*Potrero Hill*

*Dogpatch*

is now among the priciest. Its ample lofts are being replaced by designer ware-houses and tech startups. Sleek apartments are up and running near Bryant and 16th Street, with more on the way around the corner. Several new arrivals, how-ever, are celebrated by community leaders, and are local themselves: Change.org, the social justice network, is headquartered here, and has been greeted warmly by neighbors. There's also KQED, the cherished radio and public media news website that calls Potrero Hill home.

The biggest change in this neighborhood is the closure of a heroic tenant: the *San Francisco Bay Guardian*, the most influential independent newspaper in California history. Formerly headquartered on Mississippi Street, the *Guardian* recently ceased operation after almost 50 years of hard-hitting journalism. The newspaper succumbed to sinking ad revenue and other factors, after a larger media company bought it and then pulled its plug. The *Guardian*'s legacy lives on in political debates and fiery yet friendly chatter in Potrero Hill's bars and cafés.

Another change is the departure of Metronome Ballroom, the celebrated dance hall on 17th Street, where it stood for 24 years before it was priced out to make way for a higher-profile ballet company. And the arts-supply store ARCH has closed after 13 years, another indication of the shifting landscape in a Potrero Hill better known for technology startups than offbeat artists. But not all devel-opments are hot topics here—some are cold, including the ice cream shop and other new eateries coming to 18th Street between Connecticut and Texas streets, the shopping corridor. "Corridor" is actually a bit of a stretch for this small blip of shops, which has the sleepiness of a rural town.

The neighborhood is alive by day, but lights-out at night—unless you're catching a rock show at the best small music venue in San Francisco, Bottom of the Hill. The club hosts big acts on a small stage. A warehouse behind this legendary nightclub is being demolished in favor of a new apartment complex, prompting questions about future noise complaints and culture clashes. Another local landmark is Thee Parkside [sic], a scrappy dive bar on 17th Street. But nowhere is the neighborhood's rhythm more casually observed than the coffee shop Farley's.

If you're planning to live here, keep in mind that the north slope is considered safer than the south slope. Two public housing projects on the south side have seen tough times, but the projects are being replaced by mixed-income housing with 1,700 units soon, part of a larger plan bringing 9,000 new units and 30,000 new residents. The complex will feature a 40,000-square-foot community center and 7 acres of open space. It's the former home of OJ Simpson, and murals of him are still visible.

Historically, Potrero Hill housed immigrants from Ireland, Scotland, Italy, and Russia, who worked at steel and iron plants, shipyards, and a sugar refinery. Traces of this heritage include the Russian church still standing on Carolina Street, and Slovenian Hall on Mariposa Street. The 1960s turned this district into an artists' and activists' hub, but the dot-com 1990s brought tech crowds. The Safeway shopping center currently on 16th Street is the site of former Seals Stadium, the ballpark where Joe DiMaggio got his start in the 1930s.

A fast-growing hotspot within the neighborhood is **Dogpatch**, on 3rd Street from Cesar Chavez to 16th Streets, an up-and-coming site of high-end residential development, with at least five major multifamily projects currently in progress. Some residents and housing groups fear that Dogpatch's transit developments won't keep pace with the condo construction, but that doesn't stop Dogpatch developers from building high and fast. Dogpatch was recently named the city's sixth safest neighborhood (yes, sixth is pretty good in San Francisco), and it's a center of the underground jazz scene. Plenty of tech workers and anyone else who can bankroll their way here are eying Dogpatch for sun, shelter from the fog, and a hip atmosphere. To learn more about Dogpatch, follow Dogpatch Now at www.facebook.com/dogpatchnow, and visit www.mydogpatch.org.

**Website**: www.sfgov.org

**Area Code**: 415, 628

**Zip Code**: 94107, 94110, 94124

**Post Office**: Brannan Street Station, 460 Brannan St, 800-275-8777, www.usps. com

**Police Station**: Bayview Station, 201 Williams St, 415-671-2300, TTY 415-671-2346, main non-emergency number, 415-553-0123, www.sf-police.org

**Emergency Hospital**: San Francisco General Hospital, 1001 Potrero Ave, 415-206-8000, www.sfghf.org

**Library**: Potrero Branch, 1616 20th St, 415-355-2822, www.sfpl.org

**Public Schools**: San Francisco Unified School District, 555 Franklin St, 415-241-6000, www.sfusd.edu

**Community Publication**: *The Potrero View Newspaper*, 2325 3rd St, Suite 344, 415-626-8723, www.potreroview.net

**Community Resources**: Potrero Hill Neighborhood House, 953 DeHaro St, 415-826-8080, www.phnhsf.org; Potrero Hill Family Support Center, 415-795-3591, www.ymcasf.org; Potrero Hill Health Center, 1050 Wisconsin St, 415-648-3022

**Public Transportation**: MUNI, 415-701-2311, TTY 415-701-2323, www.sfmta.com: *MUNI buses and light-rail*: 10 Townsend, 3rd St T, 19 Polk, 22 Fillmore, 48 Quintara-24th St, 53 Southern Heights; *Caltrain*: 22nd St Station

# BERNAL HEIGHTS

**Boundaries: North**: Cesar Chavez St; **East**: Highway 101; **South**: Interstate 280/Alemany Blvd; **West**: San Jose Ave

In 2014, the artistic hilltop village of **Bernal Heights** grabbed global attention—whether locals liked it or not—when it was named "hottest neighborhood" in the United States by the real estate site Redfin. That's hardly news to longtime residents, who are proudly protective of the community's rustic charm, cozy gardens, and majestic views. With an easy commute in all directions, Bernal Heights is a family-centered retreat in the city's southern section, perched on a series of hills. Innovative eateries and boutiques are popping up (think Peruvian small plates and peach-lavender jam jars) alongside teashops and mom-and-pop storefronts. One of the clearest panoramas in San Francisco is found at the summit of this 440-foot-tall hill, with dazzling views of Noe Valley, the downtown skyline, and the Golden Gate Bridge.

For sights like these, be prepared to navigate narrow roads, snug sidewalks, and high costs. A few years ago Bernal Heights was considered "affordable" by San Francisco standards, but that's laughable (cryable?) now, with property values multiplying so fast that one apartment jumped 400 percent in rent in a single month in 2015—a news story that made international headlines. Rents overall are up 24 percent year-over-year, and home values are appreciating 14 percent annually.

*Bernal Heights*

However popular Bernal Heights is getting, it maintains a strong sense of independence, community activism, and unassuming warmth. In the 1960s, when the city proposed "redeveloping" (bulldozing) historic homes, locals rallied to derail the effort. Residents again banded together in the 1970s, stopping speculators from building on open space. Those same residents launched the beloved Bernal Heights Neighborhood Center, which today runs Fiesta on the Hill, a lively street party with a petting zoo, pumpkin patch, and several stages of music.

To get a feel for this community, wander along Cortland Avenue, the main hub, which feels like a pleasant mountain village. Hike up to the 26-acre park where joggers and kite-flyers run with blissed-out off-leash dogs. This park is host to an underground event called Bernal Heights Soapbox Derby, an unsanctioned race with homemade cars whose drivers, beer in hand, swerve down hairpin turns at 35 mph. The cars get clever, a reflection of this neighborhood's aesthetic: a lawn chair with wheels; a flame-shooting shopping cart; a two-person bobsled; a keg-mobile. Hundreds of spectators look on.

*Bernal Heights*

Though legally banned recently (again) and officially discontinued, rumor has it the event's not over yet.

San Francisco's oldest farmers' market is also in Bernal Heights. Founded in the 1940s, the Alemany market was part of a wartime effort to connect farmers with urban families. Today it is nicknamed "the people's market," drawing a diverse crowd on Saturday mornings for reliably ripe taro, young ginger, chestnuts, and sweet potato.

The setting is so serene that it's easy to imagine what things were like in the 1800s, when dusty pastures were grazed by goats, cows, and chickens. The first residents were Ohlone Native Americans, followed by Spanish and Mexican settlers, who lived in the region until the United States seized it in 1846. The 1906 earthquake was merciful to Bernal Heights, which has a strong bedrock foundation. Within a year, more than 500 new homes were built on the hill, attracting Italian and Irish dairy farmers and stonecutters. World War II brought a number of African-American and Asian-American families as well.

Even with today's high costs, Bernal Heights has been a community of artists and activists since the 1970s, when musicians, political cartoonists, and novelists bunked here. Bernal Heights is also the historic heartbeat of the city's lesbian community, rooted in the local bar Wild Side West. Adding to this area's cultural history is the Bernal Heights Outdoor Cinema, a crowd-pleaser (www.bhoutdoorcine.org). But the neighborhood's rural character is best felt not at any one bar or restaurant; it's felt by wandering the hills.

Architecturally, changes are happening, even if they aren't always obvious. San Francisco isn't known for basements, but in Bernal Heights, which has stringent codes against building up and modernizing facades, homeowners are building down, excavating space while maintaining period charm. The streets are lined with Victorian cottages, 1960s box-like homes, and modest bungalows. Other changes include the recently renovated library, now with an expanded children's area and designated teen room.

Though the streets are narrow, parking is usually not a challenge. Bus service in Bernal Heights is not as frequent or fast as in the neighboring Mission District. But this neighborhood is connected to the downtown area via MUNI and offers fast access to both 101 and I-280 for commuters.

To learn more about the neighborhood, visit the excellent locals' blog at bernalwood.wordpress.com, or stop by the Bernal Heights Neighborhood Center at 515 Cortland Avenue.

**Website**: www.sfgov.org

**Area Code**: 415, 628

**Zip Code**: 94110, 94112

**Post Office**: Bernal Heights Finance Station, 189 Tiffany Ave, 800-275-8777, www.usps.com

**Police Station**: Ingleside Station, 1 Sergeant John V. Young Lane, 415-404-4000, TTY 415-404-4009; main non-emergency number, 415-553-0123, www.sf-police.org

**Emergency Hospitals**: St. Luke's Hospital, 3555 Cesar Chavez St, 415-647-8600, www.cpmc.org/about/stluke; San Francisco General Hospital, 1001 Potrero Ave, 415-206-8000, www.sfghf.org

**Public Schools**: San Francisco Unified School District, 555 Franklin St, 415-241-6000, www.sfusd.edu

**Community Resources**: Bernal Heights Neighborhood Center, 515 Cortland Ave, 415-206-2140, www.bhnc.org; Alemany Farmers Market, 100 Alemany Blvd, 415-647-9423; the Writing Salon, 415-609-2468, www.writingsalons.com

**Public Transportation**: MUNI, 415-701-2311, TTY 415-701-2323, www.sfmta.com: *MUNI buses*: 9 San Bruno, 12 Folsom, 14 Mission, 23 Monterey, 24 Divisadero, 27 Bryant, 49 Van Ness-Mission, 67 Bernal Heights

# EXCELSIOR, MISSION TERRACE/OUTER MISSION, CROCKER AMAZON, INGLESIDE, VISITACION VALLEY, PORTOLA

**Boundaries:** Excelsior: **North**: Alemany Blvd; **East**: McLaren Park; **South**: Geneva Ave; **West**: Mission St; Mission Terrace/Outer Mission: **North** and **West**: Interstate 280; **East**: Mission St; **South**: San Mateo County Line; Crocker Amazon: **North** and **West**, Mission St; **North** and **East**: Geneva Ave; **South**: San Mateo County Line; Ingleside: **North**: Monterey Blvd; **East**: Interstate 280; **South**: San Mateo County Line; **West**: 19th Ave; Visitacion Valley: **North**: Mansell St; **East**: Bayshore Blvd; **South**: San Mateo County Line; **West**: McLaren Park; Portola: **North**: Interstate 280; **East**: Highway 101; **South**: Mansell St; **West**: Cambridge to Silver to Madison

Given that San Francisco is not known for affordable housing, you'll be pleasantly surprised by the bargains in these up-and-coming neighborhoods in the southern section of the city—hidden gems that many longtime San Franciscans don't even know about. Affordability and a sense of local pride have finally put the **Excelsior** on the map—literally. This neighborhood wasn't on most maps of San Francisco until recently, when community leaders persuaded cartographers to change that. Today this cluster of neighborhoods is one of the least-expensive and least-gentrified frontiers in the city. Row upon row of pastel homes line the hills; as of this writing, its houses are 40 percent cheaper than homes in more popular San Francisco neighborhoods.

One of the most diverse spots in San Francisco, the Excelsior is home to multigenerational working-class families as well as students enrolled at nearby City College. Historic Italian and German delis sit next to Vietnamese cafés and Salvadoran restaurants on Geneva Avenue and Mission Street. Diversity is even evident in the street signs: streets running east-west are named for countries, and streets running north-south are named for cities. You can live at the intersection of Paris and France, Moscow and Russia, or Naples and Italy.

Breaking news in **Visitacion Valley** is that the 20-acre site of an old factory—abandoned since 1999—is being transformed into an entirely new neighborhood, with 1,700 low- and middle-income units, as well as parks, a community center, and a modern grocery store. That's enough housing for 3,800 additional residents. When the factory closed in 1999, the site was eyed by Home Depot, but neighborhood merchants thwarted the big-box store's plans, and the new apartments will stand as one of San Francisco's largest-ever housing complexes, on Bayshore Boulevard.

Visitacion Valley doesn't offer much nightlife, but it's near neighborhoods that do. The real appeal here is scoring relatively "cheap" rentals and home purchases. Victorian flats, townhouses, and duplexes are abundant, if modestly sized.

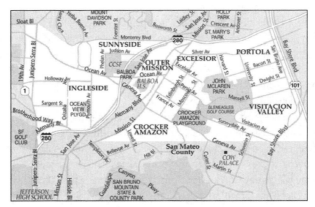

*Excelsior, Mission Terrace/Outer Mission,*
*Crocker Amazon, Ingleside, Visitacion Valley, Portola*

*Vistacion Valley*

In an effort to improve the neighborhood, one of the city's largest and most troubled public housing projects, Geneva Towers, was demolished in 1998. The 700-plus Sunnydale complex remains and continues to struggle with difficulties arising from gang activity. Challenges still plague the neighborhood, despite residents' efforts to make the streets safer. **Mission Terrace/Outer Mission** also contains hit-or-miss stuccos, duplexes, and townhouses, ranging from those that are immaculately tended to fixer-uppers. You might find a treasure in the form of an in-law tucked away in a backyard garden.

For natural outings, you've got the wilderness haven of McLaren Park, the second-largest park in San Francisco—with an amphitheater, golf course, ballparks, BBQ pits, and striking views of the skyline below, all the way to the Bay Bridge. Coyotes have taken a liking to the park, and how can you blame them? It's a pleasant spot. South of the park is the legendary Cow Palace, where the Beatles and hundreds of other big-name bands have played. The arena also hosts sports and boat shows, dog and cat exhibitions, car auctions, motorcycle races, tractor-pulls, and, true to its cowboy roots, an annual rodeo.

The hip headquarters for eating, dancing, and drinking is Mission Street from Cesar Chavez to 30th Street, which gets trendier by the minute. A few blocks away is Mitchell's Ice Cream (688 San Jose Avenue), the family-run institution where people from all around the Bay Area flock for famous flavors. Mitchell's is regularly voted "best ice cream parlor" in citywide polls.

The triangular-shaped **Crocker Amazon** sits directly south of the Excelsior. The Crocker Amazon Playground is a family-friendly weekend spot that's also home to San Francisco's first skateboard park. Crocker Amazon lines blur here with Daly City's own Crocker neighborhood boundaries. The only way to tell which city you're in is by the street signs—San Francisco's are white and Daly City's are blue.

While poised for popularity, Excelsior isn't quite there yet. It's had a rough history in spots. Street fighting and prizefighting were traditions in the past, when the neighborhood was celebrated for boxer and beloved community member

Lew Powell, California's lightweight champion in 1906. When boxing was banned in San Francisco, fighters and fans tiptoed over the county line to get their fix. In addition to athletic stardom, this community counts the Grateful Dead's Jerry Garcia as its native son. Jerry was born in the Excelsior and attended Balboa High School—as did accordion legend Carl Fortina, known for recorded scores to *The Godfather, How the West Was Won,* and *Hill Street Blues.*

Situated west of Outer Mission, **Ingleside** is a tangle of single-family homes built in the 1920s and '30s, and best known for the hilltop campus of the City College of San Francisco. Ingleside was home to one of the city's first racetracks, and today's Urbano Drive traces the old race courses. While not the safest area in the city, Ingleside is far from being the most dangerous—and it's slowly gentrifying, with a new Whole Foods on Ocean Avenue. There are a number of charming pockets along quiet streets with well-tended homes, green lawns, and sparse traffic.

Just north of Visitacion Valley, and south of Bernal Heights, is **Portola**, an area similar to Bernal Heights when it comes to housing, climate, and residential makeup. Portola has a rich Italian and Jewish heritage, much of which continues today, especially in the commercial street of San Bruno Avenue, the district's southern border with Visitacion Valley. Shopping tends toward the practical, including a butcher shop, mom-and-pop grocers, and flower shops. With McLaren Park nearby, there's plenty of open space for recreational activities.

Residents also enjoy an easy commute to downtown San Francisco to the north, and the shopping mall–rich suburbia of San Mateo County to the south. Buses run reliably along Mission Street, and the two local BART stations are Glen Park and Balboa Park.

**Website:** www.sfgov.org
**Area Code:** 415, 628
**Zip Codes:** 94112, 94134
**Post Offices:** Excelsior Station, 15 Onondaga Ave; Visitacion Valley, 68 Leland Ave; McLaren Station, 2755 San Bruno Ave, 800-275-8777, www.usps.com
**Police Station:** Ingleside Station, 1 Sergeant John V. Young Lane, 415-404-4000, TTY 415-404-4009; main non-emergency number, 415-553-0123, www.sf-police.org
**Emergency Hospital:** San Francisco General Hospital, 1001 Potrero Ave, 415-206-8000, www.sfghf.org
**Libraries:** Excelsior Branch, 4400 Mission St, 415-337-4735; Visitacion Valley, 45 Leland Ave, 415-355-2848; Portola, 380 Bacon St, 415-355-5660; Ingleside Branch, 1649 Ocean Ave, 415-355-2898, www.sfpl.org
**Public Schools:** San Francisco Unified School District, 555 Franklin St, 415-241-6000, www.sfusd.edu
**Community Publication:** *The Portola Planet,* www.portolaplanet.com; *Ingleside-Excelsior Light,* 415-215-4246, www.inglesidelight.com

**Community Resources**: Excelsior District Improvement Association, www.excelsiorsf.org; Visitacion Valley Children's Center, 325 Leland Ave, 415-585-9320; McLaren Park, Geneva and La Grande aves; Gleneagles International Golf Course, www.gleneaglesgolfsf.com

**Public Transportation**: MUNI, 415-701-2311, TTY 415-701-2323, www.sfmta.com: *Excelsior, MUNI buses*: 14 Mission, 29 Sunset, 43 Masonic, 49 Van Ness-Mission, 52 Excelsior, 54 Felton, *MUNI LRV*: J-Church, K-Ingleside, M-Ocean View; Crocker Amazon, *MUNI buses*: 14 Mission, 43 Masonic, 49 Van Ness-Mission, 88 BART shuttle; *Visitacion Valley, MUNI buses*: 9 San Bruno, 15 3rd St, 29 Sunset, 56 Rutland

# BAYVIEW/HUNTERS POINT

**Boundaries: North**: Highway 280; **East** and **South**: the Bay; **West**: Bayshore Blvd

After generations of economic decline that cast a cloud over this long-struggling neighborhood, **Bayview/Hunters Point** has risen faster and more ambitiously than any other San Francisco district in the past few years, relative to its challenges. A multibillion-dollar wave of investments has begun to transform this once-neglected area, and the signs of renewal are growing. Offering some of the warmest weather in San Francisco and easy access to the Peninsula and South Bay, Bayview/Hunters Point has started to hit its stride, thanks to the new light-rail line that carries passengers and economic opportunity into the neighborhood—part of a massive development effort. Google has pledged $3 million to a youth wellness clinic here, and is also in talks to build offices. Candlestick Park—former home of the 49ers—will soon be replaced by a 700-acre, $8 billion development project, including a 500,000-square-foot upscale shopping center and more than 6,000 new homes. Recently, a brand-new middle school, the Willie Brown Jr. Middle School (named after the former mayor), opened in a state-of-the-art facility.

*Bayview, Hunters Point*

Bayview/Hunters Point is a study in contrasts: boxy, brightly colorful two-story stuccos line the rolling hillsides with majestic views of the Bay, while a handful of exquisite Victorians hide away amid public housing projects in various states of upkeep. Tech-boom newcomers roam 3rd Street alongside families who trace their local roots decades deep, giving the area a mix of cultural and age demographics, predominantly African-American. Home prices have jumped nearly 60 percent in the past few years, but it's still less expensive in this neighborhood than anywhere else in the city. The median home price in Bayview/Hunters Point is 43 percent lower than the city's as a whole.

Plagued for years by some of the city's highest violent crime rates, Bayview/Hunters Point also struggles with health and environmental concerns resulting from its proximity to a power plant, a sewage treatment facility, and a former US Navy shipyard. A Saturday morning farmers' market at Galvez Avenue and 3rd Street is a blessing for residents who had complained about the lack of fresh produce and other healthy food options. For more than a decade, the biggest issue in Hunters Point, located in the area's southeast corner, had been the future of the 500-

*Bayview*

acre former naval shipyard. In 1867, Hunters Point became the first permanent dry dock on the Pacific Coast, and in 1939 the US Navy purchased the land for use as a dry dock and shipbuilding operation. During World War II, Hunters Point base, a ship repair yard, provided thousands of blue-collar jobs that helped send the first atomic bombs to Japan in 1945, and the Hunters Point/Bayview community boasted the highest percentage of home ownership in the city. But things slowed down in the 1960s and '70s, and in 1974 the shipyards were closed. In the decades since then, the city and the Navy were at odds over environmental cleanup and transfer of land. The Navy spent more than $100 million to help rid the area of toxins, but residents and city officials remain concerned about higher rates of cancer and asthma among children. In 2004, a major hurdle was cleared when both sides agreed to a plan to turn the land over to the city for development.

With residential and commercial expansions underway, city officials are pledging that new jobs will go to locals, driving economic growth and safety improvements. But local activists, especially in the African-American community, are concerned, and cleanup of the most polluted areas still needs to be completed. Residents debate whether the development will put low-income locals at risk of being priced out of their homes. Bayview/Hunters Point's thousands of families, including many seniors, are eager to improve the community, but are skeptical of gentrification from outside capital.

With lots of undeveloped space, Hunters Point has a surprising amount of wildlife. The stunning Candlestick Point Recreation Area—home to blue herons, possums, barn owls, seals, jackrabbits, foxes, raccoons, falcons, and red-tailed hawks—is popular with joggers and kayakers. Though still considered rough in many ways, Bayview/Hunters Point has made greater strides in the past few years than any other neighborhood in the city.

**Website**: www.sfgov.org

**Area Code**: 415, 628

**Zip Code**: 94124

**Emergency Hospital**: San Francisco General Hospital, 1001 Potrero Ave, 415-206-8000, www.sfghf.org

**Post Office**: Bayview Station, 2111 Lane St; Hunters Point: San Francisco Manual Processing Facility, 180 Napoleon St, 415-285-4647, www.usps.com

**Police**: Bayview Station, 201 Williams, 415-671-2300, TTY 415-671-2346, www.sf-police.org

**Library**: Bayview Branch, 5075 3rd St, 415-355-5757, www.sfpl.org

**Public Schools**: San Francisco Unified School District, 555 Franklin St, 415-241-6000, www.sfusd.edu

**Community Publications**: *San Francisco Bay View*, 4917 3rd St, 415-671-0789, www.sfbayview.com

**Community Resources**: Bayview Opera House, 4705 3rd St, 415-824-0386, www.bvoh.org (theater, dance, African-American center, aftercare and arts programs); Burnett Child Development Center, 1520 Oakdale Ave, 415-695-5660; SCRAP, 801 Toland St, 415-647-1746, www.scrap-sf.org; Center for Youth Wellness, 3450 3rd Street, Bldg 2, Suite 201, 415-684-9520, www.centerforyouthwellness.org; Leola M. Havard Early Education School, 1520 Oakdale Ave, 415-695-5660; Shipyard Trust for the Arts, Hunters Point Shipyard, Bldg. 101-1317, 415-822-0922; the Point, Hunters Point Shipyard, Building 101, 415-822-9675, www.shipyardtrust.org; Bayview/Hunters Point Community, www.hunterspointcommunity.com; Hunters Point Family, 1800 Oakdale Ave, 415-821-1534; Joseph Lee Recreation Center, 1395 Mendell St, 415-822-9040, www.sfrecpark.org; Candlestick Point State Recreation Area, Hunters Point Expressway, 415-671-0145, www.parks.ca.gov

**Public Transportation**: MUNI, 415-701-2311, TTY 415-701-2323, www.sfmta.com: *Light-rail*: T 3rd St. *MUNI buses*: 9 San Bruno, 19 Polk, 23 Monterey, 24 Divisadero, 29 Sunset, 44 O'Shaughnessey, 54 Felton

## SURROUNDING AREAS

Many Bay Area newcomers take one look at San Francisco's scenic hills and want to live here—and then one look at a typical asking price and roll back down the hill. San Francisco is the nation's most expensive renters' and homeowners' market, and even longtime locals are tripping over themselves in the jump to the East Bay, where things are less congested and less foggy. Many newcomers also prefer the peace and quiet of suburbs near an East Bay or Silicon Valley office. More than 7 million people live in the nine Bay Area counties of Alameda, Contra Costa, Marin, Napa, San Francisco, San Mateo, Santa Clara, Solano, and Sonoma. The Bay Area is projected to add 2.1 million people by 2040, creating a need for almost 700,000 new homes—so towns and cities beyond San Francisco are developing quickly. The counties are divided into four regions—**North Bay, East Bay, Peninsula,** and **South Bay**. The following profiles are not comprehensive, but they will help you launch your exploration of the greater Bay Area.

# NORTH BAY (MARIN, SONOMA, NAPA, SOLANO COUNTIES)

## MARIN COUNTY

Just north of San Francisco, across the Golden Gate Bridge, the pace is slower, the weather warmer, the coastline more majestic, and life more relaxed. With the Bay on the east and the Pacific Ocean on the west, Marin County's terrain is hilly and full of oaks, eucalyptus groves, and redwoods. Like San Francisco, Marin County is seeing an upswing in housing prices, fueled mostly by San Franciscans looking to buy homes north of the city. The current rise began at the end of 2012 and hasn't slowed. The average home in Marin County sells above its asking price. The farther north you go, the less expensive homes are, but the longer the commute into San Francisco. A new commuter rail system called SMART is slated for completion in late 2016 and will connect a cluster of towns running north and south—a possible sign that Silicon Valley's tech industry will jump north of San Francisco as well.

Wherever you live in Marin County, the beaches are exceptional, with very high marks for water quality (a perfect score recently from the water-quality ratings group Heal the Bay). Most of western Marin County is exhilarating, with wooded mountains that border the Pacific Ocean. From Sausalito all the way up to the Oregon state line, the windswept coastline zigs and zags, attracting sun worshippers who flock to Muir Beach and Stinson Beach—and who often clog Highway 1. Residents of Marin have one of the grandest views of the Bay Area; it is especially scenic when fog wraps around the Golden Gate Bridge. From Mount Tamalpais you can see for 100 miles in any direction. (For local hiking paths, see the **Hiking** and **Quick Getaways** sections.)

Marin County, like San Francisco, consistently ranks among the least affordable places in the nation. While the towns of Sausalito, Mill Valley, Tiburon, and Belvedere are the priciest in Marin, the towns further north—San Rafael, Corte Madera, and Novato—are slightly more affordable. With a population of 260,000, Marin County still consists largely (84 percent) of nature preserves, public lands, parks, and farms.

**Website**: www.marincounty.org

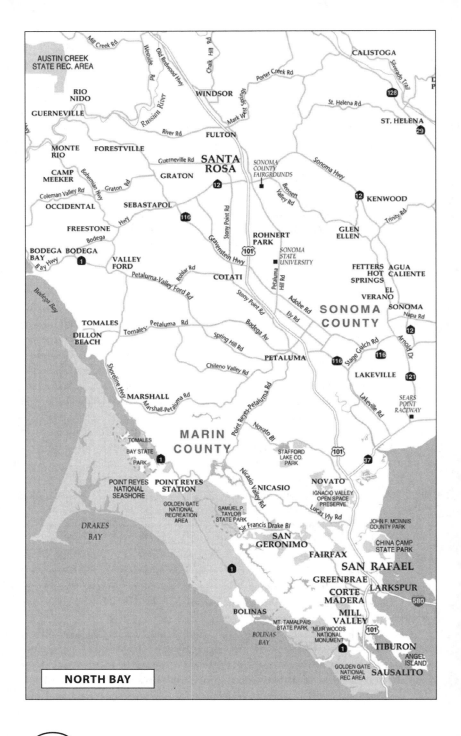

**NORTH BAY**

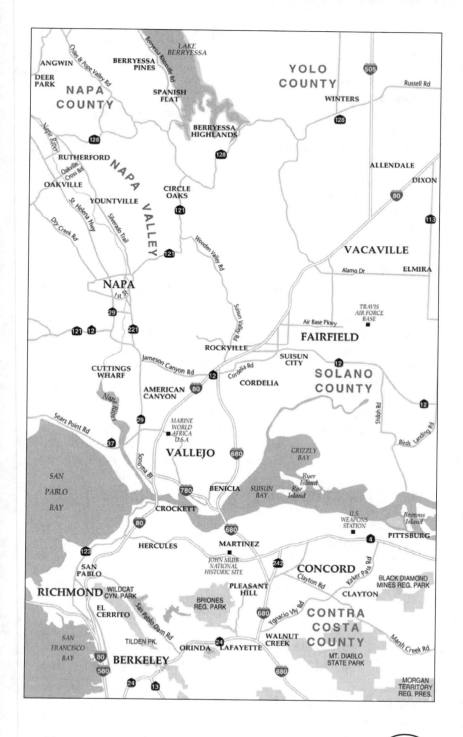

**Zip Codes**: 94965, 94941, 94920, 94901, 94925, 94945, 94930

**Area Code**: 415 and 628

**Sheriff**: Marin County Sheriff Department, 3501 Civic Center Drive, #145, San Rafael, 415-499-7250, www.marinsheriff.org

**Emergency Hospital**: Marin General Hospital, 250 Bon Air Rd, Greenbrae, 415-925-7000, www.maringeneral.org

**Library**: Main Branch, 3501 Civic Center Drive, #414, San Rafael, 415-499-6051, www.marinlibrary.org

**Public Schools**: Marin County Office of Education, 415-472-4110, www.marinschools.org

**Community Publications**: *Marin Independent Journal*, 150 Alameda del Prado, Novato, 415-883-8600, www.marinij.com; *The Ark Newspaper*, 1550 Tiburon Blvd, Tiburon, 415-435-2652; *The Coastal Post*, P.O. Box 31, Bolinas, 415-868-1600, www.coastalpost.com; Marin Scope Community Newspapers (*Mill Valley Herald, Ross Valley Reporter, Twin Cities Times, San Rafael News Pointer,* and *Marin Scope*), P.O. Box 1689, Sausalito, 94966, 415-339-8510, www.marinscope.com; *Novato Advance*, P.O. Box 8, Novato, 415-898-7084; *Pacific Sun*, 835 4th St, San Rafael, www.pacificsun.com, 415-485-6700; *Point Reyes Light*, P.O. Box 210, Point Reyes Station, 415-663-8404, www.ptreyeslight.com

**County/Community Resources**: Marin Services for Women, 415-924-5995; Bay Area Discovery Museum, Fort Baker, 557 McReynolds Rd, Sausalito, 415-339-3900; Marin Civic Center, Ave of the Flags, San Rafael, 415-499-7331; City of San Rafael Community Center, 618 B St, San Rafael, 415-485-3333; Golden Gate National Recreation Area, Fort Mason, Building 201, 415-561-4700, www.nps.gov/goga; Point Reyes National Seashore, Point Reyes, 415-464-5100, www.nps.gov/pore; Muir Woods National Monument, 415-388-2595; Mount Tamalpais State Park, 801 Panoramic Hwy, Mill Valley, 415-388-2070; Marin County Parks, 3501 Civic Center Dr Rm #260, San Rafael, 415-499-6387, www.co.marin.ca.us; Corte Madera Creek Watershed, 415-456-5052, www.friendsofcortemaderacreek.org

**Public Transportation**: *Golden Gate Transit*, 415-455-2000, www.goldengatetransit.org; *Blue & Gold Fleet*, 415-705-8200, www.blueandgoldfleet.com; *Angel Island Ferry*, 415-435-2131, www.angelislandferry.com; *RIDES for Bay Area Commuters*, 511

# SAUSALITO, MARIN CITY, MILL VALLEY, TIBURON, PETALUMA

Neatly tucked along a picturesque harbor just north of San Francisco, **Sausalito** is one of the Bay Area's most upscale and highly desirable towns, with sweeping views of the San Francisco skyline. The first town you'll see after crossing the Golden Gate Bridge, Sausalito has idyllic hillside homes stacked along curving, narrow roads. Down on the water, thousands of sailboats drift alongside 400 houseboats, some of which occasionally go on the market. Otis Redding popularized a local pastime with "(Sittin' On) The Dock of the Bay," which he wrote on a houseboat here in 1967. Today, what used to be an artists' enclave is commercialized by the crush of tourists mobbing the main street, Bridgeway. To avoid the crowds that congregate at the preciously high-end boutiques and souvenir shops, locals prefer to gather on Caledonia Street, one block east of the Bay. Away from the clicking cameras, residents enjoy an active community—from the Sausalito Women's Club, which works to improve the city, to the annual outdoor art festivals, gallery walks, yacht parties, and boardwalk games.

While San Francisco undergoes big changes in housing and culture, not much changes in Sausalito's community of proudly protective residents. When a proposal to expand the BART train system from San Francisco to Sausalito was floated, residents derailed it, worried that a local BART station would turn Sausalito into a tacked-on extension of San Francisco. Homeowners showed their pride and exclusivity by stopping a cellphone company from installing a signal-boosting antenna along the boardwalk, because the homeowners didn't want their million-dollar views of the Bay obstructed.

With a population of 7,200, Sausalito—"little willow" in Spanish—attracts new retirees and, especially today, tech executives. The community has luxurious Victorians, upscale cabins, and ranch-style houses on the hills. Many homes have gardens, and garages are at a premium. Median home prices are climbing fast, and rentals are rare and costly. Floating homes can be found in the five marinas. The community is characterized by a free-spirited '60s aesthetic; check out the Floating Homes Association's annual tour of 20 houseboats for a look. Locals commuting to San Francisco generally rely on the Sausalito Ferry or Golden Gate Transit.

Adjacent to Sausalito is **Marin City**, with far fewer residents (3,500), virtually no tourists, and much less wealth, making it a budget-friendly option. Marin City's first-ever community park has finally opened, with an amphitheater, movie nights, art installations, and a wall noting honored residents. In pop culture, this tiny city is known as the teenage home of rapper Tupac Shakur. Its first skatepark opened recently— front-page news in this low-income community eclipsed by hyper-affluent

*Sausalito*

Sausalito. Don't expect the prestige, press, or sparkle of nearby towns, as Marin City feels worlds apart—it's less developed, but its population is growing, and the easy commute to San Francisco can't be beat. With the exception of new condos on the hill, most housing is for rent down by the water.

Formerly a lumber town, **Mill Valley** has more available housing than Sausalito, and it's more diverse and less touristy. Situated northwest of Sausalito, at the foot of Mount Tamalpais, Mill Valley has an active downtown with charming amenities. The Depot Bookstore & Café is the town's heart, a gathering spot in an old train station smack in the center of town, where people chat with neighbors, or play chess or hacky sack. The square gives the community cohesion, as does the Mill Valley Market, which is ideal for hungry bikers and hikers. Just off of Highway 101 is Strawberry Village Shopping Center, with a supermarket, cafés, and boutiques. The Mill Valley Film Festival (www.calfilm.org), held each fall, has gained worldwide acclaim. It is held in the town of San Rafael. Mill Valley is also the starting gate for the region's best-known running event: the grueling, seven-mile Dipsea Race. *Smithsonian* magazine named Mill Valley the fourth-best small town in the nation recently, citing its picturesque scenery and enviable access to Mount Tam, Muir Woods, and San Francisco, as well as the local arts scene.

Many Craftsman and Victorian homes were built with exquisite redwood lumber alongside newer apartments, townhouses, and condos. With the housing boom currently racing up the coast from San Francisco, Mill Valley's residents are weary of overbuilding in this town of 14,000 people, and rallied together recently to reduce the new-unit plan from 384 to 193 in the next few years. If you can grab one, you'll have easy access to plenty of breathtaking hiking trails in the sun-soaked Marin Headlands—most enjoyably Tennessee Valley Trail, with its blackberry bushes, wild fennel, deer, and coyote.

Located 18 miles north of San Francisco, **Tiburon**—which means "shark" in Spanish—is even more upscale than Mill Valley and Sausalito, with homes priced well above Mill Valley's average. Unlike Sausalito, Tiburon is pleasant without being over-the-top precious; there's no trace of trumped-up tourist-trap T-shirt emporiums. The sophistication and serenity of Tiburon are natural, with tidy flower baskets dangling from elegant lampposts. Its population of 9,200 is larger than Sausalito's, but it's quieter here. Birds and fountains are the loudest sounds you'll hear on tiny Main Street, where car honking is unthinkable.

Tiburon juts out into the Bay, pointing the way to high-end homes on stilts along the hill. The Belvedere Peninsula has some of the fanciest homes in Marin County—many of them century-old stately mansions, and some with their own docks. Rentals are clustered on the east side, away from downtown; count yourself lucky if you score a unit with an outdoor swimming pool and hot tub on the lip of the Bay, dotted by sailboats and pelicans.

The ferry is many locals' first-choice commute to San Francisco, whose skyline is visible from the benches near the stone sidewalks. You can also catch the ferry to Angel Island, the largest island in the Bay—a 750-acre state park that is

*Mill Valley*

part wilderness and part former army base. More than 175,000 Chinese immigrants were interrogated and detained on the island in the early 1900s, when it was a checkpoint for enforcing the Chinese Exclusion Act, which prohibited Chinese from entering the country. Later, during the Cold War, nuclear missiles were based here. That history is thoughtfully told at the restored Immigration Station Museum—highly recommended for newcomers moving to this area.

Restaurants on Tiburon's Main Street, notably Sam's Anchor Café, are top social spots with outdoor patios that look onto the Bay. Tiburon recently launched its own film festival, www.tiburonfilmfestival.com, as well as a new concert series in the park. If you're a young professional looking for a singles scene, however, you won't find it here. The entire "downtown"—walkable in a matter of minutes—goes dark before 10 p.m. After that, deer tiptoe into the roads. Deer crossings before and after dusk are a signature sight in Tiburon—as are bicyclists on Paradise Loop and the path by Blackie's Pasture, along Tiburon Boulevard. If you want nightlife, seek it out in Fairfax or San Rafael.

The historic town of **Petaluma** is seven times more populous than Tiburon, and has more of a time-capsule feel than Santa Rosa, which is more modernized. About 32 miles north of San Francisco, Petaluma is a gateway to Sonoma County and San Francisco, which explains why *Travel & Leisure* magazine named it one of the nation's top-10 getaways near a major city. Petaluma is filled with Victorian homes, antique shops, country markets, and relaxed restaurants. There's a winemaking scene in the coastal hills to the west, and a waterway that connects the downtown with San Pablo Bay and then San Francisco Bay—both popular for sailing, kayaking, and fishing. Commuting by car to San Francisco can be a challenge, but it may be worth it just to live near tranquil farms tucked between old barns on picturesque, soft-green hills—with grazing horses and wandering elk.

## SAUSALITO
**Website**: www.ci.sausalito.ca.us
**Area Code**: 415, 628

**Zip Codes:** 94965, 94966
**Post Office:** 150 Harbor Dr, 800-275-8777, www.usps.com
**Police Station:** 29 Caledonia, 415-289-4170
**Library:** 420 Litho St, 415-289-4121, www.ci.sausalito.ca.us/library
**Parks, Gardens, and Open Space:** Parks and Recreation Department, 420 Litho St, 415-289-4152, www.ci.sausalito.ca.us
**Public Schools:** Sausalito Marin City School District, 630 Nevada St, Sausalito, 415-332-3190, www.sausalitomarincityschools.org

MARIN CITY
**Website:** www.marincitygov.org
**Area Code: 415, 628**
**Zip Codes:** 94965
**Post Office:** 150 Harbor Dr, 800-275-8777, www.usps.com
**Police Station:** 29 Caledonia, 415-289-4170
**Library:** 164 Donahue St, 415-332-6159, www.marinlibrary.org
**Parks, Gardens, and Open Space:** Community Services District, 630-332-1441, www.marincitygov.org/youth-recreation
**Public Schools:** Sausalito Marin City School District, 630 Nevada St, Sausalito, 415-332-3190, www.sausalitomarincityschools.org

MILL VALLEY
**Websites:** www.cityofmillvalley.org, www.millvalley.com
**Area Code:** 415, 628
**Zip Codes:** 94941, 94942
**Post Office:** 751 E Blithedale Ave, 800-275-8777, www.usps.com
**Police Station:** One Hamilton Dr, 415-389-4100
**Library:** Mill Valley Public Library, 375 Throckmorton Ave, 415-389-4292,
**Parks, Gardens, and Open Space:** Mill Valley Parks and Recreation, 180 Camino Alto, 415-383-1370, www.cityofmillvalley.org
**Public Schools:** Mill Valley School District, 411 Sycamore Ave, Mill Valley, 415-389-7700, www.mvschools.org

TIBURON
**Website:** www.ci.tiburon.ca.us
**Area Code:** 415, 628
**Zip Code:** 94920
**Post Office:** 6 Beach Rd, Tiburon, 800-275-8777, www.usps.com
**Police Station:** 1155 Tiburon Blvd, 415-789-2801
**Library:** 1501 Tiburon Blvd, Tiburon, 415-789-2665, www.bel-tib-lib.org
**Parks, Gardens, and Open Space:** Belvedere/Tiburon Recreation Department, 1505 Tiburon Blvd, Suite A, 415-435-4355, www.tiburon.org
**Public Schools:** Reed Union School District, 277A Karen Way, Tiburon, 415-381-1112, www.reedschools.org

**PETALUMA**
**Website**: www.cityofpetaluma.net
**Area Code**: 707, 628
**Zip Codes**: 94952, 94954, 94999
**Post Offices**: 120 4th St, 1601 Corporate Circle, 1150 McDowell Blvd, 800-275-8777, www.usps.com
**Police Station**: 969 N Petaluma Blvd, 707-778-4370
**Library**: 100 Fairgrounds Dr, 707-763-9801, www.sonoma.lib.ca.us
**Parks, Gardens, and Open Space**: Petaluma Community Center, 320 N McDowell Blvd, 707-778-4380
**Public Schools**: Petaluma City Schools District, 200 Douglas St, 707-778-4813, www.petalumacityschools.org; McDowell Elementary, 421 S McDowell Blvd, 707-778-4745; Sonoma County Office of Education, 5340 Skylane Blvd, 707-524-2600, www.scoe.org

# SAN RAFAEL

Situated north of Tiburon, **San Rafael** is the largest city in Marin County—and the oldest (it was founded in 1817). It's the county seat, and, to hear locals tell it, the cultural and economic capital of Marin. Compared to Sausalito and Mill Valley, rental housing here is slightly more plentiful and affordable. Architecturally, homes range from apartments to ranches, cottages, and Mediterranean villas. There are entire neighborhoods of Eichler homes. The Strand features 82 new homes on the waterfront—including condos, townhomes, and cottages—and boasts a new grocery store. And additional housing is coming to 2nd and B streets—a mixed-use residential and retail development with 41 rental homes.

Nestled beneath wooded mountains, San Rafael's claim to fame is the Marin County Civic Center, a national historic landmark designed in the 1960s by Frank Lloyd Wright. It was featured in George Lucas's *THX-1138* (look for the golden escalator). Fourth Street—San Rafael's main drag—also made its way onto the cinematic map, appearing in Lucas's *American Graffiti*.

The San Rafael-to-San Francisco commute via Highway 101 can be frustrating. Locals prefer the ferry or Golden

*San Rafael*

Gate Transit, as the ferry service is fast and scenic (board at the Larkspur Ferry Terminal). On the way out of Larkspur, the ferry passes San Quentin State Prison, as well as Alcatraz Island—the country's first military prison, which today is a tourist destination. But a lot of people who live here commute *within* the North Bay—between towns in Sonoma and Marin counties—rather than to San Francisco. In late 2016 the city will have two new train stations—part of the new SMART system (the acronym stands for Sonoma-Marin Area Rail Transit)—near Civic Center and downtown.

The community has exceptional senior housing and resources like Whistle Stop, which provides free transportation to seniors heading downtown. For crowds of all ages, San Rafael is a nightlife hub, lit up by the recent headline that Phil Lesh (of the Grateful Dead) opened a local club and restaurant—Terrapin Crossroads—where he often performs.

The city is also known for the Falkirk Cultural Center, a Queen Anne Victorian built in 1888, which hosts contemporary art exhibits, art classes, and poetry readings. Nearby you'll find the masterfully restored art-deco Smith Rafael Film Center. Called simply "the Rafael" by locals, the theater screens independent and art-house films, and plays host to the annual Mill Valley Film Festival (www.calfilm. org). With a thriving arts scene and an active nightlife set against the backdrop of pristine nature—without requiring its residents to fork over as much to live as they would in Sausalito—San Rafael is well worth exploring.

**Website**: www.cityofsanrafael.org
**Area Code**: 415, 628
**Zip Codes**: 94901, 94902, 94903
**Post Office**: 40 Bellam Blvd, San Rafael, 800-275-8777, www.usps.com
**Police Station**: 1400 5th Ave, 415-485-3000
**Library**: 1100 East St, San Rafael, 415-485-3323, www.srpubliclibrary.org
**Parks, Gardens, and Open Space:** San Rafael Parks and Recreation Commission, 618 B St, 415-485-3333, www.cityofsanrafael.org
**Public Schools**: San Rafael City Schools, San Rafael City Schools, 310 Nova Albion Way, San Rafael, 415-492-3200, www.srcs.org

## CORTE MADERA, LARKSPUR, NOVATO, HAMILTON, FAIRFAX

The slow-paced, stoic village of **Corte Madera**, which means "cut wood" in Spanish, is nestled between Mount Tamalpais to the west and Highway 101 to the east—and if you haven't heard of Corte Madera, that's just fine by locals, who prefer it calm, quiet, and restful. Slightly more affordable than higher-profile towns, this cozy spot is non-touristy, supremely friendly, and protective of its charm. In fact, residents are so content with the low profile that when a towering building with 180 apartments was constructed recently, controversy erupted. Locals likened it to a "monster." So it goes in this town of 9,300 people, who live for scenic walks through untouched nature. Five similar buildings have popped up alongside the first—the tallest towers in local history, prompting many residents, including the mayor, to question their fitness for Corte Madera's small-town character. Traffic is heavier these days, but the community remains overlooked by many Bay Area newcomers.

There's a historic square and two shopping plazas, but no official downtown. The hidden gem of Menke Park, formerly a railroad depot, is a tiny treat. And the independent bookstore Book Passage (51 Tamal Vista Boulevard) hosts literary events that draw crowds from around the Bay Area. The best commutes to San Francisco are the Larkspur Ferry or by car across the Golden Gate Bridge (half an hour).

Corte Madera and its neighbor, **Larkspur**, are the "Twin Cities," a short walk apart. Larkspur is bigger, with 12,000 people and more events around its elegant historic district on Magnolia Avenue. Leafy sidewalks frame Larkspur's library and city hall, which share a beige-and-red cottage with shingled rooftops. Picture colorful flowers and stained-glass windows against a mountain range in the distance, and you've got Larkspur. The cozy downtown is a protected treasure on the National Register of Historic Places. The town's cherished Lark Theater, an art-deco movie house from the 1930s, continues to offer sing-along nights. And a newly constructed middle school and multimillion-dollar upgrade to the police station are headlines in Larkspur, which is getting an influx of families fleeing San Francisco's housing crunch. Newcomers here are typically couples with kids, and wealthier seniors; very few single young professionals head this way.

Most housing is west of Highway 101, including the enchanting Madrone Avenue—a natural paradise that will leave you speechless. Towering above your driveway, the trees are enormous, their roots sprouting and spilling gracefully from the curbs. Some of the redwoods jut out like giants right in the middle of the street. Nearby, King Mountain Open Space has some of California's most exhilarating hiking trails. Look for the notebooks in zip-top bags—they are full of hikers' poetic comments, many of them heartwarming, some heartbreaking. You'll also

*Corte Madera*

discover the farmers' market in Larkspur Landing's outdoor shopping plaza, which also features a yoga studio, juice bar, and sushi restaurant.

A little further north, homes in **Novato**—the second most populous city in Marin County—are more affordable than Larkspur. Novato quickly outgrew its dairy and fruit orchard days when developers built condos and tract homes, but you'll also find large estates hidden in the hills. Novato has the ingredients of classic Marin suburbia, but it is set apart by having the only Costco in the county. It is also home to the $100 million Buck Center for Research in Aging. Perhaps the biggest challenge about taking up residence in sunny Novato is the commute to San Francisco. It's even longer and more arduous than the San Francisco commute from San Rafael, although the Larkspur Ferry is an excellent option. Moving here is probably realistic only if you work within the North Bay. Also notable is Novato's community hospital, ranked fourth-best in the Bay Area by the US Department of Health & Human Services' polls of patient satisfaction.

Near the edge of San Pablo Bay is old Hamilton Air Field. Opened in 1935, Hamilton Air Field was named in honor of the first American pilot to fly with the Royal Flying Corps during World War I—Lt. Lloyd Hamilton. Used at points by the Army and the Navy, the base reached its peak of activity during World War II, when it housed 20,000 servicemen. Decommissioned in 1975, Hamilton Air Field sat untouched for two decades while city officials, the community, and developers struggled to agree on a plan for the site. Finally, developers purchased the land from the government in the 1990s for $13 million and set to work on massive environmental cleanup, infrastructure rehabilitation, and new housing construction.

The airfield has since been transformed into a thriving planned community—sort of a small town within Novato, simply called **Hamilton.** Here, the very new (quiet *culs-de-sac*, new homes, outdoor trails, parks, and a large community green) blends with the very old (restored Spanish-style buildings converted for community use). Clusters of modern tract homes—from spacious luxury houses to townhomes—form the heart of Hamilton. Senior apartments, as well as some affordable housing units, are under construction, though both of these are expected to have waiting lists before completion.

Other attractions include a historic outdoor amphitheater, a large park, a community swimming pool, a history museum, a restored wetland, a handful of individual artist studios, and a home for Indian Valley Artists. Old hangars are in the process of being converted into office space. There are two large hotels here, and a free shuttle bus runs through the area. The site's military history lingers on in the form of the Coast Guard's Pacific Strike Team, which still maintains an installation in Coast Guard housing.

Away from busy Highway 101, **Fairfax** is a charming, proudly hippie-centered small town with a colorful downtown and plenty of space for hiking, biking, and horseback riding. Styling itself as one of the most progressive and eco-conscious communities in Marin County, Fairfax strictly limits development and has banned chain stores. Once a year, the community comes together for the Fairfax Festival, which has recently been expanded to include an EcoFest as well.

The Fairfax-Bolinas Road is not only scenic, but provides access to the coast. Fairfax's claim to fame is being the birthplace of the mountain bike, which was invented here in 1974. Where better to house the mountain bike hall of fame? In 2015, the town welcomed the Marin Museum of Bicycling and Mountain Bike Hall of Fame—excellently staffed, lovingly displayed, and well-embraced by the community (www.mmbhof.org).

## CORTE MADERA
**Website**: www.ci.corte-madera.ca.us
**Area Code**: 415, 628
**Zip Codes**: 94925
**Post Office**: Main, 7 Pixely Ave, Corte Madera, 800-275-8777, www.usps.com
**Police Station**: 250 Doherty Dr, Larkspur, 415-927-5150
**Library**: 707 Meadowsweet Dr, Corte Madera, 415-924-4844, www.co.marin.ca.us/depts/lb/main/corte/index.cfm
**Parks, Gardens, and Open Space:** Corte Madera Recreation Department, 498 Tamalpais Dr, 415-927-5072, www.ci.corte-madera.ca.us
**Public Schools**: Larkspur School District, 230 Doherty Dr, Larkspur, 415-927-6960, www.larkspurschools.org

## LARKSPUR
**Website**: www.ci.larkspur.ca.us
**Area Code**: 415, 628
**Zip Codes**: 94939
**Post Office**: 120 Ward St, Corte Madera, 800-275-8777, www.usps.com
**Police Station**: 250 Doherty Dr, Larkspur, 415-927-5150
**Library**: 400 Magnolia Ave, Larkspur, 415-927-5005, www.ci.larkspur.ca.us
**Parks, Gardens, and Open Space:** Larkspur Recreation, 498 Tamalpais Dr, 415-927-6746, www.ci.larkspur.ca.us
**Public Schools**: Larkspur School District, 230 Doherty Dr, Larkspur, 415-927-6960, www.larkspurschools.org

## NOVATO/HAMILTON
**Website**: www.ci.novato.ca.us
**Area Code**: 415, 628
**Zip Codes**: 94945, 94948, 94949, 94947 adding
**Post Office**: 1537 S Novato Blvd, 800-275-8777, www.usps.com
**Police Station**: 909 Machin Ave, 415-897-4361
**Library**: 1720 Novato Blvd, 415-898-4623, www.marinlibrary.org
**Public Schools:** Novato Unified School District, 1015 7th St, Novato, 415-897-4201, http://do.nusd.org
**Parks, Gardens, and Open Space:** Novato Community Services, 75 Rowland Way, #200, 415-899-8200, www.ci.novato.ca.us

<u>FAIRFAX</u>
**Website**: www.town-of-fairfax.org
**Area Code**: 415, 628
**Zip Codes**: 94930
**Post Office**: 773 Center Blvd, 800-275-8777, www.usps.com
**Police Station**: 144 Bolinas Rd, 415-453-5330, www.fairfaxpd.org
**Library**: 2097 Sir Francis Drake Blvd, 415-453-8092, www.co.marin.ca.us/library/ fairfax/index.cfm
**Parks, Gardens, and Open Space:** Fairfax Parks Department, 142 Bolinas Rd, 415-453-1584, www.town-of-fairfax.org
**Public Schools**: Ross Valley District, 110 Shaw Dr, San Anselmo, 415-454-2162, http://rvsd.marin.k12.ca.us/

## WEST MARIN COUNTY

Though much of Marin County is deliriously expensive, many homes in **West Marin** are slightly more affordable, including the coastal and tucked-away communities of **Muir Beach** (www.muirbeach.com), **Stinson Beach**, (www.stinsonbeachonline. com), **Bolinas, Nicasio, Olema, Inverness, Point Reyes Station, Tomales** (www. tomales.com), **Marshall, San Geronimo, Woodacre,** and **Dillon Beach**—though these are still pricey, even by Bay Area standards. More information on these communities can be found at www.pointreyes.org. To discourage the waves of tourists who descend upon these beach communities, residents of Bolinas have been known to tear down the street sign indicating the exit for the town.

Point Reyes National Seashore is the area's crown jewel; equally renowned is Tomales Bay, which is known for its oysters. Filmmaker George Lucas has his 3,400-acre Skywalker Ranch headquarters near Nicasio, along Lucas Valley Road. Up in Marshall, the Strauss family has been making organic milk, butter, and yogurt for

*West Marin*

years. These semi-secluded small towns offer tranquil hiking, biking, and horse-back riding, plus easy access to miles of spectacular coastline via Highway 1. In San Geronimo you'll also find a popular 18-hole golf course. Woodacre is home to the Spirit Rock Meditation Center, offering a variety of programs (5000 Sir Francis Drake Boulevard, www.spiritrock.org).

**Websites**: www.co.marin.ca.us, www.marin.org, www.pointreyes.org

**Zip Codes**: see Marin County above

**Area Code**: 415, 628

**Sheriff**: Marin County Sheriff Department, 3501 Civic Center Drive, #145, San Rafael, 415-499-7250

**Emergency Hospital**: Marin General Hospital, 250 Bon Air Rd, Greenbrae, 415-925-7000, www.maringeneral.org

**Library**: Main Branch, 3501 Civic Center Dr, San Rafael, 415-499-6056, www.marinlibrary.org

**Public Schools**: Marin County Office of Education, 415-472-4110, www.marinschools.org

**Community Publications**: *Marin Independent Journal*, 150 Alameda del Prado, Novato, 415-883-8600, www.marinij.com; *Point Reyes Light*, P.O. Box 210, Point Reyes Station, 415-663-8404, www.ptreyeslight.com; *The Coastal Post*, P.O. Box 31, Bolinas, 415-868-1600, www.coastalpost.com

**County/Community Resources**: West Marin Chamber of Commerce, 415-663-9232, www.pointreyes.org; San Geronimo Valley Community Center, 415-488-8888, www.sgvcc.org; Point Reyes National Seashore, Point Reyes, 415-464-5100, www.nps.gov/pore; Marin County Parks, 3501 Civic Center Drive Room #415, San Rafael, 415-499-6387, www.co.marin.ca.us; Golden Gate National Recreation Area, Fort Mason, Building 201, 415-561-4700, www.nps.gov/goga

**Public Transportation**: *Golden Gate Transit*, 415-455-2000, www.goldengatetransit.org

## *SONOMA COUNTY*

North and northeast of Marin County, **Sonoma County** consists of rolling, vine-yard-covered hills, dramatic coastline, seamless skies, glorious weather (most of the time), and some of the world's top chefs. Sonoma County, along with neigh-boring Napa County, is wine paradise. Hundreds of wineries dot the countryside, hosting visitors from around the world, who come to taste fine wine and learn about the art of making it. Housing is varied, ranging from apartments and condos to single-family homes and stately Victorians. You'll also find farms and ranches, mobile home parks, and summer cottages.

**Website**: www.sonoma-county.org

**Area Code**: 707

**Zip Codes**: 95403, 95404, 95405, 95406, 95476

**Sheriff**: 2796 Ventura Ave, Santa Rosa, 707-565-2650

**Emergency Hospitals**: Sutter Hospital, 3325 Chanate Rd, Santa Rosa, 707-576-4000; Palm Drive Hospital, 501 Petaluma Ave, Sebastopol, 707-823-8511; Santa Rosa Memorial, 1165 Montgomery Dr, Santa Rosa, 707-546-3210; Sonoma Valley Hospital, 347 Andrieux St, Sonoma, 707-935-5000

**Libraries**: Sonoma County Library, Petaluma Branch, 100 Fairgrounds Dr, 707-763-9801, www.sonoma.lib.ca.us

**Public Schools**: Sonoma County Office of Education, 5340 Skylane Blvd, Santa Rosa, 707-524-2600, www.scoe.org

**Community Publications**: *Santa Rosa Press Democrat*, 427 Mendocino Ave, Santa Rosa, 707-546-2020, www.pressdemocrat.com; *Marin Independent Journal*, 150 Alameda Del Prado, Novato, 415-883-8600, www.marinij.com; *Sonoma County Gazette*, 707-820-8127, www.sonomacountygazette.com; *Sonoma Index-Tribune*, P.O. Box C, Sonoma, 95476, 707-938-2111, www.sonomanews.com; *Bohemian*, serving Sonoma, Marin, and Napa Counties, 707-527-1200, www.bohemian.com; *Sonoma Valley Sun*, 707-933-0101, www.sonomasun.com

**Community Resources**: Sonoma Valley Chamber of Commerce, 651-A Broadway, Sonoma, 707-996-1033, www.sonomachamber.com; Sonoma Community Center, 276 E Napa St, Sonoma, 707-938-4626; Sonoma Valley Chorale, P.O. Box 816, Sonoma, 95476, 707-935-1576, www.sonomavalleychorale.org; Sonoma State University, E East Cotati Ave, Rohnert Park, 707-664-2880, www.sonoma.edu

**Public Transportation**: Sonoma County Transit, 800-345-7433, TTY 707-585-9817, www.sctransit.com

**Parks, Gardens, and Open Space**: Sonoma County Regional Parks, 2300 County Center Dr, 120A, Santa Rosa, 707-565-2041, www.sonoma-county.org/parks; Sonoma County Farm Trails, 800-207-9464, www.farmtrails.org

# SANTA ROSA

Recently named one of the most livable communities in the United States by the nonprofit Partners for Livable Communities, **Santa Rosa** prides itself on maintaining a small-town appeal despite a booming population. Home to the county seat and located 50 miles north of San Francisco, in central Sonoma County, the city has long been considered one of the more affordable spots to buy a home in the region, though prices have soared recently. City officials are picky about the look of new buildings and businesses, so you'll find Santa Rosa especially charming. Despite the close tabs kept on development, Santa Rosa is growing—as is traffic congestion, especially going crosstown from east to west and vice versa.

Surrounded by a handful of picturesque, lovingly restored historic neighborhoods, the downtown area comes alive every Wednesday evening from mid-May through August with the Santa Rosa Downtown Market—renowned as Sonoma

*Santa Rosa*

County's largest farmers' market. Also downtown is the Prince Memorial Greenway, a new curving terraced pedestrian and bike pathway that snakes along the banks of the Santa Rosa Creek, providing a scenic link to the city's Historic Railroad Square. In addition to scores of suburban ranch-style homes, Santa Rosa is also home to more than a dozen mobile home parks, as well as two unique spots—Valley Vista I and II—where mobile home owners own the land. To encourage upkeep and maintain affordability, the city maintains a rent control program for the private parks and offers rehabilitation loans. For a taste of local history you can visit the home, greenhouse, and gardens of horticulturist Luther Burbank or take a tour of the Charles M. Schulz Museum and Research Center, named in honor of the beloved "Peanuts" creator and longtime Santa Rosa resident (www.schulzmuseum.org).

**Website**: www.ci.santa-rosa.ca.us

**Zip Codes**: 95403, 95404, 95405, 95406

**Area Code**: 707

**Post Office**: 730 2nd St, 800-275-8777, www.usps.com

**Police**: 965 Sonoma Ave, 707-543-3600

**Library**: Santa Rosa Branch of the Sonoma County Library, 3rd and E sts, 707-545-0831, TTY 707-575-1206, www.sonomalibrary.org/branches/central.html

**Community Resources:** Downtown Market, www.srdowntownmarket.com; Sonoma County Museum, www.sonomacountymuseum.org; Wells Fargo Center for the Arts, 707-546-3600, www.wellsfargocenterarts.org

**Parks, Gardens, and Open Space:** Santa Rosa Parks and Recreation, www.ci. santa-rosa.ca.us/departments/recreationandparks; Hood Mountain Regional Park, 3000 Los Alamos Rd; Maddux Ranch Park, 4655 Lavelle Rd; Shiloh Regional Park, 5750 Faught Rd; Spring Lake Park, 5390 Montgomery Dr

# SONOMA

The town of **Sonoma**, playfully called "Slo-noma" for its tranquil, small-town feel, is the commercial heart of Sonoma Valley. Surrounded by vineyards, the entire valley is a paradise for wine lovers. The neatly manicured downtown square is the largest public square in any town in California, fostering a more cohesive community than can be found in Napa. Napa is more of a launching point for wine country, whereas Sonoma is more of a destination. On weekends, especially in the summer, the latter's population explodes as scores of tourists clog Route 12 to sample renowned cabernets, pinots, and merlots. A picture-postcard small community, rich in history, culinary treasures, and spas, Sonoma is also home to Sonoma State University. If you plan to commute to San Francisco, you'd be strained to live up here and make it work—but if you must, plan on at least one hour each way by car, factoring in traffic.

Architecturally, single-family homes, many of them ranch style, were built between 1950 and 1970. On the outskirts, you'll find older family farms, as well as regal vineyard estates. History students should visit the Mission San Francisco de Solano, or Sonoma Mission, the last and northernmost of the Franciscan missions along the California Coast. Literary crowds enjoy the serene surroundings of author Jack London's former ranch and final resting place—now an 800-plus-acre state park in nearby Glen Ellen. Heading out of the city, you'll find clusters of small towns and villages throughout the valley—many of them home to popular natural hot springs, spas, dairy farms, and award-winning wineries.

*Sonoma*

**Website**: www.sonomacity.org
**Area Code**: 707
**Zip Codes**: 95476
**Post Office**: 617 Broadway, 800-275-8777, www.usps.com

**Police**: 175 1st St W, 707-996-3601

**Library**: Sonoma Branch of the Sonoma County Library, 755 Napa St, 707-996-5217, www.sonomalibrary.org

**Parks, Gardens, and Open Space:** Sonoma Parks and Public Works Department, #1 The Plaza, 707-938-3681, www.sonomacity.org; Maxwell Farms Regional Park, 100 Verano Ave

## NAPA COUNTY

# ST. HELENA, RUTHERFORD, YOUNTVILLE, NAPA, CALISTOGA

With a mild climate, Napa Valley is wine heaven, producing hundreds of thousands of gallons of award-winning zinfandels, merlots, cabernets, pinot noirs, and chardonnays. Premier grapes are grown on the vine, then aged in casks and bottled and corked with a result rivaling—some would say surpassing—the best in France. On weekends, thousands of wine tourists take to Highway 29, the road running north-south through **Napa County**, stopping at the vineyards, wineries, and picturesque small towns of **St. Helena**, **Rutherford**, and **Yountville**. Yountville boasts more Michelin stars per capita than any other American city or town; most famously it's the serene site of French Laundry, the pioneering organic kitchen. A typical day begins with one or two tastings in the cool basement of a winery, followed by a picnic lunch in a park, then a few more wineries before dinner. A geological note about Yountville: In September 2000, a magnitude-5.2 earthquake struck Napa County, the epicenter of which was in Yountville, about six miles northwest of Napa. It caused millions of dollars of damage to buildings

*St. Helena*

*Yountville*

countywide. The same can be said of the **City of Napa**—the center of county government—which was rocked in 2014 by a magnitude-6.0 earthquake that caused $300 million in damages. The city is still rebuilding. The quake left the 1930s-era post office battered and fenced off, placing it at the top of Napa's annual Ten Threatened Treasures list. The old building still shows cracked walls, loose bricks, blasted windows, and other deep fissures that locals don't think the postal service will repair. Demolition may be the easy way out—but as of this writing, the building's future is still being debated.

Set up house here, and you can sample wine year round. In addition to ranch-style homes popular with families, a handful of mobile home parks—many of them designed especially for seniors—offer tranquil life for retirees. **Calistoga**, at the northern end of Napa Valley, is volcanic-mud-spa paradise, attracting those who just can't live without daily herbal wraps, mineral baths, massages, and mud. (For more see the **Quick Getaways** chapter.) There's also a natural geyser called Old Faithful Geyser of California (not to be confused with Yellowstone's Old Faithful) that periodically shoots hot water 60 feet into the air. The owner claims Old Faithful Geyser of California acts erratically about two to fourteen days before the area experiences a significant earthquake.

**Website**: www.countyofnapa.org
**Area Code**: 707
**Zip Codes**: 94558, 94559, 94574, 94508
**Sheriff**: 1535 Airport Blvd, Napa, 707-253-4509, TTY 707-253-4344
**Libraries**: Napa City-County Library, 580 Coombs St, 707-253-4241, www.countyofnapa.org/library
**Public Schools**: Napa Valley Unified School District, 2425 Jefferson St, Napa, 707-253-3715, www.nvusd.k12.ca.us
**Community Publications**: *The Napa Valley Register*, 1615 2nd St, Napa, 707-226-3711, www.napanews.com; *St. Helena Star*, 1200 Main St, C, St. Helena,

707-963-2731, www.sthelenastar.com; *Yountville Sun*, 6505 Washington St, Suite 4, Yountville, 707-944-5676, www.yountvillesun.com

**Community Resources**: Community Resources for Children, 5 Financial Plaza #224, Napa, 707-253-0376, www.crcnapa.org; Wildlife Rescue, P.O. Box 2571, 707-224-4295; Napa County Historical Society, 1219 1st St, 707-224-1739, www.napahistory.org; Napa Valley Museum, 55 Presidents Circle, Yountville, 707-944-0500, www.napavalleymuseum.org; Napa Community Resources Department, 1100 West St, 707-257-9529

**Public Transportation**: Caltrain, 800-660-4287; Napa Valley Transit, 800-696-6443, www.nctpa.net; Napa Valley Wine Train, 800-427-4124, www.winetrain.com

**Parks, Gardens, and Open Space**: Napa Valley Parks, 1195 3rd St, Room 310, Napa, 707-253-4580, www.co.napa.ca.us; The Petrified Forest, 707-942-6667; Old Faithful Geyser, 707-942-6463; Bothe-Napa Valley State Park, 800-444-7275; Bothe Napa Valley State Park, 5 miles north of St. Helena and 4 miles south of Calistoga on Hwy 29/128; Bale Grist Mill State Historic Park, 3369 North Saint Helena Hwy (Hwy 29)

## *SOLANO COUNTY*

East of Napa County, **Solano County** is one of the fastest-growing counties in the Bay Area, with a distinctly rural atmosphere that's seeing housing developments and new businesses springing up, from Vallejo in the southwestern corner of the county, to Vacaville and Fairfield further inland. Housing costs are below the Bay Area median, and transplants from San Francisco are arriving en masse, snatching up many of the new homes. A popular destination for rugged recreation, the county is a magnet for boating and fishing around Suisun Marsh; hiking in Lynch Canyon, Rockville Hills, and Lagoon Valley parks; and camping just about everywhere. Unlike San Francisco, Solano County actually has seasons: as high as 100° Fahrenheit in the summer and touching the 30s in the winter. Solano County also boasts its own wine country in the Suisun Valley, which includes the largest contiguous estuarine marsh in the nation.

**Website**: www.solanocounty.com

**Area Code**: 707

**Zip Codes**: 94533, 94587, 95687, 95688, 94589, 94590

**Sheriff**: 530 Union Ave, Suite 100, Fairfield, 707-421-7000

**Libraries**: Solano County Library, 1150 Kentucky St, Fairfield, 866-572-7587, www.solanolibrary.com

**Public Schools**: Solano County Office of Education, Superintendent's Office, 5100 Business Center Drive, Fairfield, 94534, 707-399-4400, www.solanocoe.net

**Community Publications**: *Vallejo Times Herald*, 440 Curtola Parkway, Vallejo, 707-644-1141; *Daily Republic*, 1250 Texas St, 707-425-4646; *Vacaville Reporter*, 318

Main St, Vacaville, 707-448-6401; *Benicia Herald*, P.O. Box 65, Benicia, 707-745-0733; *Dixon Tribune*, 145 East A St, Dixon, 916-678-5594; *River News Herald and Journal*, P.O. Box 786, Rio Vista, 707-374-6431

**Community Resources**: Six Flags Discovery Kingdom, 1001 Fairgrounds Dr, Vallejo, 707-643-6722, www.sixflags.com; Solano County Fair, 707-551-2000, www.scfair.com; Solano County Family and Children Services, 421 Executive Court North, Fairfield, 707-863-3950

**Public Transportation**: Vallejo Baylink Ferry, 707-643-3779, www.baylinkferry.com; Vallejo Transit, 707-648-4666, www.vallejotransit.com; Vacaville City Coach, 707-449-6000, www.citycoach.com; Fairfield-Suisun Transit, 707-422-2877; RIDES, 511, www.511.org

**Parks, Gardens, and Open Space:** Solano County Parks, 707-784-7514, www.solanocounty.com

## FAIRFIELD, VACAVILLE

If you want to live this far northeast and commute to San Francisco or Silicon Valley for work, think twice—unless you enjoy long hauls on highways. But if you work in the East Bay, you'll find housing bargains and natural appeal here. Halfway between San Francisco and Sacramento, along I-80 and Highway 12, **Fairfield** is a regional crossroads. It's the seat of Solano County and home to Travis Air Force Base, and it's not far from the University of California at Davis. Jelly Belly's headquarters are here, with daily tours that show why a single jellybean takes more than a week to make.

When the city of Fairfield considered selling its golf courses in 2014, residents protested and persuaded the city to back down. There's a growing sense of community cohesion that makes Fairfield increasingly appealing to San Franciscans jumping to the East Bay for housing. Moderate-priced homes are the norm, and a large apartment complex is being built with more than 300 units. Some

*Fairfield*

neighborhoods are more challenged and troubled than others when it comes to infrastructure, but Fairfield boasts an active job market and proximity to a small wine country. Except for a blanket of fog that rolls in nightly over I-80, the weather is dry and hot. Very hot.

Family-focused **Vacaville** attracts newcomers to the trails and 25 parks, several with sports fields, horseshoe pits, and BBQs. The popular Nut Tree shopping center underwent an expansion in the past few years. And Vacaville boasts the highest per-capita concentration of electric cars in the world. A major new large employer moved here in 2015 as well: ICON Aircraft, the consumer sport-plane manufacturer. Local cultural activities are more abundant here than in Fairfield, as Vacaville hosts events like a well-attended jazz festival and a farmers' market (Saturdays from 8 a.m.–noon, May through October, on Main Street between Parker and Dobbins).

Both Fairfield and Vacaville are on the upswing, as in 2015 the area broke ground on a major new train project—the Fairfield/Vacaville Train Station—a $78 million plan to widen roads to six lanes, build an overpass at the Peabody Road train tracks, and construct a station along the Capital Corridor that will run between the Bay Area and Sacramento. That's encouraging news if you plan to work in or around Sacramento, the state capital.

## FAIRFIELD
**Website**: www.fairfield.ca.gov
**Area Code**: 707
**Zip Codes**: 94533, 94587
**Post Office**: 600 Kentucky St, 800-275-8777, www.usps.com
**Police**: 1000 Webster St, 707-428-7300
**Library**: Fairfield Branch, 1150 Kentucky St, 866-572-7587, www.solanolibrary.com
**Parks, Gardens, and Open Space:** Fairfield Park Division, 1000 Webster St, 707-428-7407, www.fairfield.ca.gov; Grizzly Island State Wildlife Area, Highway 12; Rockville Hills Regional Park, 2110 Rockville Rd, Rockville

## VACAVILLE
**Websites**: www.cityofvacaville.com, www.vacavillemagazine.com, www.thereporter.com
**Area Code**: 707
**Zip Codes**: 95688, 95687
**Post Office**: 98 Cernon St, 800-275-8777, www.usps.com
**Police**: 660 Merchant St, 707-449-5231
**Libraries:** Cultural Center Branch, 1020 Ulatis Dr, 866-572-7587, www.solanolibrary.com; Town Square Branch, 1 Town Square Pl
**Parks, Gardens, and Open Space:** Vacaville Community Services Department, 40 Eldridge Ave, 707-449-5655; City of Vacaville Park Facilities, 707-449-5100

# VALLEJO

With home prices among the lowest in the Bay Area, **Vallejo**—the largest city in Solano County—has become attractive for waves of families hoping to fulfill what can seem an impossible dream in today's Bay Area—homeownership. Vallejo has started to rebound from the bankruptcy it endured in 2008. But in 2015 the city faced headlines warning of a second bankruptcy just around the corner. Economic winds continue to change, and nothing's certain yet. There are opportunities for newcomers—especially in a Bay Area booming with high rents almost everywhere else.

San Francisco is 32 miles away, and the high-speed ferry offers one of the most pleasant commutes around. Every day the ferry carries thousands to work in San Francisco (the stop is the Ferry Building), with the trip taking just under an hour each way. Commuting by car would take almost double the time.

Founded by General Mariano G. Vallejo in 1844, Vallejo originated as a shipping and naval center. A temporary state capital was built in 1852, but because of the area's lack of housing the legislature moved up to Sacramento. In 1853 a devastating flood brought the legislature back to Vallejo, but they were still dissatisfied, and moved on to Benicia—only to return later to Sacramento.

Today, Vallejo has about 42,000 households, with a median household income of $58,000—well below most Bay Area cities. Best known for being home to Six Flags Discovery Kingdom (formerly Six Flags Marine World), a large outdoor theme and animal park, Vallejo also features a farmers' market, a golf course, a yacht club, and the California Maritime Academy, a California State University School. Housing is an eclectic mix of beautifully restored Victorians, 1950s tract homes, and lavish residences in the Northgate and Hiddenbrooke Golf Course neighborhoods. In 1996, the Mare Island Shipyards closed, and the city is now in the process of converting the 5,252 acres to civilian use. Part of the conversion includes a multimillion-dollar environmental cleanup of lead-based paint, petroleum waste, and

*Vallejo*

other toxic remnants left in the shipyard. A large commercial area is on the way, and final plans call for more than 1,000 new housing units—many already completed—ranging from apartments to single-family homes, with office space, new parks, and a large area of restored open green.

With Mare Island rehabilitation underway, the city is at a crossroads. In the next few decades, the waterfront project will convert 110 acres into a thriving connected core of new housing, commercial space, and parks. A new transit center to improve bus and ferry links, complete with a massive commuter parking garage, is also scheduled, as is a waterfront promenade. Meanwhile, the downtown project will overhaul empty lots to create hundreds of new houses and thousands of square feet of retail and office space. As of this writing, the precise numbers and timeline are uncertain, as an earlier developer dropped out and the city is considering new developers. It's a start-and-stop project that will be ambitious and transformative. With so many projects in the pipeline, Vallejo is one of the fastest-developing cities in the Bay Area.

Vallejo is also one of the most diverse cities in the United States. There are several waterfront festivals and a thriving gospel scene. Downtown has become a new artists' hub, as artists are priced out of San Francisco and Oakland. Vallejo is also more of a college town than it's ever been: the California Maritime Academy (CMA) recently rolled out a new aquatics and physical education complex, and local Touro University launched a new School of Nursing in 2014. Solano Community College is also growing, having expanded several programs and facilities.

By late 2016, Vallejo will have completed the Propel Vallejo project, enhancing transportation, neighborhood improvement, and service delivery—all while facing the possibility of another bankruptcy. Stay tuned.

**Website**: www.cityofvallejo.net
**Area Code**: 707
**Zip Codes**: 94589, 94590, 94591, 94592
**Post Office**: 485 Santa Clara St, 800-275-8777, www.usps.com
**Police**: 111 Amador St, 707-648-4321
**Libraries**: John F. Kennedy Library, 505 Santa Clara St, 866-572-7587, www.solanolibrary.com; Springstowne Library, 1003 Oakwood Ave
**Parks, Gardens, and Open Space:** Greater Vallejo Recreation District, 395 Amador St, 707-648-4600, www.gvrd.org

# EAST BAY (ALAMEDA AND CONTRA COSTA COUNTIES)

## ALAMEDA COUNTY

As San Francisco's record-high costs continue to challenge newcomers and longtime locals, the **East Bay** has become the biggest and brightest frontier for homeowners in the region. Oakland is more coveted than it's ever been, topping 400,000 residents for the first time in its 150-year history. As residents jump here, so do businesses and restaurants, which reduce their rents almost in half by leaving San Francisco. **Alameda County** today is the second-fastest-growing county in California.

As San Franciscans practically trip over themselves in the rush to the East Bay, Oakland is witnessing a real estate boom and a tech-driven demographic shift. Newcomers who used to look to Oakland and Berkeley are also considering Hayward, the city of Alameda, Pinole, Union City, Fremont, and San Leandro—some of the most culturally diverse cities in Northern California. A consequence of the rush to the East Bay is that home prices are inflating quickly, but the East Bay is so much larger than San Francisco that relative bargains can still be found. Below-market-rate housing is coming in. For an updated list of affordable apartments, call 211 within Alameda County, or 888-886-9660 from elsewhere, or visit www.achousingchoices.org. Once here, for assistance and counseling with your search for below-market-rate options, consider reaching out to Eden Council for Hope & Opportunity (925-449-7340, www.echofairhousing.org).

The East Bay has dozens of towns and cities, from Crockett and Hercules at the northern end; through Pinole, Richmond, El Cerrito, Albany, Berkeley, Oakland, and Alameda in the center; to San Leandro, Castro Valley, Hayward, Union City, and Fremont on the southern end; and Livermore, Pleasanton, Dublin, Concord, Walnut Creek, Martinez, Pittsburg, and Antioch out east. The East Bay contains so many enclaves that it's difficult—and unwise—to generalize about life here. For the most part, parking is not as arduous as in San Francisco. Rents are lower, rental property is more available, and the weather is generally clearer and warmer. The biggest drawback is commuting to San Francisco by car, which newcomers and locals try to avoid. Fortunately the entire area is served well by an extensive criss-crossing network of public transit systems—including buses, trains, and Bay Area Rapid Transit (BART). Another asset is Oakland International Airport, one of the easiest-to-navigate airports in California.

The lush parks offer an array of hiking, biking, boating, picnicking, and swimming activities. Berkeley's Tilden Park, the crown jewel of the East Bay's park system, is a hiking and biking paradise, with exhilarating views. Another escape to the outdoors is Mount Diablo State Park, in eastern Contra Costa County. As the highest peak in the Bay Area, Mount Diablo is a majestic destination for hikers and campers. Oakland's Lake Merritt, beneath the downtown skyline, hosts joggers, walkers, and bikers.

The East Bay also boasts some of the top colleges and universities in the world—most prominently the University of California at Berkeley. Cal State East Bay has campuses in the Hayward hills and the Concord foothills of Mount Diablo, as well as a professional development center in Oakland. Private colleges and universities in the East Bay include Saint Mary's in the densely wooded community of Moraga, John F. Kennedy University in Orinda, and Mills College in Oakland.

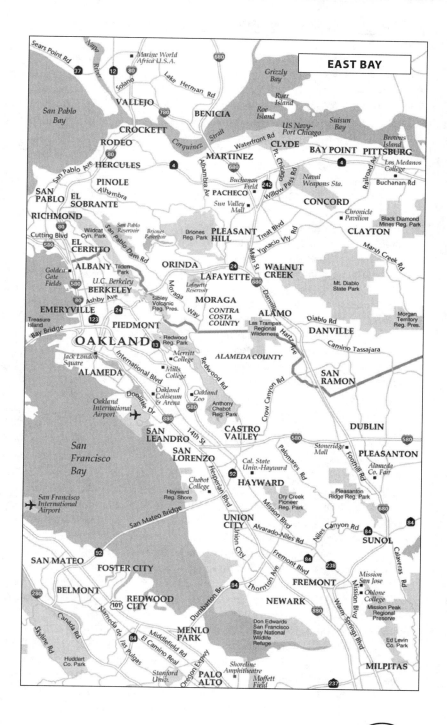

EAST BAY

**Website**: www.alameda.ca.gov
**Area Code**: 510
**Sheriff**: 1401 Lakeside Dr, 12th Floor, 510-272-6878, www.alamedacountysheriff. org
**Emergency Hospitals**: Alameda Hospital, 2070 Clinton Ave, 510-522-3700, www.alamedahospital.org; Fairmont Hospital, 15400 Foothill Blvd, San Leandro, 510-437-4800, www.acmedctr.org; Highland Hospital, 1411 E 31st St, Oakland, 510-437-4564, www.hghed.org; St. Rose Hospital, 27200 Calaroga Ave, Hayward, 510-264-4000, www.strosehospital.org; Kaiser Medical Center, 27400 Hesperian Blvd, Hayward, 510-784-4000, www.kaiserpermanente.org; Alta Bates Medical Center, 2450 Ashby Ave, Berkeley, 510-204-4444, www. altabates.com; Children's Hospital Oakland, 747 52nd St, Oakland, 510-428-3000, www.childrenshospitaloakland.org
**Library**: Alameda County Library Foundation, 2450 Stevenson Blvd, Fremont, 510-745-1500, www.aclibrary.org
**Public Schools**: Alameda County Office of Education, 313 West Winton Ave, Hayward, 510-887-0152, www.acoe.org
**Community Publications**: *Oakland Tribune*, 510-208-6300, www.insidebayarea. com/oaklandtribune (the Alameda Newspaper Group also owns the *Alameda Times-Star* and the *Fremont Argus*); *East Bay Express*, 510-879-3700, www. eastbayexpress.com; *Contra Costa Times* (covers Contra Costa and east Alameda County), 800-598-4637, www.contracostatimes.com (also owns a handful of smaller local publications, including the *Berkeley Voice, Alameda Journal,* the *Montclarion,* and the *Piedmonter*); *Berkeley Daily Planet*, 510-841-5600, www. berkeleydailyplanet.com; UC Berkeley Publications: *The Daily Californian*, www.dailycal.org; *San Leandro Times*, 510-614-1555, www.ebpublishing.com; *Fremont Bulletin*, 510-661-9920, www.fremontbulletin.com; *Tri-City Voice*, 510-494-1999, www.tricityvoice.com; *Pleasanton Weekly*, 925-600-0840, www. pleasantonweekly.com. *Alameda Sun*, 510-263-1470, www.alamedasun.com.
**County/Community Resources**: Alameda One-Stop Career Center, 510-981-7564; Bananas (childcare referrals), 510-658-7353, direct referral line: 510-658-0381, www.bananasinc.org; Alameda County Social Services Agency, 510-596-0110, alamedasocialservices.org; Eden Information and Referral for Social Services, 510-537-2710, www.edenir.org; Ohlone Community College, 510-659-6000, www.ohlone.edu; Childcare Links, 510-791-9256 www.childcarelinks.org; Alameda County Art Commission, 510-208-9646 www.acgov.org/arts
**Public Transportation**: *AC (Alameda-Contra Costa) Transit*, 510-891-4700, TTY 800-448-9790, www.actransit.org; *BART*, 510-465-2278, TTY 510-839-2278, www.bart.gov; *San Francisco Bay Ferry*, www.sanfranciscobayferry.com; *Emery-Go-Round*, 510-451-3862, next bus hotline, 510-451-3862, www. emerygoround.com; *RIDES*, 511, www.511.org; *Amtrak*, 800-USA-RAIL, TTY 800-523-6590, www.amtrak.com; *Greyhound*, 800-231-2222, TTY 800-345-3109, www.greyhound.com

**Parks, Gardens, and Open Space:** East Bay Regional Park District, 2950 Peralta Oaks Court, Oakland, 94605, 888-327-2757, TTY 510-633-0460, www.ebparks. org; maintains 62 parks throughout the region, many of them with large open areas, nature trails, and shorelines

# SAN LEANDRO, SAN LORENZO, CASTRO VALLEY, HAYWARD, FREMONT, NEWARK, UNION CITY

Housing bargains are increasingly rare in a Bay Area bursting with record-high costs, but rest assured that bargains can still be found, especially in San Leandro, San Lorenzo, and pockets of Hayward—all suburbs of Oakland. If you're looking for trendy boutiques, fashionable restaurants, and stylishly landscaped sidewalks, make a U-turn; they're not here. What you will find instead are budget-friendly sprawls where you can still get a $10 haircut, a $5 lunch, and a $1 ice cream cone. These towns are the least expensive between Oakland and San Jose. Ranked from most to least expensive, they are Fremont, Union City, Castro Valley, Newark, San Leandro, Hayward, and San Lorenzo. But that order is likely to change, as some cities build faster than others.

On the eastern shore of the Bay, **San Leandro** is a transit-rich destination of 87,000 residents, almost all in single-family households near five shopping plazas. The city is diverse in language, ethnicity, and nationality, and its infrastructure is quickly improving. Downtown San Leandro is getting an 8-acre tech campus near the BART station, slated for late 2016, to include a head-turning art installation: a 55-foot-tall steel sculpture of a woman illuminated with 2,500 LED lights—an effort to promote women's safety and equality of opportunity in the tech-competitive Bay Area. Local roads rank among the worst in the Bay Area—but not for long, as San Leandro's new half-cent tax hike is expected to haul in $10 million annually toward repaving streets and upgrading buildings. The new library at 395 Paseo Grande opened recently, almost doubling its former size, and the city's homes association is actively engaged with residents, rewarding locals who convert private lawns to drought-tolerant gardens.

Don't be surprised if you catch a fresh chocolate aroma in San Leandro, where Ghirardelli's chocolate factory and headquarters stand. Ghirardelli's is the third-oldest chocolate company in the United States, not far away from the brand-new site of the 21st Amendment beer brewery (founded in San Francisco), which has broken ground on a new site. As part of San Leandro's renewal, the city is considering tearing down businesses—don't worry, neither the chocolate factory nor the brewery are on its list—and replacing them with 354 below-market-rate housing units, a conference center, and offices near the Marina. Extra housing will mean relief for newcomers facing the merciless Bay Area housing market. You'll also find fixer-upper homes and patches of nature, but beware—this city's creek is hardly a creek at all; it's a sad cement blip with a few gulps of water. Not quite scenic—but if San Leandro fits your style and budget, you'll have access to neighborly outings, like movie nights at the little league park. And you'll be directly next to Oakland International Airport, for quick getaways. Best of all, you'll save a bundle.

Just south of San Leandro is **San Lorenzo**, also transit-rich but smaller, near interstates 880, 580, and 238. Often overlooked, this enclave is a relative bargain as well, compared to Oakland and San Francisco prices. San Lorenzo is a car-centered suburb with wide avenues, strip malls, inexpensive salons, fast food, and drive-through taquerias. Picture a dilapidated art-deco theater with a faded, fenced-off "San Lorenzo" marquee—there is plenty of history and potential here. In late 2016 the city will unveil new affordable housing for seniors, including 77 apartments directly on the bus line. Another housing development is opening nearby, with 85 units. Applications are at www.rcdhousing.org.

Adjacent to these towns is **Castro Valley**, an unassuming suburb with a much higher-rated school system than its neighbors—meaning higher home prices. If you're raising a family, Castro Valley is worth considering. It's flanked by furniture warehouses, lumberyards, and collision-repair centers—no gentrification here, not even close—and you'll live close to big cities for work and nightlife. Local fun includes the lively rodeo ranch, where rodeos are held regularly, and a village bowling alley. But avoid the rookie mistake of confusing "Castro Valley" (the town) for "*the* Castro" (the San Francisco neighborhood). Castro Valley is here in the East Bay, and is dotted with chain stores.

The scene changes as you drop south to **Hayward**, which is larger and livelier. With 150,000 residents, Hayward is the third-largest city in Alameda County—with strip malls, car dealerships, and burger joints. Kennedy Park is a treasure that is popular for birthday BBQs and graduation parties. The park has a kids' mini-train that chugs around the grass, and a petting zoo with friendly goats across from the Target shopping mall. This family-oriented city draws Filipino, Latino, and Pacific Islander families on the west side. On the east side, California State University is perched atop a hill with striking views of the Bay below. Known

*Hayward*

locally as Cal State Hayward, the campus is surrounded by the city's more spacious homes and tidier storefronts.

Many newcomers live in Hayward and commute the 25 miles northwest to San Francisco or the 30 miles south to Silicon Valley, all for the sake of home-ownership. Thanks to the San Mateo–Hayward Bridge, crossing the Bay to the Peninsula is relatively easy, despite commute-hour traffic, and the city has two BART stations. The recently redeveloped downtown shows landscaping improvements and building upgrades, and in 2015 the city pledged to convert a shoreline landfill into a solar farm, generating electricity for 1,200 homes. Keep in mind that a major fault line runs through Hayward, and there's an increasing likelihood of a devastating earthquake here, according to geologists. If "caution to the wind" is your response, then welcome to town. It's a city with a sense of humor as well: in 2015 it installed clever street signs to reduce speeding, with advisories like "Heads up! Cross the street, then update Facebook!"

South of Hayward, the cities of Fremont, Newark, and Union City make up the Tri-City Area, a trio of gentrifying suburbs absorbing the mass exodus of San Francisco families in search of more affordable suburban living. As a result, the towns are especially family-friendly, with quiet neighborhood streets and outstanding parks, as well as a new Whole Foods and upscale bakeries. All three cities lie near the eternally clogged Interstate 880, which frequently resembles a parking lot in the mornings and early evenings.

**Fremont**, the fourth-largest city in the Bay Area, is home to the largest population of Afghan-Americans in the United States. Numbering in the tens of thousands, the thriving Afghan community is known as Little Kabul, a commercial stretch of Fremont Boulevard with storefront signs in the Dari language. The city's largest population segment is children under age 14. Kids and parents head to Lake Elizabeth for boating and ballgames in the lush Central Park, which recently got new picnic tables, BBQs pits, walkways, patios, and snack bars. Next to Central Park is Washington Hospital, which broke ground in 2015 on its ambitious $339 million care center, slated for completion in 2018—the largest public works project in the district's history. The hospital is already enjoying a recent $148 million expansion. And the Fremont Tennis Center has five new kids' tennis courts.

In addition to modern department stores at the massive Pacific Commons mall, you'll find local gems like the Niles Essanay Silent Film Museum, where Charlie Chaplin made five movies, and where locals gather for Chaplin-lookalike contests. Fremont also has its own Bollywood movie theater, with samosa and chai at the concession stand.

Fremont is investing heavily in public safety (especially firefighters and police), hiring more staff than at any point since the recession of 2008. For commuters, Fremont offers easy access to Silicon Valley via the Dumbarton Bridge. The main route, Fremont Boulevard, is filled with outdoor strip malls, and it connects to the smaller town of **Newark**, which is enjoying a development push to keep pace with the building frenzy around it.

Make note of Newark (population 44,000)—it's the next up-and-coming gem in the East Bay. For one of Alameda County's smallest cities, it is on an unprecedented upswing. Two new housing developments at Enterprise Drive and Willow Street are breaking ground, including 244 single-family homes. Also underway are 77 single-family homes on the former site of an elementary school; 15 houses on Birch Street; 86 townhomes at Cedar Boulevard and Mowry School Road; and a whopping 1,200 residences in vacant land near Cherry Street and Mowry Avenue. By contrast, consider that in the previous two decades, only *four* homes were added to Newark, according to the mayor's office. That makes this 2015–16 boom historic. Newark is new. And it's less expensive than Fremont.

For shopping, the NewPark Mall is one of the busiest in the Bay Area. A little further north, **Union City** has a cluster of shopping centers near the freeway. The largest of these is Union Landing—on Alvarado-Niles Street—whose draw on weekends is a gigantic movie house with more than two dozen screens. Union City has the distinction of being one the first cities in northern California to have opened A Krispy Kreme donut shop—at one time the city drew hundreds of donut tourists, forming lines around the block. Today there's a beautifully landscaped Civic Center, whose creek is home to ducks, immaculate lawns, and sports. A bit north, near the BART station, is Shorty Garcia Park, a glistening soccer field framed by the airy hills. Union City is also safer than Hayward and San Leandro, though more expensive.

*Union City*

## SAN LEANDRO
**Website**: www.sanleandro.org
**Area Code**: 510
**Zip Codes**: 94577, 94578, 94579
**Post Offices**: 1777 Abram Ct, 800-275-8777, www.usps.com
**Police**: 901 E 14th St, 510-577-2740

**Library**: 300 Estudillo Ave, www.sanleandrolibrary.org
**Public Schools**: San Leandro Unified School District, www.sanleandro.k12.ca.us
**Parks, Gardens, and Open Space**: San Leandro Recreation and Human Services, 835 E 14th St, 510-577-3462, www.sanleandro.org/depts/rec

## SAN LORENZO
**Website**: www.alameda.ca.gov
**Area Code**: 510
**Zip Codes**: 94580
**Post Offices**: 15808 Hesperian Blvd, 800-275-8777, www.usps.com
**Police**: Alameda County Sheriff, 15001 Foothill Blvd, 510-667-7721
**Library**: 16032 Hesperian Blvd, guides.aclibrary.org
**Public Schools**: San Lorenzo Unified School District, www.slzusd.org
**Parks, Gardens, and Open Space**: Castro Valley Community Center, 18988 Lake Chabot Road, 510-888-0123, www.haywardrec.org

## CASTRO VALLEY
**Website**: www.castrovalleypage.com
**Area Code**: 510
**Zip Codes**: 94546, 94552
**Post Offices**: 20283 Santa Maria Ave, 800-275-8777, www.usps.com
**Police**: Alameda County Sheriff, 15001 Foothill Blvd, 510-667-7721
**Library**: 3600 Northbridge Ave, 510-667-7900
**Public Schools**: Castro Valley Unified School District, www.cv.k12.ca.us
**Parks, Gardens, and Open Space**: Castro Valley Community Center, 18988 Lake Chabot Road, 510-888-0123, www.haywardrec.org

## HAYWARD
**Website**: www.hayward-ca.gov
**Area Code**: 510
**Zip Codes**: 94540–94546, 94552, 94557
**Post Offices**: 822 C St; 24438 Santa Clara St; 2163 Aldengate Way, 800-275-8777, www.usps.com
**Police**: Hayward Police Department, 300 W Winton Ave, 510-293-7000
**Library**: Hayward Main Library, 835 C St, 510-293-8685; Weekes Branch, 27300 Patrick Ave, 510-782-2155, www.library.hayward-ca.gov
**Public Schools**: Hayward Unified School District, 24411 Amador St, 510-784-2600, www.husd.k12.ca.us
**Parks, Gardens, and Open Space**: Hayward Area Recreation and Park District, 1099 E St, 510-881-6700, www.haywardrec.org

## FREMONT
**Website**: www.fremont.gov
**Area Code**: 510
**Zip Codes**: 94536–94539, 94555

**Post Offices**: Fremont: 37010 Dusterberry Way; 160 J Street; 41041 Trimboli Way; 43456 Ellsworth Street; 240 Francisco Lane, 800-275-8777, www.usps.com
**Police**: Fremont Police Department, 2000 Stevenson Blvd, 510-790-6800
**Library**: Fremont Main Library, 2400 Stevenson Blvd, 510-745-1400, TTY 888-663-0660, www.aclibrary.org
**Public Schools**: Fremont Unified School District, 4210 Technology Dr, 510-657-2350, www.fremont.k12.ca.us
**Parks, Gardens, and Open Space**: Fremont Recreation Services, 3300 Capitol Ave, Building B, 510-494-4300

NEWARK
**Website**: www.ci.newark.ca.us
**Area Code**: 510
**Zip Code**: 94560
**Post Office**: Newark Post Office, 6655 Clark Ave, 800-275-8777, www.usps.com
**Library**: Newark Library, 6300 Civic Terrace Ave, 510-795-2627
**Public Schools**: Newark Unified School District, 5715 Musick Ave, 510-794-2141, www.newarkunified.org
**Parks, Gardens, and Open Space**: Newark Recreation Services, Community Center, 35501 Cedar Blvd, 510-578-4437, www.newark.org

UNION CITY
**Website**: www.unioncity.org
**Area Code**: 510
**Zip Code**: 94587
**Post Office**: Main Post Office, 33170 Alvarado-Niles Road; 3861 Smith St, 800-275-8777, www.usps.com
**Library**: Union City Library, 34007 Alvarado-Niles Rd, 510-745-1464, TTY 510-489-1655
**Parks, Gardens, and Open Space**: Leisure Services Administration, 34009 Alvarado-Niles Rd, 510-675-5329, www.ci.union-city.ca.us

# ALAMEDA

Just south of Oakland, the city of **Alameda** is an island—four islands, locals will remind you—in the East Bay, and it's fast gaining the attention of newcomers. The islands are Harbor Bay, Coast Guard Island, Ballena Isle, and the main island (Alameda), which is connected to Oakland by a number of bridges. Alameda got its start a century ago, as a resort for San Franciscans who sought mild climate and comfortable sand. The Navy had built a military base that lasted here until its closure in the 1990s. In 2011 it was transferred to the city. Today this enormous site, called Alameda Point, is undergoing a $500 million overhaul, transforming into a mix of new residential neighborhoods, shopping areas, parks, and business buildings. What developers call "Site A" at Alameda Point will include 800 new housing

*Alameda*

units—condos, flats, and townhouses—with 530 of them for rent (200 of those below market rate), and the rest for sale. Also in the works is a new ferry terminal and shuttles offering service to downtown Oakland and BART stations. Construction is ongoing, with three phases aimed for completion by 2030. You won't have to wait that long to move in; several units are already open.

Historic preservation is a top priority among locals and city officials, but this city keeps changing: residents jokingly refer to it as the place "where hipsters come to breed." Buyers from San Francisco are flooding the island, as it's an easy ferry ride—and there's no fog. Almost half of the housing is renter-occupied, and the rest is owner-occupied. Architecturally, the area has some of the most beautifully restored Victorians in the Bay Area. You'll find a few that haven't been renovated yet, and you may be lucky enough to find one at a decent price—but real estate is now keeping pace with much of the Bay Area. As neighborhoods go, the South Shore (constructed on landfill) has sweeping views, tucked along the south coast. Central Alameda has smaller Victorians, and the Fernside area, on the eastern edge, has immaculate, gorgeous 1930s storybook houses.

Alameda meets all your basic shopping needs, and not generally in the form of chain stores. Robert Crown Memorial Beach, equipped with picnic tables and showers, is a mile-and-a-half beach, excellent for beginning windsurfers and kiteboarders. Washington Park, just before the beach, has tennis courts, a baseball field, and a dog park. Taking your dogs to the beach, however, could earn you a large fine. A major new bike lane is being added to the city, running half its length, from the west side to the center, and connecting Alameda Point to the old Del Monte waterfront area. And in 2015 a cofounder of Tesla Motors announced he would move his new hybrid powertrain company, Wrightspeed, to Alameda, ditching San Jose.

**Website**: www.alameda.gov
**Area Code**: 510
**Zip Codes**: 94501, 94502

**Post Offices**: 2201 Shoreline Dr; 2 Eagle Rd; 1415 Webster St, 800-275-8777, www.usps.com

**Police**: Alameda Police Department, 1555 Oak St, 510-337-8340

**Public Schools**: Alameda Unified School District, 2200 Central Ave, 510-337-7000, www.alameda.k12.ca.us

**Community Resources**: Alameda Chamber of Commerce, 1416 Park Ave, 510-522-0414, www.alamedachamber.com; Altarena Playhouse, 1409 High St, 510-523-1553, www.altarena.org; Bill Osborne Model Airplane Field on Doolittle St, 510-747-7529; Alameda Museum and Alameda Historical Society, 2324 Alameda Ave, 510-521-1233, www.alamedamuseum.org; USS Hornet Museum, Alameda Point, Pier 3, 510-521-8448, www.uss-hornet.org; Alameda Civic Light Opera, 2200 Central Ave, 510-864-2256, www.aclo.com; Mastick Senior Center, 1155 Santa Clara Ave, 510-747-7500

**Parks, Gardens, and Open Space:** Recreation and Parks, 2226 Santa Clara Ave, 510-747-7529, TTY 510-522-7538, www.alamedaca.gov/recreation

## EMERYVILLE

For a long time, **Emeryville** was known as "that town with the only Amtrak station," because neither San Francisco nor Oakland had Amtrak. Then Emeryville was known as "that town with the only IKEA." These days Emeryville is an enviable, colorful, booming business destination, with big names in countless industries, including Pixar—the animation-film studio—and the headquarters of Jamba Juice, Clif Bar, Kodak Gallery, Electronic Arts, Peet's Coffee & Tea, AAA Northern California, and the Center for Investigative Reporting. Quite a lineup, and the parade of powerhouse names continues to grow.

Sandwiched between Oakland and Berkeley, and virtually at the foot of the Bay Bridge, Emeryville was originally an industrial area with not much else happening. By the late 1980s and early '90s, this 1.2-square-mile city set out on a path

*Emeryville*

of transformation. Industrial sites became huge shopping centers, warehouses became lofts and offices, and new apartments and condos popped up. Today more than 11,000 people call Emeryville home.

The city's free shuttle, the Emery-Go-Round, is constantly improving and expanding, transporting locals to and from BART (MacArthur Station) and Amtrak. New bike paths wind throughout the city. And Emeryville is known for its progressive daycare facility, the Child Development Center, which operates year-round and provides services for infants and toddlers whose parents are working, in training, or in school.

The city is a regional shopping magnet, drawing residents from across the East Bay to its dense core of retail plazas. There are numerous chain stores here. IKEA's 274,000-square-foot (equivalent to five football fields), do-it-yourself furniture funhouse attracts thousands of Northern Californians every day. For food, the Emeryville Public Market, which is currently undergoing a major upgrade and expansion, is a favorite for inexpensive but delicious dishes, from Korean BBQ to French crepes to Japanese noodles, served cafeteria-style. Culturally, galleries are no longer the only venues for Emeryville artists, as bus shelters now showcase locals' art, replacing the usual advertisements. The city has rolled out more than 50 public art projects. Visit www.emeryarts.org for more details.

Most of the city's newer housing takes the form of condos and townhouses within mixed-use plazas, such as the recently completed Bay Street development project. Another major effort is the Sherwin-Williams development project, converting the former paint factory into 540 new housing units and a new 2-acre park near 100,000 square feet of commercial space. You'll find single-family detached homes in "the triangle" area, on San Pablo Avenue—mostly Craftsman-style houses built in the 1920s and '30s. Waterfront living is popular at the 1970s-era Watergate condos, which offer spectacular views of the Bay. Residents also live in the 30-story Pacific Park Plaza, with hundreds of condos. Although many of Emeryville's original loft residents were artists, today it is primarily tech workers who are moving into the unique spaces created in these old industrial buildings. Median one-bedrooms ran as high as $3,200 in Emeryville in mid-2015—not that much lower than San Francisco's.

**Website**: www.ci.emeryville.ca.us
**Area Code**: 510
**Zip Code**: 94608, 94662
**Post Office**: Emeryville Branch, 1585 62nd St, 800-275-8777, www.usps.com
**Police**: Emeryville Police Department, 2449 Powell St, 510-596-3700
**Library**: Golden Gate Library, 5606 San Pablo Ave, 510-597-5023
**Public Schools**: Emery Unified School District, 4727 San Pablo Ave, 510-601-4000, www.emeryusd.k12.ca.us
**Community Resources**: Emeryville Chamber of Commerce, 5858 Horton St, Suite 130, 510-652-5223, www.emeryvillechamber.com; Emeryville Senior

Center, 4321 Salem St, 510-596-3730; Emeryville Child Development Center, 1220 53rd St, 510-596-4343; Emery-Go-Round Free Shuttle, 510-451-3862 or 511, next bus hotline: 510-451-3862, www.emeryground.com; Amtrak, 5885 Horton St, 800-USA-RAIL, www.amtrak.com; First Time Homebuyers Program, 510-596-4316.

**Parks, Gardens, and Open Space:** Emery Recreation Department, 4300 San Pablo Ave, 510-596-4300, www.ci.emeryville.ca.us

# ALBANY

Just north of Berkeley, **Albany** is one of the Bay Area's best-kept secrets, but it won't be for long. Like Emeryville, it's small—a little more than one square mile, with 20,000 residents. But unlike Emeryville, Albany has a small-town village feel. Wild turkeys will chase you here. Hobbling along on the sidewalks, the turkeys seem cartoonish—but are less funny if you're the one being chased. They have been known to flap their wings and scream to protect offspring roosting in trees. They can tear up gardens, dart in front of bicyclists, scratch car paint, and sneak snacks from outdoor pet food bowls. Whether cute or creepy or both, it's a classic part of Albany living. If you're into urban farming, know that the city also allows you to keep up to six hens (no roosters) in your yard; six hens can produce 28 eggs on average per week.

Albany's public schools are excellent. Albany High School is one of the best-rated in the Bay Area. Many parents move here just to enroll kids in schools, and then move the families out after graduation. The crime rate is among the lowest in the region, and Albany is just 30 to 50 minutes from downtown San Francisco. A few years ago, Albany was added to Nextdoor.com—a helpful website for neighborhoods—but the city didn't yet have distinct neighborhood names, so the community center's director created them. Wherever you live in Albany, housing includes single-family homes as well as apartments built in the 1940s and '50s. Plenty of people are catching on to Albany's charm, a fact reflected in the rising housing prices.

The commercial strip of Solano Avenue is shared with Berkeley. Once a railroad thoroughfare, Solano Avenue offers practical services and shopping options, all within walking distance from most parts of Albany. Among the selections are bookstores, clothing boutiques, Indian and Thai restaurants, cafés, a supermarket, and a movie theater. Each fall the mile-long stretch of Solano Avenue is closed for the Solano Avenue Stroll, a weekend festival of food, music, and entertainment. The west side of town, where I-80 and I-580 meet, is bounded by the Bay, and home to the mudflats, which are popular with bird watchers, walkers, and joggers. An extension of the Bay Trail was recently completed. If you like to play the horses, or just watch them run, Golden Gate Fields Racetrack—billed as the only horse racing track in the Bay Area—is here (510-559-7300, www.goldengatefields.com).

**Website**: www.albanyca.org
**Area Code**: 510
**Zip Code**: 94706, 94710
**Post Office**: 1191 Solano Ave, 800-275-8777, www.usps.com
**Police**: Albany Police Department, 1000 San Pablo Ave, 510-525-7300
**Library**: Albany Library, 1247 Marin Ave, 510-526-3720
**Public Schools**: Albany Unified School District, 904 Talbot Ave, 510-558-3750, www.albany.k12.ca.us
**Community Resources**: Albany Chamber of Commerce, www.albanychamber. org; Solano Avenue Association, 1563 Solano Ave, #101, 510-527-5358, www. solanoavenueassn.org
**Parks, Gardens, and Open Space:** Albany Recreation and Community Services Department, 1249 Marin Ave, 510-524-9283, www.albanyca.org

# PIEDMONT

Surrounded by Oakland, but a city in itself, **Piedmont** is one of the wealthiest communities in the East Bay—and indeed the entire Bay Area. Incorporated in 1907, only 1.8 square miles in size, and with a population hovering around 11,000, Piedmont is a tiny enclave of elegant estates, regal mansions, tennis courts, and immaculately wooded parks. This city is also known for its excellent school district. Don't go looking for an apartment here—you won't find one. As a matter of fact, relatively affordable rental property of any type is virtually nonexistent here, although Craigslist does turn up a few now and then. If the name Piedmont rings a bell, it may be because the local high school has for decades been the host of a national bird-calling contest, the winners of which were invited to appear on *The Tonight Show* and *Late Night with David Letterman*. Will Stephen Colbert have them on, too? To find out, stay tuned to Piedmont High School's Facebook page at www.facebook.com/piedmonthighschool.

**Website**: www.ci.piedmont.ca.us
**Area Code**: 510
**Zip Codes**: 94611, 94610, 94618, 94602, 94620
**Post Office**: (nearest one) 195 41st St, Oakland, 800-275-8777, www.usps.com
**Police**: Piedmont Police Department, 401 Highland Ave, 510-420-3000
**Public Schools**: Piedmont Unified School District, 760 Magnolia Ave, 510-594-2600, www.piedmont.k12.ca.us
**Community Resources**: City Hall, 120 Vista Ave, 510-420-3040; Piedmont Adult School, 510-594-2655, piedmontadultschool.org
**Parks, Gardens, and Open Space:** Piedmont Recreation Department, 358 Hillside Ave, 510-420-3070, www.ci.piedmont.ca.us

# OAKLAND

| | |
|---|---|
| UPTOWN | BROOKLYN BASIN |
| LAKE MERRITT | ADAMS POINT |
| GRAND LAKE | TEMESCAL |
| MONTCLAIR | CHINATOWN |
| ROCKRIDGE | FRUITVALE |
| KOREATOWN | DIMOND |
| JACK LONDON SQUARE | |

The East Bay's largest city, **Oakland** is transforming faster—and more controversially—than any other Bay Area city outside of San Francisco. Oakland is booming with new companies and condos catering to those fleeing San Francisco's rents, and drawn to Oakland by warmer weather, lakeside farmers' markets, thriving arts festivals, and pristine hiking trails. While developers brand this an "urban renewal," residents hear "urban renewal" as code for escalating housing prices, rising displacement of longtime locals, and a culture clash unseen in generations. Luxury high-rises are on the way, and housing protesters gather in numbers and influence, mounting campaigns against gentrification in predominantly African-American neighborhoods that shoulder the costs of the tech boom. This city is at a crossroads. Just when you thought it might bring relief from San Francisco's record-high rents, Oakland turns out to be the second-most competitive renters' market in the United States (based on rent increases, median income, vacancy rates, and percentage of income put toward housing).

Home prices in Oakland surged 133 percent between 2011 and 2015, the steepest rise in the Bay Area. And the vacancy rate in Oakland dipped below San Francisco's. Credit this rising popularity to the real estate ripple effect that's pushing eastward from San Francisco and Silicon Valley, where saturation of housing means waves of East Bay migration.

"Brooklyn by the Bay" was the *New York Times'* attempt to liken Oakland to the burgeoning borough across the bridge from Manhattan. Many Oaklanders reject the Brooklyn analogy as caricature, because locals don't consider Oakland to be in the shadows of San Francisco. Oakland is proudly, defiantly its own, alive with civic pride—as seen in the hip "Oaklandish" fashion line (www.oaklandish.com). "Warriors! Warriors!" was the chant that echoed citywide when the city's NBA team crushed the competition to become national champions in 2015. More than a million fans attended the celebratory parade. To understand Oakland beyond sports victories, look past the parades to the cries of "Hands up, don't shoot!" that shut down highway traffic during the "Black Lives Matter" protests. Consider the "Housing is a human right!" activists chaining themselves together at City Council meetings in protest against new luxury high-rises. And consider the hiphop-vegan movement (you read that right) taking root in cafés and clubs and warehouses, combining food consciousness and social messaging. All of these are characteristic of today's Oakland. Each headline—the tech crowd's arrival, the

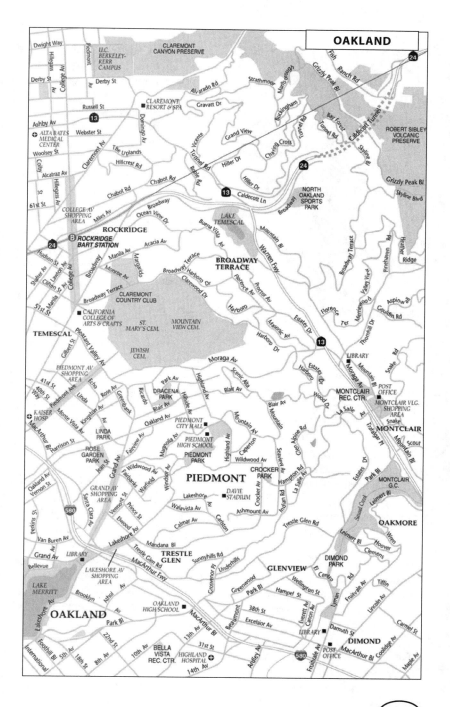

# OAKLAND

*Downtown Oakland*

soaring rents, the scenic hills, and the displacement of largely African-American communities—is part of this city's story. While industrial-chic boutiques may be a selling point, they're also a symbol of controversial change.

When it comes to housing, consider this general rule: the higher in the hills you live, the more you'll pay, thanks to spectacular Bay views. Downhill, and further west, are cheaper districts. Exhibit A: **West Oakland**, where industrial warehouses are being transformed into high-density developments. More than 1,000 condos are coming in here, making it one of the fastest-growing real estate markets around.

Historically, West Oakland became a majority-black neighborhood by the end of World War II, when black laborers migrated west from the American South for dollar-an-hour shipbuilding jobs—turning this waterfront district into the social and physical center of black life in the Bay Area. Legendary supper clubs and jazz halls hosted everyone from Billie Holiday to Miles Davis—long before the "hyphie" hip-hop movement was born here. And West Oakland was the birthplace of the Black Panther Party in the 1960s. Led by Bobby Seale and Huey P. Newton, the Panthers' marches, debates, and rallies struck a chord with the free-speech movement citywide.

Today's West Oakland is changing quickly. The neighborhood is getting 126 new condos at Filbert and Myrtle streets near West Grand Avenue, and 171 new townhouses near the historic train station, as well as a $500 million shipping and logistics center—slated to open in 2017—in the face of opposition by environmental leaders and the mayor. Coal shipments will introduce toxins into an air already polluted by nearby highways. But West Oakland is today's hottest spot for investors, who attribute its popularity to low costs, quick access to San Francisco, and the district's historic character. But developing while respecting the local communities that built this city is not easy. Stay tuned to West Oakland's developments at www.oaklandlocal.com/tags/west-oakland.

Meanwhile, the hippest new neighborhoods in Oakland—already gentrifying—are Uptown, Lake Merritt, and Temescal. **Uptown** stretches along Broadway and Telegraph between 17th and 25th streets, attracting student-artists and tech workers who enjoy its art-deco look and stylish bars. Especially popular are the Paramount Theatre, a majestic landmark, and the elegant Fox Theater, raging with rock bands. The newest hangouts for concertgoers are New Parish (www.thenewparish.com) and Duende, an intimate jazz-and-wine bar (www. duendeoakland.com). Proposals are in place for a 33-story residential tower in the heart of Uptown, with 345 apartments and almost 10,000 square feet of retail. And a new bicycle-valet station (free) is up and running at the nearby BART station.

Uptown is also home to the city's biggest vacant office tower—the former Sears building. It won't stay vacant long. The building is slated to open in late 2016 as a retail-and-office destination with a specialty market. Uptown's main street, Telegraph Avenue, fills with live music and food trucks not far from the Great Wall of Oakland—a 10,000-square-foot video projection on the side of a building, featuring new works by neighborhood artists. And Uptown is where locals stream by the thousands to events like Art Murmur—a free gallery stroll that weaves in and out of artists' studios on Telegraph Avenue between Grand and 27 streets (6–9 p.m. on the first Friday of every month, and every Saturday from 1–5 p.m.; www. oaklandartmurmur.org).

For the best of city life and scenic beauty, **Lake Merritt** is a prime option. Just moments from downtown, this three-mile lagoon is a scenic sanctuary. Home to hundreds of geese, Lake Merritt is packed with joggers and dog walkers in the morning, while at night the picturesque water lights up. Housing is getting costlier by the minute: a controversial new luxury high-rise is coming soon—a 24-story symbol of this city's housing battles. A stinging editorial in the *East Bay Express* opposed it by declaring, "We do not want a luxury high-rise apartment tower . . . We will not be manipulated or ignored by government officials and profit-driven business persons who have zero interest in the wellbeing, security, and quality of life for Black, Brown, and Asian communities . . . Gentrification is not the same as development . . . In 2015, Black residents can barely afford to live in the very city that we have helped shape." This debate will continue for the foreseeable future.

Surrounding Lake Merritt are older brick buildings from the 1920s, two- and three-bedroom homes from the 1940s and '50s, and condos from the 1960s and '70s. Lake Merritt locals who work in San Francisco enjoy a fast commute— the BART station is an easy walk. There's also a nearby Whole Foods, and in the summer the lake comes alive with canoes, kayaks, and windsurfing—while fall ushers in breezy moonlit walks and the Moon Viewing Festival.

Just north of Lake Merritt is the **Grand Lake** neighborhood—an equally hip spot that's got something that Lake Merritt doesn't: two main shopping strips that are easily strolled. Grand Avenue and Lakeshore Avenue give this neighborhood a closer-knit feel than Lake Merritt. Among its hangouts are Caña, an award-winning Cuban restaurant. Grand Lake is especially diverse in age and ethnicity, with a massive farmers' market north of the lake on Saturdays. But it's less close to the BART station. If you have a car, there's easy access to all highways, plus a "casual carpool" meeting point at the freeway's entrance.

The hippest of all Oakland neighborhoods is **Temescal**, attracting newcomers in their teens, 20s, and 30s, who stroll Telegraph Avenue's stretch of fashionable

*Lake Merritt*

dive bars and cafés. Temescal is where sidewalk chalkboards catch your eye with promises of mouthwatering mac 'n' cheese spiked with lime and chipotle. Named after a creek that's now partly underground, Temescal is best experienced by browsing the found-object vintage store East Bay Depot for Creative Reuse (4695 Telegraph Avenue, www.creativereuse.org). The neighborhood's hipness is nowhere clearer than in its pedestrian alleyways—a pair of hidden, high-end destinations with 18 shops in sites formerly used as horse stalls. As poverty deepens a few blocks away, a trendy store in the alleyways sells a basic hoodie for $170. To peek at the alleyways off 49th Street between Telegraph Avenue and Clark Street, visit www.temescalalleys.com. Meanwhile, a couple of blocks down is the Freedom Farmers' Market, which started in 2015 to support struggling farmers, on Telegraph near Claremont (every Saturday from 10 a.m.–3 p.m., June–November, www.freedomfarmersmarket.com).

Between Temescal and the downtown district is the Bay Area's largest concentration of Korean shops and businesses, popular for dakdoritang (spicy braised chicken) and pajun (flavor-packed pancakes). Dubbed **Koreatown**, this neighborhood is centered on Telegraph Avenue between 20th and 35th streets, and it's increasingly diverse and delicious. The district boasts easy access to BART and the highway.

The neighborhood of **Adams Point**, from Vernon Street to Lakeshore Avenue and MacArthur Boulevard to Grand Avenue, checks all the hipster boxes: creative cafés, young artists, tech workers, easy access to downtown, a Whole Foods, lake activities, and prime location. But the neighborhood is struggling with safety issues—a fact that is true of much of Oakland. The perks of Adams Point outnumber its pitfalls, according to the many locals who follow the neighborhood's Facebook page at www.facebook.com/groups/adamspointopen. It's a close walk from Children's Fairyland, the smile-inducing retro theme park where Walt Disney is said to have visited and drawn inspiration to create Disneyland. With boxy apartment buildings tucked between a cluster of Edwardian and Craftsmen houses,

Adams Point is coming up fast—the median sales price jumped 53 percent in a single year recently.

The ultra-fashionable **Jack London Square** neighborhood is a fancier nightlife destination on Oakland's waterfront, popular for award-winning dining and leisurely strolls. It's undergoing a $375 million upgrade to enhance its retail appeal. The neighborhood's star attraction is Yoshi's Jazz and Sushi Club (510 Embarcadero West, www.yoshis.com), a historically hip spot for all ages. Jack London Square residents enjoy a high-end farmers' market, and from here you can hop the ferry into San Francisco, or cross the street to the Amtrak station. In 2015 the popular *Sunset* magazine announced it was moving offices to Jack London Square, an indication of this neighborhood's growing prestige and investment-rich future.

Just south of Jack London Square, you'll find a new neighborhood— **Brooklyn Basin** waterfront—Oakland's largest real estate project, a $1.5 billion development that's creating 3,100 apartments, townhomes, and lofts. One-third of these will be priced below market rate. Surrounding the buildings will be 32 acres of public parks—a vibrant waterfront that developers hope will resemble Portland's Pearl District and New York's Battery Park City. One challenge facing Brooklyn Basin is its isolation from public transit, as the nearest BART station is a trek—but bicycles and cars can be used to cover the difference. Occupancy is scheduled for late 2017. (For an interactive map of Brooklyn Basin, visit www.brooklynbasin.com.)

Another up-and-coming Oakland neighborhood is **Dimond District**, centered at the intersection of MacArthur Boulevard and Fruitvale Avenue. It is many developers' "neighborhood to watch" in 2016 and beyond. The neighborhood, with a long-established Latino community, contains historic buildings, a public library, mom-and-pop shops, and two grocery stores. The district hosts the popular Oaktoberfest [sic], an outdoor fall festival luring thousands of locals with music, food, and a homebrew competition (www.oaktoberfest.org).

The **Fruitvale** district is also gaining momentum, as new residential buildings come up at 35th Avenue and East 12th Street. Many of these apartments will sell below market rate, meaning if you earn 30–60 percent of the area's median income, you're eligible. The development is part of the neighborhood's ambitious new Fruitvale BART Transit Village.

Of all the neighborhoods, many argue that **Rockridge** is Oakland's most desirable, established district for families. The streets are safe, and there are outstanding schools, easy transportation, and spacious houses—with prices in the gazillions. The shops are so chic that one, a clothing boutique on College Avenue, is even called Chic. Some students live here, but it's primarily well-paid professionals commuting to San Francisco and the South Bay. Homes are typically stucco and wood-shingled Craftsman-style bungalows with cottage gardens. Upper Rockridge (above Broadway), built during the postwar booms of the 1920s and '40s, extends into the hills northeast. Many homes destroyed in a major 1991 fire were replaced by million-dollar houses, and apartments are scarce, as the area has zoning restrictions on buildings with more than four units.

Residents of Rockridge gravitate to Rockridge Market Hall (5655 College Avenue), a European-style shopping experience near three bookstores, French and Vietnamese bistros, a kids' consignment shop, and pricy boutiques. Even the ultra-hip Smitten Ice Cream has opened a branch (look it up and drool).

Close to Rockridge is the coveted neighborhood of **Montclair**, which is quieter and calmer. Montclair is a tidy mountain village with cozy cafés and welcoming bookstores, a hillside haven for families who can afford it. In 2015 this neighborhood launched a streetscape project to improve walkways and create a community gathering space. The project invites you to purchase engraved red bricks (www.montclairbricks.com) to be embedded in the ground near Antioch Court. One hitch: due to an early curfew, there is no nightlife here. At all. Two restaurants have bars, but if you're looking for late-night performances, you'll have to travel. It's a worthy concession, considering the spectacular hikes at the top of local Shepherd Canyon Road. (For more details, visit www.montclairvillage.com.)

Another neighborhood to watch is **Golden Gate**—on the city's north side— where the main shopping strip of San Pablo Avenue includes vegan donuts, drip coffee, and a cupcake shop. The Ashby BART station is a manageable walk (about 15 minutes, tops), and most homes are Edwardian or Craftsman-style bungalows; the remainder are 1940s ranches, Victorians, and cement fixer-uppers. Developers are trying to rebrand this neighborhood as "NOBE" (North Oakland–Berkeley–Emeryville), with its own website: www.nobeneighborhood.com. So far, the "NOBE" nickname hasn't stuck.

*Montclair*

Closer to downtown Oakland, you'll find **Chinatown**, which spans 16 square blocks from Broadway to Fallon streets and 12th Street to Interstate 880. The Chinatown StreetFest is one of the Bay Area's largest Asian-American festivals, with music, dance, and more than 200 vendors across 10 blocks (www.

oaklandchinatownstreetfest.com). But Oakland's Chinatown is in transition, as landmarks keep closing. The iconic Silver Dragon restaurant bid farewell recently after almost 60 years. Silver Dragon's space is now occupied by a health clinic that serves low-income residents. For a glimpse into Chinatown, visit the neighborhood's oral-history project at www.memorymap.oacc.cc.

Culturally, this entire city is grappling with the legacy of a massive fire that struck the hills a generation ago, destroying more than 2,500 homes and killing 25 people. Responding fire trucks had trouble navigating the narrow roads. Though it's been decades since the fires, the tragedy of that disaster still haunts Oakland. Since then, the city has implemented new fire codes and built roads wide enough to allow emergency accessibility to outlying areas. And in 2015 the city was awarded $5.6 million in federal funds to thin the city's eucalyptus trees—a highly combustible nonnative species. At the same time, environmentalists are "re-oaking" Oakland by seeding new trees—a drought-tolerant native species that shelters wildlife and reduces pollution.

Politically, Oakland leans left. The city was ranked the fourth-most liberal city in the United States recently, which could explain why real estate developers here are required by law—not just urged—to install public art at the site of any new building or pay thousands of dollars in fines under a new ordinance. When it comes to education, Oakland boasts the Bay Area's best high school, according to *U.S. News & World Report* (2015): the American Indian Public High School, also ranked 12th best in the nation.

As tech crowds and condos move in, Oakland continues to see marches for housing fairness, environmental protection, and police accountability. This is one of California's most diverse cities. And as the tech boom expands Bay Area–wide, Oakland grows with it, having recently topped 400,000 residents for the first time in its 150-year history.

**Website**: www.oaklandnet.com
**Area Code**: 510
**Zip Codes**: 94601–94627, 94643, 94649, 94659, 94660–94662, 94666
**Post Office**: Oakland Main, 1675 7th St, 800-275-8777, www.usps.com
**Police**: Oakland Police Department, 455 7th St, 510-777-3333
**Libraries**: Oakland Public Library, Main Branch, 125 14th St, 510-238-3134, www.oaklandlibrary.org; Asian Branch 388 9th St, Suite 190, 510-238-3400; Brookfield Branch, 9255 Edes Ave, 510-615-5725; César E. Chávez Branch, 3301 E 12th St (services in Spanish), 510-535-5620; Dimond Branch, 3565 Fruitvale Ave, 510-482-7844; Eastmont Branch, 7200 Bancroft, Suite 211 (Eastmont Town Center), 510-615-5726; Elmhurst Branch, 1427 88th Ave, 510-615-5726; Golden Gate Branch, 5606 San Pablo Ave, 510-597-5023; Lakeview Branch, 550 El Embarcadero, 510-238-7344; Martin Luther King Branch, 6833 International Blvd, 510-615-5728; Melrose Branch, 4805 Foothill Blvd, 510-535-5623; Montclair Branch, 1687 Mountain Blvd, 510-482-7810; Piedmont Avenue

Branch, 160 41st St, 510-597-5011; Rockridge Branch, 5366 College Ave, 510-597-5017; Temescal Branch, 5205 Telegraph Ave, 510-597-5049; West Oakland Branch, 1801 Adeline St, 510-238-7352

**Public Schools**: Oakland Unified School District, 1025 Second Ave, Oakland 94606, 510-879-8200, http://webportal.ousd.k12.ca.us

**Community Publications**: *Oakland Tribune*, 510-208-6300, www.insidebayarea. com/oaklandtribune (also owns the *Alameda Times Star*, the *Fremont Argus*, and a handful of smaller local papers); *East Bay Express*, 510-879-3700, www. eastbayexpress.com; *Contra Costa Times* (covers Contra Costa and east Alameda County), 800-598-4637, www.ContraCostaTimes.com (also owns Hills News, which puts out *Berkeley Voice*, *Alameda Journal*, the *Montclarion*, and the *Piedmonter*)

**Community Resources**: Oakland Zoo, 9777 Golf Links Rd, 510-632-9525, www. oaklandzoo.org; McAfee Coliseum (Oakland–Alameda County Coliseum), 7000 Coliseum Way, 510-569-2121; Chabot Observatory and Science Center, 10000 Skyline Blvd, 510-336-7300, www.chabotspace.org; Oakland A's Baseball, 510-638-4900, www.oaklandathletics.com; Golden State Warriors Basketball, 510-986-2222, www.nba.com/warriors; Oakland Raiders Football, 510-864-5000, www.raiders.com; Oakland DMV, 5300 Claremont Avenue, 800-777-0133; Claremont Country Club, 5295 Broadway Terrace, 510-653-6789

**Cultural Resources**: Alameda County Arts Commission, P.O. Box 29004, Oakland, 94604, 510-208-9646, www.acgov.org/arts; Oakland Museum of California, 1000 Oak St, 510-238-2200, www.museumca.org; Oakland East Bay Symphony, 510-444-0801, www.oebs.org; Oakland Ballet, 510-452-9288, www.oaklandballet. org; Museum of Children's Art, 538 9th St, 510-465-8770, www.mocha.org; Pro Arts, Inc., 461 9th St, 510-763-4361, www.proartsgallery.org; California College of Arts & Crafts, 5212 Broadway, 510-594-3600, www.cca.edu

**Parks, Gardens, and Open Space**: Oakland Parks and Recreation, 250 Frank Ogawa Plaza, Suite 3330, 510-238-PARK, www.oaklandnet.com; Lake Temescal Regional Recreation Area, 6500 Broadway, 510-652-1155, www.ebparks.org/parks/temescal.htm

# BERKELEY

NORTH BERKELEY
BERKELEY HILLS
SOUTH BERKELEY
CLAREMONT, ELMWOOD
DOWNTOWN/CENTRAL BERKELEY
WEST BERKELEY

Just how progressive is the city of **Berkeley**? Try this: in 2015 the cellphone industry sued Berkeley over a new local ordinance requiring wireless companies to warn consumers that phones might exceed radiation safety standards. The phone companies claimed that the city's requirement violates the companies' own free speech by compelling the companies to convey a statement they disagree with. The irony is thick: Berkeley is the last place needing a lecture on free speech. Berkeley is the birthplace of the free-speech movement—the frontier of First Amendment activism in the 1960s. Welcome to Berkeley today, where the tech generation is writing the next political chapter.

Berkeley's radical roots—the antiwar protests, the labor movement, environmental cleanup, and countless other campaigns—are deeply established. The intellectual climate of the University of California at Berkeley is richly nourished by a top faculty and student body. Campus activism continues to define the city, even though it makes fewer headlines today. But the community surrounding the university—throughout the town—is where most of Berkeley's radical movements are launched now; the campus itself is more of a shining destination than a hotbed of liberal revolution. Among the newest debates in Berkeley is the housing shortage. As in San Francisco, short-term rentals offered by Airbnb have squeezed Berkeley's already tight housing supply. The city is clamping down on Airbnb, limiting short-term rentals to ease the burden on longtime locals, students, and newcomers.

Berkeley is adding a cluster of affordable housing downtown, where more than 1,400 new homes and 88,000 square feet of retail space are slated for 2018 completion. The downtown area is booming; its population has nearly doubled in the last decade and a half. As of 2015, Berkeley had hundreds of below-market-rate apartments spread across 25 sites. The number is growing.

**North Berkeley**, considered the quieter side of town, is home to many graduate students, professors, and young families. North on Shattuck Avenue, from Rose up to Hearst, you'll find the "Gourmet Ghetto" (its official name), replete with legendary organic restaurants and specialty shops. It was here, at 1517 Shattuck Avenue, that Alice Waters launched her pioneering organic food restaurant Chez Panisse decades ago. She has since championed organic foods in Berkeley's public

*North Berkeley*

schools. Other gourmet delights abound; stroll down Shattuck Avenue for any-thing from rosemary focaccia to Pad Thai to matzo ball soup. Intimate Walnut Square, between Walnut and Shattuck, is home to the original Peet's Coffee & Tea, at 2124 Vine Street. Additional shopping is abundant on Hopkins Street (known as "Gourmet Ghetto West").

Following Shattuck south across University Avenue, you'll hit the heart of downtown. Here you'll find a mix of shops and a centrally located BART station for easy access to San Francisco. There's also a cluster of movie theaters within a short radius. As you move away from the main drag, streets become heavily tree-lined, featuring stately Victorians and bungalows. The roads narrow, the speed limits drop, and the bike lanes abound.

Up in the **Berkeley Hills,** which run from the North Campus area east to Berke-ley's magnificent Tilden Park and north to Kensington, you'll discover scenic views with a scent of eucalyptus. To get to the Berkeley Hills, take Euclid Avenue north all the way to Grizzly Peak, coming through Tilden Park at its northernmost entrance—or start at the football stadium and follow Centennial Drive up to Grizzly Peak. Along your drive you'll see exquisite Craftsman-style homes, some with striking Bay views and majestic gardens. If you're willing to navigate the hill every day, you may be able to rent a room in one of these homes. Craigslist is your best bet.

Along Euclid Street, the higher the ascent, the more spectacular the homes. The Berkeley Rose Garden on Euclid Street (between Eunice and Bayview Place) offers enviable Bay views. For a startling sunset, try the benches at the top of the garden. Traveling up the hills via the Centennial route will bring you to the Botan-ical Gardens in Strawberry Canyon. Considered one of the world's leading gardens in terms of plant variety and quality, the gardens are home to Chinese medicinal herbs and soaring redwoods. Also on the hill is the Lawrence Hall of Science, with one of the best views of the city, as well as a first-rate public science center with hands-on educational programs.

Visitors trek from all directions to the 2,065 acres of open meadows and the

*South Berkeley*

forests of Tilden Park, with 30 miles of hiking and horse trails, an 18-hole public golf course, swimming at Anza Lake, a petting farm, a carousel, and a steam train. There are no shopping options atop the hill, so you'll need to wrap up errands before heading up.

Directly south of the campus and west of the Berkeley Hills, **South Berkeley** is predominantly populated by students, many living in dormitories, co-ops, and fraternity or sorority houses. This is the bustling area of Berkeley, with activity at all times. Some of the most architecturally exquisite homes are the large mansions that house fraternities and sororities. Architect Julia Morgan designed the outdoor Greek Theatre, and Bernard Maybeck, architect of San Francisco's Palace of Fine Arts, also made his mark on many Berkeley homes.

Much of the '60s free-speech movement and antiwar protests centered around Telegraph Avenue and Sproul Plaza. The plaza still hosts protests, as well as musicians, politicians, self-proclaimed prophets, and skateboarders. Telegraph Avenue, which begins in downtown Oakland, runs into the southern side of the campus. The Berkeley section of Telegraph is a lively shopping zone catering to students with clothing, book, and music stores. There are coffee shops, cheap eats, and cafés. Street vendors set up daily, selling handmade jewelry and tie-dyed shirts. UC Berkeley includes two top concert venues—the Greek Theatre (8,500-seat amphitheater) and the indoor Zellerbach Hall.

The bustle of campus life quiets down when you head south, away from the campus. Close to College Avenue, the **Claremont** neighborhood, bordering Oakland (east of the Elmwood District and west of the Claremont Resort), is one of Berkeley's grandest and most expensive neighborhoods. The area is named for the 22-acre resort, Claremont Hotel Club and Spa, which is so large it can be seen from across the Bay. Designed by Charles Dickey, the Claremont has tennis courts and a large outdoor swimming pool.

The **Elmwood District**, just down the street and west from the Claremont, is a pleasant area of two- and three-story brown-shingle homes surrounded by

*Claremont*

*Downtown Berkeley*

tall trees. Housing here is pricey, and to supplement income, many families find tenants for their backyard cottages, basements, or attic rooms.

**Downtown Berkeley's** civic heart is the Martin Luther King Jr. Civic Center Park, 2151 Martin Luther King Jr. Way—a stretch of green at the foot of city hall. Berkeley's main post office and library are in the 2000 block of Allston way. Though not as popular as 4th Street or College Avenue (see below), Shattuck Avenue offers a variety of shopping—from furniture, to clothing, to tiny boutiques, to toy stores and movie theaters. Downtown is home to Berkeley's theater scene, high-lighted by the Berkeley Repertory Theatre, 2025 Addison Street. Though not in downtown proper, Zellerbach Auditorium on the UC Campus also sponsors live performances, from the Kirov Ballet to John Cleese.

Downtown's central hub for mass transit includes BART (Shattuck and Center) and AC Transit. Just down the street from the BART Station, people line up early to carpool into the city (three persons in a car constitute a carpool), avoiding the steep bridge toll.

Also known as the "Flatlands," **West Berkeley** is considered a transitional area with affordable fixer-uppers, new lofts, and relatively inexpensive rents. This area is more challenged by safety concerns, but its proximity to the waterfront and the 4th Street shopping district is an asset. South of University Avenue, along the numbered streets, you'll find a cluster of warehouses and unique arts shops. Nearby San Pablo Avenue is a major route through town. Initiatives to enhance this area are well under way, including the addition of new bike routes.

Biking is extremely popular in Berkeley, which is the fourth-most popular city for bike commuters in the United States, according to the East Bay Bicycle Coalition. Even the mayor of Copenhagen—the most bike-friendly city in the world—was a special guest at Berkeley's bike happy hour in 2015, to share tips on how to make the city more "bike-able." Berkeley is also a powerhouse of literary culture: the new Bay Area Book Festival launched in 2015 as a free two-day event with hundreds of author readings, panels, and performances in a 10-block stretch of downtown

Berkeley (www.baybookfest.org). It's no wonder that Berkeley ranked sixth on the country's "best places to live" list compiled by Livability (www.livability.com).

And it's still a progressive place. While more than 30 cities and states had tried and failed to adopt soda taxes, Berkeley became the first American city to do so.

**Websites**: www.ci.berkeley.ca.us

**Area Codes**: 510, 341

**Zip Codes**: 94701, 94702, 94703, 94705, 94707, 95708, 94709

**Main Post Office**: 2000 Allston Way, Berkeley, 800-275-8777, www.usps.com

**Police**: Berkeley Police Department, 2100 Martin Luther King Jr Way, 510-981-5900, TTY 510-981-5799

**Libraries**: Berkeley Public Library, Central Branch, 2090 Kittredge St, Berkeley, 510-981-6100; Claremont Branch, 2940 Benvenue Ave, 510-981-6280; South Branch, 1901 Russell St, 510-981-6260; North Branch, 1170 The Alameda, 510-981-6250; West Branch, 1125 University Ave, 510-981-6270, www.berkeleypubliclibrary.org

**Public Schools**: Berkeley Unified School District, 2134 Martin Luther King Jr. Way, Berkeley, 510-644-6348, www.berkeley.k12.ca.us; college: www.berkeley.edu

**Community Publications**: East Bay Express, 510-879-3700, www.eastbayexpress.com; *Contra Costa Times* (covers Contra Costa and east Alameda County) 800-598-4637, www.contracostatimes.com (also owns Hills News, which puts out *Berkeley Voice, Alameda Journal*, the *Montclarion,* and the *Piedmonter); Berkeley Daily Planet*, 510-841-5600, www.berkeleydailyplanet.com; UC.Berkeley Publications: *Daily Californian*, www.dailycal.org

**Community Resources**: Berkeley Chamber of Commerce, 1834 University Avenue, 510-549-7000, www.berkeleychamber.com; Tool Lending Library, 1901 Russell St, 510-981-6101; Berkeley First Source employment program, 510-981-7550; Berkeley Art Center, 1275 Walnut St, 510-644-6893, www.berkeleyartcenter.org

**Cultural Resources**: University of California, Berkeley Art Museum, 2626 Bancroft Way, 510-642-0808, www.bampfa.berkeley.edu; Pacific Film Archive Theater, 2575 Bancroft Way, 510-642-1124, www.bampfa.berkeley.edu; Lawrence Hall of Science, Centennial Dr below Grizzly Peak, 510-642-5132, www.lhs.berkeley.edu; Judah L. Magnes Memorial Museum, 2911 Russell St, 510-549-6950, www.magnes.org; La Pena Cultural Center, 3105 Shattuck Ave, 510-849-2568, www.lapena.org; Ames Gallery of American Folk Art, 2661 Cedar St, 510-845-4949, www.amesgallery.com; Black Repertory Group, 3201 Adeline St, 510-652-2120; Julia Morgan Center for the Arts, 2640 College Ave, 510-845-8542; Berkeley Repertory Theatre, 510-647-2949, www.berkeleyrep.org

**Parks and Open Space**: Berkeley Parks Recreation and Waterfront Department, 2180 Milvia St, Third Floor, 510-981-6700, TTY 510-981-6903, www.ci.berkeley.ca.us (Berkeley Community Gardening Collaborative can be reached at 510-883-9096, www.ecologycenter.org/bcgc); Marina Experience Program/Shorebird Park and Nature Center and Adventure Playground, 160 University

Avenue, 510-981-6720; call the parks and recreation department for information about local climbing parks

## CONTRA COSTA COUNTY

**Contra Costa County**, with just over one million people, stretches along the eastern side of the East Bay hills, where the weather is warm, warmer, and warmest. The population is diverse, with all economic and cultural demographics represented. Housing options are also varied, ranging from old farmhouses and massive, gated apartment complexes to duplexes, condos, and sprawling, newly landscaped housing developments. Many apartment complexes offer swimming pools and recreation centers. Housing costs are slightly lower than most Bay Area counties.

**Website**: www.co.contra-costa.ca.us
**Area Codes**: 510, 925
**Sheriff**: 651 Pine St, 7th Floor, Martinez, 925-335-1500, www.cocosheriff.org
**Libraries**: Contra Costa County Library, Pleasant Hill/Central Branch, 1750 Oak Park Blvd, 925-646-6434, www.ccclib.org, branches throughout the county
**Emergency Hospitals**: Contra Costa Health Services: Contra Costa Regional Medical Center, 2500 Alhambra Ave, Martinez (operates community health centers in Antioch, Bay Point; Brentwood, Pittsburg, Richmond and Concord), 925-370-5000 or TTY 925-335-9959, www.cchealth.org; John Muir Medical Center, 1601 Ygnacio Valley Rd, Walnut Creek, 925-939-3000, www.johnmuirhealth.com; Mt. Diablo Medical Center, 2540 E St, Concord, 925-682-8200, www.johnmuirhealth.com; San Ramon Regional Medical Center, 6001 Norris Canyon Rd, 925-275-9200
**Public Schools**: West Contra Costa Unified School District, 1108 Bissell Ave, Richmond, 94801, 510-234-3825, www.wccusd.k12.ca.us; Contra Costa Office of Education, 77 Santa Barbara Rd, Pleasant Hill, 925-942-3388, www.cccoe.k12.ca.us
**Community Publications**: *Oakland Tribune*, 510-208-6300, www.insidebayarea.com/oaklandtribune (also owns the *Alameda Times-Star* and the *Fremont Argus*); *East Bay Express*, 510-879-3700, www.eastbayexpress.com; *Contra Costa Times* (covers Contra Costa and east Alameda County) 800-598-4637, www.contracostatimes.com. *Danville Today News*, 925-405-6397; *Community Focus* (covers Pleasant Hill, Concord, Martinez, Lafayette, and Walnut Creek) 925-335-6397, www.ourcommunityfocus.com
**Community/County Resources**: Richmond Art Center, Civic Center Plaza, 2540 Barrett Ave, 510-620-6772, www.therichmondartcenter.org; Richmond Museum of History, 400 Nevin Ave, 510-235-7387; Alvarado Adobe House and Blume House (the San Pablo Historical Society), 510-215-3046; John Muir National Historic Site, 4202 Alhambra Ave, Martinez, 925-228-8860, www.nps.

gov/jomu; Blake Garden, 70 Rincon Rd, Kensington, 510-524-2449; Martinez Marina, 925-313-0942; Contra Costa HIV/AIDS Program Resource Line, 925-313-6770; Recreation Services, City Hall, 525 Henrietta St, Martinez, 925-372-3510; Concord Police Community Action and Awareness Line, 925-671-3237

**Public Transportation:** *AC* (*Alameda-Contra Costa*) *Transit*, 510-891-4700, TTY 800-448-9790, www.actransit.org; *BART*, 510-465-2278, TTY 510-839-2278, www.bart.gov; *Benicia Transit*, 707-745-0815, *County Connection*, 925-676-7500; *RIDES*, 511, www.511.org; *Tri-Delta Transit*, 925-754-4040, *WestCat*, 510-724-7993; *Amtrak*, 800-872-7245

**Parks, Gardens, and Open Space:** East Bay Regional Park District, 2950 Peralta Oaks Ct, 510-562-PARK, www.ebparks.org, maintains 62 parks throughout the region, many with large open areas, nature trails and shorelines

# MARTINEZ, WALNUT CREEK, PLEASANT HILL, CONCORD

The city of **Martinez** is the county seat, but its downtown is pretty much lights-out after 5 p.m. There's more activity and attraction in Walnut Creek, which is far more of an upscale destination, although both towns put you at the crossroads of highways. Martinez is also the site of naturalist John Muir's historic home, a well-maintained hillside Victorian mansion that is open to the public. With a population of 37,000, Martinez boasts home prices under the county median.

**Walnut Creek**, home to 67,000 people, is shining brightly, widely considered the most desirable city in Contra Costa County. This city has more public open space per capita than any other city in California. It also boasts lively arts programs and centers, including the Lesher Center for the Arts and Bedford Gallery, with public gardens, and the Boundary Oak Golf Course. Commensurate with its desirability, housing prices run higher than its neighbors. The city's biggest project is under construction at Broadway Plaza, which is undergoing a total remodel and expansion driven by pent-up demand from the recession several years ago. It's a

*Martinez*

high-end suburban setting, whose downtown includes urban high-rise apartment living. The outlying neighborhoods are immaculately beautiful, with spacious houses on leafy streets. The city's John Muir Medical Center was ranked third-best hospital in the Bay Area in 2015, according to patient satisfaction ratings. And Walnut Creek is doing its part to conserve water during this record-long drought, by suspending public fountains until recycled water can be pumped in. The city's library also rolled out two 3D printers recently—a big draw for kids and adults alike.

**Pleasant Hill** is similarly pleasant—although it's not all hilly, despite the name. A good way to absorb the community is to meander across the downtown lawn, which is tucked behind Bed Bath & Beyond. It's an inviting, exquisitely beautiful spot with beach chairs and a dozen trendy gourmet food trucks—a crème brulee truck, a grilled-skewers truck, a lobster truck, a beer truck, and many others. Up to 800 people come out on Wednesday nights for this new ritual. It's a magnet for locals of all ages—including teens on dates, who come here from Martinez and Concord.

**Concord**, the largest city in Contra Costa County, has a population of 126,000. Houses along the corridor of Highway 680 are going up rapidly. Although housing prices are rising faster than in most areas, median home prices still skew toward the low end for the Bay Area. Concord is also home to an upper-division and graduate campus of Cal State East Bay.

For an excellent local website to learn more about these communities, visit www.claycord.com.

## MARTINEZ
**Website**: www.cityofmartinez.org
**Area Code**: 925
**Zip Code**: 94553
**Post Office**: 4100 Alhambra Ave
**Library**: 740 Court St., 925-646-2898
**Public Schools**: Martinez Unified School District, 921 Susana St., 925-313-0480, www.martinezusd.net; Mt. Diablo Unified School District, 1936 Carlotta Dr, 925-682-8000, www.mdusd.org
**Parks, Gardens, and Open Space**: Parks, Recreation and Community Services, 525 Henrietta St, 925-372-3580

## WALNUT CREEK
**Website**: www.ci.walnut-creek.ca.us
**Area Code**: 925
**Zip Code**: 94596
**Post Office**: 2070 N Broadway
**Library**: 1395 Civic Dr, 925-646-6773
**Public Schools**: Walnut Creek School District, 960 Ygnacio Valley Rd, 925-944-6850,www.wcsd.k12.ca.us; Mt. Diablo Unified School District, 1936 Carlotta Dr, 925-682-8000, www.mdusd.org

**Parks, Gardens, and Open Space**: Arts, Recreation & and Community Services Division, 1666 N Main St, 925-943-5858

PLEASANT HILL

**Website**: www.ci.pleasant-hill.ca.us
**Area Code**: 925
**Zip Code**: 94523
**Post Office**: 1945 Contra Costa Blvd
**Library**: 1750 Oak Park Blvd, 925-646-6434
**Public Schools**: Mt. Diablo Unified School District, 1936 Carlotta Dr, 925-682-8000, www.mdusd.org
**Parks, Gardens, and Open Space**: Pleasant Hill Rec, www.pleasanthillrec.com

CONCORD

**Website**: www.cityofconcord.org
**Area Code**: 925
**Zip Code**: 94519, 94520
**Post Office**: 2121 Meridian Park Blvd
**Library**: Concord Library, 2900 Salvio St., 925-646-5455
**Public Schools**: Mt. Diablo Unified School District, 1936 Carlotta Dr, 925-682-8000, www.mdusd.org
**Parks, Gardens, and Open Space**: Parks Department, 2974 Salvio St, 925-671-3404

# RICHMOND

The northernmost city in Contra Costa County, **Richmond** is known throughout the Bay Area for four characteristics above all others: savings (on housing); social infrastructure challenges (public safety has been in the headlines); proximity (the BART train is a breeze into San Francisco); and a rich history. The city was established as a shipyard town at the beginning of World War II, when ships destined for the Pacific left port from Richmond. Many residents today are descendants of those who migrated here from the American South for dollar-an-hour shipbuilding jobs in the mid-1930s and '40s. Richmond has since fallen on hard times—suffering from underemployment while nearby towns have benefitted from the tech boom. Richmond has struggled to keep pace over the years, and the city is still working to improve economically, as well as lower its high crime rates. Compared with the rest of the East Bay, rents and homeownership costs here are cheap. And Richmond boasts 32 miles of coastline—the most of any Bay Area city.

Change is coming—and relatively quickly. In 2015 this city became the first in Contra Costa County to pass rent control, joining San Francisco and Berkeley as leading cities that have adopted the measure. Rent control limits landlords to an annual rent increase equal to the rise in the local consumer price index. For newcomers who don't speak "consumer price index," all that means is that your rent can't go up an insane amount from year to year. The cost you're told when you sign your lease is pretty much the cost you'll pay the next year. While supporters of rent control claim that it protects renters against unfair eviction and surprising rent hikes, opponents say it harms landlords financially and doesn't fix the housing crisis. The new ordinance in Richmond will take effect in early 2016 if it clears opposition from the mayor's office. Rent control would then apply to 9,900 homes out of the city's 34,000 total rentals.

Richmond is also poised to become an internal hub for education, as the highly respected University of California at Berkeley plans to create a 134-acre campus—the Berkeley Global Campus—on Richmond's southern shoreline. The site will become a "living laboratory" in partnership with public universities worldwide.

Richmond has also broken ground on a cluster of new housing around the BART station, and the city has already completed 32 miles of the new San Francisco Bay Trail—a planned 500-mile multi-purpose trail winding all around the Bay.

A Richmond enclave especially worth exploring is **Point Richmond,** close to the Bay. Here you'll find a waterside artist-and-sailing community with an old-fashioned downtown. The community atmosphere is cozy, and the Richmond Yacht Club is a popular socializing spot. Many of the homes near the yacht club have their own private docks. Public swimming is available in the Richmond Plunge—the Bay Area's largest heated indoor pool, at 1 East Richmond Avenue.

*Point Richmond*

**Website**: www.ci.richmond.ca.us

**Area Code**: 510

**Zip Codes**: 94801–94808, 94820, 94850, 94875, 94530

**Post Offices**: 104 Washington Ave; 1025 Nevin Ave; 2100 Chanslor Ave; 200 Broadway, 800-275-8777, www.usps.com

**Police:** Richmond Police Department, 1701 Regatta Blvd, 510-233-1214

**Library**: Richmond Main Library, 325 Civic Center Plaza, 510-620-6561

**Public Schools**: West Contra Costa Unified School District, 1108 Bissell Ave, 510-234-3825, www.wccusd.net

**Community Resources**: Richmond Online, www.pointrichmond.com; Richmond Yacht Club, 351 Brickyard Cove, 510-237-2821; Richmond Plunge, 1 East Richmond Ave, 510-620-6820; Masquers Playhouse, 105 Park Place, 510-232-4031; Richmond City Hall, 450 Civic Center Plaza, 510-620-6509; Richmond Museum of History, 1337 Canal Blvd, 510-237-2933, www.richmondmuseum.org; Richmond Art Center (RAC), 2540 Barrett Ave, 510-620-6772, www.richmondartcenter.org; Chamber of Commerce, 3925 Macdonald Ave, 510-234-3512; Merchants Association, 510-221-9006, www.23rdsteetma.com

**Parks, Gardens, and Open Space**: Richmond Recreation and Parks, 3230 Macdonald Ave, 510-620-6793, www.ci.richmond.ca.us/recreation

# SAN RAMON, DANVILLE

Recently crowned the "best town to raise a family" in California—and the second-best in the nation—by the ranking site Niche.com (2015), **San Ramon** is gaining a whirlwind of attention among new parents, based on school ratings, safety, affordable housing, and childcare. About 25 miles east of Oakland, this sun-filled city is framed by lush pastures and trails—a beautiful backdrop to a formerly sleepy community. Today it's an active, upscale destination, with a sprawling office complex anchored by major corporations. San Ramon didn't incorporate as a city until 1983, making it a relatively new municipality with no downtown—yet. A long-anticipated downtown is set to open in 2017, including 2 million square feet of sleek shops and restaurants and a football-field-sized outdoor plaza for concerts and art installations.

Residents had tried for 20 years to add a downtown, but their effort was derailed by the 2008 financial meltdown—a setback from which this community has rebounded dramatically. Retaining San Ramon's suburban charm during today's real estate boom, the city has one of the region's highest median incomes. About 760 new houses and 170 apartments will open in 2018, plus 50 new townhomes in 2016. For budget-strapped newcomers, rest assured that 25 percent of all new housing is required to be sold below market rate. You'll also find two-, three-, and four-bedroom houses built in the 1980s—many with spacious backyards and neatly landscaped front lawns.

San Ramon is just moments away from picturesque Mount Diablo—at 3,849 feet, it's the area's highest peak, and is dotted with unusual rock formations and wildflowers. On weekends, campers and horseback riders flock here from throughout the Bay Area to scale the summit, where you can view more than half of California's 58 counties. On clear days, according to park authorities, you can also see more of the Earth's surface than is viewable from any other peak in the world except Mount Kilimanjaro. San Ramon's creeks, however, are a concern. They can cause serious flooding during heavy rain—a distant problem, given the

*San Ramon*

ongoing drought. Consider purchasing flood insurance if you buy a home here, in case rain ever returns.

The city's commercial core is a 585-acre office park called Bishop Ranch, anchored by the corporate headquarters of Chevron, and regional offices of Toyota, Ford, and 600 other companies. Tens of thousands of jobs are expected to be added here over the next decade. To prepare for it, City Hall is relocating to a brand-new building in the downtown area.

As part of the Tri-Valley area, which is known for wealthy enclaves, lush golf courses, and local wineries, San Ramon shares services with the cities of Pleasanton, Livermore, Dublin, and Danville, each connected to San Francisco, Oakland, and San Jose via two major highways, I-680 and I-580. These highways resemble a parking lot during commute hours. A BART station would be helpful, but none exists in San Ramon. If you rely on trains, consider nearby Dublin and Pleasanton, which have BART access.

Just north of San Ramon is **Danville**, a pristine, exclusive, pleasant village where American flags mark the leafy downtown—yes, Danville has a downtown, a magnet for San Ramon locals who don't. Danville is decked out with spotless patios and floral gardens. Even the public library is a masterpiece, an exquisite structure with village charm, set back from an immaculate lawn that's bathed in sun. Just when you think Danville couldn't get prettier, you find out there's a $2 million "beautification" project along Hartz Avenue, almost completed. How can you improve on spotless? Danville found a way. This village is transforming its historic hotel into 16 condos with a handful of restaurants and boutiques—one of the biggest projects in decades. Shopping plazas skew heavily toward high-end dance rooms, yoga studios, health clubs, and day spas.

For housing, you'll find upscale modern estates and 1950s ranch-style houses that are (or will soon be) upgraded. You'll pay slightly higher taxes to retain the higher-quality schools in Danville than nearby towns, as this community is very affluent, safe, and sunny. The Alamo-Danville Newcomers club and Danville

Women's Club are increasingly active, hosting lively outings for women of all ages (www.alamodanvillenewcomers.com and www.danvillewomensclub.org). To learn more about Danville's community projects, visit www.danvilleimprovements.com.

A note to naturalists: each fall is tarantula mating season here, offering an unusually memorable sight—thousands of the arachnids—if you hike Mount Diablo State Park nearby. Just watch where you step.

### SAN RAMON

**Website**: www.ci.san-ramon.ca.us

**Area Code**: 925

**Zip Code**: 94582, 94583

**Post Office**: 12935 Alcosta Blvd, 800-275-8777, www.usps.com

**Police**: 2220 Camino Ramon, 925-973-2700, www.ci.san-ramon.ca.us/police

**Library**: 100 Montgomery St, 925-973-2850, www.ccclib.org

**Public Schools**: San Ramon Valley Unified, 699 Old Orchard Dr, Danville, 925-552-5500, www.srvusd.k12.ca.us

**Community Resources**: San Ramon Olympic Pool and Aquatic Park, 9900 Broadmoor Dr, 925-973-3240; Senior Center, 9300 Alcosta Blvd, 925-973-3250; San Ramon Royal Vista Golf Course and San Ramon Golf Club, 9430 Fircrest Ln, 925-828-6100, www.sanramongolfclub.com; The Bridges Golf Club, 9000 South Gale Ridge Rd, 925-735-4253, www.thebridgesgolf.com; Child Day Schools and Hidden Canyon School, 18868 Bollinger Canyon Rd, 925-820-2515; San Ramon Historical Foundation, www.sanramonhistoricfoundation.org

**Community Publications**: *Tri-Valley Herald*, 510-208-6300, www.insidebayarea.com/trivalleyherald; *San Ramon Observer*, www.sanramonobserver.org

**Public Transportation**: *County Connection*, 925-676-7500, www.cccta.org; *AC (Alameda-Contra Costa) Transit*, 510-891-4700, TTY 800-448-9790, www.actransit.org; *BART*, 510-465-2278, TTY 510-839-2278, www.bart.gov; *Amtrak*, 800-USA-RAIL, TTY 800-523-6590, www.amtrak.com, *ACE (Altamont Commuter Express)*, 800-411-RAIL, www.acerail.com

**Parks, Gardens, and Open Space**: San Ramon Parks and Recreation and Community Center, 925-973-3200, www.ci.san-ramon.ca.us/parks; San Ramon Community Center at Central Park, 12501 Alcosta Blvd, 925-973-3350

### DANVILLE

**Website**: www.danville.ca.gov

**Area Code**: 925

**Zip Code**: 94506, 94526

**Post Office**: 2605 Camino Tassajara, 800-275-8777, www.usps.com

**Police**: 510 La Gonda Way, 925-314-3700, www.ci.danville.ca.us

**Library**: 400 Front St, 925-837-4889, www.ccclib.org

**Public Schools**: San Ramon Valley Unified, 699 Old Orchard Dr, Danville, 925-552-5500, www.srvusd.k12.ca.us

**Community Resources**: Chamber of Commerce, 117 Town & Country Dr, 925-837-4400, www.danvilleareachamber.com; Blackhawk Automotive Museum, 3700 Blackhawk Plaza Cir, 925-736-2277, www.blackhawkmuseum.org; Discover Danville Association, 925-339-8330, www.discoverdanvilleca.com; Danville Village Theatre, 233 Front St, 925-314-3463, www.villagetheatreshows.com; Eugene O'Neill National Historic Site, 1000 Kuss Rd, 925-838-0249, www.nps.gov/euon; All Wars Memorial, 1000 Sherbrune Hills Rd, 925-314-3450, www.allwarsmemorial.org

**Community Publications**: *Tri-Valley Herald*, 510-208-6300, www.insidebayarea.com/trivalleyherald

**Public Transportation**: *County Connection*, 925-676-7500, www.cccta.org; *AC (Alameda-Contra Costa) Transit*, 510-891-4700, TTY 800-448-9790, www.actransit.org; *BART*, 510-465-2278, TTY 510-839-2278, www.bart.gov; *Amtrak*, 800-USA-RAIL, TTY 800-523-6590, www.amtrak.com, *ACE (Altamont Commuter Express)*, 800-411-RAIL, www.acerail.com

**Parks, Gardens, and Open Space:** Danville Community Center, 925-314-3400, www.danville.ca.gov/services/recreation-services

## LAFAYETTE, MORAGA, ORINDA

Known as "Lamorinda"—*LA*fayette, *MOR*aga, and Or*INDA*— this highly desirable trio of villages is popular among families drawn to the area's top-notch schools, quiet creeks, rolling hills, and secluded parks. The towns' hiking trails are so breathtaking that you can easily forget you're just a short BART ride from downtown Oakland and San Francisco.

Orinda is more expensive than Lafayette, which is more expensive than Moraga. But all three towns are similarly scenic and safe. Set against the Berkeley-Oakland hills, Orinda's downtown is divided into two parts—the Village District and the Theater District—by a freeway and the BART tracks, making it less than intuitive to find your way around. But new signage is coming in 2016. What sets Orinda apart is that it is all hills—whereas Walnut Creek, for example, is considerably flatter. The charming atmosphere creates a spectacular stage for the Shakespeare performances that are top attractions among locals. Deer, wild turkeys, soaring birds—they're all common around the town's 31 miles of creeks and 32 native plant species. Orinda's wild turkeys escort (or chase) you home on occasion—a running joke throughout the town. And in 2014 the town's library added a new teens-only space, designed with the help of teens themselves.

All three towns—Orinda, Moraga, Lafayette—have some of the best-rated schools in California. This is especially true of Orinda, whose high school ranks in the top 60 of all 1,000 high schools in California, and the top 4 percent of high schools in the nation. *Forbes* named Orinda one of "America's friendliest towns" recently. A big challenge Orinda faces, however, is road quality, as local roads received a "poor" rating from the Metropolitan Transportation Commission. But there's a multimillion-dollar, 10-year road plan underway (the city repaired more than 20 roads in 2015).

The wooded, secluded community of **Moraga** is similarly picturesque. The town is trying to keep pace with the flurry of downtown developments nearby by expanding its own downtown. But a growing chorus of residents opposes the development, hoping to keep the town's semi-rural character by gathering signatures to halt the construction. Residents also showed up in force to rally in support of the beloved Rheem Theatre, which was facing closure due to a 60 percent increase in rent. The community continues to search for ways to hold onto the theater: many residents have started a GoFundMe campaign to keep it running. The theater is an art-deco masterpiece, home to the acclaimed California Independent Film Festival (CAIFF).

Like Orinda, Moraga is known for its schools—consistently among the best in California, according to *U.S. News & World Report*. Many newcomers move here just for the schools. Just one new house was built in 2015, and only one was constructed a few years before that. Locals like the town's rustic, slow pace. Some projects in Moraga take 25 years to get off the ground. Most of its landscape is stunningly beautiful open space owned privately, including the 600-acre rolling hills of the Carr Ranch, which will soon become public. On most days the loudest sound you'll hear is a quiet bird chirp.

**Lafayette** has more activities and a bigger downtown than both Orinda and Moraga. Lafayette is considered a happy medium—popular for the Glenn Seaborg Consortium, which hosts daily events with distinguished speakers. The town is flush with new housing. There are dozens of developments either recently completed or nearing completion, including 44 single-family homes on Deer Hill Road; eight single-family luxury homes on Lucas Drive; 49 below-market-rate senior-citizen rentals on Mt Diablo Boulevard; and, most impressive, 81 rentals where Mt Diablo Boulevard meets Dewing Ave, directly south of the BART station. This last is scheduled for completion in 2017. A mix of upscale dining and casually hip eateries is part of the downtown strip known as Restaurant Row.

Summers in all three towns—Orinda, Moraga, Lafayette—can be sweltering (unlike San Francisco). And in a sign of solidarity, the Orinda Arts Council has been renamed the Lamorinda Arts Council, which coordinates art activities across the three communities.

## ORINDA

**Website**: www.cityoforinda.org
**Area Code**: 925
**Zip Code**: 94563
**Post Office**: 29 Orinda Way, 800-275-8777, www.usps.com
**Police**: 22 Orinda Way, 925-254-6820, www.cityoforinda.org

**Library**: 26 Orinda Way, 925-254-2184, www.ccclib.org

**Public Schools**: Orinda Union School District, 925-254-4901, www.orindaschools. org

**Community Resources**: Orinda Theatre, 4 Orinda Theatre Sq, 925-254-9065, www.lamorindatheatres.com, California Shakespeare Theater, 100 California Shakespeare Theatre Way, 510-548-9666, www.calshakes.org; Lamorinda Arts Council, lamorindaarts.org; Chamber of Commerce, 26 Orinda Way, 925-254-3909, www.orindachamber.org; Orinda Starlight Village Players Theatre, 28 Orinda Way, 925-528-9225, www.orsvp; Meadow Swim and Tennis Club, 20 Heather Ln, 925-254-3861, www.gomeadow.com

**Community Publications**: *Lamorinda Weekly*, www.lamorindaweekly.com

**Public Transportation**: *County Connection*, 925-676-7500, www.cccta.org; *AC (Alameda-Contra Costa) Transit*, 510-891-4700, TTY 800-448-9790, www. actransit.org; *BART*, 510-465-2278, TTY 510-839-2278, www.bart.gov; *Amtrak*, 800-USA-RAIL, TTY 800-523-6590, www.amtrak.com, *ACE (Altamont Commuter Express)*, 800-411-RAIL, www.acerail.com

**Parks, Gardens, and Open Space**: Parks & Recreation, 28 Orinda Way, 925-253-4202, www.cityoforinda.org

## MORAGA

**Website**: www.moraga.ca.us

**Area Code**: 925

**Zip Code**: 94563

**Post Office**: 460 Center St, 800-275-8777, www.usps.com

**Police**: 329 Rheem Blvd, 925-284-5010, www.police.moraga.ca.us

**Library**: 1500 St Mary's Rd, 925-376-6852, www.ccclib.org

**Public Schools**: Moraga School District, 1540 School St, 925-376-5943, www. moraga.k12.ca.us

**Community Resources**: Rheem Theatre, 16 Moraga Ln, 350 Park St, 925-388-0752, www.lamorindatheatres.com; Hacienda de las Flores, 2100 Donald Dr, 925-888-7045, www.moragahacienda.com; Saint Mary's College Museum of Art, 1928 Saint Mary's Road, 925-631-4000, www.stmarys-ca.edu

**Community Publications**: *Lamorinda Weekly*, www.lamorindaweekly.com

**Public Transportation**: *County Connection*, 925-676-7500, www.cccta.org; *AC (Alameda-Contra Costa) Transit*, 510-891-4700, TTY 800-448-9790, www. actransit.org; *BART*, 510-465-2278, TTY 510-839-2278, www.bart.gov; *Amtrak*, 800-USA-RAIL, TTY 800-523-6590, www.amtrak.com, *ACE (Altamont Commuter Express)*, 800-411-RAIL, www.acerail.com

**Parks, Gardens, and Open Space**: Parks & Recreation, 329 Rheem Blvd, 925-888-7045, www.moraga.ca.us/dept/park-rec

## LAFAYETTE

**Website**: www.ci.lafayette.ca.us

**Area Code**: 925

**Zip Code**: 94563
**Post Office**: 29 Orinda Way, 800-275-8777, www.usps.com
**Police**: 3675 Mt Diablo Blvd #130, 925-284-5010
**Library**: 3491 Mt Diablo Blvd, www.ccclib.org
**Public Schools**: Lafayette School District, 3477 School St, www.lafsd.k12.ca.us
**Community Resources**: Community Resources: Glenn Seaborg Learning Consortium, 3491 Mt Diablo Blvd, 925-385-2280, www.lafayettelib.org; Community Center, 500 St. Mary's Rd, 925-284-2232, www.ci.lafayette.ca.us/visitors/community-center; Chamber of Commerce, 925-284-7404, www.lafayettechamber.org
**Community Publication**: *Lamorinda Weekly*, www.lamorindaweekly.com
**Public Transportation**: *County Connection*, 925-676-7500, www.cccta.org; *AC (Alameda-Contra Costa) Transit*, 510-891-4700, TTY 800-448-9790, www.actransit.org; *BART*, 510-465-2278, TTY 510-839-2278, www.bart.gov; *Amtrak*, 800-USA-RAIL, TTY 800-523-6590, www.amtrak.com, ACE (Altamont Commuter Express), 800-411-RAIL, www.acerail.com*
**Parks, Gardens, and Open Space**: Recreation Programs, 925-284-2232, www.ci.lafayette.ca.us

## ADDITIONAL CITY WEBSITES—CONTRA COSTA COUNTY

**Antioch:** www.ci.antioch.ca.us
**El Cerrito:** www.el-cerrito.ca.us
**Hercules:** www.ci.hercules.ca.us
**Livermore:** www.cityoflivermore.net
**Oakley:** www.ci.oakley.ca.us
**Pinole:** www.ci.pinole.ca.us
**Pittsburg:** www.ci.pittsburg.ca.us
**Pleasanton**: www.cityofpleasantonca.gov
**San Pablo:** www.ci.san-pablo.ca.us

# THE PENINSULA (SAN MATEO COUNTY AND NORTHERN SANTAW CLARA COUNTY)

## SAN MATEO COUNTY

Part of the beauty of Bay Area life is how quickly you can reach rugged coastline and serene nature just minutes from San Francisco. **San Mateo County** is a clear winner in that category. Known as "the Peninsula," San Mateo County is directly south of San Francisco. It's hard to imagine what this area was like just a century ago when only a few towns dotted the road between San Francisco and San Jose. The enclaves of Belmont, Hillsborough, Woodside, Atherton, and Palo Alto were

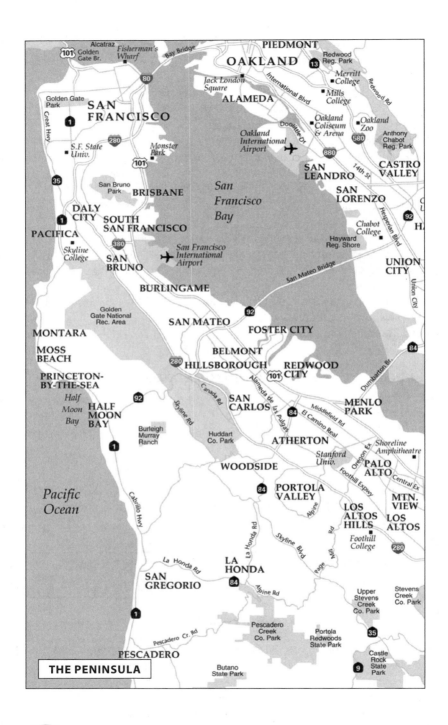

THE PENINSULA

not boomtowns, but rather garden spots with estates where wealthy San Franciscans relaxed in tranquil surroundings and glorious weather.

Today San Mateo County—which became independent of San Francisco in 1856—consists of 21 cities, many of them booming with tech headquarters. The eastern half of San Mateo County offers easy access to Interstate 280 and Highway 101.

Filled with spacious single-family homes and an array of outdoor shopping malls, San Mateo County combines cozy suburbia with jagged hiking trails. The most populous city, Daly City, borders San Francisco and marks the beginning of the suburbs. Here at the northernmost edge, longtime San Francisco "bedroom communities" like San Bruno and South San Francisco are attracting more newcomers with the development of condos and townhouses. A little further south are San Mateo (the city), Burlingame, and Belmont, where the price of homes has been edging up fast. Neatly tucked between San Francisco to the north and Silicon Valley to the south, commuter traffic flows heavily in both directions, and can be rough.

San Francisco International Airport (SFO) is on the bay side of the Peninsula, in the South San Francisco/Millbrae/San Bruno area. The airport is a madhouse practically every day. It is notorious for attracting a perpetual blanket of fog, causing frequent delays. The Peninsula is also served by the Caltrain commuter service and several bus lines, including Sam Trans (the San Mateo County bus service), which runs to San Francisco. By far the most exciting development in recent years is the expansion of BART service. Rather than terminating in Daly City, the trains reach Colma, San Bruno, South San Francisco, Millbrae, and SFO. The newer stops offer excellent park-and-ride options for commuters headed into San Francisco or the East Bay.

People living in the East Bay commute to San Mateo County and Silicon Valley via the San Mateo–Hayward Bridge or the Dumbarton Bridge (to Fremont). As more people move east in search of more affordable homes, traffic has grown considerably. The San Mateo–Hayward Bridge was widened in hopes of alleviating the strain, but traffic along Highway 92—the route that crosses the bridge—still moves at a slow crawl during peak times. From the late afternoon into the evening, cars are backed up from the ocean to the Bay (and sometimes vice versa).

To the west is the ocean-side edge of San Mateo County, trimmed with Highway 1, one of the most strikingly beautiful roadways in the world, tracing the Pacific coastline from the beach town of Pacifica to the pumpkin patches of Half Moon Bay and the boardwalk of Santa Cruz. Be on the lookout for gray whales and dolphins. The coastline is often blanketed with fog, giving the beaches a surreal atmosphere.

Housing costs are swelling out of control, however. In 2015 only 29 percent of residents in San Mateo County were able to afford a basic home, as median prices for entry-level houses topped $1.1 million. A one-bedroom rental here averages $2,500 per month—a jump of 63 percent between 2009 and 2015. But that's still far lower than San Francisco's rental median. The numbers in 2015 also showed that in San Mateo County, Section 8 subsidized housing was virtually impossible to find. Newcomers with housing vouchers have a tough time getting rentals because landlords prefer renters with cash—and although the vouchers are like cash, landlords typically shy away from the required paperwork. In response to the housing crisis, county leaders have called for increased rent protections in Redwood City, Burlingame, Mountain View, and Fremont. Officials have also budgeted $30 million to build more affordable housing.

**Website**: www.co.sanmateo.ca.us

**Area Code**: 650

**Sheriff:** San Mateo County Sheriff's Office, 400 County Center, Redwood City, 650-365-4911

**Emergency Hospitals**: San Mateo Medical Center, 222 W 39th Ave, San Mateo, 650-573-2222; Sequoia Hospital, 170 Alameda de las Pulgas, Redwood City, 650-369-5811, www.sequoiahospital.org; Seton Medical Center, 1900 Sullivan Ave, Daly City, 650-992-4000, seton.dochs.org; Stanford Medical Center, 300 Pasteur Dr, Stanford, 650-723-4000, www.stanfordhospital.org

**Library:** Peninsula Library System, 25 Tower Rd, San Mateo, 650-780-7018, www.plsinfo.org

**Public Schools:** San Mateo County Office of Education, 101 Twin Dolphin Dr, Redwood City, 650-802-5300, www.smcoe:k12.ca.us

**Community Publication:** *San Mateo County Times,* 650-348-4321, www.insidebayarea.com/sanmateocountytimes; *Daily Post,* serving Palo Alto, 650-328-7700, www.padailypost.com

**Community Resources:** San Mateo County Convention and Visitors Bureau, 111 Anza Blvd, Suite 410, Burlingame, 650-348-7600, www.smccvb.com; TIES (information, advice, and resources for seniors and disabled), 800-675-8437 or 650-573-3900, TTY 711

**Public Transportation:** *RIDES,* 511, www.511.org; *Caltrain,* 800-660-4287, TTY 415-508-6448, www.caltrain.com; *SamTrans,* 800-660-4287, TTY 650-508-6448, www.samtrans.com

**Parks, Gardens, and Open Space:** San Mateo County Park and Recreation Department, 455 County Center, 4th Floor, Redwood City, 650-363-4020, www.co.sanmateo.ca.us/portal/site/parks

# DALY CITY, COLMA

Billing itself as the "gateway to the Peninsula"—and the "gateway to San Francisco" if you're heading north—**Daly City** is immediately south of San Francisco, just off of Interstate 280. After the 1906 earthquake and fire, many San Franciscans sought refuge in the open countryside of Daly City, which was incorporated five years later. Today this 7.5-square-mile city is the most populous community in the county, with more than 105,000 residents.

Among locals, Daly City is even more notorious for its blanket of fog than its big-city neighbor to the north. It's frequently cool and gray here even when the sun is shining on all of San Francisco. But for those who don't mind wearing sweaters every day, this town offers family-oriented living just minutes from San Francisco's attractions—at a fraction of the price. The large, deeply rooted Filipino-American community has a rich history in all corners of Daly City, and the neighborhoods are increasingly diverse across cultural backgrounds. Daly City's BART station ensures easy access to downtown San Francisco, and for those driving to the station, BART provides 1,400 parking spaces. The spaces fill up quickly, so arrive early or look for parking on a nearby street. San Francisco Airport is under ten minutes away, a convenience—but also a noise nuisance if you prefer a neighborhood free of overhead rumble. If you're commuting to Silicon Valley, it takes anywhere from 40 minutes to two hours, depending on traffic.

Daly City is far less expensive than San Francisco; it's one of the most affordable cities in San Mateo County. Apartments, duplexes, townhouses, condos, and single-family terraced homes can be found throughout, and many hillside houses have ocean and Bay views.

For those who can afford it, the desirable neighborhood of **Westlake**, bordering San Francisco, has its own shopping plaza, and is within minutes of Lake Merced. To the west, you'll find single-family and newer luxury homes perched atop steep cliffs overlooking the crashing waves of the Pacific. In recent years, several hillside spots have had trouble with erosion, and even landslides; consider asking for a geological assessment before settling here.

One of the area's major shopping malls, the Serramonte Shopping Center, is found in Daly City. Home Depot, Nordstrom Rack, and a second Target (in case the one at Serramonte doesn't cut it for you) are south on I-280, at the Metro Shopping Center in the neighboring city of **Colma**, whose most notable characteristic is a fact about its 17 cemeteries: Colma has more deceased people than living people. The town's buried population is 1.5 million; its living population is 1,800.

*Daly City*

Locals refer to Colma as the "city of the dead," as cemeteries make up 73 percent of its 2.25 square miles.

But there's more to Colma than chilling demographics. There's a popular multiplex cinema packed every Friday and Saturday night just off the freeway, as well as two popular fast food pit stops—In-N-Out Burger and Krispy Kreme Doughnuts. Locals here enjoy easy access to three golf courses, including Lake Merced Country Club, which also features tennis courts. Although there's a ton of coastline, there's little coastal access here, so determined dog walkers and joggers frequent paths down to the city's only beach, Thornton.

## DALY CITY
**Website**: www.dalycity.org
**Area Codes**: 415, 650
**Zip Codes:** 94014, 94015
**Post Office:** 1100 Sullivan Ave, 800-275-8777, www.usps.com
**Police Station:** Daly City Police Department, 333 90th St, 650-991-8119
**Emergency Hospital:** Seton Hospital, 1900 Sullivan Ave, 650-992-4000, www.setonmedicalcenter.org
**Library:** Serramonte Main Library, 40 Wembley Dr, 650-991-8023, www.dalycitylibrary.org
**Public Schools:** Jefferson Elementary School District, 101 Lincoln Ave, 650-746-2400, www.jsd.k12.ca.us; Jefferson Union High School District, 699 Serramonte Blvd, #100, 650-550-7900, www.juhsd.k12.ca.us
**Community Resources:** Daly City-Colma Chamber of Commerce, 355 Gellert Blvd, Suite 138, 650-755-3900, www.dalycity-colmachamber.org; Doelger Senior Center, 101 Lake Merced Blvd, 650-991-8012, www.doelgercenter.com
**Parks, Gardens, and Open Space:** Parks and Recreation Department, 111 Lake Merced Blvd, 650-991-8015, www.ci.daly-city.ca.us/city_services/depts/park_rec/index.htm

## COLMA
**Website**: www.colma.ca.gov
**Area Codes**: 650
**Zip Codes:** 94014
**Post Office:** 7373 Mission, 800-275-8777, www.usps.com
**Police Station:** 1199 El Camino Real, 650-997-8321
**Emergency Hospital:** Seton Hospital, 1900 Sullivan Ave, 650-992-4000, seton.dochs.org
**Library:** Serramonte Main Library, 40 Wembley Dr, 650-991-8023, www.dalycitylibrary.org
**Public Schools:** Jefferson Elementary School District, 101 Lincoln Ave, 650-746-2400, www.jsd.k12.ca.us; Jefferson Union High School District, 699 Serramonte Blvd, #100, 650-550-7900, www.juhsd.k12.ca.us

**Community Resources:** Daly City-Colma Chamber of Commerce, 355 Gellert Blvd, Suite 138, 650-755-3900, www.dalycity-colmachamber.org; Doelger Senior Center, 101 Lake Merced Blvd, 650-991-8012, www.doelgercenter.com
**Parks, Gardens, and Open Space:** Parks and Recreation Department, 1520 Hillside Blvd, 650-985-5678, www.colma.ca.gov

# PACIFICA

Just 15 miles from San Francisco, this rugged beach town is where scenic trails, breathtaking bluffs, and powerful ocean waves mark the end of urban living and the start of natural retreats. **Pacifica** (population 39,000) is no longer a small coastal town in San Francisco's shadows. The word is out, and people have flocked here, especially young professionals and established families who enjoy frequent fog (Pacifica's nickname is Fog City) and windswept hikes through forested canyons. Ironically, Pacifica, which means "peace" in Spanish, is only five miles from San Francisco International Airport, and flights can be heard overhead at night. Don't look for the town center, because it doesn't exist. What you will find instead is a string of 11 shopping enclaves, and a dispersed community atmosphere—quiet, friendly, welcoming. Near the water's edge, Rockaway Beach Plaza, the Pacific Manor area, and Pedro Point—with cozy waterside cafés, seafood restaurants, antique stores, and surfboard shops—welcome you in flip-flops. Other plazas, like the Linda Mar Shopping Center east of Highway 1, have an outdoor-strip-mall feel.

If you prefer T-shirt weather, look elsewhere. The wind snaps. Except in times of drought, storms can rattle the windows, lending an aura of excitement to the coast's sights, sounds, and eucalyptus scent. Major change has finally arrived in the form of Devil's Slide, the former motorway that now has a new, picture-perfect walking trail above the ocean. This 1.3-mile walkway is one of the state's most impressive coastal redesigns in the past half century, with staggeringly beautiful views—ideal for recreational hikers, bikers, and dog walkers.

*Pacifica*

People move to Pacifica for one reason, to be close to the ocean. But the town is not far from nightlife, if you have a car. You'll find a variety of unfussy apartments and houses, many overlooking the Pacific. Architecturally, homes are typically California ranch style, with a handful of Queen Anne Victorians, beach shacks, and limited two-story luxury houses. Boxy 1970s-style apartment buildings, scattered throughout town, attract young workers who commute via Highway 1 and Interstate 280 to San Francisco every morning. While not much to look at on the outside, many of these apartments have small balconies perfect for kicking back with a drink and a book (and a very warm sweater) and taking in the ocean vistas.

A few years ago, newcomers who couldn't afford San Francisco could move to Pacifica and grab a spacious house for the price of a studio in the big city. That's not so easy today. Pacifica's prices are jumping, though not to San Francisco levels. Parking is abundant here, and freeway access is a breeze. But the nearby tech boom and housing frenzy have finally affected Pacifica's mixed-income working-class roots, adding heavy competition and cost.

The town has rolled out a free weekend shuttle service; download the new iPacifica mobile app for real-time departures. Pacifica is also the fourth-richest marine habitat in the world, as well as one of the best fishing spots in California. There's an abundance of outdoor activities, including surfing, scuba diving, fishing (spearfishing too), paragliding, tennis, archery, golf, and horseback riding. Most of the sandy shores aren't nearly as crowded as those in nearby Half Moon Bay. The same goes for public parks, except at the end of September, when the city hosts thousands of visitors at the annual Pacific Coast Fog Fest—a street fair with music, food, and artists' booths.

As stoic as Pacifica is, it includes a minor-league football team—the national champion Pacifica Islanders. There's also an active senior center, offering housing and meal assistance, and the Pacifica Resource Center, which helps families in need of food, shelter, clothing, and agency referrals.

**Website:** www.cityofpacifica.org

**Area Code:** 650

**Zip Code:** 94044

**Post Office:** 50 W Manor Dr, 800-275-8777, www.usps.com

**Police Station:** 2075 Coast Hwy, 650-738-7314

**Libraries:** Pacifica Library, 104 Hilton Way, Pacifica, 650-355-5196; Sanchez Library, 1111 Terra Nova, 650-359-3397

**Public Schools:** Pacifica School District, 375 Reina Del Mar, 650-738-6600, www.pacificasd.org

**Community Resources:** Pacifica Resource Center, 1809 Palmetto Ave, 650-738-7470; Pacifica Performances, 1220A Linda Mar Blvd, 650-355-1882, www.pacificaperformances.org; Pedro Point Surf Club, pedropoint.typepad.com

**Community Publications:** *Pacifica Tribune*, 650-359-6666, www.pacificatribune.com

**Beaches, Parks, Gardens, and Open Space:** Parks, Beaches & Recreation Department, 1810 Francisco Blvd, 650-738-7381

# HALF MOON BAY

When the fog lifts—and it occasionally does—on this upscale beachfront town 25 miles south of San Francisco, you'll see some of the most spectacular coastline in California. Salty air permeates **Half Moon Bay**'s community of 12,000 people, who proudly enjoy the stretches of sandy beaches, jagged cliffs, grazing horses, and artichoke farms. It's a rustic retreat, increasingly popular with highly paid tech workers and independent artists, who move here for the seaside atmosphere, which feels worlds apart from nearby cities. Hiking trails hug the coast, pelicans soar above the ocean, and dozens of surfers congregate at sunrise. Half Moon Bay is the oldest town in San Mateo County, dating to the 1840s. The World Championship Pumpkin Weigh-Off comes here annually—a festive crowd-pleaser whose winner recently tipped the scales at more than 2,000 pounds.

Alongside this town's historic landmarks are pricy, charming galleries and wine-and-cheese shops tucked between specialty stores like an olive oil tasting station. But Half Moon Bay continues to struggle with city finances, rebounding from the brink of bankruptcy after the recession and other local setbacks. The biggest industry here—tourism—flatlined just when the city was battling costly missteps in development. But recovery is steady, and housing prices are back to all-time highs. A $23 million library is underway, and a $2 million upgrade is coming to a creek bridge. New benches are installed on the coastal trail, and in 2014 Half Moon Bay earned the "most improved roads" award from the Metropolitan Transportation Commission. A multimillion-dollar push is also underway to improve bicyclist safety on the beautiful stretch of Highway 1 overlooking the coast.

Don't let this low-key beachside spot fool you: there are billions of dollars concentrated here, but not always visibly. There's a cliffside Ritz-Carlton tucked

*Half Moon Bay*

away near the ocean, and in a recent controversy, a local tech billionaire bought and privatized a beach near Half Moon Bay. He denied access to locals, who hauled him to court to keep the beach public. The public won, securing a court order forcing the owner to let the public back in. The line between privacy rights and public access—between new tech influence and natural resources—shapes conversation in Half Moon Bay (just as it does across the Bay Area).

Median home prices topped $1 million recently, and housing under $600,000 is increasingly hard to find, accounting for just 13 percent of recent sales. Most houses are owner-occupied, and few are rented out. If you find a spot you can afford, grab it. You'll enjoy eucalyptus-scented walks to roadside markets, and a farmers' market at Shoreline Station (Saturdays, May to December). But don't expect late-night parties. Many locals' idea of a big night out here is a community stroll—literally. Called the Passeggiata, after the Italian tradition of the evening promenade, an official Friday night stroll has been sanctioned by the city, and is announced by downtown banners. Chatting and walking in the evenings: that's about as mischievous and rambunctious as weekends get in Half Moon Bay.

Recreation opportunities include golf courses and plenty of access to beaches for horseback riding, surfing, biking, eating fresh-caught seafood, and whale watching—as well as whale burials. A dozen whales mysteriously washed ashore in the past few years, fascinating scientists and confounding residents.

Nearby, you'll find a cluster of smaller, semirural coastal towns, including El Granada, Montara, Moss Beach, and a fishing village known affectionately as Princeton-by-the-Sea. Home to Pillar Point Harbor, this little hotspot attracts daredevil surfers who tackle 50-foot waves at the Mavericks surf spot, which hosts an annual contest for pros worldwide. A little further south on Highway 1 is Año Nuevo State Reserve, the world's largest breeding colony of northern elephant seals.

**Website:** www.hmbcity.com

**Area Code:** 650

**Zip Codes:** 94018, 94019, 94038

**Post Office:** 500 Stone Pine Rd, 800-275-8777, www.usps.com

**Police Station:** 537 Kelly Ave, 650-726-8288

**Library:** Half Moon Bay Library, 620 Correas St, 650-726-2316, www.halfmoon baylibrary.org

**Public Schools:** Cabrillo Unified School District, 498 Kelly Ave, 650-712-7100, www.cabrillo.k12.ca.us

**Community Resources:** The Coastsider, www.coastsider.com; Coastside Children's Programs, 494 Miramontes Ave, 650-726-7413, www.coastsidechildren.org; Coastside Opportunity Center, 99 Ave Alhambra, Half Moon Bay, 650-726-9071

**Community Publications:** *Half Moon Bay Review*, 650-726-4424, www.hmbreview.com

**Beaches, Parks, Gardens, and Open Space:** Parks and Recreation Department, 535 Kelly Ave, 650-726-8297, www.hmbcity.com

# SOUTH SAN FRANCISCO, SAN BRUNO, BRISBANE

Wander the modest one-street downtown of **South San Francisco** and you'd never guess you're standing in the world's largest hub of biotech companies. 150 of them are based here, in what locals call "South City." Sprawled across 11 million square feet and growing fast, the tech companies are out of sight from the downtown sidewalks, which feel pleasantly stuck in the 1950s and '60s. But that's changing quickly. A retail and housing boom are underway to match the city's biotech growth, making this a fast-rising outpost of San Francisco proper—just 10 minutes away. If you crave proximity to the big city while saving a bundle on rent, South San Francisco is worth exploring.

Signs of renewal are everywhere. At least 15 restaurants have opened within blocks of each other recently, reflecting an upswing in the community's Filipino, Korean, Jamaican, and Vietnamese newcomers, alongside the more established Mexican and Italian communities. Condos and apartment rentals are rising along Grand, Linden, and Miller avenues, including 1,000 new units in the next few years, several of them luxury—a first for this low-key town—and a handful below market rate. South City is a transit-rich option, with a BART station, new ferry routes, and a $55 million upgrade coming to the Caltrain station. Living here puts you within very easy reach of San Francisco's Mission District nightlife (there's not much of that in South San Francisco). There's no prestige, however—the community has the compact feel of post–World War II tract homes. But hidden gems are scattered in the hills beneath San Bruno Mountain. Many streets are repaved, and the city will soon turn its attention to the parks, which, residents agree, badly need an upgrade. Help is coming: the city recently dedicated millions of dollars to fund new playgrounds in 2016 and beyond.

For a deeper dive into the neighborhoods of South San Francisco, veer off Grand and El Camino to the colorful piñata stores, Catholic churches, and Middle

*South San Francisco*

Eastern cafés. You'll see truck-repair shops and warehouses, a stark contrast to the sleek new office towers popping up across town.

Your biggest neighbor, Genentech—the world's leading biotech company, located east of Highway 1—has headquarters that resemble a sci-fi movie set. The company's campus is growing. With 11,000 employees, Genentech commendably invests millions in the community, including a new biotech building for a local high school, as well as donations of lab equipment, computers, and iPads to classrooms. That level of community outreach stands in contrast to many of the tech companies in San Francisco and Silicon Valley, whose relationships to local communities are less reciprocal.

Also known as the "Industrial City," South San Francisco was home to a steel boom a century ago—thus the massive sign that still reads "South San Francisco, The Industrial City" (today it should probably read "South San Francisco, The Biotech City"). Commercial rent here is half of San Francisco's. This is also where your flight actually lands when you arrive at San Francisco International Airport (SFO)—so airplane noise is a given, and should be considered if you are sensitive to sound. In general, the western portion near Interstate 280 is more expensive than the vibrant lower south side, near Highway 101.

Nearby, the city of **San Bruno** continues its home-building frenzy, adding new condos, townhouses, and luxury homes, including more than 80 apartments and 7,000 square feet of retail space on San Mateo Avenue. Twelve miles south of San Francisco, San Bruno—home of YouTube—attracts crowds of young professionals. Lured by the potential to own their own condos—a near impossibility for many newcomers in San Francisco—high-paid young families are arriving here in droves, attracted by the convenient BART station and the recently completed mall makeover. San Bruno recently raised building heights from 50 to 90 feet downtown, allowing for some 4,000 new jobs and 3,800 new residents.

San Bruno the city took its name from San Bruno the mountain. In the 1820s, the land was part of a grant given by the Mexican government to Jose Antonio

*San Bruno*

Sanchez for his military service. Sanchez's heirs lost their claim to the land in the 1840s, but their legacy lived on when the Tanforan Racetrack, named for Sanchez's grandson-in-law, opened in 1899. Though it has since burned down, the site of the racetrack is thought of fondly by residents: the first San Mateo County flight took off from here. But there are disturbing memories too. The track was converted into a World War II assembly center for Japanese Americans, many of whom lost their homes, jobs, and lives when they were forcibly relocated to internment camps—one of which was right here in San Bruno.

Today Tanforan is the site of a shopping center in the heart of the city's rapidly transforming commercial core. Nearby you'll find the San Bruno Towne Center (a 24-acre shopping plaza); the BART station; and Bayhill Drive, home to an 80-acre office park. Walmart.com is also headquartered in San Bruno.

You'll also find the Crossing, a 20-acre former US Navy site that has been converted into a lively, high-density village of hundreds of new apartments. East San Bruno consists of two- and three-bedroom single-family homes from the 1950s and '60s clustered on narrow side streets off of San Bruno Avenue (one of the city's older commercial thoroughfares). The area east of Highway 101 is dominated by the airport and businesses—long-term parking lots, car rental agencies, and hotels. If you don't mind the sound of jets roaring overhead, you can find some of the Peninsula's most affordable single-family homes here.

To the west, you'll find woody, winding roads and more expensive homes, some with sweeping views of the Bay below. Skyline Boulevard offers access to trails at Milagra and Sweeney Ridges, and links up with Highway 1 to carry you to nearby Pacifica's beaches in minutes. A good resource for continuing education, Skyline Community College is also here, and it has just rolled out a new four-year degree program.

Downtown San Bruno, with its 1950s time-warp feel, stretches along San Mateo Avenue, filled with small eateries and shops, and one of the Peninsula's few casino-style card rooms. The avenue had struggled to keep pace with newer shopping centers on nearby El Camino Real, but the languishing strip has finally come alive.

A natural gem, San Bruno Mountain (outside city limits) is one of the largest urban open spaces in the country, with 3,300 undeveloped acres. Home to the rare Mission Blue butterfly, the mountain is covered with hundreds of wildflowers in the spring. Curve around Guadalupe Canyon Road to the mountain's northern slope, and you'll find the tight-knit community of **Brisbane** (www.ci.brisbane.ca.us). With its old-fashioned downtown area, small-town vibe, and hillside homes, Brisbane is a well-kept secret—and residents want it to stay that way. But the area is catching on. Brisbane was eyed for an Olympic stadium recently. The entire San Mateo County continues to gain popularity as the surrounding areas are saturated with tech-boom newcomers.

## SOUTH SAN FRANCISCO

**Websites**: www.ssf.net, www.everythingsouthcity.com
**Area Codes**: 415, 650

**Zip Codes**: 94080
**Post Offices**: 322 Linden Ave; 36 Chestnut Ave, 800-275-8777, www.usps.com
**Police Station**: SSF Police Department, 333 Arroyo Dr, Suite C, 650-877-8900
**Public Schools**: South San Francisco High, 400 B St, 650-877-8754; El Camino High, 1320 Mission Rd, 650-877-8806; Buri Buri Elementary, 120 El Campo Dr, 650-877-8776; Ponderosa Elementary, 295 Ponderosa Rd, 650-877-7725
**Library**: Main Library, 840 W Orange Ave, 650-829-3860, www.ssflibrary.net
**Parks, Gardens, and Open Space**: Parks and Recreation Department, 33 Arroyo Dr, 650-829-3800, www.ssf.net/377/parks-recreation

## SAN BRUNO
**Website:** www.sanbruno.ca.gov
**Police:** 1177 Huntington Ave, 650-616-7100
**Area Code**: 650
**Zip Code**: 94066
**Post Office:** 1300 Huntington Ave, 800-275-8777, www.usps.com
**Library:** 701 Angus Ave West, 650-616-7078, www.ci.sanbruno.ca.us/Library
**Police Station:** 1177 Huntington Ave, 650-616-7100
**Public Schools:** San Bruno Park School District, 500 Acacia Ave, 650-624-3100, www.sbpsd.k12.ca.us; San Mateo Union High School District, 650 N Delaware St, 650-558-2299, www.smuhsd.k12.ca.us
**Community Resources:** Recreation Services Department, 567 El Camino Real, 650-616-7180, San Bruno Mountain Watch, 44 Visitacion Ave, Brisbane, 415-467-6631, www.mountainwatch.org; San Bruno Senior Center, 1555 Crystal Springs Rd, 650-616-7150; Skyline Community College, 3300 College Dr, 650-738-4100, www.skylinecollege.edu
**Parks, Gardens, and Open Space:** Parks Department, 251 City Park Way, 650-616-7180; San Bruno Mountain Park, 555 Guadalupe Canyon Pkwy

## BURLINGAME, SAN MATEO, BELMONT

The moment you step foot in **Burlingame's** upscale downtown—halfway between San Francisco and Palo Alto—you'll understand why this high-end suburb tops the United States in the most million-dollar home sales per zip code. This town's stretch of chic runs along Burlingame Avenue, popular with high-paid newcomers, from tech executives to investors and families who can afford this small village with big-name shops. There's even a new branch of the hip-as-it-gets Delfina Pizzeria. Homes in Burlingame are beyond elegant, but luxury isn't the only appeal; Burlingame's proximity to San Francisco and Silicon Valley is its greatest asset, followed by amenities and top schools, including 19 preschools.

Known as the City of Trees, Burlingame boasts 18,000 towering trees—so treasured that the city prohibited cutting, injuring, or destroying them. On the east edge, residents enjoy long stretches of water, with sports parks. A multi-year

*Burlingame*

renovation was just completed, widening the sidewalks and adding new lighting downtown, where the parking lots are being eyed as possibilities for below-market-rate housing—part of Burlingame's affordable-housing push, given the booming housing prices throughout the Bay Area. And the City Hall building will soon undergo a $12 million seismic retrofit.

Along California Drive is the PEZ Museum—yes, the PEZ Museum—a pop-culture paradise in a tiny storefront. It features hundreds of PEZ dispensers—every version ever made, purportedly—including the world's largest. And the historic train station was recently converted into a local history museum, with treasures transporting you to a time when street signs warned, "Look out for the Locomotive," and police wagons had open-air canopies. If you want to live in this highly desirable town, come prepared: houses sell well above asking price, and the median home sales price recently was just shy of $2 million.

The city of **San Mateo** has a more diverse population in a variety of homes, from traditional ranches to Mediterranean-style houses and new condos, with

*San Mateo*

*Belmont*

enormous mansions mixed in. The new Bay Meadows development, on a former racetrack next to the Caltrain station, will include more than 1,100 housing units, 750,000 square feet of office space, and 18 acres of public parks, scheduled for completion in 2020. Once the banking capital of the Peninsula, San Mateo is now a popular community for Silicon Valley tech commuters. A mini renaissance is taking place in the town's once-languishing downtown, where a wave of top restaurants and a new centrally located movie theater and revamped transit center have brought life to the area. In the heart of downtown, Central Park draws visitors from throughout the Peninsula.

**Belmont** has some of the highest prices in the region surpassed only by Hillsborough, Woodside, Atherton, and Burlingame. On the west side of town, most homes are nestled in the lush hillside, and it's not unusual to find deer trolling through your backyard in the evening. The entrance to Crystal Springs Reservoir and the San Francisco Watershed area, with winding waterside trails popular with bicyclists and joggers throughout the Peninsula, is just a few moments away off Highway 92 just west of I-280. The town is primarily residential, with shopping concentrated in a few short blocks along El Camino Real, the Peninsula's main commercial thoroughfare. Residents typically head south to the cluster of upscale eateries and boutiques on Laurel Street in neighboring San Carlos.

## BURLINGAME
**Website:** www.burlingame.org
**Area Code:** 650
**Zip Code:** 94010
**Post Office:** 220 Park Rd, 800-275-8777, www.usps.com
**Police Station:** 1111 Trousdale Dr, 650-777-4100
**Library:** Burlingame Library, 480 Primrose Rd, 650-558-7400
**Public Schools:** San Mateo Union High School District, 650 N Delaware St, 650-558-2299, www.smuhsd.org; Burlingame School District, 1825 Trousdale Dr, 650-259-3800, www.bsd.k12.ca.us

**Community Resources:** Burlingame Chamber of Commerce, 650-344-1735, burlingamechamber.org; Burlingame Historical Society, www.burlingamehistorical.org

**Parks, Gardens, and Open Space:** Parks and Recreation Department, 850 Burlingame Ave, 650-558-7200

## SAN MATEO

**Website:** www.cityofsanmateo.org
**Area Code:** 650
**Zip Codes:** 94401, 94402
**Post Office:** 1630 S Delaware St, 800-275-8777, www.usps.com
**Police Station:** 2000 S Delaware St, 650-522-7700
**Library:** San Mateo Public Library, 55 W Third Ave, 650-522-7800; Hillsdale Branch, 205 W Hillsdale Blvd, 650-522-7880; Marina Branch, 1530 Susan Ct, 650-522-7890
**Public Schools:** San Mateo-Foster City School District, 51 West 41st Ave, 650-312-7777, www.smfc.k12.ca.us; San Mateo Union High School District, 650 N Delaware St, 650-558-2299, www.smuhsd.org
**Community Resources:** Poplar Creek Golf Course, 1700 Coyote Point Dr, 650-522-4653, www.poplarcreekgolf.com; Coyote Point Recreation Area, Coyote Point Dr, 650-573-2592
**Parks, Gardens, and Open Space:** Parks & Recreation, 1900 O'Farrell St, 650-522-7400, www.cityofsanmateo.org

## BELMONT

**Website:** www.belmont.gov
**Area Code:** 650
**Zip Code:** 94002
**Post Office:** 640 Masonic Way, 800-275-8777, www.usps.com
**Police Station:** Belmont Police Department, One Twin Pines Ln, 650-595-7400
**Library:** Belmont Library, 1110 Alameda de las Pulgas, 650-591-8286
**Public Schools:** Belmont-Redwood Shores School District, 2960 Hallmark Dr, 650-637-4800, www.belmont.k12.ca.us; San Mateo Union High School District, 650 N Delaware St, 650-558-2299, www.smuhsd.org
**Community Resources:** 1870 Art Center, 1870 Ralston Ave, 650-595-9679, www.1870artcenter.org; Belmont Community Players, 1835 Belburn Ave, 650-599-2720, www.belmontcommunityplayers.org; Belmont Historical Society, 650-593-4213; Notre Dame de Namur University, 1500 Ralston Ave, 650-508-3500, www.ndnu.edu
**Parks, Gardens, and Open Space:** Parks & Recreation, 30 Twin Pines Ln, 650-595-7441

# FOSTER CITY

The fastest-growing suburb just south of San Francisco, **Foster City** is landscaped with lagoons and brimming with biotech companies moving their headquarters here, making this town the Bay Area's newest biotech hub. The *largest* biotech suburb is still the city of South San Francisco, but Foster City is joining the ranks. Waterways curve along Foster City's residential neighborhoods, giving hundreds of apartments a waterside view. There's no nightlife—not even one standalone bar in town—so locals head to San Mateo at night. Still, with 19 tidy parks across 100 acres, this up-and-coming town of 33,000 people has more parks per capita than any other city in California.

Visa's headquarters are in Foster City, and Gilead Sciences is expanding its massive campus, as is Illumina, the gene-sequencing firm, adding thousands of employees between the two companies. That's a familiar headline in a region booming with tech expansion: sleepy suburb awakes, cranes move in. It's trace-able primarily to the proximity of Silicon Valley and San Francisco. Foster City is just arriving to the party.

For budget-minded newcomers, below-market-rate apartments are avail-able, including one- and two-bedroom units at Marlin Cove, Foster's Landing, Marimar, and Plaza at Triton Park, each reserved for low- and middle-income ten-ants. Seniors earning less than half of the area's median income can apply to live at Foster Square apartments, a sleek spot under construction next to City Hall. Waiting lists are growing, making Foster City a catch-it-while-you-can option.

Socially, the city is still finding its way forward, searching for a sense of iden-tity and personality. Put plainly, it is not much to look at yet. There's no downtown and no main gathering spot, but there's a new $4 million teen center overlooking the water—with video games, homework rooms, art rooms, and basketball courts alongside a skatepark. Sorry, Foster City doesn't have a high school, but it does contain a handful of elementary and middle schools. A hip new gourmet food-truck event is gaining popularity in Ryan Park on Wednesdays, with live music and a beer garden.

Demographically, one third of households include children, and the top-rated Jewish day school in the South Bay is in Foster City—part of the North Peninsula Jewish Campus, a 12-acre community center with sports, educational classes, and social events for 10,000 members.

Foster City wasn't even a city before the 1960s, when it was founded on land-fill in the marshes of the Bay. Landfill makes the city highly prone to liquefaction during an earthquake—cause for concern among homeowners. And a rising sea level puts homes at risk of inundation. But neither has stopped hundreds of new-comers from buying condos along the water, a popular watersports spot. One of the best-rated launching points for kitesurfers and windsurfers in the Bay Area is at 3rd Avenue past Coyote Point, and swimming is allowed in the lagoons—but watch for kayaks behind you.

Safety is another big draw. Foster City was ranked eighth-safest suburb in the Bay Area in 2015.

**Website:** www.fostercity.org

**Area Code:** 650

**Zip Code:** 94404

**Post Office:** 1050 Shell Blvd, 800-275-8777, www.usps.com

**Police Station:** 1030 E Hillsdale Blvd, 650-286-3300, www.fostercity.org/police

**Library:** 1000 E Hillsdale Blvd, 650-574-4842, www.smcl.org

**Public Schools:** San Mateo-Foster City School District, 51 West 41st Ave, 650-312-7777, www.smfc.k12.ca.us

**Community Publication:** *Foster City Islander*, 650-574-5952, www.fostercityislander.com

**Community Resources:** Community Resources: North Peninsula Jewish Campus and Ronald C. Wornick Jewish Day School, 800 Foster City Blvd, 650-378-2600, www.wornickjds.org; Community Center, 1000 E. Hillsdale Blvd, 650-286-2500, www.fostercity.org; Chamber of Commerce, 650-286-3205, www.fostercity.org; Hillbarn Theatre, 1285 W. Hillsdale Blvd, 650-349-6411, www.hillbarntheatre.org

**Parks, Gardens, and Open Space:** Parks & Recreation, 610 Foster City Blvd, 650-286-3200, www.fostercity.org/parksandrecreation

## HILLSBOROUGH, ATHERTON, WOODSIDE

Consistently ranked the wealthiest and safest town in all of California, **Hillsborough** has the highest concentration of new tech millionaires and billionaires in the United States. It's no surprise that the Peninsula would have secluded, exclusive towns like this one, envied for its elegance and majestic views. Hillsborough is heavily mansioned, with grand estates set back from the road. It also has the

*Hillsborough*

highest income of all American towns with populations above 10,000 people. Except for the town hall, there's not much infrastructure. And there are no stores and businesses, as zoning doesn't allow it. Most locals do their shopping at upscale boutiques and chains in Burlingame, although Hillsborough recently rolled out a new mobile app for event calendars and announcements. Search for "Hillsborough CA" in your app store, and enjoy a fantasy move-in.

If you dream of calling **Atherton** home, you'll need similarly deep pockets. Home to Google pioneer Eric Schmidt and investment mogul Charles Schwab, Atherton is the most expensive zip code in the United States, as of 2015—with home prices up 40 percent annually. Facebook leader Sheryl Sandberg sold her home here for nearly $10 million recently, and President Obama has popped in for fundraisers. Most Atherton estates are secluded behind thick foliage and entrance gates, not far from **Woodside**, which has more of a country feel with its natural streams, wildflowers, and towering redwoods. At the heart of Woodside is a tidy town center that resembles a trading post from the Wild West era, with an old-fashioned general store and charmingly scuffed sidewalks—but not for long. In 2015 the town got busy replacing 25,000 square feet of deteriorated asphalt,

*Woodside*

and a town remake is on the way, with new sites for the library, police department, and administration building. You'll frequently see horses tied up in front of Woodside's Roberts Market—founded in 1889. The bulletin board out front is a kind of community clearinghouse, where you'll find everything from landscaping services, to thoroughbreds for sale, to ads looking for experienced live-in nannies.

Many of Woodside's estates have substantial lots, and stables are common here—but more CEOs than cowboys live here today. Rich in natural beauty, Woodside is also one of the biggest water consumers—and water wasters—in California. Given the current drought, the town's water district could face fines up to $10,000 a day if it doesn't cut water use by 35 percent.

Locals' crowning glory is the 973-acre Huddart Park on King's Mountain Road, with wandering wooded trails and wide grassy meadows. The sharply curving Highway 84 connects the town to busier suburban life in Redwood City to the northeast, and with Highways 101 and I-280. Heading southwest, Highway 84 carries you through the redwoods to the Pacific Ocean.

## HILLSBOROUGH
**Website:** www.hillsborough.net
**Area Code:** 650
**Zip Code:** 94010
**Post Office:** 220 Park Rd, Burlingame, 800-275-8777, www.usps.com
**Police Station:** Police Department, 1600 Floribunda Ave, 650-375-7470
**Libraries:** Burlingame Library, 480 Primrose Rd, 650-558-7444; San Mateo Library, 55 W 3rd Ave, 650-522-7802
**Public Schools:** Hillsborough City School District, 300 El Cerrito Ave, 650-342-5193, www.hcsd.k12.ca.us; San Mateo Union High School District, 650 North Delaware St, 650-558-2299, www.smuhsd.org
**Community Resources**: *Town Newsletter*, www.hillsborough.net; also see **Burlingame** above
**Parks, Gardens, and Open Space:** Public Works and Parks Department, Municipal Service Center, 1320 La Honda Rd, 650-375-7444, www.hillsborough.net/depts/pw/parks.asp

## ATHERTON
**Website:** www.ci.atherton.ca.us
**Area Code:** 650
**Zip Code:** 94027
**Post Office:** 3875 Bohannon Dr, Menlo Park, 800-275-8777, www.usps.com
**Police Station:** Atherton Police Department, 83 Ashfield Rd, 650-688-6500
**Library:** Atherton Public Library, 2 Dinkelspiel Station Ln, 650-328-2422
**Public Schools:** Menlo Park City School District, 181 Encinal Ave, Atherton, 650-321-7140, www.mpcsd.k12.ca.us; Sequoia Union High School District, 480 James Ave, Redwood City, 650-369-1411, www.seq.org
**Community Resources**: *The Almanac*, 650-854-2626, www.AlmanacNews.com; Holbrook-Palmer Park and Carriage House, 150 Watkins Ave, 650-752-0534
**Parks, Gardens, and Open Space:** Public Works, 93 Station Ln, 650-752-0535; Holbrook-Palmer Park, 150 Watkins Ave, 650-752-0534

## WOODSIDE
**Website:** www.woodsidetown.org
**Area Code:** 650
**Zip Code:** 94062
**Post Office:** 1100 Broadway St, Redwood City, 800-275-8777, www.usps.com
**Sheriff:** San Mateo County Sheriff's Office, 400 County Center, Redwood City, 650-364-1811

**Library:** Woodside Library, 3140 Woodside Rd, Woodside, 650-851-0147, www.woodsidelibrary.org

**Public Schools:** Woodside Elementary School District, 3195 Woodside Rd, 650-851-1571; Sequoia Union High School District, 480 James Ave, Redwood City, 650-369-1411,www.seq.org

**Community Resources:** *The Almanac*, 650-854-2626, www.almanacnews.com; Kings Mountain Art Fair (held annually on Labor Day weekend), 650-851-2710, www.kingsmountainartfair.org; Filoli Center and Gardens, 650-364-8300, www.filoli.org; Horse Park, 650-851-2140, www.horsepark.org; the Woodside Store and history museum, 650-851-7615

**Parks, Gardens, and Open Space:** Huddart Park, 1100 King's Mountain Rd, 650-851-1210; Wunderlich Park, Woodside Rd, 650-851-1210

# MENLO PARK

### SHARON HEIGHTS

Beyond the dozens of American flags waving from this affluent community's downtown awnings, you'll see a town so manicured and pleasant that you might not notice there's an enormous giant behind you. It's growing bigger every minute. Facebook's towering headquarters, which expanded here in 2015, include a 430,000 square-foot upgrade with a 9-acre rooftop park. As the city's largest employer, Facebook has thousands of employees in this small town, many of whom shuttle here on company buses from San Francisco (30 miles away), giving this suburb an increasingly high profile—and steep housing costs.

Not every resident "likes" the city's chief tenant, but many locals do support Facebook even as protestors gather occasionally to voice dissent on a range of topics, including the connection between Facebook's expansion and the city's rising rents. Facebook moved from Palo Alto to Menlo Park in 2011, and the company got into the local housing business when it partnered on a new apartment

*Menlo Park*

complex within walking distance of its campus. Known as Anton Menlo and located at 3639 Haven Avenue, it's the biggest local housing development in two decades.

It's no coincidence that **Menlo Park** was ranked in the top 10 in *Money* magazine's "Best Places for the Rich and Single" to live. Stroll along Santa Cruz Avenue, and you'll absorb this quintessential Silicon Valley scene in and around the trendy boutiques, home-furnishing stores, and elegant shaded eateries, with train whistles in the distance. New outdoor dining is on the way, as the city council recently voted to fund more sidewalk cafés.

Public swimming pools and tennis courts mark the city's 19 square miles, which include a duck pond behind the police station. A cluster of venture capitalists and researchers—including Stanford's Linear Accelerator Center, which smashes atoms in its world-renowned laboratory—are stationed on Sand Hill Road. The headquarters of *Sunset* magazine was once here, but in 2015 the editors announced they were moving their operation to an up-and-coming neighborhood in Oakland—yet another sign of fast changes throughout the Bay Area.

Menlo Park got its name in 1854 when two settlers purchased 640 acres and built an estate, printing "Menlo Park" on the gate. The town transformed from an agricultural center to a military camp housing tens of thousands of soldiers, establishing a strong infrastructure. Today you'll find a variety of housing styles, from 1950s apartments to Eichler homes to ranch-style houses. Newer apartments continue to arrive, including—as of 2016—almost 200 units at Greenheart Housing (777 Hamilton Avenue) and 146 units at GrayStay Housing (3649 Haven Avenue). The neighborhoods west of Highway 101 are more upscale: **Sharon Heights**, near the golf course, is known for serene mountain views. With Stanford University one town over, Menlo Park is home to many professors and employees, and some students—but mostly tech workers. Across a creek and past the stately 1,000-year-old redwood called "El Palo Alto" is the northernmost reach of Santa Clara County.

Managing environmental impact is high on the city's list of priorities. New improvements include solar-panel installation on gyms and community centers, and a water-pump station replacement. Parking is relatively easy, as most homes have garages, and access to San Francisco and Silicon Valley is quick via Interstate 280 on the west side, and via Highway 101 near the waterfront. The East Bay is accessible across the Dumbarton Bridge, and commuter trains are popular.

Menlo Park also boasts a renowned surgical center—the top-rated hospital in the Bay Area in 2015, according to patient satisfaction data compiled by the US Department of Health & Human Services.

**Website:** www.menlopark.org
**Area Code:** 650
**Zip Code:** 94025
**Post Office:** 3875 Bohannon Dr, 800-275-8777, www.usps.com
**Police Station:** 701 Laurel St, 650-330-6317
**Library:** 800 Alma St, 650-330-2500, www.menlopark.org/library

**Public Schools:** Menlo Park City School District, 181 Encinal Ave, Atherton, 650-321-7140, www.mpcsd.k12.ca.us; Sequoia Union High School District, 480 James Ave, Redwood City, 650-369-1411, www.seq.org

**Community Resources:** Menlo Park Chamber of Commerce, 650-325-2818 www.menloparkchamber.com; *The Almanac*, 650-854-2626, www.almanacnews.com; Horse Park, 650-851-2140, www.horsepark.org

**Parks, Gardens, and Open Space:** Community Services Department, 701 Laurel St, 650-330-2200

## REDWOOD CITY

Located halfway between San Francisco and San Jose, **Redwood City** is one of the fastest-growing residential and commercial hotspots in the Bay Area. Big tech companies are increasingly bringing their headquarters to this wooded, charming town. Silicon Valley's saturation of tech offices has sent companies scrambling up the Peninsula in search of a new town, and Redwood City—the county seat—is it. Dismissed for decades as "Deadwood City"—a sleepy snooze-town—Redwood City today is on the rise, with construction moving ahead on major office buildings. Box, the cloud storage giant, moved downtown recently, as part of the largest commercial expansion in Redwood City's history. Google is also taking up new offices here—nearly a million square feet by the waterfront. And Shazam, the name-that-tune mobile app leader, moved its headquarters downtown. (Keep in mind that "downtown" in Redwood City means a walkable blip of small-town boutiques.)

To get a feel for this community, take a seat on any patio under the trees that shade Broadway Street. To one side, you'll see the majestic Courthouse Square, which doubles as a performance space on Tuesdays (when lightshows are projected) and again on Fridays (when concerts fill the square). The town is getting younger, as late-night activities multiply and highly paid tech workers move

*Redwood City*

in. But that's hard news for low- and middle-income families priced out of their homes. To stem the effects of displacement, the city recently funded 40 assistance programs for below-market-rate housing. And many people in Redwood City oppose the town's growth; there's a new Facebook group called "Redwood City Residents Say: 'What?'" which denounces the tech boom. Redwood City's own monthly magazine, *Spectrum*, is leading the charge against the building frenzy. Its publisher assigned blame to the tech companies for "invading our downtown" and causing "too much traffic and too much congestion." That's how contentious and fast the growth is. When *Redwood City Climate Magazine* began publishing in 2015, its first issue carried a massive headline: "Looking at the Building Boom." Meanwhile, $29 million of public funds are going to sidewalk repairs, pavement resurfacing, pipeline improvements, and turf replacement.

The curved, tree-lined streets are filled with post–World War II two- and three-bedroom homes with green lawns and spacious backyards. You'll find kids on skateboards and bikes cruising down quiet residential streets or playing ball at the eclectic mini-parks that zigzag through town. Docktown Marina has an alluring houseboat scene—70 of them—docked at the end of Maple Street. And heading west into Emerald Hills, you'll find homes with spectacular views surpassing the million-dollar mark, and a few older country houses with stables and good acreage. A semi-secret swimming spot popular with kids, Emerald Lake is open in summers to neighborhood residents. In the western hills, you'll discover hiking trails and wildflowers at Edgewood Park. Cañada College, located just off of I-280, is an excellent community resource.

Another hidden gem is Sigona's, Redwood City's best farmers' market, which operates year-round on a busy strip away from downtown. In 2015, Sigona's was voted best farmers' market in the Bay Area. The renovated Fox Theatre (founded in 1929) keeps a historic vibe with a variety of big-name theater and music programs—including the Silicon Valley Ball, a new four-venue party hosted recently by Kathy Griffin. On the edge of downtown, you'll find the public library in a converted firehouse, and Sequoia High School. Originally built as a feeder for Stanford University, this large campus with pristine lawns, majestic trees, and tiled rooftops is among the most impressive public high school campuses you'll ever see. And Summit Preparatory High School, nearby, was ranked the seventh-best high school in California by *U.S. News & World Report* in 2015.

Heading east, you'll find a busy commercial strip across Middlefield Road, with delicious and inexpensive taquerias. Homes here are cheaper, but not by much. Heading east of Highway 101, you'll find Redwood Shores, a relaxing green space with tract homes and major tech presence. Built on landfill, Redwood Shores offers scenic Bay views, lagoons, and plenty of trails. Software powerhouse Oracle is located here. Insider's tip: if you move to Redwood Shores, sign up with Tragon Research's focus-group taste tests, which pay you to sample ice cream, soda, coffee, and other ready-to-launch products in exchange for your opinions (350 Bridge Parkway, 800-291-1907, www.tragon.com).

**Website:** www.redwoodcity.org

**Area Code:** 650

**Zip Code:** 94061–5

**Post Office:** 855 Jefferson Ave; 1100 Broadway St; 800-275-8777, www.usps.com

**Police Station:** 1301 Maple St, 650-780-7100

**Library:** 1044 Middlefield Rd, 650-780-7018, www.rcpl.info

**Public Schools:** Redwood City School District, 750 Bradford St, 650-423-2200, www.rcsd.k12.ca.us; Sequoia Union High School District, 480 James Ave, Redwood City, 650-369-1412, www.seq.org

**Community Resources:** Redwood City San Mateo County Chamber of Commerce, 650-364-1722; www.redwoodcitychamber.com; Cañada College, 4200 Farm Hill Blvd, 650-306-3100, www.canadacollege.net

**Parks, Gardens, and Open Space:** Parks, Recreation, and Community Services Department, 1400 Roosevelt Ave, 650-780-7250

## NORTHERN SANTA CLARA COUNTY

Two decades ago, **Santa Clara County** was one of the fastest growing counties in the Bay Area. A decade later, it was one of the fastest shrinking areas in the United States, struggling under the recession and in the aftermath of the dot-com bust. Today it's swinging again, higher than ever, booming with record-high prices and popularity. Both Palo Alto and Mountain View are part of Santa Clara County, but they're also considered part of the amorphous Silicon Valley—a term coined by Don Hoefler, a writer for the weekly *Electronic News*. He'd used the name in 1971 to describe the electronic firms that were growing in Santa Clara County. But the northern end of the county has its own distinct feel.

If you're considering moving to Palo Alto, Cupertino, or Los Gatos—each extremely expensive—keep in mind that it's more cost-effective to rent than buy a home here. The median home price in these towns is nearly 30 times the local rents.

For Santa Clara County resources, see the **South Bay** section.

# PALO ALTO

OLD PALO ALTO

CRESCENT PARK

PROFESSORVILLE DISTRICT

COLLEGE TERRACE

FOREST AVENUE

BARRON PARK

MIDTOWN

DOWNTOWN NORTH

VENTURA

EAST PALO ALTO

Pristine hiking trails and prestigious schools are among the countless reasons **Palo Alto** has become a hotspot for families. This city ranked fifth among best American cities to live in, according to the ratings site Livability.com in 2015.

(Just one year earlier, it was ranked first.) The city, whose name means "tall tree" in Spanish, recently installed a 31-mile dark-fiber ring around town for superfast Internet access—a characteristic breakthrough in a community that's passionate about technology, arts, education, and late-night ice-cream socials.

Palo Alto's star is Stanford University, which accepts just 5 percent of applicants, casting a competitive shadow over the standout students at Palo Alto High School, which is among the Bay Area's top high schools. Located 35 miles south of San Francisco, the city's downtown—upscale and friendly—stays open later than Menlo Park's and Mountain View's. Crowds come here from across the region for the hip hangouts and trendy wine bars. Despite its small size relative to San Francisco and San Jose, Palo Alto boasts more than 30 parks, two community centers, seven libraries (including a new children's library), a first-rate hospital, and the elegant Stanford Shopping Center, which recently added electric car-charging stations. The city's brightest developments include the new Magical Bridge Playground, the nation's most inclusive park, designed for kids of all abilities. The park, part of the impressive new Mitchell Park Community Center, features a treehouse and swings, and welcomes kids in and out of wheelchairs.

Living near the university offers distinct advantages, including excellent performances, public lectures, and picturesque trails—especially the hike around the immensely popular Stanford Dish, a 3.3-mile paved loop path in the hills above the campus. Stanford is currently building a new Perimeter Trail for public use, complementing the palm-lined grounds of the 8,200-acre campus. Locals turn out in droves for the award-winning Stanford Jazz Festival and Workshop, a national treasure of performance and education (www.stanfordjazz.org).

While education is the heart of Palo Alto, tech companies are its economic engine: Hewlett-Packard began in a one-car garage at 367 Addison Avenue, in 1939. This garage is now a historical landmark with a plaque describing it as "the birthplace of Silicon Valley." With its headquarters still in Palo Alto, today Hewlett-Packard has about 300,000 employees worldwide—a drop of 50,000 in the past half-decade, as the company tightens its workforce amid competition from tech leaders saturating Silicon Valley. The 700-acre Stanford Research Park has 140 tech companies, including Tesla Motors, whose driverless cars have just hit Bay Area roads.

For housing, you'll find a variety of options across more than a dozen neighborhoods, each with its own charm. Oregon Expressway divides the city, and generally speaking the neighborhoods north of it are more established and expensive. On the north side, **Old Palo Alto** and **Crescent Park** have magnificent mansions, including the homes of Facebook cofounder Mark Zuckerberg, former San Francisco 49ers quarterback Steve Young, and the late Steve Jobs, cofounder of Apple—it's an ideal neighborhood if you've got millions lying around. Also on the north side is **Professorville District**, so named because it is home to many Stanford faculty members. Another popular neighborhood is **College Terrace**, nestled between Stanford University and Stanford Research Park, which is home to a mix of students, professional engineers, musicians, and retirees.

Slightly north of Professorville is **Forest Avenue**, with newer apartments and many condos. This neighborhood attracts a younger crowd, many of whom frequent the nearby Whole Foods and St. Michael's Alley—a club where Joan Baez used to sing. South of Oregon Expressway, where apricot orchards used to grow, is the largest community of Eichler homes, built from 1949 to 1970. Joseph Eichler crafted these homes with open designs (minimal interior walls in their living space), shallow pitched roofs, and glass walls.

One of the quirkiest neighborhoods is **Barron Park**, just west of El Camino and south of Stanford. Barron Park has a rural feel: there are no sidewalks, and you'll find towering trees and grazing donkeys (yes, donkeys) as well as mailboxes detached from the homes. Until recently, it was known for its mobile-home park, Buena Vista, which closed in 2014, causing great controversy among locals. The 4.6-acre park's closure dealt a blow to the city's affordable housing, as it had housed 400 working-class residents. In its place will be luxury condos.

Finding housing in late summer is difficult, as you'll be competing with Stanford students. Prospective homebuyers are looking cautiously but increasingly at **East Palo Alto**, an area recovering from a history of higher crime and poverty rates. But East Palo Alto is substantially turning around, and bargain-hunters are buying fast. A large shopping plaza near Highway 101, just off of University Avenue, includes IKEA and Home Depot. New homes are going in, with prices significantly lower than those in Palo Alto. Facebook itself (headquartered a few

*College Terrace*

towns away) has reached out to East Palo Alto, recently constructing a tech building for a local high school, including 3D printers and computers—a sign of Facebook's community engagement at a time when gaps are widening between local tech giants and the impoverished margins of Silicon Valley. The East Palo Alto Fair Rent Coalition is a treasure—a recommended resource if you're looking for below-market-rate rentals and housing help.

More than 67,000 residents call Palo Alto home, and thousands commute to the city, bringing rush hour to a frequent standstill. The median home price in Palo Alto (not including less-expensive East Palo Alto) has surpassed $2.5 million, and in 2015 the median rental for a one-bedroom exceeded $2,800. It's far more cost-effective to rent than buy a home here, as the price-to-rent ratios are higher in Palo Alto than anywhere else in the Bay Area. Almost half of Palo Alto's homes are rentals.

The area known as **Downtown North**, walkable from Stanford University, used to be primarily single grad students and professionals but now sees an influx of large families. New houses are being constructed, including garden apartments and duplexes. The median home price is the millions. The neighborhood of **Midtown** is another family-centered destination, with a handful of childcare and preschool options, a beloved Halloween haunted house tradition, and condo prices lower than nearby districts. A slightly more affordable neighborhood is **Ventura**, bounded by Oregon Expressway, Alma Street, West Meadow Drive, and El Camino Real, where rentals include a mix of cottages and Spanish- and English-style revivals.

If you're exploring Palo Alto in further depth, pick up a copy of *Info Palo Alto*, an excellent local directory published by the *Palo Alto Weekly*.

**Websites:** www.pafd.org, www.paloaltoonline.com
**Area Code:** 650
**Zip Codes:** 94301, 94302, 94303, 94304, 94306, Stanford University 94309
**Post Office:** 380 Hamilton Ave, 800-275-8777, www.usps.com
**Police Station:** 275 Forrest Ave, 650-329-2413
**Public Schools:** Palo Alto Unified School District, 25 Churchill Ave, 650-329-3700, www.pausd.org
**Libraries:** Palo Alto Children's Library, 1276 Harriet St, 650-329-2436; Main Library, 1213 Newell Rd, 650-329-2436
**Community Publications:** *Palo Alto Weekly*, www.paloaltoonline.com
**Community Resources:** Junior Museum and Zoo, 1451 Middlefield Rd, 650-329-2111; Lucie Stern Community Center, 1305 Middlefield Rd, 650-463-4900; Cubberley Community Center, 4000 Middlefield Rd, 650-329-2418; Stanford University, 650-723-2300, www.stanford.edu
**Parks, Gardens, and Open Space:** Parks Division, 3201 E Bayshore Rd, 650-496-6962

## MOUNTAIN VIEW

Take any seat along **Mountain View**'s downtown steps, and brace yourself: you're about to see a self-driving car move by. If you search online for the phrase "self-driving car, Mountain View," you'll learn why. Better yet, ask Google yourself, by knocking on the company's Googleplex doors in this town where the company is headquartered, and ask how Google's driverless masterpiece is coming along. Mountain View is home to the search-engine powerhouse, which has expanded in so many directions that it's no longer surprising when the company breaks ground. Google dominates Mountain View's landscape and culture. The company

*Mountain View*

has invested millions in local housing, building an apartment complex close to its headquarters. These new apartments are designed for tenants in the $40,000 salary range, with average rents at $1,100—staggeringly low, by Bay Area standards, but with a growing wait list. That's one of several ways that Google engages with Mountain View's community, situated 40 miles south of San Francisco and eight miles north of San Jose. There's also a slew of new subsidized rentals in the pipeline—below-market-rate studios and one- and two-bedroom units. (For listings, visit www.mountainview.gov/subsidizedrentalmap.)

For a town that originated as a stagecoach stop in 1850, a lot has happened to this 7-square-mile city. Today it's one of the most populated cities in Silicon Valley, with more than 70 restaurants downtown, from tapas to Thai to Indian to Italian. Intel started in Mountain View before it moved to Santa Clara, and NASA's Ames Research Center is also based in Mountain View. The population and job market boomed here during the dot-com heyday, and then quickly shrank when the economy turned sour, before rebounding higher than ever.

The town is predominantly home to young tech professionals. According to the city, a majority of the population is between 20 and 44. The popular 660-acre Shoreline Park includes a golf course, bike and jogging trails, and a lake, which is often jumping with windsurfers, paddle-boaters, and shore-side picnickers. The outdoor Shoreline Amphitheatre hosts top festivals, and downtown along Castro Street is the center of social life by day and night.

Apartments dominate the housing mix, highlighted by Craftsman-style bungalows and several Eichler homes. During the dot-com boom of the '90s, a number of small single-family condos and townhouses were added to the housing pool. And the real estate rush is growing, especially in the downtown area. Neighborhoods are changing citywide, driven by the development of residential and commercial sites. Special incentives have been given—in the form of additional floor space and higher densities—to projects located near the transit center.

Nearby, the Mountain View Center for the Performing Arts hosts acclaimed performances in a newly rebuilt area centered on Castro and Church streets.

Moffett Federal Airfield, now decommissioned, is also in Mountain View; some of the complex continues to be used by NASA and federal agencies, and when the president flies into Silicon Valley, Air Force One typically lands at Moffett Airfield. The city is exploring various alternatives for Moffett's future. One idea is to convert a portion of it into a large mixed-use site for research and residential housing.

**Website:** www.mountainview.gov
**Area Code:** 650
**Zip Codes:** 94040, 94041, 94043, 94035, 95002
**Post Office:** 1768 Miramonte Ave, 800-275-8777, www.usps.com
**Police Station:** 1000 Villa St, 650-903-6395
**Library:** 585 Franklin St, 650-903-6337
**Public Schools:** Mountain View Whisman School District, 750-A San Pierre Way, 650-526-3500, www.mvwsd.k12.ca.us; Mountain View Los Altos Union High School District, 1299 Bryant Ave, 650-940-4669, www.mvla.net
**Communication Publications:** *Mountain View Voice*, www.mountainviewonline.com
**Community Resources:** Mountain View Center for the Performing Arts, 500 Castro St, 650-903-6000; Mountain View Community Center, 201 S Rengstorff Ave, 650-903-6407; Shoreline Amphitheatre, 1 Amphitheatre Pkwy, 650-967-3000, www.theshorelineamphitheatre.com
**Parks, Gardens, and Open Space:** Community Services Department, Recreation Division, 201 S Rengstorff Ave, 650-903-6326

# LOS ALTOS

**LOS ALTOS HILLS**
**LOYOLA CORNERS**

As exclusive and elegant a place as you are likely to find in Silicon Valley, **Los Altos** is set in the lush, hot foothills just west of Mountain View. It's quieter and pricier than Mountain View, and is an elite home to tech executives and other high-paid professionals. The cozy village atmosphere includes spotless boutiques along Main Street, where many residents are on first-name basis with baristas and corner grocers. Stately houses here have even larger yards than in most towns nearby—and if you don't have mansion-level millions, you might still have a shot at newer rentals near the San Antonio Shopping Center on El Camino.

To the west, the hills offer a sweeping backdrop with majestic views. The beautiful hillside homes are a "secret" so poorly kept that investors across the world are buying up these houses in cash, sight unseen, and letting the properties sit empty as long-term investments—a competitive reality that's a new challenge for local families in today's housing boom. Nowhere is this truer than the adjoining community of **Los Altos Hills**, the city's wealthier, more secluded, and more elite district. Here you'll find multimillion-dollar estates nestled between towering trees, sharply

*Los Altos*

twisting roads, and long, private drives. Incorporated in the 1950s to preserve the charms of rural life, Los Altos Hills is where homes have a mandated minimum lot size of one acre—and several homes surpass that margin many times over. Mixed with the mansions, you'll find a handful of stables and family farms.

A biker's, walker's, and horseback rider's haven, Los Altos Hills has 63 miles of roadside and off-road trails known as the pathway system. Open space is vast, and outdoor gems abound, including the 75-acre Byrne Preserve and the 165-acre Rancho San Antonio Preserve. The town also owns a public horseback-riding arena, Town Riding Ring, which is free and open to all. **Loyola Corners** is an even quieter neighborhood within Los Altos, with the convenience of the tranquil Loyola Corners shopping plaza.

To fit in with locals, say you'll meet them at "the Quad," local lingo for the four corners downtown where residents meet up on Second and Main streets—where a bakery and Starbucks sit opposite a new restaurant on the site of a former Jamba Juice and an Italian deli. The six-block downtown triangle includes a farmers' market that is packed on Thursdays from May to September. You'll find it on State Street, where parking is routinely tight during lunch hours.

Education is top-notch in Los Altos, including the award-winning School for Independent Learners, an acclaimed, small program with personalized courses geared to individual students' learning needs. For activities, Hillview Community Center has a variety of recreation and cultural programs, while Foothill College—spread out across a picturesque hillside campus—offers first-rate theater performances and a renowned community radio program, KFJC 89.7 FM. Because these communities cherish the small-town atmosphere and rural, upscale living, Los Altos and Los Altos Hills are short on big-name department stores and megaplex theaters. Residents head downhill to Mountain View for bulk shopping and nightlife.

**Website:** www.losaltoshills.ca.gov
**Area Code:** 650

**Zip Codes:** 94022–94024
**Post Office:** 100 1st St, 800-275-8777, www.usps.com
**Police Station:** 1 N San Antonio Rd, 650-947-2770
**Library:** 13 S San Antonio Rd, 650-948-7683, www.sccl.org/locations/los-altos
**Public Schools:** Los Altos School District, 650-947-1150, www.lasdschools.org
**Community Publications:** *The Los Altos Town Crier*, www.losaltosonline.com
**Community Resources:** Los Altos Chamber of Commerce, 321 University Ave, 650-948-1455, www.losaltoschamber.org; Los Altos Village Association, www.downtownlosaltos.org; Town Riding Ring, www.lahha.org; Foothill College, www.foothill.fhda.edu
**Parks, Gardens, and Open Space:** Los Altos Recreation Department, 97 Hillview Ave, 650-947-2790; Los Altos Hills Recreation Department, 26379 Fremont Rd, 650-941-7222, www.losaltoshills.ca.gov

## SOUTH BAY (SOUTHERN SANTA CLARA COUNTY)

"Silicon Valley" won't appear on many maps—the area is officially "**Santa Clara County**"—but that didn't stop HBO from launching the hit series "Silicon Valley" in 2014, a spot-on spoof of a tech valley that has transformed this region into the world's digital headquarters. Silicon Valley is so fast-moving that before you reach the end of this sentence, its secretive software masterminds will have tested a thousand new apps, built a dozen new campuses, traded a few top executives, and changed your life—and then changed it again. Change is constant here, so don't be surprised if you soon see private drones hovering silently overhead, pedestrians talking into their wrists, and motorists checking email in their eyelids—all technologies that Google promises are coming. Living in Silicon Valley means stepping into the newest frontier of experience—a southern stretch of the Bay Area that extends all the way to Gilroy (and sometimes beyond, depending on who you ask). The median income of Silicon Valley's tech workers exceeded $121,000 in 2015. That figure is growing, but it is barely enough to make rent in this region. Just a slim percentage of residents in Santa Clara County can afford to buy basic, entry-level homes. The area currently has the hottest job market in the nation. As always in the Bay Area, Craigslist—invented in San Francisco—is your ultimate resource for rental listings.

Beyond technology, Santa Clara County is also breaking ground politically: in 2015 the county proposed creating an Office of Lesbian, Gay, Bisexual, Transgender & Queer Affairs as part of the Office of the County Executive. The county, which includes San Jose, estimates that the LGBT community accounts for more than 2 million residents. As Silicon Valley makes progress technologically, the area is just beginning to keep pace with San Francisco politically (though in that respect it is ahead of the curve nationally).

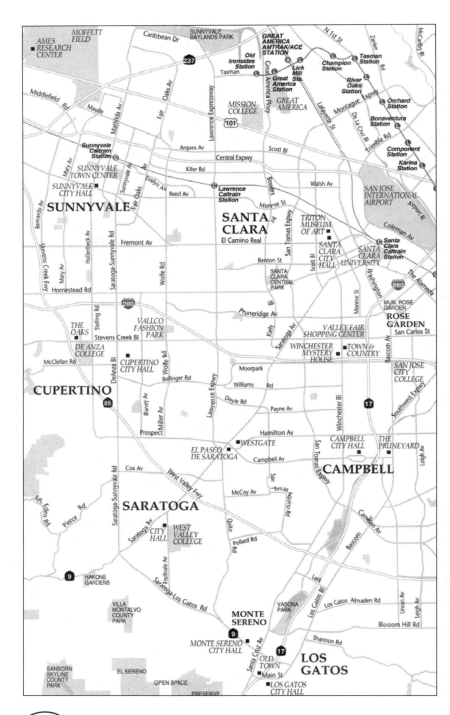

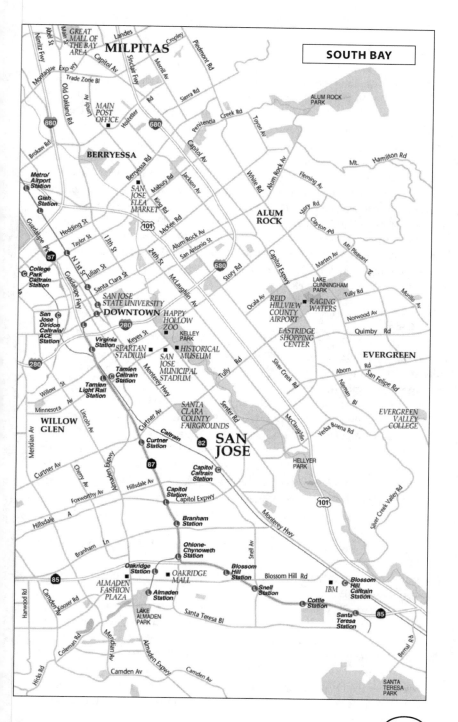

Weather-wise, you'll find Santa Clara County is more Los Angeles than San Francisco, especially in the summer. Away from the cooling Pacific fog, the sky here is blue and the air warm at least 300 days a year. Tank tops, shorts, and flip-flops are everyday wear for half of the year. The Mediterranean climate is ideal for agriculture, which attracted early settlers, beginning with Ohlone Native Americans. Spanish settlers came to Santa Clara County in 1777 and established El Pueblo de San Jose de Guadalupe, now known as San Jose. The community raised crops and cattle for the Spanish presidios (army bases) located in San Francisco and Monterey. After Mexico declared independence from Spain in 1821, San Jose became a Mexican town. Several years later, with the signing of the Treaty of Guadalupe Hidalgo, all of California joined the United States. In 1849, at the start of the Gold Rush, San Jose was declared the first state capital. The state capital was moved to Vallejo a few years later, and eventually to Sacramento. By some estimates, the city of San Jose grew from 95,000 to 909,000 between 1950 and 1999. Today the population is more than 1 million.

**Website**: www.sccgov.org

**Area Code**: 408

**Zip Codes**: 95109–13, 95116, 95119, 95125, 95126, 95128, 95129, 95133, 95134, 95136, 95141, 95148, 95150–95192

**Sheriff**: Office of the Sheriff, 55 W Younger Ave, San Jose, 800-211-2220

**Emergency Hospitals**: Santa Clara Valley Medical Center, 751 S Bascom, San Jose, 408-885-5000; San Jose Regional Medical Center, 225 N Jackson Ave, San Jose, 408-259-5000; O'Conner Hospital, 2105 Forest Ave, San Jose, 408-947-2500; Good Samaritan Hospital, 2425 Samaritan Dr, San Jose, 408-559-2011; Kaiser Santa Teresa, 250 Hospital Pkwy, San Jose, 408-972-7000; Kaiser Santa Clara, 710 Lawrence Expy, Santa Clara, 408-851-1000; Community Hospital of Los Gatos, 815 Pollard Rd, Los Gatos, 408-378-6131; Saint Louise Regional Hospital, 9400 No Name Uno, Gilroy, 408-848-2000; Stanford Hospital, 300 Pasteur Dr, Stanford, 650-723-4000; El Camino Hospital, 2500 Grant Road, Mountain View, 650-940-7000

**Library**: Santa Clara County Library, 14600 Winchester Blvd, Los Gatos, 408-293-2326 ext 3001or 800-286-1991, www.sccl.org

**Public Schools**: Santa Clara County Office of Education, 1290 Ridder Park Dr, San Jose, 408-453-6500, www.sccoe.org

**Community Publications**: *San Jose Mercury News*, 888-688-6400, www.mercurynews.com; *Metro*, 408-298-8000, www.metroactive.com; *Silicon Valley-San Jose Business Journal*, 408-295-3800, www.bizjournals.com/sanjose

**Community Resources**: Symphony Silicon Valley, 467 S 1st St, 408-286-2600, www.symphonysiliconvalley.org; Opera San Jose, 345 S 1st St, 408-437-4450, www.operasj.org; Ballet San Jose-Silicon Valley, 40 N 1st St, 408-288-2820; Lick Observatory, 19 miles east of San Jose on Highway 130 on top of Mount Hamilton, 408-274-5061, www.ucolick.org; Fujitsu Planetarium, 21250 Stevens

Creek Blvd, DeAnza Community College Campus, Cupertino, 408-864-8814, www.planetarium.deanza.edu; Tech Museum of Innovation, 201 S Market St, 408-294-8324, www.thetech.org

**Public Transportation:** *Santa Clara Valley Transportation Authority (SCVTA)*, 408-321-2300, www.vta.org; *Traffic and Transit Assistance*, 511, www.511.org; *Caltrain*, 800-660-4287, www.caltrain.com

# SAN JOSE

DOWNTOWN SAN JOSE
ALUM ROCK
JAPANTOWN
NAGLEE PARK
ROSE GARDEN
BURBANK/BUENA VISTA
FRUITDALE

WILLOW GLEN
EVERGREEN
EDENVALE/GREAT OAKS
SANTA TERESA
ALMADEN VALLEY
CAMBRIAN PARK

Though San Francisco gets all the attention, **San Jose** is the largest city in the Bay Area and currently boasts more job opportunities per capita than any other city in the United States. A fast-growing city of 1 million residents, San Jose is the third largest destination in California. By sheer size alone, this city can seem daunting to newcomers wondering where and how to start looking. Each neighborhood's characteristics are quickly changing. Contrasts within San Jose have never been sharper: while the city enjoys the fastest job growth in the country, it also struggles with a housing crisis. Until 2015, San Jose had the largest homeless encampment in the country—an eastside area dubbed locally "the Jungle." In the shadows of Silicon Valley, the Jungle's hundreds of homeless were kicked out recently when city officials dismantled and shut down the 75-acre homeless site. Today it's undergoing a multiyear conversion to hiking trails, stirring local controversy over the deepening challenge of available housing in tech-centered Silicon Valley.

What this means for newcomers depends on your budget, political perspective, employment status, and transit needs. San Jose's enormous size means it has more homeownership opportunities than anywhere else in the Bay Area. The city's employment grew 25 percent in 2015 alone, and its hourly wages rose 14 percent. Those numbers include the nearby towns of Sunnyvale and Santa Clara—also major engines of growth—but even counted by itself, San Jose's portion of that rise is impressive. Storefronts that sat empty during the recession have rebounded. There is a drawback, however: San Jose is ranked third "worst" for renters, as the city's median rent jumps 12 percent year over year, with a vacancy rate under 4 percent.

San Jose has dozens of neighborhoods, some officially recognized on maps and others existing only in nods of agreement between residents. Among the better-known neighborhoods are the downtown area, Rose Garden, Naglee Park,

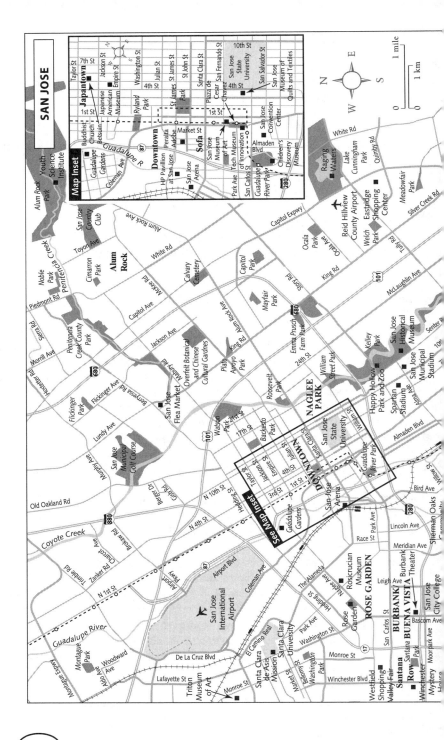

# SAN JOSE

**Map Inset**

Japantown
Downtown
Sofa

San Jose Museum of Art
Tech Museum of Innovation
Children's Discovery Museum
San Jose Convention Center
San Jose Museum of Quilts and Textiles
San Jose State University

Guadalupe Gardens
HP Pavillion at San Jose
San Jose Arena
Guadalupe River Park

Buddhist Church Betsuin
Japanese American Museum
Peralta Adobe
Market St
Ryland Park
St James Park
Plaza de Cesar Chavez
San Fernando St
Santa Clara St
San Salvador St
10th St
4th St
1st St
Taylor St
7th St
Jackson St
Empire St
Washington St
Julian St
St James St
St John St
San Jose State

Alum Rock Park
Youth Science Institute
Alum Rock Creek
San Jose Country Club

See Map Inset

San Jose International Airport
Guadalupe River
Montague Park
Woodward Park

Coyote Creek
Old Oakland Rd

Piedmont Rd
Sierra Rd
Morrill Ave
Hostetter Rd
Penitencia Creek County Park
Noble Park
Penitencia Creek
Cimarron Park
Alum Rock
Toyon Ave
White Rd
Capitol Ave
Jackson Ave
Berryessa Rd
McKee Rd
Calvary Cemetery
Capitol Park
Mayfair Park
Story Rd
King Rd
Capitol Expwy
Reid Hillview County Airport
Ocala Park
Ocala Ave
Welch Park
Eastridge Shopping Center
Lake Cunningham Park
Quimby Rd
White Rd
Meadowfair Park
Silver Creek
Raging Waters
Tully Rd

Flickinger Park
Lundy Ave
Murphy Ave
San Jose Municipal Golf Course
Flickinger Ave
McKee Rd
San Jose Flea Market
Overfelt Botanical and Chinese Cultural Gardens
Arroyo King Rd
Plata Park
Roosevelt Park
24th St
Emma Prusch Farm Park
William Street Park
Happy Hollow Park and Zoo
Spartan Stadium
San Jose Municipal Stadium
Kelley Park
San Jose Historical Museum
McLaughlin Ave
Senter Rd

Murphy Ave
N 1st St
N 4th St
N 10th St
Berryessa Rd
Coyote Rd
Brokaw Rd
Trimble Rd
Zanker Rd
Charcot
De La Cruz Blvd
Airport Blvd
Airport Pkwy
Coleman Ave
Race St
Guadalupe Gardens
Watson Park 24th St
17th St
Backesto Park
Taylor St
Jackson St
Empire St
Julian St
Santa Clara St
4th St
1st St
3rd St
N 10th St
Helding Rd
San Jose State University
San Jose Arena
Guadalupe River Park
William St
Almaden Blvd
Bird Ave
Park Ave
Lincoln Ave
Meridian Ave

DOWNTOWN
NAGLEE PARK

Park Ave
The Alameda
Santa Clara de Asis Mission
Santa Clara University
Park Ave
Washington St
Monroe St
Winchester Blvd
Triton Museum of Art
Lafayette St
Alto Ave
Monroe St
Bellomy St
Washington Park
Market St
Heding St
Naglee Ave
Rosicrucian Museum
Rose Garden
ROSE GARDEN
San Carlos St
Leigh Ave
Bascom Ave
Moorpark Ave
Santana Row
Santana Park
Westfield Valley Fair
Westfield Shopping Mall
San Jose City College
Burbank Theater
BURBANK
BUENA VISTA
Mystery House
Sherman Oaks
Santa Clara St
El Camino Real

N
W        E
S

0        1 mile
0        1 km

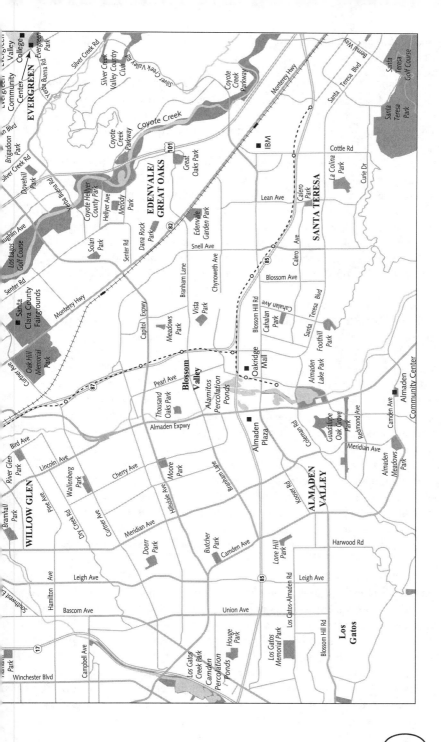

Willow Glen, Evergreen, Santa Teresa, Almaden Valley, Japantown, Burbank/Buena Vista, and Edenvale/Great Oaks. Each neighborhood feels less cramped than those in other Bay Area cities. As a general rule, the further you live from downtown, the more suburban the neighborhoods—with larger yards, quieter streets, and bigger strip malls.

The oldest neighborhood is **Naglee Park**, which stands in the city's central core, just east of San Jose State University. It's bordered by Highway 280 to the south, Coyote Creek to the east, 10th Street to the west, and Santa Clara Street to the north. The neighborhood is named after General Henry Naglee, who owned a 140-acre estate that still stands, surrounded by classic Victorian and Craftsman-style homes, and stately mansions dating from the early 1900s, some of them divided into apartments and duplexes. You'll also find clusters of apartments from the 1970s and '80s. Naglee Park residents amble through the playground at William Street Park and attend the annual Bark in the Park Festival for dogs, hosted here each September. The area was given an upgrade recently, with a new elementary school and symphony. Newcomers eyeing houses along the creek should keep in mind that it sometimes overflows in winter months.

The **Rose Garden** neighborhood is centrally located west of downtown, bordered by Alameda Roadway on the east, Interstate 880 on the northwest, and Naglee Avenue on the north. The area takes its name from the majestic rose garden at Dana and Naglee avenues—a popular spot for morning strolls. Also nearby (1660 Park Avenue) is the Rosicrucian Egyptian Museum and Planetarium, an award-winning attraction. Housing choices include exquisite Queen Anne Victorians, some Tudor-style homes, contemporary apartments, and many new condos. With San Jose State University nearby, students gravitate here—as do plenty of professionals, and those interested in architectural preservation, a trend led by the Rose Garden Neighborhood Preservation Association (www.rgnpa.org). The main drawback in the Rose Garden neighborhood is its proximity to the airport and Caltrain tracks, both of which may present noise concerns.

Exiting the freeway, you might easily miss **Burbank**, even though its main drag, West San Carlos Street, is the gateway to downtown. The neighborhood, bounded roughly by 2nd Street, I-280, McLaughlin Avenue, and Phelan Avenue, consists of single-family houses, apartments, and new condos. Within walking distance of downtown, Burbank has the advantage of being quiet in the evenings. West San Carlos Street is a kind of mini antique alley, with eclectic furnishings and vintage gems. The community comes out for the annual Burbank Neighborhood Jamboree, which dates back to 1948 and hosts antiques shows, hot-rod collections, and more inflatable bounce-houses and games than kids can count. Nearby, the **Buena Vista** neighborhood has a cluster of historic bungalows with handcrafted features built between 1906 and 1930. The **Fruitdale** area, just south of Buena Vista, is named for the fruit orchards (especially plum trees) that used to grow here. These days a cluster of mixed-income houses, shopping malls, and sleek apartments have replaced the orchards, and San Jose City College is located here, making Fruitdale a magnet for students.

One of the city's most desirable and colorful family retreats is **Willow Glen**, just southwest of downtown and easily accessible by the light-rail system. If you can afford to grab a spot in this exclusive neighborhood, strongly consider it. Named after the trees along its creeks and river, this neighborhood used to be the *town* of Willow Glen before incorporating into San Jose, and it still has a self-contained atmosphere. Founded in 1927, the town was annexed by San Jose just 9 years later, and today there's an active Willow Glen Neighborhood Association. The newly paved Los Gatos Creek Trail is warmly welcoming to strollers and bicyclists. Architecturally, Victorians appear side by side with Eichlers, Tudors, ranch homes, and Mediterranean-style stuccos. Several older houses were recently torn down in favor of larger lots, but residents work tirelessly to preserve the old-fashioned charm. Wandering these leafy sidewalks, you'll spot lovely lawns and well-tended gardens filled with colorful flowers. Many Willow Glen families have been here for generations, so turnover isn't as high as in neighboring areas.

Southeast of downtown San Jose, on the eastern side of Highway 101, awaits **Evergreen**, a newly developed area. Much of the housing is no older than a few decades, and you'll find spacious homes with three, four, and even five bedrooms. Set against the arid hills, Evergreen Community College (3095 Yerba Buena Road), is an excellent local resource, with tranquil fields and a picturesque pond on the edge of campus—an inviting spot to relax and feed the ducks. Just south of campus is the golf course, Silver Creek Valley Country Club, and a gated community with 1,500 Mediterranean-style homes. Evergreen feels a world away from bustling downtown San Jose, and residents typically like it that way. New corner malls satisfy all the basics for shopping and banking, and the main thoroughfare, Yerba Buena Road, links the neighborhood with nearby Highway 101.

The Edenvale, Great Oaks, and Santa Teresa neighborhoods are clustered near the end of the light-rail system. In the southeast corner of the city, just north of

*Downtown San Jose*

the Blossom Hill overpass, sit **Edenvale** and **Great Oaks**. Built on the site of an old racetrack, many of Edenvale's and Great Oaks' streets are named after racehorses. Great Oaks Park forms the boundary between the two communities. Homes tend toward ranch-style, single-family abodes. Resources are a little sparse, but there's a local shopping center and new skate park. Both neighborhoods are part of an ongoing revitalization effort to improve resources, make neighborhoods cleaner and safer, and better connect them to one another. For outdoor adventure, head north of Edenvale to Coyote Hellyer County Park, located along Coyote Creek and Coyote Road.

**Santa Teresa** is bordered by Blossom Hill Road on the north, Santa Teresa Boulevard on the west, and Monterey Road on the east. Most homes here were built in the 1960s, though new developments have been added. A scenic expanse of green is nestled nearby in the 1,688-acre Santa Teresa County Park, along Santa Teresa's southern border. For a view of the sprawling city and surrounding mountains, climb Coyote Peak. The practical single-family tracts in these southeastern neighborhoods provide much of the housing for employees of the Almaden Research Center—an IBM Research facility on a 700-acre campus in the nearby valley.

The neighborhood of **Almaden Valley** is one of the city's most desirable hotspots—an affluent destination with a rural, newer feel, and it's one of San Jose's most recent areas to see development. No wonder Almaden Valley is—ready for this?—currently the sixth most competitive neighborhood in the United States for homebuyers. It's arguably the most immaculately landscaped location in Northern California, filled with zigzagging hiking paths and bright-green pastures. Tucked along the city's southernmost edge, it's bordered by Almaden Expressway to the north, the Santa Teresa foothills to the east, Guadalupe Road to the west, and the city limits to the south. In recent years the area has boomed with multimillion-dollar mansions. Many lifelong locals are in shock over this neighborhood's home values. Almaden Lake Park, at the intersection of Almaden Expressway and Coleman Avenue, has a sandy beach and swim area, which comes in handy on hot summer days. Also on the lake are kayaks, paddleboats, and windsurfers. Sitting atop Los Capitancillos Ridge, the 4,100-acre Quicksilver County Park is home to vast open meadows, wildflowers, and 33 miles of hiking trails. The Almaden Expressway connects residents to state routes 85 and 87. For more information on the neighborhood, contact the Almaden Valley Community Association (www. avca-sj.org). For a bit of history, head beyond the city limits about 11 miles south to find the remnants of a mining town. Known as New Almaden, this little village, home to the Almaden Quicksilver Mining Museum, is like a living time capsule.

By contrast, **downtown San Jose** is a monument to twenty-first-century tech culture: billions of dollars have been pumped into the downtown area, creating museums, convention centers, theaters, a light-rail system, fountains, tech offices, restaurants, and shopping areas. More than 90 tech businesses have moved in, spurring new apartment towers and an impressive new City Hall, on West Santa Clara Street. The *San Jose Mercury News*, the city's daily newspaper, moved its headquarters downtown in late 2015—a sign of the district's comeback. And nearly 1,000 new apartments are in the pipeline near the downtown Greyhound station and across from City Hall. That's an enormous rebound from a recession that had presumably sounded the death knell for the city's core just a few years ago.

The city's resurgence is picking up speed. Apple itself recently grabbed its first major San Jose office building, along Orchard Parkway, and tech giant Samsung Semiconductor expanded on North 1st Street—a historic street that bustled with dot-com companies during the 1990s, before the economic meltdown wiped them out. For nightlife, however, there's a hitch: downtown isn't yet the place to be. Frankly, it's bleak, by many locals' standards. Plenty of younger professionals still jump in their cars to head up to San Francisco for nights out, even though San Jose's main commercial streets, Market and First, are packed with new restaurants.

Still, there's a state-of-the-art cultural arts complex—home to a performing arts center, civic auditorium, and convention center—and a handful of theaters around edges of downtown. The trendy southern edge of downtown is dubbed **SoFA** (South First Area). A new apartment tower is coming—a 24-story high-rise dubbed "Gateway Tower," at South Market and East Williams streets, a key access point to downtown. The area is pedestrian-friendly, and a monthly art walk passes in and out of eclectic galleries.

An acclaimed downtown highlight is the Tech Museum of Innovation, one of the Bay Area's premier science museums, exploring robotics, genetics, space exploration, and microchip technology. The museum boasts hundreds of hands-on exhibits. On Thursday evenings locals line up for live concerts in the Plaza de Cesar Chavez. And on Friday afternoons from May through November, the farmers' market spreads out on San Pedro Street between Santa Clara and St. John streets.

Also in the heart of downtown—from Highway 880 at the north to Highway 280 at the south—is Guadalupe River Park, a three-mile ribbon of lush land with many options for family entertainment, including the Children's Discovery Museum, a carousel, and the rapidly expanding Guadalupe Gardens along the banks of the Guadalupe River. A little further west you'll find the idyllic Chinese Cultural Garden (368 Educational Park Drive, 408-251-3323, www.chineseculturalgarden.org).

The Chinese garden is especially impressive and important as a historic window onto the legacy of Chinese heritage in San Jose. This city used to have five Chinatowns, but today it has none. Each Chinatown was devastated by mysterious fires or discriminatory zoning laws targeting Chinese immigrants over the decades. From constructing the railroads to building the levees, Chinese laborers created the infrastructure for today's Silicon Valley. These days, the city's Chinese community is thriving again, as festivals and arts groups multiply, including the acclaimed Cantonese Opera Association of Silicon Valley (www.coasv.com); Chinese Performing Artists of America (www.chineseperformingarts.org); and Chinese Historical & Cultural Project (www.chcp.org).

San Jose also boasts the largest Vietnamese population of any city outside of Vietnam—a rich history told powerfully at San Jose's pioneering Viet Museum (www.vietmuseum.org), which opened a few years ago. This is the first Vietnamese museum in the United States, and is housed in an elegant Victorian built in 1877. Cultural diversity is a point of pride in this city, whose **Japantown**—from 1st Street to the west, Taylor Street to the north, 8th Street to the east, and Empire Street to the south—is a destination neighborhood with single-family houses and a cluster of new condos. Japantown is also home to mouthwateringly good family-owned restaurants and bakeries; line up for homemade tofu at the San Jose Tofu Company (175 Jackson Street, 408-292-7026). Also be sure to check out the Japanese American Museum of San Jose (535 North 5th St, www.jamsj.org) and the Buddhist Church Betsuin (640 North 5th Street, www.sjbetsuin.com)—a historic temple that's frequently crowded. Every Sunday morning, rain or shine, residents pack Japantown's farmers' market on Jackson Street between 6th and 7th streets.

A local treasure on the west side of San Jose is the Winchester Mystery House (525 South Winchester Boulevard, www.winchestermysteryhouse.com), where waves of visitors wander a dizzying maze of seemingly endless hallways, trapdoors, and staircases that lead to nowhere. Designed by the eccentric heiress to the Winchester rifle fortune to ward off the spirits of those killed by guns, the house is an impressive estate of gardens that get spooky on Friday the 13th and on Halloween.

Near the Winchester Mystery House, you'll find ultra-chic **Santana Row**, an enormously popular shopping and dining district boasting some of Bay Area's finest restaurants and designer boutiques, as well as luxury townhomes and flats. Not far away, nestled within Alum Rock Canyon—in the foothills of the Diablo Mountain range—is Alum Rock Park (16240 Alum Rock Avenue). San Jose's oldest and largest park, at 720 acres, Alum Rock Park is home to Youth Science Institute, which houses a variety of live animals and hosts kids' camps. The Mexican Heritage Plaza and Cultural Center (www.mhplaza.com), is also housed in **Alum Rock**, as is the last vestige of Little Portugal.

The city also boasts 59 mobile-home parks, housing 35,000 residents in almost

*Alum Rock*

11,000 mobile homes. But one of those mobile-home parks, Winchester Ranch Mobile Home Park—a popular site for senior citizens—was sold in 2015 and may face closure soon—but not without a court battle. Stay tuned. As lack of affordable housing is a growing challenge for San Jose, public safety is as well: this city *was* one of the safest in Silicon Valley, but today San Jose is one of the most dangerous, as citywide budget cuts have reduced the police department's ranks. By 2016, the police department is projected to shrink to two-thirds the size it was in 2008.

As big as San Jose is, the city is, by necessity, a city of contrasts—of trends both exciting and daunting. If you're considering moving here, devote as many days you can to absorbing each neighborhood firsthand.

**Website:** www.sanjoseca.gov

**Area Codes:** 408

**Zip Codes:** 95109–13, 95116, 95119, 95125, 95126, 95128, 95129, 95133, 95134, 95136, 95141, 95148, 95150, 95151, 95192

**Post Office:** 1750 Lundy Ave, San Jose, 800-275-8777, www.usps.com

**Police:** 201 W Mission St, 408-277-8900

**Library**: Dr. Martin Luther King, Jr. Library, 150 E San Fernando St, 408-808-2000, www.sjlibrary.org

**Public Schools**: San Jose Unified School District, 855 Lenzen Ave, 408-535-6000, www.sjusd.org

**Community Publications:** *San Jose Mercury News*, 408-920-5662, www.mercurynews.com; *San Jose Post Record*, 408-287-4866; Metro, 408-298-8000, www.metroactive.com; *Silicon Valley-San Jose Business Journal*, 408-295-3800, sanjose.bizjournals.com

**Cultural Resources:** Peralta Adobe, 154 W Saint John St, 408-993-8300; History Park at Kelley Park, 1650 Senter Rd, 408-287-2290, www.historysanjose.org; Japanese American Museum of San Jose, 535 North 5th St, www.jamsj.org; Santa Clara de Asis Mission, 500 El Camino Real; Santa Clara University, 408-554-4023, www.scu.edu/mission; San Jose Museum of Quilts and Textiles, 520 S 1st St, 408-971-0323, www.sjquiltmuseum.org; San Jose Museum of Art, 110 S Market St, 408-271-6840, www.sjmusart.org; San Jose Institute of Contemporary Art, 560 S 1st St, 408-283-8157, www.sjica.org; Lick Observatory, 19 miles east of San Jose on Highway 130 on top of Mount Hamilton, 408-274-5061, www.ucolick.org; Tech Museum of Innovation, 201 S Market St, 408-294-8324, www.thetech.org; American Musical Theater of San Jose, 408-453-7100, www.amtsj.org; Cantonese Opera Association of Silicon Valley, www.coasv.com; Chinese Performing Artists of America, www.chineseperformingarts.org; Chinese Historical & Cultural Project, www.chcp.org; Opera San Jose, 345 S 1st St, 408-437-4450, www.operasj.org; Ballet San Jose, 40 N First, 408-288-2120, www.balletsanjose.org; San Jose Convention and Cultural Facilities (Center for the Performing Arts, Parkside Hall, Civic Auditorium, Montgomery Theater, McEnery Convention Center), 150 W San

Carlos St, 408-792-4194, www.sanjose.org; Children's Discovery Museum of San Jose, 180 Woz Way, 408-298-5437, www.cdm.org; Buddhist Church Betsuin, 640 North 5th Street, www.sjbetsuin.com;

**Residential and Commercial Resources:** San Jose Silicon Valley Chamber of Commerce, 101 W Santa Clara St, 408-291-5250, www.sjchamber.com; Almaden Community Center, 6445 Camden Ave, 408-268-1133; Evergreen Community Center, 4860 San Felipe Rd, 408-270-2220; Sherman Oaks Community Center, 1800A Fruitdale Ave, 408-292-2935; Rose Garden Neighborhood Preservation Association, P.O. Box 59838, www.rgnpa.org; Willow Glen Neighborhood Association, P.O. Box 7706, 408-294-9462, www.wgna.net; Japantown Neighborhood Association, www.jtownneighbors.org

**Parks, Gardens, and Open Space:** Parks, Recreation and Neighborhood Services, 200 E Santa Clara St, 408-535-3570, www.sanjoseca.gov/prns; Emma Prusch Farm Park, 647 S King Rd; Alum Rock Park, 15350 Penitencia Creek Rd; Overfelt Gardens (and Chinese Cultural Gardens), 2145 Mckee Rd; Almaden Lake Park, 6099 Winfield Blvd, 408-277-5130; Kelley Park (Japanese Friendship Gardens and Happy Hollow Park and Zoo, 1300 Senter Rd, 408-277-3000, www.happyhollowparkandzoo.org are also located here); Heritage Rose Garden, 715 Spring St, 408-298-7657; Lake Cunningham Park, 2305 S White Rd, www.lakecunningham.org

## SUNNYVALE

The 24 square miles of **Sunnyvale** are home to more tech companies than any other city in the world. In the past millisecond, that distinction might have changed, as today's center of gravity in the tech world moves quickly between Silicon Valley towns. Each time you look up around the Bay Area, there's a new town claiming "it" status among tech cities. Given Sunnyvale's strong local economy, sparkling parks, and excellent safety record, it's no surprise that it consistently ranks as one

*Sunnyvale*

of the safest midsize towns in the United States. Yahoo is headquartered here, and Lockheed Martin, Network Appliance, and hundreds of other tech giants operate locally. But don't go looking for Sunnyvale on Yahoo Maps. Yahoo discontinued its map services in 2015—a concession to the more popular maps offered by Google, headquartered one town over, in Mountain View. The competitive clash between Google and Yahoo is a sort of mirror of the residential rivalry between Sunnyvale and Mountain View. Sunnyvale claims to be the "heart" of Silicon Valley—which is true, if you go by size. With 150,000 residents, Sunnyvale is today's second-most populous city in the region, larger than Palo Alto and Cupertino combined.

Sunnyvale is coming up fast. It's one of the most in-demand Silicon Valley communities. The town borders Cupertino, where the new Apple "spaceship" campus is being built. And Sunnyvale is also home to research labs belonging to Mercedes-Benz, which is testing self-driving cars around town.

With Sunnyvale's large size come extra public services and outstanding green space, including an 18,500-square-foot skatepark that's among the 18 award-winning parks, which include ponds, fountains, ballparks, and swimming pools. Tennis is enormously popular here, with 51 tennis courts—16 of which are lighted—at the Sunnyvale Municipal Tennis Center. The town also boasts a unified Department of Public Safety, whose personnel are trained as firefighters, police officers, and EMTs, and are able to respond to emergencies in any of the three roles.

Houses range from multi-story condos, to red-tiled Mediterranean-style homes, to multimillion-dollar mansions. The city has more than 1,100 Eichler homes, characteristic of Sunnyvale's modernist aesthetic. And the downtown area is shining with a new City Plaza, new office buildings, and a 20-screen movie theater. Historic Murphy Avenue includes a handful of new restaurants and shops, as well as a popular Saturday morning farmers' market (Murphy Avenue at Washington Avenue). Recently completed projects include the upscale new Transit Station and Plaza del Sol (200 West Evelyn Avenue), which symbolizes the city's agricultural past with large, colorful fruit sculptures. Generations ago, this town's first developer— Walter Crossman—was onto something when he dubbed this agricultural farmland the "city of destiny"—prophetic words. While Google and Yahoo grapple over office space here, Amazon is jumping into the Sunnyvale land grab by building a new drive-up store—the first in the world. Order groceries at Amazon.com, then schedule a drive-through pickup.

Apple also jumped into the action in 2014, leasing 290,000 square feet of new offices in Sunnyvale. Apple's seven new buildings are projected to house 1,450 workers, making it even more competitive for residential newcomers to find affordable housing. Heading into 2016, Sunnyvale's median home prices broke the $1 million mark.

**Website:** www.sunnyvale.ca.gov
**Area Codes:** 408
**Zip Codes:** 94086, 94087, 94089, 94089

**Post Office:** 580 N Mary Ave, Sunnyvale, 800-275-8777, www.usps.com

**Police:** 700 All America Way, 408-730-7100

**Library:** Main Library, 665 W Olive Ave, Sunnyvale, 408-730-7300, www.sunnyvale. ca.gov

**Public Schools:** Sunnyvale School District, 819 W Iowa Ave, Sunnyvale, 408-522-8200, www.sesd.org

**Community Publication:** *Sunnyvale Sun*, 408-200-1000, www.sunnyvalesun.com

**Community Resources:** Sunnyvale Chamber of Commerce, 260 S Sunnyvale Ave, 408-736-4971, www.svcoc.org; Sunnyvale Community Center Theater, 550 E Remington Dr, 408-733-6611; Sunnyvale Volunteer Resources, 408-730-7533

**Parks, Gardens and Open Space:** Parks and Recreation Department (and Sunnyvale Community Center), 550 E Remington Dr, 408-730-7350, www. sunnyvale.ca.gov

## LOS GATOS, MONTE SERENO

Spotless downtown parks, spacious backyards, and luxurious hillside houses are increasingly common in Silicon Valley towns fueled by the tech scene, and **Los Gatos** is a prime destination for tech millionaires and billionaires. Tucked away just east of the Santa Cruz Mountains, off of Highway 17, this upscale and picturesque community of 31,000 people is especially desirable among top-paid professionals. Stroll along the downtown sidewalks, and you'll see exquisite picnic spots and colorful flower baskets on elegant lampposts. And just when you thought Los Gatos couldn't get more dreamlike, along comes this: a small, inconspicuous Lamborghini showroom—across from the Bentley showroom—each blending in with the adjacent boutiques, tidy antique stores, and spas. This is high-end homeownership at its most shining, with easy access to nature.

If you can afford Los Gatos—given the median home sales price of $1.6

*Monte Sereno*

*Los Gatos*

million, going into 2016—you'll enjoy woodsy roads with new homes, especially in the Blossom Hill Manor area. Among the lots are a 20-room mansion formerly owned by Apple co-founder Steve Wozniak, with a koi pond, a pool fed by a waterfall, and mesmerizing views of the mountains. More modest, early-1900s Victorians are on offer, but many home prices have escaped gravity.

Culturally, Los Gatos has enjoyed major changes, including the opening in 2015 of the New Museum Los Gatos (NUMU), one of the brightest interactive museums in the Bay Area. The two-story museum has rotating exhibitions, ranging from social justice and technology to local art history, in a 16,000-square-foot space formerly occupied by the library. (The new library opened a few doors down recently.) NUMU houses the MakerSpace—a drop-in studio for families to create their own art.

Los Gatos is also where Netflix is headquartered. Two new Netflix buildings are under construction, making this elegant village the world's center of streaming video. As Netflix expands here, expect more tech employees to join you in the housing hunt.

Throughout the year, the Los Gatos Creek Trail draws cyclists, runners, and walkers along its 5-mile path, which winds up hills and around Lexington Reservoir, with majestic views. For family outings, the 150-acre Vasona Park is popular for picnics and jogging. Next to Vasona Park is Oak Meadow Park, which features a colorful carousel. Those with pets should head to the newly renovated Los Gatos Creek County Dog Park.

For an even more upscale area—yes, it's possible—visit the town of **Monte Sereno** (population 3,500), right next to Los Gatos. An older, more established community, it's similarly known for multimillion-dollar mansions on spacious, picturesque lots. Unlike Los Gatos, this community is entirely residential, with no commercial zoning—meaning no stores or businesses are allowed to "distract" from the scenic surroundings. It's no wonder that John Steinbeck was able to concentrate long enough, and creatively enough, to write the *Grapes of Wrath* here in 1939.

<u>LOS GATOS</u>
**Website:** www.losgatosca.gov
**Area Code:** 408
**Zip Codes:** 95030, 95031, 95032
**Post Office:** 101 S Santa Cruz Ave, 408-395-7526, www.usps.com
**Police:** 110 E Main St, 408-354-8600
**Library:** 110 E Main St, 408-354-6891, www.losgatosca.gov
**Public Schools:** Los Gatos Union School District, 17010 Roberts Rd, 408-335-2000, www.lgusd.org
**Community Publications**: *Los Gatos Weekly Times*, www.mercurynews.com; *Los Gatos Magazine*, www.losgatosmagazine.com
**Community Resources:** Community Resources: New Museum Los Gatos (NUMU), 106 E. Main St, 408-354-2646, www.numulosgatos.org; Arts & Culture Commission, 110 E. Main St, 408-354-6834, www.losgatosca.gov; Addison-Penzak Jewish Community Center, 14855 Oka Rd, 408-357-7429, www.apjcc.org; Los Gatos Recreation, 123 E. Main St, 408-354-8700, www.lgsrecreation.com; Chamber of Commerce, 10 Station Way, 408-354-9300, www.losgatoschamber.com
**Parks, Gardens, and Open Space:** Department of Parks and Public Works, 110 E Main St, in the Los Gatos Town Hall Complex, 408-399-5781, www.losgatosca.gov; Los Gatos Creek County Dog Park, 1250 Dell Ave, 408-356-2729

<u>MONTE SERENO</u>
**Website:** www.montesereno.org
**Area Code:** 408
**Zip Codes:** 95030
**Post Office:** 101 S Santa Cruz Ave, 408-395-7526, www.usps.com
**Police:** 110 E Main St, 408-354-8600
**Library:** 110 E Main St, 408-354-6891, www.losgatosca.gov
**Public Schools:** Los Gatos Union School District, 17010 Roberts Rd, 408-335-2000, www.lgusd.org
**Community Resources:** City Hall, 18041 Los Gatos Saratoga Rd, 408-354-2805, www.montesereno.org
**Parks, Gardens, and Open Space:** 18041 Los Gatos Saratoga Rd, 408-354-2805, www.montesereno.org

# CUPERTINO, CAMPBELL

Cupertino and Campbell are increasingly desirable choices in the South Bay. Each is a suburban paradise, with lush parks filled with sun, birds, trails, and festivals. Campbell (41,000 people) is smaller, with a cohesive community in its historic downtown. Cupertino is more spread out, with no agreed-upon downtown. Strip malls are common in Cupertino, whose flagship resident is Apple. The tech giant's presence helps explain why Cupertino is one of the richest towns in the United States.

From iWatches and iPhones to iPods and iPads, **Cupertino** may as well change its name to iCupertino. Apple is everywhere, but it's not this town's only star. Education is another big attraction. Recently named the second-best town in California to raise a family—and the fifth best in the United States—by the ranking site Niche.com, Cupertino has schools so prestigious that hundreds of parents move here just to enroll their kids in school; many of them move away after graduation. Residents call it "prestige poaching." Schools routinely rank in the highest percentiles nationwide. In the end, Cupertino's identity is divided: tech workers shuttle back and forth from San Francisco, staying close to Apple's campuses while they are in town, and rarely mingling with local families.

Diversity is growing, with a residential majority of immigrants from China and India—communities especially present in shopping plazas with award-winning eateries. Cupertino recently became the first city in Northern California to have an Asian-American majority in the city council, and the town's Silicon Valley Korean School is the world's largest Korean school outside of South Korea.

Apple looms so large that even Cupertino's housing is shaped by the company's presence. Proposals are in place to expand an apartment building within walking distance of Apple's campus by 600 more units—the densest housing site in city history. Construction is slated to begin in 2017. The property, called the Hamptons, sits near Interstate 280 and Wolfe Road. For below-market-rate housing, the city requires a portion of all new housing to remain "affordable," but the inventory is low and the waiting lists long.

Wherever you live in Cupertino, Apple is never far away: it's expanding so fast that it's building a new "spaceship" campus to complement its One Infinite Loop complex. The new site is a whopping $5 billion stretch of 2.8 million square

*Cupertino*

feet—enough to house 13,000 employees, with a thick layer of 7,000 trees and 1,000 bicycles for workers. Community leaders express mixed feelings. Some welcome the upgrade, while others call it extravagant—as though Apple is setting out to build another country within Cupertino.

Consider that the city had just 500 homes in 1950, and today it contains closer to 20,000. For nightlife, residents typically head to San Jose, a manageable drive away. To the west of Saratoga Sunnyvale Road sit the lush Cupertino foothills, home to mansions. Outdoor enthusiasts have plenty of hiking and biking, while shoppers head to the Vallco department stores—but not for long: the mall will soon be demolished in favor of condos.

The farmers' market in Cupertino Square is bustling every Friday. Just before Highway 85, you'll find De Anza Community College and the Flint Center, which features Broadway plays, concerts by the San Francisco Symphony, and other performances. Bargain hunters head to the De Anza Flea Market, held on the first Saturday of every month at 21250 Sevens Creek Boulevard. The swimming and picnic facilities at the 60-acre Blackberry Farm, including a golf course, are popular with locals—as is the sleek new Bay Club Gym (10101 North Wolfe Road). If you want a less-expensive workout, explore Cupertino Sports Center (21111 Stevens Creek Boulevard), with a fitness center, racquetball, and tennis courts.

**Campbell**, by comparison, is less tech-dominated, and more walkable. Strolling the old Campbell Avenue is a pleasant pastime that gives you a strong sense of local character: flower baskets, wine bars, Irish pubs, Italian restaurants, and vintage-clothing stores. The strip is developing fast, with new patios fashioned after upscale Los Altos. But Campbell isn't chic or showy. Insider's tip: one of the Bay Area's best small record stores is here: On the Corner (530 E Campbell Ave), with hard-to-find jazz and rock gems.

Like Cupertino, Campbell has an excellent public safety record and an outstanding school system. Prospect High School recently completed its gym modernization, tennis-court renovation, and construction of a performing arts center.

*Campbell*

The school hosts a farmers' market on Saturdays, but the bigger and more popular farmers' market is on Campbell Avenue every Sunday morning—rain or shine.

Not to be outdone in recreation, Campbell has a sprawling outdoor community center with skate parks, soccer and tennis facilities, a theater, a swimming pool, a fitness center, and a football field with a running track. A new concert series has come to Orchard City Green (adjacent to City Hall) on Thursday nights during the summer.

## CUPERTINO

**Website:** www.cupertino.org
**Zip Codes:** 95014, 95015
**Area Codes:** 408
**Post Office:** 21701 Stevens Creek Blvd, Cupertino, 800-275-8777, www.usps.com
**Police:** Santa Clara County Sheriff's Office West Valley Division, 1601 S De Anza Blvd, 408-868-6600
**Library:** Cupertino Library, 10800 Torre Ave, 408-446-1677, www.sccl.org/cupertino
**Public Schools:** Cupertino Union School District, 10301 Vista Dr, Cupertino, 408-252-3000, www.edline.net/pages/cupertino_union_sd
**Community Publication:** *Cupertino Courier*, 408-200-1000, www.mercurynews/cupertino
**Community Resources:** Cupertino Chamber of Commerce, 20455 Silverado Ave, 408-252-7054, www.cupertino-chamber.org; De Anza Community College, 21250 Stevens Creek Blvd, 408-864-5678, www.deanza.edu; Quinlan Community Center and Cupertino Historical Museum, 10185 N Stelling Rd, 408-777-3120; De Anza College Flint Center for the Performing Arts, 21250 Stevens Creek Blvd, 408-864-8820; Asian-Americans for Community Involvement, 408-975-2730; Cupertino Sports Center, 21111 Stevens Creek Blvd, 408-777-3160; Fujitsu Planetarium, De Anza Community College, 21250 Stevens Creek Blvd, 408-864-8814, www.planetarium.deanza.edu
**Parks, Gardens, and Open Space:** Parks and Recreation Department (and Quinlan Community Center), 10185 N Stelling Rd, 408-777-3110, www.cupertino.org; Blackberry Farm Golf Course, 22100 Stevens Creek Blvd, 408-253-9200

## CAMPBELL

**Website:** www.ci.campbell.ca.us
**Area Codes:** 408
**Zip Code:** 95008
**Post Office:** 500 W Hamilton Ave, 800-275-8777, www.usps.com
**Police:** 70 N 1st St, 408-866-2121
**Library:** Campbell Library, 77 Harrison Ave, 408-866-1991, www.santaclaracountylib.org/campbell
**Public Schools:** Campbell Union School District, 155 N 3rd St, Campbell, 408-364-4200, www.campbellusd.k12.ca.us

**Community Publications:** *Campbell Express*, 408-374-9700, www.campbell express.com; *Campbell Times*, 408-494-7000, www.campbelltimes.com; *the Campbell Reporter*, 408-200-1000, www.mercurynews.com/campbell

**Community Resources:** Campbell Community Center, 1 W Campbell Ave, 408-866-2105; Campbell Chamber of Commerce, 1628 W Campbell Ave, 408-378-6252, www.campbellchamber.com

**Parks, Gardens, and Open Space:** Recreation and Community Services, 1 W Campbell Ave #C-31, 408-866-2105, www.ci.campbell.ca.us

# SARATOGA

Nestled in the foothills of the Santa Cruz Mountains, 10 miles west of San Jose, **Saratoga** is an elegant village with wooded trails, idyllic creeks, and oak-lined streets—a quintessential set of South Bay characteristics. But what sets this town apart is what it does not have: chain stores. Residents are so protective of Saratoga's downtown charm that when a Subway sandwich shop tried to open recently, the city refused. This 12-square-mile enclave of 31,000 people is decidedly upscale—and like Los Gatos, it offers quick access to pristine nature. Saratoga was recently named the second-safest city in California—and the 12th safest in the United States. As of 2015, Saratoga is in the running for a prestigious national beautification award from America in Bloom, a competition between 42 cities. As part of the town's beautification boost, it set a goal of 2,015 trees by the year 2015. Mission accomplished. The community recently won a $4.2 million state grant for beautification and safety, including 16 landscaped medians, green bike lanes, bus shelters, and audible signals for the visually impaired. There's also a lively Facebook page dedicated to Saratogans' passion for nature and landmarks, named "You Know You're From Saratoga, CA When . . ."

For a glimpse into Saratoga's old-town charm, stroll downtown and notice the heritage plaques marking the entrances to lavish boutiques on Big Basin Avenue.

*Saratoga*

And note the controversy over Measure Q—the most hotly contested initiative in generations here—which would have limited commercial buildings to two stories. Could Saratogans handle a three-story building? By a close margin, the measure was defeated, paving the way for three-story buildings—a turning point in this slow-changing town. The breathtaking Hakone Gardens are the oldest and most treasured Japanese gardens in the Western Hemisphere. Created in 1918, the gardens are poised for renovation, including two new buildings. For summer concerts, hundreds head to Mountain Winery. Another landmark is Montalvo Arts Center, a 175-acre estate with gardens, a bird sanctuary, and nature trails—a great setting for big-name concerts and plays in the outdoor amphitheater. Montalvo was built in 1912 by James Duval Phelan, a three-term mayor of San Francisco and the state's first popularly elected United States Senator.

Proximity to the Santa Cruz redwoods put Saratoga on the map by the mid-1800s, when the town had become a thriving lumber center, and later an agriculture paradise. Wealthy San Franciscans flocked here for cottages, and today the area is considered an extension of Silicon Valley. Architecturally you'll find ranch-style estates and two-story Victorians, but beware the price tag: the median home in 2015 topped $2.3 million. This is no surprise when you consider the land value and location. Influential architect Julia Morgan (best known for the Hearst Castle) designed the Saratoga Foothill Club in 1915. And rock climbers come from across the Bay Area to Castle Rock State Park, where overnight backpackers, day hikers, horseback riders, and mountain bikers enjoy 32 miles of trails.

**Website:** www.saratoga.ca.us

**Area Code:** 408

**Zip Code:** 95070

**Post Office:** 14376 Saratoga Ave, 800-275-8777, www.usps.com

**Sheriff:** Santa Clara County Sheriff's Office West Valley Division, 408-868-6690

**Library:** Saratoga Library, 13650 Saratoga Ave, 408-867-6126, www.santaclaracountylib.org/saratoga

**Community Publication**: *Saratoga News*, 408-200-1000, www.mercurynews.com/saratoga

**Community Resources**: Hakone Gardens, 21000 Big Basin Way, 408-741-4994, www.hakone.com; Mountain Winery, 14831 Pierce Rd, 408-741-2822, www.mountainwinery.com; Montalvo Arts Center, 15400 Montalvo Rd, 408-961-5800, www.montalvoarts.org; West Valley Community College, 12000 Fruitvale Ave, 408-867-2200, www.westvalley.edu

**Public Schools**: Saratoga Union School District, 20460 Forrest Hills Dr, 408-867-3424, www.saratogausd.org

**Parks, Gardens and Open Space**: Saratoga Parks and Recreation (also the Saratoga Community Center), 19655 Allendale Ave, 408-868-1249

# SANTA CLARA

A global spotlight is shining on the city of **Santa Clara**, which in 2015 was crowned by Livability.com as the 7th most livable city in the country—rising from its previous position as 16th. Outstanding schools, a strong job market, and family-centered services attract waves of new graduates and well-paid families, as well as senior citizens. That's a sharp reversal from a few years ago, when this city's trajectory was tilting down in the aftermath of the recession. This town is growing fast, and is no longer in the shadows of Cupertino and Mountain View. Santa Clara has new claims to fame: the San Francisco 49ers moved here in 2014, acquiring the brand-new $1.3 billion Levi's Stadium. It's the first NFL site to earn the LEED gold award for eco-friendly design. Super Bowl 50 landed here in February 2016, adding to this city's popularity—and traffic.

The new football stadium sits along the highway, generating millions of dollars and hundreds of jobs for the local community. But the 49ers took a publicity hit when the team tried to convert a kids' soccer field into a VIP parking lot. Protective parents were furious, rallying to the soccer field's defense and sacking the 49ers' efforts, prompting the NFL team to extend a $3 million peace offering to the kids to improve youth sports fields. Families in Santa Clara flex their influence, typically with a smile.

Also underway is a $400 million entertainment and hotel complex owned by football great Joe Montana, across from Levi's Stadium. And the International Swimming Hall of Fame is moving to Santa Clara—a natural fit for a town whose swimmers have won more than 70 Olympic medals. The new Northside Branch Library is also a success, and the city's new Thomas Barrett Park is a well-maintained enclave in the South of Forest neighborhood. What sets Santa Clara apart, above all, is its electric supplier—Silicon Valley Power—which earned the US Department of Energy's top award for innovation and customer benefits by keeping electric costs among the lowest in California. If you move here, your

*Santa Clara*

electric bill will drop to half of those in nearby towns. But you'll spend a bundle for housing itself: the median home in Santa Clara is around $1 million, keeping pace with Silicon Valley. Dozens of below-market-rate rentals are available, but there are wait lists. For an up-to-the-minute directory, consult the housing department at City Hall (1500 Warburton Ave, 408-615-2490, www.santaclaraca.gov), or visit www.affordablehousingportal.org.

Amid Santa Clara's housing growth, there's also a growth in homeless-ness—countless families priced out of their homes. The town is taking steps to give exceptional, personalized attention, notably to mothers living with their babies in cars—a chilling reality in the shadows of Silicon Valley's wealth. That is a grim aspect of Bay Area life, where tech success obscures the hardships of lower-income locals. If you can afford it here, you'll enjoy an abundance of natural beauty—including 32 exquisite parks, with sports and picnic areas. Most popular is 52-acre Central Park, which fans out along Saratoga Creek. The park hosts an art and wine festival each September, drawing 50,000 people, and a new BBQ cham-pionship. For a serene stroll, visit Ulistac Natural Area, a 40-acre preserve with wooded areas, grasslands, and wetlands. Another family attraction is California's Great America rollercoaster park, with some of the scariest rides on Earth. And the stretch of El Camino Real that runs through Santa Clara is widely acclaimed as the hub of the Bay Area's best Korean food—packed with 350 Korean-American-owned businesses.

But as family-friendly as Santa Clara is, this is still Silicon Valley—which means all tech, all the time. Intel's headquarters are here, alongside Texas Instruments and Applied Materials. The Intel Museum is a crowd-pleaser, tracing the birth and rise of the microchip. Nearby is Santa Clara University, the oldest university in Cal-ifornia, founded in 1851—sprawled immaculately across the eastern corner of the city. Growing communities of Chinese, Korean, and Indian immigrants are rooted here, with shops and cultural centers reflecting a wide range of traditions.

Senior citizens are in excellent hands in Santa Clara, as an acclaimed 45,000-square-foot senior center is free to residents aged 50 and older, offering assistance in housing, health, food, transportation, and taxes. On Saturday morn-ings year round, locals of all ages flock to the farmers' market—a nice complement to the Whole Foods that is slated to open soon, in a massive, 50,000-square-foot part of Santa Clara Square.

**Websites:** www.santaclaraca.gov, www.sccgov.org (county site); www.facebook. com/cityofsantaclara; @santaclaracity

**Zip Codes:** 95050, 95051

**Post Office:** 1200 Franklin Mall on Jackson St, 800-275-8777, www.usps.com

**Police:** 601 El Camino Real, 408-615-4700, www.scpd.org

**Library:** Central Park Library, 2635 Homestead Rd, 408-615-2900

**Public Schools:** Santa Clara Unified School District, 1889 Lawrence Rd, 408-423-2000, www.santaclarausd.org

**Community Publications:** *Santa Clara Weekly*, 408-243-2000, www. santaclaraweekly.com; Santa Clara Visitor's Bureau, 1850 Warburton Ave, 800-272-6822, www.santaclara.org

**Community Resources:** Santa Clara Convention and Visitor's Bureau, 1850 Warburton Ave, 408-244-9202; Triton Museum of Art, 1505 Warburton Ave, 408-247-3754; Intel Museum, 2200 Mission College Blvd, 408-765-0503; Santa Clara Players Theatre, 1511 Warburton Ave, 408-248-7993; Louis B. Mayer Theatre, Santa Clara University, corner of Lafayette and Franklin Sts, 408-554-4015; California's Great America amusement park, Great America Parkway off of Hwys 101 and 237, 408-988-1776, www.cagreatamerica.com, Santa Clara University, 500 El Camino Real, 408-554-4000, www.scu.edu; Mission Community College, 3000 Mission College Blvd, 408-988-2200, www.missioncollege.org

# MILPITAS

Set against the hilly, arid backdrop of Mount Diablo to the north and Copernicus Peak to the south, this growing community of 70,000 has abundant attractions and transportation, including the largest outdoor mall in Northern California. The Great Mall's 1.4 million square feet are a bargain hunter's paradise, with factory outlets and department stores across from a converted Ford Motor plant. It's one of many draws that make **Milpitas** the 11th best city in California to raise a family, according to the ranking site Niche.com, which made that designation in 2015.

Milpitas has one of Santa Clara County's highest home-ownership rates—more than 75 percent of households are owner-occupied—thanks to the real estate rush in nearby San Jose and Silicon Valley. Tech companies are coming to Milpitas—including software giant Cisco Systems, which helps Milpitas to rank first in the nation among tech towns, with the largest percentage of residents employed in the industry.

Milpitas has no central downtown, however—so if you want one, try elsewhere. Instead you'll find a cluster of shopping plazas—many of them treasures for those who crave Indian, Chinese, Vietnamese, Korean, and Thai food and products. The popular Indian movie theater Serra, at 200 Serra Way, is thumping every night with dance parties and screenings. The city has a majority-Asian population—more than 60 percent—and central hangouts like Ulferts Center—a mix of Chinese salons, wellness centers, and shops carrying a lifetime supply of dried sea cucumber, dried scallop, dried ginseng . . . dried *everything*, all stored in per-pound buckets that come with shovels. Dig in, or head to Northern California's largest Asian market center, Milpitas Square.

Recent repairs to Main Street's sidewalks and pavement are a sign of investments in the city's growing profile. With all the large-scale projects underway, don't be surprised if you find more modern architecture than old charmers—from single-family ranch-style homes to an endless wave of condos and townhomes.

Half a decade ago, suffering from a recession, the median home value fell to a dreamlike $450,000. That dream is long over; currently, you're looking at a record-high $730,000 median (a 14 percent rise from the year before). But that's still hundreds of thousands lower than San Francisco. With today's housing boom, you can pay $1 million for a Milpitas house with a backyard the size of an IKEA coffee table, at best. Know this going in, and be prepared for competition.

Among the city's 25 large parks—with several mini-parks scattered throughout—is Ed Levin County Park, with 1,539 acres of hiking trails, lawn-chair fishing, a golf course, and enormous open areas, including an off-leash dog park. From Monument Peak, you'll get sweeping views of both the valley below and the southern part of the Bay. Murphy Park is popular with kids, while Hidden Lake Park is a serene place to relax alongside ducks.

Milpitas, which means "little cornfields" in Spanish, is relatively young as Bay Area cities go—about 60 years old. A stopping point on the road between San Jose and Oakland, the area first attracted settlers in the 1850s—most of them farmers tending to orchards and fields of sugar beet, peas, and corns. The town proved it could go it alone when locals defeated a ballot measure that would have turned the city into an annexed arm of San Jose in the 1960s. Milpitas leaders likened their battle for independence to the American Revolutionary War, dubbing themselves the "Milpitas Minutemen." Today a minuteman symbol engraved on the city seal pays tribute to that legacy, and a kind of friendly rivalry exists with San Jose.

Milpitas has easy access to three highways: I-680, I-880, and Highway 237, putting it within short commuting distance of the East Bay and Silicon Valley—though the commutes are brutal during peak hours. And Milpitas's traffic cops mean business if you even *slightly* exceed the speed limit. They'll get you every time, as many locals can attest. To help alleviate traffic madness, the city urges commuters to carpool at least once a week (visit www.511.org for more information).

Fortunately, a sleek, efficient light-rail system now extends to Milpitas, greatly improving commute options. Better still, a local BART stop is currently in the construction phase, with final completion scheduled for 2018.

**Website:** www.ci.milpitas.ca.gov
**Area Code:** 408
**Zip Codes:** 95035, 95036
**Post Office:** 450 S Abel St, 800-275-8777, www.usps.com
**Police:** 1275 N Milpitas Blvd, 408-586-2400
**Library:** Milpitas Library, 40 N Milpitas Blvd, 408-262-1171, www.sccl.org
**Public Schools:** Milpitas Unified School District, 1331 E Calaveras Blvd, 408-635-2600, www.musd.org
**Community Resources:** Milpitas Community Center, 457 E Calaveras Blvd, 408-586-3210; Milpitas Sports Center, 1325 E Calaveras Blvd, 408-586-3225; Rainbow Children's Theatre (performances at the Milpitas Community Center),

457 E Calaveras Blvd, 408-586-2777; Milpitas Chamber of Commerce, 828 N Hillview Drive, 408-262-2613, www.milpitaschamber.com

**Parks, Gardens, and Open Space:** Recreation Service Department, 457 E Calaveras Blvd (and Milpitas Community Center), 408-586-3210, www.ci.milpitas.ca.gov

FROM COASTAL WILDLIFE TO PRISTINE PARKS, RUGGED HILLS TO THRIVING arts festivals, this tiny slice of California is one of the country's most desirable places to live. Forget "one of"—it is *the* most desirable, considering the highest-in-the-nation housing costs and record-low inventory. Brace yourself, as San Francisco in 2015 was crowned the "worst" city for renters, according to *Forbes* magazine and countless other publications. The real estate ripple effect set in motion by San Francisco and Silicon Valley is spreading across the East Bay, South Bay, Peninsula, and North Bay. Three of the country's most competitive neighborhoods for homebuyers are in San Francisco (the Sunset, the Castro, and Bernal Heights). Housing hopes and tensions are at all-time highs, as demand soars. The area's tech job market, thriving arts community, academic excellence, and start-up-friendly business climate make the Bay Area an economic powerhouse. For newcomers, moving here means gearing up for high rents and high risk—with the possibility of high reward.

There are bright spots. In an effort to meet the growing need for affordable housing, state and local authorities have banded together—prompted by local activists—to create a variety of housing initiatives toward a better balance between market-rate and below-market-rate housing, though that dream isn't fulfilled yet. A number of cities have implemented programs to attract and retain residents of all economic means, through first-time homebuyer assistance programs. But let's not sugarcoat this: the Bay Area housing market is hyperventilating. So are thousands of hopeful homebuyers—so in addition to the tips below, take to the Internet and self-educate, using these pointers as guidance.

In San Francisco, a majority of the city's population are renters, and many live with roommates to bring costs down. Homebuyers are increasingly considering condos, townhouses, and tenancies-in-common (TIC) ownership. Just be aware of Homeowner Association (HOA) dues, which essentially pay for the upkeep of the building but can top hundreds per month, in addition to the mortgage. If you dream of owning a home here, you'll need to be a bit creative. Housing options in the Bay Area are immensely varied. San Francisco's most distinctive dwellings are wood-framed Victorian homes, many of which have been remodeled and turned into flats with two to four units per building. You'll also find a large number of Edwardians—each a castle containing dozens of units. Here in quake country, wood-framed buildings, especially if they are built on rock, are safest because they are more flexible when the earth moves. Virtually every large building in San Francisco has been highly reinforced against the next big earthquake—but not all. If you're especially worried about earthquakes, steer clear of homes built on landfill (like the Marina District of San Francisco, or Foster City near San Mateo); landfill acts like gelatin during a long-duration quake. See the **Emergency Preparedness** chapter for more on this topic.

## APARTMENT HUNTING

### DIRECT ACTION

One word: Craigslist. The website started in the Bay Area, where it is headquartered and has millions of local users. It is by far the most popular website for local apartment listings. Also recommended are the new mobile apps Padmapper, Hotpads, and Lovely—free tools that help you find an apartment through location mapping, sourcing their data primarily from Craigslist. Many newcomers may be used to looking for rental ads on coffee shop, grocery store, and laundromat bulletin boards. Drop that idea. The Bay Area is all Craigslist all the time. For up-to-the-minute housing commentary, also visit www.curbed.com, www.redfin.com, and www.socketsite.com.

Sifting through the mountains of rental ads and advice can be a full-time job. Energetic newcomers should start with those websites and ask everyone they know for word-of-mouth referrals. If this seems like too much work, check below under **Rental Agents, Relocation Services, and Roommate Services**.

### NEWSPAPER CLASSIFIED ADS

As prehistoric as newsprint has become in the world of digital everything—especially in the Bay Area, where Craigslist was invented—a few sellers still post ads to newspapers' print editions. "Newspaper classifieds" is a phrase you won't hear much in today's Bay Area, but a few small-town newspapers still carry housing classifieds in the Bay Area, which a local real estate agency can point you toward. Still, your best bet is to familiarize yourself with the listings at Craigslist (www.craigslist.org).

### OTHER RENTAL PUBLICATIONS

Many property owners still pay to list their units in glossy guides that are free to prospective renters. These guides, available in racks at supermarkets, bus and

BART stations, and many street corners, are designed to make each property look like a paradise. Keep in mind that while many of them are as charming and glistening as they look in the ads, these units are typically located in large apartment complexes and towers.

Here are just two of these glossies:

- *Apartment Guide* covers San Francisco and the greater Bay Area (www.apartmentguide.com)
- *Rental Guide* covers San Francisco and the greater Bay Area (415-929-7733, www.rentalguide.com)

## RENTAL AGENTS, RELOCATION SERVICES, ROOMMATE SERVICES

The demand for housing is at an all-time high, and vacancy rates are at record lows—a tough trend that many analysts predict will continue, owing to the Bay Area's growing confidence after the recession, as well as the strength of Silicon Valley's and San Francisco's tech markets. Finding a home is challenging, statistically and anecdotally. For newcomers who want expert help, a rental agency is a worthwhile investment.

When it comes to professional services, the most popular option is to sign up with a listing service that typically charges a fee for access to an extensive bank of rentals. Listings are accessible online and updated daily. Some agencies will also run a credit report for you and put together a renter's resume when you sign up. Rental agencies that offer a more customized approach may do the footwork to find you a place and create lists but also charge a percentage of the first month's rent. If you have friends or coworkers in the area, ask if they can recommend an agency, or look at the user reviews at www.yelp.com (where dedicated reviewers crank out write-ups of everything from apartment complexes to oversized burritos from the corner food truck). A word of advice: always ask for a clear description of fees and services before entering into any binding agreements. In addition to Yelp, you can find passionate and free reviews by tenants at www.apartmentratings. com—a vibrant community of former and current renters.

For pet owners, www.peoplewithpets.com and www.sfrent.net are great places to start looking for tolerant landlords. The Bay Area in general is pet-friendly (see the **Pets** section in the **Getting Settled** chapter), although pet owners typically pay more for the privilege. In its apartments section, Craigslist also has a handy search function for animal lovers. Below is a partial list of Bay Area rental agencies; check Yelp and www.yellowpages.com for more listings.

### SAN FRANCISCO
- **American Marketing Systems Inc.** specializes in high-end furnished and unfurnished apartments and vacation rentals (2800 Van Ness Ave, 800-747-7784, 510-339-1419, www.amsires.com).

- **Apartment Guide** offers rental listings (www.apartmentguide.com).
- **ApartmentRatings.com,** making slumlords across the nation nervous, is the largest rating resource for rental apartments (www.apartmentratings.com).
- **Craigslist,** by far the most popular and all-inclusive listings resource, features an endless list of apartments, houses, sublets, and parking spaces, and is updated daily (www.craigslist.org).
- **Move** is a national website that includes listings for apartment rentals all around the Bay Area (www.move.com).
- **The Rental Source,** a rental listings site, charges a $25 application fee and $25 credit-report fee (2013 16th St, 415-771-7685, www.therentalsource.com).
- **Roommate Express** is a national roommate-matching service with Bay Area listings; a fee applies (800-487-8050, www.roommateexpress.com).
- **Roommates.com** is a roommate-finder with listings for cities across California; basic membership is free, and choice membership costs $5.99 for 3-day trial, with better deals for extended membership (www.roommates.com).
- **Sabbatical Homes,** a resource for the traveling academic, includes home exchanges and rentals in the Bay Area (www.sabbaticalhomes.com).
- **Saxe Real Estate,** a competitor of Craigslist, is also free but less comprehensive (1999 Van Ness Ave, 415-474-2435; www.saxerealestate.com).
- **SF Gate,** the website of the *San Francisco Chronicle* newspaper, lists rentals and homes for sale (www.sfgate.com/realestate).
- **SF Real Estate Services** is a large database of higher-end condo rentals and houses for sale (150 Lombard St, Suite 1 #1, 415-788-4488, www.sfres.com).
- **SF Rent** specializes in renting pet-friendly Victorian apartments, and requires references and a $30 application fee (1201 Fulton St, 415-861-0777, www.sfrent.net).
- **SF State University Housing** provides housing resources for students, faculty, and visiting scholars (800 Font Blvd, Mary Ward Hall, SFSU Campus, 415-338-1067, www.sfsu.edu/~housing).
- **Trinity Management Services** specializes in short-term furnished rentals and long-term unfurnished rentals on the pricier side (1145 Market St, 415-433-3333, www.trinitymanagement.com).
- **UCSF Campus Housing Office** rents university housing to undergrads, post-docs, clinical fellows, and faculty (500 Parnassus Ave (for Parnassus) and 1505 4th St (for Mission Bay), 415-476-2231 and 415-514-4550 respectively, www.campuslifeservices.ucsf.edu/housing).

## EAST BAY & NORTH BAY

- **Apartment Guide,** see above for description, www.apartmentguide.com
- **ApartmentRatings.com,** see above for description, www.apartmentratings.com
- **Craigslist,** see above for description, www.craigslist.org
- **Move,** see above for description, www.move.com
- **Roommate Express,** see above for description, 800-487-8050, www.roommateexpress.com

- **Roommates.com**, see above for description, www.roommates.com
- **Sabbatical Homes**, see above for description, www.sabbaticalhomes.com
- **Tenant Finders**, 3483 Golden Gate Way, Suite 217, Lafayette, 925-939-2200, www.tenantfinders.com

### PENINSULA
- **Apartment Guide**, see above for description, www.apartmentguide.com
- **ApartmentRatings.com,** see above for description, www.apartmentratings.com
- **Craigslist**, see above for description, www.craigslist.org
- **Move**, see above for description, www.move.com
- **Roommate Express**, see above for description, 800-487-8050, www.roommateexpress.com
- **Roommates.com**, see above for description, www.roommates.com
- **Sabbatical Homes**, see above for description, www.sabbaticalhomes.com
- **HIP-Homesharing** is a rental agency specializing in shared housing for people with special needs, low-income family assistance, and rehabilitation of properties in San Mateo County. Call to set up an interview (364 S Railroad Ave, San Mateo, 650-348-6660, www.hiphousing.org).

### SOUTH BAY
- **Apartment Guide**, see above for description, www.apartmentguide.com
- **ApartmentRatings.com,** see above for description, www.apartmentratings.com
- **Bay Rentals** is a service that claims 95 percent success rate in placing customers. They have exclusive listings from contacts in the property management industry; basic service contracts ($50) are for 30 days and include detailed listings and daily updates (900 S Winchester Blvd #9, San Jose, 800-706-7878, www.bayrentals.com).
- **Craigslist**, see above for description, www.craigslist.org
- **Move**, see above for description, www.move.com
- **Roommate Express**, see above for description, 800-487-8050, www.roommateexpress.com
- **Roommates.com**, see above for description, www.roommates.com
- **Sabbatical Homes**, see above for description, www.sabbaticalhomes.com

## SUBLETS

Like most housing answers in the Bay Area, your best bet for subletting—and virtually all else—is to start with a search on Craigslist, which lists countless sublets daily. Subletting allows you to rent a room on a short-term basis while the original tenant is away. In San Francisco, subletting is common, but most leases prohibit tenants from subletting without the landlord's approval. If it can be arranged, speak to the landlord before signing with a tenant, or at least ask the tenant if sub-letting is technically allowed. If you find a room, apartment, or a house to sublet, you'll need to vacate the premises when the original tenant returns. You're not considered to be the legal tenant until entering into a separate agreement with the landlord. For those choosing to stay, the landlord can require you to sign a new lease at a higher rent than what you had been paying.

Subletting from a "master tenant" who is the sole lease signer and who lives on the premises is most common, but typically must be approved by the landlord. While it's illegal for master tenants to charge you more than the rent they pay to the landlord, in practice this does happen, so ask upfront if they're charging more than they themselves pay—but ask delicately or you'll tick them off, and may lose their interest. The master tenant has the right to evict you with 30 days' written notice for any reason. For more information, visit www.hrcsf.org/subletting_basic.html.

## SHARING

Considering the record-high cost of rent, the top universities, and the countless Victorian flats—with odd-shaped rooms and formal dining rooms that double as bedrooms—sharing is ubiquitous in the Bay Area. Housemate situations can be challenging, so carefully consider the dynamics by meeting the occupants first. You'll find lots of households comprised solely of nonsmoking tenants, or cat-loving tenants, or strictly vegetarian tenants, or other lifestyle-mandatory housemates in search of likeminded tenants; search Craigslist by keyword.

There are two ways to enter into lease agreements with roommates. Lessees can be "co-tenants," which means that whoever signs the lease with the landlord has equal rights and responsibilities. This is only bad if living together doesn't go well. Because everyone has signed the lease, everyone has the right to remain in the house and no one can force anyone else to go. The other lease option is to appoint a master tenant, who signs the lease, pays the rent in one check, and deals with the landlord. The other roommates are then considered sub-tenants. Should you, as a sub-tenant, be unable to pay your share of the rent, the landlord cannot go after you, but your roommate can. In fact, the master tenant can evict you with 30 days' written notice, regardless of cause. This type of situation can vary if living in San Francisco, which has strict rent control laws that protect ten-ants' rights. Check out the San Francisco Tenants Union, www.sftu.org, which is a great resource for legal information. The Tenants Union holds a series of "tenant bootcamps"—free workshops educating renters on how to fight unlawful evic-tions and prevent displacement.

Housemate situations can build lifelong friendships or place you in a few months of living hell. It's wise to agree on some boundaries, create chore wheels, and put some agreements in writing—but don't rush to that level of formality with potential housemates without feeling out the dynamics first.

If you don't mind paying a fee to find a roommate, hire a roommate service (see **Rental Agents, Relocation Services, and Roommate Services**). The fee to match you with a roommate can exceed $100. If you'd rather not pay the roommate referral service fee, there are free alternatives. Chief among them is Craigslist (commit Craigslist to memory for all your listings needs). As always, be careful and skeptical about roommate-wanted ads, and don't commit before both meeting and verifying the person and place. Consider looking the person up on Facebook and other social media to start; that may sound sneaky, but it's just due diligence.

## CHECKING IT OUT

Books and websites tell you only so much about neighborhoods and housing. Get out and walk around. Find people who live in the area and strike up a conversation. Check the city's or town's website, and keep a running checklist of wants and needs and deal breakers. Some points to consider:

- Are the kitchen appliances clean and in working order? Do the stove's burners work?
- Check the windows—do they open, close, and lock? Do the bedroom windows open onto a noisy or potentially dangerous area?
- Is the water pressure strong enough? Try turning on the shower and sink.
- Do the electrical outlets work?
- Are there any signs of insects or other pests?
- Are there laundry facilities in the building, or is there a laundromat nearby?
- Do you feel comfortable outside? Will you feel safe at night? Is there secured parking? How many spaces? If two, are they tandem (one car blocking the other) or side by side? Is there an extra fee for parking? What about public transportation and shopping?
- Are you responsible for paying gas, water, or electricity?
- Watch for discrimination. The California Legislature has declared that "the opportunity to seek, obtain and hold housing without unlawful discrimination is a civil right." It is illegal for landlords to discriminate on the basis of race, color, religion, gender, sexual orientation, marital status, national origin, ancestry, familial status, source of income, or disability.

If you're buying a home, all questions of functionality and cleanliness must be disclosed in the seller's disclosure package.

Ed Sacks' *Savvy Renter's Kit* contains a thorough renter's checklist. The California Department of Consumer Affairs also maintains useful documents and checklists at www.dca.ca.gov/publications/landlordbook.

## STAKING A CLAIM

When you view a rental, come *prepared*. Bring your checkbook, a copy of your credit report, and a completed rental application so that if the place looks good, you can hold it with a deposit immediately. Competition is fierce, and crowded open houses are the norm. Landlords often want references from your previous residences, as well as your basic employment information. Landlords can request nonsmokers, prohibit pets other than a service dog, and bar you from having overnight guests for more than a certain number of nights per year. (If you think you'll have lots of visitors, watch out for a lease containing such a clause, as this may not bode well for your tenant-landlord relationship.)

## LEASES/RENTAL AGREEMENTS & SECURITY DEPOSITS

For a preview of what Bay Area leases or rental agreements look like, take a trip to any well-stocked office supply store. Standard lease and rental agreements are sold in tear-off pads. Or search online for "rental agreement" and your city's name. You'll get a glimpse at how most landlords handle deposits, rent due dates and grace periods, appliances, and pets.

The law requires that a lease of one year or more be in writing. Every lease must specify a termination date. If the termination date isn't included, the tenant and landlord are considered to have entered into a month-to-month rental agreement. An oral agreement to rent for more than one year is considered a month-to-month rental agreement, not a lease. Unless it's a fixed-term lease, the lease will convert to a month-to-month rental agreement at the conclusion of the first tenancy period. Rarely, a landlord might ask you to sign another yearlong lease.

It is customary and acceptable for California landlords to require upfront charges, including a fee for running a credit check (not refundable), the first month's rent, possibly last month's rent (which differs from a security deposit, also required), a key deposit, and a pet deposit. If the property manager asks for last month's rent, keep in mind it must be used for just that. That way, when you give your 30 days' notice of intent to vacate, you're paid up. No lease may include nonrefundable deposits. In California all deposits are returnable if all agreed-to conditions are met. In some cities, landlords are required to pay interest on security deposits at the termination of the lease if the unit was held for longer than a year. If your security deposit is not returned within three weeks of your vacancy date, you can talk to a tenants' rights organization or seek recourse in small claims court— don't hesitate, as small claims courts in the Bay Area are especially sympathetic to tenants. If your landlord is withholding deposit unlawfully, you may be entitled to triple that amount in damages. If you are a co-tenant or sub-tenant, the landlord does not have to return your portion of the security deposit directly to you. The deposit on the unit is returned only when the entire unit is vacated, which means you will have to get your part of the deposit from the co-tenants or master tenant.

If you have to break a lease, there are ways to mitigate the situation, making it less contentious and less costly. If you need to move out before the lease is up, the landlord must make an effort to rent your unit, and he or she may not double-dip—meaning the landlord may not accept rent from you and a new tenant at the same time. When breaking a lease, be careful and savvy. Give the landlord written notice of intent as far in advance as possible. If you can, try to find a new tenant for your unit, making sure the new person is financially capable of taking on the responsibility. If you know that your old unit has been rented and you are still being held responsible for the lease, take action. Speak to the new tenant, photograph a new name on your old mailbox, and seek help from a tenants' organization (see below).

## RENT AND EVICTION CONTROL

Before you've secured a place, be aware that San Francisco has a Rent Stabilization and Arbitration Ordinance that offers protection against some rent increases. The ordinance does not apply to post-1979 apartment units, government-regulated housing, and short-term residential hotels. For units covered by the ordinance, landlords are allowed to raise the rent once a year, beginning on the anniversary of your move-in date, as long as a 30-day written notice is given. The amount by which the rent may be raised is determined by the San Francisco Rent Board and is announced each March. By law it will always be between 0 and 7 percent. In early 2016 the rate stood at 1.9 percent.

San Francisco saw a staggering 55 percent increase in evictions between 2010 and 2015, as landlords tried to jack up rents to market rates. With evictions on the rise, many newcomers join a local tenants' union to safeguard their rights. The San Francisco Tenants Union has an excellent anti-eviction mapping project at www.antievictionmappingproject.net/buyouts.html.

San Francisco and Berkeley have stringent eviction protection for tenants. In San Francisco there are 16 "just cause" reasons for eviction, and in Berkeley there are 12. For a comprehensive list of causes, visit www.sftu.org/justcauses (San Francisco); for Berkeley, visit www.ci.berkeley.ca.us/Rent_Stabilization_Board/Home/Evictions.aspx. A newer quirk is landlords' use of the Ellis Act, a state law permitting owners to evict tenants on the grounds that they're permanently removing rental units from the market. Highly controversial, the law was meant to relieve the strain of management for retiring apartment owners, but it has been exploited by developers in lucrative markets like San Francisco. The landlord must evict the entire building and keep it off market for five years. But a loophole in the law allows developers to convert the property into condos and sell the resulting units at a much higher value. Anti-gentrification groups have fought this ordinance with varying degrees of success. The sale of property, the expiration of a rental agreement, or a change in the Federal Section 8 status of a unit does *not* constitute "good cause" for eviction.

A comprehensive source of information on the legal aspects of tenancy, *California Tenants' Rights*, is published by Berkeley-based Nolo Press, www.nolo.com. Nolo also publishes the *California Landlord's Law Book*, for those on the other side of the rental wall. Knowing the rights and responsibilities of both sides may prove valuable when it comes time to sign on the dotted line, and again when you're ready to move out, as security deposits, apartment cleaning, and repairs become potential issues of concern. To view the California Civil Code, visit www.leginfo.ca.gov.

If you're in need of help, try these offices:

- **Bay Area Legal Aid** has offices across the region, and is headquartered at 1735 Telegraph Ave in Oakland; call for a pre-screening (510-663-4755, www.baylegal.org).
- **Berkeley Rent Stabilization Board**, 2125 Milvia St (510-981-7368, www.ci.berkeley.ca.us/rent)
- **California State Department of Fair Employment and Housing**, 1515 Clay St, Suite 701, Oakland (510-622-2973 or 800-884-1684); 2570 N 1st St, Suite 480, San Jose (408-325-0344, www.dfeh.ca.gov)
- **East Palo Alto Rent Stabilization Program,** 650-853-3114, www.ci.east-palo-alto.ca.us
- **Eviction Defense Center**, 995 Market St #1200, San Francisco (415-947-0797, www.evictiondefense.org)
- **Just Cause San Francisco and Oakland** advocates for low-income tenants (510-763-5877, www.cjjc.org).
- **Legal Aid Society Housing Counseling Program**, 480 N. 1st St (408-283-1540, www.legalaidsociety.org)
- **Project Sentinel** specializes in landlord-tenant disputes across the lower Bay Area (888-324-7468, www.housing.org).
- **San Francisco Rent Board**, 25 Van Ness Ave, Suite 320, San Francisco (415-252-4600, www.sfrb.org)
- **San Francisco Tenants Union**, 558 Capp St, San Francisco (415-282-6622, www.sftu.org)
- **San Jose Rental Rights and Referrals**, 200 E Santa Clara St, San Jose (408-975-4480, www.sjhousing.org)

## LANDLORD/TENANT RIGHTS & RESPONSIBILITIES

California landlords must rent premises that are sanitary and functional, with adequate containers for garbage and recycling. Floors, hallways, and railings must be in working condition, and there must be safe heating facilities and hot- and cold-running water, as well as plumbing, electricity, gas, effective waterproofing, unbroken windows and doors, and functioning locks.

Landlords are not allowed to enter your premises without giving 24 hours' notice and receiving your permission, unless an emergency threatens damage to the unit. You must permit the landlord to enter to make repairs, and to show the apartment to prospective buyers, tenants, contractors, and appraisers. The landlord is not allowed to harass you verbally or physically or make threats. A landlord can neither lock you out of the premises until you have been legally evicted nor turn off utilities in an attempt to pressure you to vacate without due process.

Tenants are responsible for maintaining the premises in working and sanitary condition, for paying the rent on time, and for following the rules written in the lease.

Rental situations in the Bay Area vary widely, from renting a typical apartment in a complex to renting an attic room in someone's home. To learn more about local ordinances, read *California Tenants: A Guide to Residential Tenants' and Landlords' Rights and Responsibilities* at www.dca.ca.gov/publications/landlordbook/catenant.pdf.

## RENTERS INSURANCE

Renters insurance provides relatively inexpensive coverage against theft, water damage, fire, and in many cases, personal liability. In this earthquake-prone area, try to find a policy that covers earthquake damage to personal possessions. Shop around, as insurance rates vary considerably.

One website worth considering is www.insure.com, which compares plans and costs. Most large insurance companies offer renters insurance. If you own a car, a good option is to see if your auto insurance carrier also provides renters insurance.

## BUYING

Many hopeful homebuyers come to the Bay Area only to get sticker shock—especially today, when the median cost of homes in San Francisco exceeds $1.225 million, an all-time high. But the interest rate is the lowest it's ever been. While it's good to have a clear idea of what you want, you may need to make concessions—in neighborhood and size. Before searching, make a list of top priorities. Think about neighborhood, commute, parking, schools, number of bedrooms and bathrooms. Consider your lifestyle. If you're the Bay Area's next top chef, is the kitchen spacious enough? Do you need a dedicated parking spot? If you're looking for a fixer-upper, consider how much time, money, and effort you can afford to put in. Drafting this list will let your real estate agent focus on what's important to you. But before meeting with a real estate agent, do footwork on your own. Investigate the cost of a given neighborhood, and compare it to your financial situation. Good resources to check locally are www.paragon-re.com, www.curbed.com, www.redfin.com, and www.trulia.com, as well as www.fsbo.com, an online DIY home-buying and selling website that demystifies homeownership.

## ONLINE RESOURCES—HOUSE HUNTING

Searching online for a home before you arrive in the Bay Area is a good way to get a handle on prices and inventory. Homes in today's booming Bay Area sell faster than ever—many as quickly as they're listed—but searching ahead will give you an idea of what's on the market. Keep in mind that asking prices are just starting points in bidding wars these days, so don't expect to get any home at its list price. The fastest-growing sites for real estate analysis and neighborhood news in the

Bay Area are www.curbed.com, www.redfin.com, and www.socketsite.com. A handful of sites to get you started:

- **www.craigslist.org**, by far the most popular listings site in the Bay Area
- **www.curbed.com,** excellent neighborhood news and real estate commentary with original reporting and a witty style
- **www.cyberhomes.com,** home listings and pertinent real estate information
- **www.homefair.com**, real estate listings, moving tips, and salary calculators
- **www.homeseekers.com**, a database system of the Multiple Listing Service (MLS)
- **www.marinhousing.org**, a highly respected source of information about housing affordability in Marin County
- **www.mls.com**, Multiple Listing Service (MLS), with home listings and real estate information
- **www.move.com**, lists houses, apartments, and roommates; also includes moving tips
- **www.msn.com/en-us/money/realestate**, home-buying site with information on houses, financing, moving, and home improvement
- **www.paragon-re.com**, top-notch Bay Area real estate resource for sales, commentary, and data
- **www.realestate.yahoo.com**, lists homes for sale, mortgage loans, community profiles, listings for home inspectors, real estate agents, title companies, and more
- **www.realtytimes.com**, nice national real estate news site that provides local information
- **www.redfin.com**, widely respected, reliable source for housing commentary, data, and all things real estate
- **www.socketsite.com**, San Francisco real estate tips and trends
- **www.zillow.com**, lists homes for sale, real estate advice, and lots of local information
- **www.ziprealty.com**, claims to be the first online real estate brokerage to host online transactions

## CONDOS, CO-OPS, TENANCIES-IN-COMMON

In the Bay Area, detached single-family homes are plentiful but expensive. Alternative housing options include condos, co-ops, and tenancies-in-common.

**Condos** are communal associations or cooperative developments where the co-owners share interest and responsibility for the common areas (elevator, garden, laundry room, and hallways), but hold sole ownership of their unit. Condos are common in the Bay Area, and new ones (especially luxury condos) are rapidly being built—a construction frenzy that's controversial in today's Bay Area, where mass displacement has become a severe concern.

A **co-op** is a corporation; owners hold shares in the property and have voting rights. An owner has the right to sell those shares, but the board members or fellow co-op members reserve the right to refuse to sell to someone they consider undesirable. Co-op residences are generally in larger, older buildings.

With **tenancies-in-common**, known as TICs, co-owners usually buy an existing building of two to six units. By law, co-owners must live on the premises. Co-owners own a percentage of the building, but while they enjoy exclusive use of their unit, they do not own it outright. In San Francisco, TICs are a popular option for newcomers who want out of the San Francisco rental market but can still afford to purchase a traditional single-family home. San Franciscans concerned about the shrinking supply of affordable rentals have opposed the recent rise in condo and TIC conversions. Laws governing TICs shift and flow according to political currents, and you should pursue a full understanding of up-to-date regulations regarding these complex housing contracts if considering this option.

## FINDING A REAL ESTATE AGENT

Yes, you'll need one. While it's possible to find a house or condo on your own, you're better off with the help of an expert, especially in this heavily competitive Bay Area housing market. Most homes are bought through a real estate agent because of the complex financial and legal points of the transaction.

The best way to find a real estate agent is through word of mouth. The second-best is to search reviews of real estate agents online. Check www.yelp.com, www.trulia.com, and www.redfin.com by Bay Area neighborhoods, and as simple as it sounds, run an online search for "real estate reviews Bay Area"—a straightforward first step for up-to-the-minute local reviews. Also visit open houses to meet agents. Talk to several agents before choosing one, and look for someone who will represent you as a buyer—a buyer's broker. A buyer's broker works exclusively for prospective homebuyers, while a traditional broker works for the home seller, even though they show buyers around. A broker working for you will bargain on your behalf to negotiate the lowest price, while a traditional broker's job is just the opposite—to get the seller the most money possible. Make sure that whomever you choose seems trustworthy and has a good reputation (and excellent online reviews).

## HOMEOWNERS INSURANCE

If you're buying a new home and financing with a mortgage, homeowners insurance is a required part of the process. Factors that insurers consider when determining your policy rate include the house's fire resistance—wood frames cost more to insure than masonry structures—and your location. Living in a high-theft neighborhood or far from a fire hydrant or fire station will add to your policy cost.

Earthquake insurance in the Bay Area is a smart idea. In 1994, as a result of the costly Northridge earthquake, many insurance companies stopped writing new homeowner's and renter's policies, and some pulled out of California altogether. In response, the state established the **California Earthquake Authority (CEA)** in 1996, providing basic earthquake-damage coverage. Insurance companies in California are required either to supply their own earthquake coverage to policyholders or offer the CEA's policy. For more information about the CEA, visit www.earthquakeauthority.com or call 888-423-2322. For answers to any other insurance questions, contact the **California Department of Insurance** at www.insurance.ca.gov.

The most common type of earthquake insurance is an add-on to a standard homeowners insurance policy. Typically there's a deductible of 5 to 10 percent (and sometimes 15 percent) of the value of the home. Separate deductibles may apply to contents and structure. An important coverage includes temporary living expenses, which pays for a motel and meals if you have to vacate your home. There's usually no deductible on this coverage. The annual cost of residential earthquake insurance is normally about $1.50 to $3 per $1,000 of coverage on the structure.

To learn more about earthquake insurance, ask your insurance agent or contact the California Department of Insurance (www.insurance.ca.gov, 800-927-4357).

If you're considering buying an older home, find out if it's been retrofitted. Retrofitting won't guarantee your home will escape an earthquake damage-free, but reinforced structures withstand shocks better, reducing damage in quakes. For shaking maps and information on making your home safer, visit resilience.abag.ca.gov. The **US Geological Survey**, www.usgs.gov, also offers a wealth of information on earthquake safety.

## ADDITIONAL RESOURCES—HOUSE HUNTING

Popular resources for homebuyers in the Bay Area:

- **Emily Landes, blog.sfgate.com/ontheblock/author/elandes,** an outstanding columnist for the *San Francisco Chronicle*'s website, known as *SFGate*; original reporting, commentary, and data analysis presented in an engaging, authoritative style
- **How to Buy a House in California**, 15th edition (Nolo Press), by George Devine, Ira Serkes, and Ralph E. Warner
- **www.edf.org**, maintained by the Environmental Defense Fund, with information about toxic waste surrounding homes—a wise thing to check, since the entire Bay Area once had a heavy military presence

H AVING FOUND AND SECURED A PLACE TO LIVE, YOU NOW HAVE THE task of getting your stuff here (and probably storing some of it, because Bay Area homes aren't as spacious as reruns of "Full House" make them seem).

## TRUCK RENTALS

First, are you moving everything yourself, or hiring someone else to do it for you? If you're going solo, rent a vehicle, load it up, and hit the road. Search for truck rentals at www.yelp.com and www.yellowpages.com and call around and compare; always ask about any specials. Below is a short list of national truck rental companies. Most of them offer one-way rentals as well as packing accessories and storage facilities. Boxes can be purchased from a local big-box store. If you're cost-conscious, scavenge them yourself; musical instrument stores and liquor stores are perennial favorites for free small and mid-sized boxes.

If you plan to move during the peak moving months (May through September), call well in advance—at least a month ahead of your move. Saturday is a popular moving day, so you may be able to find cheaper rates if you book a different day.

Once you're on the road, keep in mind that your rental truck is a tempting target for thieves. If you must park it overnight or for an extended period—more than a couple of hours—find a safe place, preferably somewhere well-lit and easily observable by you, and do your best not to leave anything of particular value where it can be seen. Make sure you lock the back door and, if possible, use a steering wheel lock or other easy-to-purchase safety device.

A few national self-moving companies:

- **Budget**, 800-462-8343, www.budgettruck.com
- **Penske**, 888-996-5415, www.pensketruckrental.com

- **Ryder**, 800-297-9337, www.ryder.com (now a Budget company, still operating under the Ryder name)
- **U-Haul**, 800-468-4285, www.uhaul.com

## COMMERCIAL FREIGHT CARRIERS AND CONTAINER-BASED MOVERS

If you'd rather not drive a truck and also don't want to hire a full-service mover, there's a third option: hire a commercial freight carrier to deliver a trailer or container to your home. You pack and load as much as you need, and the carrier delivers your trailer or container to its destination. In some cases, this option is cheaper than renting and driving a truck yourself, especially considering cost of fuel. **ABF U-Pack Moving** (www.upack.com, 800-355-1696) uses commercial 28-foot freight trailers. ABF charges by the linear foot, and you only pay for the linear feet you use (subject to a minimum charge). When you've finished loading, you install a plywood bulkhead; ABF fills the remaining space with freight, which is unloaded before the trailer is delivered to your new home.

ABF, **PODS** (www.pods.com, 877-770-7637), **Door-to-Door Storage and Moving** (www.doortodoor.com, 888-366-7222), and several other companies offer container-based moves. With this type of move, the carrier delivers plywood, metal, or fiberglass cubes or other containers to your home. You can take a few days—sometimes a full month—to load the containers; when you're done loading, the company picks up the containers, transfers them to flatbed trucks, moves them to your destination city, and delivers them to your new home. You generally pay only to transport the containers you use, and unlike a truck, the containers can be stored at either end of the journey. A set of containers has smaller storage capacity than a large truck, however, so this option may not work for people with extra-large houses full of furniture. Some large furniture may not fit inside the containers. If you have to move long or tall items, ask the company for its containers' *interior* dimensions before you commit.

If you aren't moving an entire house and can't estimate how much truck space you need, keep in mind this general guideline: two to three furnished rooms equal a 15-foot truck; four to five rooms, a 20-foot truck.

## MOVERS

### INTERSTATE

The best way to find a trusted mover is by **personal recommendation**. Absent that, turn to www.yelp.com for user reviews, or check out one of the hundreds of more or less helpful moving sites.

Also check www.movingscam.com, another user-driven consumer review website. If you're a member of Angie's List, www.angieslist.com, you'll find lists of moving companies rated by members. You might ask a local real estate agent, who may steer you toward a good mover or tell you which ones to avoid. Members of the American Automobile Association (AAA) have a valuable resource in **AAA's Consumers Relocation Services**, which assigns a personal consultant to handle every detail of your move free of charge, and offers savings from discounts arranged with premier moving companies. Visit www.aaa.com or call 800-922-8228.

Another good resource for avoiding or minimizing problems is California-based **MoveRescue** (800-832-1773, www.moverescue.com), which offers pre-move education and consumer assistance, all aimed at helping you avoid being scammed.

*Beware:* since 1995, when the federal government eliminated the Interstate Commerce Commission, the interstate moving business has degenerated into a wild and mostly unregulated industry with thousands of unhappy, ripped-off customers annually. (There are so many reports of unscrupulous carriers that we no longer list movers in this book.) You're pretty much on your own when it comes to finding an honest, hassle-free mover, which is why we can't emphasize enough the importance of carefully researching and choosing who will move you.

To guide your search for an **interstate mover**, a few general recommendations:

First, gather the names of a half-dozen movers and make sure they are licensed by the **US Department of Transportation's Federal Motor Carrier Safety Administration** (**FMCSA**). With the movers' Motor Carrier (MC) numbers in hand, call 866-637-0635 or 202-385-2423 (if you'd like to speak to an agent) or go online to www.safer.fmcsa.dot.gov to see if the carriers are licensed and insured. If the companies you're considering are federally licensed, your next step is to check with the **Better Business Bureau**, www.bbb.org, in the state where the moving companies are licensed, as well as with the state's consumer protection boards or attorneys general (in California call the Department of Consumer Affairs, 800-952-5210, or visit www.dca.ca.gov). Also check FMCSA's **Household Goods Consumer Complaint** at nccdb.fmcsa.dot.gov, which maintains complaints filed against interstate movers. Assuming there is no negative information, you can move to the next step: asking for references. Particularly important are references from customers who experienced moves similar to yours. If a moving company is unable or unwilling to provide references, eliminate it from your list. Unscrupulous movers have been known to give phony references, falsely singing the mover's praises—so talk to more than one reference and ask questions. If something feels fishy, it probably is. One way to learn more about a prospective mover: ask them if they have a local office (they should) and then drop in and check it out.

Once you have at least three movers you feel comfortable with, ask for price quotes (always free). Best is a binding "not-to-exceed" quote, which should of course be in writing. This will require an on-site visual inspection of what you are shipping. If you have *any* doubts about a prospective mover, drop it from your list before you invite a stranger into your home to catalog your belongings.

FMCSA regulations require movers to supply several documents to consumers before executing a contract. These include two booklets: *Important Information for Persons Moving Household Goods (within California)*, which must be provided at the first in-person contact between the consumer and the mover, and *Your Rights and Responsibilities When You Move*; a concise and accurate written estimate of charges; a summary of the mover's arbitration program; the mover's customer complaint and inquiry handling procedure; and the mover's tariff containing rates, rules, regulations, and classifications. For more about FMCSA's role in handling household goods, visit www.protectyourmove.gov.

## ADDITIONAL MOVING RECOMMENDATIONS

- If someone recommends a mover, get names (salesperson, drivers, loaders). Moving companies don't move people, people do.
- Price, while important, isn't everything—especially when you're entrusting all of your worldly possessions to strangers.
- Legitimate movers charge by the hour for local moves (under 100 miles), and by weight/mileage for long-distance moves. Be wary if the mover wants to charge by the cubic foot.
- Ask about the other end—subcontracting increases the chance that something could go wrong.
- In general, ask questions. If you're concerned about something, ask for an explanation in writing. If the mover seems impatient with your questions, drop them. If you change your mind about a mover after you've signed on the dotted line, write a letter or email explaining that you've changed your mind and that you won't be using its services. Better safe than sorry.
- Ask about insurance. The "basic" 60-cents-per-pound industry standard coverage is not enough. If you have homeowners or renters insurance, check to see if it covers your belongings during transit. If not, ask your insurer if you can add coverage for your move. Otherwise consider purchasing "full replacement" or "full value" coverage from the carrier— it's the most expensive coverage, but it's probably worth it. Trucks get into accidents, they catch fire, they get stolen—if such insurance seems pricey to you, ask about a $250 or $500 deductible. This can reduce your cost substantially while still giving you much better protection in case of a catastrophic loss.
- Whatever you do, ***do not*** mislead a salesperson/estimator about how much and what you are moving. Make sure you tell prospective movers about how far they'll have to transport your stuff to and from the truck, as well as any stairs, driveways, obstacles, and long paths. The clearer you are with your mover, the better he or she will be able to serve you.
- If you plan to pack by yourself, you'll save money—but if something is damaged you may not be able to file a claim for it. On the other hand, if you hire movers to pack for you, they may not treat your belongings as well as you will.

They will certainly do it faster, however. Depending on the size of your move and whether you're packing yourself, you'll need more boxes, tape, and packing material than you expect. Mover boxes, while not cheap, are typically sturdy. Sometimes a mover will give a customer free used boxes. It doesn't hurt to ask. Most important, **don't** wait to pack until the last minute. And be sure to ask the mover about weight or size restrictions on boxes.

- Transport all irreplaceable items—jewelry, photographs, work documents—personally. *Do not* put them in the moving van! Consider sending less precious items by FedEx or UPS.
- Ask your mover what is not permitted in the truck: usually anything flammable or combustible, as well as certain types of valuables.
- Although movers will place numbered labels on your possessions, you should make a numbered list of every box and item going in the truck. Detail box contents and take photographs of anything of particular value. Repeat: *take photographs*. Don't skip this step. Once the truck arrives on the other end, you can check off every piece and know for sure what did (or did not) make it. In case of claims, this list can be invaluable. Even after the move, keep it; it can be surprisingly useful.
- Movers are required to issue you a "bill of lading." Do not hire a mover who doesn't use them.
- During the busy season (May through September), demand can exceed supply, and moving may be more expensive than during the rest of the year. If you must relocate during the peak moving months, book service well in advance—a month at least, more if possible.
- Listen to what the movers say; they are professionals with expert advice about packing and preparing. Be ready for the truck on both ends—don't make them wait. Not only will it irritate your movers, but it may cost you. Understand that surprises beyond a carrier's control happen on the road (e.g., weather and accidents) and your belongings may not get to you on the day promised.
- Treat your movers well, especially those actually loading and unloading your stuff. Offer to buy them lunch, and tip them if they do a good job.
- Before moving pets, attach a tag to your pet's collar with the new address and phone number. Your pet should travel with you. Never plan on moving a pet inside a moving truck. For more on moving with pets, you might want to look into **The Pet-Moving Handbook: Maximize Your Pet's Well-Being and Maintain Your Sanity**, by Carrie Straub, published by First Books, www.firstbooks.com.
- Be prepared to pay the full moving bill upon delivery. Some carriers accept Visa and MasterCard but it's a good idea to get it in writing that you'll be permitted to pay with a credit card, as the delivering driver may not be aware of this and may demand cash. Unless you routinely keep thousands in greenbacks on you, you could have a problem getting your stuff off the truck.

# INTRASTATE AND LOCAL MOVERS

The **California Public Utilities Commission (CPUC)**, www.cpuc.ca.gov, regulates the licensing, rates, and rules of the household moving industry in California. All moving companies must be insured and licensed to provide services in California. To verify a mover's certification, contact CPUC (415-703-2782) or the **California Moving and Storage Association (CMSA)** (800-672-1415, www.thecmsa.org) and have the mover's CAL-T number (listed on the mover's literature) ready. CMSA is a nonprofit that offers references to legitimate movers and provides information to help consumers avoid "bandit movers" (movers who engage in unlawful practices or bully customers into outrageous prices once the move has started). According to the CMSA, 80 percent of the calls they receive involve complaints about bandit movers. The CMSA advises against booking online or over the phone without investigating the company's physical address or confirming that it is licensed (with a CAL-T number) with the CPUC. For moves within California, CPUC regulations require all movers to provide clients with a written "not to exceed" price before the move. This price must be clearly disclosed on your Agreement for Service form. The mover will have you sign this form before the move begins.

## CONSUMER COMPLAINTS—MOVERS

If a move goes badly and the moving company is at fault, file a written claim with the mover for loss or damage. If this doesn't work and it's an intrastate move, call 800-894-9444 or visit www.cpuc.ca.gov to file a complaint with the CPUC. If the mover is a CMSA member, the CMSA will intervene on the consumer's behalf if there is a problem.

If your grievance is with an interstate carrier, your choices are limited. Interstate moves are regulated by the Federal Motor Carrier Safety Administration (FMCSA) (888-368-7238, www.fmcsa.dot.gov), an agency under the Department of Transportation, with whom you can file a complaint against a carrier. While FMCSA's role in the regulation of interstate carriers has historically been concerned with safety issues rather than consumer issues, in response to the upsurge in unscrupulous movers and unhappy consumers, it recently issued a set of rules "specifying how interstate household goods (HHG) carriers (movers) and brokers must assist their individual customers shipping household goods." According to its consumer page, carriers in violation of the rules can be fined, and repeat offenders may be barred from doing business. On the other hand, "FMCSA does not have statutory authority to resolve loss and damage of consumer complaints, settle disputes against a mover, or obtain reimbursement for consumers seeking payment for specific charges. Consumers are responsible for resolving disputes involving these household goods matters." The agency cannot represent you in an arbitration dispute to recover damages for lost or destroyed property, or enforce a court judgment. If you have a grievance, your best bet is to file a complaint against a mover with FMCSA and with the Better Business Bureau (www.bbb.org) in the state where the moving company is licensed, as well as with that state's attorney general or consumer protection office. To seek redress, hire an attorney.

## STORAGE WAREHOUSES

Storage facilities come in handy when you're shipping furniture without an apartment to receive it. The CPUC regulates short-term storage (under 90 days) but not long-term or self-storage. If your mover maintains storage warehouse facilities in the city, as many do, you'll want to store with them. Some offer one month's free storage. Search www.yelp.com for "storage" and shop around for the best and most convenient deal. Below are a few major moving-and-storage companies. Listing here does *not* imply endorsement by First Books.

- **Caremore Moving and Storage** is a full-service option in San Francisco (415-822-8547, www.caremoremoving.com).
- **Door-to-Door Storage** delivers cargo containers to you for packing, then transports the containers back to its facilities in the Bay Area, or to your desired location (888-366-7222, www.doortodoor.com/storage).
- **Public Storage** has locations throughout the Bay Area for self-service storage and truck rentals (800-567-0759, www.publicstorage.com).

## SELF-STORAGE

Self-storage is a problem-solver for Bay Area newcomers and longtime locals—especially in San Francisco, where landlords frequently rent garage space separately (for homes that have it) to monthly parkers. Rates are higher in the Bay Area than in most places in the country: expect to pay at least $70 a month for a 5' x 5' (25 sq ft) space, and $200 a month for a 10' x 10' space (100 sq ft)—and so on. If you're looking for lower rates, inquire with the storage facility for move-in specials, upper-floor discounts, or other incentives. Check www.groupon.com for deeper discounts.

As you shop around, check the facility for cleanliness and security. Does the building have sprinklers in case of fire? Does it have carts and hand trucks for moving in and out? Does it bill monthly or automatically charge the bill to your credit card? Access should be 24-hour, or nearly so. Some units are air-conditioned—an asset if you plan to visit your locker in the summer in the East Bay or South Bay. Is the area well-lit at night? Is there a security guard on-site at all times? Is the rental month-to-month, or is there a minimum lease? Is it easily accessible from your home?

A word of warning: unless you no longer want your stored belongings, pay your storage bill and pay it on time. Storage companies may auction the contents of delinquent customers' lockers.

Here are a few self-storage companies in the Bay Area. For more options, check www.yelp.com for local reviews:

- **AAAAA Rent-A-Space** offers student and senior discounts, with locations in Foster City and Moraga (650-341-2964, www.5Aspace.com).
- **American Storage** is a popular option in San Francisco (415-824-2338, www. americanstorage-ca.com).
- **Bay Area Self Storage** has locations in Redwood City, San Carlos, San Mateo, and San Jose (650-288-1189, www.bayareaseflstorage.com).
- **Mobile Mini, Inc.** delivers storage containers from 5′ x 8′ to 40′ x 10′ (866-344-4092, www.mobilemini.com).
- **Public Storage** has a variety of locations throughout the Bay Area, offering pick-up and delivery services at certain locations (866-863-4838, www. pspickup.com).

## CHILDREN AND MOVING

Moving can be hard on kids. The American Medical Association reports that children who move often are more likely to suffer from depression, low self-esteem, and aggression. Academic performance can suffer as well. Here are several steps you can take to reduce stress on your children:

- Talk about the move with your kids. Be honest but positive. Listen to their concerns. To the extent possible, involve them in the process.
- Make sure children have their favorite possessions on the trip.
- **Plan** social activities on the other end. Your kids may feel lonely in your new home, and activities can ease the transition. If you move during the summer, enroll your kids in a local camp (check with the YWCA or YMCA), giving them the opportunity to make new friends.
- Try to schedule your move during the summer so your kids can start their new school at the beginning of the term.
- If possible, before the move, spend time doing fun things in the area to which you are moving, such as visiting a local playground or playing ball in a park or checking out the neighborhood stores. With any luck your kids will meet some other children their own age.

**First Books** (www.firstbooks.com) offers two helpful resources for children. For those aged 6–11, *The Moving Book: A Kids' Survival Guide* by Gabriel Davis is an excellent gift. Younger kids will appreciate *Max's Moving Adventure: A Coloring Book for Kids on the Move* by Danelle Till. For general guidance, read *Smart Moves: Your Guide Through the Emotional Maze of Relocation,* by Nadia Jensen, Audrey McCollum, and Stuart Copans.

## TAXES AND MOVING

If your move is work-related, some or all moving expenses may be tax-deductible—keep those receipts. Though eligibility varies, the cost of moving yourself, your family, and your belongings is tax deductible even if you don't itemize. The criteria: your move must be employment-related; your new job must be more than 50 miles away from your current residence; and you must be at the new location for at least 39 weeks during the first 12 months after your arrival. If you take the deduction and then fail to meet the requirements, you will have to pay the IRS back (unless you were laid off through no fault of your own or transferred again by your employer). It's a good idea to consult a tax expert regarding IRS rules related to moving. Or, if you're a confident soul, get a copy of IRS Form 3903 (www.irs.gov/pub/irs-pdf/f3903.pdf) and do it yourself.

## ADDITIONAL RELOCATION AND MOVING INFORMATION

- **First Books** publishes relocation resources and information on moving to Atlanta, Boston, Chicago, Dallas–Ft. Worth/Houston/Austin, Los Angeles, Minneapolis–St. Paul, New York City, Portland, the San Francisco Bay Area, Seattle, and Washington, D.C., as well as China and London, England. See also the *Newcomer's Handbook® for Moving to and Living in the USA* (www.firstbooks.com).
- **American Auto Transporters, Inc.** offers help moving your car (800-800-2580, www.shipcar.com).
- **BestPlaces** compares quality-of-life and cost-of-living data for cities in the United States (www.bestplaces.net).
- *How to Survive a Move*, edited by Jamie Allen and Kazz Regelman, is a **Hundreds of Heads** guide (www.hundredsofheads.com). Divided into sections ranging from planning a move to packing tips, moving with kids, and worst moves ever, this easy-to-digest book provides the perspectives of hundreds of people who've lived through the experience.
- **Moversguide.usps.com** includes relocation information from the United States Postal Service.
- **The Riley Guide** is an online moving and relocation clearinghouse that lists other moving and relocation guides and websites, offers links to sites that cover cost of living and demographics as well as directories of schools, real estate, and health care (www.rileyguide.com).
- *Steiner's Complete How-to-Move Handbook*, by Clyde and Shari Steiner, is an excellent general guidebook.
- **Worldwide ERC** is a global employee relocation agency—"ERC" stands for Employee Relocation Council (703-842-3400, www.worldwideerc.org).
- **www.moving.com** is a planning resource.
- **www.mymove.com** offers relocation calculators and coupons for your move.
- **www.nerdwallet.com** is an invaluable resource (headquartered in San Francisco), with tips on budgeting your relocation expenses.

ONE OF YOUR FIRST STEPS UPON ARRIVING TO THE BAY AREA IS SET-
ting up checking and perhaps savings accounts—a generally painless
process and sometimes a rewarding one, as banks offer cash incentives
for doing so. The Bay Area has no shortage of banks, savings and loans, and credit
unions that want—even crave—your business.

Banks offer a variety of accounts, from no-fee checking and savings with a siz-
able minimum balance to inexpensive service if you do all your banking by ATM.
Shop around for the best deal—read the expert comparisons at www.nerdwallet.
com, a financial website headquartered in San Francisco. If you're in a rush during
the move, sign up with one of the big banks; you can always change later if you
find a better deal. Keep in mind that smaller banks may have fewer fees than their
colossal counterparts, while offering you a more navigable bureaucracy to deal
with when you need help.

## CHECKING ACCOUNTS

Setting up a checking account should be quick, as long as you have photo identification with your signature and an address. Some banks prefer to see that you've
had an account at another financial institution, but most will not require it. Many
banks offer free checking accounts, though most require you to maintain a minimum balance to avoid monthly service fees. When you open an account, ask the
teller for a full description of your new account, including minimum balances,
available services, fees, and reward points (and how to redeem them). Also ask
for a map of the bank's local ATM locations to avoid racking up painful penalties
for using another institution's ATMs. You'll typically be issued temporary checks
on the spot, for use until printed ones arrive, usually within a week to 10 days. But
many merchants don't like to accept non-printed checks. Stay on the safe side by
keeping enough cash on hand to meet basic needs for two weeks. Chances are
you'll also get a debit/ATM card when you open your account. The card usually

arrives in the mail within 7 to 10 days, ready to use. Most accounts can be linked to each other and to the card, making it easy to bank without ever going into a branch. And most banks offer mobile apps for depositing checks by sending photos of the checks through your smartphone at no additional charge.

## SAVINGS ACCOUNTS

Savings accounts differ from bank to bank, in terms of fees, interest, required minimum balances, and reward points. A savings account can be linked to a checking account to provide overdraft protection—usually for a fee—and a savings account can easily be accessed through mobile apps on your smartphone, without ever setting foot in a bank branch.

## AREA BANKS

Here's a list of some of the Bay Area's biggest banks and their main offices. Visit their websites to find branches closer to home or work.

### SAN FRANCISCO

- **Bank of America**, 345 Montgomery St, 800-622-8731, www.bankofamerica.com
- **Bank of the West**, 180 Montgomery St, 800-488-2265, www.bankofthewest.com
- **California Bank and Trust**, 465 California St, 415-875-1500, www.calbanktrust.com
- **Chase**, 401 California St, 800-788-7000, www.chase.com
- **Citibank**, 1399 Post St, 800-627-3999, www.citibank.com
- **First Republic Bank**, 111 Pine St, 800-392-1400, www.firstrepublic.com
- **Union Bank of California**, 1675 Post St, 415-202-0350, www.uboc.com
- **US Bank**, 2601 Mission St, 800-872-2657, www.usbank.com
- **Wells Fargo**, 1266 Market St, 800-869-3557, www.wellsfargo.com

### NORTH BAY

- **Bank of America**, 1000 4th St, San Rafael, 800-622-8731, www.bankofamerica.com
- **Bank of Marin**, 50 Madera Blvd, Corte Madera, 415-927-2265, www.bankofmarin.com
- **Bank of the West**, 1313 Grant Ave, Novato, 800-488-2265, www.bankofthewest.com
- **US Bank**, 3200 Northgate Dr, San Rafael, 800-872-2657, www.usbank.com
- **Wells Fargo**, 715 Bridgeway, Sausalito, 800-869-3557, www.wellsfargo.com

## EAST BAY

- **Bank of America**, 1500 Park St, Alameda, 510-273-5531; 2129 Shattuck Ave, Berkeley, 510-273-5466; 300 Lakeside Dr, Oakland, 510-273-5118; 1400 E 14th St, San Leandro, 510-649-6600, www.bankofamerica.com
- **Bank of the West**, 1969 Diamond Blvd, Concord, 925-689-4410; 11100 San Pablo Ave, El Cerrito, 510-235-2980; 2127 Broadway, Oakland, 510-444-5636, www.bankofthewest.com
- **Mechanics Bank**, Lake Merritt Plaza Building, 155 Grand Ave, Oakland, 510-251-6106; 1350 N Main, Walnut Creek, 925-210-8170, www.mechanicsbank.com
- **Union Bank of California**, 2333 Shattuck Ave, Berkeley, 510-843-6353; 3223 Crow Canyon Road #100, San Ramon, 925-866-0422; 1970 Franklin St, Oakland, 510-891-9505, www.unionbank.com
- **US Bank**, 2424 Santa Clara Ave, Alameda, 800-872-2657, www.usbank.com
- **Wells Fargo**, 1221 Broadway, Oakland, 510-891-2011, www.wellsfargo.com

## PENINSULA

- **Bank of America**, 530 Lytton Ave, Palo Alto, 650-566-8331, www.bankofamerica.com
- **Chase**, 300 Hamilton Ave, Palo Alto, 650-853-2602, www.chase.com
- **First National Bank of Northern California**, 6600 Mission St, Daly City, 650-992-8800, www.fnbnorcal.com
- **Union Bank**, 400 University, Palo Alto, 650-859-1200, www.unionbank.com
- **US Bank**, 1105 El Camino Real, Menlo Park, 650-617-8330, www.usbank.com
- **Wells Fargo**, 400 Hamilton Ave, Palo Alto, 650-330-8135, www.wellsfargo.com

## SOUTH BAY

- **Bank of America**, 2611 N 1st St, San Jose, 408-983-0588; 2905 Stevens Creek Blvd, Santa Clara, 408-557-6508; 921 E Arques Ave, Sunnyvale, 408-983-0588, www.bankofamerica.com
- **Bank of the West**, 2395 Winchester Blvd, Campbell, 408-379-9954; 50 W San Fernando St, San Jose, 408-947-5005; 1705 El Camino Real, Santa Clara, 408-261-1861; 800-488-2265, www.bankofthewest.com
- **Chase**, 55 W Santa Clara St, San Jose, 408-291-3331, 800-788-7000, www.chase.com
- **Union Bank**, 990 N 1st St, San Jose, 408-279-7400, www.uboc.com
- **US Bank**, 1099 Lincoln Ave, San Jose, 408-287-2710, 800-872-2657, www.usbank.com
- **Wells Fargo**, 121 Park Center Plaza, San Jose, 408-277-6535, 800-869-3557, www.wellsfargo.com

## CREDIT UNIONS

Some of the Bay Area's best financial deals are found at credit unions. A credit union's goal is to offer affordable, bank-like services, including checking and savings accounts, and low-interest loans. On the downside, credit unions offer fewer locations than banks and don't have easily accessible teller machines. You'll have to pay a fee when using a non–credit union ATM. Generally, credit-union membership is available through group affiliation—often your workplace or residence. To see if your company sponsors one, check www.ccul.org for a list of dozens of Bay Area credit unions, or try:

- **Marin County Federal**, 30 N San Pedro Rd #115, San Rafael, 415-499-9780, www.marincu.org
- **Pacific Service Credit Union**, 245 Market St #1A, San Francisco, 888-858-6878, www.pacificservice.org
- **PremierOne Credit Union**, 140 Asbury St, San Jose, 408-294-8800, www.premieronecu.org

## ONLINE BANKING

All major banks in the Bay Area offer mobile apps and websites that let you deposit checks straight from your smartphone by taking snapshots of the checks and submitting the photos securely. You'll receive email confirmations when the checks are cleared, and the physical checks stay with you; no need to visit the bank for deposits. Transfers, bill payments, and even loan applications can be done on banks' websites, and soon, on their mobile apps. Security is relatively reliable, but while banks encrypt your personal information and password, you should take standard precautions. Don't share your password with anyone, and change it often; don't send confidential information over unsecured Wi-Fi networks; and restrict your bank interactions to private computers and phones—never use a computer with a shared network, such as a work computer or one at an Internet café.

## CREDIT REPORTS

To see your personal credit report, visit www.annualcreditreport.com, where you can obtain a free credit report once a year from each of the three main credit bureaus (Equifax, Experian, and TransUnion). It's best to get a copy from each service, because each company's report may be different. If you discover any inaccuracies, contact the service immediately and request that it be corrected. By law the companies must respond to your request within 30 days. Note: checking your credit report too frequently can adversely affect your credit rating.

You can also visit or call each bureau individually:

- **Equifax**, P.O. Box 740241, Atlanta, GA 30374, 800-685-1111, www.equifax.com

- **Experian**, P.O. Box 2002, Allen, TX 75013, 888-397-3742, www.experian.com
- **TransUnion**, 2 Baldwin Place, P.O. Box 2000, Chester, PA, 19022, 800-888-4213, www.transunion.com

# TAXES

## FEDERAL INCOME TAX

All the forms you'll need from the Internal Revenue Service (IRS) can be found at www.irs.gov/formspubs, but the IRS still maintains offices in the Bay Area, where you can pick up forms to file your income tax return and get answers to tax questions. Tax forms are also available at most post offices and libraries during filing season (January–April), and at the Federal Building in San Francisco (450 Golden Gate Ave, 415-553-8990).

IRS taxpayer assistance centers can help clarify tax laws and answer questions about your return, tax account, and letters you've received from the IRS. The centers are open for walk-in assistance, and no appointment is necessary. You can also get help by calling 800-829-1040 (individuals) or 800-829-4933 (businesses).

Stop by one of the IRS assistance centers listed below (all are open Monday–Friday, 8:30 a.m.–4:30 p.m.) for more information and to set up an appointment:

- **Oakland**: 1301 Clay St, 510-637-2487
- **San Francisco**: 450 Golden Gate Ave, 415-522-4061
- **San Jose:** 55 S Market St, 408-817-6747
- **Santa Rosa:** 777 Sonoma Ave, 707-523-0924
- **Walnut Creek**: 185 Lennon Ln, 925-935-9308

If you have ongoing unresolved issues with the IRS, contact the Taxpayer Advocate Service (510-637-2703 or 408-817-6850, www.irs.gov/advocate).

## ELECTRONIC INCOME TAX FILING

Electronic tax filing is a convenient alternative for countless Bay Area residents, who download or purchase tax software using an online tax service, or hire an accredited agency. Electronic filers receive their refunds in about half the time it takes for people who file through the mail, according to the IRS. E-filing also costs less and is more accurate.

To find out more about tax-filing software, search for "tax software reviews" online. **Turbo Tax** (turbotax.intuit.com) and **H&R Block** (www.hrblock.com) are just a few of many that are available.

For more information on electronic filing, visit **IRS E-file** at www.irs.gov/efile, which includes convenient payment options and direct deposit for those expecting a return, and also has a list of software brands and websites for both federal and state returns.

## STATE INCOME TAX

California residents file state tax form 540, 540-2EZ, 540-ES, or additional forms found at www.ftb.ca.gov/forms. Much of the information for your California taxes comes directly from your completed federal return. State income tax forms and answers to your tax questions can be found at State Franchise Tax Board offices:

- **San Francisco**: 121 Spear St, Suite 400, Monday–Friday, 8 a.m.–5 p.m.
- **Oakland:** 1515 Clay St, Suite 305, Monday–Friday, 8 a.m.–5 p.m.

For information and assistance with state taxes, visit www.ftb.ca.gov or call 800-852-5711. The state tax filing deadline is the same as federal tax deadlines: April 15. Tax forms are available at post offices and libraries during tax season (January–April). You can also file online at the Franchise Tax Board's website, www.ftb. ca.gov/online/calfile.

## SALES TAX

Local sales tax throughout the Bay Area ranges from 7.625 to 10 percent. It has risen over the years to help fund the BART transit system and to pay for earthquake damage repairs.

## STARTING OR MOVING A BUSINESS

The Bay Area is the world's fastest engine of wealth creation, as countless tech and biotech companies are turning up more quickly here than anywhere else on the planet. With top talent, the Bay Area is a magnet for starting a business or moving your existing business.

If your business involves sales of tangible personal property, you'll have to apply for a seller's permit from the **California Board of Equalization** (www.boe. ca.gov, 800-400-7115). This website provides information about doing business in California, including employer tax forms and the *California Employer's Guide*. The Board of Equalization's information center can also answer your tax questions.

To protect your investment you should consider hiring a local attorney to help you through the maze of state rules and regulations, especially if you are moving your business from another state. Resources include:

- **California Department of Finance** 916-445-3878, www.dof.ca.gov
- **California State Franchise Tax Board**, the agency to contact regarding payroll, unemployment insurance, and disability insurance taxes (800-852-5711, www. ftb.ca.gov)
- **Chambers of Commerce**: Berkeley, 1834 University Ave (510-549-7000, www.berkeleychamber.com); Oakland, 475 14th St (510-874-4800, www. oaklandchamber.com); San Francisco, 235 Montgomery St, 12th floor (415-392-4520, www.sfchamber.com); San Jose, 101 W Santa Clara St (408-291-5250,

www.sjchamber.com); for additional locations, search online for your town name and "Chamber of Commerce"

- **Internal Revenue Service**, for information about an employer tax ID number (800-829-1040, www.irs.gov)
- **Referral Service of the San Mateo County Bar Association**, 650-369-4149, www.smcba.com
- **Renaissance Entrepreneur Center,** a Bay Area nonprofit dedicated to helping low-income women and men start and run their own businesses, with offices in San Francisco, East Palo Alto, San Rafael, and Richmond (www.rencenter.org)
- **San Francisco Bar Association Lawyer Referral Service**, 415-982-1600, www.sfbar.org
- **Service Corps of Retired Executives (SCORE)**, one-on-one counseling for starting a new business, free of charge (800-634-0245, www.score.org)
- **SF OEWD, Mayor's Office of Economic and Workforce Development,** a resource for businesses looking to expand or relocate in San Francisco (415-554-6969, www.oewd.org)
- **State Bar of California**, 415-538-2000, www.calbar.ca.gov
- **United States Small Business Administration (SBA)**, information on starting and financing a business (800-827-5722, www.sba.gov)

A T LAST! YOU'VE NAVIGATED THE SEA OF HOUSING LISTINGS, OUTBID your competition, and secured a place to call home. Time to set up utilities and basic services and settle in. You may want to subscribe to the local paper (online or in print), find a doctor, get a library card, and register to vote. Details follow.

## UTILITIES

### GAS & ELECTRICITY

To transfer existing service to your name or initiate gas and electric service, call **Pacific Gas & Electric Company (PG&E)**, available 24 hours a day at 800-743-5000. PG&E covers San Francisco, the North Bay, the East Bay, and parts of the South Bay and the Peninsula. If you're speech or hearing impaired, the TTY number is 800-652-4712 (also available 24 hours). The website is www.pge.com. The city of Santa Clara has its own electric service, **Silicon Valley Power**, while PG&E provides gas. To learn about setting up service, contact Silicon Valley Power at 408-615-2300 (www.siliconvalleypower.com). The municipally owned and operated company recently added an eco-friendly option, **Santa Clara Green Power**, which offers residents the option of choosing 100 percent renewable energy from wind and solar power sources. Silicon Valley Power estimates the additional monthly cost for going green at about $7.50 for the average Santa Clara household. For more information check out the website listed above and click on the "Green Power" icon. The **City of Palo Alto Utilities (CPAU)** (www.cityofpaloalto.org/gov/depts/utl, 650-329-2161) is the only municipal utility in California that operates city-owned utility services that include electric, fiber-optic, natural gas, water, and wastewater collection.

If you have questions about utilities, contact the **Public Advisor's Office** in San Francisco (866-849-8390) or visit the **California Public Utilities Commission's** website (www.cpuc.ca.gov). When you move into a new place, check to see if the water heater's pilot light is on. If it isn't, follow directions on the heater for lighting the flame—or if you're nervous about doing it yourself, call your landlord or PG&E, and have them do it. While you're looking at the water heater, check to see if it is strapped to the wall. Many post-quake fires are started by ruptured gas lines to water heaters, and attaching the heater to the wall is an important safety precaution that is required in earthquake country. (See **Emergency Preparedness** for more details.)

# TELEPHONE

Gone are the days when the only Bay Area choice for landline telephone service was AT&T, as cellphone companies like Verizon and cable companies like Comcast have jumped into the business. Compare plans, prices, and reviews at www.cnet.com (based in San Francisco), an acclaimed journalistic resource for all things tech.

A deposit is generally not required, and if additional hardware doesn't need to be installed at your new residence, the phone companies will waive the line connection charge. Basic phone service includes unlimited local calls, but not long-distance charges. It also doesn't include the additional maze of taxes, fees, and surcharges levied onto the bill.

## LONG-DISTANCE SERVICE

Landline phones still exist, even in today's smartphone-laden Bay Area. Below are the biggest long-distance service providers available locally. For comparisons of long-distance and wireless calling plans, visit www.cnet.com; see also the **Telecommunications Research and Action Center** (www.fairness.com).

- **AT&T**, 800-288-2020, www.att.com
- **Comcast**, 800-934-6489, www.comcast.com
- **Verizon**, 800-837-4966, www.verizon.com

## CELLPHONE SERVICES

Almost everyone in California carries a smartphone or basic cellphone, and there are as many mobile carriers as makes and models of phones. The market is changing rapidly, so your best bet (for all tech analysis) is to visit www.cnet.com for up-to-the-minute reviews and call around to determine which service and pricing structures meet your needs. San Francisco-based **TURN (The Utility Reform Network)** offers useful consumer information for choosing a plan, switching plans, keeping your old phone number, and deciphering phone charges (www.turn.org). Here are the Bay Area's largest cellphone providers:

- **AT&T**, 800-331-0500, www.wireless.att.com
- **MetroPCS**, 888-863-8768, www.metropcs.com
- **Sprint**, 866-866-7509, www.sprint.com

- **T-Mobile**, 1-800-866-2453, www.t-mobile.com
- **Verizon Wireless**, 800-922-0204, www.verizonwireless.com

Most businesses that sell cellphones can activate them for you on the spot. Many give you the phone for free if you sign up and pay for a service contract with the company they represent. Scattered around the Bay Area are mini-stores that carry all the latest products and services. Check the local malls, shopping strips, or www.yelp.com for reliable reviews.

## AREA CODES

- **415 and 628:** all of San Francisco, parts of the lower North Bay, and the northeast corner of San Mateo County. 415 is the master number; 628 was overlaid in 2015.
- **510:** the inner East Bay: Alameda County—including Berkeley, Oakland, Alameda, Emeryville, Albany, Piedmont, Hayward, Fremont, Newark, and Union City; some parts of western Contra Costa County, including Richmond.
- **707:** the upper North Bay: Sonoma County, including Santa Rosa and Sonoma; Napa County, including Napa, St. Helena, Yountville, and Calistoga; and Solano County, including Vacaville, Vallejo, and Fairfield.
- **925:** the outer East Bay: Contra Costa County, including Walnut Creek, Martinez, San Ramon, Dublin, and Pleasant Hill, among others.
- **650 and 628:** the Peninsula: San Mateo County, including parts of Daly City, South San Francisco, San Bruno, Millbrae, Burlingame, San Mateo, Pacifica, Half Moon Bay, Belmont, San Carlos, Redwood City, Woodside, Atherton, Menlo Park; some parts of northern Santa Clara County, including Palo Alto and Mountain View.
- **408 and 669:** the South Bay: Santa Clara County, including San Jose, Santa Clara, Sunnyvale, Campbell, Milpitas, Cupertino, Saratoga, and Los Gatos.
- **916:** Sacramento, the state capital, and surroundings.

## WIRELESS HOTSPOTS (WI-FI)

Hundreds of businesses, libraries, and public parks across the Bay Area offer free wireless. If you need access while waiting for home-service installation, the place to start is www.wififreespot.com. In this tech-centric part of California you'd be hard-pressed to find a coffee shop that doesn't have free wireless. Another method popular with newcomers is to find a motel parking lot around any of the major airports. Google recently gave $600,000 to San Francisco to install free Wi-Fi in 31 parks. Efforts like that are multiplying; connect to #SFWIFI for free Wi-Fi.

## ONLINE SERVICE PROVIDERS

For a complete list of Internet service providers and user-submitted reviews in the Bay Area, narrow the results by location at www.yelp.com and read seasonally updated reviews at www.cnet.com. A few of the top companies:

- **AT&T**, 800-288-2020, www.att.com
- **Comcast**, 800-COMCAST, www.comcast.com
- **Juno**, 800-879-5866, www.juno.com
- **Net Zero**, 888-349-0029, www.netzero.net
- **Sonic Net**, 707-522-1000, www.sonic.net
- **Verizon,** 800-440-8000, www.verizon.com
- **Webpass,** 800-932-7277, www.webpass.net
- **ZR Net**, 415-920-2226, www.zrnetservice.com

## DIRECTORY ASSISTANCE

Many websites provide phone listings and websites—not just Google. Consider the following:

- **www.411.com**
- **www.anywho.com**
- **www.switchboard.com**
- **www.superpages.com**
- **www.whitepages.com**
- **www.yellowpages.com**

## CONSUMER PROTECTION—UTILITY COMPLAINTS

In California, utility rates and practices relating to telephones, electricity, and gas are governed by the state **Public Utilities Commission (PUC)**. The San Francisco Public Utilities Commission handles water issues. Officials at both organizations strongly suggest you take your complaints first to the utility involved. If you don't get satisfaction there, the PUCs will listen to you.

- **California PUC**, 505 Van Ness Ave, San Francisco, 415-703-2782, www.cpuc. ca.gov
- **San Francisco PUC**, 1155 Market St #4, 11th Floor, San Francisco, 415-551-3000, www.sfwater.org

If you have problems, there is a public watchdog organization that keeps tabs on the effectiveness of each PUC. It's called **TURN (The Utility Reform Network)**, and can be found at 711 Van Ness Ave in San Francisco (415-929-8876, www.turn.org).

With the proliferation of service providers comes the inevitable rise in scams. If you look at your phone bill and see calls you didn't make or changes that were made without your approval, and your service provider and state attorney general's office cannot assist you, contact the **Federal Communications Commission's Consumer Center** (888-225-5322, www.fcc.gov), or the **Federal Trade Commission** (877-382-4357, www.ftc.gov), to file a complaint.

See the **Helpful Services** chapter for more consumer protection tips.

# WATER

Water has never been more scarce—and political—than it is today in the Bay Area. The worst local drought in more than two millennia entered its fifth consecutive year in 2016—a crisis so dire that the governor declared a state of emergency in 2015 and mandated a 25 percent statewide reduction in water use. A new law prohibits the use of potable water to wash sidewalks and driveways, or in non-re-circulating fountains, or to irrigate lawns within 48 hours after rainfall. Violations are punishable by fines of up to $500 each day. Want water when you go out to eat? Speak up, as restaurants are not allowed to serve it unless you ask. These emergency regulations are in effect through early 2016 and are subject to extension by the State Water Board. If this historic drought has ended by the time you're reading this, consider it a blessing. Either way, consult the **Water Conservation** section in the **Green Living** chapter for conservation tips, and for daily drought updates visit www.ppic.org/water, www.saveourwater.com, and www.waterboards.ca.gov.

Several water districts serve the Bay Area (see list below). Accounts and billing are handled either through the water district or by your city's municipal services. Bay Area renters generally are responsible for paying for water except in San Francisco apartments and multi-unit flats, where usually the landlord pays.

The United States Congress enacted the Safe Drinking Water Act in 1974; the act, amended since then, set up a comprehensive program for monitoring drinking water. Among many provisions, the act banned future use of lead pipe and lead solder in public drinking systems, set up a monitoring system, mandated greater protection of groundwater sources of drinking water, and streamlined enforcement procedures to ensure that suppliers comply with the Safe Drinking Water provisions. The Environmental Protection Agency (EPA) added amendments that include stronger consumer protections, strengthened regulatory rules, and provided for states to access federal funds when implementing clean water actions. About 85 percent of San Francisco's water supply comes from **Hetch Hetchy Reservoir** (www.hetchhetchy.org), a remote area of Yosemite National Park in the Sierra Nevada Mountains. Because of its pristine source, the quality of San Francisco's water is higher than most cities; however, it's not entirely sterile or free of all organisms. The other 15 percent of San Francisco's water comes from watersheds in San Mateo, Santa Clara, and Alameda counties. To preserve water quality and improve local service, the San Francisco Public Utilities Commission has embarked on a massive program to repair and upgrade its regional water system.

Outside of San Francisco, about two thirds of the state (25 million people) obtains water from the San Francisco Bay and the Sacramento Delta (northeast of Contra Costa County) through a series of pumps and canals. In the South Bay, concern remains over water contamination caused by the gasoline additive methyl tertiary butyl ether (MTBE), which is mixed with gasoline to make it burn cleaner. When scientists discovered that MTBE can contaminate groundwater and isn't as readily removable as other contaminates, the governor at the time ordered a statewide phase-out of the additive. MTBE is now officially banned, and massive cleanup efforts have taken place across the state. Nevertheless, areas that were impacted, like the Santa Clara Valley Water District, are still keeping a watchful eye on water supplies to determine whether further action is necessary. The likelihood of having MTBE in the groundwater may depend on how close you live to a gas station. If you are within 1,000 feet, check with the station to find out if they have ever had any leaks or spills. If you are moving to the South Bay, contact the **Santa Clara Valley Water District** (408-265-2600, www.valleywater.org) for more information about MTBE. Another good source of information is the State Water Resources Control Board (916-341-5455, www.swrcb.ca.gov).

If you're moving to San Francisco and are concerned about the quality of tap water, contact the **San Francisco PUC** at 415-551-3000, www.sfwater.org. Those outside of San Francisco can contact the **Water Quality Control Board, San Francisco Bay Region**, 1515 Clay St, Suite 1400, Oakland, 510-622-2300, www.waterboards. ca.gov/sanfranciscobay, which offers an annual report on water quality.

For further questions on tap water quality, contact the **California Department of Public Health** (916-558-1784, www.cdph.ca.gov), the **US Environmental Protection Agency Safe Drinking Water Hotline** (800-426-4791, water.epa.gov/ drink/hotline), or the **Water Quality Association** (630-505-0160, www.wqa.org). Information regarding home water filtration systems is covered in Environmental Protection Agency reports at www.water.epa.gov.

To set up water service, contact one of the following water districts or municipal services:

- **Alameda County Water District**, 43885 S Grimmer Blvd, Fremont, 510-668-4200, www.acwd.org
- **California Water Service Co.** (serves San Carlos, San Mateo, South San Francisco, Woodside, Los Altos, and some areas of Cupertino, Menlo Park, Mountain View, and Sunnyvale), 650-917-0152, www.calwater.com
- **City of Palo Alto Utilities (CPAU)**, 250 Hamilton Ave, Palo Alto, 650-329-2161, www.cpau.com
- **City of Sonoma Public Works**, #1 The Plaza, Sonoma, 707-938-3332, www.sonomacity.org
- **Contra Costa Water District**, 1331 Concord Ave, Concord, 925-688-8000, www.ccwater.com
- **East Bay Municipal Utility District**, 375 11th St, 866-403-2683, www.ebmud.com
- **Marin Municipal Water District**, 220 Nellon Ave, Corte Madera, 415-945-1455, www.marinwater.org
- **North Marin Water District**, 999 Rush Creek Pl, Novato, 415-897-4133, www.nmwd.com
- **San Francisco Water Department**, 1155 Market St, San Francisco, 415-551-3000, www.sfwater.org

- **San Jose Municipal**, 3025 Tuers Rd, San Jose, 408-535-3500, www.sjmuniwater. com, and Great Oaks Water, 15 Great Oaks Blvd, Suite 100, 408-227-9540, www. greatoakswater.com
- **San Jose Water Company** (serves Campbell, Los Gatos, and Saratoga, and parts of the cities of San Jose and Cupertino), 110 W Taylor St, San Jose, 408-279-7900, www.sjwater.com
- **Santa Clara Valley Water District**, 5750 Almaden Expy, San Jose, 408-265-2600, www.valleywater.org
- **Santa Rosa Water District**, 707-543-4200, www.ci.santa-rosa.ca.us/ departments/utilities
- **Sonoma County Water Agency**, 404 Aviation Blvd, Santa Rosa, 707-526-5370, www.scwa.ca.gov

## GARBAGE, RECYCLING, AND COMPOSTING

In San Francisco landlords pay for garbage collection for apartments, and for some duplexes and single-family homes. Homeowners must order and pay for disposal service; the collection fee is based on how many trashcans you fill up each week. All cities provide a bulk pickup option—typically twice a year—that allows home-owners or renters to hand off bulky garbage. The best way to determine your garbage service provider is to contact your city's public works department or one of the following companies:

- **Acterra**, 650-962-9876, www.acterra.org
- **Marin Sanitary Services**, 415-456-2601, www.marinsanitary.com
- **Recology, 415-875-1000,** www.recology.com
- **Republic Services (newly merged with Allied Waste),** 650-756-1130, www.republicservices.com
- **South San Francisco Scavenger**, 650-589-4020, www.ssfscavenger.com
- **StopWaste**, 510-891-6500, www.stopwaste.org

Curbside recycling collection is included in the cost of garbage pickup. In San Francisco, residents of apartment buildings with fewer than five units are responsible for picking up the approved plastic containers themselves. Land-lords are responsible for setting up recycling programs if the building has five or more units. Landfill space is scarce in the Bay Area, making recycling all the more important. To find out more about recycling in the Bay Area, contact:

- **Marin Recycling Center**, 415-453-1404, www.marinsanitary.com
- **Palo Alto Zero Waste Program,** 650-496-5910, www.cityofpaloalto.org/gov/ depts/pwd/zerowaste
- **Recology San Francisco**, 415-330-1400, www.recologysf.com
- **RecycleWorks** (for San Mateo County), 888-442-2666, www.recycleworks.org
- **San Francisco Environment**, 415-355-3700, www.sfenvironment.org

- **Santa Clara County Recycling Hotline**, 800-533-8414, www.recyclestuff.org
- **StopWaste**, 877-786-7927, www.stopwaste.org

**Earth911.com** offers a wealth of information on recycling, including what items can and cannot be recycled, how to find local recycling centers, and instructions for dealing with hazardous waste. For information on beverage container collection centers, call the **California Department of Conservation** at 800-732-9253. For composting tips in the Bay Area, visit www.urbanwormcomposting.org.

# AUTOMOBILES

## DRIVER'S LICENSES

If you moved from out-of-state and want to drive in California, you have 10 days from arrival to apply for a local driver's license from the Department of Motor Vehicles (DMV). While there's no penalty for filing late, and no method for law enforcement to determine your residency status, if you're pulled over for a traffic violation after the 10-day grace period, the officer can cite you if you admit to living in California for more than 10 days. Bring your current driver's license and a birth certificate or passport for proof of age to your DMV appointment. If the name you use is different than the one on this document, you'll also need to provide a marriage certificate, or a dissolution of marriage, adoption, or name change document that shows your current name.

The DMV will ask you to complete an application, provide your social security number, and pass a vision test. You'll also be required to pass a written test on traffic laws and road signs. You have three chances to pass this test, which has 36 questions. To give yourself a quick refresher course, take a sample test on the DMV's website, www.dmv.ca.gov/pubs/interactive/tdrive/exam.htm. Once you pass, you'll have your thumbprint scanned and your picture taken. Your new license will be mailed to you. In the meantime, the DMV will issue an interim license good for 60 days. When driving with an interim license, always keep a valid photo ID handy (i.e., an out-of-state driver's license or a passport).

A note to international newcomers: if your license is from another country, you'll be required to take a driving skills test.

A driver's license costs $33 and is good for up to four years, expiring on your birthdate. If you're moving to the Bay Area from within California, you have 10 days to notify the DMV of your address change; visit www.dmv.ca.gov. Effective 2015, the designation "veteran" is available to be printed on driver's licenses for military veterans.

The DMV also handles the issuance of **state identification cards**. To get one, bring a birth certificate or passport and provide your social security number. The fee is $28 and the card is valid for six years. Seniors can get free ID cards that are good for 10 years.

## AUTOMOBILE REGISTRATION & INSURANCE

If you bring your car into California, be prepared to jump through bureaucratic hoops. The Golden State sets the national standard for exhaust emissions on vehicles and has strict laws to regulate these gases. New cars that are 49-state legal cannot be imported into California unless they have more than 7,500 miles on them. The car must be smog-checked and inspected by the DMV or a law enforcement officer. The DMV requires that emission control devices on your car operate correctly; any non-diesel vehicle that is four years old or older must pass an emissions test. Most service stations will do the test for less than $60. When you've received emission certification, bring it along with your automobile registration and checkbook to the nearest DMV. Registration is good for one year and can vary in cost—sometimes in the hundreds of dollars for newer cars. Note that the DMV will not accept payment via credit cards. Cash, check, money order, and ATM/debit cards are accepted.

Newcomers from out-of-state may be surprised to learn that vehicles in California are *required to have both rear and front license plates*. Driving without a front plate is illegal here, and while enforcement is spotty, the ticket can be expensive and time-consuming, because in addition to the fine, a violation requires a daytime trip to a police station for verification of compliance.

All California drivers must carry liability insurance on their vehicles and show proof of coverage when registering an automobile at the DMV. Insurers have estimated that 30 to 40 percent of the drivers on California roads are not properly covered, although avoiding this mandate has become increasingly difficult because the DMV is rapidly digitizing and communicating with insurers.

## DMV OFFICES

The DMV in San Francisco is notorious for long lines. If you can, spare yourself this frustration and go instead to the DMV in Marin County or San Mateo County. Wherever you go, make an appointment beforehand (www.dmv.ca.gov)—it may mean the difference between a half-hour wait and a four-hour wait. When heading to your appointment, show up early—they won't wait for you! Information about business hours, driver's license requirements, and vehicle registration can be found at www.dmv.ca.gov.

### SAN FRANCISCO & NORTH BAY
- **Corte Madera**, 75 Tamal Vista Blvd
- **Novato,** 936 7th St
- **San Francisco**, 1377 Fell St

### EAST BAY
- **Concord**, 2070 Diamond Blvd
- **El Cerrito**, 6400 Manila Ave

- **Fremont**, 4287 Central Ave
- **Hayward**, 150 Jackson St
- **Oakland**, 501 85th Ave; 5300 Claremont Ave
- **Walnut Creek**, 1910 N Broadway

### PENINSULA & SOUTH BAY
- **Daly City**, 1500 Sullivan Ave
- **Redwood City**, 300 Brewster Ave
- **San Jose**, 111 W Alma Ave
- **San Mateo**, 425 N Amphlett Blvd
- **Santa Clara**, 3665 Flora Vista Ave

# PARKING

## SAN FRANCISCO

Parking spaces are some of the most sought-after real estate in San Francisco—a city that rakes in $90 million in parking-ticket revenue annually. Chances are good that you're getting a parking ticket here—the costliest parking ticket in the nation. But here are some tips on how to keep those chances low.

Many neighborhoods require parking permits, which allow residents and guests to park without time limits. Drivers without a permit are required to move cars frequently, usually after two hours. If you're not sure if your neighborhood requires a parking permit, check for signs posted along the street. Also check the sign to see when street sweeping happens, as illegally parked vehicles on street-sweeping days will be slapped with a ticket of up to $74 (count yourself lucky if it's no more than that).

Word of advice: leave nothing—absolutely nothing—of value in your car. Break-ins are common in the Bay Area—San Francisco especially, where car van-dalism jumped 40 percent in one year recently. Shattered glass is as common a sight on local sidewalks as caked-in gum and half-smoked cigarettes. Also, new-comers to the steep streets of San Francisco may not be familiar with "curbing" their front wheels on an incline. In this mountainous city, it's the law, and will merit a $58 ticket if not done properly. Runaway vehicles are a real danger. When parking downhill with a grade of more than 3 percent, it is required that the front wheels touch the curb and that tires are turned toward the sidewalk. When parking uphill, tires must be turned outward from the curb. Don't forget this—you *will* get tick-eted if you don't curb your wheels.

San Francisco recently introduced parking smartcards that can be purchased at local retail businesses—supplementing and perhaps someday replacing the old coin-only kind (which is still available in the meantime). The city is also consid-ering a new tax on credit card payments at meters, so stay tuned to local headlines.

**Residential Parking Permits** are available at the SFMTA Customer Service

Center (11 South Van Ness Ave, 415-701-3000, www.sfmta.com). To get your permit, bring valid car registration that shows your new address, which means you'll first need to visit the nearby DMV. Also bring another proof of address: your lease, a utility bill with your address on it, a bank statement, or a personal check. Your driver's license is not an acceptable proof of residency. The full-fledged parking permit is good for a year and will set you back $111. For more information on the program, visit www.sfmta.com and search for "parking permits," or call 415-554-5000.

When it comes to parking in downtown San Francisco, your choices are limited to meters or parking garages. The latter are numerous but certainly the costliest option. Fees vary, averaging about $30 a day. For parking information in San Francisco, visit www.sfmta.com. Here are just a few of San Francisco's downtown parking garages:

- **Ellis-O'Farrell Garage**: 123 O'Farrell St, 415-986-4800, 925 spaces
- **5th and Mission Garage**: 5th and Mission St, 415-982-8522, www.fifthandmission.com, 2,500+ spaces
- **Portsmouth Square Garage**: 733 Kearny St, 415-982-6353, www.sfpsg.com, 500+ spaces
- **St. Mary's Square Garage**: 433 Kearny St, 415-956-8106, 600+ spaces
- **Sutter-Stockton Garage**: 444 Stockton St, 415-982-8370, 1,800+ spaces
- **Union Square Garage**: 333 Post St, 415-397-0631, 900+ spaces

If lots are full or closed, try the new SpotHero mobile app that launched in 2014 in San Francisco (www.spothero.com/san-francisco). Other parking-assistance apps are popping up in the mobile market, so check your smartphone's app store by searching for "San Francisco parking." If you park at metered spaces, check the postings several times over. The only people faster at their jobs than the meter readers are the tow-truck operators they call. **To pay a parking citation**, visit www.sfgov.org/onlineservices.

## COLORED CURBS

You'll need to memorize the meaning of painted curbs:

- **Red:** Fire zone—don't even think of parking here
- **Yellow:** Commercial loading zone only, for times posted
- **White:** Passenger pick-up or drop-off and valet only
- **Green:** Temporary parking only, as posted (usually 20–30 minutes)
- **Blue:** Disability parking only; special placard required

## PARKING FINES

Almost everything is more expensive in San Francisco, and that's true of parking tickets too—they're the most expensive in the United States, and the prices keep rising. The city issues thousands of tickets every month, and meter readers troll the streets as if entering a goldmine. Enforcement is strict. If you get a ticket, pay it right away. Delaying payment will increase your fine—doubling and in some cases tripling what you owe. Below is a list of fees for common violations as of 2016.

- Failure to block wheels (curbing your tires) $62
- Meter violation outside of downtown $66
- Meter violation downtown $76
- Parking in a red zone $103
- Parking in a white zone $103
- Parking in a yellow zone $88
- Parking in a green zone $76
- Parking on a sidewalk $110
- Failure to move car for street sweeper $66
- Residential permit zone violation $76
- Blocking a bike lane $119
- Blocking a driveway $103 (If a resident calls to complain, you can also be towed)
- Double parking $110
- Abandoned vehicle $229
- Parking in a bus zone $279
- Blocking wheelchair access ramp $279
- Illegally parking in a blue (handicapped) zone $880

## SURROUNDING AREAS

Fortunately parking is easier outside of San Francisco, and there is plenty of street parking in most cities and towns, much of it without meters, and some of it without any posted regulations. In fact, many people move out of San Francisco just for the parking. To obtain a residential parking sticker in Sausalito, call the **Sausalito Parking Authority** (415-289-4149). Most of the other cities in Marin County do not require parking stickers. For information on parking tickets, towing, and other unpleasantness in the North Bay, contact the Transportation Authority of Marin (415-226-0815, www.tam.ca.gov).

In the East Bay, Oakland residents should contact **Oakland Department of Public Works** (510-238-3099, www.oaklandnet.com) or the **Traffic Division of the Superior Court** (510-627-4701, www.alameda.courts.ca.gov). In Berkeley, contact the **Residential Preferential Parking (RPP) Program** Finance Customer Service Center (510-981-7200, www.ci.berkeley.ca.us). For UC Berkeley call the **UC Berkeley Parking and Transportation Office** (510-643-7701). In other towns and cities, search online for City Hall's website.

In the South Bay/Peninsula, call **Palo Alto Parking Permits** (650-329-2317, www.cityofpaloalto.org) or **San Mateo Parking Permits, Residential & City Parking Facilities** (650-522-7300, www.cityofsanmateo.org). In San Jose, contact **Residential Parking Permits** (408-535-3850, www.sanjoseca.gov).

2222

## GETTING YOUR TOWED CAR BACK

If your car is towed in San Francisco, call **DPT Tow Line** (415-865-8200) to find out why it was towed and what you need to do (read: how much of your life's savings you have to pay) to get it back. Most towed cars are held at **AutoReturn** (450 7th Street, 415-865-8200, 7 days / 24 hours). To obtain your vehicle's release you must appear in person with photo identification and pay not only the towing cost and ticket(s) but also any outstanding tickets written against the vehicle, and storage costs. (Yikes!)

In surrounding Bay Area counties, if your car is missing, call the local police station first, and they'll tell you the name of the towing company contracted by that city. Police department numbers are listed at the end of the neighborhood profiles.

# OFFICIAL DOCUMENTS

## VOTER REGISTRATION

Registering to vote in the Bay Area is easy, as voter registration drives bring the process to you—along downtown sidewalks, in malls, at farmers' markets, and in public transit facilities. You can also register by visiting the **Registrar of Voters** or **Elections Department** in the county where you live, or by heading to the California Secretary of State's **voter registration website** (www.sos.ca.gov/elections/elections_vr.htm). The voting age is 18, but in San Francisco, the Board of Supervisors is considering a proposal to lower the age to 16.

You can register with any political party in California, sign up as an independent, or decline to state a party affiliation. Voters may cast their ballots in person or via absentee ballot. If you want to vote absentee, allow ample time, usually about a month, for them to receive your forms in the mail. Your registrar's office will tell you what the cut-off date is for sending in an absentee ballot.

Voter registration offices in each of the nine Bay Area counties:

- **Alameda**, 1225 Fallon St, Oakland, 510-272-6933, www.acgov.org
- **Contra Costa**, 555 Escobar St, Martinez, 925-335-7800, www.co.contra-costa.ca.us
- **Marin**, 3501 Civic Center Dr, San Rafael, 415-499-6456, www.marincounty.org
- **Napa**, 900 Coombs St, Room 256, Napa, 707-253-4321, www.countyofnapa.org
- **San Francisco**, City Hall, Room 48, San Francisco, 415-554-4375, www.sfelections.org
- **San Mateo**, 40 Tower Rd, San Mateo, 650-312-5222, www.sfcare.org
- **Santa Clara**, 1555 Berger Dr, Building 2, San Jose, 408-299-8683, www.sccvote.org
- **Solano**, 675 Texas St, Fairfield, 707-784-6675, www.solanocounty.com
- **Sonoma**, 435 Fiscal Dr, Santa Rosa, 707-565-6800, vote.sonoma-county.org

## LIBRARY CARDS

San Francisco has one of the finest public libraries in the world. Opened in 1996, **the main library** (415-557-4400, 100 Larkin St, www.sfpl.org), located across the Civic Center plaza from City Hall, holds more than one million books, magazines, and research tools. It also provides Wi-Fi access and multimedia resources. Library cards are free, and you don't have to be a San Francisco resident to get one. Just bring ID and something else with your mailing address on it, like a utility bill. The card is valid at all San Francisco library branches; addresses and phone numbers are listed in the Neighborhoods section of this book. The San Francisco main library is easy to get to; it's a short walk through the United Nations Plaza from the Civic Center BART/MUNI station. For information on local branch libraries throughout the Bay Area, see the town listings, and for specialty libraries, see the **Cultural Life** chapter.

## PASSPORTS

You must apply in person for new passports. A number of post offices and city halls are set up to provide this service; check iafdb.travel.state.gov for the office closest to you. You'll need to bring two identical 2" x 2" photographs, proof of US citizenship (birth certificate, social security card, old passport), and a valid photo ID (driver's license, state ID card, military ID). You'll also need to fill out the application at the passport office. The fee for a new passport is $140, and there's an "execution fee" of $25. For more information contact the **National Passport Information Center** (877-487-2778, TTY 888-874-7793, www.travel.state.gov).

If you need to renew your passport, do so by mail. Fill out the renewal application (DS-82) at www.travel.state.gov and send it along with your old passport, 2" x 2" photos, and a check for $110 made out to the US Department of State, at the following address: National Passport Processing Center, P.O. Box 90155, Philadelphia, PA, 19190-0155.

Passports take about six weeks to arrive by mail—but they can take longer, so it's a good idea to apply well in advance. If you need a passport sooner, you can pay $60 to expedite the process—plus overnight charges there and back. Expedited passports should arrive within three weeks. If you've been called out of the country on an emergency, it is possible to get a passport sooner—in some cases a same-day turnaround, but it will cost extra for speedy service. If this is the case, your first step should be to call the **National Passport Information Center** (see number above). You can also contact the **San Francisco Passport Agency** at 877-487-2778 for assistance in making an appointment. The services at this office are reserved for those in need of expedited service. The San Francisco Passport Agency, at 95 Hawthorne Street, 5th Floor, is open Monday–Friday from 8:30 a.m.–1:30 p.m. for appointments only. If you are outside San Francisco, check with your local city hall. In San Jose, the **Santa Clara County Recorders Office** (County Government Center, East Wing, 70 West Hedding Street, 408-299-5688, www.sccgov.org/sites/rec/Pages/Office-of-the-Clerk-Recorder.aspx) can process your passport application within 10 to 14 days. Passports are good for 10 years (for adults).

# BROADCAST AND PRINT MEDIA

## BROADCAST TELEVISION STATIONS

Broadcast television reception in the Bay Area is reliably strong, unless you live in a particularly hilly area, in which case cable is the way to go. If you don't want cable, a standard roof antenna can help pull in most of the stations listed below. Apartment dwellers may want to consider getting a pair of "rabbit ears"—a small indoor antenna that sits on top of the television set.

| Channel | Call Letters | Network | Location |
|---------|--------------|---------|----------|
| 2 | KTVU | Fox | Oakland |
| 4 | KRON | Independent | San Francisco |
| 5 | KPIX | CBS | San Francisco |
| 7 | KGO | ABC | San Francisco |
| 9 | KQED | PBS | San Francisco |
| 11 | KNTV | NBC | San Jose |
| 14 | KDTV | Univision | San Francisco |
| 20 | KOFY | KOFY-TV | San Francisco |
| 26 | KTSF | Independent | San Francisco |
| 32 | KMTP | Minority Television Project | San Francisco |
| 36 | KQED | Plus Public | San Jose |
| 44 | KBCW | CW | Bay Area |
| 48 | KSTS | Telemundo | San Jose |
| 50 | KEMO | Azteca America | Santa Rosa |
| 66 | KFSF | Univision | Vallejo |

## CABLE AND SATELLITE TELEVISION

If broadcast television (listed above) doesn't provide you with adequate options, get cable or a satellite dish. Cable and satellite are available throughout the nine Bay Area counties. Satellite availability is limited if there are large objects in the path of a signal. Each provider offers various packages based on how many channels you wish to receive.

Some of the largest local providers:

- **AT&T**, 800-331-0500, TTY 866-241-6567, www.att.com
- **Comcast**, 800-266-2278, www.comcast.com
- **Direct TV**, 800-531-5000, TTY 800-779-4388, www.directv.com
- **Dish Network**, 888-825-2557, www.dishnetwork.com

## RADIO STATIONS

There are almost 100 radio stations within the nine-county Bay Area. AM reception is fairly consistent throughout the area, with no special equipment needed. FM reception can be spotty, especially if you live in a hilly area of San Francisco (that is, most of the city), the East Bay, or the North Bay. You can also stream online or on your smartphone through Pandora (www.pandora.com), Spotify (www.spotify.com), Rhapsody (www.rhapsody.com), or iTunes (www.itunes.com; a streaming version of this service was rolled out by Apple in 2015).

## AM

San Francisco
- **KNBR 680** Talk, sports
- **KCBS 740** News
- **KGO 810** News, talk, sports
- **KNEW 960** Liberal talk
- **KSFO 560** Conservative talk
- **KIQI 1010** Spanish
- **KSRO 1350** News, talk, sports
- **KVTO 1400** Cantonese

East Bay
- **KDYA 1190** Gospel
- **KMKY 1310** Children, Disney
- **KNEW 910** Talk
- **KQKE 960** Liberal Talk Radio
- **KVTO 1400** Cantonese

North Bay
- **KDYA 1190** Gospel
- **KSRO 1350** News, talk, sports
- **KRRS 1460** Spanish

Peninsula & South Bay
- **KTCT 1050** Sports
- **KSJX 1500** Vietnamese
- **KLIV 1590** News
- **KZSF 1370** Spanish
- **KTCT 1050** Talk, sports
- **KLOK 1170** Spanish

## FM

San Francisco
- **KQED 88.5** Public radio news, information (NPR)
- **KPOO 89.5** Music, talk, variety, listener-sponsored

- **KUSF 90.3** College, alternative rock, multicultural
- **KCSM 91.1** Jazz
- **KALW 91.7** News and information (NPR, BBC, CBC)
- **KSJO 92.3** Spanish
- **KRZZ 93.3** Spanish
- **KPFA 94.1** News, information, variety
- **KYLD 94.9** Urban top 40
- **KUIC 95.3** Adult contemporary
- **KBWF 95.7** Modern country
- **KOIT 96.5** Light rock
- **ALICE 97.3** Modern adult contemporary
- **KISQ 98.1** Classic soul
- **KUFX 98.5** Modern rock
- **KFRC 99.7** Adult contemporary
- **KBRG 100.3** Romantic, Spanish
- **K101 101.3** Adult contemporary
- **KBLX 102.9** Adult contemporary
- **KKSF 103.7** Smooth jazz
- **KFOG 104.5** Adult alternative rock
- **KITS 105.3** Modern rock
- **KMEL 106.1** Hip hop
- **KSAN 107.7** Classic rock

East Bay
- **KALX 90.7** College, alternative rock
- **KKDV 92.1** Adult contemporary
- **KPFA 94.1** Public radio liberal news, culture

North Bay
- **KJZY 93.7** Jazz
- **KVRV 97.7** Classic rock
- **KSXY 98.7** Popular top 40

Peninsula & South Bay
- **KBAY 94.5** Soft rock
- **KVRV 97.7** Classic rock
- **KEZR 106.5** Adult contemporary
- **KFJC 89.7** Alternative rock
- **KZSU 90.1** Eclectic music

## MEDIA LANDSCAPE

The Bay Area said goodbye in 2014 to the most influential weekly newspaper in California history—the **San Francisco Bay Guardian**, which ceased operation after 48 years as the most progressive journal for political reporting and arts coverage. But locals quickly said hello to a stack of new glossies, websites, and mobile apps that are redefining the media landscape. The *Guardian* was one of the world's longest-running weeklies—an independent voice that tackled corruption scandals with hard-hitting investigations before losing financial footing and succumbing to shrinking ad revenue. The largest Bay Area news group today, the **San Francisco Media Company**—which owns the *San Francisco Examiner* and *SF Weekly*—bought the *Guardian* in a last-minute attempt to keep it afloat, but the honeymoon was short-lived; the *Guardian* was shuttered on October 15, 2014, a day that lives in a kind of journalistic infamy in these parts. You can still browse the *Guardian*'s archives at www.sfbg.com, but the newspaper's closure signals a new height of consolidation in Bay Area media ownership, which means newcomers will have to search for other sources of independent journalism.

There is a silver lining to the *Guardian*'s demise, however: its former editor, Tim Redmond, resurfaced at an excellent new website, **www.48hills.org**, the most significant newcomer to San Francisco news, packed with solid reporting and insight. The **SF Weekly** and **East Bay Express** continue to hum along as strong alternative weeklies with outstanding arts coverage, and the **San Francisco Chronicle, Oakland Tribune, San Jose Mercury News**, and **Contra Costa Times** are your major dailies, though there are several others (see below).

With the popularity of **reddit**—the San Francisco–based online message board—as well as Tumblr, Twitter, and Facebook, it's harder today for long-form journalism to get attention in the Bay Area. Even the *New York Times* made a go of it by ramping up Bay Area coverage in special sections, but the local news industry is at a crossroads. The hip news site **Bold Italic** (www.bolditalic.com), which had great San Francisco reporting and readership, shut down abruptly in 2015 when its parent company abandoned it without explanation. The resulting outcry from readers was loud and clear, and new investors stepped in to revive the site, giving it fresh energy and a new look. It is now a go-to website for cultural reporting. On the other hand, San Francisco's print edition of the **Onion**, the satirical masterpiece—staffed locally and filled with Bay Area arts coverage—bit the dust recently.

New to the scene are **Edible San Francisco**, a popular print and online magnet for the fashionable food crowd (www.ediblesf.com); the **California Sunday Magazine**, a *New Yorker*-style cultural magazine (www.californiasunday.com); and **Callisto Media**, a new paradigm of book publishing that's transforming the news industry through an innovative *Lightning Guides* series of topical books (www.callistomedia.com, based in Berkeley). Among those at the helm of the *Lightning Guides* series is the exceptional Elizabeth Castoria, an award-winning Bay Area writer and editor who was previously editorial director at *VegNews* magazine (www.vegnews.com, based in San Francisco).

Consider yourself briefed. For more magazines, newspapers, websites, and media developments in the Bay Area, consider the following sites:

- **Asian Week**, news, commentary, and event calendars (415-397-0220, www.asianweek.com)

- *The California Sunday Magazine*, a new cultural publication delivered through select newspapers (www.californiasunday.com)
- *Contra Costa Times*, published daily with East Bay listings, focusing on Concord, Walnut Creek, Pleasant Hill, Martinez, Richmond, Hercules, Benicia, Antioch, Pittsburg, and Bay Point areas; also owns Hills Newspapers and a handful of smaller local publications including the *Berkeley Voice*, *Alameda Journal*, the *Montclarion*, and the *Piedmonter* (925-943-8235, www.contracostatimes.com)
- *Daily Post*, serving Palo Alto (650-328-7700, www.padailypost.com)
- *East Bay Express*, a free weekly alternative paper focusing on the East Bay; great resource for arts & culture listings; found in newsstands and at cafés (510-879-3700, www.eastbayexpress.com)
- *East Bay Monthly*, distributed free throughout the East Bay (510-238-9101, www.themonthly.com)
- *Edible San Francisco; Edible Silicon Valley*, sleek new quarterly magazines centered on local food culture (415-322-3615, www.ediblesanfrancisco.com; 650-206-8394, www.ediblesiliconvalley.com)
- *48 Hills,* highly influential source of progressive political and social commentary in the Bay Area, launched in 2014; a scaled-down but sharp reincarnation of the *San Francisco Bay Guardian* (www.48hills.org)
- *India Currents*, distributed free throughout the Bay Area, based in San Jose (408-324-0488, www.indiacurrents.com)
- **KQED.org**, excellent, award-winning website covering politics, arts, and cultural events throughout the Bay Area; highly recommended (www.kqed.org)
- *Los Gatos Magazine*, 408-213-9552, www.losgatosmagazine.com
- *Marin Independent Journal*, published daily with listings for Marin, Sonoma, and Napa counties (415-883-8600, www.marinij.com)
- *Metro*, the South Bay's alternative weekly (408-298-8000, www.metroactive.com/metro)
- *Oakland Tribune*, published daily with a focus on the East Bay, especially Oakland, Berkeley, and Alameda (510-208-6300, www.insidebayarea.com/oaklandtribune)
- *Pacific Sun*, a free, weekly alternative with listings for Marin County; found in newsstands and cafés; good for rentals and roommate listings (415-485-6700, www.pacificsun.com)
- *Pakistan Times*, 415-740-6300, www.pakistantimesusa.net
- *San Francisco Bay View*, national newspaper of black culture and progressive politics based in San Francisco (www.sfbayview.com)
- *San Francisco Business Times*, 415-989-2522, www.bizjournals.com/sanfrancisco.
- *San Francisco Chronicle*, the most-read newspaper in the area; includes listings for San Francisco, North Bay, East Bay, Peninsula counties, and some surrounding areas (415-777-1111, www.sfgate.com)

- *San Francisco Examiner*, free daily newspaper covering local news (866-733-7323, www.sfexaminer.com)
- *San Francisco Magazine*, glossy lifestyle magazine, San Francisco (415-398-2800, www.sanfranmag.com)
- *San Jose Mercury News*, published daily; most extensive listings for the South Bay as well as much of the Peninsula and southern East Bay (408-920-5000, www.mercurynews.com)
- *San Mateo County Times*, listings for the Peninsula (650-348-4321, www.insidebayarea.com/sanmateocountytimes)
- *Santa Rosa Press Democrat*, published daily; listings for Sonoma, Marin, and Napa counties (707-546-2020, www.pressdemocrat.com)
- *7 x 7*, San Francisco lifestyle, fashion, food, design, celebrity magazine (888-260-4269, www.7x7.com)
- *SF Arts Monthly*, extensive arts calendar online and in print (415-956-5200, www.sfarts.org)
- *SF Evergreen*, San Francisco's only print publication focused on cannabis and marijuana news and culture (415-536-8100, www.sfevergreen.com)
- SFist, daily arts and entertainment coverage (www.sfist.com)
- *SF Station*, popular website covering San Francisco nightlife, with an events calendar (www.sfstation.com)
- *SF Weekly*, free weekly alternative paper with San Francisco listings; great for arts & culture events; published Wednesdays; found citywide at newsstands and cafés (415-536-8100, www.sfweekly.com)
- *Sierra*, top-rated publication on nature, environmental politics, and conservation, published by the Sierra Club (www.sierraclub.com)
- *Sonoma*, magazine of arts, dining, and wine (855-850-0991, www.sonomamag.com)
- *The Voice* magazine, Solano and Napa counties' only bilingual magazine, in English and Spanish (www.issuu.com/thevoicemagazine707)
- *Where San Francisco*, glossy monthly magazine with cultural calendars and local spotlights (www.wheretraveler.com/san-francisco)

## FINDING A PHYSICIAN

Like finding a place to live in the Bay Area, finding a physician isn't easy. First consider your needs—are you looking for a pediatrician, family physician, OB/Gyn, or all of the above? Are you interested in an MD or an osteopath? Perhaps most important, does your health plan limit whom you can see? In the Bay Area you'll find top-notch care at the **University of California San Francisco Medical Center** (505 Parnassus Avenue, 415-476-1000, www.ucsfhealth.org), famous for its pioneering work in pediatrics, high-risk obstetrics, organ transplantation, cancer care, cardiac care, neurosurgery, and orthopedics. The most popular way to find a good doctor is through word of mouth—talking to coworkers, friends, neighbors, or other doctors. To assist in your search, check the reviews at www.checkbook.org/reviews/ca/san-francisco-bay-area/doctors, which lists the Bay Area's outstanding physician specialists; there is a charge for the service. See the **Helpful Services** chapter for more information. To determine if a physician is board certified, check with the American Board of Medical Specialties Board Certification Verification (www.abms.org).

If you're strapped for cash while in transition, **Health Right 360** (www.healthright360.org, formerly the Haight Ashbury Free Clinic), offers free primary health care and specialty care, including podiatry, chiropractic care, pediatrics, HIV testing, comprehensive HIV treatment services, and community information and referral services. Health Right 360's clinics welcome everyone who walks through the door (588 Clayton St, San Francisco). But the clinic is unable to treat emergency medical problems, such as broken bones, severe bleeding, trauma, abdominal pain, and so on. For emergency medical problems, go immediately to the nearest hospital emergency room.

Another popular resource for free, confidential sexual health tests is **San Francisco City Clinic** (356 7th St, 415-487-5500, www.sfcityclinic.org). In the East Bay, the **Berkeley Free Clinic** is an excellent resource (2339 Durant Ave, 510-548-2570, www.berkeleyfreeclinic.org). For additional free medical centers, visit the invaluable chart at www.freeprintshop.org/download/medical_english.pdf.

Hopefully you'll never need the following: the **Medical Board of California** (2005 Evergreen Street, Suite 1200, Sacramento, 800-633-2322, www.mbc.ca.gov) and the **Osteopathic Medical Board of California** (1300 National Drive, Suite 150, Sacramento, 916-928-8390, www.ombc.ca.gov) are the two state organizations that handle complaints against medical professionals in California.

# PETS

## PET LAWS & SERVICES

To measure just how pet-friendly the Bay Area is, consider this headline from 2015: when a new dog festival dubbed "Poochella" was scheduled to launch in San Francisco, the event's host was denied a permit by city officials because of concerns about overcrowding, as 30,000 spectators and dog owners had said they'd show up—far more than the site could handle. The postponed festival is now set to start in 2016 at a larger park—with a dog photo booth, dog adoptions, dog fashion show, music, and food trucks. If you're bringing your pet to the Bay Area, you're in good company. Learn about leash laws and immunizations by contacting one of the hundreds of local pets groups. **SF Dog** (San Francisco Dog Owners Group, 415-339-7461, www.sfdog.org) has a comprehensive list of dog-friendly areas, events, and contact numbers. Your local courthouse can provide details about pet licenses and local leash laws. Additional pet services include the countless pet sitters, walkers, and boarding and grooming establishments in the Bay Area. Search www.yelp.com for "pet services."

You and your dog can take MUNI together, but your dog must pay her own way (no joke—you'll have to pay an additional fare for your dog) and wear a muzzle. Non-service animals cannot ride during peak hours on weekdays from 5–9 a.m. and 3–7 p.m. Guide dogs can ride all public transit at no charge and do not need to be muzzled. For more information, visit www.sfmta.com/getting-around/accessibility/animals-muni or call 415-701-2311. Also noteworthy is **Pets are Wonderful Support (PAWS)**, an organization dedicated to people with AIDS and their pets; visit www.pawssf.org to volunteer and for more information. The *Dog Lover's Companion to the San Francisco Bay Area* by Maria Goodavage provides valuable information for the best places to explore, sleep, and eat with your dog in the Bay Area; there's also a glossy quarterly magazine devoted to dogs, called *Bark* (www.thebark.com), based in Berkeley.

Below is a select list of animal shelters, adoption services, and rescue and resource groups:

## SAN FRANCISCO
- **Animal Care & Control**, 1200 15th St, 415-554-6364, www.sfgov.org/acc
- **Northern California Family Dog Rescue**, www.norcalfamilydogrescue.org
- **Pets Are Wonderful Support (PAWS)**, www.pawssf.org
- **Pets Unlimited Adoption Center** (recently merged with San Francisco SPCA), 2343 Fillmore St, 415-568-3058, www.petsunlimited.org
- **Rocket Dog Rescue**, 415-756-8188, www.rocketdogrescue.org
- **SF DOG (Dog Owners Group)**, 415-339-7461, www.sfdog.org
- **SF Society for the Prevention of Cruelty to Animals (SPCA)**, 201 Alabama St, 415-554-3000, www.sfspca.org

## NORTH BAY
- **All Creatures Main**, 415-456-1941, www.allcreaturesmarin.org
- **Humane Society of the North Bay**, 1121 Sonoma Blvd, Vallejo, 707-645-7905, www.hsnb.org
- **Humane Society of Sonoma County**, 5345 Highway 12 West, Santa Rosa, 707-542-0882 www.sonomahumane.org
- **Marin County Humane Society**, 171 Bel Marin Keys Blvd?, Novato, 415-883-4621, www.marinhumanesociety.org
- **Napa County Humane Society**, 3265 California Blvd, 707-255-8118, www.napahumane.org
- **Second Chance Rescue**, 415-506-0161, www.hopalong.org

## EAST BAY
- **Alameda Animal Shelter**, 1590 Fortmann Way, Alameda, 510-337-8565, www.alamedaanimalshelter.org

- **Alameda County Animal Control**, 4595 Gleason Dr., Dublin, 925-803-7040, www.ci.dublin.ca.us
- **Antioch Animal Services**, 300 L St, Antioch, 925-779-6989, www.ci.antioch. ca.us/citysvcs/antiochanimalsvcs
- **Benicia-Vallejo Humane Society**, 1121 Sonoma Blvd, Vallejo, 707-645-7905, www.bvhumane.org
- **Berkeley Animal Care Services**, 1 Bolivar Dr., Berkeley, 510-981-6600, www. ci.berkeley.ca.us
- **Berkeley-East Bay Humane Society**, 2700 9th St, Berkeley, 510-845-7735, www.berkeleyhumane.org
- **Contra Costa County Animal Services**, 4800 Imhoff Pl, Martinez, 925-335-8300, www.ccasd.org
- **Contra Costa Humane Society**, 171 Mayhew Way, Pleasant Hill, 925-279-2247, www.cchumane.org
- **East Bay Animal Rescue and Refuge**, 925-429-2785, www.ebarr.org
- **East Bay SPCA**, 8323 Baldwin St, Oakland, 510-569-0702, www.eastbayspca.org
- **Furry Friends Rescue**, 510-794-4703, www.furryfriendsrescue.org
- **Hayward Animal Services**, 16 Barnes Ct., Hayward, 510-293-7200
- **Home at Last Animal Rescue**, 510-981-0890, www.homeatlastrescue.org
- **Milo Foundation**, 220 South Garrard Blvd,, Point Richmond 510-900-2275, www.milofoundation.org
- **Oakland Animal Services**, 1101 29th Ave, 510-535-5602, www.oaklandanimalservices.org
- **Tony La Russa's Animal Rescue Foundation**, 2890 Mitchell Dr, Walnut Creek, 925-256-1273, www.art.net
- **Tri-Valley SPCA Maddie's Adoption Center**, 4651 Gleason Dr, Dublin, 925-479-9670 www.eastbayspca.org

## PENINSULA & SOUTH BAY
- **Homeless Cat Network**, 650-286-9013, www.homelesscatnetwork.org
- **Humane Society Silicon Valley**, 901 Ames Ave, Milpitas, 408-262-2133, www.hssv.org
- **Peninsula Cat Works**, 650-329-9570, www.peninsulacatworks.org/index.php
- **Peninsula Humane Society**, 12 Airport Blvd, San Mateo, 650-340-8200, www.peninsulahumanesociety.org
- **A Safe Haven For Cats**, 270 Redwood Shores Pkwy, Redwood City, 650-802-9686, www.safehavenforcats.com
- **San Jose Animal Care Center**, 2750 Monterey Rd, San Jose, 408-578-PAWS, www.sanjoseanimals.com
- **Silicon Valley Animal Control Authority**, 3370 Thomas Rd, Santa Clara, 408-764-0344, www.svaca.com

## FINDING A VETERINARIAN/EMERGENCY HOSPITALS

To alleviate the cost of veterinarian bills, consider health coverage for your pet. Contact the national organization **Veterinary Pet Insurance** (888-899-4874, www.petinsurance.com) or the pet HMO **Pet Assure** (888-789-7387, www.petassure.com). Most neighborhoods have at least one vet. To limit your travel time, try a vet in your area first. The best way to get the inside scoop on vets is to frequent the dog park and talk to neighborhood owners. Reading the reviews at www.yelp.com is another great option. In addition to adoption services, the **San Francisco SPCA** (201 Alabama St, 415-554-3000, www.sfspca.org) also runs a full-service animal hospital and operates a spay-neuter clinic. For additional sites across the Bay Area, contact the **California Veterinary Medical Association** (www.cvma.org).

If your pet has ingested anything poisonous, contact **ASPCA National Animal Poison Control Center** (24-hour emergency information service at 888-426-4435); there is a $65 charge for a visit. You can also go straight to an emergency pet hospital at the following locations:

### SAN FRANCISCO

- **Animal Internal Medicine and Specialty Services**, 1333 9th Ave, 415-566-0540, www.aimss-sf.com
- **Balboa Pet Hospital**, 3329 Balboa St, 415-752-3300, www.balboapethospital.com
- **Pets Unlimited Veterinary Hospital**, 2343 Fillmore St, 415-563-6700, www.sfpethospital.com
- **San Francisco Veterinary Specialists**, 600 Alabama St, 415-401-9200, www.cvaspecialtyvets.com

### NORTH BAY

- **Calistoga Pet Clinic**, 2960 Foothill Blvd, Calistoga, 707-942-0404, www.calistogapetclinic.net
- **Madera Pet Hospital**, 5796 Paradise Dr, Corte Madera, 415-924-1271, www.vcahospitals.com/madera-pet
- **Pet Emergency Center**, 901 E Francisco Blvd, San Rafael, 415-456-7372, www.pescm.com
- **San Francisco Veterinary Specialists**, 901 E Francisco Blvd, 415-455-8317,
- **South Novato Veterinary Hospital**, 7077 Redwood Blvd, Novato, 415-897-8200, www.novatovets.com

### EAST BAY

- **All Bay Animal Hospital**, 1739 Willow Pass Rd, Concord, 925-687-7346, www.allbayanimalhospital.com
- **Berkeley Dog and Cat Hospital**, 2126 Haste St, Berkeley, 510-848-5041, www.berkeleydogandcat.com

- **Pet Emergency Treatment Service of Berkeley**, 1048 University Ave, 510-548-6684, www.petsreferralcenter.com

## PENINSULA & SOUTH BAY
- **Adobe Animal Hospital**, 396 1st St, Los Altos, 650-948-9661, www.adobe-animal.com
- **Mayfair Veterinary Hospital**, 2810 Alum Rock Ave, San Jose, 408-258-2735, www.alumrockanimalhospital.com
- **Skyline Pet Hospital**, 170 Skyline Plaza, Daly City, 650-756-4877, www.skylinepethospital.com
- **Stanford Pet Clinic**, 4111 El Camino Real, Palo Alto, 650-493-4233, www.vcahospitals.com/palo-alto

## OFF-LEASH AREAS

San Francisco is a dog lover's paradise. This city has more dogs than kids, according to the Animal Care & Control Department and the latest US census figures. Berkeley is the birthplace of *Bark* magazine (www.thebark.com). And the greater Bay Area continues to add off-leash dog runs. See the list below for off-leash locations. Every morning and evening, the sandy shores of Fort Funston, Ocean Beach, and Crissy Field are packed with Golden Retrievers, Labs, and German Shepherds jogging alongside their owners. Some dogs are on leash, as the new rules require, while many others—in open defiance of the rules—are not.

Created in 1979, the Golden Gate National Recreation Area's pet policy allowed dogs to run off-leash in these areas, as well as at North Baker Beach, Fort Miley, and Lands End. But in 2001, amid protests, the National Park Service abruptly revoked this privilege, citing concerns about sensitive habitats, bird life, and eco-restoration. Many dog owners have refused to comply. Luckily there's a host of neighborhood parks and fenced runs available.

A note about etiquette: off-leash does not mean out of control. Dogs must always be under your direct supervision and under strict voice control. This is especially important in unfenced off-leash areas. You should always carry a leash, and consult with fellow dog owners before releasing yours into a pack. And always—*always*— carry waste bags and pick up after your pet.

For more information about off-leash dog rules, contact the city's Recreation and Park Department (415-831-2700, www.sfrecpark.org). Also visit the excellent www.sfdog.org.

## SAN FRANCISCO DESIGNATED OFF-LEASH AREAS
- **Alamo Square Park**, western half of the park, along Scott Street between Hayes and Fulton sts
- **Alta Plaza Park**, second park terrace, Clay Street between Scott and Steiner sts
- **Bernal Heights**, trails wind along the top of the hill, Bernal Heights Blvd

- **Buena Vista Park**, green spot with great city views, trails, and open runs, Buena Vista West at Central Ave
- **Corona Heights**, upper field with fenced area near the base of the hill, adjacent to Randall Museum (closed for renovation until fall 2016), Roosevelt Way, and Museum Way
- **Dolores Park**, south of tennis courts, north of soccer field, 18th St between Church and Dolores sts
- **Douglass Park**, 26th and Douglass sts
- **Eureka Valley Park**, fenced area, 19th St and Collingwood, east of baseball diamond
- **Golden Gate Park**, four off-leash areas: southeast section bounded by Lincoln Way, King Dr, 2nd and 7th aves; northeast section at Stanyan and Grove sts; south central area bounded by King Dr, Middle Dr, 34th and 38th aves; fenced training area in the north central area near 38th Ave and Fulton
- **Lafayette Park**, near Sacramento St between Octavia and Gough sts
- **Lake Merced**, north side of lake provides lots of space for free roaming, Lake Merced Blvd and Middlefield Dr
- **McKinley Square**, western slope, San Bruno Ave and 20th St
- **McLaren Park**, two off-leash areas: top of hill at Shelly Dr and Mansell St; south section via 1600 block of Geneva or 1600 block of Sunnydale—dogs must remain outside of sensitive habitat area
- **Mountain Lake Park**, east end of park, north of Lake St at 8th Ave
- **Potrero Hill Mini-Park**, 22nd St between Arkansas and Connecticut sts
- **St. Mary's Park**, lower park terrace, fenced area, Murray Ave and Justin Dr
- **Stern Grove**, north side, Wawona St between 21st and 23rd aves
- **Upper Noe Park**, fenced area adjacent to ball field, Day and Sanchez sts

## UNOFFICIAL OFF-LEASH AREAS

There's quite a bit of controversy over some of San Francisco's leash laws, especially at Fort Funston, Crissy Field, and Ocean Beach. Duboce Park (Duboce and Steiner streets) has been an "unofficial" dog park for years, although it has never been legally designated for off-leash use.

## BAY AREA OFF-LEASH AREAS

Outside of San Francisco, check out **South Bay Pet Talk** (www.southbaypettalk.com) for events and off-leash locations throughout the area.

## EAST BAY

- **Black Diamond Mines Regional Preserve**, 5175 Somersville Rd, Antioch
- **Briones Regional Park**, 2537 Reliez Valley Rd, Martinez
- **Cesar Chavez Park**, 11 Spinnaker Way, Berkeley
- **Chabot Regional Park**, 9999 Redwood Rd, Castro Valley

- **Crown Memorial State Beach**, Alameda
- **Del Mar Dog Park**, Del Mar Dr at Pine Valley Rd, San Ramon
- **Dracena Park**, 130 Dracena, Piedmont
- **Drigon Dog Park**, fake fire hydrants, a dog-bone-shaped walkway, jumps, tunnels, separate small dog and large dog areas (Mission Blvd and 7th St, Union City)
- **East Bay Regional Parks**: the majority of parks in this district allow off-leash dogs in most open space and trail areas (with some exceptions) as long as they're under control at all times, and the owner is carrying a leash. A popular option is the dog-swimmable shoreline at Lake Del Valle, and the puppy paradise Point Isabel, which has its own set of guidelines (see below). For detailed dog rules, off-leash areas, park listings, and trail maps, visit www.ebparks.org.
- **Hardy Dog Park**, fenced, off-leash, 2.16 acres, 491 Hardy St, Oakland
- **Las Trampas Regional Wilderness**, Danville
- **Lake Elizabeth Dog Park**, at Central Park and Lake Elizabeth, fenced area near softball camp side of the lake, off Stevenson Blvd (40000 Paseo Padre Pkwy, Fremont)
- **Leona Heights Park**, Campus and Canyon Oaks drs
- **Livermore Canine Park**, Murdell Lane, Livermore
- **Lower Washington Park**, recently expanded to a half acre (8th and Westline, Alameda)
- **Marina Park**, Marina and Fairway, San Leandro
- **Memorial Park—Dog Run**, 1.3-acre fenced dog run within Memorial Park, Bollinger Canyon Rd at San Ramon Valley Blvd, San Ramon
- **Newhall Dog Park**, areas for big and small dogs (Ayers and Turtle Creek rds, Concord)
- **Ohlone Dog Park** (Martha Scott Benedict Memorial Park), dogs allowed off-leash in entire park (Grant St and Hearst Ave, Berkeley)
- **Paso Nogal Park**, Paso Nogal Rd and Morello Ave, Pleasant Hill
- **Piedmont Park**, 711 Highland Avenue, Piedmont
- **Point Isabel Regional Shoreline** offers 21 acres of run-free shoreline; the official off-leash area is along the south side of the canal (Central Ave, exit I-80 East or I-580 West, Richmond, www.pido.org). Point Isabel Dog Owners and Friends, a dog owner membership group, provides biodegradable waste bags, publishes a newsletter, and sponsors monthly cleanups.
- **Redwood Regional Park**, 7867 Redwood Rd, Oakland
- **San Lorenzo Community Park**, half-acre site on the west side of the 30-acre park (1970 Via Buena Vista, San Lorenzo)
- **Sunol Regional Wilderness**, 1895 Geary Rd, Sunol
- **Tilden Regional Park**, Berkeley, 2501 Grizzly Peak Blvd

## NORTH BAY

- **Alston Park/Canine Commons**, Dry Creek Rd, Napa
- **Bayfront Park**, popular 2-acre dog park, Camino Alto and Sycamore Ave, Mill Valley

- **Camino Alto Open Space Preserve**, end of Escalon Dr, West of Camino Alto, Mill Valley
- **DeTurk Roundbarn Park**, 819 Donahue St, Santa Rosa
- **Doyle Park Dog Park**, fenced dog park is behind the stadium, 700 Hoen Ave, Santa Rosa
- **Field of Dogs**, fenced two-thirds of the area behind Marin Civic Center (San Rafael, 3540 Civic Center Dr, www.fieldofdogs.org)
- **Galvin Dog Park**, in Don Galvin Park, next to Golf Course (3330 Yulupa Ave, Santa Rosa)
- **Larkspur—Piper Park**, 250 Doherty Dr (behind police station)
- **Marin Headlands Trails**, several entrances, one at the Coastal Trail off Bunker Rd, near Rodeo Beach, Marin
- **Mc Dog**, within John F. McInnis County Park (Highway 101 to Smith Ranch Rd, San Rafael)
- **Northwest Community Dog Park**, Marlow off Gurneville Rd, Santa Rosa
- **Remington Dog Park** (also known as Sausalito Dog Park), fenced area within the Martin Luther King Park (Bridgeway and Ebbtide Ave, Sausalito)
- **Rincon Valley Dog Park**, in Rincon Valley Community Park, fenced pond area for dogs, separate fenced large and small dog areas (5108 Badger Rd, Santa Rosa)
- **Rocky Memorial Dog Park**, Sonoma County's biggest dog park (West Casa Grande Road, Petaluma)
- **Rodeo Beach and Lagoon**, from the Marin Headlands Visitor Center, follow the sign west, Sausalito
- **San Pedro Mountain Open Space Preserve**, North Point San Pedro Rd, at Meriam Dr, San Rafael
- **Terra Linda–Sleepy Hollow Divide Open Space Preserve**, end of Ridgewood Dr, San Rafael

## PENINSULA
- **Bedwell Bayfront Park**, Bayfront Expressway and Marsh Rd, Menlo Park
- **Bayside Park**, 1125 Airport Blvd, Burlingame
- **Boothbay Park**, Boothbay Ave and Edgewater Lane, Half Moon Bay
- **Cipriani Dog Park**, 2525 Buena Vista Ave, Belmont
- **Coastside Dog Park**, Wavecrest Rd near the Smith Field ball fields, off Highway 1 (Half Moon Bay, coastdogs.org)
- **Esplanade Beach**, enter by stairs at the end of Esplanade, north of Manor Drive, Pacifica
- **Foster City Dog Exercise Area**, 600 Foster City Blvd, Foster City
- **Foster City Dog Park**, Foster City Blvd and Bounty Dr, Foster City
- **Greer Park**, West Bayshore Rd and Amarillo St, Palo Alto
- **Heather Dog Exercise Area**, Portofino and Melendy drs, San Carlos
- **Hoover Park**, 2901 Cowper Street, Palo Alto

- **J. Pierce Mitchell Dog Run**, 600 East Meadow, Palo Alto
- **John Lucas Greer Park**, 1098 Amarillo Road, Palo Alto
- **Mitchell Park**, 3800 Middlefield Rd, Palo Alto
- **San Bruno Dog Run**, fenced area, Maywood and Evergreen, San Bruno
- **Seal Point Park Dog Park, San Mateo**
- **Shoreline Dog Park**, Shoreline Recreation Area, east end of Shoreline Blvd, Mountain View
- **Shores Dog Park**, Radio Road off Redwood Shores Parkway, Redwood City

### SOUTH BAY

A great resource for dog parks in the South Bay is **www.wagntrain.com/dog_parks.htm**. For the newest San Jose parks, visit **www.sjparks.org/dogparks.asp**.

- **Hellyer Park**, an enclosed acre near the Shadow Bluff picnic area (101 to Hellyer Ave, San Jose)
- **Las Palmas Park**, Russet and Danforth drs, Sunnyvale
- **Lincoln Park**, fenced area (Wabash and West San Carlos, San Jose)
- **Miyuki Dog Park**, small dirt enclosed area (Miyuki Dr and Autotech Ln, off Santa Theresa Blvd, San Jose)
- **Mountain View Dog Park**, corner of North Road and Shoreline, Mountain View
- **Percolation Ponds**, off-leash running and swimming (Noble Ave north of Piedmont, San Jose)
- **Santa Clara Dog Park**, 3450 Brookdale Dr, Santa Clara
- **Watson Dog Park**, San Jose's first official dog park, with a separate fenced small dog area, benches, picnic tables and grass (E Jackson and 22nd, San Jose)

## A WORD ABOUT SAFETY

As scenic and bubble-protected as many newcomers believe the Bay Area to be, the region suffers from the same crime risks as most areas in the country. Below are a few urban safety tips:

- Walk with determination, and remain aware of your surroundings at all times.
- If you're carrying a handbag or backpack, do so with the strap across your chest. But if someone demands what you're carrying, give it up!
- On the street, you do not owe a response to anyone. This may seem callous but it is better to err on the side of bad manners than bad judgment.
- Never get into a car with a stranger (unless it's an Uber, Lyft, Sidecar, or other ridesharing service—in which case, knock yourself out).
- On the bus, ride in the front, next to the driver.
- Keep clear of abandoned/deserted areas; if you must go into an area that you suspect is unsafe, do so in the daytime and, if possible, with someone else.
- **Always** lock your house (and your bike).
- If you like to jog, find a running partner, particularly if you run at night.

- Know where the local police and fire stations are located.
- If something happens to you or if you witness a crime, notify the police immediately.

Neighborhood Watch programs are on the increase throughout the Bay Area, but they're not in every community yet. Check with the police department in your neighborhood to find out if a watch program exists—if not, you may want to take the lead and set one up yourself. You can also visit the neighborhood watch website at www.ncpc.org, which gives safety tips. The District Attorney's office launched a community DA program where district attorneys in San Francisco volunteer in their own neighborhoods and share their expertise.

The San Francisco Police Department is looking for volunteers to assist in crime prevention, neighborhood policing, and other areas. For more information, contact the Reserve Coordinator (850 Bryant Street, Room 535, San Francisco, 415-553-1643), or fill out a request for information at the police department's website (www.sfgov.org/police).

In San Francisco and across the Bay Area, crime statistics are available online and can help you pinpoint areas with high crime rates. In San Francisco, visit www.sf-police.org and search for "compstat." If you *are* a victim of a crime, contact the police. For family violence, the crisis hotline is 800-799-7233 (non-emergency) or 911 for emergencies. For more listings, see **Crisis Lines** in the **Useful Phone Numbers and Websites** chapter.

If you have a complaint against a police officer in San Francisco, contact the Office of Citizen Complaints (415-241-7711 or TTY 415-241-7770). In Oakland contact the Citizens' Police Review Board (510-238-3159). In San Jose, contact the Office of the Independent Police Auditor (408-794-6226). You can also contact the police department in question directly.

N OW THAT YOU'VE FOUND A PLACE TO HANG YOUR HAT, AND YOU'VE taken care of some of the basics, like turning on electricity, it's time to make your new place feel like home. This chapter covers appliance rentals, domestic services, finding an automobile repair shop, and receiving and sending packages, as well as services for people with disabilities, information for international newcomers, and more.

## RENTAL SERVICES

Most Bay Area rental apartments come with all of the necessities—refrigerator, stove, and so on—with one exception. Your odds of getting a washer and dryer in San Francisco are 50/50 at best—especially if you opt, as many do, for an older Victorian or Edwardian flat. If you'd rather not haul your laundry to the laundromat with all your neighbors, you might consider renting a washer and dryer. Always be sure to check with your landlord first about logistics—where to hook it up, and who will pay for the increased water (the owner, if you're lucky) and electricity (almost always you). If you're lucky you may be able to convince your landlord to purchase one instead. It's worth a try.

If you're buying a house or condo, and wind up missing an appliance (or want to replace an old one), or if you find yourself in a studio rental with a "partial kitchen," look into appliance rental options. For major appliance rental, contact **Rent-A-Center**, which has various locations in the Bay Area (800-655-5510, www. rentalcenter.com).

## DOMESTIC SERVICES

### HOUSEKEEPING

Depending on how many hours you spend at work, domestic details like house cleaning can easily fall by the wayside. Rest assured—the Bay Area has countless freelancers and businesses that would be more than happy to clean your couch and counters for a fee. Housekeepers used to advertise on bulletin boards at laundromats, coffeehouses, grocery stores, and college campuses, but like most things in the Bay Area, Craigslist listings eclipse the old platforms. Check www.craigslist.org for housekeeping ads, and check www.yelp.com for reviews. In San Francisco, the North Bay, the Peninsula, and the South Bay, **Parents Place** has a bulletin board full of ads posted by people looking for housecleaning and childcare jobs; for Parents Place locations, visit www.parentsplaceonline.org. A few listings to get you started:

## SAN FRANCISCO
- **City Maids**, 415-665-6633, www.sfcitymaids.com
- **Maid Green**, 415-839-6105, www.maidgreensf.com
- **Marvel Maids**, 877-627-8358, www.marvelmaids.com
- **Merry Maids**, 415-221-6243 or 800-637-7962, www.merrymaids.com
- **Self-Help for the Elderly**, free temporary at-home assistance for qualified seniors and the disabled, particularly in Chinatown but also across the Bay Area (415-677-7600, www.selfhelpelderly.org)

## NORTH BAY
- **Merry Maids**, 415-455-9191 or 800-637-7962, www.merrymaids.com
- **Molly Maid**, 415-454-3600, www.mollymaid.com

## EAST BAY
- **Dana's Housekeeping**, 510-654-6880, www.danashousekeeping.com
- **Marvel Maids**, 877-627-8358, www.marvelmaids.com
- **Merry Maids**, 510-521-5878, 510-614-6243, or 800-637-7962, www.merrymaids.com

## PENINSULA
- **City Maids**, 415-665-6633, www.sfcitymaids.com
- **Marvel Maids**, 877-627-8358, www.marvelmaids.com
- **Merry Maids**, 650-572-8200 or 800-637-7962, www.merrymaids.com

## SOUTH BAY
- **Complete Cleaning**, 408-248-4162
- **Marvel Maids**, 877-627-8358, www.marvelmaids.com
- **Merry Maids**, 408-978-6273 or 800-637-7962, www.merrymaids.com

## PEST CONTROL
There are generally far fewer pests in the Bay Area than in many other parts of the country. Some older buildings, especially those with restaurants on the premises, are

pest-prone. Ants, fleas, roaches, and other visitors can show up if you live near the beach, at ground level, or have pets. In warmer, damper regions, mosquitoes can be a nuisance. Alameda, San Mateo, Santa Clara, Marin, Sonoma, Napa, Solano, and Contra Costa counties have mosquito abatement programs. Some homes also suffer from termites; if you are in the market to buy a house, have it inspected for termites. In more rural areas, ticks, raccoons, opossums, and skunks can be a problem.

Now for the wakeup call: bed bugs. They're here—everywhere in the Bay Area, especially in San Francisco, where reported cases have soared recently. They're costly and challenging to exterminate. A good preventative approach is to check www.bedbugregistry.com before moving into any new home to see if previous or current tenants have reported cases of bed bugs at a given property. Stay on the safe side and check that website. If you do get bed bugs, consider hiring the best-rated pest-control agency in the Bay Area: **Scent Tek** (415-933-0880, www.scent-tek.com).

If you're renting your place, it is the landlord's responsibility to keep your premises free from vermin, although keeping your home or apartment clean always helps. Nontoxic and humane means of controlling pests are available. Check www.yelp.com for listings.

## MAIL SERVICES

If you're in between addresses but still need a place to get your mail, dozens of businesses will rent you a mailbox. You can also rent mailboxes at your local post office. In San Francisco, try the following services—and search www.yelp.com for other locations in the Bay Area:

- **Jet Mail**, 2130 Fillmore St, 415-922-9402, www.fillmoreshop.com
- **Mail Access**, 2261 Market St, 415-626-2575, www.mailaccess.us
- **Mail Boxes Etc. (MBE)** and **UPS Stores**: 268 Bush St, 415-765-1515; 3701 Sacramento St, 415-221-9882; 601 Van Ness Ave, 415-775-6644; 2443 Fillmore St, 415-922-6245; 1032 Irving St, 415-566-2660; multiple other San Francisco and Bay Area locations; to find the store nearest you, visit www.theupsstore.com or www.mbe.com
- **Postal Annex**, 100 1st St, 415-882-1515; 350 Bay St #100, 415-772-9022, www.postalannex.com

For mailing services, packaging help, faxing, and copying, try:

- **FedEx**, 1967 Market St, 415-252-0864; 1155 Harrison St, 415-552-4628; 1800 Van Ness Ave, 415-292-2500; 100 California St, 415-834-0240; 369 Pine St, 415-834-1053, www.fedex.com

## MAIN POST OFFICES

Neighborhood post offices are listed at the end of each neighborhood profile.

Check there for the one nearest you. For postal rates, post office locations, zip codes, and more, contact the post office (www.usps.com, 800-275-8777) or try the post offices listed below:

### SAN FRANCISCO & NORTH BAY

- **San Francisco**, 1300 Evans Ave (Monday–Friday, 7 a.m.–8:30 p.m.; Saturday, 8 a.m.–2 p.m.)
- **San Rafael**, 40 Bellam Boulevard (Monday–Friday, 8:30 a.m.–5 p.m.; Saturday, 10 a.m.–1 p.m.)
- **Santa Rosa**, 730 2nd St (Monday–Friday, 8 a.m.–6 p.m.; Saturday, 10 a.m.– 2 p.m.)

### EAST BAY

- **Berkeley**, 2000 Allston Way (Monday–Friday, 9 a.m.–5 p.m.; Saturday, 9 a.m.–3 p.m.)
- **Concord**, 2121 Meridian Park Blvd (Monday–Friday, 9 a.m.–6 p.m.; Saturday, 9 a.m.–2 p.m.)
- **Emeryville**, 1585 62nd St (Monday–Friday, 8:30–5 p.m.; Saturday, 8 a.m.–2 p.m.)
- **Walnut Creek**, 2070 N Broadway (Monday–Friday, 8:30 a.m.–5 p.m.; closed Saturday)

### PENINSULA & SOUTH BAY

- **Palo Alto**, 2085 E Bayshore Rd (Monday–Friday, 8:30 a.m.–5 p.m.; closed Saturday)
- **San Mateo**, 1630 S Delaware St (Monday–Friday, 8:30 a.m.–5 p.m.; Saturday, 9 a.m.–12:30 p.m.)
- **San Jose**, 1750 Lundy Ave (Monday–Friday, 8:30 a.m.–8 p.m.; closed Saturday)

## JUNK MAIL

Everyone gets it, and most hate it. There are a number of strategies for curtailing the onslaught. Try writing a note, including your name and address, asking to be purged from the **Direct Marketing Association's list** (Direct Marketing Association's Mail Preference Service, P.O. Box 9008, Farmingdale, NY 11735). This may work, although some catalog companies need to be contacted directly with a purge request. Another option is to call the **"Opt-out" line** at 888-567-8688 and request that the main credit bureaus not release your name and address to interested marketing companies pushing "pre-approved" credit and insurance offers. To keep telemarketers at bay, register your home and cellphone numbers with the **National Do Not Call Registry** (888-382-1222, TTY 866-290-4236, www.donotcall.gov).

## SHIPPING SERVICES

- **DHL Worldwide Express**, 800-225-5345, www.dhl.com
- **FedEx**, 800-463-3339, www.fedex.com

- **United Parcel Service (UPS)**, 800-742-5877, www.ups.com
- **US Postal Service Express Mail**, 800-275-8777, www.usps.com

## AUTOMOBILE REPAIR

Everything is going great: you scored a place to live and a job. And then your car starts smoking. Or the brakes give out on a steep hill in the Bay Area. After calling your auto insurance company (and the police if necessary), you'll need a reputable auto repair shop. Choosing one isn't a breeze, no matter where you live. The most popular way to find a trusted repair place is to check www.yelp.com for user-submitted service reviews and locations in your area, and to ask coworkers and neighbors. Going to your auto dealer, while generally a reliable option, can be expensive. Remember, it's always a good idea to check with the **Better Business Bureau** (see below under **Consumer Protection**) to find out if any complaints have been filed against a service station you are considering using.

### AAA (AMERICAN AUTOMOBILE ASSOCIATION)

Co-founded more than a century ago by San Francisco resident Jim Wilkins—proprietor of the Cliff House—the American Automobile Association (AAA) began as an automobile club when only a dozen self-propelled vehicles navigated the hills of San Francisco. Today, more than 54 million people belong to AAA. As a member, you receive 24-hour emergency road service, free maps, travel services, discounts at numerous hotels, DMV services, and more. If you run out of gas or have a flat tire or blown transmission, AAA will rescue you; call their **Emergency Road Service Number** at 800-AAA-HELP (800-222-4357). You can also call 800-922-8228 to find an office near you, or visit California AAA at www.csaa.com.

AAA also publishes a popular travel and culture magazine called *VIA* (headquartered in the Bay Area), with excellent road trip tips and feature stories (www.viamagazine.com).

## CONSUMER PROTECTION

The *Bay Area Consumers' Checkbook* is a pro-consumer guide published by the Center for the Study of Services. It's a nonprofit magazine, free of advertising, created to advise consumers on services' and products' qualities and prices. The quality of information is excellent. Articles can be ordered online at www.checkbook.org/reviews/ca/san-francisco-bay-area or by calling 510-763-7979. A subscription to the magazine is $34 for two years.

For consumer protection information about utilities, see **Consumer Protection—Utility Complaints** in the **Getting Settled** chapter.

Got problems with a merchant? Several agencies monitor consumer businesses and take action when necessary. Read contracts before you sign them, save all receipts and canceled checks, get the names of telephone sales and service people, and check a contractor's license number with the Department of Consumer Affairs for complaints. Sometimes you still get stung: a dry cleaner returns your blue suit but now it's purple and he shrugs. A shop reneges on a promise to refund an expensive gift. Your landlord fails to return your security deposit when you move (common in the Bay Area). After $898 in repairs to your automobile's engine, the car now vibrates, and the mechanic claims innocence. Negotiations fail, even though you have the appropriate documents in hand. You're angry and embarrassed because you've been had. Here's where to turn:

- **Better Business Bureau: San Francisco**, Alameda, Contra Costa, San Mateo, and Marin counties, 510-844-2000; Santa Clara and Santa Cruz counties, 408-278-7400; maintains consumer complaint files about businesses; also research businesses at www.bbb.org/greater-san-francisco
- **California Attorney General**, maintains a public inquiry unit that reviews consumer complaints, 800-952-5225, TTY 800-735-2929, www.ag.ca.gov
- **California Department of Consumer Affairs**, state agency that investigates consumer complaints, 800-952-5210, TTY 800-326-2297, www.dca.ca.gov
- **Contractors State License Board**, 800-321-2752, www.cslb.ca.gov
- **San Francisco District Attorney**, maintains a consumer protection unit that investigates and mediates consumer-business disputes, 415-553-1751, www.sfdistrictattorney.org

## MEDIA-SPONSORED CALL FOR ACTION PROGRAMS

The following are consumer advocacy and public investigation programs offered by Bay Area news media:

- **Chronicle Watch** (*San Francisco Chronicle*), San Francisco, chroniclewatch@sfchronicle.com, www.facebook.com/sfchronwatch
- **KGO Seven On Your Side**, San Francisco, 415-954-8151, www.abc7news.com/7onyourside

## LEGAL MEDIATION/REFERRAL PROGRAMS

For a full list of licensed mediation programs, visit www.dca.ca.gov/consumer/mediation_programs.shtml. A few trusted resources:

- **The Bar Association of San Francisco**, 310 Battery St, San Francisco, 415-982-1600, www.sfbar.org
- **Community Boards**, 901 Van Ness Ave, Suite 2040, San Francisco, 415-920-3820, www.communityboards.org
- **East Bay Community Mediation**, 1968 San Pablo Ave, Berkeley, 510-548-2377, www.seedscrc.org

## LEGAL ASSISTANCE TO THE ELDERLY

- **Legal Assistance to the Elderly**, 995 Market St, San Francisco, 415-538-3333, www.laesf.org

## SMALL CLAIMS COURTS

The maximum amount of money you can sue for in small claims court is $7,500, and in accordance with state law, you cannot sue more than twice in a calendar year for more than $2,500 in small claims court.

The **California Department of Consumer Affairs** maintains a helpful website, www.dca.ca.gov/publications/small_claims, with information on small claims courts for each county. A few to get you started:

- **Alameda County**, www.alameda.courts.ca.gov
- **Contra Costa County**, www.cc-courts.org
- **Marin County**, www.marincourt.org
- **Napa County,** www.napa.courts.ca.gov/divisions/small-claims
- **San Francisco County**, www.sfsuperiorcourt.org/divisions/small-claims
- **San Mateo County**, www.sanmateocourt.org
- **Santa Clara County**, www.sccsuperiorcourt.org
- **Solano County**, www.solanocourts.com
- **Sonoma County**, www.sonomasuperiorcourt.com

# SERVICES FOR PEOPLE WITH DISABILITIES

Long before the Americans with Disabilities Act, the Bay Area's sensitivity to the needs of all individuals was raised by a group of ability-challenged college applicants who fought for admission to the Berkeley campus of the University of California. Their efforts, in the 1960s and '70s, not only achieved many of the group's goals but also gave rise to the **Independent Living Center**, which now boasts nationwide offices that offer training and rehabilitation services, as well as referrals to support groups and organizations.

**Lighthouse for the Blind and Visually Impaired** provides assistance, equipment, support, and referrals (www.lighthouse-sf.org). Fully trained guide dogs are available through **Guide Dogs for the Blind** (welcome.guidedogs.com), which is based in Marin County. **The Hearing and Speech Center of Northern California** provides testing, education, support, and referrals to the hearing impaired (www.hearingspeech.org).

A great resource for accessible sports in the Bay Area can be found at the **Bay Area Outreach & Recreation Program**, a Berkeley nonprofit (www.borp.org), which features year-round activities for youth and adults. Several helpful organizations:

- **The Arc of San Francisco**, 1500 Howard St, 415-255-7200, www.thearcsf.org

- **Bay Area Outreach & Recreation Program,** 600 Bancroft Way, Berkeley, 510-849-4663, www.borp.org
- **Center for Independent Living**, various locations in Oakland and Berkeley, 510-763-9999, www.cilberkeley.org
- **Deaf & Disabled Telecommunications Program**, provides free service to the hearing disabled, 877-546-7414, TTY 800-867-4323, ddtp.cpuc.ca.gov
- **Deaf Services of Palo Alto**, Palo Alto, 650-856-9262, www.dspa.org
- **Guide Dogs for the Blind**, 350 Los Ranchitos Rd, San Rafael, 800-295-4050, welcome.guidedogs.com
- **Hearing and Speech Center**, 1234 Divisadero St, San Francisco, 415-921-7658, TTY 415-921-8990, www.betterhearing.org
- **Independent Living Resource Center**, 649 Mission, 3rd Floor, San Francisco, 415-543-6222, TTY 415-543-6698, www.ilrcsf.org
- **Lighthouse for the Blind & Visually Impaired**, 214 Van Ness Ave, 415-431-1481; TTY 415-431-4572, www.lighthouse-sf.org
- **Pomeroy Recreation & Rehabilitation Center**, 207 Skyline Blvd, 415-665-4241, www.janetpomeroy.org
- **Support for Families of Children with Disabilities**, 2601 Mission St, 415-920-5040, www.supportforfamilies.org

## GETTING AROUND

All BART stations are wheelchair accessible with elevators at every station, and discount tickets are available. Most public buses throughout the Bay Area are also equipped to handle wheelchairs by use of ramps and lifts. For more information on transit options for the disabled, call the appropriate transit agency (BART, MUNI, AC Transit, SamTrans, and Caltrain are listed in the **Transportation** chapter). Wheelchair rentals are available at medical equipment and supply businesses. You can also purchase new and used wheelchairs; search www.yelp.com for reviews by location.

Applications for parking permits are available at any local **Department of Motor Vehicles** and online at www.dmv.ca.gov—or you can request to have an application mailed to you by calling 800-777-0133. Once you complete the application, it must be signed by your doctor and brought to any local DMV office or returned by mail to the address listed on the application. There is no fee for disabled placards.

## COMMUNICATION

The **California Telephone Access Program** offers free assistance devices for hearing-, speech-, mobility-, and visually impaired individuals—from amplified phones to voice enhancers, large-button phones, and more. **TTY** is a small telecommunications device with a keyboard for typing and a screen for reading conversations. TTY is sometimes also referred to as **TDD (Telecommunications**

**Device for the Deaf)**. Experts will visit your home to install the equipment and help train you to use it. To get started contact TTY 800-806-4474 or Voice: 800-806-1191; for services in Spanish TTY 800-896-7670, or Voice: 800-949-5650; for service in Hmong: 866-880-3394; or Cantonese: 866-324-8754; or Mandarin: 866-324-8747. You can also drop by the walk-in center, **CTAP Berkeley Service Center** (3075 Adeline, Suite 260, Berkeley, open Monday through Friday, 9 a.m.–6 p.m., ddtp.cpuc.ca.gov/Berkeley.aspx).

California has a telephone relay service that provides a communication system for the hearing- and speech-impaired. The operator will contact your party and relay your conversation. **Speech-to-Speech Relay Service (STS)** assists those who can hear but have a speech disability and use a voice synthesizer or voice enhancer. A trained operator re-voices what's being said by the STS user. The STS user hears the other party's voice directly. No special telephone equipment is required. This service is free except for any toll charges. Also available is an online relay service at the websites listed below.

- **TTY**: 800-735-2922 or 711
- **STS**: 800-854-7784 or 711
- **Websites**: www.purple.us, www.sprintip.com
- **Voice**: 877-546-7414 or 711

If you need help with sign language, contact the following organizations, which usually require one week's notice: **Bay Area Communication Access** (415-356-0405, TTY 415-356-0376, www.bacainterp.com) and **Hands On Bay Area** (415-541-9616, www.handsonbayarea.org).

## HOUSING

Some of the organizations listed above can help you with accessible housing, including the **Independent Living Resource Center** in San Francisco and the **Center for Independent Living** in Oakland and Berkeley.

## INTERNATIONAL NEWCOMERS

Immigration rules and regulations have become increasingly strict, as national security concerns escalate. If you are relocating from abroad, visit the United States consulate in your home country to find out how to prepare. The consulate will provide you with information specific to your situation—applications for permanent residency, guest worker programs, and student visas, as well as information on green cards, naturalization, political asylum, and citizenship.

A variety of helpful information can be found at the **US Citizen and Immigration Services'** website, www.uscis.gov. Contact USCIS national customer service at 800-375-5283 or TTY 800-767-1833. For further assistance, schedule an appointment with **USCIS**. Below are addresses of local USCIS district and satellite offices:

- **Asylum Office**: 75 Hawthorne St, #303S, San Francisco, 415-293-1234
- **Oakland Application Support Center**: 2040 Telegraph Ave, Oakland
- **San Francisco District Office**: 444 Washington St, San Francisco
- **South Bay Office**: 1887 Monterey Rd, San Jose

Once you've settled in, consider getting in touch with the consulate from your home country. The consulate can be a useful starting point for information on community groups and organizations, as well as assisting with questions about your move to the United States. For United States citizens planning to travel abroad—especially for work or school—the consulate is the place to learn about rules and regulations and visas. Below are the major offices in San Francisco:

## INTERNATIONAL CONSULATES IN SAN FRANCISCO

- **The British Consulate General**, 1 Sansome St, Suite 850, 415-617-1300, www.ukinusa.fco.gov.uk
- **The Consulate General of Australia**, 575 Market St, 415-644-3620, usa.embassy.gov.au/whwh/SanFranCG.html
- **The Consulate General of Brazil**, 300 Montgomery St, Suite 300, 415-981-8170, saofrancisco.itamaraty.gov.br/en-us
- **The Consulate General of Canada**, 580 California St, 415-834-3180, www.can-am.gc.ca
- **The Consulate General of Chile**, 870 Market St, Suite 1058, 415-982-7662, www.chileabroad.gov.cl/san-francisco
- **The Consulate General of China**, 1450 Laguna St, 415-852-5900, www.chinaconsulatesf.org
- **The Consulate General of Ecuador**, 235 Montgomery St, Suite 934, 415-982-1819, www.ecuador.us/info/consulate.htm
- **The Consulate General of El Salvador**, 507 Polk St, Suite 280, 415-771-8524, www.elsalvadorsf.org
- **The Consulate General of France**, 88 Kearny St, 415-397-4330, www.consulfrance-sanfrancisco.org
- **The Consulate General of Germany**, 1960 Jackson St, 415-775-1061, www.germany.info
- **The Consulate General of Greece**, 2441 Gough St, 415-775-2102, www.mfa.gr/usa/en/consulate-general-in-san-francisco
- **The Consulate General of Guatemala**, 544 Golden Gate Ave #100, 415-563-8319, www.minex.gob.gt
- **The Consulate General of Honduras**, 870 Market St, Suite 449, 415-392-0076
- **The Consulate General of India**, 540 Arguello Blvd, 415-668-0683, www.cgisf.org
- **The Consulate General of Indonesia**, 1111 Columbus Ave, 415-474-9571, www.kemlu.go.id

- **The Consulate General of Ireland**, 100 Pine St, 415-392-4214, www. consulateofirelandsanfrancisco.org
- **The Consulate General of Israel**, 456 Montgomery St, Suite 2100, 415-844-7500, www.israeliconsulate.org
- **The Consulate General of Italy**, 2590 Webster St, 415-292-9200, www. conssanfrancisco.esteri.it
- **The Consulate General of Japan**, 275 Battery St, Suite 2100, 415-780-6000, www.sf.us.emb-japan.go.jp
- **The Consulate General of the Republic of Korea**, 3500 Clay St, 415-921-2251, usa-sanfrancisco.mofa.go.kr/english
- **The Consulate General of Luxembourg**, 1 Sansome St, Suite 830, 415-788-0816, sanfrancisco.mae.lu
- **The Consulate General of Mexico**, 532 Folsom St, 415-354-1700, www.sre.gob. mx/sanfrancisco
- **The Consulate General of Peru**, 870 Market St, Suite 1075, 415-362-5185, www.consuladoperu.com
- **The Consulate General of the Philippines**, 447 Sutter St, 415-433-6666, www. philippinessanfrancisco.org
- **The Consulate General of Portugal**, 3298 Washington St, 415-346-3400, www. secomunidades.pt/web/saofrancisco
- **The Consulate General of the Russian Federation**, 2790 Green St, 415-928-6878, www.consulrussia.org
- **The Consulate General of the Republic of Singapore**, 595 Market St, Suite 2450, 415-543-4775, www.mfa.gov.sg/sanfrancisco
- **The Consulate General of Spain**, 1405 Sutter St, 415-922-2995, www.maec.es/consulados/sanfrancisco
- **The Consulate General of Sweden**, 505 Sansome St, 415-788-2631, www. swedenabroad.com/en-GB/Embassies/San-Francisco
- **The Consulate General of Switzerland**, 456 Montgomery St, Suite 1500, 415-788-2272, www.eda.admin.ch/sf
- **The Consulate General of Ukraine**, 530 Bush St, Suite 402, 415-398-0240, www.ukrconsul.org
- **The Consulate General of Vietnam**, 1700 California St, Suite 430, 415-922-1707, www.vietnamconsulate-sf.org
- **The Royal Norwegian Consulate General**, 575 Market St, Suite 3950, 415-882-2000, www.norway.org/embassy/sanfrancisco

## IMMIGRATION RESOURCES

- **Bureau of Immigration and Customs Enforcement**, www.ice.gov
- **Customs & Border Protection**, www.cbp.gov
- **Department of Homeland Security**, www.dhs.gov
- **General Government Questions**, 800-333-4636, www.usa.gov

- **Social Security Administration**, 800-772-1213, www.ssa.gov
- **US Bureau of Consular Affairs**, www.travel.state.gov
- **US Bureau of Citizenship and Immigration Services** (green cards, visas, government forms), www.uscis.gov
- **US Department of State, Visa Services**, travel.state.gov

## IMMIGRATION PUBLICATIONS

Several publications for immigrants are found at www.uscis.gov/newimmigrants, including useful information on your rights and responsibilities, as well as the steps to becoming a US citizen. Another helpful publication is the ***Newcomer's Handbook for Moving to and Living in the USA***, by Mike Livingston (First Books).

## MOVING PETS TO THE USA

- ***The Pet-Moving Handbook*** (First Books) covers domestic and international moves by car, airplane, ferry, and train, with a primary focus on cats and dogs.
- **Cosmopolitan Canine Carriers,** based in Connecticut (800-243-9105, www.caninecarriers.com), has been shipping dogs and cats worldwide for more than 25 years. Contact them with questions or concerns regarding air transportation arrangements, vaccinations, and quarantine times.

## GAY & TRANSGENDER LIFE

When the US Supreme Court ruled in 2015 that same-sex marriage is a guaranteed right nationwide, it sparked more than parties and parades and marriage permits. It stirred pride across generations—particularly in San Francisco, which has led the national gay-rights movement. At the forefront are leaders like the **Lesbian, Gay, Bisexual & Transgender Center of San Francisco**, known simply as "The Center," which opened its doors in 2002 at the corner of Market Street and Laguna. Today the spacious facility—proudly flying the rainbow flag—provides a variety of programs for the LGBT community and its allies, including parenting classes, HIV support groups, and a range of arts activities and presentations. The Center also has a drop-in youth center, a large auditorium for special events, a senior space, a reading room, an art gallery, a bulletin board with dozens of resources, child care, offices for a handful of nonprofit groups, a computer room, a café, and a roof terrace. To learn more, drop by 1800 Market Street, call 415-865-5555, or visit www.sfcenter.org.

Another exceptional local resource is **Lyric**, a below-the-radar nonprofit for at-risk youth in the gay, lesbian, and transgender communities (127 Collingswood Street in San Francisco, 415-703-6150, www.lyric.org). Lyric is especially important, as almost 30 percent of homeless youth under the age of 25 are LGBT in San Francisco. For gay and lesbian-centered nightlife, dance clubs, comedy, and theater, the Castro, the Mission, and SOMA neighborhoods are the places to go—but not exclusively, as today's Bay Area shows growing acceptance of sexual orientations and gender identities in a variety of neighborhoods and cities. For the leather-loving crowd, a handful of SOMA clubs are at your service, including the Stud, one of the oldest gay bars around, which frequently draws a crowd of all backgrounds to its popular dance nights at 399 9th St (www.thestud.com, 415-863-6623).

South of San Francisco, popular LGBT clubs include **King of Clubs** in Mountain View (893 Leong Drive, www.koclubs.com, 650-969-6366), featuring cabaret, drag, and goth-industrial nights. **Lido Nightclub**, in San Jose (30 S 1st St, www.lidonightclubsj.com), is acclaimed for its Latino bar and Asian disco, and hosts anything-goes throw-downs. One of the longest-running gay bars in the region is **Mac's Club**, a mellower dive bar frequented by legions of locals at 39 Post St in San Jose, 408-288-8221.

The biggest gay celebration is the annual **Gay Pride Parade** in June (www.sfpride.org). Festivities are held all over the Bay Area. See **A Bay Area Year** for month-by-month events, festivals, and websites. Also in June, check out **the International Lesbian & Gay Film Festival**, put on annually by Frameline (415-703-8650, www.frameline.org). For a tour through the evolution of queer politics, culture, and identity in the Bay Area and nationally, visit the new GLBT History Museum, the nation's first museum of gay, lesbian, and transgender history, which opened a few years ago in the Castro district (4127 18th St, www.glbthistory.org/museum, 415-621-1107). For LGBT-friendly worship, check out the **Gay and Lesbian** section of **Places of Worship** in the **Getting Involved** chapter.

In 2015, the Bay Area also celebrated the news of San Francisco's first high school college-prep course on gay history—a rarity in public schools nationwide. And Santa Clara County plans in 2016 to create an **Office of Lesbian, Gay, Bisexual, Transgender & Queer Affairs**, part of the executive branch in a county where LGBT residents number in the millions. Meanwhile, technology moves at lightning speed in the gay-rights community, as the University of California at San Francisco launches an ambitious study of gay health using information from iPhones to create the largest database of physical issues unique to gay and transgender individuals. The smartphone study—called the **Pride Study**—uses a mobile app to gather data; to learn more and participate, visit www.pridestudy.org.

## PUBLICATIONS

- **Bay Area Reporter** has been around for almost 50 years, with the largest circulation to LGBT readers in the Bay Area's nine counties. It offers entertainment listings, hard news, sports, classifieds, personals, and more (44 Gough St #204, San Francisco, 415-861-5019, www.ebar.com.)
- **Curve** is a glossy magazine with lesbian-related news, politics, style, travel, social issues, and entertainment content (www.curvemag.com).
- **Pink Spots** is a directory of resources for the LGBT community (www.gaypinkspots.com).

- **San Francisco Bay Times** is another free weekly LGBT newspaper offering news, reviews, employment listings, therapy ads, and support groups (415-626-0260, www.sfbaytimes.com).

## BOOKSTORES

- **Books Inc.** has an acclaimed selection of local and global literature (2275 Market St, San Francisco, 415-864-6777, www.booksinc.net).
- **Modern Times** is a progressive bookstore with a wide range of LGBT literature (888 Valencia St, 415-282-9246, www.mtbs.com).

   **For additional** bookstores and businesses across the Bay Area, visit www.gaycities.com.

RAISING CHILDREN IN THE BAY AREA IS REWARDING WHEN YOU CONsider the countless arts festivals and youth museums surrounded by coastal playgrounds, onsite daycare centers, after-school programs, and top colleges and universities. Education across the region, however, is currently perched between two extremes: struggling scores statewide, and the world's best public universities.

In 2015, UC Berkeley was named the planet's top public university by *U.S. News & World Report*—but long before your 2-year-old thinks about college applications, you might want a nursery. The keys are research and persistence. Start with the following tips.

## PARENTING PUBLICATIONS

First, pick up a copy of **Bay Area Parent**, the free monthly magazine that includes a calendar of events and articles on parenting resources in all nine counties of the Bay Area. The same company publishes several related publications, including *Camps & Activities, Family Fun, Teen Focus,* and *Education & Enrichment Guide.* To read articles or subscribe, visit www.bayareaparent.com. **Parents' Press** offers online magazines for parents at www.parentspress.com (875-A Island Dr, Suite 421, Alameda, 510-748-9122). Also reach for **Parenting on the Peninsula** at www.ponthep.com (650-477-2579).

## DAYCARE

The best way to find a great daycare provider is by referral from someone you know and trust—but short of that, contact the **California Child Care Resource & Referral Network** (111 New Montgomery Street, 7th floor, San Francisco,

415-882-0234, www.rrnetwork.org), which provides referrals to childcare agencies throughout California. **The National Association for the Education of Young Children (NAEYC)** can also provide a list of accredited daycare centers and nurseries in your area (www.naeyc.org, 202-232-8777).

Newcomers affiliated with a Bay Area university may have access to a university-operated referral agency or university-run childcare center. Inquire at the student services desk of your university. Sometimes graduate student divisions provide referrals and services. For a childcare referral agency in your area, consider the following:

## SAN FRANCISCO & NORTH BAY

- **Children's Council of San Francisco**, childcare resource and referral (445 Church St, 415-276-2900, www.childrenscouncil.org)
- **Marin Child Care Council**, 555 Northgate Dr, Suite 105, San Rafael, 415-472-1092; childcare referral line: 415-479-2273, www.mc3.org
- **Wu-Yee Children's Services**, serving San Francisco's Cantonese-speaking community, with several childcare centers in the Tenderloin, Chinatown, and Visitacion Valley (888 Clay St, Lower Level, Joy Lok Family Resource Center, San Francisco, 94108, 415-677-0100, www.wuyee.org)

## EAST BAY

- For childcare referrals in Alameda County contact **Bananas** (5232 Claremont Ave, Oakland, 510-658-7353, www.bananasbunch.org)
- For referrals in Hayward, San Leandro, and the Tri-Cities area, contact **4Cs of Alameda County** (22351 City Center Dr, Suite 200, Hayward, 510-582-2182, www.4c-alameda.org); childcare referral lines: 510-582-2182 (Hayward, San Leandro, San Lorenzo, and Castro Valley) and 510-713-2557 (Fremont, Newark, and Union City).
- In Contra Costa County, contact **Contra Costa Child Care Council** (2280 Diamond Blvd, Suite 500, Concord, 925-676-5437, www.cocokids.org)

## PENINSULA & SOUTH BAY

- **Child Care Coordinating Council of San Mateo County (4Cs)**, 2121 El Camino Real, Suite A-100, San Mateo, 650-655-6770, www.thecouncil.net
- **Community Child Care Council of Santa Clara County**, 2515 N 1st St, San Jose, 95131, 408-487-0747; childcare referrals: 408-487-0749, www.4c.org

## WHAT TO LOOK FOR IN DAYCARE

When searching for the best place for your child, be sure to visit prospective daycare providers—preferably unannounced. Look for safety, cleanliness, and caring attitudes on the part of daycare workers. Check that the kitchen, toys, and furniture are clean and safe. Observe the other kids at the center. Do they seem happy?

Are they well-behaved? Ask for the telephone numbers of other parents who use the service and talk to them before committing. It's a good idea to request a daily schedule—look for both active and quiet time, and age-appropriate activities. As the temperate weather in the Bay Area allows for year-round outdoor sports, games, and field trips, make sure the childcare curriculum includes them.

Keep in mind that being licensed doesn't guarantee quality. If you think a provider might be acceptable, check to see if they're licensed, and read reviews online by looking them up on Google and Yelp. To see if a daycare is licensed, check the online registry of the **California Community Care Licensing Division** (www.ccld.ca.gov) or contact the **California Child Care Resource & Referral Network** (111 New Montgomery Street, 7th floor, San Francisco, 415-882-0234, www.rrnetwork.org), or any of the referral agencies listed above.

For drop-in childcare, try a **KidsPark Center**, which has locations near major shopping malls in Silicon Valley (Oakridge and Valley Fair) and accepts children aged 2–11 (www.kidspark.com, 408-213-0973). In 2015, rates were $7.75 per hour for one child, with discounted rates for siblings. **KidsPark** also charges a one-time $25 registration fee per family. While reservations are not necessary, it's a good idea to call first to be sure they have room on a particular day.

## NANNIES

Many agencies can assist you in finding a qualified nanny. In San Francisco and Marin counties, **Aunt Ann's In-House Staffing** (415-749-3650, www.in-housestaffing.com) matches families with baby nurses, nannies, and babysitters. Another useful resource is **Town and Country Resources** (www.tandcr.com, 415-567-0956 in San Francisco, 650-326-8570 in Palo Alto). They place childcare and household professionals in homes, including nannies, baby nurses, personal assistants, housekeepers, and cooks.

Be sure to check all references before hiring someone. Many parents run background checks on prospective nannies. **Trustline** (800-822-8490, www.trustline.org), a nonprofit background checking agency and registry, conducts fingerprint searches through both FBI and California Department of Justice records, and name searches for child-abuse reports. This service is available to all prospective childcare employers, but keep in mind that searches usually take three to four weeks to complete.

If you hire a nanny without using an agency, you'll need to take care of taxes, disability, unemployment insurance, and social security. For information, call 800-NANITAX or check www.4nannytaxes.com.

## AU PAIRS

The United States Information Agency oversees organizations that offer au pair services, which connect you with young adults for a year of in-home childcare and light housekeeping, in exchange for airfare, room and board, and a weekly stipend. The program offers a valuable cultural exchange between the host family and the au pair, as well as flexible childcare schedules for parents. In the Bay Area, many au pairs come from Poland, Germany, France, Scandinavia, Russia, and China, as well as other countries. The agencies run background checks before making placements, and orientation and training sessions once the placements have been made. A few of the top agencies to contact to learn more about au pairs:

- **Agent Au Pair**, 415-376-0202, www.agentaupair.com
- **Au Pair Care**, 800-428-7247, www.aupaircare.com
- **Au Pair in America**, 800-928-7247, www.aupairinamerica.com
- **Cultural Care Au Pair**, 800-333-6056, www.culturalcare.com
- **Interexchange, Au Pair USA**, 800-479-0907 or 800-287-2477, www.interexchange.org/au-pair-usa

## SCHOOLS

Choosing a school can feel like a job in itself—factor in moving to a new city, and it can be a stressful proposition. Add to that the reputation of California public schools for overcrowding and underfunding, and the search can be intimidating. Many newcomers rush to the conclusion that the only chance to get a great well-rounded education is to shell out briefcases of money for an expensive private school. Breathe easier: today's Bay Area offers countless schooling possibilities, including an excellent public charter program, public and private year-round schooling centers, and myriad private options. Case in point is the exceptional Fusion Academy (www.fusionacademy.com), a network of alternative new schools for grades 6–12, with a one-to-one student-teacher ratio. The academy's network is growing, with several schools around the Bay Area—a new one just opened in Silicon Valley.

Today's tech boom means creative new resources for education in the Bay Area, including www.coursera.com, founded in 2012 by Stanford University professors and based in the Bay Area. **Coursera** makes university courses available for free online, as does **Khan Academy** (www.khanacademy.com), based in Mountain View. **Udacity** is another bright light in the Bay Area's online education galaxy, providing customized courses on software engineering from the world's top tech talent. An additional resource is **EdSurge** (www.edsurge.com), a one-stop shop for all education-technology content.

If there's one tool to recommend for picking the best school in the Bay Area, it's **GreatSchools** (www.greatschools.org). Bookmark it. Repeat: *bookmark it*. GreatSchools is an authoritative ratings site that lets you compare schools' test scores, programs, facilities, student body size, teacher qualifications, and other comprehensive data. Another helpful tool is www.familiesbythebay.com, a directory of private schools.

## CHOOSING A SCHOOL

Quantitative measures such as graduation rates and test scores are essential, but just as important are subjective impressions and feelings you and your child gain from visiting a prospective school. In addition to searching www.greatschools.org, consider these crucial ingredients. When visiting a school, ask yourself:

- Am I comfortable here? Will my child be comfortable?
- Does the school feel safe? Are the bathrooms clean and functional?
- Does this school meet my child's learning style? Are elementary-age students moving around naturally but staying on task?
- What are the halls like in junior high and high schools when classes change? Are students interacting with one another and teachers as their class changes?
- Are students actively engaged in discussions or projects? Is student work displayed?
- Ask elementary teachers about reading and math groups and whether kids move up as they build skills.
- Ask about special programs offered to assist new students with their transition to their new school.
- Check for after-school or enrichment activities.
- Ask if parents are encouraged to volunteer in the classroom.
- Look at the faculty and curriculum as well as facilities and equipment. Are adults a presence in all parts of the building? Are the computer labs up-to-date with enough computers? Are instructional materials plentiful and new? Do textbooks cover areas you think are important? Does the school have a clearly articulated mission statement? Can teachers articulate the school's mission and educational philosophy? Do you see opportunities in art, music, and science?
- Inquire about field trips to the Bay Area's museums.
- Finally, if the school you're visiting is near one of the Bay Area's colleges and universities, ask if there are collaborative programs that bring in college students for presentations and talks.

That's a lot of questions, but with research and visits you'll find a good match. (And again, remember that source for reviews: www.greatschools.org.)

To find out about public schools' accountability programs, funding, and reform efforts in California, as well as district and school-by-school breakdowns of recent test scores and campus rankings, visit the **California Department of Education's** website (www.cde.ca.gov).

To familiarize yourself with Bay Area schools, also consult the nonprofit **EdSource** (www.edsource.org), based in Oakland. If your head isn't already swimming, you can find additional facts and figures at **Ed-Data** (www.ed-data.k12.ca.us), a joint effort between the state and EdSource to provide accessible data to parents. **SchoolMatch** (www.schoolmatch.com), based in Mountain View, maintains a database of information on student-teacher ratios, test scores, and per-pupil spending for public and private schools.

## PRESCHOOLS

Preschools—typically for children ages 3 to 5—offer kids a chance to start off on the right foot at a critical period of development. The Bay Area has some of the country's top-rated preschools. The most popular have waiting lists, so as a newcomer it's a good idea to do thorough research and sign up as far in advance as possible. There's a range of programs available—from co-ops offering parent participation and education, to Montessori, which is characterized by an emphasis on kids' independence, individuality, and freedom within limits. To find accredited programs, contact the **National Association for the Education of Young Children (NAEYC)** (202-232-8777, www.naeyc.org). The national **Head Start** program (www.nhsa.org, 703-739-0875) helps low-income families and children ages five and younger.

Proposition 10, the California Children and Families Act of 1998, helps fund early childhood development services to children up to five years of age. For information about programs contact **California Children & Families Commission** (916-263-1050, www.ccfc.ca.gov).

## BAY AREA PUBLIC SCHOOLS

Public schools in the Bay Area are still rebounding from the recession of 2008 and 2009, when classroom overcrowding, struggling test scores, and shrinking funds dominated the local news. With the booming tech scene in today's Bay Area, public schools have made some impressive strides, especially the **San Francisco Unified School District** (www.sfusd.edu). SFUSD has ramped up its arts, music, sports, food, and financing resources, as well as its outdoor activities and career counseling. Decades ago California spent more on public schools than did most American states. Due to property tax cuts set in motion by Proposition 13 in the 1970s, California's spending on schools dropped painfully from one of the highest per-pupil spending levels to near the bottom of that list a few years ago. And performance went with it. California's median student achievement on national standardized tests ranks low. Despite efforts to reduce class size, focusing first on K–3, California still has one of the nation's highest student-teacher ratios.

In the late 1980s, California voters passed Proposition 98 to guarantee that minimum school funding levels were met. But the "guarantee" has proven less than solid as the state continues to rebound from fiscal crisis. Districts are contending with spiraling health care and retirement benefit costs. To save funds, some districts have cut back on support staff—school librarians, and secretaries—and cut extracurricular and enrichment programs. A number of districts with declining enrollments have closed down campuses entirely, while other districts have regained momentum.

On the bright side, a number of counties and cities have banded together and taken it upon themselves to pass bond initiatives to help upgrade and retrofit ailing buildings, provide new equipment, and build science centers and recreation facilities for their local schools. And tech giants like Google and Genentech have launched philanthropic wings designed to spur local growth and improve public schools. Parent groups and concerned residents have also chipped in to keep art and music programs, which have often landed on the chopping block. In San Francisco, initiatives were approved to restore public school arts, physical education, and other extras cut by state funding, and add funds for after-school activities, childcare subsidies, and additional programs. Innovative efforts are under way to help educate the state's large ESL (English as a Second Language) population.

California has a dizzying array of assessment tests and performance evaluations that confuse even education experts. How a school measures up can been seen in the annual Academic Performance Index (API) report, which measures tests results on an overall scorecard. Looking at the API, you'll see district and school-by-school test scores as well as overall rankings. To see how your neighborhood schools stack up, visit www.cde.ca.gov/ta/ac/ap/apireports.asp.

In 1994, Bay Area public schools adopted an open enrollment policy, which (space permitting) offers a student the option to enroll in any public school in his/her district, if parents believe that the school within a student's immediate vicinity is not right for their child. With top schools, particularly high schools, there are often waiting lists, and open spots are granted by lottery. If your transfer request is declined, you can appeal to the governing district school board.

Throughout the Bay Area, the length of the academic year is becoming more flexible. You can decide whether a traditional ten-month or the newly adopted yearlong academic program is the best for your child. In the past few decades, California public education has seen the soaring growth and funding of the charter school movement. Unlike most public schools, charter schools—which are bound by their own charter agreements—are free from some traditional regulations. A charter school is a public program created by a group of individuals— teachers, parents, community leaders—that must have the local school district's approval. Many charter schools promote innovative teaching methods, expand the learning base beyond the classroom, and encourage parent-community involvement. Charter school enrollment is voluntary, and isn't determined by location, which means parents can select any school where space allows. Because charter schools are designed with freedom and flexibility, in some cases they have been spectacularly successful. In other cases the standards haven't been high enough. California charter school students are required to take part in the Standardized Testing and Reporting Program. If students don't perform at a certain level, the school may be closed. For more information about charter schools, consult the **California Charter School Association** (atwww.ccsa.org).

# BAY AREA SCHOOL DISTRICTS

In addition to the school information at the end of each neighborhood listing earlier in this book, the following organizations will provide details about referrals, enrollment, testing, and special programs:

- **San Francisco Unified School District**, 555 Franklin St, 415-241-6000, www.sfusd.edu
- **Marin County Office of Education**, 1111 Las Gallinas Ave, San Rafael, 415-472-4110, www.marinschools.org
- **Alameda County Office of Education**, 313 W Winton Ave, Hayward, 510-887-0152, www.acoe.org
- **Fremont Unified School District**, 4210 Technology Dr, Fremont, 94538, 510-657-2350, www.fremont.k12.ca.us
- **Hayward Unified School District**, 24411 Amador St, Hayward, 510-784-2600, www.husd.k12.ca.us
- **Oakland Unified School District**, 1025 Second Ave, Oakland, 510-879-8200, www.ousd.k12.ca.us
- **Contra Costa County Office of Education**, 77 Santa Barbara Rd, Pleasant Hill, 925-942-3388, www.cccoe.k12.ca.us
- **San Mateo County Office of Education**, 101 Twin Dolphin Dr, Redwood City, 650-802-5300, www.smcoe.org
- **Santa Clara County Office of Education**, 1290 Ridder Park Dr, San Jose, 408-453-6500, www.sccoe.k12.ca.us

## PRIVATE AND PAROCHIAL SCHOOLS

Private schools are more popular in the Bay Area than almost anywhere else in the country. San Francisco has the country's third-highest percentage of students enrolled in private schools from 1st through 12th grades. That's 24 percent of the area's children. San Mateo and Marin counties have 18 percent; Santa Clara has 12 percent; Alameda has 11 percent; Napa and Contra Costa have 10 percent; Sonoma has 8 percent; and Solano has 7 percent (according to www.trulia.com). If you're prepared to finance your child's studies, you'll find no shortage of excellent options. To find a private school that suits your needs, visit www.bayareakidfun.com/k-12-schools-bay-area, which lists schools' information, locations, and links. Other helpful publications include *Peterson's Private Secondary Schools* (www.petersons.com), *The Handbook of Private Schools* (www.privateschoolsearch.com), *Private High Schools of the San Francisco Bay Area* (by Betsy Little and Paula Molligan), and *Private Schools of San Francisco & Marin Counties (K-8): A Parents' Resource Guide* (by Susan Vogel).

## PRIVATE SCHOOLS

- **Fusion Academy**, alternative personalized schools with one-to-one and flexible scheduling; various locations in the Bay Area (www.fusionacademy.com)

- For information on Montessori schools, contact **Montessori Schools of California** (16492 Foothill Blvd, San Leandro, 510-278-1115, www.montessorica.com)
- For **Waldorf schools**, consider the following:
  - San Francisco Waldorf School: K–8 (2938 Washington St, 415-931-2750); high school (470 West Portal Ave, 415-431-1712); www.sfwaldorf.org
  - Marin County, 755 Idylberry Rd, San Rafael, 415-479-8190, www.marinwaldorf.org
  - East Bay, 3800 Clark Rd, El Sobrante, 94803, 510-223-3570, www.eastbaywaldorf.org
  - Silicon Valley, Waldorf School of the Peninsula K-8, 11311 Mora Dr, Los Altos, 650-948-8433, www.waldorfpeninsula.org
- **Challenger Schools** (888-748-1135, www.challengerschool) are known for their engaging approach to elementary and middle school education. Their mission is to prepare "children to become self-reliant, productive individuals; to teach them to think, speak, and write with clarity, precision, and independence; and to inspire them to embrace, challenge, and find joy and self-worth through achievement."

## PAROCHIAL SCHOOLS

- Information regarding Catholic schools in San Francisco, San Mateo, and Marin counties is provided by the **Archdiocese of San Francisco Department of Catholic Schools** (1 Peter Yorke Way, San Francisco, 415-614-5660, www.sfcatholicschools.org).
- The **Archdiocese of Oakland, Department of Catholic Schools** (2121 Harrison St, Oakland, 510-628-2154, www.csdo.org) provides information for Alameda and Contra Costa counties.
- In the South Bay, contact the **Archdiocese of San Jose, Office of Education** (1150 N 1st St, San Jose, 408-983-0185, www.dsj.org).
- For information on **Jewish education** in the Bay Area, visit www.jewishresourceguide.com (click the top-right magazine icon), where you'll find *The Resource: A Guide to Jewish Life in the Bay Area*, which provides listings and information on all the Jewish schools in the Bay Area.

Admission to private schools can be highly competitive, so the sooner you learn about admission deadlines and open houses the better. The registration process begins as early as October of the year prior to the desired academic start date. Be sure to visit schools to hear about their teaching methodologies. As private schools aren't required to follow state standards (though most do), a visit can give insight into the admissions process. Many parents and children have a visceral reaction when walking into a school, and can often sense whether it is "right" for them. Since private schooling is expensive and signing up for a private program is an arduous task, finding a natural match between child and school is immeasurably important.

## HOMESCHOOLING

Homeschooling is increasingly popular in the Bay Area. Many parents believe that they—with intimate knowledge of their kids' psychological and intellectual needs—are better suited to design an educational program that is engaging and rigorous. If you have time to plan and implement a comprehensive study program for your children, many organizations can assist you. For homeschooling information and support, consult the **HomeSchool Association of California** (www.hsc.org), which provides information, monitors legislation, and cultivates connections among homeschoolers. Another helpful organization is **California Homeschool Network** (www.californiahomeschool.net), which provides facts about homeschooling and works to protect the rights of homeschooling families.

## ADDITIONAL PARENTING RESOURCES

- **La Leche League** provides a wealth of information on breastfeeding, and runs support groups at locations throughout the Bay Area (www.llli.org).
- **Parents Place** offers weekly drop-in playgroups for children five and under (1710 Scott St, San Francisco, 415-359-2454, www.parentsplaceonline.org). A variety of programs are also available in Palo Alto (650-688-3040), San Rafael (415-491-7958), and Sonoma (707-571-8131).
- **Petit Appetit** is a resource for preparing all-natural food for babies and toddlers, and offers classes, cookbooks, and food services (415-601-4916, San Francisco, www.petitappetit.com).
- **Support for Families of Children with Disabilities** offers support groups for children, siblings, and parents—some in Spanish or Cantonese—as well as a parent mentor program, workshops, a drop-in center, a resource library, a help line, short-term counseling, and a newsletter (415-282-7494, 1663 Mission St, www.supportforfamilies.org).
- **Las Madres Neighborhood Playgrounds** is a South Bay group that hosts baby days in local parks, with field trips, parties, educational speaker nights, classes, discounts, Mom's Night Out, Couple's Night Out, babysitting co-ops, sit 'n play groups, and more (877-527-6237, San Jose, www.lasmadres.org).
- **Parents Helping Parents** is a family resource center serving parents of special-needs kids; it offers an extensive network of referrals, support groups, community events, and online tools (1400 Parkmoor Ave, San Jose, 408 727-5775, www.php.com).
- **Special Parents Information Network (SPIN)**, based in Santa Cruz, has a wealth of online information, with links to support services throughout California for parents of children with special needs (www.spinsc.org).

## HIGHER EDUCATION

The Bay Area has the best public university in the United States, according to the

Center for World University Rankings, which in 2015 crowned the University of California at Berkeley the best nationally—and the seventh-best in the world. Stanford University ranks second-best in the world among universities of any kind, private or public. And the University of California at San Francisco is rated sixth-best public university in the country, based on educational quality, alumni satisfaction and achievement, and quality of faculty. The Bay Area is renowned for higher education. Whether you're looking to enroll in a bachelor's, master's, or PhD program; are pursuing continuing education; or are interested in a lecture series or stage performance, the possibilities are endless. A few of the many colleges and universities:

## SAN FRANCISCO

- **Golden Gate University** offers a private, accredited program in the downtown area, with both graduate and undergraduate programs in business, law, and public administration (536 Mission St, 415-442-7000, www.ggu.edu).
- **San Francisco State University** offers undergraduate and graduate degrees, and is one of the largest schools in the state's university system (1600 Holloway Ave, 415-338-1111, www.sfsu.edu).
- **University of California at San Francisco** is renowned for health sciences research, patient care, and education (500 Parnassus Ave, 415-476-9000, www.ucsf.edu).
- **University of California Hastings College of the Law** is consistently ranked one of the top law schools in the country (200 McAllister St, www.uchastings.edu).
- **University of San Francisco**, founded in 1855 by Jesuit leaders, was San Francisco's first institution of higher learning. It offers undergraduate and graduate degrees in nursing, business, education, law, and other disciplines (2130 Fulton St, 415-422-5555, www.usfca.edu).

## NORTH BAY

- **Dominican University of California**, affiliated with the Catholic Church, is known for its counseling psychology, education, and music programs; it offers bachelor's and master's degrees (50 Acacia Ave, San Rafael, 415-457-4440, www.dominican.edu).
- **Sonoma State University**, founded in 1960, is one of the youngest universities in the California State University system. Located 50 miles north of San Francisco, with a 220-acre campus, the school offers degrees and certificates in a variety of disciplines (1801 E Cotati Ave, Rohnert Park, 707-664-2880, www.sonoma.edu).

## EAST BAY

- **California State University, East Bay** (formerly California State University, Hayward) has two main campuses—one on a hilltop overlooking the city of Hayward to the west, and the other in the Concord foothills of Mt. Diablo (25800 Carlos Bee Blvd, Hayward, 510-885-3000, and 4700 Ygnacio Valley Rd, Concord, 925-602-4700; www.csuhayward.edu).

- **John F. Kennedy University** has locations in Berkeley, Pleasant Hill, and Campbell, and offers courses geared to adult students pursuing degrees in counseling, library or museum arts, management, law, and liberal arts (www.jfku.edu).
- **Mills College**, founded in 1852, is the oldest women's college in the western United States, with a rich history of excellence in the fields of liberal arts and science. The college offers undergraduate and graduate degrees (5000 MacArthur Blvd, Oakland, 510-430-2255, www.mills.edu).
- **Saint Mary's College** is based in the hilly, wooded, secluded community of Moraga. Classes are small and instruction excellent, with undergraduate and graduate degrees (1928 St Mary's Rd, Moraga, 925-631-4000, www.stmarys-ca.edu).
- **University of California, Berkeley**, crowned the country's best public university in 2015 by the Center for World University Rankings, has long been considered the finest school in the UC system. Founded in 1868 and sprawled across a 1,500-acre wooded urban campus, it has top-notch facilities, faculty, and courses in hundreds of disciplines, at both undergraduate and graduate levels. Admission competition is stiff, to say the least: Berkeley admitted 17 percent of applicants in 2014 (510-642-6000, www.berkeley.edu).

## PENINSULA & SOUTH BAY

- **San Jose State University**, in the heart of Silicon Valley, offers the nation's only undergraduate nuclear science lab, a deep-sea research ship, and centers for the study of Beethoven and John Steinbeck (1 Washington Sq, San Jose, 408-924-2000, www.sjsu.edu).
- **Santa Clara University**, founded in 1851 by the Jesuits, is recognized as California's oldest institution of higher learning. Today it's known for law, business, and engineering schools (500 El Camino Real, Santa Clara, 408-554-4000, www.scu.edu).
- **Stanford University**, the world's second-best university, according to 2015 rankings by the Center for World University Rankings, is located in scenic Palo Alto, at the northern end of Silicon Valley. It is known for excellence in arts and sciences, and for a highly regarded faculty and facilities—including its medical center. Stanford's hospital is the Bay Area's fifth best, according to the US Department of Health & Human Services' database of patient satisfaction; the new Stanford hospital is scheduled to open in 2018 (450 Serra Mall, 650-723-2300, www.stanford.edu).

## SURROUNDING AREAS

- **University of California at Davis**, about 70 miles northeast of San Francisco and 15 miles west of Sacramento, is a top-rated research university offering undergraduate and graduate degrees in a range of fields, and is based in a beautiful college town that is known as one of the most bicycle-friendly communities in the nation (1 Shields Ave, Davis, 530-752-1011, www.ucdavis.edu).
- **University of California at Santa Cruz**, an idyllic beachside campus with deer roaming freely on the hilltop fields, has an exceptional academic reputation and renowned research teams, including one of the world's leading planetary science programs (1156 High St, Santa Cruz, 831-459-0111, www.ucsc.edu).

THE BAY AREA IS A SHOPPER'S PARADISE—AND A WINDOW SHOPPER'S nightmare, given that so many irresistibly good choices can cause indecision. Whether you prefer shopping in familiar chain stores or independent shops, they're all here, from secondhand stores to department megastores to flea markets—and, because of the mild climate, garage and yard sales year round.

## MALLS/SHOPPING CENTERS

A few of the most popular:

### SAN FRANCISCO

- **Embarcadero Center**, 1 Embarcadero Center, 415-772-0700, www.embarcaderocenter.com
- **Ghirardelli Square**, 900 N Point St, 415-775-5500, www.ghirardellisq.com
- **Japan Center**, Post St between Webster and Laguna, 415-567-4573, www.sfjapantown.org
- **Metreon**, 135 4th St, 415-369-6000, www.shoppingmetreon.com
- **Stonestown Galleria**, 3251 20th Ave, 415-759-2626, www.stonestowngalleria.com
- **Westfield San Francisco Centre**, 865 Market St, 415-495-5656, www.westfield.com/sanfrancisco

### NORTH BAY

- **Larkspur Landing Shopping Center**, Larkspur Landing Circle, Larkspur, 415-461-5700, www.marincountrymart.com
- **Northgate Mall**, Los Ranchitos Rd and Las Gallinas Ave, San Rafael, 415-479-5955, www.shopatnorthgate.com
- **Strawberry Village**, Redwood Highway Frontage Rd, Mill Valley, www.strawberryvillage.com

- **Town Center**, 100 Corte Madera Town Center, Corte Madera, 415-924-2961, www.shoptowncenter.com
- **The Village**, Hwy 101 and Paradise Dr, Corte Madera, 415-924-8557, www.villageatcortemadera.com

## EAST BAY
- **Bayfair Mall**, 15555 14th St, San Leandro, 510-357-6000, www.shopbayfair.com
- **Hilltop Mall**, 2200 Hilltop Mall Rd, Richmond, 510-223-1933, www.shophiltop.com
- **Jack London Square**, Broadway and Embarcadero, Oakland, 866-295-9853, www.jacklondonsquare.com
- **NewPark Mall**, 2086 Newpark Mall, Newark, 510-794-5523, www.newparkmall.com
- **Sun Valley**, 1 Sunvalley Mall, Concord, 925-825-0400, www.shopsunvalley.com
- **The Willows**, 1975 Diamond Blvd, Concord, 925-825-4001, www.willowsshopping.com

## PENINSULA
- **Hillsdale Mall**, 60 31st Ave, San Mateo, 650-345-8222, www.hillsdale.com
- **Serramonte Center**, Serramonte Blvd and I-280, Daly City, 650-301-3360, www.serramontecenter.com
- **The Shops at Tanforan**, 1150 El Camino Real, San Bruno, 650-873-2000, www.theshopsattanforan.com
- **Stanford Shopping Center**, 660 Stanford Shopping Center, Palo Alto, 650-617-8200, www.stanfordshop.com
- **Town & Country Village**, El Camino Real and Embarcadero Rd, Palo Alto, 650-325-3266, www.tandcvillage.com

## SOUTH BAY
- **Great Mall of the Bay Area**, 447 Great Mall Dr, Milpitas, 408-956-2033, www.simon.com/mall/great-mall
- **Oakridge Mall**, 925 Blossom Hill Rd, San Jose, 408-578-2912, www.westfield.com/oakridge
- **The Pruneyard**, 1875 S Bascom Ave, Campbell, 877-367-0006, www.thepruneyard.com
- **Santana Row**, San Jose, 408-551-4611, www.santanarow.com
- **Westfield Valley Fair Mall**, Santa Clara, 408-248-4451, www.westfield.com/valleyfair

## OUTLET MALLS

Whether outlet malls offer more affordable merchandise than elsewhere is debatable, especially with online options. What's certain is that their popularity has soared. Check www.outletsonline.com for more information. In the South Bay, the city of Gilroy is renowned for its outlets, clustered along Highway 101. Below are a few of the Bay Area's most popular outlet malls:

- **Gilroy Premium Outlets**, 681 Leavesley Rd, Highway 101 at Leavesley exit, Gilroy, 408-842-3729, www.premiumoutlets.com/gilroy
- **Great Mall of the Bay Area**, 447 Great Mall Dr, Milpitas, 408-956-2033, www.simon.com/mall/great-mall
- **Marina Square**, 1201 Marina Blvd, San Leandro,.www.marinasquarecenter.com
- **Vacaville Commons**, 321 Nut Tree Rd, Vacaville, www.premiumoutlets.com/vacaville

## DEPARTMENT STORES

- **Gump's**, the height of elegance in San Francisco department stores, stocks furniture and other home accessories with special attention to impeccable display—and the service is top-notch (135 Post St, 415-982-1616, www.gumps.com).
- **JC Penney** is a national department store chain that sells just about everything you'll need—and stuff you won't—for your home; it has numerous Bay Area locations (www.jcpenney.com).
- **Macy's** has a Union Square store that is reportedly the second-largest in the nation, behind the flagship store in Manhattan. You can fully stock your closets and furnish your home. Bay Area locations include San Francisco (Union Square, Stockton & O'Farrell sts, 415-397-3333), Peninsula (1 Serramonte Center, Daly City, 650-994-3333), East Bay (Bayfair Mall, San Leandro, 510-357-3333), North Bay (Northgate Mall, San Rafael, 415-499-5200, www.macys.com).
- **Neiman-Marcus**, the opulent retailer, carries expensive accessories and has an extensive gourmet department (150 Stockton St, San Francisco, 415-362-3900; 400 Stanford Shopping Center, Palo Alto, 650-329-3300, www.neimanmarcus.com).
- **Nordstrom**, a Seattle-based retailer, is staffed by employees who have a reputation for being helpful, courteous, and knowledgeable about products; merchandise ranges from shoes and clothing to jewelry and cosmetics, though no home furnishings. Most popular are the women's shoe sales. Bay Area locations include: San Francisco: Westfield Shopping Centre (the second-largest Nordstrom in the United States), 865 Market St, 415-243-8500; Stonestown Galleria, 285 Winston Dr, 415-753-1344; Peninsula: Hillsdale Mall, San Mateo, 650-570-5111; North Bay: The Village at Corte Madera, 1870 Redwood Hwy, Corte Madera, 415-927-1690; East Bay: 1200 Broadway Plaza, Walnut Creek, 925-930-7959.
- **Saks Fifth Avenue** is an upscale retailer with clothing, jewelry, cosmetics—a new 40,500-square-foot location opened in 2015 on Market St off 5th, in San Francisco, complementing the original store at 384 Post St (415-986-4300, www.saksfifthavenue.com).

## DISCOUNT DEPARTMENT STORES AND OUTLETS

Discount chains **Target, Kmart**, and **Wal-Mart** all do business (and plenty of it) throughout the Bay Area. Below are a few local discount outlet stores:

- **Nordstrom Rack**, 555 9th St, San Francisco, 415-934-1211; Metro Shopping Center, 81 Colma Blvd, Colma, 650-755-1444; the discount rack for all the Nordstrom stores, www.nordstrom.com
- **The North Face Outlet**, 1238 5th St, Berkeley, 510-526-3530
- **Rochester Big & Tall**, for men, 700 Mission St, San Francisco, 415-982-6455; 319 S Winchester Blvd, San Jose, 408-244-8255; 1337 N Main St, Walnut Creek, 925-407-1000, www.rochesterclothing.com

## COMPUTERS/ELECTRONICS/APPLIANCES

The computer was invented in the Bay Area, the birthplace and headquarters of the digital revolution. Experts aren't hard to find. This list includes some top-rated computer and electronics retailers; check www.yelp.com for additional options.

- **Apple Store**, One Stockton St, San Francisco, 415-392-0202; 3251 20th Ave, Stonestown Shopping Center, San Francisco, 415-242-7890; 1301 Burlingame Ave, Burlingame, 650-340-1167; 1516 Redwood Hwy, Corte Madera, 415-927-5820; 5656 Bay St, Emeryville, 510-350-2400; 451 University Ave, Palo Alto, 650-617-9000; 925 Blossom Hill Rd, Oakridge Shopping Center, San Jose; 408-362-4930; 1129 S Main St, Walnut Creek, 925-210-2020; 2855 Stevens Creek Blvd, Santa Clara, Valley Fair Shopping Center, 408-551-2150, www.apple.com/retail
- **We Fix Macs**, 1245 Laurelwood Rd, Santa Clara, 408-850-3300; 3159 El Camino Real, Palo Alto, 650-813-6161; www.allmac.com
- **Best Buy**, 1717 Harrison St, San Francisco, 415-626-9682; 2675 Geary Blvd, San Francisco, 415-409-4960; 200 Colma Blvd, Colma, 650-756-8711; 1250 El Camino Real, San Bruno, 650-244-5139; 180 Donahue St, Marin City, 415-332-6529; 3700 Mandela Pkwy, Emeryville, 510-420-0323; 1127 Industrial Rd, San Carlos, 650-622-0050; 3090 Stevens Creek Blvd, San Jose, 408-241-6040; for more Bay Area locations visit www.bestbuy.com
- **Fry's**, 340 Portage Ave, Palo Alto, 650-496-6000; 600 E Hamilton Ave, Campbell, 408-364-3700; 1077 East Arques Ave, Sunnyvale, 408-617-1300; 550 E Brokaw Rd, San Jose, 408-487-1000, www.frys.com

## BEDS, BEDDING & BATH

A few of the Bay Area's well-rated stores:

- **Bed Bath and Beyond**, numerous locations, www.bedbathandbeyond.com
- **Duxiana**, 1803 Fillmore St, San Francisco, 415-673-7134, www.dux.com
- **Earthsake**, 1772 4th St, Berkeley, 510-559-8440, www.earthsake.com

- **Mancini's Sleepworld**, 2950 Geary Blvd, San Francisco, 415-750-0500; 3806 El Camino Real, San Mateo, 650-212-0200; www.sleepworld.com
- **Mattress Discounters**, multiple locations, 800-289-2233, www.mattressdiscounters.com
- **McRoskey Mattresses**, 1687 Market St, San Francisco, 415-861-4532; 220 Hamilton Ave, Palo Alto, 650-327-1966; www.mcroskey.com
- **Scheuer Linens**, 340 Sutter St, San Francisco, 415-392-2813, www.scheuerlinens.com
- **Warm Things**, 3063 Fillmore St, San Francisco, 415-931-1660; 6011 College Ave, Oakland, 510-428-9329; www.warmthingsonline.com

## CARPETS & RUGS

- **Carpet Connection**, 1460 Egbert Ave, San Francisco, 415-550-7125, www.carpetconnection-sfbayarea.com
- **Claremont Rug Company**, 6087 Claremont Ave, Oakland, 510-654-0816, www.claremontrug.com
- **Conklin Brothers**, 1801 S Grant St, San Mateo, 650-432-6063, www.conklinbros.com
- **Cost Plus World Market**, 2552 Taylor St, San Francisco, 415-928-6200; 890 Jefferson Ave, Redwood City, 650-701-1820; 101 Clay St, Oakland, 510-834-4440, www.worldmarket.com
- **The Floor Store**, 5327 Jacuzzi St, Suite 2A, Richmond, 510-527-3203, www.floorstores.com
- **Pier 1 Imports**, 3535 Geary Blvd, San Francisco, 415-387-6642; 2501 El Camino Real, Redwood City, 650-364-6608; 20610 Stevens Creek Blvd, Cupertino 408-253-4512; 1009 Blossom Hill Rd, San Jose, 408-978-9555, www.pier1.com

## FURNITURE

There are one billion furniture stores in the Bay Area, more or less. To list them all would be lunacy, so start instead with this select list of well-reviewed favorites—and be sure to check www.yelp.com for additional highlights:

- **Cort Furniture Clearance Center**, 2925 Meade Ave, Santa Clara, 408-727-1470; 426 El Camino Real, San Bruno, 650-615-0406; 1240 Willow Pass Rd, Concord, 925-609-9127, www.cort.com/furniture
- **Crate & Barrel**, 55 Stockton St, San Francisco, 415-982-5200; Stanford Shopping Center, Palo Alto, 650-321-7800,; Hillsdale Shopping Center, San Mateo, 650-341-900; 301 Santana Row, San Jose, 408-247-0600; Crate & Barrel Outlet Store, 1785 4th St, Berkeley, 510-528-5500; for more Bay Area stores check out www.crateandbarrel.com

- **Design Plus,** stylish consignment gallery with excellent furniture, 333 8th St, San Francisco, 415-800-8030; 733 Francisco Blvd East, San Rafael, 415-455-8165, www.designplusgallery.com
- **Flegel's,** 1654 2nd St, San Rafael, 415-454-0502; 870 Santa Cruz Ave, Menlo Park, 650-326-9661, www.flegels.com
- **Hoot Judkins,** offers a wide selection of finished and unfinished furniture at reasonable prices; 1269 Veterans Blvd, Redwood City, 650-367-8181; 1400 El Camino Real, Millbrae, 650-952-5600, www.hootjudkins.com
- **IKEA,** various locations throughout the Bay Area, including 4400 Shellmound St, Emeryville, 510-420-4532; 1700 E Bayshore Road, East Palo Alto, 650-323-4532, www.ikea.com
- **Nest,** San Francisco: 2300 Fillmore St, 415-292-6199; 2340 Polk St, 415-292-6198, www.nestsf.com
- **Noriega Furniture,** 1455 Taraval St, San Francisco, 415-564-4110, www.noriegafurniture.com
- **Scandinavian Designs,** 317-South B St, San Mateo, 650-340-0555; 2101 Shattuck Ave, Berkeley, 510-848-8250; 1212 4th St, San Rafael, 415-457-5500, www.scandinaviandesigns.com
- **The Wooden Duck,** 1823 Eastshore Hwy, Berkeley, 510-848-3575; 1848 4th St, San Rafael, 415-453-0345, www.thewoodenduck.com
- **Z Gallerie,** 2154 Union St, San Francisco, 415-567-4890; 1731 4th St, Berkeley, 510-525-7591; 215 Corte Madera Town Center, 415-924-3088; 378 Santana Row, San Jose, 408-615-9863, www.zgallerie.com

## HOUSEWARES

If shopping online at Overstock.com and Amazon.com doesn't meet your needs, try a few of these crowd-pleasers:

- **Bed, Bath & Beyond,** various locations throughout the Bay Area, including 555 9th St, 415-252-0490, www.bedbathandbeyond.com
- **Cost Plus World Market,** 2552 Taylor St, 415-928-6200, www.worldmarket.com
- **Crate & Barrel,** 55 Stockton St, San Francisco, 415-982-5200; Stanford Shopping Center, Palo Alto, 650-321-7800; Hillsdale Shopping Center, San Mateo, 650-341-900; 301 Santana Row, San Jose, 408-247-0600; Crate & Barrel Outlet Store, 1785 4th St, Berkeley, 510-528-5500, for more Bay Area stores visit www.crateandbarrel.com
- **IKEA,** 4400 Shellmound St, Emeryville, 510-420-4532; 1700 E Bayshore Rd, East Palo Alto, 650-323-4532; www.ikea.com
- **Pier One Imports,** Pier One Imports, 3535 Geary Blvd, San Francisco, 415-387-6642; 2501 El Camino Real, Redwood City, 650-364-6608; 20610 Stevens Creek Blvd, Cupertino 408-253-4512; 1009 Blossom Hill Rd, San Jose, 408-978-9555, www.pier1.com

- **Pottery Barn**, 2390 Market St, San Francisco, 415-861-0800; 2100 Chestnut St, 415-441-1787; for other Bay Area locations check www.potterybarn.com
- **Sur La Table,** 77 Maiden Ln, San Francisco, 415-732-7900; Ferry Building Marketplace, 415-262-9970; 1806 4th St, Berkeley, 510-849-2252; 23 University Ave, Los Gatos, 408-395-6946; cookware, kitchenware, linens, small appliances, and tableware; www.surlatable.com
- **Williams-Sonoma**, 340 Post St, San Francisco, 415-362-9450; 2 Embarcadero Center, San Francisco, 415-421-2033; Stonestown Galleria, San Francisco, 415-242-1473; Hillsdale Mall, San Mateo, 650-574-2818; 180 El Camino Real, Palo Alto, 650-321-3486; The Village, Corte Madera, 415-924-6799, www.williams-sonoma.com
- **The Wok Shop**, 718 Grant Ave, 415-989-3797, San Francisco, www.wokshop.com

## HARDWARE/PAINTS/WALLPAPER/GARDEN CENTERS

By far the most well-reviewed independent hardware store in the Bay Area is **Cliff's Variety**, cherished for its long family history and Castro Street community-mindedness. Find it at 479 Castro St, San Francisco (415-431-5365, www.cliffsvariety.com). For additional resources, consider these favorites:

### ACE HARDWARE STORES

- **Cole Hardware**, various San Francisco locations, all highly rated, 415-753-2653, www.colehardware.com
- **Discount Builders Supply**, 1695 Mission St, 415-621-8511, www.discountbuilderssupplysf.com
- **Fredericksen Hardware & Paint**, 3029 Fillmore St, 415-292-2950, www.fredericksenhardwareandpaint.com
- **Standard 5 & 10**, 3545 California St, 415-751-5767, www.standard5n10.com

### TRUE VALUE HARDWARE STORES

- **Creative Paint**, 5435 Geary Blvd, 415-666-3380, www.truevalue.com
- **Sunset Hardware**, 3126 Noriega St, 415-661-0607, www.truevalue.com
- **True Value Hardware**, 2244 Irving St, 415-753-6862, www.truevalue.com

### GARDENING STORES

- **Broadway Terrace Nursery**, 4340 Clarewood Dr, Oakland, 510-658-3729, www.broadwayterracenursery.com
- **Flora Grubb Gardens,** highly rated, 1634 Jerrold Ave, 415-626-7256, www.floragrubb.com
- **Native Here Nursery**, focuses on California native plants, 101 Golf Course Dr, Berkeley, 510-549-0211, www.nativeherenursery.org

- **Sloat Garden Centers,** a full range of garden supplies, plants and trees, classes, and friendly, helpful advice; 3rd Ave between Geary and Clement, San Francisco, 415-752-1614; 2700 Sloat Blvd, San Francisco, 415-566-4415; 2000 Novato Blvd, Novato, 415-897-2169; 1580 Lincoln Ave, San Rafael, 415- 453-3977; www.sloatgardens.com
- **Summer Winds Garden Center,** 4606 Almaden Expy, San Jose, 408-266-4400; 725 San Antonio Rd, Palo Alto, 650-493-5136, www.summerwindsca.com

## HOME IMPROVEMENT CENTERS

- **Orchard Supply Hardware (OSH),** 2245 Gellert Blvd, South San Francisco, 650-878-3322; 900 El Camino Real, Millbrae, 415-873-5536; 1151 Anderson Dr, San Rafael, 415-453-7288; 1025 Ashby Ave, Berkeley, 510-540-6638, www.osh.com
- **Home Depot,** 2 Colma Blvd, Colma, 650-755-9600; 2001 Chess Dr, San Mateo, 650-525-9343; 1125 Old County Rd, San Carlos, 650-592-9200; 1781 E Bayshore, East Palo Alto, 650-462-6800; 1933 Davis St, San Leandro, 510-636-9600; 11939 San Pablo Ave, El Cerrito, 510-235-0800; www.homedepot.com

## SECONDHAND SHOPPING

*The Advertiser,* a free weekly circular, lists treasures sold by individuals or at flea markets; the publication can be picked up at supermarkets and newsstands, or perused online by visiting www.sfadvertiser.com. Craigslist (www.craigslist.org, founded and headquartered in San Francisco) is your one-stop shop for everything conceivable—and most things inconceivable.

A few other good places for bargain hunting:

- **Berkeley Outlet,** 711 Heinz Ave, Berkeley, 510-549-2896, www.berkeleyoutlet. com
- **Community Thrift Store,** 623 Valencia St, San Francisco, 415-861-4910, www. communitythriftsf.org
- **Cottrell's Moving and Storage,** 150 Valencia St, San Francisco, 415-431-1000
- **Goodwill,** numerous locations throughout the Bay Area, www.goodwill.org
- **Home Consignment Center,** 863 E Francisco Blvd, San Rafael, 415-456-2765, many other locations in the Bay Area, www.thehomeconsignmentcenter.com
- **Hospice by the Bay Thrift Shop,** 910 Lincoln Ave, San Rafael, 415-459-4686; 910 Grant St, Novato, 415-893-9036, www.hospicebythebay.org
- **Mickey's Monkey,** vintage furniture, 218 Pierce St, San Francisco, 415-864-0693
- **Out of the Closet,** 100 Church St, San Francisco, 415-252-1101, many other Bay Area locations with cheap vintage and used clothing; www.outofthecloset.org
- **People's Bazaar,** 3258 Adeline St, Berkeley, 510-655-8008; www.peoples-bazaar.com
- **Repeat Performance,** 2436 Fillmore St, San Francisco, 415-563-3123, vintage

- **Salvation Army**, 1500 Valencia St, 415-401-0698, has multiple Bay Area locations; www.salvationarmyusa.org
- **St. Vincent de Paul Society**, 6256 Mission St, Daly City, 650-992-9271, has multiple Bay Area locations; www.svdpusa.org
- **Thrift Center**, 1060 El Camino Real, San Carlos, 650-593-1082
- **Thrift Town**, 2101 Mission St, 415-861-1132, www.thrifttown.com
- **Town School Closet**, 1850 Polk St, 415-929-8019, www.townschoolclothescloset.org

## FLEA MARKETS

- **Alameda Point Faire,** 2900 Navy Way, Alameda, 510-522-7500, www.alamedapointantiquesfaire.com
- **Alemany Flea Market**, 100 Alemany Blvd, San Francisco, 415-647-2043
- **Berkeley Flea Market**, Saturdays and Sundays, 7am-7pm, 1937 Ashby Ave, Berkeley, 510-644-0744, www.berkeleyfleamarket.com
- **Coliseum Public Market**, 5401 Coliseum Way, Oakland, 510-534-0325, www.westwinddriveins.com
- **Midgley's Country Flea Market**, 2200 Gravenstein Hwy South, Sebastopol, 707-823-7874, www.mfleamarket.com
- **Norcal Swap Meet**, Laney College, Oakland, 510-769-7266, www.laney.edu
- **San Jose Flea Market**, Wednesday and Friday through Sunday, from dawn to dusk; a huge flea market with live music, produce, food stands, and playgrounds; 1590 Berryessa Road, San Jose, 408-453-1110 or 800-BIG FLEA, www.sjfm.com

## ANTIQUES

The Bay Area is a paradise of antique stores, especially in Napa and Sonoma. The 400 block of Jackson Street in San Francisco's financial district has a high concentration of them. Most of the Jackson Street dealers are members of the Antique Dealers Association of California, and if they don't have what you're looking for they can steer you in the right direction. Market Street at Franklin has lower-priced antique shops. Sacramento Street in Presidio Heights has an array of fine antique shops. And in Marin County, San Anselmo has a small antique row along Sir Francis Drake Boulevard.

# FOOD

It's an experience most Bay Area locals have had: biting into a mouthwatering, locally grown heirloom tomato; or a perfectly ripe cherry sourced one town over; or a wood-fired pizza blistered in a 900-degree oven for 90 seconds, with an airy interior under pinches of mozzarella and basil so good you'll lose all self-control. The Bay Area specializes in irresistibly fresh ingredients. San Francisco has more farmers' markets and restaurants per capita than any other city in the country. Local sustainable produce is so fashionable it's become a fetish in Northern California. The garlic capital of the world, Gilroy, is a few hours south of San Francisco. The artichoke capital of the world, Castroville, is close by. And the world's pumpkin capital and strawberry capital, Half Moon Bay and Watsonville, respectively, are at your doorstep. It's possible to eat enviably well on a tight budget. The Bay Area's let-vegetables-speak-for-themselves movement isn't the only philosophy in town, but it has sparked a revolution, which makes sense in a region blessed with pristine farms. Today's historic drought has hit farmers hard, costing California farmers $1.5 billion annually, but farmers' markets are still top-notch.

Formal dining is also award-winning here: there's no shortage of Michelin-winning masterpieces at lavish organic restaurants, and everything in between, from coastal kitchens' tasting menus to Vietnamese pho and banh mi, handmade Japanese soba noodles, freshly baked Russian poppy buns, and sizzling tandoori sea bass.

First, contain yourself: it is poor etiquette to drool, unless you're on line at one of the new gourmet food trucks parading across the Bay Area as part of a network called **Off the Grid**. (Track the trucks' locations on your smartphone by downloading the mobile app; search the app store for "Off the Grid Markets.")

Vegetarian and vegan restaurants are multiplying—consider **Republic of V** (1624 University Ave, Berkeley, www.republicofvegan.com) and **Pepples Donuts** (6037 San Pablo Ave, Oakland, www.pepplesdonuts.com), which are both enormously popular. For a good tour through vegan life beyond recipes, read the outstanding commentary in a new book by Bay Area author Elizabeth Castoria, *How to Be Vegan: Tips, Tricks, and Strategies for Cruelty-Free Eating, Living, Dating, Travel, Decorating, and More* (www.elizabethcastoria.com). And look up the local pioneer Miyoko Schinner (www.miyokoskitchen.com), who is popularizing vegan cheese (cultured nut products), alongside Bay Area companies **Kite Hill** (www.kite-hill.com) and **Fromagerie Esseme** (www.fromagerieesseme.com). Think smoked pecan, sharp cashew, and creamy macadamia.

Scientists in Oakland and Sunnyvale recently formed the **Real Vegan Cheese** group, which bioengineers vegan cheese and in 2014 won the International Genetically Engineered Machine competition. Also newsworthy on the organic food front is **Millennium** (www.millenniumrestaurant.com), an upscale vegan restaurant that moved recently from San Francisco to Rockridge. For the latest insight on vegetarianism and veganism in the Bay Area, visit **www.vegansaurus. com**, **www.bayareaveg.org**, and **www.vegnews.com**. For meat eaters, just walk outside in any direction and follow the aromas of blissful dim sum (**Koi Palace** in Daly City), Ethiopian berbere chicken (**Zeni** in San Jose), citrus ceviche (**Limón** in San Francisco), flame-kissed Korean beef (**Jin Mi** in San Francisco), crispy Thai salmon rolls (**Chili Cha Cha 2** in San Francisco), and vinegar-spiked Indian vindaloo (**Darbar** in Palo Alto). Search Google Maps by cuisine and read **www.sf.eater.com** and **www.ediblesanfrancisco.com** for insider commentary, guides, and food maps. For chat boards about Bay Area food, visit **Chow.com** (www.chowhound. chow.com/boards/1).

A strong selection of budget groceries, imported goods, and natural-food markets spells good news for newcomers. Budget shoppers head to **Foods Co.**, **Food 4 Less**, **Grocery Outlet**, **Smart & Final**, and **Pak-N-Save**. The next level includes **Safeway**, **Lucky**, and **SaveMart**. **Trader Joe's** offers an array of high-quality foods, as well as beers and wines, for reasonable prices. **Andronico's** reigns supreme at the high end. **Whole Foods** is the big-chain health food store, and **Mollie Stone's** is a more local natural-food chain. **Rainbow Grocery** (www. rainbow.coop) is a bulk-food paradise in San Francisco, and **Berkeley Bowl** is similarly cherished in Berkeley, now with two locations (www.berkeleybowl.com). Also head over to **Serious Eats** online (www.seriouseats.com); the site's managing culinary editor, James Kenji López-Alt, recently moved to San Francisco from New York, and has an avid following wherever he goes.

If all else fails, order in. At least one new restaurant opens every week in San Francisco, and delivery services are multiplying, with websites and mobile apps to keep you spoon-fed by services like www.spoonrocket.com, www.delivery. com, www.grubhub.com, www.orderahead.com, www.doordash.com, www. munchery.com, and www.blueapron.com.

## SPECIALTY GROCERS

### SAN FRANCISCO

- **Bi-Rite**, fashionable spot for locally sourced fruit, vegetables, seafood, meat, and more—all organic and exceptionally good, 3639 18th St, 415-241-9760, and 550 Divisadero St, 415-551-7900, www.biritemarket.com
- **Chinese food markets**, featuring some of the best produce in town, Irving St in the Sunset, and Clement St in the Richmond District; the top rated is New May Wah, 707 Clement St, 415-221-9826
- **Cost Plus World Market**, a discount clearing house for nonperishable imports with a variety of wines, beers, teas, and chocolates, as well as housewares; 2552 Taylor St, 415-928-6200, www.worldmarket.com
- **Ferry Building Marketplace**, dozens of high-end specialty shops, including the North Bay's Cowgirl Creamery Cheese Shop, Acme Bread Company, and the San Francisco Fish Company, with an outdoor waterside plaza that hosts one of the Bay Area's most popular farmers' markets (see details below); Embarcadero at Market St, 415-983-8000, www.ferrybuildingmarketplace.com
- **Good Life Grocery**, friendly Bernal Heights shop with a good selection of produce, fine cheeses, and wines; 448 Cortland Ave, 415-648-3221
- **Lucca Ravioli**, traditional Italian deli with exceptional homemade ravioli and delicious tomato focaccia; 1100 Valencia St, www.luccaravioli.com

- **Mollie Stone's,** a large, upscale natural-foods shop with a wide selection, and several additional locations throughout the area; 2435 California St, 415-567-4902, www.molliestones.com
- **Rainbow Grocery,** popular, eco-friendly, worker-owned co-op with a vast selection of bulk products from grains to pastas to teas, organic produce, a huge vitamin and mineral selection, and an amazing olive bar (you'll have to go elsewhere for your meat though); 1745 Folsom St, 415-863-0620, www.rainbowgrocery.org
- **Whole Foods,** natural-food giant offering a wide array of bulk products, a large prepared foods area, a decent house brand, popular salad bar, and everything to meet your basic grocery needs; various locations, www.wholefoodsmarket.com

### NORTH BAY
- **Mill Valley Market,** 12 Corte Madera, Mill Valley, 415-388-3222
- **Mollie Stone's,** 100 Harbor Dr, Sausalito, 415-331-6900; Bon Air Shopping Center, Greenbrae, 415-461-1164; www.molliestones.com
- **Whole Foods,** various locations, 415-451-6333; www.wholefoodsmarket.com

### EAST BAY
- **Berkeley Bowl,** 2020 Oregon St, Berkeley, 510-843-6929, and 920 Heinz Ave, Berkeley, (510) 898-9555; a beloved local favorite that draws shoppers from throughout the Bay Area, offers bulk foods, organic produce, seafood, and a wide variety of goods and great prices
- **Cheese Board Collective,** 1504 Shattuck Ave, 510-549-3183, www.cheese-boardcollective.coop; popular Berkeley co-op with a rotating variety of freshly baked breads, a wide selection of cheeses, and a tasty pizza place a few doors down at 1512 Shattuck Ave
- **Cost Plus World Market,** 101 Clay St, Oakland, 510-834-4440, www.worldmarket.com
- **G.B. Ratto and Co,** 821 Washington St, Oakland, 510-832-6503
- **Market Hall,** 5655 College Ave, Oakland, 510-250-6000; specialty stores for wine, coffee, tea, pasta, produce, poultry, meat, and fish
- **Monterey Market,** 1550 Hopkins, Berkeley, 510-526-6042; incredible produce
- **Monterey Fish Market,** 1582 Hopkins St, Berkeley, 510-525-5600
- **New India Bazaar,** extraordinary array of Indian ingredients, from Kashmiri chili to kasoori methi (dried fenugreek) and amchoor (mango) powder, with locations in Milpitas, Dublin, Fremont, Santa Clara, Sunnyvale, and Pleasanton, www.newindiabazar.com
- **Pacific East Mall,** 3288 Pierce St, Richmond, 510-527-3000
- **Whole Foods,** various locations, www.wholefoodsmarket.com

## PENINSULA & SOUTH BAY

- **Cosentino's Vegetable Haven**, South Bascom and Union aves, San Jose, 408-377-6661; vegetables, bulk items, ethnic condiments
- **Cost Plus World Market**, 423 Serramonte Blvd, Daly City, 415-994-7090
- **Draeger's**, 1010 University Ave, Menlo Park, 650-324-7700; imported cheeses, deli, produce, and wine
- **Mollie Stone's**, 164 South California Ave, Palo Alto, 650-323-8361; 1477 Chapin Ave, 650-558-9992, Burlingame; 22 Bayhill Shopping Center, San Bruno, 650-873-8075; 49 W 42nd Ave, San Mateo, 650-372-2828, www.molliestones.com
- **New India Bazaar**, see description above; locations in Milpitas, Dublin, Fremont, Santa Clara, Sunnyvale, and Pleasanton, www.newindiabazar.com
- **Takahashi**, 221 S Claremont St, San Mateo, 650-343-0394; Southeast Asian, Hawaiian, and more
- **Whole Foods**, various locations, www.wholefoodsmarket.com

## WAREHOUSE SHOPPING

**Costco**, www.costco.com, a giant in the club-shopping world, has cavernous warehouse-type facilities stacked floor to ceiling with restaurant-trade items like gallon jars of olives, more mayonnaise than you can suck down in a lifetime, family cases of chopped tomatoes, pet food, tires, cleaning supplies, clothing, and pharmaceuticals. Basic membership costs $55 a year, and there are dozens of locations around the Bay Area.

## FARMERS' MARKETS

The Bay Area boasts some of the world's most productive farmland in and surrounding the nine counties, from the San Joaquin Valley to Sonoma, Salinas, and Monterey, and farmers' markets offer delicious, inexpensive deals with free samples. Below is a handful of local favorites, but this list is not comprehensive; see the neighborhood descriptions above for additional markets, and for a full list, visit www.cafarmersmkts.com/find-your-farmers-market.

### SAN FRANCISCO

- **100 Alemany Blvd**, Saturday, dawn to dusk, year round
- **Ferry Building Marketplace**, Ferry Building, Tuesday, 10 a.m.–2 p.m.; Saturday 8 a.m.–2 p.m.
- **Fillmore Farmers' Market**, O'Farrell and Fillmore sts at the Fillmore Center Plaza, Saturday 9 a.m.–1 p.m., year round
- **United Nations Plaza**, Market St (between 7th and 8th sts), Sunday and Wednesday 7 a.m.–5 p.m., year round

## CONTRA COSTA COUNTY

- **El Cerrito**, El Cerrito Plaza, corner of San Pablo and Fairmont aves, Tuesday and Saturday, variable times, year round.
- **Kensington**, Oak View Ave at Colusa Circle, Saturday, 10 a.m.–2 p.m. year round
- **Moraga**, corner of Moraga Road and Moraga Way, Sunday, 9 a.m.–1 p.m., year round
- **Pinole**, corner of Fernando Ave and Pear St, Saturday, 9 a.m.–1 p.m. year round
- **Richmond**, Civic Center and McDonald, Friday, 8 a.m.–5 p.m., year round; and Nevin Plaza, Wednesday, 10 a.m.–2 p.m., summer and fall; and Park Place, 4–8 p.m., summer and fall
- **San Pablo,** City Hall parking lot, San Pablo Ave, 10 a.m.–2 p.m., June–September

## MARIN COUNTY

- **Corte Madera**, Village Shopping Center, Wednesday, noon–5 p.m., year round
- **Novato**, downtown (Grant Ave between Reichert and Machin aves), Tuesday, 4 p.m.–8 p.m., April–September
- **San Rafael**, Civic Center parking lot, Sunday and Thursday, 8 a.m.–1 p.m., year round
- **Sausalito**, Bridgeway and Tracy, Friday, 4 p.m.–8 p.m., May–October

## SAN MATEO COUNTY

- **Belmont,** Caltrain parking lot, Sunday
- **Burlingame**, Park Road and Burlingame Ave, Sunday, 9 a.m.–1:30 p.m., and Thursday, 3–7 p.m., May through November
- **Daly City**, Serramonte Center, Thursday, 9 a.m.–1 p.m., and Saturday, 10 a.m.–2 p.m., year round
- **Menlo Park**, Crane and Chestnut, Sunday, 9 a.m.–1 p.m., year round
- **Millbrae**, 200 Broadway, Saturday, 8 a.m.–1 p.m., year round
- **Redwood City**, Arguello between Marshall and Brewster sts, Saturday, 8 a.m.–noon, summer
- **San Carlos**, Laurel and Cherry sts, Thursday, 4–8 p.m., seasonal

## ALAMEDA COUNTY

- **Alameda**, Haight Ave at Webster St, Alameda, Tuesday and Saturday, 9 a.m.–1 p.m., year round
- **Berkeley**, Saturday Berkeley Farmers' Market, 2151 Martin Luther King Jr. Way, Saturday, 10 a.m. to 3 p.m., year round; North Berkeley Farmers' Market, Shattuck Ave at Rose St, Thursday, 3–7 p.m.; South Berkeley Farmers' Market, Adeline and 63rd sts, Tuesday, 2–6:30 p.m., year round
- **El Cerrito,** El Cerrito Plaza, Tuesday and Saturday, 9 a.m.–1 p.m., year round
- **Oakland**, Freedom Farmers' Market, 5316 Telegraph Ave, Oakland, Saturday 10 a.m.–3 p.m.; Fruitvale Farmers' Market, Fruitvale BART station, 3401 East 12 St, Sunday, 10 a.m.–3 p.m.; Grand Lake Farmers' Market, Grand and Lake Park aves,

Saturday, 9 a.m.– 2 p.m.; Jack London Square Farmers' Market, Webster and Water sts, Sunday, 10 a.m.–2 p.m., year round; Montclair Village Farmers' Market, LaSalle and Moraga aves, Sunday 9 a.m.–1 p.m.; Old Oakland Farmers' Market, 9th St between Broadway and Clay sts, Friday, 8 a.m.–2 p.m.; Temescal Farmers' Market, DMV parking lot, 5300 Claremont Ave, Sunday, 9 a.m.–1 p.m.; Uptown Oakland Farmers' Market, 1 Kaiser Plaza, Wednesday, 10 a.m.–2 p.m., year round
- **Richmond**, 24th St and Barrett Ave, Friday, 8 a.m.–5 p.m., year round

## SANTA CLARA COUNTY
- **Cupertino**, Cupertino Square parking lot, Wolfe Rd at I-280, Friday, 9 a.m.–1 p.m., year round
- **Palo Alto**, Hamilton and Gilman, Saturday, 8 a.m.–noon, May–December
- **San Jose downtown**, Jackson between Sixth and Seventh, Sunday, 8 a.m.–noon, year round
- **Vallejo**, Georgia and Marin sts, Saturday, 9 a.m.–1 p.m., year round

## SONOMA COUNTY
- **Bodega Bay**, 2255 Highway 1, Sunday, 10 a.m.–2 p.m., May–October
- **Healdsburg**, North and Vine (Purity Lot), Saturday, 9 a.m.–noon, May–November, and Wednesday, 3:30–6 p.m., June–October
- **Petaluma**, 320 N McDowell Ave, Tuesday, 10 a.m.–1:30 p.m., year round

## NAPA COUNTY
- **Calistoga**, Washington Street (Sharpsteen museum plaza), Saturday, 8:30 a.m.–noon, year round
- **Napa downtown**, 500 1st St (Oxbow parking lot), Tuesday and Saturday, 8 a.m.–12:30 p.m., May–October
- **St. Helena**, Crane Park, Friday, 7:30 a.m.–noon, May–October

# COMMUNITY GARDENS

If you've got time and energy, forget the fruit markets and grow your own instead. San Francisco, Berkeley, Oakland, and surrounding towns have excellent soil and sun for the purpose (when the fog lifts, which it sometimes does). The area is highlighted by a variety of community gardens, ranging from dense urban forests in larger city parks to tiny backyards at local schools and community centers. You'll be assigned a plot of your own to care for, and there're sometimes a waiting list. But urban gardening is a breezy way to get outdoors and meet likeminded neighbors. For information about community gardens in San Francisco, visit www.sfrecpark.org and search for "community gardens."

## SAN FRANCISCO
- **Adam Rogers Garden**, 1220 Oakdale Ave

- **Alemany Farm,** 700 Alemany Blvd
- **Alioto Park Community Garden,** Capp and 20th sts
- **Arkansas Friendship Garden,** 22nd St between Arkansas and Connecticut sts
- **Arlington Community Garden,** Arlington St and Highland Ave
- **Bernal Heights Garden,** Bernal Heights Blvd between Gates and Banks sts
- **Brewster-Rutledge (Miller Memorial),** Brewster and Costa sts
- **Brooks Park,** Ramsell and Shields sts
- **Clipper Community Garden,** Clipper St near Grandview Ave
- **Connecticut St Garden,** 22nd and Connecticut sts
- **Corwin St Community Garden,** Corona Heights Park, 16th and Flint sts
- **Crags Court Garden,** end of Crags Ct, off Berkeley Way
- **Golden Gate Park Community Garden,** Frederick St and Arguello Blvd
- **Good Prospect Garden,** Prospect St and Cortland Ave
- **Hooker Alley (Nob Hill) Garden,** Mason St between Bush and Pine sts
- **Howard & Langton Mini Park Community Garden,** Langton and Howard sts
- **Kid Power Park Community Garden,** 45 Hoff St
- **Koshland Park Community Garden,** Page and Buchanan sts
- **La Grande Community Garden,** end of Dublin St near Russia St
- **Lessing and Sears Community Garden,** Lessing and Sears sts
- **McLaren Park Garden,** Leland Ave and Hahn St
- **Michelangelo Community Garden,** Greenwich St between Jones and Leavenworth sts
- **Noe Beaver Garden,** Noe and Beaver sts
- **Ogden Terrace Community Garden,** Ogden St between Prentiss and Nevada sts
- **Page & Laguna (aka Rose/Page) Community Garden,** Page and Laguna sts
- **Page St Community Garden,** 438 Page St
- **Palega Community Garden,** 500 Felton St
- **Park Street Garden,** end of Park St (Bernal Cut Path)
- **Potrero Del Sol Community Garden,** San Bruno Ave and 20th St
- **Potrero Hill Community Garden** (at MicKinley Square), San Bruno Ave and 20th St
- **States Street (Corona Heights Community Garden),** 100 States St
- **Treat Commons Community Garden** at Parque Ninos Unidos, 23rd St and Treat Ave
- **Victoria Manalo Draves Community Garden,** Folsom and Sherman sts
- **Visitacion Valley Garden,** Arleta St, between Alpha and Rutland sts
- **White Crane Springs Garden,** 7th Ave, near Lawton St
- **Wolfe Lane Community Garden,** Rutledge and Mullen

## BEYOND SAN FRANCISCO

For information on Community Gardens in **Oakland**, contact the Ecology Center, 568 Bellevue Ave, Oakland, www.ecologycenter.org, 510-238-2197.

- **Allendale**, 3711 Suter St, Oakland
- **Arroyo Viejo**, 79th Ave and Arthur St, Oakland
- **Bushrod**, 584 59th St, Oakland
- **Dover**, Dover St between 57th and 58th
- **Fitzgerald Park Urban Farm**, Corner of 34th and Peralta sts
- **Golden Gate**, 1068 62nd St, Oakland
- **Lakeside Horticultural Center Kitchen Garden**, 666 Bellevue Ave, Oakland
- **Marston Campbell**, between 16th and 18th sts and Market and West sts, Oakland
- **Temescal**, 876 47th St; Verdese Carter, 96th and Bancroft aves, Oakland

**Berkeley** is very community garden–friendly and many schools have educational gardens; to find out more, contact **Berkeley Community Gardening Collaborative** (Berkeley, 510-883-9096, www.ecologycenter.org/bcgc).

- **BYA Community Garden**, Allston Way between Bonar and West sts, Berkeley
- **Karl Linn Community Garden**, Peralta Ave and Hopkins St, Berkeley
- **Northside Community Gardens**, Northside Ave and Hopkins St, Berkeley
- **Ohlone Community Garden**, Hearst and McGee aves, Berkeley
- **People's Park Gardens**, Bowditch St between Dwight Way and Haste St, Berkeley
- **Peralta Community Art Garden**, Peralta Ave near Hopkins St, Berkeley
- **South Berkeley Community Garden**, Martin Luther King Jr. Way and Russell St, Berkeley
- **UC College of Natural Resources Garden**, Walnut and Virginia sts, Berkeley
- **West Berkeley Senior Center**, Senior Gardening, 1900 6th St, Berkeley

For **San Jose** visit www.sjcommunitygardens.org. In other cities, contact the local parks and recreation department for information on community gardening programs.

## FOOD DIVERSITY

"Food diversity" has become redundant in a Bay Area where food is as diverse as the neighborhoods themselves, which have everything you'd crave in a single row of restaurants. The old category "ethnic cuisine" has fallen forever out of use in a Bay Area bursting with creative food communities north, south, east, and west: a mouthwatering Sardinian restaurant next to an irresistible Indian chaat house, next to Greek, French, Russian, and Thai cafés. Each of these restaurants may incorporate aspects of the others. Not long ago you'd have to stick to one neighborhood for coriander-infused Vietnamese pho (Polk Street in San Francisco), another for roasted Mexican menudo (the Mission District), a separate corner entirely for perfectly seasoned Pakistani saag aloo methi (the Tenderloin), another for Szechuan claypots (Chinatown), and somewhere else completely for ginger-ponzu Japanese salmon (Japantown in San Francisco and San Jose). That's all changed. With more restaurants per capita than any other area in the United

States, and more farmers' markets, the Bay Area is less defined by food distinctions per neighborhood than by innovation.

For the latest restaurants in today's fast-changing Bay Area, read the reviews, features, and columns in the newspapers, magazines, websites, and mobile apps listed in the **Media Landscape** section above. And if you're frozen with indecision, just follow the food trucks network **Off the Grid** (www.offthegridsf.com), which launched in 2010 and currently includes more than 175 truck vendors rolling through the Bay Area.

## WINES

In case your schedule or tolerance doesn't allow for visiting the country's most renowned wine getaway (Napa and Sonoma counties)—where 600-plus wineries await—you can always try these warehouses:

- **Beltramos**, 1540 El Camino Real, Menlo Park, 650-325-2806, www.beltramos.com
- **BevMo!**, multiple Bay Area locations, www.bevmo.com
- **Cost Plus World Market**, 2552 Taylor St, San Francisco, 415-928-6200; Westlake Center, Daly City, 415-994-7090; 101 Clay St, Oakland, 510-834-4440, www.worldmarket.com
- **The Jug Shop**, 1590 Pacific Ave, San Francisco, 415-885-2922, 800-404-9548, www.thejugshop.com
- **K&L Wine Merchants**, 3005 El Camino Real, Redwood City, 877-559-4637; 638 4th St, San Francisco, 415-896-1734, www.klwines.com
- **The Wine Stop**, 1300 Burlingame Ave, Burlingame, 650-342-5858, www.thewinestop.com

J UST WHEN IT SEEMED AS IF THE BAY AREA COULDN'T GET MORE CRE-
atively diverse in its music, film, and dance festivals, along come new
generations and genres that remind you why you moved here. The possibilities in the Bay Area are as endless as the lines outside the rock clubs, jazz halls,
underground parties, symphony spaces, and university stages. Artistic diversity
is part of the Bay Area's appeal. You'll have no trouble finding museum events,
dance groups, comedy open mics, and improv nights—but you may have trouble
deciding which to attend first.

The most comprehensive listings of Bay Area events used to be found in
the *San Francisco Chronicle*'s "Datebook" section and online at www.sfgate.com.
That's changed. Today there is no central clearinghouse for event calendars in and
around the Bay Area; instead, there are countless, competing websites, and you'll
just have to bookmark them all. For the best and brightest in event calendars, see
the sections below and the **Media Landscape** section above. Also see the highlight of special events in **A Bay Area Year**, later in this book.

Tickets for most events and performances may be purchased at the venue box
offices. For same-day discount tickets to San Francisco theater productions and
full-price tickets to other events, check out the **TIX Bay Area** booth on the east side
of Union Square, where last-minute open seats are sold for half-price. Although
choices are limited, you can score great bargains (350 Powell St, 415-433-7827,
www.tixbayarea.org). Also check out Brown Paper Tickets, www.brownpaper-
tickets.com, which bills itself as the first and only fair-trade ticketing company.
Another option is www.stubhub.com, trusted for tickets to sold-out events but
notoriously pricy. Other ticket agencies are listed at www.yelp.com by location.

## CONTEMPORARY MUSIC

From the rock concerts of the counterculture '60s to the first Asian-American
jazz festival in the country (San Francisco, 1981) and the rise of Oakland's hyphy

hip-hop scene, the Bay Area has been pioneering the sounds and sights of count-less musical revolutions. Long gone are the days of Grateful Dead festivals, and longer gone are the blues chants of the local laborers who built the railroads. But that musical history is still rich in the Bay Area—and made richer by the culture clashes we see today: tech companies moving in are eyed skeptically by artists who respond to rising housing costs by composing ballads about displacement. Tech blips and beeps are heard in new electronic music by local DJs. And more and more locals are discovering the timeless beauty of music at the Stanford Jazz Workshop, the Fillmore Jazz Festival, and the innovative sounds of local legends Jon Jang (piano), Mark Izu (bass), Francis Wong (saxophone), Anthony Brown (drums), Akira Tana (also drums), and countless others who break ground and plant new flags in the music scene.

As San Francisco's rents topped the nation in 2015, local nightclubs faced threats of eviction and inched closer to extinction—but it's not quite an existential crisis yet. Clubs and amphitheaters abound. It is true that some cherished venues closed recently—Café du Nord, Elbo Room, Red Devil Lounge, Lexington Club, Jazz at Pearl's, Yoshi's San Francisco, Rasselas Jazz, and Café Cocomo—many of them pushed out by condo developers and dance clubs. But in a resounding victory for clubgoers, San Francisco passed a measure in 2015 to protect nightclubs from noise complaints by prohibiting neighbors from filing complaints as long as the clubs operate within their entertainment permits. A collective "phew" is still heard throughout the local scene. Beyond the clubs, you'll find underground rock bands playing word-of-mouth shows in the caves at the old Sutro ruins by the ocean.

For hip-hop, dance clubs, rowdy pick-up bars, and late-night clubbing, SOMA is your spot. About a decade ago the area became the target of "cleanup" efforts by city officials. Frequent raids by the police and feds ushered in tighter restric-tions on club operating hours and shut down many of the city's most popular clubs. To this day it's difficult to get an after-hours license in San Francisco, so you'll be hard pressed to find anything (legally) open after 2 a.m. The best-known exception is **Ten 15**, a massive multi-tier dance club with DJs spinning in every room. Long lines form every Friday when the club is open later than the rest (1015 Folsom Street, www.1015.com). For the latest on local bands, shows, and venues, check out the alternative weeklies—*SF Weekly* (www.sfweekly.com), *East Bay Express* (www.eastbayexpress.com), and *Metro Silicon Valley* (www.metroactive.com)—as well as **SF Station** (www.sfstation.com), **SFist** (www.sfist.com), **SFGate** (www.sfgate.com), and the local publications listed at the end of each neighbor-hood description in this book, and in the **Media Landscape** section. To catch local emerging rock bands and fast-rising out-of-town acts, keep close watch of the calendar at **Bottom of the Hill** in San Francisco (www.bottomofthehill.com) and the **Stork Club** in Oakland (www.storkcluboakland.com)—and, above all, keep an eye on **Noise Pop**, the annual indie rock festival (www.noisepop.com).

If you're a fan of arena rock, the name Bill Graham will be familiar to you. Graham, the prolific Bay Area concert promoter, is best remembered for his promotion of San Francisco psychedelic rockers the Grateful Dead and Jefferson Airplane, first at local art spaces and later at the Fillmore. These days his legacy lives on in the venues he popularized, bringing big-time rock acts to the Fillmore and the Warfield, as well as the large, centrally located Civic Center, now officially renamed the **Bill Graham Civic Auditorium** (www.billgrahamcivicauditorium.com).

In the East Bay, the **Oakland Coliseum** (officially called the O.co Coliseum, though no one refers to it that way) is one of the Bay Area's premier outdoor sites for big-name pop stars; it also has an indoor stage. A number of other outdoor venues are used for concerts—chief among them **Shoreline Amphitheatre** in Mountain View and the **Concord Pavilion** (formerly Sleep Train Pavilion) in Concord. Both have covered seating up front, close to the stage, and loads of uncovered lawn behind the seats. Bring a blanket and stretch out. Though it's not outdoors, the **SAP Center** in San Jose (formerly HP Pavilion) gets icons like Madonna.

Jazz and blues used to be the hallmarks of North Beach and the Fillmore District, but today's jazz scene is dispersed across the Bay Area, including the cozy **Red Poppy Art House** (www.redpoppyarthouse.org), the lively **Amnesia** (www.amnesiathebar.com), the academically rigorous **Jazzschool** (www.jazzschool.org), the iconic **Stanford Jazz Workshop** (www.stanfordjazz.org), the biggest-name-in-the-Bay-Area **Yoshi's** (www.yoshis.com—the Oakland club, not the San Francisco outpost, which closed in 2015), and **Kuumbwa Jazz** (www.kuumbwajazz.org). To really learn the history of music in the Bay Area, run an online search for "Edsel Matthews" and "Koncepts Cultural Gallery," and buckle up. Then search for "Keystone Korner" and "San Francisco."

Wherever you go, be forewarned—there is no smoking indoors in public places in San Francisco (or anywhere in California, for that matter). Smoking is officially banned in restaurants, bars, and clubs throughout the state. Of course a handful of places have figured out a way around the law by providing suction fans or indoor-outdoor combination rooms.

For the latest on who's playing where and when, consult the publications and websites listed earlier in this section.

## BAY AREA CONCERT HALLS & NIGHTCLUBS

The following list will help you get started, though it is by no means comprehensive. Call ahead: here today, gone tomorrow is often the case in this fast-paced scene.

### SAN FRANCISCO

- **Bill Graham Civic Auditorium,** a treasured landmark with 6,000 seats in a majestic setting, has hosted the Grateful Dead, Janis Joplin, the Who, and other revolutionary musicians over the years. Today it is a major destination for international tours (99 Grove St, 415-624-8900, www.billgrahamcivicauditorium.com).
- **Bimbo's 365 Club,** an intimate retro club, has had tons of local appeal since 1931; shows are produced by the city's best team of showrunners, including

the masterful Harry Duncan, a longtime producer of soul, funk, jazz, blues, and roots reggae (1025 Columbus Ave, 415-474-0365, www.bimbos365club.com).

• **Biscuits & Blues** features blues and soul of all styles and sensibilities; a full-service restaurant upstairs that serves Cajun cuisine, including jambalaya and fried chicken; and a raw oyster bar (401 Mason St, 415-292-2583, www.biscuitsandblues.com).

• **The Boom Boom Room** is an iconic destination for West Coast blues, jazz, funk, and rock; it was founded by Mississippi blues great John Lee Hooker (1601 Fillmore, 415-673-8000, www.boomboomroom.com).

• **Bottom of the Hill** is a long-reigning champion of indie rock that hosts up-and-coming locals and touring favorites; the outdoor patio is the place to mix and mingle, and to escape the noise (1233 17th St, 415-621-4455, www.bottomofthehill.com).

• **The Edinburgh Castle** offers a tiny stage with a friendly pub atmosphere, excellent beer, and banter; its support of emerging bands makes it a great place to check out local rock groups. The venue hosts a handful of intimate but popular dance nights, and drinkers square off for a test of wits at the Castle Quiz trivia night every Tuesday at 8:30 p.m. (950 Geary St, 415-885-4074, www.thecastlesf.com).

• **The Fillmore** is an ornate, old-fashioned hall that was closed for several years after being ravaged by the 1989 earthquake. Walls lined with posters and photos from its rock glory days provide a suitable backdrop for today's big acts; the upstairs lounge hosts DJs and smaller acts that play between sets on the main stage, plus a snack bar to soothe late-night cravings. Arrive early to snag one of the premier balcony tables (1805 Geary Blvd, 415-346-6000, www.thefillmore.com).

• **The Great American Music Hall** is San Francisco's longest-running music spot, and was voted sixth best club in the nation by *Rolling Stone* recently; it's a safe bet for the greatest rock acts in the city (859 O'Farrell St, 415-885-0750, www.slimspresents.com).

• **Hotel Utah** is a dive in the best sense of the word, with bar-style rock and blues bands (500 4th St, 415-546-6300, www.hotelutah.com).

• **The Independent** is a top-act venue featuring indie rock, electronica, jazz, and reggae (628 Divisadero St, 415-771-1421, www.theindependentsf.com).

• **Plough & Stars**: voted "Best Irish Pub" by the *SF Weekly*, this club offers a variety of imported pints and live Irish music Tuesday through Sunday. Admission is free most nights, with a cover charge on Friday and Saturday (116 Clement St, 415-751-1122, www.theploughandstars.com).

• **Slim's** was opened decades ago by R&B legend Boz Scaggs; it's a mid-size club in the heart of SOMA, and features rock, hip hop, jazz, and blues acts, both local and touring (333 11th St, 415-522-0333, www.slims-sf.com).

• **The Warfield Theatre**: originally a vaudeville venue, today the Warfield is a 2,300-seat rock and pop club in the heart of the mid-Market Street district, with top touring musicians from around the world (982 Market St, 415-245-0900, www.thewarfieldtheatre.com).

## NORTH BAY

- **The Empress Theatre** features velvet seats, a dance floor, and a creatively lit stage in a historic landmark built in 1911 and upgraded in 2008, after two decades of dormancy following the 1989 earthquake (330 Virginia St, 707-552-2400, Vallejo, www.empresstheatre.org).
- **McNear's Mystic Theatre**: name a genre—any genre—and you're likely to find it on this grand-marquee theater's impressive calendar, with big-name touring musicians in a cozy town atmosphere (23 Petaluma Blvd N, Petaluma, 707-765-2121, www.mystictheatre.com).
- **19 Broadway** offers a lineup that ranges from rock to ragas and blues to bebop (19 Broadway, Fairfax, 415-459-1091, www.19broadway.com).
- **The Phoenix Theatre**, as punk as punk gets in the North Bay, features up-and-coming Bay Area musicians (201 Washington St, Petaluma, 707-762-3565, www.thephoenixtheatre.com).
- **Sweetwater Music Hall** is newly renovated with an improved sound system but the same great reputation for soul, rock, punk, and open mics (19 Corte Madera Ave, Mill Valley, 415-388-3850, www.sweetwatermusichall.com).
- **The Uptown Theatre** features internationally renowned musicians, comedians, and authors in a majestic setting (1350 3rd St, Napa, 707-259-0123, www.uptowntheatrenapa.com).

## EAST BAY

- **Ashkenaz** is known for all-ages local rock, hip hop, funk, blues, and country shows (1317 San Pablo Ave, Berkeley, 510-525-5054, www.ashkenaz.com).
- **Café Van Kleef**, a longtime favorite for local jazz and blues, is one of the best spots in the Bay Area (1621 Telegraph Ave, 510-763-7711, Oakland, www.cafevankleef.com).
- **Concord Pavilion (formerly Sleep Train Pavilion)** is a 12,500-seat amphitheater featuring festivals of chart-toppers in pop, rock, soul, and hip hop (2000 Kirker Pass Rd, Concord, 925-676-8742, www.theconcordpavilion.com).
- **Duende** is an intimate new jazz spot with a wine bar and a Spanish-inspired menu, and is on the rise in Oakland's hip uptown district (468 19th St, 510-893-0174, www.duendeoakland.com).
- **The Fox**, a newly restored, pristine art-deco palace, hosts the biggest-billed musicians across genres (1807 Telegraph Ave, 510-302-2250, Oakland, www.thefoxoakland.com).
- **Freight & Salvage** presents rock, blues, pop, and country in a coffeehouse setting (1111 Addison St, Berkeley, 510-644-2020, www.thefreight.org).
- **The Greek Theatre**, an 8,500-seat amphitheater operated by UC Berkeley, can be found near the football stadium (2001 Gayley Road, Berkeley, 510-548-3010, www.thegreektheatreberkeley.com).

- **La Pena Cultural Center** features hip-hop and soul, and is deeply rooted and respected in Berkeley's artist-activist community (3105 Shattuck, Berkeley, 510-849-2568, www.lapena.org).
- **The Oakland Coliseum & Arena**: when professional sports teams aren't head-lining here, the world's top-name touring musicians are (Hegenberger Rd and I-880, Oakland, 510-569-2121, www.coliseum.com).
- **The New Parish**, a hip small spot, has rising credibility among indie concertgoers in the fast-growing uptown district (579 18th St, Oakland, www.thenewparish.com).
- **The 924 Gilman Street Project** is an all-ages punk club credited with helping establish the Foo Fighters, Green Day, and today's newer bands (924 Gilman, Berkeley, www.924gilman.org).
- **The Starry Plough**—a small, friendly pub—features local rock, country, and genre-crossing musicians (3101 Shattuck Ave, Berkeley, 510-841-0188, www.thestarryplough.com).
- **The Stork Club** is a dive bar with an indie-magnet stage and lots of credibility among fans of local and touring punk (2330 Telegraph Ave, Oakland, 510-444-6174, www.storkcluboakland.com).
- **Yoshi's**, a renowned jazz club in the heart of Jack London Square, is where the giants of jazz play when they come to town; shows are top-notch, and you can enjoy award-winning sushi and classic Japanese entrees during the performance (510 Embarcadero West, Oakland, 510-238-9200, www.yoshis.com).

## PENINSULA & SOUTH BAY

- **Cow Palace**: when slick car shows and medical marijuana conventions aren't taking over this massive stadium, it is home to the biggest award-winning musicians in the world (Geneva Ave and Santos St, Daly City, 415-404-4111, www.cowpalace.com).
- **J.J.'s Blues** offers blues, rock, and hip-hop (3439 Stevens Creek Blvd, San Jose, 408-243-6441).
- **Kuumbwa Jazz Center**—one of California's most acclaimed, historic, and wel-coming jazz spots—is an intimate setting entering its fifth decade with top musicians. It is notable for its lineup of lyrical Hammond B-3 organists (320 Cedar St #2, Santa Cruz, 831-427-2227, www.kuumbwajazz.org).
- **Los Altos Grill** features jazz and fine dining on Tuesday and Thursday (233 3rd St, Los Altos, 650-948-3524—no website; call for lineup).
- **The Montalvo Arts Center**, based in an Italian mansion nestled in the Santa Cruz Mountains foothills, is coveted by concertgoers (15400 Montalvo Rd, Sara-toga, 408-961-5800, www.montalvoarts.org).
- **The Pioneer Saloon** is a dive bar offering country and rock (2925 Woodside Rd, Woodside, 650-851-8487, www.pioneer-salon.com).

- **SAP Center at San Jose**: Madonna and other pioneering performers take center stage when the arena's main attraction—the San Jose Sharks hockey team—isn't playing (525 W. Santa Clara St, San Jose, 409-287-7070, www.sapcenter.com).
- **Shoreline Amphitheatre**: as many as 22,500 people pack this amphitheater for dozens of top-billed festivals (One Amphitheatre Pkwy, Mountain View, 650-851-8487, www.theshorelineamphitheatre.com).
- **The Stanford Jazz Festival and Workshop** is world-renowned for jazz superstars and up-and-coming generations of younger musicians, with small and large performances and educational workshops (Stanford University campus, open to the public, 650-736-0324, www.stanfordjazz.org).

## SWING

Swing is on the upswing and has been for the last several years in the Bay Area, where a historically underground youth movement has caught the imagination of new generations. Today there are numerous swing bands, street fairs, and swing clubs, and the old nightclubs hire young swing bands that attract waves of dancers in their 20s and 30s. Vintage clothing stores have run out of original 1940s swing attire, so designers are making their own replicas of everything from zoot suits for men to floral-print rayon for women. Almost every venue hosts pre-event dance classes for beginners, so there's no excuse not to lindy or balboa. Check out the Lindy List (www.lindylist.com) for Bay Area–wide classes and happenings.

## MUSIC—SYMPHONIC, OPERATIC, CHORAL

### SAN FRANCISCO & NORTH BAY

- The **San Francisco Symphony** is one of the country's premier orchestras, performing to packed houses and critical acclaim. Renowned conductor Michael Tilson Thomas runs the show with an innovative approach: along with showcasing Beethoven and Mozart as well as classics of American music, the symphony has paired with unusual partners (like heavy metal and pop stars) for sold-out shows. At home, the San Francisco Symphony and Chorus perform separately and in tandem at their glittering Louise M. Davies Symphony Hall. Opened in 1980, the structure underwent an acoustic upgrade in 1992. The concert hall and box office are located in the Civic Center area (201 Van Ness Ave, 415-864-6000, www.sfsymphony.org).
- The **San Francisco Opera** performs at the War Memorial Opera House, right across Van Ness Avenue from City Hall, and north of Davies Symphony Hall. It features many of the opera world's biggest stars in lavish productions. Tickets are on the expensive side, and go fast, but rush tickets can be purchased the day of the show at the box office (301 Van Ness Ave, 415-864-3330, sfopera.com). No budget? Catch free performances in Stern Grove, Golden Gate Park, Yerba Buena Gardens, and the San Francisco Giants' AT&T ballpark during the summer.

- San Francisco's **Kronos Quartet** is a revered favorite, specializing in modern experimental music. If you like contemporary chamber and jazz traditions, Kronos comes highly recommended. Visit www.kronosquartet.org.

- Up-and-coming classical musicians can be discovered at the **San Francisco Conservatory of Music,** a premier teaching and performing institution housed in a beautiful venue at 50 Oak Street. Frequent concerts feature classical and contemporary solo and ensemble performers (415-864-7326, www.sfcm.edu).

- **San Francisco Community Music Center** is an excellent neighborhood spot for taking low-pressure music classes and catching inexpensive, sometimes free performances by students, instructors, and acclaimed professionals (544 Capp St, 415-647-6015, www.sfcmc.org).

- At the striking Frank Lloyd Wright–designed Civic Center in San Rafael you can hear the **Marin Symphony.** For calendars and tickets, visit www.marinsymphony.org or call 415-479-8100.

## EAST BAY

In Contra Costa County the **Lesher Center for the Arts** (1601 Civic Drive, Walnut Creek, 925-943-7469, www.lesherartscenter.org) houses performance companies such as the **Contra Costa Chamber Orchestra** and the **Center REPertory Company.** The East Bay offers countless similarly acclaimed groups. To get you started:

- **West Edge Opera (formerly Berkeley Opera),** 3055 Hillegass Ave Berkeley, 510-841-1903, www.berkeleyopera.org
- **Berkeley Symphony Orchestra,** 1942 University Ave, Berkeley, 510-841-2800, www.berkeleysymphony.org
- **Oakland East Bay Symphony,** 2025 Broadway, the Paramount Theatre, Oakland, 510-444-0801, www.oebs.org

## PENINSULA & SOUTH BAY

In and around Stanford University you can hear **Stanford Symphony Orchestra, Symphonic Chorus,** and **Chamber Chorale,** as well as the highly recommended **Stanford Jazz Workshop,** which does a world-class job of integrating genres and generations; visit events.stanford.edu and www.stanfordjazz.org for a full events calendar.

- **Cupertino Symphonic Band,** various locations, 408-262-0471, www.netview.com/csb
- **Opera San Jose,** the California Theatre, 345 S 1st St, San Jose, 408-437-4450, www.operasj.org
- **Palo Alto Chamber Orchestra,** various locations, Palo Alto, 650-856-3848, www.pacomusic.org
- **Palo Alto Philharmonic,** various locations, www.paphil.org
- **San Jose Wind Symphony,** various locations, 408-927-7597, www.sjws.org
- **Symphony Silicon Valley,** performances at the California Theatre, 345 S 1st St, 408-286-2600, www.symphonysiliconvalley.org
- **West Bay Opera,** Lucie Stern Theatre, Palo Alto, 650-424-9999, www.wbopera.org

# DANCE

Dancers and dance fans in the Bay Area are spoiled for choice by the abundance of award-winning companies and styles (from Celtic to Native American to Korean to Russian to Balkan to Scottish and more). The outstanding publication *In Dance* is your top source for dance events and culture in the Bay Area. Check it out at www.dancersgroup.org/indance.

## SAN FRANCISCO & NORTH BAY

- **Amnesia**, a stylish Mission District dive bar, is a hotspot for dance nights presided over by DJ Primo, and known for danceable slow jams and Motown magic on Saturdays once or twice a month (853 Valencia St, San Francisco, 415-970-0012, www.amnesiathebar.com).
- Balancoire, which means "swing" in French, is a popular nightclub-restaurant with a disco ball and a lively swing session every Wednesday called Cat's Corner (2565 Mission St, San Francisco, 415-920-0577, www.balancoiresf.com).
- **Copious Dance Theater**, founded recently, bridges styles and sensibilities with outstanding performances by top talent, including the exceptionally creative Laura Sharp, a shining presence in the Bay Area's modern dance community (26 7th St, 5th Floor, San Francisco, 818-724-7524, www.copiusdance.org).
- **Dance Mission Theater**, run by Dance Brigade, hosts a variety of shows—from performances by the resident contemporary company to Afro-Cuban festivals. It's a popular spot to take classes in everything from hip hop to salsa to modern dance to Brazilian (3316 24th St, 415-826-4441, www.dancemission.com).
- **Fat Chance Belly Dance**, a San Francisco institution, performs tribal-style belly dancing at a variety of festivals and events, as well as offering drop-in dance classes, for women only, at the studio (670 S Van Ness Ave, San Francisco, 415-431-4322, www.fcbd.com).
- **The Knockout** features first and third Fridays of rare soul records, and a dance floor of impressive moves and outfits (3223 Mission St, San Francisco, 415-550-6994, www.theknockoutsf.com).
- **Marin Ballet** celebrated its 50th anniversary in grand style recently, and continues to perform top programs with exceptional creativity (100 Elm St, 415-453-6705, www.marinballet.org).
- **Michael Smuin**, formerly a choreographer with the San Francisco Ballet, started his own company, Michael Smuin Ballet, which, years after he passed away, lives on brightly and strongly. Excitement for the company: in 2015 the group bought its first-ever home, a dance space in the Potrero Hill neighborhood where the Metronome Ballroom had flourished before the lease expired. The Smuin Ballet performs contemporary and classical pieces often reworked with a modernist touch. Visit www.smuinballet.org for more information.
- **ODC Theater** (formerly the Oberlin Dance Collective) performs acclaimed modern dance at ODC Dance Commons (351 Shotwell St, 415-863-6606, www.

odcdance.org, and elsewhere); they also put on the popular "Velveteen Rabbit" for children each December at Yerba Buena Center for the Arts.

- **Raw Dance** is one of the Bay Area's most impressive modern dance companies of any size; a tight-knit group that's phenomenally talented and groundbreaking in many areas of performance and concept. One of the group's longtime talents, Laura Sharp, is a featured dancer in Copious Dance Theater (see listing above), another outstanding choice for modern dance. For more information on Raw Dance, visit www.rawdance.org.
- **Safehouse Arts** (formerly Kunst-Stoff Arts), offers local dance performances designed to reenergize the mid-Market Street arts district (1 Grove St, 415-518-1517, www.safehousearts.org).
- **The San Francisco Ballet** is a small company with a big reputation—it's the longest-running full-time professional ballet company in the nation. The ballet season follows the opera season, starting with the perennially popular "Nutcracker" in November and proceeding throughout the late winter and spring. Performances are at the War Memorial Opera House at Van Ness and Grove. For performance and ticket information call 415-865-2000, or visit www.sfballet.org.
- **Theatre Flamenco of San Francisco** enlivens the Spanish dancing scene (1144 Rhode Island, 415-826-2477).
- Other modern dance troupes include **Deborah Slater Dance Theatre** (415-267-7687), **Margaret Jenkins Dance Company** (415-861-3940), and **Footloose Dance Company** and **Shotwell Studios** (415-289-2000, www.ftloose.org). This is only a partial list. New companies form, combine, and move in all the time.
- **Verdi Club** is an elegant ballroom that transports you to the 1920s, '30s, and '40s—and earlier, as it was established in 1913—with welcoming swing nights popular with twentysomething and thirtysomething crowds (2424 Mariposa St, San Francisco, www.verdiclub.net).

### EAST BAY

- **Axis Dance Company** is a contemporary ensemble including dancers with disabilities who create and perform original works (1428 Alive St, Suite 200, Oakland, 510-625-0110, www.axisdance.org).
- **Bissap Baobab**, a Senegalese hangout, provides timba and salsa dancing in a lively atmosphere (381 15th St, Oakland, 510-817-4722, www.bissapbaobaboakland.com).
- **BrasArte**, a lively destination for traditional Brazilian dance, is open to all skill levels (1901 San Pablo Ave, Berkeley, 510-528-1958, www.brasarte.com).
- **Cal Performances** presents renowned dancers who perform through UC Berkeley at the Greek Theatre, Hertz Hall, and Zellerbach Auditorium (510-642-9988; www.calperformances.org).
- **Julia Morgan Theatre** offers a variety of arts programs in a historic building designed by the celebrated architect Julia Morgan (2727 College Ave, Berkeley, 510-845-6830, www.berkeleyplayhouse.org).

- **Oakland Ballet Company** celebrated its 50th anniversary in 2015, marking half a century of pioneering programs and performances and ushering in a new era of acclaimed ballet (2201 Broadway, Suite 206, 510-893-3132, www.oaklandballet.org).

### PENINSULA & SOUTH BAY

- **Ballet San Jose** showcases classic and contemporary works; the ballet school's educational outreach program is dedicated to serving young audiences (40 N 1st St, San Jose, 408-288-2800, www.balletsj.org).
- **Peninsula Ballet Theatre** presents a variety of classical ballet performances, including an annual rendition of the *Nutcracker* (1880 S Grant St, San Mateo, 650-342-3262, www.peninsulaballet.org).
- **San Jose Dance Theatre** hosts classics and children's favorites, including *Alice in Wonderland*, *Sleeping Beauty*, *Beauty and the Beast*, and the *Nutcracker* (408-286-9905, www.sjdt.org).

# THEATER

Beyond the traveling Broadway productions and celebrity one-offs that parachute into town for sold-out weekends, the Bay Area is home to a vibrant community of playwrights who have spent time cultivating their own styles and transforming the art. The scene is centered commercially around the theater district two blocks west of Union Square on Geary Street, where you'll find the Curran and Geary theaters. The Curran stages musicals as well as shows being prepared for travel, while the Geary plays host to one of the most respected companies around, the American Conservatory Theatre (ACT). The Golden Gate Theater, in the nearby Tenderloin neighborhood, stages big, splashy musicals. The surrounding streets are stricken by poverty, homelessness, and devastation—a fact that puts many newcomers off. If possible, stick with the crowd when traveling through this area, and learn more about the Tenderloin's culturally rich history by reading the **Tenderloin** neighborhood description earlier in this book.

Once you leave the theater district, productions have a less commercial, more experimental feel, and there are many to choose from. Several highlights:

### SAN FRANCISCO

- **African-American Shakespeare Company** and **AfroSolo Theatre Company,** 762 Fulton St, 415-762-2071, www.african-americanshakes.org
- **American Conservatory Theater (ACT)**, 415 Geary St, 415-749-2228, www.act-sf.org
- **Brava! For Women in the Arts**, 2781 24th St, 415-641-7657, www.brava.org,
- **Club Fugazi**, home of the immensely popular *Beach Blanket Babylon*, 678 Beach Blanket Blvd, 415-421-4222, www.beachblanketbabylon.com
- **CounterPULSE**, 1310 Mission St, 415-626-2060, www.counterpulse.org

- **Curran**, 445 Geary Street, 415-551-2000, www.shnsf.com
- **Eureka Theatre**, 215 Jackson St, 415-788-7469, www.theeurekatheatre.com
- **Exit Theatre**, 156 Eddy St, 415-673-3847, www.theexit.org
- **Golden Gate Theatre**, 1 Taylor St, 415-551-2050, www.shnsf.com
- **Intersection for the Arts**, 925 Mission St, 415-626-2787, www.theintersection.org
- **Lorraine Hansberry Theatre**, 777 Jones St, 415-345-3980, www.lhtsf.org
- **Magic Theatre**, Fort Mason, Building D, 415-441-8822, www.magictheatre.org
- **Marines Memorial Theatre**, 609 Sutter Street, 415-447-0188, www.marinesmemorialtheatre.com
- **New Conservatory Theatre Center**, 25 Van Ness Ave, 415-861-8972, www.nctcsf.org
- **Orpheum**, 1192 Market St, 888-746-1799, www.shnsf.com
- **San Francisco Playhouse**, 450 Post St, 415-677-9596, www.sfplayhouse.org
- **Theatre Rhinoceros**, 2926 16th St, 415-861-5079, www.therhino.org
- **Young Performers Theatre**, Fort Mason Center, 415-346-5550, www.ypt.org

## NORTH BAY
- **Marin Shakespeare Company**, 415-499-4488, www.marinshakespeare.org
- **Marin Theatre Company**, 397 Miller Ave, Mill Valley, 415-388-5208, www.marintheatre.org
- **Mountain Play Association**, Mt Tamalpais State Park, 415-383-1100, www.mountainplay.org
- **The Playhouse**, 27 Kensington Rd, San Anselmo, 415-456-8555, www.playhousesananselmo.org

## EAST BAY
- **Actors Ensemble of Berkeley**, 1301 Shattuck Ave, 510-841-5580, www.aeofberkeley.org
- **Aurora Theatre Company**, 2081 Addiston St, Berkeley, 510-843-4822, www.aurotheatre.org
- **Berkeley Repertory Theatre**, 2025 Addison St, Berkeley, 510-647-2900, www.berkeleyrep.org
- **Black Repertory Group**, 3201 Adeline St, Berkeley, 510-652-2120; www.blackrepertorygroup.com
- **Contra Costa Civic Theatre**, 951 Pomona Ave, El Cerrito, 510-524-9132; www.ccct.org
- **Diablo Theatre Company (formerly Diablo Light Opera Company)**, Lesher Center for the Arts, 1601 Civic Center Dr, Walnut Creek, 925-943-7469, www.dloc.org
- **East Bay Center for the Performing Arts**, 339 11th St, Richmond, 510-234-5624, www.eastbaycenter.org

- **Lesher Center for the Arts**, 1601 Civic Dr, Walnut Creek, 925-943-7469, www.lesherartscenter.org
- **Shotgun Players**, the nation's first all-solar-powered theater company, 1901 Ashby Ave, 510-841-6500, www.shotgunplayers.org

## PENINSULA & SOUTH BAY

- **Broadway by the Bay**, San Mateo Performing Arts Center, 600 North Delaware St, San Mateo, 650-579-5565, www.broadwaybythebay.org
- **City Lights Theater Company**, 529 S 2nd St, San Jose, 408-295-4200, www.cltc.org
- **Louis B. Mayer Theatre**, Santa Clara University, Santa Clara, 408-245-2978, www.ctcinc.org
- **Palo Alto Players**, 1305 Middlefield Rd, Palo Alto, 650-329-0891, www.paplayers.org
- **San Jose Stage Company**, 490 S 1st St, San Jose, 408-283-7142, www.thestage.org
- **Santa Clara Players**, 1511 Warburton Ave, Santa Clara, 408-248-7993, www.scplayers.org
- **Shady Shakespeare**, Sanborn Skyline County Park, 16055 Sanborn Rd, Saratoga, 408-264-3479, www.shadyshakes.org
- **TheatreWorks**, Mountain View Center for the Performing Arts, 500 Castro St, and Lucie Stern Theater, 1305 Middlefield Rd, Palo Alto, 650-463-1960, www.theatreworks.org

# MOVIES

Mainstream theaters, some of them still offering bargain matinees in the afternoon, show the latest blockbusters and aren't hard to find on your smartphone's maps app. Below is a list of harder-to-find art houses that specialize in foreign and alternative films:

## SAN FRANCISCO

- **Artists' Television Access**, 992 Valencia St, 415-824-3890, www.atasite.org
- **Balboa**, 3630 Balboa St, 415-221-8184, www.balboamovies.com
- **Castro Theatre**, 429 Castro St, 415- 621-6120, www.castrotheatre.com
- **Clay**, 2261 Fillmore St, 415-267-4893, www.landmarktheatres.com
- **Embarcadero**, 1 Embarcadero Center, Promenade Level, 415-267-4893, www.landmarktheatres.com
- **Four Star**, 2200 Clement St, 415-666-3488, www.lntsf.com
- **Oddball Films**, 275 Capp St, 415-558-8112, www.oddballfilms.blogspot.com
- **Opera Plaza**, 601 Van Ness Ave, 415-267-4893, www.landmarktheatres.com
- **Presidio,** 2340 Chestnut St, 415-776-2388, www.lntsf.com

- **Roxie**, the city's longest-running theater, built in 1909, 3117 16th St, 415-863-1087, www.roxie.com
- **Sundance Kabuki**, 1881 Post St, 415-346-3243, www.sundancecinemas.com
- **Victoria**, 2961 16th St, 415-863-7576, www.victoriatheatre.org
- **Vogue**, 3290 Sacramento St, 415-346-2228, www.voguesf.com

**SURROUNDING BAY AREA**
- **Albany Twin**, 1115 Solano Ave, Albany, 510-525-4531, www.landmarktheatres.com
- **Aquarius Theatre,** 430 Emerson St, Palo Alto, 650-327-3241, www.landmarktheatres.com
- **California Theatre**, 2113 Kittredge St, Berkeley, 510-848-0620, www.landmarktheatres.com
- **Camera 12 Cinemas**, 201 S 2nd St, San Jose, 408-998-3300, www.cameracinemas.com
- **Christopher B. Smith Rafael Film Center**, 1118 4th St, San Rafael, 415-454-1222, www.cafilm.org
- **Guild Theatre**, 949 El Camino Real, Menlo Park, 650-566-8367, www.landmarktheatres.com
- **Los Gatos Cinemas**, 43 N Santa Cruz Ave, Los Gatos, 408-399-9800, www.losgatostheatre.com
- **New Pacific Film Archive Theater**, 2725 Bancroft Ave, Berkeley, 510-642-0808, www.bampfa.berkeley.edu
- **Piedmont Theatre**, 4186 Piedmont Ave, Oakland, 510-985-1252, www.landmarktheatres.com
- **Shattuck Cinemas**, 2230 Shattuck Ave, Berkeley, 510-644-2992, www.landmarktheatres.com
- **Stanford Theater**, 221 University Ave, Palo Alto, 650-324-3700, www.stanfordtheatre.org

For a lineup of acclaimed film festivals, see the section **A Bay Area Year**.

## COMEDY

The untimely passing of Robin Williams continues to be mourned around the Bay Area—the comedian was a local fixture for decades. While his presence continues to loom large, the Bay Area celebrates newer generations of talent from near and far—from passers-through like Louis CK, Sarah Silverman, Dave Chappelle, and Mitch Fatel, to the many locals cracking jokes and smiles full-time, like Joseph Andre, Andrew Moore, Justin Gomes, David Gborie, and Keith D'Souza. A few stages and events to get you started:

- **Cobb's**, 915 Columbus Ave, San Francisco, 415-928-4320, www.cobbscomedyclub.com

- **Comedy on the Square**, various locations, 415-646-0776, www.comedyonthesquare.com
- **Punch Line**, 444 Battery St, San Francisco, 415-397-7573, www.punchlinecomedyclub.com
- **Rooster T. Feathers**, 157 W El Camino Real, Sunnyvale, 408-736-0921, www.roostertfeathers.com

Visit www.comedyday.org/sfcomedy/events and www.sylvanproductions.com for more comedy listings across the Bay Area.

## MUSEUMS

The Bay Area is blessed with outstanding art museums, from the marquee destinations like San Francisco Museum of Modern Art (SFMOMA)—set to reopen in 2016 after a massive multiyear renovation and expansion—as well as the de Young Museum in Golden Gate Park, the Oakland Museum of California, and the brilliantly renovated Museum of the African Diaspora. Many smaller art museums and galleries are packed throughout the region. A snapshot:

### ART, CULTURAL & HISTORY MUSEUMS

#### SAN FRANCISCO & NORTH BAY

- **The African-American Art & Culture Complex**, a popular resource and reflection of the Bay Area's richly diverse cultural heritage and progressive arts community, is located in a 34,000-square-foot facility that houses a gallery, three exhibition spaces, a 203-seat theater, dance studios, and a recording studio (762 Fulton St, San Francisco, 415-922-2049, www.aaacc.org).
- **The Asian Art Museum**—featuring art from China, Korea, Japan, South and Southeast Asia, the Himalayas, West Asia, and the United States—is the largest institution of Asian art and culture on the West Coast (200 Larkin St, San Francisco, 415-581-3500, www.asianart.org).
- **The Beat Museum**, 540 Broadway St, San Francisco, 415-399-9626, www.kerouac.com
- **The Cable Car Museum** gives audiences a close look at the history and design of San Francisco's iconic cable cars (1201 Mason St, 415-474-1887, www.cablecarmuseum.org).
- **The Center for Sex & Culture** promotes healthy sexual knowledge and the art of empowerment (1349 Mission St, San Francisco, www.sexandculture.org).
- **The Charles M. Schulz Museum** honors the cartoonist and one-time Santa Rosa resident through original art, memorabilia, and other cartoonists' tributes (2301 Hardies Ln, Santa Rosa, 707-579-4452, www.schulzmuseum.org).
- **The Chinese Culture Center** is based inside the Hilton Hotel (750 Kearny St, 3rd Floor, San Francisco, 415-986-1822, www.c-c-c.org).

- **The Chinese Historical Society of America** contains the nation's largest Chinese-American historical institute archives—fitting, given that San Francisco's Chinatown is the largest and oldest in the country (965 Clay St, San Francisco, 415-391-1188, www.chsa.org).
- **The Contemporary Jewish Museum**, 736 Mission St, San Francisco, 415-655-7800, ww.wthecjm.org
- **The De Young Museum**, located in Golden Gate Park since 1917, has recently been dramatically transformed (it reopened in 2005), and features a stunning observatory tower as well as American works across cultures and regions. Also featured are African, European, and Asian art. The museum is the site of many lectures and gala events (Golden Gate Park, 50 Hagiwara Tea Garden Drive, San Francisco, 415-750-3600, www.famsf.org/deyoung).
- **The Falkirk Cultural Center**, 1408 Mission Ave, San Rafael, 415-485-3328, www.falkirkculturalcenter.org
- **The GLBT History Museum** is North American's first museum dedicated to gay, lesbian, bisexual, and transgender history (4127 18th St, San Francisco, 415-621-1107, www.glbthistory.org/museum).
- **The Headlands Center for the Arts**, 944 Fort Barry, Sausalito, 415-331-2787, www.headlands.org
- **The Legion of Honor**, a stunningly beautiful building perched atop a hill in Lincoln Park, was given to the city in 1924 as a monument to the state's war dead. The collection features European art from the medieval era to the present. Free on the first Tuesday of the month (100 34th Ave, San Francisco, 415-750-3600, www.famsf.org/legion).
- **The Marin Museum of Bicycling**, 1966 Sir Francis Drake Blvd, Fairfax, 415-450-8000, www.mmbhof.org
- **The Maritime Museum**, Hyde St Pier, San Francisco, 415-561-6662, www.maritime.org
- **The Mexican Museum**, the first museum in the United States to focus on Mexican and Mexican-American artists, is located at Fort Mason, 2 Marina Blvd, Building D; in 2019 the museum will move to 706 Mission St, San Francisco (415-202-9700, www.mexicanmuseum.org).
- **The Museo Italo Americano**, Fort Mason, 2 Marina Blvd, Building C, San Francisco, 415-673-2200; free for children 11 and under
- **The Museum of the African Diaspora** recently emerged in outstanding, sparkling form after a $1.3 million redesign, and continues to celebrate and explore the art, culture, and history of the African diaspora, including an interactive theater and immersive exhibitions. Kids 12 and younger are free (685 Mission St, 415-358-7200, San Francisco, www.moadsf.org).
- **The Museum of Craft and Design,** 2569 3rd St, San Francisco, 415-773-0303, www.sfmcd.org
- **The Musée Mécanique** is a coin-operated antique arcade on the waterfront (Pier 45, Shed A, San Francisco, www.museemecaniquesf.com).

- **The Museum of Performance and Design**, 893B Folsom St, San Francisco, 415-255-4800, www.mpdsf.org
- **The National Japanese American Historical Society**, 1684 Post St, San Francisco, 415-921-5007, www.njahs.org
- **The San Francisco Museum of Modern Art (SFMOMA),** one of the most popular destinations in the Bay Area, features exhibitions by top modernists. The museum reopens in early 2016 after a highly anticipated multiyear renovation and expansion costing $610 million. Free on the first Tuesday of the month (151 3rd St, San Francisco, 415-357-4000, www.sfmoma.org).
- **The San Francisco Filipino Cultural Center Museum** is currently under construction at 814 Mission St, San Francisco (415-252-9701, www.thesffcc.com).
- **The Tenderloin Museum** is a major new museum (opened in 2015) dedicated to the history and future of the Tenderloin neighborhood in San Francisco (398 Eddy St, 415-830-4640, www.tenderloinmuseum.org).
- **The USS Pampanito** allows audiences to wander aboard a restored World War II submarine (Pier 45, San Francisco, 415-775-1943, www.maritime.org/pamphome).
- **The Western Railway Museum**, 5484 Highway 12, between Suisin City and Rio Vista, Solano County, 707-374-2978, www.wrm.org
- **The Yerba Buena Center for the Arts** is free the first Tuesday of the month (701 Mission Street, San Francisco, 415-978-2700, www.ybca.org).

## EAST BAY

- **The African-American Museum and Library at Oakland**, 659 14th St, Oakland, 510-637-0200, www.oaklandlibrary.org/locations/african-american-museum-library-oakland
- **The Berkeley Art Museum and Pacific Film Archive** is a premier institution for art installations and films in an impressive new building one block from the downtown Berkeley BART station (Center and Oxford, Berkeley, 510-642-1475, www.bampfa.berkeley.edu).
- **The Judah L. Magnes Memorial Museum** features Jewish art and objects, and admission is free for children under 12 (2911 Russell St, Berkeley, 510-549-6950, www.magnes.org).
- **The Museum of Art and Digital Entertainment**, 610 16th St, Oakland, 510-210-0291, www.themade.org
- **The Oakland Museum of California** is a highly recommended center for California art and history (1000 Oak St, 510-318-8400; www.museumca.org).
- **The Pacific Pinball Museum**, 1510 Webster St, Alameda, 510-769-1349, www.pacificpinball.org

## PENINSULA & SOUTH BAY

- **The California History Center**, 21250 Stevens Creek Blvd, DeAnza College Campus, Cupertino, 408-864-8987, www.deanza.edu/califhistory

- **The Cantor Arts Center** features modern painting, sculpture, and photography; the highlight here is the outdoor Rodin Sculpture Garden, with 20 bronze statues by Auguste Rodin (328 Lomita Dr, Palo Alto, 650-723-4177, www.museum.stanford.edu).
- **The Cupertino Historical Museum**, 10185 N Stelling Rd, Quinlan Community Center, Cupertino, 408-973-1495
- **The de Saisset Museum of Art and History**, Santa Clara University, 500 El Camino Real, Santa Clara, 408-554-4528, www.scu.edu/desaisset
- **The Marin History Museum**, 1125 B St, San Rafael, 415-454-8538, www.marinhistory.org
- **Movimiento de Arte y Cultura Latino Americana (MACLA)**, 510 S 1st St, San Jose, 408-998-2783, www.maclaarte.org
- **The Museum of American Heritage**, 351 Homer Ave, Palo Alto, 650-321-1004, www.moah.org
- **The New Museum Los Gatos (NUMU),** a top pick, opened in 2015 with forward-looking multimedia exhibitions about Bay Area arts and culture (106 E Main St, Los Gatos, 408-354-2646, www.numulosgatos.org).
- **The Palo Alto Art Center**, 1313 Newell Rd, Palo Alto, 650-329-2366, www.cityofpaloalto.org/gov/depts/csd/artcenter
- **The San Jose Museum of Art**, 110 S Market St, San Jose, 408-271-6840, www.sjmusart.org
- **The San Jose History Park at Kelley Park**, 1650 Senter Rd, San Jose, 408-287-2290, www.historysanjose.org
- **The San Jose Institute of Contemporary Art**, 560 S 1st St, San Jose, 408-283-8155, www.sjica.org
- **The San Jose Museum of Quilts and Textiles** showcases contemporary and traditional quilts and textile design (520 S 1st St, San Jose, 408-971-0323, www.sjquiltmuseum.org).
- **The San Mateo County History Museum** is located in the courthouse at 2200 Broadway, Redwood City (650-299-0104, www.historysmc.org).
- **The Saratoga Historical Museum**, 20450 Saratoga-Los Gatos Rd, Saratoga, 408-867-4311, www.saratogahistory.com
- **The Tech Museum of Innovation**, 201 S Market St, San Jose, 408-294-8324, www.thetech.org
- **The Triton Museum of Art**, 1505 Warburton Ave, Santa Clara, 408-247-3754, www.tritonmuseum.org

## SCIENCE MUSEUMS & ZOOS

The Bay Area is one of the world's top scientific research centers, home to the Lawrence Livermore and Lawrence Berkeley laboratories, medical research facilities at UCSF, and the Stanford University Medical Center. In Silicon Valley and elsewhere in the Bay Area, the next generation of biotechnology and wireless everything is being developed. Below is a partial list of entertaining and educational hotspots:

## SAN FRANCISCO

- **Aquarium of the Bay**, at the tourist magnet of Pier 39, takes you through a long viewing tunnel with the aquarium's residents gliding by you in all directions (2 Beach St, 415-623-5300, www.acquariumofthebay.org).
- **The California Academy of Sciences** has been completely rebuilt and upgraded and now features some of the most innovative displays of tropical rainforests, aquariums, and reptile tanks—more than 26 million specimens. The facility includes the Morrison Planetarium, the Steinhart Aquarium, the Kimball Natural History Museum, and a four-story rainforest. One of the most popular attractions is the fish roundabout, including sharks, bat rays, and eel in a 100,000-gallon tank (55 Music Concourse Dr, 415-379-8000, www.calacademy.org).
- **The Exploratorium**, recently relocated to a massive new waterfront location, offers a hands-on scientific experience for all ages, with hundreds of exhibits, many of them interactive, and all highly educational (Pier 15, Embarcadero at Green St, 415-528-4444, www.exploratorium.edu).
- The **San Francisco Botanical Garden** celebrated its 75th anniversary in 2015; it is a treasured home to more than 50,000 plants (in Golden Gate Park, 1199 9th Ave, 415-661-1316, www.sfbotanicalgarden.org).
- **The San Francisco Zoo**, covering 100 acres, is best known for koalas and gorillas—although a growing chorus of protestors has urged the zoo to reflect on its treatment of animals, as a baby gorilla was crushed recently by an automatic door, prompting investigations and boycotts; also, the zoo's chimpanzee treatment has jeopardized the institution's accreditation (Sloat Blvd at 47th Ave, 415-753-7080, www.sfzoo.org).

## NORTH BAY

- **Bay Area Discovery Museum**, hands-on museum for kids and youthful adults (557 McReynolds Rd, Sausalito, 415-339-3900, www.baykidsmuseum.org)
- **Bay Model Visitor Center**, presented by the US Army Corps of Engineers (2100 Bridgeway, Sausalito, 415-332-3871, www.spn.usace.army.mil)
- **Space Station Museum**, 464 Ignacio Blvd, Novato, 415-524-3940, www.thespacestationca.org

## EAST BAY

- **Lawrence Hall of Science**, Centennial Dr, Berkeley, 510-642-5132, www.lawrencehallofscience.org
- **Oakland Zoo**, 9777 Golf Links Rd, 510-632-9525, www.oaklandzoo.org
- **UC Berkeley Botanical Gardens**, 200 Centennial Dr, 510-643-2755, www.botanicalgarden.berkeley.edu

## PENINSULA AND SOUTH BAY

- **Children's Discovery Museum of San Jose**, 180 Woz Way, 408-298-5437, www.cdm.org

- **Computer History Museum**, one of the largest collections of computing artifacts in the world, in the heart of where the microchip was invented (1401 N Shoreline Blvd, Mountain View, 650-810-1010, www.computerhistory.com)
- **Hiller Aviation Museum**, 601 Skyway Rd, San Carlos, 650-654-0200, www.hiller.org
- **Intel Museum**, 2200 Mission College Blvd, Santa Clara, 408-765-0503, www.intel.com/museum
- **Lick Observatory**, 7281 Mount Hamilton Rd, 408-274-5061, www.ucolick.org
- **Fujitsu Planetarium**, 21250 Stevens Creek Blvd, De Anza College Campus, Cupertino, 408-864-8814, www.planetarium.deanza.edu
- **NASA Ames Research Center**, Moffett Field, Mountain View, 650-604-6274, www.nasa.gov/centers/ames
- **Stanford Linear Accelerator**, 2275 Sand Hill Rd, Menlo Park, 650-926-2204, www.slac.stanford.edu
- **The Tech Museum of Innovation**, 201 S Market St, San Jose, 408-294-8324, www.thetech.org

## DISCOUNTS

For local discounts on restaurants, attractions, activities, and anything else you'll crave in the Bay Area, there's no easier way to score inexpensive front-row seats or hour-long massages than by signing up for alerts from Groupon (www.groupon.com), LivingSocial (www.livingsocial.com), Amazon Local (www.local.amazon.com), and similar coupon sites. The Bay Area turns to these sites almost religiously, and budget-minded newcomers can find great deals daily. Download their mobile apps for notifications.

## CULTURE FOR KIDS

If the rollercoaster hills and colorful sights of the Bay Area aren't enough to keep kids entertained, don't panic—there's an astonishing wealth of experimental, historical, and art museums, and hundreds of dance, theater, poetry, and musical events aimed at or composed by children. During the holidays the **San Francisco Ballet** performs its version of *The Nutcracker,* and **ODC** (Oberlin Dance Company) performs a modern version of the *Velveteen Rabbit.* A small sample of the countless cultural options:

### SAN FRANCISCO

- **The Exploratorium**, the **San Francisco Zoo**, and the **Aquarium of the Bay** are kid wonderlands; see descriptions above under **Science Museums & Zoos.**
- **The Randall Junior Museum**, a favorite among children; features an earthquake exhibit, live animals, art and science programs, films, lectures, concerts, and plays. The museum is closed for upgrades and will reopen in late 2016 after

an extensive, multimillion-dollar renovation (199 Museum Way, 415-554-9600, www.randallmuseum.org).

- **Yerba Buena Gardens** offers gardens, waterfalls, and fountains full of birds, alongside an ice-skating rink, a colorful bowling alley, a playground, and a merry-go-round; at the other end is the **Sony Metreon** (415-369-6000, www. metreon.com), a high-end multiplex movie theater, with restaurants, shops, and arcades (4th and Mission sts, www.yerbabuenagardens.com).
- **The Children's Creativity Museum (formerly Zeum)**, part of the larger arts complex at Yerba Buena Gardens, includes hands-on science and technology exhibits for kids (221 4th St, 415-820-3320, www.creativity.org).

### SURROUNDING BAY AREA

- **Berkeley Youth Orchestra**, 1587 Franklin St, Oakland, 510-698-2296, www.berkeley-youth-orchestra.org
- **Billy Jones Wildcat Railroad**, 233 Blossom Hill Rd, Los Gatos, 408-395-7433, www.bjwrr.org
- **Children's Discovery Museum of San Jose**, 180 Woz Way, 408-298-5437, www.cdm.org
- **CuriOdyssey (formerly Coyote Point Museum for Environmental Education)**, 1651 Coyote Point Dr, San Mateo, 650-342-7755, www.curiodyssey.org
- **Emma Prusch Farm Park**, 647 S King Rd, San Jose, 408-926-5555, www.pruschfarmpark.org
- **Happy Hollow Park and Zoo**, 1300 Senter Rd, San Jose, 408-277-3000, www.happyhollowparkandzoo.org
- **Marin Dance Theatre**, 1 St. Vincents Dr, San Rafael, 415-499-8891, www.mdt.org
- **Oakland Symphony Youth Orchestra**, 1428 Alice St, Oakland, 510-832-7710, www.oyo.org
- **Palo Alto Junior Museum and Zoo**, 1451 Middlefield Rd, Palo Alto, 650-329-2111, www.friendsjmz.org
- **Winchester Mystery House**, 525 S Winchester Blvd, San Jose, 408-247-2101, www.winchestermysteryhouse.com
- **Young People's Symphony Orchestra**, 2345 Channing Way, Berkeley, 510-849-9776, www.ypsomusic.org

## LITERARY LIFE

The Bay Area's legacy of illustrious authors doesn't stop at humorist Mark Twain, noir master Dashiell Hammett, legendary columnist Herb Caen, jazz chronicler Ralph Gleason, and poets Sonia Sanchez, Daphne Muse, and Ishmael Reed. Beyond the iconic novelists Jack London and Amy Tan, there are thousands of bright lights. San Francisco was a stomping ground of Allen Ginsberg, Amiri Baraka, Ed Bullins, and Jack Kerouac, while in the 1970s Armistead Maupin began a series that shined a light on San Francisco life, and eventually became the famed *Tales of the City*.

But those who think the Bay Area's glory days as a writers' haven are gone should take a closer look. A new community of novelists, essayists, poets, and publishers commands national attention, and community spaces like **826 Valencia**, which offers free writing workshops for teens, and the **Grotto**, a writers' collective, are immeasurably influential.

Below you'll find a list of some of the best-loved independent bookstores (many of which host regular readings); cafés and clubs with storytelling and open-mic nights; writers' groups; literary publications; and annual events.

## BOOKSTORES

Excellent independent bookstores are holding up in the Bay Area. While books were once assumed to be on the endangered species list, the picture today looks brighter, as e-book sales have plateaued, and independent bookstores are back in business. Check indie bookstore bulletin boards or get on their email lists for upcoming event calendars. Below is a small sample of local bookstores—once you move here you'll quickly discover dozens more. Particularly worth checking out: the university towns of Palo Alto and Berkeley.

- **Adobe Book Shop**, 3130 24th St, San Francisco, 415-864-3936, www.adobe-backroomgallery.com
- **Alexander Book Co.**, a three-level store in the heart of the Financial District, specializes in African-American literature and children's books, and also maintains a large poetry collection (50 2nd St, San Francisco, 415-495-2992, www.alexanderbook.com).
- **Book Passage** is known for its readings, writing workshops, and great support of local authors (51 Tamal Vista Blvd, Corte Madera, 415-927-0960 and 1 Ferry Building, San Francisco, 800-999-7909, www.bookpassage.com).
- **Booksmith** offers a wide collection of new and used books, as well as a substantial magazine section and celebrity author readings (1644 Haight St, San Francisco, 415-863-8688, www.booksmith.com).
- **Bound Together Books** specializes in anarchist and progressive books (1369 Haight St, San Francisco, 415-431-8355, www.boundtogetherbooks.wordpress.com).
- **Builders Booksource** sells architectural, design, and construction books for the novice and professional (1817 4th St, Berkeley, 510-845-6874, www.buildersbooksource.com).
- **City Lights Bookstore**, the legendary Beat Generation hangout founded by San Francisco's first poet laureate, Lawrence Ferlinghetti, was the nation's first paperback bookstore. Its creaky wooden floors and endless shelves are probably the best place to browse late in the evening, with an excellent collection of fiction, a poetry room upstairs, and a nook dedicated to magazines. The store

showcases local authors, operates its own publishing house, and hosts frequent poetry and fiction events (261 Columbus Ave, San Francisco, 415-362-8193, www.citylights.com).

- **Dog Eared Books** features a great collection of used fiction, from the classics to recent works (900 Valencia St, San Francisco, 415-282-1901, www.dogeared-books.com).
- **Green Apple Books and Music**; two words: the best. This is the undisputed champion of Bay Area bookstores, with a huge selection of used books—among them a wide fiction selection, including small presses; a large magazine collection; and used CDs, DVDs, and videos. Sell your own used books here for decent credit or cash exchanges (506 Clement St, San Francisco; annex at 520 Clement St, 415-387-2272; and an impressive new outpost at 1231 9th Ave, 415-742-5833, www.greenapplebooks.com).
- **Kepler's Books** boasts a highly knowledgeable staff, frequent author events, a children's section, and an expansive collection of fiction and nonfiction. It stays open late and is conveniently located next to an outdoor café (1010 El Camino Real, Menlo Park, 650-324-4321, www.keplers.com).
- **Marcus Books**, a legendary, beloved store specializing in African-American, African, and Caribbean literature, has an iconic branch that closed recently in the Fillmore District of San Francisco, but is reopening in a to-be-determined location nearby. The second store remains open at 3900 Martin Luther King Jr. Way, Oakland (510-652-2344, www.marcusbookstores.com).
- **Modern Times** hosts frequent author events and has a large left-leaning politics section; it occasionally presents music events as well (888 Valencia St, San Francisco, 415-282-9246, www.moderntimesbookstore.com).
- **Moe's Books**, an East Bay favorite, features an outstanding, huge collection of used fiction and nonfiction on several floors (2476 Telegraph Ave, Berkeley, 510-849-2087, www.moesbooks.com).
- **Nolo Press Outlet Bookstore** publishes a variety of easy-to-read legal guides (950 Parker St, Berkeley, 510-549-1976, www.nolo.com).
- **Omnivore Books on Food** is a highly respected, welcoming destination for excellent books on food (3885a Cesar Chavez St, San Francisco, 415-282-4712, www.omnivorebooks.com).
- **William Stout** specializes in books on architecture and design (804 Montgomery St, San Francisco, 415-391-6757, stoutbooks.com).

## BOOKSTORE CHAINS

In the battle of book heavyweights, the two big chains—Borders and Barnes & Noble—couldn't both survive in today's era of smartphone purchases. Borders threw in the towel, closing all Bay Area shops in 2011, leaving Barnes & Noble to scrap for your book bucks. Here's what's left of the major chains locally, in case Powells.com and Amazon.com don't satisfy you:

- **Barnes & Noble**, San Bruno, Emeryville, El Cerrito, Corte Madera, San Mateo, Redwood City, Walnut Creek, Dublin, Antioch, San Jose; for hours and addresses, visit www.barnesandnoble.com
- **Books Inc.**, San Francisco, Palo Alto, Alameda, Berkeley, Burlingame, Mountain View, Palo Alto, San Francisco International Airport terminals 2 and 3; for hours and addresses, visit www.booksinc.net

## RESOURCES

- **826 Valencia**, author Dave Eggers' strange pirate shop in the front and writing center in the back offers free youth writing classes and occasional adult workshops and events, and is also home to literary publication *McSweeney's*. The flagship location is 826 Valencia St (415-642-5905), and a new storefront will open in 2016 in San Francisco's Tenderloin district at 180 Golden Gate Ave (www.826valencia.org).
- **Bay Area Book Fest**, launched in 2015, is a free two-day event with hundreds of authors, panels, and performances throughout a 10-block stretch of downtown Berkeley (www.baybookfest.org).
- **Berkeley Poetry Slam**, a popular open-mic that showcases up-and-coming poets and spoken-word artists, draws crowds from throughout the Bay Area; it is held every Wednesday at the Starry Plough (3101 Shattuck Ave, Berkeley, www.thestarryplough.com).
- **City Arts & Lectures** brings top talent and offbeat cult favorites to town for packed lectures at the newly restored Nourse Theater (275 Hayes St, San Francisco, 415-392-4400, www.cityarts.net).
- **Commonwealth Club** hosts a range of impressive guests, from political heavyweights to cultural icons and literary giants (555 Post St, San Francisco, 415-597-6700, www.commonwealthclub.org).
- **Friends of the San Francisco Public Library** offers a way to get involved with your local library, and operates two book bays with excellent deals (710 Van Ness Ave, San Francisco, 415-626-7500; www.friendssfpl.org).
- **The Grotto** is a writers' collective whose members frequently offer workshops and seminars at various locations, including a multimedia series in conjunction with SF Public Library (490 2nd St, San Francisco, www.sfgrotto.org).
- Every year, **Litquake**, a weeklong extravaganza of fiction and nonfiction, celebrates local literary life with readings by some of the Bay Area's best-known authors (various locations, www.litquake.org).
- **Oakland Book Festival**, an acclaimed new festival, was launched in 2015 at Oakland's City Hall (www.oaklandbookfestival.org).
- **Selected Shorts** is a public radio broadcast of actors reading short stories by notable authors (Saturdays at 8 p.m., KQED 88.5 FM).
- **Writers with Drinks** is a spoken-word variety show hosted at 7:30 p.m. on the second Saturday of every month at the Make Out Room (3225 22nd St, San Francisco, 415-647-2888, www.writerswithdrinks.com).

## SPECIALTY LIBRARIES

**The San Francisco Public Library** is San Francisco's main library, and hosts excellent programs throughout the year—from author readings and poetry workshops for teens to film screenings, all free (100 Larkin Street, www.sfpl.org, 415-557-4400).

Home to top-tier universities, including Stanford and the University of California at Berkeley, and a cutting-edge scientific research facility at UCSF, the Bay Area offers several specialty libraries and research centers. Some of the highlights:

- **The Alliance Française** maintains a large library of French books, videos, CDs, and magazines, as well as works in French with accompanying English translations. Alliance also offers a variety of French language classes and programs. Library is open to all, but borrowing privileges are reserved for members and students enrolled in classes (1345 Bush St, San Francisco, 415-775-7755, www.afsf.com).
- **The Asian Art Museum Library**, a rich collection of well-known and hard-to-find books on Asian art and culture, is masterfully curated by the museum's longtime librarian, John Stucky, who is exceptionally knowledgeable and respected by students and scholars across the Bay Area (200 Larkin St, 4th Floor, San Francisco, 415-581-3500, www.asianart.org).
- **The Bureau of Jewish Education**, 639 14th Ave, San Francisco, 415-751-6983, www.bjesf.org
- **The Foundation Center and Library;** nonprofits, artists, students, and scholars turn here first for information about grants and special funding opportunities. Anyone can use the library, which is filled with helpful resource materials; the staff is extremely knowledgeable. The online database is available on a first-come, first-served basis, and there are also frequent specialized workshops (312 Sutter St, Suite 606, San Francisco, 415-397-0902, www.foundationcenter.org/sanfrancisco).
- **The Holocaust Center of Northern California** features an extensive archive, part of the Tauber Holocaust Library (2245 Post St, San Francisco, 415-449-3717, www.hcnc.org).
- **The Hoover Institution Library and Archives** offers a mind-boggling collection of firsthand historical accounts recording major political, social, and economic transformations, with more than 1.6 million volumes, 60 million archive documents, and 100,000 original political posters. The institute is free and open to the public, but borrowing privileges are reserved for Stanford students, faculty, and research affiliates. The reading tower is worth a trip for spectacular views of the Peninsula (434 Galvez Mall, Palo Alto, 650-723-3563, www.hoover.org/library-archives).
- **The Japanese American National Library** is an invaluable resource for the preservation of primary and secondary source material related to Japanese Americans (1619 Sutter St, San Francisco, 415-567-5006, www.janlibrary.org).
- **The San Francisco Law Library** houses a wealth of legal documents and information on various aspects of federal and state law. Access is free to the public, but borrowing privileges are reserved for members of the state bar in good

standing and practicing law in San Francisco; judges of courts within San Francisco; and municipal, state, and federal officers. If you meet these requirements, you may qualify for a library card (1145 Market St, 4th floor, San Francisco, 415-554-1772, www.sflawlibrary.org).

WATCH WHERE YOU STEP IN THE BAY AREA: YOU'RE BOUND TO TRIP over the hundreds of championship trophies won by locals (most recently the Golden State Warriors, 2015 NBA champions). The San Francisco Giants won three World Series in five years recently, and the list of luminaries and victories continues. From professional to recreational sports, the Bay Area is one of the world's best urban playgrounds, with sandy beaches, wide-open hills, nearby mountain ranges, and ocean activities both leisurely and treacherous. Surfing (with a wet suit) at Ocean Beach is one option, as well as kayaking, windsurfing, or rowing—though probably not in the ocean. Biking, hiking, and running in Golden Gate Park, the Presidio, or Mount Tamalpais are popular choices; bird watching at the Palo Alto Baylands is catching on.

## PROFESSIONAL

Sports fans here are blessed (some might say cursed, depending on the year) with teams in all of the majors: baseball, basketball, football, hockey, and soccer. For the latest, consult the sports section of the *San Francisco Chronicle*, *Oakland Tribune*, *Marin Independent Journal*, or *San Jose Mercury News*—or visit your team's website.

### BASEBALL

One of the most intense rivalries in the Bay Area rages between the National League **San Francisco Giants** and the American League **Oakland Athletics** (the A's). Passions run high on both sides. Among the most popular matches are the interleague games where the Giants and the A's face off against each other. The last time the A's and Giants met in the World Series was in 1989, a series disrupted by the October 17th Loma Prieta earthquake that rattled Candlestick Park. (The game was canceled, and the A's went on to win the series four games to three.)

- **San Francisco Giants** (National League): three-time champions within five years recently, the Giants play in the waterside AT&T Park (24 Willie Mays Plaza, San Francisco, 415-972-2000, www.sfgiants.com). It's a gorgeous 41,000-seat ballpark completed in March 2000. Purchase tickets at sanfrancisco.giants.mlb. com or the stadium's windows.
- **Oakland Athletics** (American League): A's fans have a reputation for throwing a good party, and the bleachers—where you can catch the game for a mere $13— can get rowdy, especially during tense night games. If this is your idea of a fun night out, track down tickets at oakland.athletics.mlb.com or the Oakland Coliseum ticket windows (Oakland Coliseum, 7000 Coliseum Way, 510-638-4900).

## BASKETBALL

The NBA champion **Golden State Warriors** rose to the top of the basketball world in 2015, but while the champs' home games are currently in Oakland, the team is rumored to be leaving Oakland for a new San Francisco arena in time for the 2018–2019 season. Strong opposition to the team's move is mounting—but odds are that San Francisco will get the team soon, so keep your eyes open. Tickets can be purchased at the Oakland arena's ticket office or by calling 888-479-4667 or visiting www.nba.com/warriors.

## FOOTBALL

Similar to the baseball rivalry between the A's and the Giants, competition between the **Oakland Raiders** and the **San Francisco 49ers** is fierce. These teams, two of the most successful franchises in the NFL (though not recently), rarely play each other because they are in different conferences. But when they do, the air is thick with anticipation and the cheers are passionate and riotous.

- The **Raiders** play at Oakland (Oracle) Coliseum, but for how long? There's talk of the Raiders ditching Oakland—just like the NBA's Golden State Warriors. But it's anyone's guess where they will move to. Catch them while you can. (Oakland Coliseum, 7000 Coliseum Way, 510-864-5000, 800-RAIDERS, www.raiders.com.)
- The **San Francisco 49ers** kissed San Francisco goodbye in 2014, hauling the team's headquarters down to the sparkling new Levi's Stadium in Santa Clara— one of the most eco-friendly, tech-focused stadiums in the nation. For tickets visit www.levisstadium.com or call 415-GO-49ERS. (Levi's Stadium, 4900 Marie P. DeBartolo Way, Santa Clara.)

## HOCKEY

The **San Jose Sharks** of the NHL are the Bay Area's ice hockey locals, whose pre-season starts in September, and whose season runs until April in the SAP Center at San Jose (formerly HP Pavilion), affectionately known as the "Shark Tank." Tickets for the Sharks are available at the arena ticket office, 408-998-8497, or www.sharks.nhl.com.

## HORSE RACING

Just across the Bay Bridge from San Francisco you can place bets at **Golden Gate Fields**, at 1100 Eastshore Highway, in the city of Albany. Entrance fees range from $1 to $15, depending on the day and the location of your viewing stand. For more information call 510-559-7300 or visit www.goldengatefields.com.

## SOCCER

The year 1996 brought professional soccer to the Bay Area for the first time in years, in the form of Major League Soccer's San Jose Clash. At the inaugural match against DC United, the Clash won, 1-0. Today, the renamed **San Jose Earthquakes** play at the new Avaya Stadium (1123 Coleman Ave), which opened in 2015. The season runs from March through October. For tickets call 408-556-7700 or visit www.sjearthquakes.com.

# COLLEGE SPORTS

Probably the most closely watched and fiercely debated college game in the Bay Area is football's annual grudge match between the **University of California Golden Bears** and the **Stanford Cardinal**. The big game is usually a spirited event that sells out fast, so get your tickets early.

Another popular attraction is the Stanford women's basketball team. Under Coach Tara VanDerveer, this is one of the best teams in the country. **Stanford University** plays basketball at Maples Pavilion and football at Stanford Stadium, both on the university campus in Palo Alto. For tickets call 650-723-4591 or visit www.gostanford.com. The **University of California at Berkeley** plays basketball in the Haas Pavilion and football at Memorial Stadium, both on the Berkeley campus. For tickets call 800-462-3277 or visit www.calbears.com.

The following schools also stage sporting events:

- **Cal State East Bay**, 510-885-3000, www.csueastbay.edu
- **San Francisco State University**, 415-338-2218, www.sfstategators.com
- **San Jose State University**, 877-757-8849, www.sjusspartans.com
- **Santa Clara University**, 408-554-4063, www.santaclarabroncos.com
- **St. Mary's College**, 925-631-4392, www.stmarys-ca.edu/athletics

# PARTICIPANT SPORTS & ACTIVITIES

From kitesurfing in Foster City to snowboarding in Lake Tahoe and soccer in San Jose, San Francisco, and Oakland, the Bay Area is a haven for athletes. Crissy Field in the Golden Gate National Recreation Area is home to some of the world's best windsurfing, and Mount Tamalpais and the Marin Headlands have serene hiking and biking trails. Area **Parks and Recreation Departments** can assist you with locations and hours of access:

- **California Department of Parks and Recreation**, Sacramento, 800-777-0369, www.parks.ca.gov
- **East Bay Regional Park District**, 2950 Peralta Oaks Court, Oakland, 888-327-2757, TTY 510-633-0460, www.ebparks.org
- **Marin County Parks**, 3501 Civic Center Dr, Room #260, San Rafael, 415-499-6387, www.visitmarin.org
- **Mid-Peninsula Regional Open Space District**, 330 Distel Circle, Los Altos, 650-691-1200, www.openspace.org
- **Napa Valley Parks**, 1195 3rd St, Room 310, Napa, 707-259-5933, www.napaoutdoors.org
- **San Francisco Recreation and Parks Department**, 501 Stanyan St, San Francisco, 415-831-2700, www.parks.sfgov.org
- **San Mateo County Park and Recreation Department**, 455 County Center, 4th Floor, Redwood City, 650-363-4020, www.parks.smcgov.org
- **Santa Clara County Park and Recreation**, 298 Garden Hill Dr, Los Gatos, 408-355-2200, www.sccgov.org
- **Solano County Parks**, 707-347-2097, parkreservations.solanocounty.com
- **Sonoma County Regional Parks**, 2300 County Center Dr, 120A, Santa Rosa, 707-565-2041, parks.sonomacounty.ca.gov

Parks and recreation departments for specific cities can be found at the end of each Neighborhood listing earlier in the book.

## BASEBALL & SOFTBALL

Whether you swing for the fences with a grimacing game face and inelegant grunts, or plant yourself on the bench without breaking a sweat, you'll find dozens of softball and baseball leagues around the Bay Area welcoming players of all skill levels. The **Northern California Amateur Softball Association** sponsors slow- and fast-pitch adult and junior leagues. Visit www.norcalasa.org. For **Little League** contact www.littleleague.org, and for **Pony Baseball and Softball** contact www.pony.org.

City parks and recreation departments are good resources for baseball and softball games. (See above and also see **Neighborhood** listings.)

## BASKETBALL

The Bay Area has basketball leagues for professionals and recreational players, both men and women. From sharp-elbow competition to leisurely touch passes, the leagues welcome everyone; check with your town's parks and recreation department (see above) or try your community gym or health club, which may have its own league. **Dream League** (www.dreamleague.org) runs programs for at-risk teens. The **San Francisco Gay Basketball Association**—the world's oldest gay basketball league, www.sfgba.com—runs the **Castro League** at various locations. **YMCA** branches throughout the Bay Area offer organized youth programs and pick-up games for all ages (www.ymcasf.org). If pickup games are your calling card, strut around your new neighborhood and spot the nearest court—almost every town in the Bay Area has a pickup contest.

## BICYCLING

Biking trails throughout the Bay Area offer mesmerizing ocean views and pristine mountain scenery. One of the most acclaimed recent developments is the installation of a biking and walking trail ringing the entire Bay Area. While only portions of the Bay Trail have been built so far, it's an impressive accomplishment. For a map, visit www.baytrail.org.

A new bike-sharing service called **Bay Area Bike Share** has boomed since its introduction in 2013, first with 700 bikes at 70 docking stations in San Francisco, Palo Alto, San Jose, Redwood City, and Mountain View. The subscription service lets you rent bikes for short rides and drop them off elsewhere. This service has been so popular that a tenfold expansion was approved in 2015—meaning more than 7,000 bicycles will be on hand by 2017, and available in the East Bay for the first time. The program's expansion will make the Bay Area's bike-sharing the second largest in the nation. The expansion will mean 4,500 bikes in San Francisco, 1,000 bikes in San Jose, 850 in Oakland, 400 in Berkeley, and 100 in Emeryville. For details, visit www.bayareabikeshare.com.

By California law, bike riders younger than 18 must wear a helmet. Violators are subject to fines. A proposed law in 2015 would have made California the first state to require adult bike riders to wear helmets, but the bill was gutted under pressure from opposition. Bicycle activism is growing in the Bay Area, where, since 1992, the "critical mass" campaign has taken to the streets on the last Friday of every month, sparking a national movement. Hundreds, sometimes thousands gather at Justin Herman Plaza in San Francisco and bike en masse through city streets to raise awareness of the environmental and social values of biking. The monthly ride has police escorts to protect riders from irate drivers who resent the inevitable delays.

Some of the best biking in San Francisco is in Golden Gate Park, along Embarcadero and Golden Gate Promenade beneath the south end of the Golden Gate Bridge. The stretch runs from the Marina to Fort Point. For more information on trails, bike groups, and resources, contact the **San Francisco Bicycle Coalition** (8335 Market St, 10th Floor, 415-431-BIKE, www.sfbike.org).

The Peninsula and the South Bay have more than 440 miles of biking trails. On the **Peninsula**, the Long Ridge Open Space Preserve provides majestic views and grassy hills for some of the area's best single-track riding. The trail parallels Skyline Blvd between Page Mill Road and Highway 9. Another popular ride runs along Montebello Road just off Stevens Canyon Road in **Cupertino**, where you'll find creeks and steep hills near the Ridge Winery. Upper Stevens Creek County

Park is a similarly spectacular ride with steep canyons and forests. For biking tips in the mid-Peninsula, contact the **Silicon Valley Bicycle Coalition** (96 N 3rd St, Suite 375, San Jose, 408-287-7259, www.bikesiliconvalley.org). Another excellent resource is the **Trail Center**, www.trailcenter.org.

Taking your bike across to the **East Bay** and **Marin County** from San Francisco is fairly easy, as the BART system accommodates bikes during non-commute hours. Most public bus systems also accommodate bikes, as do ferries that crisscross the Bay. Riding your bike across the Golden Gate Bridge is a popular and rewarding rite of passage for newcomers and longtime locals, even those who don't have a bike—rent one at one of the many bike rental shops along Fisherman's Wharf and North Beach, including Bike and Roll (899 Columbus Ave, San Francisco, 415-229-2000, www.bikeandroll.com). Marin Headlands and Mount Tamalpais are the most cherished destinations for riders up north. While you're north, ride by the new **Mountain Bike Hall of Fame** in the Marin County city of Fairfax—the birthplace of mountain biking. The intimate, impressive new museum opened in 2015, and it's already a beloved destination (1966 Sir Francis Drake Blvd, Fairfax, 415-450-8000, www.mmbhof.org). For more tips contact the **Marin County Bicycle Coalition** (www.marinbike.org). In the East Bay your best bets for bike adventures and advocacy are **Bike East Bay** (www.bikeeastbay.com), **Rock the Bike** (www.rockthebike.com), and **Bicycle Trail Council for the East Bay** (www.btceb.org). For exceptional trails in the East Bay, your first stops are Tilden Park (see the **Hiking section** of this book), Redwood Regional Park, Wildcat Canyon, and Briones Park.

Bike thefts are a growing crisis in the Bay Area, so be sure to register with www.safebikes.org and www.stolenbicycleregistry.com, and always use U locks (not just cable locks). And remember, it's illegal to ride on the sidewalk if you're over 13 years old.

## BOWLING

Piled-high nachos, handcrafted cocktails, and 7-10 splits are on offer at countless upscale bowling alleys in the Bay Area, but many newcomers prefer to keep casual at the old-fashioned bowling dives. A few popular alleys are listed below, ranging from glow-in-the-dark to creaky-floored favorites (check their websites' photos for ambiance):

- **The Rooftop at Yerba Buena Center Gardens Ice Skating and Bowling Center**, 750 Folsom St, San Francisco, 415-820-3541; www.skatebowl.com
- **Presidio Bowling Center**, 93 Moraga Ave, in Park Presidio , San Francisco, 415-561-2695, www.presidiobowl.com
- **Albany Bowl**, 540 San Pablo Ave, Albany, 510-526-8818, www.thealbanybowl.com
- **Southshore Lanes**, 300 Park St, Alameda, 510-523-6767, www.amf.com/southshorelanes

- **Bel Mateo Bowl**, 4330 Olympic Ave, San Mateo, 650-341-2616, www.belmateobowl.com
- **Fourth St Bowl**, 1441 N 4th St, San Jose, 408-453-5555, www.4thstreetbowl.com
- **Moonlite Lanes**, 2780 El Camino Real, Santa Clara, 408-296-7200, www.amf.com/moonlitelanes
- **Sea Bowl**, 4625 Coast Highway, Pacifica, 650-738-8190, www.seabowl.com

For additional bowling alleys in your new town, check listings and reviews at Yelp. com.

## CHESS

From casual games with friendly chatter to grueling competitions in clubhouses, chess is growing in the Bay Area. One longtime scene, however, has bitten the dust: in the past, dozens of players would gather day and night around tables on **Market Street** near the corner of 5th Street in San Francisco—a 30-year tradition that attracted masters of all economic backgrounds. Police shooed them away—highly controversially—in favor of window-shopping tourists and a bicycle-sharing station. But those players have resurfaced at **Yerba Buena Gardens' outdoor tables,** which have built-in game boards. If you're looking for a strong pick-up match, start there. The tables are located on the southwest side of the gardens, near the pedestrian bridge, and there's nowhere better to relax on a sunny afternoon.

In the North Bay, the **Depot in Mill Valley** has permanent chess tables set up throughout the square. Donated by famed local music promoter Bill Graham, the tables are busy with pick-up games of both casual and speed chess, from afternoon until evening.

A good first stop for chess-loving newcomers is **the Northern California Chess Association** at www.calchess.org. Cal Chess maintains lists of active local clubs, events, and tournaments. Below are a few club contacts to get you started. For more information also try the **US Chess Federation**, www.uschess.org, as well as www.meetup.org (search for "chess") and www.bayareachess.com.

- **Fremont Chess Club**, meets Fridays at 8 p.m. at 3375 Country Dr, Fremont, www.newfremontchessclub.org
- **Kolty Chess Club**, meets Thursday evenings at the Campbell United Methodist Church, Campbell, koltychess.blogspot.com
- **The Mechanics' Institute Chess Room**, daily drop-in games, Tuesday night marathons, programs for children, 57 Post St, San Francisco, 415-393-0110, www.chessclub.org
- **San Mateo-Burlingame Chess Club**, meets Thursdays at 7 p.m. at the Lions Hall Building, 990 Burlingame Ave, Burlingame, www.chess.com/club/burlingame-chess-club

If you're interested in chess lessons try one of the following or look under "chess instruction" at www.yelp.com.

- **Academic Chess**, classroom and after-school programs, 415-412-4040, www.academicchess.com
- **The Berkeley Chess School**, teaches chess in Bay Area schools, runs summer camps, and offers Friday night chess games, 1845 Berkeley Way, 510-843-0150, www.berkeleychessschool.org

## FENCING

The art of the foil attracts many newcomers in the Bay Area. Start by contacting the **Northern California Division of the United States Fencing Association**, www.norcalfence.org, which keeps a list of local fencing teachers and information on competitions. **The Bay Cup**, www.thebaycup.net, sponsors Bay Area fencing competitions for kids and adults at all skill levels, and keeps a list of active clubs and fencing camps. Another source of information is www.fencing.net, a national website with tips on techniques, tournaments, and equipment, as well as chat forums. Below is a handful of clubs; many colleges have competitive fencing teams, and a few parks and recreation departments also offer classes. Contact your local parks and recreation department for offerings in your neighborhood.

### SAN FRANCISCO & NORTH BAY
- **Golden Gate Fencing Center**, 2417 Harrison St, 415-626-7910, www.gofencing.com
- **Halberstadt Fencers' Club**, 621 S Van Ness Ave, 415-863-3838, www.halberstadtfc.com
- **La Spada Nimica**, 309 Todd Way, Mill Valley, 415-388-8939, www.fencing.franklurz.com
- **Marin Fencing Academy**, 827 4th St, San Rafael, 415-454-1559, www.marinfencing.com
- **Massialas Foundation at Halberstadt**, 2530 Taraval St, 415-441-0521, www.fencingusa.com
- **Coastside Fencing Club**, 3201 Balboa St, 415-518-8869, www.coastsidefencers.net

### EAST BAY
- **East Bay Fencers' Gym**, 1429 Martin Luther King Jr Way, Oakland, 510-451-2291, www.eastbayfencers.com
- **Fremont Fencers**, 3355 Country Dr, Centerville Community Center, Fremont, 510-791-4324, www.fremontfencers.com
- **Pacific Fencing Club**, 2329 Santa Clara Ave, Alameda, 510-814-1800, www.pacificfencingclub.com

- **Sport Fencing Center**, 5221 Central Ave #9, Richmond, 510-528-5110, www.sportfencingcenter.com
- **Sword Play Fencing Academy**, 1061 Shary Circle, Suite A-1, Concord, 925-687-9883, www.swordplayfencing.net

## PENINSULA & SOUTH BAY

- **Accademia di Scherma Classica**, 14 Bancroft Rd, Burlingame, 650-401-3838, www.scherma.org
- **California Fencing Academy**, 5289F Prospect Rd, San Jose, 408-865-1950, www.calfencingacademy.com
- **Cardinal Fencing** (Stanford Fencing Club), 341 Galvez St, Stanford, 650-444-1972, www.cf.iteqx.com
- **The Fencing Center**, 1290 S 1st St, San Jose, 408-298-8230, www.fencing.com
- **First Place Fencing Club**, 835-B E San Carlos Rd, San Carlos, 650-592-1619, www.firstplacefencing.com

## FISHING

Handwritten "Gone Fishing" signs are still found on business doors in the Bay Area, where lakes, boardwalks, and oceans call hundreds of locals in search of bass, perch, trout, and catfish. In San Francisco, spots include the pier near Crissy Field in the Presidio, and piers near Fisherman's Wharf. Lake Merced in Oakland is stocked, but water quality can vary depending on season. Check the **Lake Merced Task Force**'s website (www.lmtf.org) for up-to-date conditions. Lake Anza, north of Berkeley in Tilden Park, is open for fishing throughout the year. Oakland's Lake Temescal, next to the junction of highways 24 and 13, periodically has rainbow trout, largemouth bass, red-eared sunfish, bluegill, and catfish. And the pier in Pacifica is another favorite of many residents —it stinks but it's somehow popular.

For those more interested in fishing on the open ocean, check www.sfsportfishing.com, where Bay Area commercial fishing fleets have pooled charter information onto one page. The website lists boats leaving from Fisherman's Wharf, Emeryville Marina, Berkeley Marina, Half Moon Bay, Point San Pablo, Sausalito, and San Rafael. The **California Department of Fish and Game** (www.wildlife.ca.gov), requires you to obtain a license to fish—but be advised that because of the virtual collapse of the salmon runs along the Pacific Northwest, fishing for salmon has been banned in California. Local fisherman, however, are retooling to focus on other species.

If you're planning to cook your catch, be aware of high mercury levels, PCBs, and other chemicals found in the Bay— health officials advise adults to eat no more than two servings per month of fish caught in the Bay. Striped bass over 35 inches long—as well as croakers, surfperches, bullheads, gobies, and shellfish from the Richmond Harbor Channel—should not be eaten at all. Pregnant women, nursing mothers, and children should not eat more than one serving of

Bay fish per month. They should avoid entirely striped bass over 27 inches. These guidelines do not apply to anchovies, herring, and smelt from the Bay. For more information visit www.dfg.ca.gov.

## ULTIMATE FRISBEE AND DISC GOLF

Contact the local **Ultimate Players Association**, 800-872-4384, www.usaultimate. org, for Bay Area ultimate frisbee groups and games. For disc golfers, San Francisco has a new 18-hole course in **Golden Gate Park**, at Marx Meadow between 25th and 30th avenues on the north side of the park off Fulton Street. For details contact the **San Francisco Disc Golf Club**, www.sfdiscgolf.org, which lists courses throughout the Bay Area.

## GOLFING

Where better than the Bay Area for the World Golf Championship? The event landed in San Francisco in 2015, drawn here by the scenic surroundings and cultural attractions throughout the area. Golf courses range widely across the Bay Area. A few highlights:

### SAN FRANCISCO
- **Gleneagles**, 9-hole course in McLaren Park (2100 Sunnydale Ave, 415-587-2425, www.gleneaglesgolfsf.com)
- **Golden Gate Park Golf Course**, 9-hole course, a good spot for beginning golfers (970 47th Ave, Golden Gate Park, 415-751-8987, www.goldengateparkgolf.com)
- **Harding Park**, the most popular public course in San Francisco, hosts a variety of competitions. Located near the beach, it features an 18-hole tournament course and 9-hole practice course (99 Harding Rd, 415-664-4690, www.tpc.com/tpc-harding-park).
- **Lincoln Park Golf Course**, a local favorite, is an 18-hole course that offers sweeping views of the Golden Gate Bridge. Walk the nearby Lands End trail after your game and take in the latest exhibition at the Legion of Honor museum. (300 34th Av, 415-221-9911, www.sfrecpark.org/destination/lincoln-park/lincoln-park-golf-course.)
- **Presidio Golf Club**, which is not just for high-ranking military officers anymore, is an 18-hole course set in the lush Presidio National Park, and now open to the public (300 Finley Rd, in Park Presidio, 415-561-4653, www.presidiogolf.com).

### NORTH BAY
- **Indian Valley Golf Club**, 18 holes, instruction, bar and grill (3035 Novato Blvd, Novato, 415-897-1118, www.indianvalleygolfclub.com)
- **Mare Island Golf Course**, recently expanded into an 18-hole course (1800 Club Dr, Vallejo, 707-562-4653, www.mareislandgolfclub.com)

- **McInnis Park Golf Center**, 9 holes, golf academy, driving range, miniature golf course, batting cages, and a restaurant (350 Smith Range Rd, San Rafael, 415-492-1800, www.mcinnisparkgolfcenter.com)
- **Mill Valley Golf Course**, 9 holes (280 Buena Vista Ave, Mill Valley, 415-388-9982, www.cityofmillvalley.org)
- **Napa Municipal Golf Course at Kennedy Park**, 18 holes (2295 Streblow Dr, Napa, 707-255-4333, www.playnapa.com)
- **Peacock Gap Golf & Country Club**, 18 holes, two putting greens, driving range, instruction, and a restaurant (333 Biscayne Dr, San Rafael, 415-453-4940, www.peacockgapgolf.com)
- **San Geronimo Golf Course**, 18 holes (5800 Sir Francis Drake Blvd, San Geronimo, 415-488-4030, www.golfsangeronimo.com)
- **Stone Tree**, new 18-hole championship course (9 StoneTree Lane, Novato, 415-209-6090, www.bayclubs.com/stonetree)

### EAST BAY

- **Chuck Corica Golf Course**, two 18-hole courses, par 3 executive course, putting greens, restaurant, and lighted driving range (1 Clubhouse Memorial Rd, Alameda, 510-747-7800, www.alamedagolf.com)
- **Lake Chabot Golf Course**, 27 holes, panoramic views (11450 Golf Links Rd, Oakland, 510-351-5812, www.lakechabotgolf.com)
- **Metropolitan Golf Links**, driving range (10051 Doolittle Dr, Oakland, 510-569-5555, www.playmetro.com)
- **Montclair Golf Course**, 9-hole course (2477 Monterey Blvd, Oakland, 510-482-0422, www.montclairgolfshop.com)
- **Tilden Park Golf Course**, 18-hole course (10 Golf Course Dr, Berkeley, 510-848-7373, www.tildenparkgc.com)

### PENINSULA & SOUTH BAY

- **Blackberry Farm**, 9-hole course (22100 Stevens Creek Blvd, Cupertino, 408-253-9200, www.blackberryfarmgolfcourse.com)
- **Cinnabar Hills**, 27-hole course (23600 McKean Rd, San Jose, 408-323-7814, www.cinnabarhills.com)
- **Coyote Creek,** two 18-hole courses (1 Coyote Creek Golf Dr, San Jose, 408-463-1400, www.coyotecreekgolf.com)
- **Crystal Springs**, 18-hole championship course, tournaments, and a restaurant (6650 Golf Course Dr, Burlingame, 650-342-4188, www.playcrystalsprings.com)
- **Deep Cliff Golf Course**, 18-hole course (10700 Clubhouse Lane, Cupertino, 408-253-5357, www.playdeepcliff.com)
- **Half Moon Bay Golf Links**, two 18-hole championship courses, ocean views, lessons, and a restaurant (2 Miramontes Point Rd, Half Moon Bay, 650-726-1800, www.halfmoonbaygolf.com)

- **Mariner's Point Golf Center**, 9-hole bayside course (2401 E 3rd Ave, Foster City, 650-573-7888, www.marinerspoint.com)
- **Palo Alto Municipal Golf Course (soon to be renamed Baylands Golf Links)**, 18-hole championship course, lighted driving range, and a restaurant (1875 Embarcadero, Palo Alto, 650-856-0881, www.bradlozaresgolfshop.com)
- **Poplar Creek Golf Course**, 18-hole course, junior golfer program, and a restaurant (1700 Coyote Point Dr, San Mateo, 650-522-4653, www.poplarcreek-golf.com)
- **San Jose Municipal Golf Course**, 18-hole course (1560 Oakland Rd, San Jose, 408-441-4653, www.sjmuni.com)
- **Santa Clara Golf and Tennis Club** offers Santa Clara residents preferential rates and tee time sign-ups for its municipal 18-hole course (5155 Stars & Stripes Dr, Santa Clara, 408-980-9515, www.santaclaragc.com).
- **Sharp Park Golf Course**, 18-hole course (1 Sharp Park Rd, Pacifica, 650-359-3380, 650-359-3380, www.sfrecpark.org/destination/sharp-park/sharp-park-golf-course)
- **Shoreline Golf Links**, 18-hole course (2600 North Shoreline Blvd, Mountain View, 650-903-4653, www.shorelinelinks.com)

## HIKING

Windswept hikes with exhilarating views of the ocean are standard in a Bay Area so naturally appealing that it'll never grow old—and neither will you if you hike the steeper trails in the **Marin Headlines**, one of the most rewarding spots north of San Francisco. Before heading there, consider starting with the **Golden Gate Bridge walk** (the Bridge is about a mile and a half long). Longer hikes can be found at **Presidio National Park**. **Crissy Field** is a walking-and-running hotspot within San Francisco. **Point Lobos** is a paradise of surreal chunks of land jutting straight out of the Pacific—a highly recommended sight from the flatter, safer trails that are feet away. Another enjoyable option for an afternoon is taking the ferry to Angel Island, to hike the island. **Mount Tamalpais** in Marin County and **Tilden Park** in the Oakland/Berkeley hills are also well worth exploring. And drive further north (about 90 minutes) to **Point Reyes National Seashore** for exceptional views. Keep going north to **Redwood National Park** for the world's tallest trees.

An exciting addition to the local hiking options is **Devil's Slide**, the spectacular new 1.3-mile coastal trail that opened in 2014, high above the crashing waves of the Pacific, with views of vultures, hawks, and falcons soaring over gray whales and sea lions. The trail welcomes hikers, runners, bicyclists, dog walkers, and horseback riders.

If you can afford to escape for longer than a day, visit California's largest redwood park, **Humboldt Redwoods State Park**, where 53,000 acres include some of the world's tallest trees. And schedule time for **Yosemite National Park**, about a four-hour drive to the east, in the Sierra Nevada Mountains—but wait until the fall or early spring to avoid the summer tourist season. The most consistently crowded part is Yosemite Valley. For park information contact **Yosemite National Park** (209-372-0200, www.nps.gov/yose). **Lake Tahoe** and the **Sierras**, a monument to hiking—the highest peak in the contiguous United States is nearby Mount Whitney—are also about four hours away. Consult with the **Forest Service** for the best hikes (707-562-8737, www.fs.fed.us/r5), and flip through the book *Best Hikes Near San Francisco*, by Linda Hamilton.

## HORSEBACK RIDING

Public trails and riding areas abound on the coast in and around Half Moon Bay, as well as the wooded hills of Woodside, Portola Valley, and Marin County. East Bay regional parks (see details below) offer irresistible trails, and on the peninsula, **Huddart Park** is a popular riding spot. Whether you're an expert or beginner, saddle up at any of the popular Half Moon Bay stables, which offer guided rides along the water's edge. In the North Bay, the **National Golden Gate Recreation Area** has spectacular horse-friendly coastal trails, and **Miwok Stables** in Mill Valley (415-383-8048, www.miwokstables.com) runs guided rides in the park. For extraordinary riding options north of San Francisco—surrounded by pristine pastures near Tamales Bay—drive north and keep your eyes open. If you don't spot them from the road, search for them on Google Maps in the area.

In the East Bay, trail rides are offered at **Las Trampas Stables** in San Ramon (925-862-9044, www.lastrampasstables.com), and at **Tilden Regional Park** in Berkeley. For more options, contact East Bay Parks (888-327-2757, www.ebparks.org).

## KAYAKING, KITEBOARDING

Kayaking and kiteboarding are becoming more popular in the Bay Area, which has majestic spots for both. If you're looking for lessons, check for discounts at www.groupon.com and www.livingsocial.com. It's best to kayak early in the morning, when the water is more likely to be calm. The secluded, relatively quiet waters of Tomales Bay, in Marin County, are protected from the pounding waves of the Pacific and the winds of nearby Inverness, making Tomales Bay one of the most popular spots for kayaking; contact **Tomales Bay State Park** (415-669-1140, www.parks.ca.gov/tomalesbay). Kiteboarding is especially active in Foster City, where dozens of kiteboarders turn out daily. A few of the best-rated options:

- **Blue Waters Kayaking**, Tomales Bay, 12944 Sir Francis Drake Blvd, Inverness, and 19225 Shoreline Hwy, Marshall, 415-669-2600, www.bluewaterskayaking.com
- **Boardsports School & Shop**, locations in San Francisco, Alameda, and Coyote Point, 415-385-1224, www.boardsportsschool.com
- **Cal Adventures**, 2301 Bancroft Way, Berkeley, 510-642-4000, www.recsports.berkeley.edu/outdoor-adventures
- **California Canoe & Kayak**, 409 Water St, Oakland, 510-893-7833, www.calkayak.com

- **Environmental Traveling Companions**, Fort Mason Center, Building C, San Francisco, 415-474-7662, www.etctrips.org
- **KGB Kiteboarding**, 3310 Powell St, Emeryville, 510-967-8014, www.kgbswag.com
- **Kite the Bay**, various locations, 415-295-KITE, www.kitethebay.com
- **Kite415**, 3rd Ave at Lakeside Dr, Foster City, and Oyster Point Park, 425 Marina Blvd, South San Francisco, 415-244-8007, www.kite415.com
- **Sea Trek Kayak**, 2100 Marinship Way, Sausalito, 415-332-8494, www.seatrek.com

## RUNNING

Running clubs in the Bay Area are open to all levels—from those looking to get in decent shape to those training for marathons. Most have an annual membership fee (usually in the $20–$30 range), which helps support the club.

- **Golden Gate Running Club** offers Sunday morning runs in the park, followed by brunch, and is open to all ability levels. Track workouts are Wednesday nights at Kezar Stadium, San Francisco (415-921-6833, www.goldengaterunningclub.org).
- **Excelsior Running Club**, Tuesday and Thursday 6 p.m. track runs at Kezar Stadium; Sunday morning Golden Gate Park and Bay Area trail runs; competitive teams (650-703-7412, www.runexcelsior.org)
- **Lake Merritt Joggers and Striders** hosts runs at Lake Merritt in Oakland every fourth Sunday at 9 a.m. On the morning of San Francisco's Bay to Breakers (see below), the club sponsors an alternative race in the Berkeley Hills—the Tilden Tough Ten, the first race in the renowned Triple Crown Trail Championship (510-644-4224, www.lmjs.org).
- **Palo Alto Run Club**, runs on Sundays and Wednesdays, Lucie Stern Community Center, 1305 Middlefield Rd, Palo Alto (www.parunclub.com)
- **Pamakid Runners Club**, weekly fun runs and racing team practices at Kezar Stadium, San Francisco (415-333-4780, www.pamakids.org)
- **San Francisco Dolphin South End Runners**, open to all levels; walkers welcome (415-978-0837, www.dserunners.com)
- **San Francisco FrontRunners**, club for the LGBT community and friends, with weekly runs and brunches; open to walkers (415-846-5494, www.sffrontrunners.com)
- **San Francisco Road Runners Club**, weekend runs at Marina Green divided into pace groups, training programs for beginners and marathon and half-marathon runners; Tuesday and Thursday track runs at Kezar Stadium, distance runs throughout San Francisco and Marin County (415-273-5731, www.sfrrc.org)
- **Stevens Creek Striders**, runs every Saturday morning in Stevens Creek County Park, followed by breakfast, with additional days seasonally, Cupertino (www.stevenscreekstriders.org)

- **Tamalpa Runners**, holds regular runs on Mt. Tamalpais; racing teams for road, cross-country, and distance trips; coaching and youth activities, Mill Valley (www.tamalparunners.org)

## RACES

- **Bay to Breakers**, San Francisco's moveable Mardi Gras, includes as many (or more) costumed revelers as serious racers, and begins with a massive hail of tortilla throwing. The race runs from east to west through the city—a distance of 12K—each May (415-359-2800, www.baytobreakers.com).
- **Bridge to Bridge**, 5K and 12K routes from the Bay Bridge to the Golden Gate Bridge, each October, San Francisco (www.bridgetobridge.com)
- **Escape from Alcatraz**, a mesmerizing June triathlon, starts with a 1.5-mile swim from Alcatraz Island in the San Francisco Bay, proceeds with a 18-mile bike ride along the Great Highway and through Golden Gate Park, and concludes with an 8-mile run through Golden Gate National Recreation Area, finishing at the Marina Green (www.escapefromalcatraztriathlon.com).
- **Rock 'n' Roll San Francisco Half Marathon**, a moveable party from downtown to Ocean Beach each April, in San Francisco (www.runrocknroll.com)
- **San Francisco Marathon**, includes a shorter half-marathon and 5K run/walk option, July (888-958-6668, www.runsfm.com)
- **Marina Bay Half Marathon and 5K** starts and finishes each June at the Craneway Pavilion: 1414 Harbour Way S, in Richmond (www.marinabayhalfmarathon.com).
- **Napa Valley Marathon,** napavalleymarathon.org

## TRAILS

In addition to the spectacular new Bay Trail (www.baytrail.org), which circles the entire Bay Area—or will, when construction is completed—below are a few trails with stunningly lush landscapes:

### SAN FRANCISCO

- **The Coastal Trail** runs from the Golden Gate Bridge just more than 9 miles south through China Beach, Lands End, the Cliff House, Lake Merced, and Fort Funston (www.californiacoastaltrail.info).
- **The Embarcadero** is a long palm-lined promenade stretching along the Bay from the Ferry Building to Fisherman's Wharf for a few miles.
- **Golden Gate Park**, the city's main park, has several trails—paved and dirt. A 7.4-mile loop wraps the perimeter of the park; a 2-mile loop circles Stow Lake and goes up Strawberry Hill (www.sfrecpark.org/parks-open-spaces/golden-gate-park-guide).
- **Golden Gate Promenade**, a 3.5-mile multi-use path at Crissy Field, is extremely popular with joggers, walkers, bicyclists, and dog walkers; the paved path starts a little past the Yacht Harbor and ends near the Fort Point Coast Guard Station.

This run offers fantastic views of the Bay and the Golden Gate Bridge. If you're feeling ambitious, run or walk across the bridge for dramatic, unforgettable views (www.presidio.gov).

- **Lake Merced** is a 4.5-mile paved and dirt loop alongside the water at Lake Merced Boulevard and Skyline (www. sfrecpark.org/destination/lake-merced-park).
- **Ocean Beach**: run or walk on the sand or along the esplanade, both of which are flat. If you've got endurance, head up to the Cliff House for sweeping views and a strenuous workout (www.parksconservancy.org).

For more trails, contact the Golden Gate National Recreation Area (415-561-4700, www.nps.gov/goga), or the San Francisco Recreation and Park Department (415-831-2700, www.parks.sfgov.org). Also visit www.everytrail.com and www.alltrails.com.

## PENINSULA AND SOUTH BAY

- **Devil's Slide Trail** is a stunning new trail of 1.3 miles converted from a former segment of Highway 1, with breathtaking views of crashing waves and hide-and-seek sea lions. It is also part of the California Coastal Trail (www.devilsslidecoast.org).
- **Edgewood Park** is a network of hillside trails trekking up and down amid dense forested areas and open grasslands; in the spring, the fields are blanketed with colorful wildflowers, and docent-led walking tours are available every Saturday and Sunday mornings during peak season. The main park entrance is at Edgewood Rd off I-280 in Redwood City (www.co.sanmateo.ca.us).
- **Huddart Park**, set in the hills with lush redwoods, offers several trails of varying length and difficulty. The entrance is at the top of Kings Mountain Road in Woodside (parks.smcgov.org/huddart-park).
- **Rancho San Antonio Open Space Preserve**, popular with runners and hikers, offers more than 20 miles of scenic, hilly trails; Cristo Rey Dr off Foothill Expy in Mountain View (www.openspace.org/preserves/rancho-san-antonio).
- **San Bruno Mountain** consists of multiple trails snaking up and down, with a 1,314 foot summit that boasts pristine views. Wildflowers and butterflies abound in the spring. Entrance is at Guadalupe Canyon Parkway in Brisbane (parks.smcgov.org/san-bruno-mountain-state-county-park).
- **Sawyer Camp Trail**, a waterside loop and one of the most popular trails on the peninsula, is paved with some dirt areas, and is mostly flat; the scenic trail winds around the blue waters of Crystal Springs Reservoir, and mile markers are posted. Entrance is at Skyline Boulevard and Highway 92 in San Mateo (parks.smcgov.org/sawyer-camp-segment).
- **Stanford University** features countless paved trails that weave through the Palo Alto palm tree–lined campus; routes are popular with bikers and walkers (www.stanford.edu).

- **Sweeney Ridge** offers steep and rolling coastal hills with ridges overlooking the peninsula and the Pacific Ocean. Its three trails cover about 10 miles—the Sweeney Ridge Trail is the easiest, and is located in Pacifica (www.cityofpacifica.org).

For more Peninsula trails, contact the **San Mateo County Park and Recreation Department** (650-363-4020, www.parks.smcgov.org); for more South Bay trails, contact Santa Clara County Park and Recreation (408-355-2200, www.sccgov.org).

## EAST BAY

- **Briones Reservoir Loop**, in the Orinda Hills, is a 13.5-mile favorite for hikers seeking a challenge—and rewards, as the wildflowers and colorful trees frame striking views from serene stops over the reservoir (www.redwoodhikes.com/eastbay/brionesreservoir).
- **Coyote Hills Regional Park** offers vistas of the Bay, marshlands, hills, and multiple trails. The Alameda Creek Trail is a popular, paved 12-mile trail along the south side of the creek from the mouth of Niles Canyon west to the Bay. There's an additional 3.5-mile loop, making the run (or walk) from Niles Canyon through Coyote Hills and back again feel like a marathon (8000 Patterson Ranch Rd, Fremont, www.ebparks.org).
- **Crockett Hills Regional Park**, a moderate hike along five miles of creek-side bliss, is surrounded by butterflies and majestic oaks; Crockett (www.ebparks.org/parks/crockett_hills).
- Nimitz Way (part of Tilden Park) is one of the most popular multi-use pathways in the East Bay; it's an 8-mile trail starting at Inspiration Point, with exceptionally beautiful views (Wildcat Canyon Rd, Tilden Park, Berkeley, www.ebparks.org).

For more information on East Bay trails, contact the **East Bay Regional Park District** (510-562-PARK, www.ebparks.org).

## NORTH BAY

- **Dipsea Trail** is a 7.1-mile trail from Mill Valley to Stinson Beach. The best-known trail in the North Bay, with twisting dirt trails curving among shady trees, Dipsea guides you through Mt. Tamalpais State Park, Muir Woods National Monument, and the Golden Gate Recreational Area (www.dipsea.org).
- **King Mountain Open Space** offers some of the state's most enchanting, serene hiking trails. Look for the mountaintop notebooks in zip-top bags with hikers' comments—many of them heartwarming, and some heartbreaking (Larkspur, www.marincountyparks.org).
- **Marin Headlands**, with more breathtaking trails than you can count, includes several that are near Point Bonita Lighthouse and Hawk Hill, with spectacular views of San Francisco and the Golden Gate Bridge (www.nps.gov/goga/marin-headlands.htm).

- **Tennessee Valley** is packed with deer, coyote, and raptors. Follow the main trail to the beach and back, about 4 miles total. To get there, take Highway 1 exit off 101 and follow the signs (www.nps.gov/goga/planyourvisit/tennessee_valley.htm).

For more information on Marin County trails, contact the **Golden Gate National Recreation Area** (415-561-4700, www.nps.gov/goga), or Marin County Parks (415-499-6387).

## ROCK CLIMBING

A few of the popular climbing gyms in the Bay Area:

- **Berkeley Ironworks**, 800 Potter St, Berkeley, 510-981-9900, www.touchstoneclimbing.com/ironworks
- **Mission Cliffs**, 2295 Harrison St, San Francisco, 415-550-0515, www.touchstoneclimbing.com/mission-cliffs
- **Planet Granite Rock Climbing**, 924 Old Mason St, San Francisco, 415-692-3434; 100 El Camino Real, Belmont, 650-591-3030; 815 Stewart Dr, Sunnyvale, 408-991-9090, www.planetgranite.com
- **Vertex Climbing Center**, 3358 Coffey Lane, Santa Rosa, 707-573-1608, www.climbvertex.com
- Several parks in Berkeley also have excellent outdoor climbing:
- **Contra Costa Rock Park**, 869-A Contra Costa Ave
- **Cragmont Rock Park**, 960 Regal Rd
- **Glendale La Loma Park**, 1339 La Loma Ave
- **Great Stoneface Park**, 1930 Thousand Oaks Blvd
- **Grotto Rock Park**, 879 Santa Barbara Rd
- **Indian Rock Park**, 1950 Indian Rock Ave
- **Mortar Rock Park**, 901 Indian Rock Ave
- **Remillard Park**, 80 Poppy Lane

For more venues contact the **Berkeley Parks, Recreation, and Waterfront Department** (1947 Center St, 510-981-5150, www.ci.berkeley.ca.us/prw).

## SAILING

When the America's Cup sailing competition convened here in 2013—and the local team won the international trophy—sailing enjoyed a profile boost among residents, many of whom learned that sailing is sensational in these parts. Throughout the year the Bay Area has various sailing regattas. Many yacht clubs have summer sailing programs for kids, and adult classes for beginners. For information on sailing schools, contact the nonprofits and clubs below or search www.yelp.com by location.

- **Cal Sailing Club**, nonprofit membership sailing club that offers lessons at the Berkeley Marina (124 University Ave, Berkeley, www.cal-sailing.org)

- **Lake Merritt Boating Center,** offers beginner, intermediate, and advanced sailing classes, as well as youth programs and summer camps at Lake Merritt—windsurfing, kayaking, canoeing, and rowing programs are also available at the lake (568 Bellevue Ave, Oakland, 510-238-2196, www.oaklandnet.com)
- **Robert W. Crown Memorial Beach,** a shoreline gem that offers sailboard rentals and lessons during summer weekends (8th St and Otis Dr, Alameda, 510-562-PARK, www.ebparks.org)
- **Sailing Education Adventures,** this nonprofit offers beginning and advanced classes for adults, and youth summer sailing camps (310 Harbor Dr, Sausalito, www.sfsailing.org)
- **Shoreline Lake Boathouse,** sailing, windsurfing, and kayaking lessons, plus summer sailing camps on a 50-acre lake (3160 North Shoreline Blvd, Mountain View, 650-965-7474, www.shorelinelake.com)

## SCUBA AND FREE DIVING

Bay Area waters are not even close to warm, so grab a thick wetsuit when you scuba dive in Monterey Bay. If you have strong lungs, try free diving (diving without a tank) for abalone off the northern coast of California, by Mendocino. Make sure to secure a fishing license if you catch abalone or any fish. Also familiarize yourself with the rules regarding size and limits. Contact the **Department of Fish and Game** (916-227-2245, www.wildlife.ca.gov) for more information.

- **Any Water Sports,** 1344 Saratoga Ave, San Jose, 408-244-4433, www.anywater.com
- **Bay Area Scuba,** 390 Lang Rd, Burlingame, 650-544-4092, www.bayareascuba.com
- **Diver Dan's,** 2245 El Camino Real, Santa Clara, 408-984-5819, www.diverdans.com
- **Monterey Bay Harbormaster,** 831-646-3950, Monterey, www.monterey.org

Visit www.scubasanfrancisco.com and www.scubamonterey.com for additional listings.

## SKATING—ROLLER, IN-LINE, ICE

Every Friday night, in-line skaters, sometimes more than 500 at a time, meet at San Francisco's Ferry Building to tour the city on wheels. Skating is increasingly popular in San Francisco, especially on weekends in Golden Gate Park. If you don't own skates, head to Fulton Street along the northern end of the park in the morning and look for the brightly colored rent-a-skate vans. Alternatively, plenty of skate shops are more than happy to outfit you. A handful of highlights:

### SAN FRANCISCO
- **DLX SF Skateboards,** 1831 Market St, 415-626-5588, www.slxsf.com
- **FTC Skate Shop,** 1632 Haight St, 415-626-0663, www.ftcsf.com
- **Golden Gate Park Skate & Bike,** 3038 Fulton St, 415-668-1117, www.goldengateparkbikeandskate.com

- **Skates on Haight**, 1818 Haight St, 415-752-8375, www.skatesonhaight.com
- **Yerba Buena Center Gardens Ice Skating**, 750 Folsom St, 415-820-3532, www.skatebowl.com

### NORTH BAY

- **Adrenaline Zone Sports**, 124 Calistoga Rd, Santa Rosa, 707-538-7538
- **Brotherhood Board Shop**, 1240 Mendocino Ave, Santa Rosa, 707-546-0660, www.brotherhoodboard.com
- **Snoopy's Home Ice**, 1667 West Steele Lane, Santa Rosa, 707-546-7147, www.snoopyshomeice.com

### EAST BAY

- **Golden Skate**, 2701 Hooper Dr, San Ramon, 925-820-2525, www.thegoldenskate.com
- **Oakland Ice Center**, 519 18th St, Oakland, 510-268-9000, www.oaklandice.com

### PENINSULA & SOUTH BAY

- **Belmont Iceland**, 815 Country Rd, Belmont, 650-592-0533, www.belmonticeland.com
- **Sharks Ice at San Jose**, 1500 S 10th St, San Jose, 408-279-6000, www.sharksiceatsanjose.com
- **Nazareth Ice Oasis**, 3140 Bay Rd, Redwood City, 650-364-8090, www.iceoasis.com
- **Redwood Roller Rink**, 1303 Main St, Redwood City, 650-369-5559, www.redwoodrollerrink.com
- **The Winter Lodge**, 3009 Middlefield Rd, Palo Alto, 650-493-4566, www.winterlodge.com

## SKATEBOARDING

When the X Games came to San Francisco years ago, kids and adults of all ages packed the bayside bleachers for a chance to see legends like Tony Hawk take on seemingly impossible vertical feats. Today that waterside legacy lives on in the summertime at Pier 7, which, while not a sanctioned spot, is a popular gathering place for skaters. Years after shouting the mantra "skateboarding is not a crime," and tangling with frustrated office building owners over sleek and inviting staircases and benches, skateboarding is finally getting its due, and its own public space. Skate parks are popping up throughout the Bay Area, offering skaters a place to flip kick freely—and legally. Below is a just a glimpse of locals' favorite spots; check with your parks and recreation department to find the park closest to you, or visit www.sfskateboarding.wordpress.com, www.sfskateclub.com, www.sk8parklist.com, www.thrashermagazine.com, and www.skateboarding.com.

## SAN FRANCISCO

- **Balboa Skate Park**, Ocean and San Jose aves, www.sk8parkatlas.com/sanfranciscobalboa.html
- **Crocker Amazon Skate Park**, Geneva Ave and Moscow St, 415-831-2700, www.sfrecpark.org/destination/crocker-amazon-playground
- **SOMA West Skate Park**, San Francisco's newest park; opened in 2015 on Duboce Ave between Mission and Valencia sts, under the freeway (www.sfdpw.org)

## NORTH BAY

- **Marin City Skate Park**, 133 Drake Ave, Marin City, 415-332-1441, www.marincitycsd.org
- **Mill Valley Skate Park**, 180 Camino Alto, Mill Valley, 415-383-1370, www.cityofmillvalley.org
- **Novato Skate Park**, 15,000-square-foot park, bowls, walls, curbs, stairs, rails, and ramps, 1200 Hamilton Parkway, at Sport Court Island, Novato (415-493-4753, www.novato.org)
- **Santa Rosa Skate Park,** pool-style features, concrete half acre, three bowls connected by runs, fun box, curb, **1700** Fulton Rd, at Youth Community Park, Santa Rosa (707-543-3737, www.srcity.org)

## EAST BAY

- **Antioch Skate Park**, 4701 Lone Tree Way, at Prewett Family Park, Antioch (925-779-7070, www.ci.antioch.ca.us)
- **Berkeley Skate Park**, 18,000 square feet, double bowl, ramps, Harrison and 5th sts, Berkeley (510-981-6700, www.ci.berkeley.ca.us)
- **City View Skate Park**, recently revamped with design input from local skateboarders, this 15,000-square-foot park has a bowl, banks, a pyramid, ledges, and excellent views (1177 W Redline Ave, Alameda Point, Alameda, 510-747-7529)
- **Kennelly Skate Park**, Moraga Ave off of Pleasant Valley Rd, Piedmont (510-420-3070, www.ci.piedmont.ca.us)
- **Livermore Skate Park**, 11,000 square feet, bowls, fun box, pyramid, rails; east end of Pacific Ave, in Sunken Gardens Park, Livermore (925-373-5700, www.larpd.org/parks/skatepark.html)
- **Pleasanton Skateboard Track**, 10,000 square feet, at the front of a 105-acre sports park, 5800 Parkside Dr, Pleasanton (925-931-5340, www.cityofpleasantonca.gov)

## PENINSULA & SOUTH BAY

- **Campbell Skatepark**, pyramid, quarter pipe, fun box, rails, half pipe, 1 West Campbell Ave, Campbell (408-866-2105, www.ci.campbell.ca.us)

- **Derby Skatepark**, a classic—one of the world's first public skate parks, with a long concrete snake run and bowls, 508 Woodland Way, Santa Cruz (831-420-5270, www.cityofsantacruz.com)
- **Foster City Skate Park**, one of the newest skate parks in the Bay Area, 670 Shell Blvd, Foster City (650-286-3254, www.fostercity.org)
- **Greer Skateboard Park**, popular three-bowl complex, 1098 Amarillo Ave, in Greer Park, Palo Alto (650-329-2390, www.cityofpaloalto.org)
- **Mountain View Skatepark**, ramp, quarter pipe, mini half pipe, fun box, rails, 201 S Rengstorff Ave at Crisanto Ave, northwest corner of Rengstorff Park, Mountain View (650-903-6331, www.mountainview.gov)
- **Phil Shao Memorial Skatepark**, 13,000 square feet, bowl, concrete features; St. Francis St off Jefferson St, in Red Morton Park, Redwood City (650-780-7250)
- **Sunnyvale Skatepark**, 18,500 square feet, massive bowl, vertical and street course elements; local favorite, 540 Fair Oaks Ave, in Fair Oaks Park, Sunnyvale (408-730-7751, www.sunnyvale.ca.gov)

## SKIING

Sierra Nevada ski resorts, including Lake Tahoe, are a four-hour drive east of the Bay Area, along Interstate 80 and Highway 50. If you don't own skis, several local merchants will rent everything you need to hit the slopes or cross-country ski trails in style, including the national chain **REI** (Recreational Equipment Incorporated), with various locations throughout the Bay Area (www.rei.com). Also check **Sports Basement**, 1590 Bryant Ave, San Francisco (415-575-3000, www.sportsbasement. com). For additional outfitters, search www.yelp.com by location.

## SKYDIVING

Many dive centers await the interested daredevil. Try one of the resources below for information about skydiving lessons, equipment, instructors, and how not to lose your lunch while plummeting from the safety of a perfectly fine plane:

- **Bay Area Skydiving,** 925-634-7575, www.bayareaskydiving.com
- **NorCal Skydiving**, 220 Airport Rd, Colverdale, 888-667-2259, www.norcalskydiving.com
- **Skydive Lodi Parachute Center**, 23597 N Highway 99, Acampo, 209-369-1128, www.parachutecenter.com
- **Skydive Monterey Bay**, 721 Neeson Rd #1, Marina, 888-229-5867, www.skydivemontereybay.com

Remember to check www.groupon.com and www.livingsocial.com for skydiving discounts across the Bay Area.

## SOCCER

Soccer is enormously popular in the Bay Area, where hundreds of organized games and pickups are on offer daily; contact your local parks and recreation department (see earlier listings). The **Palo Alto Adult Soccer League (PAASL)**, for men and women ages 25 and over, has an informative website about soccer options in the Bay Area (www.paasl.org). Many pickup games are so crowded that participation may be limited to the first 20 players to arrive. For youth, the **American Youth Soccer Organization (AYSO)** is the main organization with kids' teams throughout the region (800-872-2976, www.ayso.org).

## SWIMMING

For those rare days when it's actually warm enough to swim outdoors here, try one of these locations or visit www.parks.sfgov.org for more information. Hours vary, so call ahead. Below is a select handful of public-pools:

- **Albany Pool**, 1311 Portland Ave, Albany, 510-559-6640, www.ausdk12.org
- **Alameda Swim Center**, 2256 Alameda Ave, Alameda, 510-522-8107, www.alamedaislanders.org
- **Angelo Rossi**, Arguello Blvd and Anza St, 415-666-7014, San Francisco, www.sfrecpark.org
- **Coffman Swimming Pool**, 1701 Visitacion Ave, San Francisco, 415-337-9085, www.sfrecpark.org
- **El Cerrito Swim Center**, 7007 Moeser Lane, El Cerrito, 510-559-7011, www.el-cerrito.org
- **Garfield Pool**, 1271 Treat St, San Francisco, 415-695-5001, www.sfrecpark.org
- **Hayward Plunge**, 24176 Mission Blvd, Hayward, 510-881-6703, www.haywardrec.org
- **Hamilton Recreation Center**, Geary Blvd and Steiner St, San Francisco, 415-292-2001, www.sfrecpark.org
- **Martin Luther King Jr. Swimming Pool**, 5701 3rd St, San Francisco, 415-822-2807, www.sfrecpark.org
- **McNears Pool**, 201 Cantera Way, San Rafael, 415-499-6979, www.marincountypark.org
- **Mill Valley Community Center Pool**, 180 Camino Alto, Mill Valley, 415-383-1370, www.cityofmillvalley.org
- **Sava Swimming Pool**, 2699 19th Ave, San Francisco, 415-753-7000, www.sfrecpark.org

**Lake Anza**, north of Berkeley, has a sandy beach sheltered from the wind, with picnic grounds nearby. There's an entrance fee to the swim area, which has changing rooms and a refreshment stand. The lake is open for fishing throughout the year.

Originally constructed as a storage lake for drinking water, **Lake Temescal**, next to the junction of highways 24 and 13 in Oakland, was opened to the public in 1936 and today is an urban oasis popular for swimming, fishing, sunbathing, and picnicking. Lifeguards are on duty during posted periods, and a snack stand is nearby. Many facilities are accessible to the disabled, and picnic areas dot the eight acres of lawn. For more information about Temescal, call 510-562-PARK. One of the most popular yet secluded swimming destinations is **Bass Lake**, which requires an hour to hike from the car park—but you're rewarded with a timelessly fun rope swing that launches you into the lake (1 Bear Valley Road, Point Reyes Station, www.nps.gov). Meanwhile, if you're a strong and courageous swimmer, consider joining the **Alcatraz Challenge Swim** from the old prison island to the San Francisco shore in June and August (www.tricalifornia.com).

People do actually swim in the San Francisco Bay, and some more than once. Shivering? Shrug it off. Many intrepid souls belong to **the Dolphin Club** (502 Jefferson St, 415-441-9329, www.dolphinclub.org). After a bitingly cold dip, enjoy the club's sauna and shower facilities.

## TENNIS AND RACQUET SPORTS

San Francisco alone boasts 140 public tennis courts, most of them operating on a first-come, first-served basis. At the east end of **Golden Gate Park** are 21 courts that may be reserved by calling 415-753-7100. There are also several private clubs in and around San Francisco, including **Bay Club** (370 Drumm St, 415-616-8800, and 645 5th St, 415-777-9000, www.bayclubs.com), as well as the **California Tennis Club** (1770 Scott St, 415-346-3611, www.calclubtennis.com). The **Presidio YMCA** gives access to numerous courts throughout Park Presidio (415-447-9622, www.ymcasf.org). For more information about public tennis and lessons in San Francisco, call 415-751-5639. And for courts outside San Francisco in the Bay Area, contact your local parks and recreation department (see above for listings).

## VIDEO ARCADES

Whether your game is Ms. Pac-Man or first-generation Super Mario, you can show off your joystick skills at dozens of arcades and mini-golf lands across the Bay Area. A handful of the most popular:

### SAN FRANCISCO
- **Free Gold Watch**, wall-to-wall pinball machines—the most in San Francisco (1767 Waller St, 415-876-4444, www.freegoldwatch.com)
- **Metreon**, 135 4th St, San Francisco, 415-369-6000, www.shoppingmetreon.com
- **Musée Mécanique**, highly recommended antique arcade on the waterfront (Pier 45, Shed A, San Francisco, www.museemecaniquesf.com)
- **Pier 39**, San Francisco, www.pier39.com

<u>EAST BAY</u>
- **Escapade Family Entertainment Center**, in the Public Market (Emeryville, 510-653-3323)
- **Pacific Pinball Museum,** Alameda

<u>PENINSULA & SOUTH BAY</u>
- **Capitol Flea Market**, a great market to find rare, inexpensive video games (3630 Hillcap Ave, San Jose, 408-225-5800)
- **Great Mall**, 447 Great Mall Dr, Milpitas, 408-956-2033, www.simon.com/mall/great-mall
- **Milpitas Golfland**, 1199 Jacklin Rd, 408-263-6855, www.golfland.com/milpitas
- **Nickel City**, 1711 Branham Lane, San Jose, 408-448-3323, www.nickelcitysanjoseca.com
- **Santa Cruz Boardwalk**, 400 Beach St, Santa Cruz, 831-423-5590, www.beachboardwalk.com
- **Town and Country Billiards**, 1 San Pedro Rd, Daly City, 650-992-7900

## VOLLEYBALL

Whether you're a pro looking to join an indoor tournament team or a parent trying to sign your kids up for outdoor summer fun, the Bay Area has you covered. Many parks and recreation departments offer lessons, leagues, and special summer camps. Start with the **Northern California Volleyball Association** (72 Dorman Ave, San Francisco, 415-550-7582, www.ncva.com). Also visit www.volleyball.org/bay_area.

- **City Beach Volleyball** sponsors tournaments and runs two volleyball facilities that offer indoor and outdoor classes (4020 Technology Pl, Fremont, 510-651-2500, and 2911 Mead Ave, Santa Clara, 408-654-9330, www.citybeach.com/sports).
- **Industrial Volleyball League** organizes indoor volleyball competitions on the Peninsula and in the South Bay; open play for individuals and teams on Friday nights in the large gym at Wilcox High School (3250 Monroe St, Santa Clara; 947 Emerald Hill Rd, Redwood City, 650-365-2666, www.ivlinc.com).

## WINDSURFING

Where there's wind and water, there's windsurfing. San Francisco has some of the world's best. The inexperienced should take instruction before heading out, as understanding the Bay's tides and currents is key to staying safe. Check www.iwindsurf.com for updates on wind speed and direction. Locals' favorite spots for riding the wind include **Crissy Field/Golden Gate Bridge** (415-561-4700, www.nps.gov/goga), and **Candlestick Point Recreation Area** (415-671-0145, www.sfparksalliance.org) in San Francisco; **Crown Beach** in Alameda (510-562-7275, www.parks.ca.gov); and **Brannan Island State Park,** home of Windy Cove, in the Sacramento Delta (916-777-6671, www.parks.ca.gov).

A few of the best-rated windsurfing clubs and outfitters:

- **Cal Sailing Club**, 124 University Ave, Berkeley, www.cal-sailing.org
- **Cal Adventures**, 2301 Bancroft Way, Berkeley, 510-642-4000, www.recsports.berkeley.edu/outdoor-adventures
- **Helm Ski and Windsurf**, 333 N Amphlett Blvd, San Mateo, 650-344-2711, www.helm-sport.com
- **San Francisco Boardsailing Association**, www.sfba.org
- **Shoreline Lake Boathouse,** 3160 N Shoreline Blvd, Mountain View, 650-965-7474, www.shorelinelake.com
- **WOW: Women on Water**, Crown Beach, Alameda, 415-385-1224, www.uswindsurfing.org/wow/wowhome.htm

## YOGA

Hundreds of yoga studios with thousands of classes and events attract millions of locals throughout the Bay Area, making California a top frontier for all things yoga, as well as a battleground for yoga's political identity. Consider the history: San Francisco was the first destination for yoga when it reached the United States from South Asia generations ago. After decades of popularization and commercialization, yoga has transformed from its ancient spiritual roots to its mega-marketed symbolism in today's San Francisco. For a glimpse into the tug of war over yoga's heritage, search online for "Pardon My Hindi" and "San Francisco yoga," and let local artist and historian Chiraag Bhakta educate us all with substance and style on where yoga came from and where it's heading. Chiraag's research is illuminating, and his perspective is powerful. The Bay Area's yoga circles and artistic community are stronger for hearing his voice on the subject.

A selection of top yoga centers to get you started:

### SAN FRANCISCO
- **Bikram Yoga**, 1336 Polk St, 415-673-8659, www.bikramyoganobhill.com; for other San Francisco locations visit www.funkydooryoga.com
- **Integral Yoga**, 770 Dolores, 415-821-1117, www.integralyogasf.org
- **Iyengar Yoga Institute of San Francisco**, 2404 27th Ave, 415-753-0909, www.iyisf.org
- **Mindful Body**, 2876 California St, 415-931-2639, www.themindfulbody.com
- **Yoga Society of San Francisco**, 2872 Folsom St, 415-285-5537, www.yssf.com
- **Yoga Tree**, multiple locations, 415-626-9707, www.yogatreesf.com

### NORTH BAY
- **Bikram Yoga San Rafael**, 1295 2nd St, San Rafael, 415-453-9642, www.sanrafaelyoga.com

- **Yoga Center of Marin**, 142 Redwood Ave, Corte Madera, 415-927-1850, www.yogacenterofmarin.com
- **Yogaworks**, 2207 Larkspur Landing Circle, Larkspur, 415-925-2440, www.yogaworks.com

### EAST BAY

- **4th Street Yoga**, 1809C 4th St, Berkeley, 510-845-9642, www.4thstreetyoga.com
- **Funky Door Yoga**, 2567 Shattuck Ave, Berkeley, 510-204-9642 (Bikram), www.funkydooryoga.com
- **Piedmont Yoga Studio**, 3966 Piedmont Ave, Piedmont, 510-652-3336, www.piedmontyoga.com

### PENINSULA & SOUTH BAY

- **Willow Glen Yoga**, 1188 Lincoln Ave, San Jose, 408-289-9642, www.willowglenyoga.com
- **Yoga Source**, 158 Hamilton Ave, Palo Alto, 650-328-9642, www.yogasource.com

## HEALTH CLUBS, GYMS, YMCAS

A select list of health clubs to get you started:

### SAN FRANCISCO

- **Active Sports Clubs (formerly Club One)**, various locations, 415-337-1010, www.activesportsclubs.com
- **Bay Club**, 150 Greenwich St, 415-433-2200, www.bayclubs.com/sanfrancisco
- **Crunch**, various locations, 888-227-8624, www.crunch.com
- **Curves**, designed for women, 608 Portola Dr, 415-759-9103, www.curves.com
- **24 Hour Fitness**, various locations, 800-204-2400, www.24fitness.com
- **YMCA**, various locations, 415-586-6900, www.ymcssf.org
- **YWCA**, 1830 Sutter St, 415-397-6886, www.ywca.org

### NORTH BAY

- **Anytime Fitness**, locations in Novato, Petaluma, Sonoma, Rohnert Park, San Rafael, 415-898-1166, www.anytimefitness.com
- **Body Kinetics of Mill Valley**, 639 E Blithedale Ave, Mill Valley, 415-380-8787, www.bodykineticsmarin.com
- **24 Hour Fitness**, locations in Larkspur, Petaluma, Vallejo, Rohnert Park, 415-925-0333, www.24fitness.com

### EAST BAY

- **Curves**, designed for women, locations throughout the East Bay, 925-600-9612, www.curves.com

- **In Forma**, 23 Orinda Way, #A, Orinda, 925-254-6877, www.informaorinda.com
- **YMCA**, locations throughout the East Bay, 510-451-8039, www.ymcaeastbay.org

## PENINSULA & SOUTH BAY

- **Bay Club**, locations throughout the Peninsula and South Bay, 408-402-7600, www.bayclubs.com
- **Curves**, designed for women, locations in Los Alto and San Carlos, www.curves.com
- **Optimum Results**, locations in San Jose, Campbell, Mountain View, 650-941-9148, www.optimumresults.com
- **Prime Physique Fitness**, 3635 Union Ave, San Jose, 408-558-1800, www.primephysique.com
- **YMCA**, locations throughout the Peninsula and South Bay, 650-856-9622, www.ymcasv.org

## PARKS

GOLDEN GATE PARK GETS ALL THE ATTENTION, BUT BEYOND THAT urban destination awaits a profusion of semi-hidden parks throughout the Bay Area, with equally beautiful—at times more beautiful—wildflowers and windswept walks so peaceful you'll be surprised to learn you're just a short drive from downtown. These little havens, some of them perched atop hillsides, are ideal for family outings and solo journeys. In San Francisco alone there are 230 parks.

If you're interested in national parks beyond the Presidio Park, discussed below, refer to **National Parks** in the **Quick Getaways** chapter.

## SAN FRANCISCO

### GOLDEN GATE PARK

The idea to create a large park in San Francisco originated in the mid-1860s as city leaders considered how to wrest control of an enormous sandy stretch of land occupied by settlers. Today this area stretches three miles from its eastern border of Stanyan Street to the Pacific Ocean—a park so picturesque it's an iconic symbol of San Francisco's balance between urban destination and natural escape. The park is half a mile wide, and it marks the boundary between the Richmond district to the north and the Sunset district to the south.

The rolling sand dunes of the 1800s have been transformed into green fields and wooded groves, with wild bison (yes, there are bison in San Francisco). The park's designer, William Hammond Hall, had noticed a horse's barley nosebag fall to the sand and eventually saw that the barley had sprouted. Hall took note of its possibilities and started planting barley, grass, and other plants throughout the sandy areas, setting in motion a landscaping frenzy that led to the park's development. Hall is also credited with keeping traffic moving slowly through the park by insisting on the design of park roads that twisted and turned.

Hall appointed John McLaren as assistant superintendent, and by 1890 McLaren became superintendent and continued the park's transformation. Today Golden Gate Park is the city's 1,017-acre playground, seven days a week. It's enormous—New York's Central Park comes in at a mere 843 acres. Foggy or clear, you'll find joggers, skaters, bike riders, and dogs strolling leisurely along the lush trails. The meadows and groves are popular picnic sites, and the park boasts several streams, baseball diamonds, soccer fields, tennis courts, playgrounds, an antique carousel, two art museums, a science museum, an aquarium, a Japanese tea garden, and more.

For further information or reservations visit www.sfrecpark.org.

- **Boating** (Stow Lake), 415-752-0347
- **Botanical Garden**, 415-661-1316
- **De Young Art Museum**, 415-750-3600
- **Golf** (9-hole course), 415-751-8987
- **Japanese Tea Garden**, 415-752-1171
- **Lawn bowling**, 415-753-9298
- **Park Senior Center**, 415-666-7015
- **Permits & Reservations**, 415-831-5500
- **Sharon Arts Studio**, 415-753-7004
- **Tennis** (21 courts), 415-753-7001

## PRESIDIO NATIONAL PARK

At the northern tip of San Francisco, the 1,480-acre Presidio is a scenic destination scented by eucalyptus, cypress, and pine—a natural and cultural treasure that boasts San Francisco's only overnight campground. Only recently made part of the National Park system, the Presidio was originally settled by the Spanish in 1776 and functioned as a military post before, a century later, serving as a training base for Union troops in the Civil War and—in the aftermath of the 1906 earthquake that decimated much of San Francisco—as a refuge for displaced residents. The park became a command center during World War II, and it wasn't until 1994 that the National Park Service assumed control from the Army. It's now part of the Golden Gate National Recreation Area and boasts 24 miles of the city's best wooded trails with ocean vistas. Bikers, hikers, and dog walkers populate the paths that zigzag through the groves, while windsurfers and kite surfers head for Crissy Field. Locals also fish for bass and perch at the pier near Fort Point.

The park's social center, the Presidio Officers' Club, reopened in 2014 after a three-year $30 million upgrade, and it now includes an impressive archaeology lab and cultural hub with exhibition space, and a newly renovated visitors' center nearby. The park's 469 elegant buildings evoke the area's rich history, and the new Inn at the Presidio, which opened in 2012, is the park's first public lodging. A second hotel is slated for completion in 2017.

The San Francisco arm of Lucas Films runs the Letterman Digital Arts Center, a multimedia mega-complex here, and local organizations and businesses have offices in the park. The Presidio is also a residential area with houses and apartments, available primarily to those who work here. For more information on the park's activities and ameneties, call the visitors' center at 415-561-4323. Golfers interested in teeing off in the park should visit www.presidiogolf.com (or call 415-561-4653). And bowling is popular at the park's 12-lane alley, between Moraga and Montgomery streets (www.presidiobowl.com, 415-561-2695). Visit the Presidio's website at www. nps.gov/prsf and check the **Sports and Recreation** chapter for more details.

### ADDITIONAL SAN FRANCISCO PARKS

- **Sigmund Stern Memorial Grove**, 19th Ave and Sloat Blvd, 415-252-6252, www.sfrecpark.org/destination/sigmund-stern-recreation-grove
- **Harding Park**, popular public golf course, Harding Dr off Skyline Dr, 415-664-4690, www.tpc.com
- **McLaren Park**, University and Woolsey sts, 415-239-5378, www.sfparksalliance.org
- **Dolores Park**, Dolores and 18th sts, www.sfrecpark.org/destination/mission-dolores-park
- **Balboa Park**, Ocean Ave and San Jose St, www.sfrecpark.org/destination/balboa-park
- **Glen Canyon Park**, Bosworth St and O'Shaughnessy Blvd, www.sfrecpark.org/venue/glen-canyon-park
- **Crocker Amazon**, Moscow St and Italy Ave, www.sfrecpark.org/destination/crocker-amazon-playground

Most San Francisco neighborhoods have parks with playgrounds, tennis courts, and secluded sunbathing groves. **Washington Square Park** in North Beach, **Alamo Square Park** at Fulton and Scott streets, **Lafayette Park** and **Alta Plaza** in Pacific Heights, and **Buena Vista Park** in the Haight are just a few. For more parks and recreational opportunities in your area, visit the **San Francisco Recreation & Park Department** (www.sfrecpark.org, 415-831-2700).

## BEYOND SAN FRANCISCO—BAY AREA PARKS

The park system throughout the Bay Area is vast and varied. Included here are city, county, and national parks—there are too many parks to list completely but the following will get you started. For additional parks in the western United States, contact the **National Park Services** (415-623-2100, www.nps.gov).

### NORTH BAY

Part of the Golden Gate National Recreation Area, the ruggedly scenic **Marin**

**Headlands** are on the Marin side of the Golden Gate Bridge, offering spectacular views of the city, the bridge, the ocean, the patches of fog rolling through the area. Hiking, camping, and mountain biking are popular here, and it's only moments from the city. A mosaic of geological processes—tectonic shifts, erosion, wave action, weather—over 140 million years has made this a stunningly beautiful getaway. Near Rodeo Beach you'll find the Marine Mammal Center (415-289-SEAL, www.marinemammalcenter.org), which provides shelter and medical assistance to elephant seals and sea lions. For more details about the Marin Headlands, contact the visitors' center in Sausalito (415-331-1540, www.nps.gov/goga/marin-headlands.htm).

In the center of the Bay is **Angel Island State Park**, a recommended destination where visitors arrive by ferries from Tiburon, San Francisco (at Pier 41, Fisherman's Wharf), and Vallejo. The island is richly evocative of its past: more than 175,000 Chinese immigrants were interrogated and detained here in the early 1900s, when Angel Island was an immigration checkpoint used to enforce the Chinese Exclusion Act, which prohibited Chinese from entering the country at the time. Later, during the Cold War, nuclear missiles were based here. That history is thoughtfully told at the restored Immigration Station Museum, which is highly informative for newcomers. Before and after the museum, there's no shortage of inviting spots for hiking, picnicking, and camping. For more information about Angel Island, visit www.angelisland.org.

**Mount Tamalpais** (elevation 2,572 feet), in Mount Tamalpais State Park, is Marin's highest peak, featuring 50 miles of hiking and biking trails. On clear days the views of the Bay and San Francisco are unbeatable, especially from Trojan Point and Pantoll. You can also see the Farallon Islands, some 25 miles out to sea. For more details about Mount Tamalpais, visit www.parks.ca.gov or call 415-388-2070. On your way to Mount Tamalpais, you'll pass **Muir Woods**, a towering grove of ancient redwoods that are mesmerizing and humbling—and also increasingly popular with tourists, so expect a crowd. Visit in the winter when there are fewer visitors and lots of lush foliage. For more information visit www.nps.gov/muwo.

**Samuel P. Taylor State Park**, 15 miles west of San Rafael on Sir Francis Drake Boulevard, offers 2,700 acres of hilly forested countryside, complete with hiking trails, fire roads, and a paved bike trail. The redwood groves and Papermill Creek make the area a popular camping spot. To reserve a campsite (there are 61 to choose from), contact Reserve America at 800-444-7275 (www.reserveamerica.com).

Nestled between the towns of Bolinas and Tomales, **Point Reyes National Seashore** boasts 80 miles of coastline and 70,000 acres of pristine wilderness; take your pick of paths and take a contemplative breath while standing on granite rocks formed up to 90 million years ago. Amid its rugged bluffs, wooded canyons, dense forests, and open meadows, you'll find spectacular hiking, biking, camping, bird watching, and whale watching. Mountain lions live here, so contact the visitor center at 415-464-5100 before venturing out. In 1995 a fire destroyed 13,000 acres of the park. Though you can still see the fire's effects, most of the area has recovered. During today's record-long drought, however, wildfires are a heightened concern, so be mindful about the risk of campfires. Also be sure to reserve campsites ahead of time.

To learn more about parks in Marin County, visit www.marincountyparks.org/depts/pk.

## EAST BAY

The East Bay's parks, especially in the Berkeley and Oakland hills, are more stoic and serene than San Francisco's. Call the **East Bay Regional Park District** at 888-327-2757 for information, or visit www.ebparks.org. In Berkeley, the Aquatic Park, at Seventh and Heinz streets, features a kite-flying contest at Berkeley Marina, off University Avenue in Berkeley. But the crown jewel here is **Tilden Park**, which is many newcomers' first stop in the East Bay. Located in North Berkeley, it offers floral hiking trails as well as Anza Lake for swimming (see **Sports and Recreation** for swimming details), a merry-go-round, miniature trains, a golf course, a steam train, and a petting zoo.

Tucked away in Oakland are several impressively landscaped havens. **Lake Temescal Recreation Area** (510-652-1155, www.ebparks.org/parks/temescal) has a reservoir for swimming and trout or bass fishing. Just a few miles from downtown Oakland, **Redwood Regional Park** offers stately redwoods, horseback riding, a swimming pool, and picnic areas. At **Anthony Chabot Regional Park** you can row along the 3,315-acre lake—no swimming allowed, however. To reserve one of the 75 campsites, visit www.ebparks.org/parks/anthony_chabot. Another welcoming Oakland Park is the 425-acre **Joaquin Miller Park**, off Highway 13 on Joaquin Miller Road, with plenty of hiking trails.

In Richmond, **Wildcat Canyon** offers hiking trails that are less crowded than many other Bay Area trails.

In Alameda, **Crown Memorial Beach** (Shoreline Drive, 510-521-7090) is popular for leisurely walks as well as windsurfing and kitesurfing. The **Crab Cove Visitor Center** offers marine education and tide pooling; call 510-521-6887 for details.

In Contra Costa County, the most magical, eye-popping attraction is the 19,000-acre **Mount Diablo State Park**, which is exceptional for hiking, camping, mountain biking, and sweeping views (www.stateparks.com/mount_diablo_state_park_in_california.html, 925-837-2525).

Between the cities of Martinez and Lafayette is the hilly **Briones Regional Park**, whose 6,117 acres offer 45 miles of trails through meadows and wooded areas, among lakes and waterfalls.

## PENINSULA

In San Mateo County, along Highway 1 from Pacifica to Santa Cruz, the coastline is stunning, the waves enormous, and the beachcombing unbeatable. Some of the largest sharks in the world patrol this area, but attacks are rare, and surfers by the thousands ride the waves fearlessly along this stretch of magnificent coast.

About 55 miles south of San Francisco is the **Año Nuevo State Reserve**, which hosts the world's largest breeding colony of northern elephant seals. Every year the elephant seals mate and give birth to 75-pound pups along the sand dunes. Breeding season is from December to late March, and organized sighting trips are popular among locals (www.parks.ca.gov/anonuevo/).

On the Bay, the **Coyote Point County Recreational Area** has a well-reviewed nature museum, along with swimming, boating, windsurfing, and kite-boarding. Windsurfing is also popular a few miles south of Coyote Point and near the San Francisco Airport, especially in Foster City. **Crystal Springs Reservoir** (13 miles south of San Francisco, on Interstate 280) is another refuge, with trails for hiking, biking, and horseback riding. The reservoir holds 22 billion gallons of Hetch Hetchy water for delivery to San Francisco and northern peninsula towns.

At **Huddart County Park** in Woodside, you'll find groves of redwoods. To reserve a picnic area, visit reservations.eparks.net, or call 650-363-4021. The park also features a playground designed for the physically challenged. Additional San Mateo County Parks are **Memorial Park**, where you can fish for trout, plunge into a swimming hole, hike, bike, and visit a nature museum; 7,500-acre **Pescadero Creek County Park,** with clear ocean views; and **Sam MacDonald County Park,** with 42 miles of hiking trails.

For more information on **San Mateo's County Parks** contact parks.smcgov. org or call 650-363-4020.

### SOUTH BAY

Santa Clara County's 28 parks range from bustling playgrounds to rustic retreats; contact **Santa Clara Department of Parks and Recreation** (www.parkhere.org, 408-355-2200). Below is just a sample.

The 3,600-acre **Sanborn Skyline County Park**, nestled in the Santa Cruz Mountains between the city of Saratoga and Skyline Boulevard, is a steep wooded area with camping, an outdoor theater, and a youth hostel; call 408-867-9959 for more information. You'll also find Silicon Valley's only outdoor Shakespearean company, Shady Shakespeare (www.shadyshakes.org). **Stevens Creek County Park**, in Cupertino (408-867-3654), is popular for riding or biking around its reservoir. Within the city of San Jose is **Alum Rock Park** (408-794-7275), which has mineral springs as well as hiking, biking, and horse trails.

Bird watchers from all over the country flock to **Palo Alto's Baylands Preserve**, featuring 2,000 acres of bird-beckoning salt marsh. It's a magnet for 100 species of birds, including white egrets and California clappers. In the fall and winter, the tiny black rail makes its appearance. For more details visit www.city-ofpaloalto.org.

With more than 87,000 acres, **Henry Coe State Park** is the largest state park in northern California. Plenty of people come to mountain bike, backpack, camp, fish, and ride horses. Sprawled across Morgan Hill (south of San Jose), the park has blue oaks, ponderosa pines, wild pigs, deer, and birds.

# BEACHES

If you think all California beaches are soft-sanded paradises of sun and temperate water, erase that image from your mind. Those are southern California beaches. Northern California beaches are frequently encased in fog, with bitterly cold water and an undertow that's extremely dangerous. Although Bay Area beaches do host hardy surfers and sunbathers, many local beaches are more akin to those on the North Sea—places to walk with a stick and a dog and warm clothing.

Because it is often encased in fog, the coastline rarely gets very warm, even by mid-afternoon. **San Francisco** nevertheless boasts scenic, mesmerizing beaches for lazing around with a blanket, a book, and a game. Dog walkers head to **Fort Funston**, south of **Ocean Beach**, and nudists throw caution (and more) to the wind at **Lands End** (on the northern edge of Lincoln Park). **China Beach**, a few steps away from popular **Baker Beach**, is a secluded stretch of sand adjacent to the upscale Seacliff neighborhood. Daring swimmers willing to endure the frigid Bay take the plunge at the beach in **Aquatic Park,** near Fisherman's Wharf.

In **Marin County, Stinson Beach** takes the crown as the Bay Area's most popular beach. It's so popular that on summer weekends you'll find thousands of vehicles (and inevitable traffic jams) on Highway 1 along the coast north of San Francisco, as city dwellers set out in search of peace and quiet (but don't necessarily find it). Keep in mind that the car trip includes a winding coastal road, which can make even the sturdiest stomach queasy, but can also delight passengers with cinematic views of the ocean. For clothing-optional beaches in Marin try **Muir Beach**, just before Stinson. Just past Stinson is the town of Bolinas, which has a small beach popular for surfing.

The **San Mateo County** coastline offers quieter beaches, perfect for avoiding the crowds. Head south from San Francisco down Highway 1, through **Pacifica** and **Half Moon Bay,** and keep your eyes peeled for a beach that fits the bill. Remember, though, that the water is cold and the currents are strong. For more details visit www.parks.ca.gov.

## SAN FRANCISCO & NORTH BAY

- **Ocean Beach**: San Francisco's main beach is a long, sandy shoreline stretching flatly along the city's western edge, a few steps from the foot of Golden Gate Park. Packed with sunbathers on rare days when the fog lifts and the skies are warm, Ocean Beach is popular year-round with surfers, hang-gliders, kite fliers, strollers, joggers, and dog walkers (officially on-leash). High winds that kick sand into your food and face are part of the fun. On summer evenings, the beach is lit up (on the northern end only) with campfires. Waters are icy and the waves are rough, so swimming is hazardous. *Rip currents are extremely strong here.* Many people have drowned, so be cautious. But sunbathing and bonfires are safe and welcoming (www.parksconservancy.org/visit/park-sites/ocean-beach.html).

- **Baker Beach**: Smaller than Ocean Beach but far more picturesque, Baker Beach is nestled at the bottom of the deeply wooded Point Lobos, just beneath the Golden Gate Bridge—offering exquisite views of the bridge and the Marin Headlands. Toward the foot of the bridge is the nude portion of the beach (www.parksconservancy.org/visit/park-sites/baker-beach.html).
- **Point Reyes**, one of the Bay Area's greatest destinations, with 100 square miles of beaches, forests, marshes, and coastal trails, is popular for weekend hiking, kayaking, biking, bird watching, picnicking, and camping. The rough ocean currents make swimming dangerous, but many intrepid water-lovers take the cold plunge at Bass Lake—dubbed by the park service as the best unofficial place to take a dip. The hike to Bass Lake via the Coastal Trail can be challenging in spots (415-464-5100, www.nps.gov/pore).
- **Tomales Bay State Park**, a 2,000-acre park right next to Point Reyes, is home to four protected, surf-free beaches, making it a prime spot for swimming, boating, and kayaking. Find it four miles north of Inverness on Pierce Point Road (415-669-1140, www.parks.ca.gov).
- **Stinson** is a well-loved 3-mile sandy stretch and adjoining 51-acre park. Both are packed with families in the summer. Swimming is permitted, and lifeguards are on duty from May through October. There are countless picnic tables and a snack bar during peak season, plus restrooms and showers. To avoid the crowds, visit on a weekday. Take Highway 1 to the Stinson Beach exit (www.nps.gov/goga/stbe.htm).
- **Red Rock, a popular clothing-optional beach half a mile south of Stinson Beach**, is located at Milepost 11 on Highway 1. There's a turnout for parking, but no signs. It's about a 15-minute hike down a steep trail, but there are no facilities at Red Rock Beach, and poison oak is reportedly rampant, so wear shoes on the trail and use caution. Then join neighbors for nude Scrabble on the sand.

For more information on San Francisco and Marin County beaches, contact the **Golden Gate National Recreation Area** (San Francisco, 415-561-4700, www.nps.gov/goga).

## PENINSULA, SOUTH BAY & EAST BAY BEACHES

- **Half Moon Bay State Beach**, a half-mile west of Highway 1 on Kelly Avenue, is actually three beaches in one—Dunes (end of Young Avenue off Highway 1), Francis (end of Kelly Avenue in Half Moon Bay), and Venice (end of Venice Boulevard off Highway 1). Francis Beach has a campground for tents and RVs, and reservations are recommended. Contact Half Moon Bay Beaches (650-726-8819, www.parks.ca.gov) for more information. Campsite reservations must be made through Reserve America (800-444-7275, www.reserveamerica.com).
- **San Gregorio State Beach** is a favorite for families and school field trips. San Gregorio's clay cliffs and caves, hiking trails, and picnic facilities make it an

idyllic adventure. Find it 10.5 miles south of Half Moon Bay on Highway 1 (www.
parks.ca.gov, 650-726-8819).

- **Año Nuevo State Reserve**, fifty-six miles south of San Francisco, is a rocky point
that juts out into the ocean and is home to the largest mainland northern elephant seal breeding colony in the world. During breeding season, December
through March, access is available by guided walks only—but it is well worth a
day trip (www.parks.ca.gov, 650-879-2025).

- **Montara State Beach** boasts one of the country's best hostels, tranquilly set
at the lighthouse 20 miles south of San Francisco, on Highway 1. The tide pools
and fishing are unbeatable. The paths down to the beach are steep, and dogs
are allowed on leash only. For information contact the hostel at www.norcal-
hostels.org/montara or 650-728-7177.

- **Pacifica**, a handful of spectacular beaches, includes Linda Mar (also known as
Pacifica State Beach), which runs along a wide curving mouth. Kids typically
enjoy what locals call the world's most beautiful Taco Bell, while the wave-
pounded shores at nearby Rockaway are favorites with surfers. All of Pacifica's
beaches are accessible from Highway 1 (www.cityofpacifica.org, 650-738-7381).

- **Pescadero State Beach** features sandy shores, rocky cliffs, and picnic tables
that make it a hotspot for families in the summer; arrive early for the tide pools.
Across the highway, Pescadero Marsh Natural Preserve is a bird-watching destination. The beach is 15 miles south of Half Moon Bay on Highway 1 (www.parks.
ca.gov, 650-879-2170).

- **Robert W. Crown Memorial State Beach**, the city of Alameda's 2.5-mile sandy
playground, is well-equipped for family picnics, BBQs, and windsurfing. Swimming is permitted year-round. Rental sailboards and lessons are available on
summer weekends (www.ebparks.org, 888-327-2757).

L IVING ON THE WEST COAST IS REWARDING BUT NOT WITHOUT RISK. While storms are not usually a problem here—especially during this ongoing drought—one does have to prepare for the possibility of earthquakes. There are precautions to take, including establishing a family emergency plan and creating a stock of supplies (see the end of this chapter). Keep the following resources on hand:

- **American Red Cross Bay Area Chapter,** 415-427-8000 (disaster preparedness information), or 24-hour disaster dispatch at 866-272-2237, www.redcross.org
- **California Office of Emergency Services**, 916-845-8510, www.caloes.ca.gov
- **Federal Emergency Management Agency (FEMA)**, 800-621-FEMA, TTY 800-462-7585, www.fema.gov

## EARTHQUAKES

Newcomers' biggest fear about the Bay Area—apart from the soaring housing costs—tends to be earthquakes. While many natives aren't too frightened by the swaying caused by small temblors, no one is fully prepared for the proverbial big one. An outstanding new quake-preparedness website, www.sf72.org, is a wise place to start, and is the local hub for emergency readiness.

San Francisco has been victimized by devastating earthquakes twice in the past century: in 1906 and 1989. In 1906 the 7.8-magnitude quake leveled buildings and sparked fires that engulfed and destroyed much of the city, killing thousands of people—the highest death toll from a natural disaster in California history. The 1989 Loma Prieta quake killed fewer but brought down a section of a major East Bay freeway, dislodged part of the San Francisco–Oakland Bay Bridge, sparked fires in the Marina district, and brought that year's World Series to an abrupt, albeit temporary, halt. The question now is when—not if—the next quake will strike. Experts say there is a 99.7 percent chance that the big one—an ominous shaker of magnitude 6.7 or greater—will occur somewhere in California by 2038. If you choose to settle down in earthquake country, you might be unsettled soon—but there are steps you can take to keep you, your family, and your home safe.

## HOME PREPARATION AND INSURANCE

Simple steps to make your home a bit safer include fastening big appliances and equipment to desks and counters. Large furniture like bookcases should be bolted to the wall. Small items like fragile collectibles should be taped or glued to their shelves or stuck with clay or museum wax. Strap the water heater to the wall. Earthquake supply and hardware stores are happy to sell what you need to do this. For information about retrofitting your home contact the **California Earthquake Authority**, 916-325-3800, www.earthquakeauthority.com. Additional tips on seismic safety are found at www.resilience.abag.ca.gov.

Bolted wood frame buildings (such as Victorians) are considered safer, and steel-reinforced concrete buildings (like downtown skyscrapers) are also reasonably safe, unless they're built on landfill, which is subject to liquefaction. The most dangerous building during a quake is one made of non-reinforced masonry. For this reason, brick buildings can no longer be constructed in San Francisco, though a handful of older ones remain. Dozens of San Francisco buildings are still being retrofitted following the 1989 earthquake. You might want to find out whether the building you live or work in has been retrofitted or bolted.

If you're buying a home in California the seller is required by law to tell you if the property is on or near an earthquake fault line. Before buying, engage the services of a civil engineer to give your prospective home the once-over, just to make sure it's as safe as it can be. If that sounds like a headache to arrange, ask your real estate agent to advise you. Rental property owners are not required to disclose information about nearby faults to prospective tenants.

Property owners are strongly advised to buy a homeowners insurance policy that covers quake damage. The California Insurance Commissioner requires that companies selling homeowners and rental policies in California must also offer quake insurance. To learn more about earthquake coverage, ask your insurance agent or contact the **California State Department of Insurance** (800-927-HELP (4357), www.insurance.ca.gov).

## WHAT TO DO DURING AN EARTHQUAKE

- If you're inside when it strikes, remember the life-saving line—duck, cover, and hold. Get under a strong table or desk. Cover your head and face to protect them from broken glass and falling debris. Hold onto the table or desk and be prepared to move with it. Stay there until the shaking stops. Do not run outside. Stay away from windows, and avoid elevators and stairwells. Keep a lookout for falling objects.
- If you're driving when the earthquake strikes, pull over. Stay away from bridges, overpasses, power lines, and large buildings. Remain in your car and wait for the shaking to stop.

- If you're outside, go into an open area away from trees, power lines, and buildings.
- If you're in a crowded public area, stay calm, do not jam the exit, and avoid elevators and stairwells. Look for a safe place to duck and cover until passage is clear.

## AFTER THE SHOCK

- First, see if your natural gas line is leaking. If you detect a leak, and *only* if you detect a leak, turn the shutoff valve. Remember this: don't turn the gas off if you don't think it's leaking. The gas company will be busy fixing numerous emergency problems following the earthquake, so it could be days before someone can get to those who shut things off unnecessarily. If your water is working, fill the tub and sinks with water. Although the pipes are running now they may not later, and you can use this water for drinking and washing. Check outside for downed utility lines, and turn on the radio for instructions and news reports. Your smartphone may or may not get service.
- Stay calm, help others, make sure all household members and pets are accounted for. Keep the radio on for emergency announcements. To leave roads clear for emergency vehicles, avoid driving. Check gas, water, electrical, and sewer lines, and turn off anything that appears to be leaking or broken. Report any problems immediately to your utility company.
- Check your home for damages—paying attention to the roof, foundation, and chimneys, as well as cracked walls.
- Look for downed power lines; steer clear and warn others to stay away.
- Brace yourself for aftershocks.
- If you must leave your home, leave a note telling others where you are.
- If you haven't found your pets, remember to leave food and water accessible before leaving your home to search, in case they run back. Leave the toilet seat up, fill the bathtub, open cans of food, and tear open entire bags of dry food. It might be several days before you are allowed to return.

## BASIC EARTHQUAKE FACTS: BAY AREA FAULTS

The biggest and baddest of all Bay Area faults—and the source of greatest anxiety—is the San Andreas. This master fault spans almost the entire length of California. The San Andreas is more than 800 miles long, and at its greatest depth it dips 10 miles beneath the surface. Two of the continent's great tectonic plates, the Pacific and the North American, meet here, creating what geologists call a "strike slip fault." Earthquakes in the Bay Area result from the pressure buildup and strain as the plates push against one another. From the San Andreas, a network of smaller faults splinter off, weaving in and out from inland areas along the coast. These smaller faults include Rodgers Creek, Concord–Green Valley, Greenville, Hayward, San Gregorio, and Calaveras.

For more insight into the science of earthquakes, and up-to-the-minute information on quakes worldwide, visit the US Geological Survey at www.usgs.gov.

Other **earthquake information sources:**

- **American Red Cross Bay Area Chapter,** 415-427-8000 (disaster preparedness information), or 24-hour disaster dispatch at 866-272-2237, www.redcross.org
- **California Earthquake Authority,** for seismic safety and earthquake insurance information, 916-325-3800, www.earthquakeauthority.com
- **California Office of Emergency Services,** 916-845-8510, www.caloes.ca.gov
- **California Seismic Safety Commission,** publishes "The Homeowner's Guide to Earthquake Safety" as well as other materials on quake preparedness, 916-263-5506, www.seismic.ca.gov
- **Federal Emergency Management Agency (FEMA)**, 800-621-FEMA, TTY 800-462-7585, www.fema.gov
- **Northern California Earthquake Data Center at UC Berkeley Seismology Laboratory**, www.ncedc.org
- **US Geological Survey**, measures quakes and offers a trove of information on all things seismic, www.usgs.gov

## DISASTER KITS AND SAFETY PLANS

Aside from luck, the secret to surviving a disaster is the adage "be prepared." Keep a basic disaster kit at home and in your trunk. Remember to store supplies away from areas likely to be damaged in a big earthquake. The kit should include the following:

- Water (at least one gallon per person, per day, for several days)
- Food for each family member and your pets (canned goods such as stew, beans, soup, evaporated milk, cereal, granola bars, nuts, dried fruit, and cookies)
- Water purification tablets
- Smartphone chargers and extra batteries
- Non-electric can opener
- Flashlights and extra batteries
- Portable radio and extra batteries
- Blankets, sleeping bags, pillows
- Camping stove or BBQ with plenty of appropriate fuel
- Swiss Army knife or similar tool
- Cooking and eating utensils, paper plates, cups
- Tent
- Small bottle of chlorine bleach
- Toiletries—including toilet paper, feminine hygiene products, contact lens supplies, and diapers
- Waterproof matches
- Plastic garbage bags and ties
- Toys, games, cards, crosswords, paper and pencils, books

- Markers to scrawl a message on the front of the building door (or ruins) if you must leave
- Sturdy shoes
- Rain gear
- Sunglasses and sunscreen
- Dust masks
- Cold weather clothing, gloves, scarves, hats
- Fire extinguisher
- Whistle
- Pet carrier and photos of your pets to identify them if they take off
- A basic tool kit, with hammer, pliers, wrench, and other tools for minor repairs
- Cash (bank ATMs may not work after a big temblor, and merchants may not accept credit cards)
- First aid kit, including the following:
- Plastic adhesive strips
- ACE bandages
- Gauze pads and tape
- Scissors
- Tweezers
- Safety pins
- Chemical ice packs
- Cotton balls or swabs
- Aspirin or the equivalent
- Antibiotic ointments
- Hydrogen peroxide
- Rubbing alcohol
- Insect repellent
- Thermometer
- Over-the-counter medications for diarrhea and upset stomach
- First aid manual
- Prescription medications that are not past their expiration dates

Is your head swimming yet? Once you've gathered everything together, put it all in a container like a big plastic can with a lid, and stash it in a place that's not likely to be buried in a quake. If you live in a house, the backyard may be best. If you live in an apartment building you'll have to be creative when it comes to protecting your kit.

Several Bay Area stores sell earthquake preparedness equipment. Here are a few:

- **Earthquake Supply Center**, 3095 Kerner Blvd, San Rafael, 415-459-5500, www. earthquakesupplycenter.com

- **Earth Shakes**, 1004 Oak Grove, Burlingame, 650-548-9065, www.earthshakes. com
- **REI—Recreational Equipment Inc.**, 840 Brannan St, San Francisco, 415-934-1938; 1338 San Pablo Ave, Berkeley, 510-527-4140; 1119 Industrial Rd, San Carlos, 650-508-2330; other locations throughout the Bay Area, www.rei.com

As you put your disaster kit together you should also come up with a family (or neighbor) emergency plan:

- Assign someone outside the Bay Area to be your call-center contact—a clearinghouse for family information. Make sure each family member knows the number. Phone lines and wireless service may not be working for a few days—keep trying; eventually they will be restored.
- Should your home suffer severe damage, create a planned meeting place like the local high school football field or park, or a department store parking lot—someplace that isn't likely to come tumbling down during an initial quake or any aftershocks.

THE VIRTUES OF VOLUNTEERING AND COMMUNITY ENGAGEMENT ARE central to the Bay Area, and now that you've found a place to live, unpacked, and settled into your new home, it's time to explore your neighborhood by pitching in however you can. This chapter lists a variety of options for participation.

## VOLUNTEERING

Giving back to the community—especially in today's Bay Area, where fortunes are made as quickly as they're lost—is a rewarding and mutually enriching experience. Whether you're skilled at building houses, caring for the elderly, tutoring underprivileged children, or canvassing neighborhoods (bilingual skills can be especially helpful), there's a volunteer project for you. Volunteering in your new community can also help make the transition to an unfamiliar place less stressful.

### VOLUNTEER REFERRAL SERVICES

If you know the place you'd like to volunteer with, call directly and inquire about opportunities. The agencies below can put you in touch with the many organizations and people in need of your assistance:

- **Center for Volunteer and Nonprofit Leadership**, 65 Mitchell Blvd, Suite 101, San Rafael, 415-479-5710, www.centerforleadershipmarin.org
- **HandsOn Bay Area**, 1504 Bryant St, San Francisco, 415-541-9616, www.handsonbayarea.org
- **Hayward Area Volunteer Services**, 4901 Breakwater Ave, Hayward, 510-670-7270, www.haywardrec.org
- **Volunteer Center of San Francisco** and San Mateo Counties, 1675 California St, San Francisco 415-982-8999, www.thevolunteercenter.net

- **Volunteer Center of the East Bay**, serving Contra Costa and Alameda counties, 700 Ygnacio Valley Rd, #140, 925-472-5760, 510-232-0163, www.volunteereastbay.org

## HOW YOU CAN HELP

### THE HUNGRY AND THE HOMELESS

Scores of volunteers are needed to assist the Bay Area's growing homeless population, from monitoring and organizing the shelters to providing medical and legal help. Other tasks include ministering to psychiatric and social needs, raising money, and caring for children in the shelters. Many people solicit, organize, cook, and serve food throughout the Bay Area. Others deliver meals to the homeless and the homebound. Visit www.freeprintshop.org for up-to-the-minute charts showing locations and contact information.

### CHILDREN

If encouraging and empowering children strikes a chord with you, you can tutor in and out of schools, become a big brother or sister, teach music and sports in shelters or at community centers, run activities in the parks, entertain children in hospitals, or accompany kids on weekend outings. Schools, libraries, community associations, hospitals, and other facilities providing activities and guidance for children are all worth exploring.

### HOSPITALS

The need for volunteers in both city-run and private hospitals is growing: from interpreters to laboratory personnel to admitting and nursing aides. Assistants in crisis medical areas—emergency rooms and intensive care units especially—are wanted if you have the skills. Volunteers are also needed to work with victims of sexual assault.

### THE DISABLED AND THE ELDERLY

Many newcomers read and even sing to those who may not be able to, as well as help to prevent birth defects and assist the developmentally delayed and disabled. There are ample reasons to make regular visits to the homebound elderly, bring hot meals to them, and teach everything from nutrition to arts and crafts in senior centers and nursing homes.

### EXTREME CARE SITUATIONS

Helping with suicide prevention, Alzheimer's and AIDS patients, rape victims, and abused children is a special category demanding a high level of attention and a high number of volunteers. If you have the abilities and values to reach out and alleviate immediate suffering, lend a life-saving hand by contacting the Bay Area's many outreach groups. (See listings above.)

## ARTS

Museums are constantly in need of volunteers to lead tours or lend a hand in countless ways. Often these positions come with perks. Libraries, theater groups, and ballet companies have plenty of tasks on rolling deadlines, and fundraising efforts also require volunteers to make phone calls and prepare emails.

## PLACES OF WORSHIP

The Bay Area's diversity is evident in its multitude of churches, temples, ashrams, mosques, and other houses of worship—as well as the growing number and influence of atheist groups. Below are a few relevant organizations. To find a place of worship or atheist community close to your new home, word of mouth is best—ask neighbors and local merchants—and also check the reviews at www.yelp.com under "atheists," "churches," "synagogues," "mosques," and so on.

### ATHEIST GROUPS

- **Atheists of Silicon Valley**, meetings throughout Silicon Valley, www.godlessgeeks.com
- **Contra Costa Atheists & Freethinkers**, Pleasant Hill, www.meetup.com/contra-costa-atheists-and-freethinkers
- **East Bay Atheists**, 510-222-7580, www.eastbayatheists.org
- **Freedom From Religion Foundation**, 608-256-8900, www.ffrf.org
- **Rossmoor Atheists and Agnostics**, Walnut Creek, 925-464-7879, www.rossmooratheists.info
- **San Francisco Atheists**, 900 Bush St, #210, San Francisco, www.sfathiests.com

### CHURCHES

#### BAPTIST
- **Bay Area Baptist Church**, 2929 Peralta Blvd, Fremont, 510-797-8882, www.bayareabaptist.org
- **Community Baptist Church of San Jose**, 2215 Curtner Ave, Campbell, 408-371-6200, www.cbcsj.org
- **Ebenezer Baptist Church**, 275 Divisadero St, San Francisco, 415-431-0200, www.ebcsf.org
- **First Chinese Baptist Church of San Francisco**, 15 Waverly Pl, San Francisco, 415-362-4139, www.fcbc-sf.org.
- **Lakeshore Avenue Baptist Church**, 3534 Lakeshore Ave, Oakland, 510-893-2484, www.labcoakland.org
- **Third Baptist Church**, 1399 McAllister St, San Francisco, 415-346-4426, www.thirdbaptist.org

## EASTERN ORTHODOX
- **Ascension Cathedral**, 4700 Lincoln Ave, Oakland, 510-531-3400, www.groca.org
- **Greek Orthodox Cathedral of the Annunciation**, 245 Valencia St, San Francisco, 415-864-8000, www.annunciation.org
- **Greek Orthodox Cathedral of the Ascension**, 4700 Lincoln Ave, Oakland, 510-531-3400, www.groca.org
- **Holy Virgin Cathedral**, 6210 Geary Blvd, San Francisco, 415-221-3255, www.sfsobor.com
- **Nativity of Christ Greek Orthodox Christian Church**, 1110 Highland Dr, Novato, 415-883-1998, www.nativityofchrist.org
- **Russian Orthodox Church of Our Lady of Kazan**, 5725 California St, San Francisco 415-752-2502, www.kazanchurch.org
- **St. Nicholas Greek Orthodox Church**, 1260 Davis St, San Jose, 408-246-2770, www.saintnicholas.org

## EPISCOPAL
- **Grace Cathedral**, perched high atop Nob Hill, is a towering cathedral with spectacular stained glass windows and soaring vaults that frame not just individual prayer but also popular concerts of jazz, gospel, and other genres, as well as the largest free yoga sessions in San Francisco. Strolling through the outdoor labyrinth and the majestic Huntington Park across the street is a meditative, peaceful experience. There are several other Episcopal churches throughout the Bay Area, but Grace Cathedral is a sight to behold for all visitors (1100 California St, San Francisco, 415-749-6300, www.gracecathedral.org).

## JEHOVAH'S WITNESSES
Jehovah's Witnesses in the Bay Area can contact the Kingdom Hall of Jehovah's Witnesses at 501 Fulton St, San Francisco (415-252-7082). To find your local hall, visit www.jw.org.

## LATTER DAY SAINTS/MORMON
Even if you're not a member of the Church of Jesus Christ of Latter Day Saints, the **Mormon Temple**, 4770 Lincoln Avenue, Oakland (510-531-3200, www.lds.org), is well worth a visit for its architectural splendor. Built in the 1960s and nested high in the Oakland hills overlooking the Bay, this impressive temple and its five spires dominate the skyline and can be seen from miles away. The congregation is large, made up of many ethnicities and nationalities. The temple itself is reserved for religious services, but the exquisitely kept grounds and visitors' center are open to the public.

## LUTHERAN
- **St. Mark's Lutheran Church**, 1111 O'Farrell St, San Francisco, 415-928-7770, www.stmarks-sf.org

- **St. Matthew's Lutheran Church**, 3281 16th St, San Francisco, 415-863-6371, www.stmatthews-sf.org
- **St. Paul Lutheran Church**, 1658 Excelsior Ave, Oakland, 510-530-6333, www.stpaul-lutheran.com
- **West Portal Lutheran Church and School**, 200 Sloat Blvd, San Francisco, 415-661-8402, www.westportallutheran.org
- **Zion Lutheran Church and School**, 495 9th Ave, San Francisco, 415-221-7500, www.zionsf.org

## METHODIST

There are many Methodist churches throughout the Bay Area. To find one near you, visit www.umc.org. One of the most active is San Francisco's **Glide Memorial Methodist Church,** which features food giveaways, recovery meetings, classes, and housing programs (330 Ellis St, San Francisco, 415-674-6000, www.glide.org).

## PRESBYTERIAN

- **Calvary Presbyterian Church**, 2515 Fillmore St, San Francisco, 415-346-3832, www.calvarypresbyterian.org
- **Menlo Park Presbyterian Church**, 950 Santa Cruz Ave, Menlo Park, 650-323-8600, www.mppc.org
- **Noe Valley Ministry**, 1021 Sanchez St, San Francisco, 415-282-2317, www.noevalleyministry.org
- **The Old First Presbyterian Church**, 1751 Sacramento St, San Francisco, 415-776-5552, www.oldfirst.org

## QUAKER

Known for promoting fellowship, solidarity, justice, and spirituality, the Quakers, also known as the Religious Society of Friends, have an active meeting house and school in San Francisco, at 250 Valencia St (415-565-0400, www.sffriendsschool.org). The San Francisco Friends hold an open-to-all silent peace vigil in front of the Federal Building at Golden Gate and Larkin streets every Thursday at noon. The San Francisco meeting house holds regular worship services every Sunday at 11 a.m.; newcomers are encouraged to attend the orientation held beforehand at 10:40 a.m. To learn more, contact **San Francisco Friends Meeting** (www.sfquakers.org). Outside of San Francisco, find the meeting house nearest you by visiting www.quakerfinder.org.

## ROMAN CATHOLIC

There are hundreds of Catholic churches in the Bay Area. For a comprehensive list, visit www.thecatholicdirectory.com, as well as the San Francisco Archdiocese (1 Peter Yorke Way, San Francisco, 415-614-5500, www.sfarchdiocese.org). For churches throughout the South Bay, contact the Archdiocese of San Jose (1150 N 1st St, #100, San Jose, www.dsj.org). Numerous Bay Area churches offer services in Italian, Chinese, Tagalog, French, Spanish, Latin, Vietnamese, Korean, and more. A few to get started:

- **The Cathedral of St. Mary of the Assumption,** 1111 Gough St, San Francisco, 415-567-2020, www.stmarycathedralsf.org
- **Mission Dolores**, the oldest building in San Francisco (dating to 1776), tucked on the edge of Dolores Park (3321 16th St, San Francisco, 415-621-8203, www.missiondolores.org)
- **St. Augustine**, 400 Alcatraz Ave, Oakland, 510-653-8631, www.staugustineoakland.com
- **St. Christopher**, 1576 Curtner Ave, San Jose, 408-269-2226, www.saintchris.com
- **St. Dominic's**, 2390 Bush St in San Francisco, 415-567-7824, www.stdominics.org
- **St. Ignatius**, Fulton and Parker sts, San Francisco, 415-422-2188, www.stignatiussf.org
- **St. Vincent de Paul**, 35 Liberty St, Petaluma, 707-762-4278, www.svpch.org

## SEVENTH-DAY ADVENTIST
Seventh-day Adventist churches are located throughout the Bay Area, including churches dedicated to Chinese, Japanese, Latin American, and Russian communities. A popular starting point is the **San Francisco Central Seventh-day Adventist Church** (2889 California St, San Francisco, 415-921-9016, www.sfcentral.org). To find a church or school in your town, visit www.adventistdirectory.org.

## UNITARIAN UNIVERSALIST
Known for progressive social activism and embrace of individuals from various religious backgrounds, Unitarian Universalist churches are active throughout the Bay Area. For a comprehensive directory, visit www.uua.org or start with the **First Unitarian Universalist Church and Center** (1187 Franklin St, San Francisco, 415-776-4580, www.uusf.org).

## JEWISH CONGREGATIONS
The **Jewish Community Center** (3200 California St, San Francisco, 415-292-1200, www.jccsf.org) offers education classes and workshops, social and singles events, programs for interfaith couples and families, preschools, after-school programs, a teen center, summer camps, youth sports classes, and dance, music, and ceramics instruction. In the Peninsula and the South Bay, the **Oshman Family Jewish Community Center** (3921 Fabian Way, Palo Alto, 650-223-8700, www.paloaltojcc.org) is a highly popular option for classes and community events, as is **Foster City's Peninsula Jewish Community Center** (800 Foster City Blvd, Foster City, 650-212-7522, www.pjcc.org).

The **Jewish Community Federation** (www.sfjcf.org) is an excellent resource for volunteer opportunities and trips to Israel, as is *Resource: A Guide to Jewish Life in the Bay Area* (www.jewishresourceguide.com/chapter/5), which maintains a thorough list of congregations, organizations, and social events. Also bookmark www.jweekly.com for information on Jewish cooking, classifieds, and a calendar of events. There are hundreds of Jewish congregations in the Bay Area. Below are just a few:

## CONSERVATIVE

- **Beth Sholom**, 301 14th Ave, San Francisco, 415-221-8736, www.bethsholomsf.org.
- **Congregation Beth Ami**, 4676 Mayette Ave, Santa Rosa, 707-360-3000, www.bethamisr.org
- **Congregation Beth David**, 19700 Prospect Rd, Saratoga, 408-257-3333, www.beth-david.org
- **Congregation Netivot Shalom**, 1316 University Ave, Berkeley, 510-549-9447, www.netivotshalom.org

## ORTHODOX

- **Am Echad,** 1504 Meridian Ave, San Jose, 408-267-2591, www.amechad.org
- **Chabad Jewish Center of Oakland & Piedmont**, 3008 Lakeshore Ave, Oakland, 510-545-6770, www.jewishoakland.org
- **Chabad of Noe Valley**, 3771 Cesar Chavez, San Francisco, 415-648-8000, www.chabadnoevalley.org

## PROGRESSIVE REFORM

- **Congregation Sha'ar Zahav**, a progressive reform synagogue for people of all sexual identities, 290 Dolores St, San Francisco, 415-861-6932, www.shaarzahav.org

## RECONSTRUCTIONIST

- **Keddem Congregation**, 3900 Fabian Way, Palo Alto, 650-494-6400, www.keddem.org
- **Or Zarua**, various locations in Berkeley, www.orzaruaeastbay.org

## REFORM

- **Beth Israel Judea**, 625 Brotherhood Way, San Francisco, 415-586-8833, www.bij.org
- **Congregation Emanu-El**, 2 Lake St, San Francisco, 415-751-2535, www.emanuelsf.org
- **Rodef Sholom**, 170 N San Pedro Rd, San Rafael, 415-479-3441, www.rodefsholom.org
- **Temple Sherith Israel**, one of the oldest synagogues in the United States, 2266 California St, San Francisco, 415-346-1720, www.sherithisrael.org
- **Temple Sinai**, 2808 Summit St, Oakland, 510-451-3263, www.oaklandsinai.org

## ISLAMIC CENTERS

Mosques, Islamic community centers, libraries, schools, and political and social groups abound in the Bay Area. In San Francisco, consider starting with the **Islamic Society of San Francisco** (20 Jones St, San Francisco, www.islamsf.com). In the South Bay, contact the **Muslim Community Association of the San Francisco Bay Area** (408-727-7277, www.mcabayarea.org). The **South Bay Islamic Association** (408-947-9389, www.sbia.net) offers extensive details on Bay Area mosque locations, schools, elder groups, restaurant listings, charities, and more.

## SIKH TEMPLES

The Bay Area has several Sikh temples (gurdwaras), the most notable of which is **Sikh Center of San Francisco Bay Area,** also known as **Gurdwara Sahib**. Based in in El Sobrante, it is located a few miles northwest of Richmond. The city of Stockton lays claim to North America's first Sikh gurdwara (1930 S Grant St, Stockton, 209-625-7500, www.stocktongurdwarasahib.org), which opened in 1912. In San Jose, visit **Sikh Gurdwara Sahib** (3636 Murillo Ave, San Jose, 408-274-9373, www.san-josegurdwara.com).

## BUDDHIST AND HINDU CENTERS

### BUDDHISM

The **San Francisco Buddhist Center** (37 Bartlett St, San Francisco, 415-282-2018, www.sfbuddhistcenter.org) is an excellent resource for newcomers wanting to learn about the many Buddhist centers in the Bay Area.

Bay Area Zen Buddhist centers offer stoic, sheltered environments for ceremonies, meditations, meals, and chanting to members and non-members. The beloved **Zen Center** (300 Page Street, San Francisco, 415-863-3136) and Marin County's **Green Gulch Farm Zen Center** (1601 Shoreline Highway, Muir Beach, 415-383-3134), are the most cherished of the many centers in the Bay Area. (Produce grown at Green Gulch is used at the exquisite Green's vegetarian restaurant in Fort Mason.) For information and links to local centers, visit www.sfzc.org.

### HINDUISM

To practice the traditions of Hinduism and learn about its past and present, visit **BAPS Swaminarayan Sanstha** (950 Avalon Ave, San Francisco, 415-469-9121, www.baps.org), and the **Vedanta Society of Northern California** (2323 Vallejo St, 415-922-2323, www.sfvedanta.org), which both offer lectures, scripture classes, a bookshop, and a library. In the East Bay, one of the popular resources is the **Hindu Temple and Cultural Center** (3676 Delaware Dr, Fremont, 510-659-0655, www.fremonttemple.org). For newcomers to the Peninsula and South Bay, visit **Vaidica Vidhya Ganapathi Center** (32 Rancho Dr, San Jose, 408-226-3600, www.vvgc.org).

## RELIGIOUS CENTERS WELCOMING OF ALL SEXUAL ORIENTATIONS

- **A Common Bond** is a support network for current and former Jehovah's Witnesses who identify as gay, lesbian, bisexual, and transgender; the group began in San Francisco and has expanded nationally (www.gayxjw.org).
- **Congregation Sha'ar Zahav** is a progressive reform synagogue for people of all sexual identities (290 Dolores St, San Francisco, 415-861-6932, www.shaarzahav.org).
- **Dignity San Francisco** is a supportive group for gay, lesbian, and transgender individuals and allies in and beyond the Catholic community (1329 7th Ave, 415-681-2491, www.dignitysanfrancisco.org).
- **Metropolitan Community Church** offers social activities and counseling. The parishioners also serve meals and provide showers for the homeless, and tutor children at the Harvey Milk Civil Rights Academy (1300 Polk St, San Francisco, 415-863-4434, www.mccsf.org).
- **Most Holy Redeemer Church** offers services, reconciliation, and AIDS support groups (100 Diamond St, San Francisco, 415-863-6259, www.mhr.org).
- **St. Francis Lutheran**: this church was expelled from mainstream Lutheranism for adopting welcoming, progressive policies toward LGBT members. It currently offers several help groups, elder meetings, and bingo (152 Church St, San Francisco, 415-621-2635, www.st-francis-lutheran.org).
- **St. Paul Lutheran Church**, 1658 Excelsior Ave, Oakland, 510-530-6333, www.stpaul-lutheran.com

## RELIGIOUS STUDIES

**The Graduate Theological Union**, nicknamed Holy Hill, includes the Pacific School of Religion, the Bade Museum (of religious works), and the Flora Lamson Hewlitt Library, as well as several other religious centers and schools of theology. It hosts a packed calendar of lectures, presentations, and public prayer services (2400 Ridge Rd, Berkeley, 510-649-2400, www.gtu.edu).

## THE MISSIONS

Spanish missionaries reached California in the 1700s, and several sites remain popular portals into local history. Some are active, consecrated churches; others are crumbling remnants. A few highlights:

- **Mission Dolores**, the oldest and best-known building in San Francisco (dating to 1776), tucked on the edge of sun-soaked Dolores Park (3321 16th St, San Francisco, 415-621-8203, www.missiondolores.org)
- **Mission San Jose**, reconstructed at 43300 Mission Blvd, Fremont, www.missionsanjose.org

- **Mission San Rafael**, 1104 5th Ave, San Rafael, 415-456-3016, www.saintraphael.com
- **Mission Soledad**, 36641 Fort Romie Rd, Soledad, 831-678-2586, www.missionsoledad.com
- **Mission Carmel**, 3080 Rio Rd, Carmel, 831-624-1271, www.carmelmission.com

Visit the **California Missions Resource Center** at www.missionscalifornia.com to learn more.

# GREEN LIVING

C ALIFORNIA HAS BEEN ON THE FOREFRONT OF ENVIRONMENTAL STEW-
ardship since the 1970 passage of the California Environmental Quality
Act (CEQA), which required developers to disclose the potential environmental impact of projects, and in many cases required them to mitigate damages
to the environment. Most states follow less stringent federal guidelines. CEQA
set the stage for an ongoing existential battle between California and the federal government with regard to environmental standards. Tellingly, today's federal
guidelines on fuel-efficiency standards, adopted by the Obama administration,
are a carbon copy of California's tough regulations—a testament to California's
leadership in green living. As a result of these efforts, California residents generally
enjoy clean air, long stretches of undeveloped waterways, and tax incentives to
"green" their lives.

## GREENING YOUR HOME

The simplest way to go green is to reduce the size of your home—probably not
too hard for hopeful homeowners in today's Bay Area, which is prohibitively
expensive for those seeking large lots. Many "eco-homes"—look for the distinctive solar panels—have sprung up here recently. If you're a do-it-yourselfer in the
market for a dwelling that uses limited resources efficiently, read on.

### GREEN REMODELING

A good starting point is www.sfenvironment.org, which lists approved green
businesses and suppliers. Many Bay Area homes are in dire need of basic improvements that will save you money on energy costs. Insulation and fans in the
attic, dual-pane windows, high-efficiency toilets, modern water heaters, central
heating/cooling units, and Energy Star-rated appliances were all typically left out
of pre-1970s construction. Upgrading to modern systems can pay off big in the

long run, and is considered the cheapest method of improving energy consumption, because older technologies are obsolete and expensive.

For basic building supplies, lumber, and innovations like "wheatcore" doors (which contain pressed wheat straw under a veneer of hardwood), contact these suppliers, as well as big-box retail home-improvement chains:

- **Ashby Lumber (ACE)**, 824 Ashby Ave, Berkeley, 510-843-4832; 2295 Arnold Industrial Way, 925-689-8999, Concord, www.ashbylumber.com
- **Discount Builders Supply**, 1695 Mission St, San Francisco, 415-621-1830, www.discountbuilderssupplysf.com
- **Ecohome Improvement**, 2617 San Pablo Ave, Berkeley, 510-644-3500, www.ecohomeimprovement.com
- **Golden State Lumber**, 1100 Anderson Dr, San Rafael, 415-454-2532, www.goldenstatelumber.com

For recycled building materials:

- **Habitat for Humanity**, 2619 Broadway, Oakland, 510-251-6304, www.habitatebsv.org
- **The ReUse People**, 9235 San Leandro Blvd, Oakland, 510-383-1983, www.thereusepeople.org
- **Urban Ore**, 900 Murray St, Berkeley, 510-841-7283, www.urbanore.com

## LANDSCAPING

Landscaping with plants indigenous to the area, and ones that don't require a lot of water—especially critical during this historic drought—is a smart way to go green. San Francisco–based Bay Natives Nursery (www.baynatives.com) is a great resource for drought-tolerant gardening. For the South Bay, try Yerba Buena Nursery in Woodside (www.yerbabuenanursery.com). Both are excellent repositories of plant species that thrive in the Bay Area climate and soils. Also visit www.bayfriendlycoalition.org/bfguidedetail.shtml.

A few full-service options:

- **A Scape Artist**, 1195 Pine Ave, San Jose, 650-759-2455, www.ascapeartistonline.com
- **Ploughshares Nursery**, 2701 Main St, Alameda, 510-755-1102, www.ploughsharesnursery.com
- **St. John Landscapes**, 1635 Le Roy Ave, Berkeley, 510-848-5673, www.stjohnlandscapes.com

## ENERGY EFFICIENCY

Energy efficiency is a high priority among progressive communities in the Bay Area, and newcomers can learn why by visiting www.energy.ca.gov and www.coolcalifornia.org, which together provide troves of information on improving energy use. The government offers incentives—often in the form of tax breaks—for homeowners and businesses that adopt these improvements. Flex Your Power (www.fypower.org) is a great resource for these programs. For federal standards regarding appliances, and a wealth of information and shopping advice, visit www.energystar.gov.

## RENEWABLE ENERGY

Most of the Bay Area's utility companies provide a method of purchasing green power. Check the **Getting Settled** chapter for contact information for your local electrical provider. California also has innovative programs for newcomers who mount solar panels on their roofs. The California Solar Initiative offers informative solar-energy tips (www.gosolarcalifornia.ca.gov, 415-355-5586).

# WATER CONSERVATION

With the exception of high housing costs, nothing generates more headlines and controversy in the Bay Area than the worst drought California has witnessed in 1,200 years—an ongoing crisis so severe that the state mandated a 25 percent emergency reduction in water use, in effect through early 2016 and subject to extension. Water conservation isn't just a progressive rallying point; it's the law, strictly enforced and costly to test. Don't even think about luxuriating while exfoliating in that hour-long shower anymore. To size up the severity of the drought, consider that it's costing California farms $1.5 billion annually. Contracts between states and cities over the past century have divided water ownership into fractional and fiercely competing parties. Cities across the Bay Area run advertising campaigns begging consumers to turn off the tap while brushing their teeth. Meanwhile, farm cooperatives post ads reminding citizens of the value of locally grown food, which requires locally available water. As California is a major producer of nuts, fruits, vegetables, rice, and wine, the politics of water veers quickly to the politics of trade, individual property rights, and the protection of endangered species.

As the drought wears on, several Bay Area cities have also canceled Fourth of July fireworks and replaced grass fields with artificial turf to reduce watering needs. To pitch in with conservation during the worst drought in recent history, consider these tips:

- When rinsing dishes, don't leave water running between each item
- Turn water off while brushing teeth
- Shorten showers by several minutes
- For baths, fill the tub halfway
- Wash only full loads of clothes, and run the dishwasher only when full
- Reduce irrigation cycles, and adjust sprinklers to avoid overspray onto sidewalks and driveways
- Replace part of your lawn with drought-resistant plants

For tips and updates, consult these excellent resources:

- www.saveourwater.com
- www.ppic.org/water
- www.waterboards.ca.gov

## GREEN PRODUCTS AND SERVICES

Many companies have joined the green revolution and purport to be the latest innovation in environmental excellence. These claims have led to the creation of competing standards—ASTM, LEED, Green Globes, and other rating systems—with regard to environmental impact and friendliness of the product or service to the ecosystem. There isn't yet a universal standard for measuring the "greenness" of these things, so due diligence is required from the consumer. Check out www.buildinggreen.com and search for "Behind the Logos" to access a 2014 article detailing the latest standards on the market.

## GREENER TRANSPORTATION

With the Bay Area's wide-ranging public transportation systems, many residents forgo a car and ride the rails, buses, and boats that crisscross the area. Check the **Transportation** section for car sharing and other transportation options.

Freeways are eternally clogged around here, particularly during peak commute times, so carpooling is a viable option if HOV (High-Occupancy Vehicle) lanes are available. Generally you can use this lane if two or more people are in the car. Motorcycles can use this lane with a single rider. For more information, follow the excellent local news coverage by transportation reporter Michael Cabanatuan of the *San Francisco Chronicle*, at www.sfgate.com/author/michael-cabanatuan, and on Twitter (@ctuan). Also check dmv.ca.gov, and the Air Resources Board (www.arb.ca.gov) for more information.

For service to your hybrid vehicle, check out the innovative Luscious Garage (www.lusciousgarage.com), housed in a converted building in San Francisco.

### ALTERNATIVE FUELS

California has the highest demand for hybrid vehicles—with more than 3,500 alternative fueling stations—but care should be taken when traveling across the state to ensure options are available. A handy website (www.afdc.energy.gov/states/ca) solves this problem by listing everything from electrical charging outlets to biodiesel gas stations (click "Stations in California"). Purchasing cars or trucks that use these fuels encourages manufacturers and the government to continue production—and will, in time, reduce the cost associated with them.

## BY CAR

CALIFORNIA IS WIDELY KNOWN FOR ITS CAR CULTURE, AND NOT JUST IN Los Angeles. Northern California—and San Francisco especially—is car cluttered. If you're planning to live or work in San Francisco, having a car can be more a hindrance than a help, with merciless traffic and the staggering price of gas and parking tickets (the nation's highest in 2016). Living car-free in San Francisco is common, thanks to an excellent public transit that makes getting around easy and inexpensive. Living car-free outside the city, however, is a different story. Many newcomers outside San Francisco, Oakland, and San Jose rely on cars. Despite the efforts of alternative transportation advocates, there's a history of poor regional planning, abysmal connections, and sparse suburban options that have left locals who live or work outside San Francisco with little choice but to drive. Bay Area freeways are crowded every weekday morning, afternoon, and evening—often to the point of gridlock. Millions of residents commute by car here, and a majority drive alone. The eastern span of the Bay Bridge, connecting San Francisco to the East Bay, is still not completely rebuilt, as busted bolts and other gaffes pose continuing challenges. With ongoing construction near the bridges, you'll face several obstacles to travelling by car. For the latest news on car travel, follow the excellent articles by transportation reporter Michael Cabanatuan of the *San Francisco Chronicle* (at www.sfgate.com/author/michael-cabanatuan, and on Twitter, @ctuan).

Meanwhile, Bay Area transportation planners have been struggling to handle the rapidly expanding population of cars on local freeways, as well as neighborhood activists who don't want a freeway in their backyards—and the planners seem to be making an impact, albeit slowly. The number of solo drivers has been decreasing slowly, as the stress- and money-saving option of carpooling becomes more popular. BART, the rail system, has become a way of life for many newcomers and locals, and there are plans to extend it, improving links between Santa Clara and Alameda counties. With plans inching forward throughout the region to create "transit corridors"—stronger connections between BART, Caltrain, light rail, ferries, buses, shuttles, bike lanes, and pedestrian paths—commuters have eco-friendly options.

For details on transit fares, routes, and schedules, as well as ridesharing, bicycling, and trip planning, visit www.511.org or call 511 within the Bay Area. Also check out www.sfpark.org, which offers a mobile app with real-time parking information using GPS.

## TRAFFIC

It cannot be said enough. The Bay Area has some of the most brutal traffic in the country, particularly if you commute from the South Bay to San Francisco. Some routes are particularly problematic—most notoriously the dreaded Bay Bridge commute, which backs up not only Interstate 80 but also the connecting highways, as well as several city blocks starting in the late afternoon. To alleviate bottlenecking and bumper-to-bumper madness, CalTrans teamed up with city authorities in late 2015 to launch the long-anticipated I-80 Smart Corridor Project—a network of ramp meters and real-time electronic signs alerting drivers to traffic conditions. For more information, visit www.80smartcorridor.org.

Replacing the South Bay as the new heart of the Bay Area's traffic woes, the East Bay now boasts some of the Bay Area's worst commutes along Interstate 580, in eastern Alameda County. If taking BART is not feasible—as happened a few years ago, when the service went on strike—the travel information line 511 (no area code needed) will give up-to-the-minute highway condition reports for the entire Bay Area. Or tune into KALW-FM at 91.7, KGO-AM at 810, and KCBS-AM at 740, during morning and afternoon commute hours. The free mobile app **Waze** (www.waze.com) is the most popular community-based traffic and navigation app, and real-time traffic incidents are overlaid on **Google Maps** as well (maps.google.com).

## CARPOOLING

**511 Rideshare** is a free carpool and vanpool matching service. To be matched with fellow commuters on a similar work schedule, call the service at 511 or check www.rideshare.511.org. Throughout the Bay Area you'll find carpool lanes—also called diamond or HOV (high-occupancy vehicle) lanes—on major freeways. The number of passengers required and the hours of lane use vary; call 511 for details or check your route for posted information. The Bay Area has 150 park-and-ride lots, where you can leave your car and meet up with a carpool.

## CAR SHARING

If you don't own a car but need a set of wheels for day trips and errands, a number of hourly car-sharing services can meet your needs in the Bay Area. **City CarShare** maintains a fleet of vehicles—from hybrids to minivans—that can be picked up and dropped off at a variety of locations (415-995-8588, www.citycarshare.org). Other popular options are **Zipcar** (415-495-7478, www.zipcar.com) and **Getaround**, which offers peer-to-peer car sharing (866-438-2768, www.getaround.com).

## CAR RENTALS

All the big rental names are represented in the Bay Area, most with numerous locations. Here are a few:

- **Alamo**, 877-222-9075, www.alamo.com
- **Avis**, 800-230-4898, www.avis.com
- **Budget**, 800-527-0700, www.budget.com
- **Dollar**, 800-800-3665, www.dollar.com
- **Enterprise**, 800-261-7331, www.enterprise.com
- **Hertz**, 800-654-3131, www.hertz.com
- **National**, 877-222-9058, www.nationalcar.com
- **Thrifty**, 800-847-4389, www.thrifty.com

## TAXIS AND RIDESHARING

Anyone who has to get around a big city quickly knows that the big three ride-sharing apps—**Uber**, **Lyft**, **Sidecar**—are growing. Since launching in 2009, Uber has drawn heavy criticism for using controversial tactics to poach thousands of passengers and drivers from competitors. But the company appears to have found ways to improve its reputation in the Bay Area. E-hailing a ride, after all, is more convenient than tapping your foot until a yellow cab intuits your need. Remember to enroll in each service by using a referral code to get your first rides free; check www.retailmenot.com for codes.

While ridesharing apps like Uber and Lyft are enormously popular in the Bay Area—both companies are headquartered in San Francisco—don't count out the traditional yellow taxis just yet. Cabs are everywhere in the Bay Area. San Francisco's oldest taxi company, DeSoto Cab, recently rebranded its entire fleet as part of the new **Flywheel** app, getting in on the smartphone action. You'll be doing yourself and the Bay Area's taxis a service by downloading this app.

To score a traditional yellow taxi the old-fashioned way, call ahead, as waving one down isn't as easy as in other cities. Try the following:

### SAN FRANCISCO
- **Flywheel** (including the taxis formerly known as **DeSoto**), 877-691-2170, www.flywheel.com
- **Luxor Cab**, 415-282-4141, www.luxorcab.com
- **Veteran's Cab**, 415-552-1300
- **Yellow Cab**, 415-333-3333, www.yellowcabsf.com

## NORTH BAY

- **Happy Cab**, 415-455-4555
- **Marin Door-to-Door,** 415-457-2717, www.marindoortodoor.com
- **North Bay Cooperative Taxi**, 415-258-2800, www.northbaytaxi.com
- **Yellow Cab of Marin County**, 415-453-6030

## EAST BAY

- **Berkeley Yellow**, 510-528-9999, www.yellowexpresscab.com
- **DeSoto Cab and Yellow Cab**, 925-935-1234, www.contracostayellowcab.com
- **Veteran's Cab**, 510-533-1900

## PENINSULA & SOUTH BAY

- **American Cab**, 408-988-3300, www.american-cab.com
- **Merit Taxi**, 650-571-0606, www.merittaxi.com
- **Yellow Cab of Silicon Valley,** 408-777-7777, www.yellowcheckercab.com
- **United Cab**, 408-971-1111, www.unitedcabco.com

# BY BIKE

Despite the steep hills and distractingly beautiful views, there's an enormously popular bicycling community in the Bay Area, as thousands of bicyclists commute on a network of flat bike lanes. Everything you need to know about bicycling here can be found at www.bicycling.511.org: routes, rack locations, lock tips, group contacts, and maps. For rules of the road, see the bicycling guide at www.bicycling.511.org/pdf/bike_guide_en.pdf. Also make sure to purchase lights and a helmet.

Police are stepping up enforcement of bike laws, so don't roll through that stop sign anymore; tickets are expensive. San Francisco has a "vision zero" plan to end all traffic deaths by 2024, meaning bicyclists are now scrutinized as carefully as motorists. While it's true that motorists are more lethally dangerous and faulted for two-thirds of severe and fatal traffic collisions in San Francisco, the entire Bay Area is eyeing bicyclists for shared responsibility. Bikes are allowed on all BART trains, with the following restrictions: not on crowded cars (there must be enough room to accommodate you and your bicycle); not on the first car; and not on the first three cars from 7–9 a.m. and 4:30–6:30 p.m. There's no extra cost to bring your bike. BART is also in the process of adding nearly 300 new eLocker stations throughout the Bay Area, including 84 spaces at West Oakland station and 130 free valet bike spaces at Oakland's 19th Street station. Most ferries and buses (not all) accommodate bikes. But be forewarned: most city bus racks can only hold two bicycles at a time. Bikes are not allowed on cable cars, historic streetcars, and light-rail vehicles.

For updates on the fast-changing bike rules and safety tips in the Bay Area, visit the **California Department of Transportation** at www.dot.ca.gov/hq/tpp/offices/bike. Also visit:

- **Alameda Cycle Touring Club**, www.actc.org
- **Bay Area Bicycle Coalition**, www.bayareabikes.org
- **Bay Area Velo Girls**, www.velogirls.com
- **Berkeley Bicycle Club**, www.berkeleybike.org
- **Bike East Bay**, www.bikeeastbay.org
- **Different Spokes**, the Bay Area's largest bike club dedicated to gay, lesbian, and transgender riders, www.dssf.org
- **Marin County Bicycle Coalition**, www.marinbike.org
- **Marin Cyclists**, www.marincyclists.com
- **Napa County Bicycle Coalition**, www.napabike.org
- **San Francisco Bicycle Coalition**, www.sfbike.org
- **Silicon Valley Bicycle Coalition**, www.bikesiliconvalley.org
- **Sonoma County Bicycle Coalition**, www.bikesonoma.org
- **Western Wheelers** (based in the Peninsula), www.westernwheelers.org
- **Women's Mountain Bike & Tea Society**, www.wombats.org

Mark your calendar for the last Friday of every month, when **Critical Mass**, a large group of bicyclists, gathers at the Ferry Building in downtown San Francisco to ride the city and raise awareness of biking as a form of transportation (www.sfcriticalmass.org). Also note that the annual World Naked Bike Ride is a popular party each March, open to all riders—as bare as you dare. For information, visit www.worldnakedbikeride.org. To learn more about bicycling in the Bay Area, see the **Sports and Recreation** chapter.

## PUBLIC TRANSPORTATION

Fourteen major transit agencies accept the Clipper Card, a reloadable smartcard that'll save you a bundle. Participating agencies include AC Transit, BART, Caltrain, City Coach, FAST, Golden Gate Transit, Marin Transit, MUNI, San Francisco Bay Ferry, SamTrans, SolTrans, Vine, VTA, and Park with Clipper (garages in San Francisco). Learn more at www.clippercard.com.

### BAY AREA RAPID TRANSIT (BART)

Bay Area Rapid Transit—everyone calls it BART—boasts the longest-running train fleet in the United States. It's a high-speed, above- and belowground system that runs between San Francisco, the East Bay, and San Mateo County, and through one of the world's longest underwater tunnels. BART transports more than 420,000 passengers daily, and has a reputation for being clean and quiet but not reliably on time. Delays are frequent, and given the single shared track in San Francisco, one delay slows the entire Bay Area. Compared to New York and Chicago, however, BART is blissfully clean: less grime, far fewer rodents, and better-kept trains. BART's future is bright: at least 775 new train cars will start arriving in late 2016.

Currently BART runs five lines on more than 100 miles of track between 44 stations, split between surface, elevated, and subway stations. Trains run week-days from 4 a.m. to midnight, Saturdays from 6 a.m. to midnight, and Sundays from 8 a.m. to midnight. Want 24-hour subway service? Tough luck. 92 percent of passengers name BART's midnight cutoff as their top complaint, but extending the service would mean creating a second underground tube while the existing tube undergoes nightly maintenance. There's talk of that happening—but it would be a $10 billion commitment, and is most likely years away.

Although BART doesn't reach Silicon Valley, it may soon: $150 million in federal funding has already been secured for this project. Don't hold your breath, but stay tuned.

Fares are based on distance traveled, starting at $1.85 one way (hold onto your ticket to exit). Discount tickets (62.5 percent off) for senior citizens, children 5–12 years old, persons with disabilities (a proper ID is required), and students on a chaperoned field trip are sold at participating banks, retailers, social service agencies, and other community-based organizations. These tickets are not sold at any of the BART stations. For locations to purchase discount tickets, visit www.bart.gov/tickets/sales/retailsales.

BART stations are also transfer points for local buses, making it fairly easy to get anywhere in the Bay Area on public transit. You can pick up free transfers from BART stations in San Francisco and Daly City for discounts on connections with MUNI. All BART stations are wheelchair accessible. Bicycles are allowed on BART (see **By Bike** above for details). For schedule and fare information, visit www.bart.gov or drop by the customer service windows at any station, or call 510-465-2278 (Oakland, Berkeley, San Leandro), 415-989-2278 (San Francisco, Daly City) or 650-992-2278 (South San Francisco/San Bruno/San Mateo); TTY 510-839-2220.

## SAN FRANCISCO MUNICIPAL TRANSPORTATION AGENCY (MUNI)

San Francisco's public transportation system boasts a variety of vintage and new vehicles, including electric buses and trolleys (some of them stylishly historic), light rail, and the renowned cable cars that chug and clang their way up and down rollercoaster hills. The nation's eighth-largest transit system, MUNI operates 80 lines, several of them express, serving 700,000 passengers daily. Service is available 24 hours a day on select lines only. The adult fare is $2.25 one way, with discounts for seniors, disabled passengers, and kids. Cable car rides cost $7 (discounts for seniors also available). Exact change is required on all MUNI vehicles except cable cars, and transfers are available on all MUNI lines. A monthly pass costs $24 for seniors, youths, and disabled people, and $70 for everyone else. If you take BART and then MUNI, you can get a 25-cent discount on your bus ride. Just stop off before exiting the BART gates near the add-fare machine to pick up a transfer discount coupon.

In 2015 the long-awaited E-Embarcadero line became a reality, running weekends along the San Francisco waterfront, from the foot of the Embarcadero freeway to the Ferry Building, Fisherman's Wharf, and Fort Mason. The line's launch fulfills a three-decades-long struggle to make it happen. In 2016 the line will run daily. To combat MUNI's reputation for unreliable buses and unpleasant conditions, MUNI was granted a record-high $1 billion budget boost for 2016, for new buses, light-rail vehicles, and station improvements. For real-time bus updates while waiting at a station, visit www.nextmuni.com.

For more information on MUNI, call 311 (inside San Francisco), 415-701-2311, or TTY 415-701-2323, or visit www.sfmta.com for a detailed map. Call 415-701-4485 or TTY 415-701-4730 for information about services for passengers with disabilities.

## ALAMEDA-CONTRA COSTA TRANSIT (AC)

AC Transit, the bus system connecting the East Bay to San Francisco, serves Alameda and Contra Costa counties. Widely used are the rush-hour express routes from San Francisco to Oakland, Berkeley, Alameda, Emeryville, Richmond, and elsewhere in the East Bay. AC Transit also connects with all East Bay BART stations. Single-ride tickets are $2.10 for adults or $4.20 if you cross the Bay; for seniors, disabled passengers, and kids under 18, it's $1.05, and $2.10 if crossing the Bay. A new day pass is available ($5 for adults and $2.50 for seniors, disabled passenger, and youth). To contact AC Transit, call 511 and say "AC Transit" for the main menu, then say "customer relations" (TTY 800-735-2929, www.actransit.org).

## SAN MATEO COUNTY TRANSIT (SAMTRANS)

SamTrans provides Peninsula residents with local bus service as well as routes to downtown San Francisco and the San Francisco International Airport, making it easy for passengers to travel to and from the airport entirely on public transit. Stops include Atherton, Burlingame, Colma, Daly City, East Palo Alto, Foster City, Half Moon Bay, Hillsborough, Menlo Park, Millbrae, Pacifica, Palo Alto, Redwood City, San Bruno, San Carlos, San Mateo, and South San Francisco. Adult fares for single rides range from $2–5; for seniors, disabled passengers, and kids under 18, it's $1–2.50. Day passes for adults are $5; for seniors, disabled passengers, and kids under 18 the day pass is $3–3.75. Monthly passes are also available. For more information, visit www.samtrans.com, or call 800-660-4287, TTY 650-508-6448.

## GOLDEN GATE TRANSIT (GGT)

Golden Gate Transit provides local bus service for Marin and Sonoma County communities, as well as commuter bus and ferry service between Marin and Sonoma counties and downtown San Francisco (see below). Fares are calculated by distance traveled. For more information, visit www.goldengatetransit.org or call 511 within the Bay Are—or, from outside the area, 415-455-2000, TTY 711.

## ADDITIONAL BUS SERVICES

When it opens in 2017, the new **Transbay Transit Center** will become San Francisco's long-promised "Grand Central Station of the West"—a hub for long-range bus service and regional bus systems, including **AC Transit** (Alameda and Contra

Costa counties), **WestCAT** (western Contra Costa County, north of Oakland), **SamTrans** (San Mateo County), and **Golden Gate Transit** (Marin and Sonoma Counties). Additional services include **Contra Costa County Connection**, which provides local bus service in Contra Costa County (925-676-7500, www.countyconnection.com); and **Santa Clara Valley Transportation Authority** (VTA), which offers bus and light-rail service in the South Bay (408-894-9908, TDD 408-321-2330, www.vta.org).

## FERRIES

### EAST BAY

Providing a waterway link for East Bay residents who want to travel to downtown San Francisco, the **San Francisco Bay Ferry** is a convenient and scenic option seven days a week from Oakland's Jack London Square and Alameda's Main Street and Harbor Bay, as well as Vallejo's and South San Francisco's terminals. Ridership rose 36 percent between 2012 and 2014, as ferries helped to alleviate the congestion of land-based mass transit. The ferries dock in San Francisco at the Ferry Building, AT&T Park, and Pier 41 (near Fisherman's Wharf). Food and beverage service is available. As of 2016, a one-way fare ranges from $1.50 (for a short hop between Alameda and Oakland) to $6.40 for adults, and $3.20 for seniors, disabled passengers, and youth under 19. Kids under 5 are free. Clipper Cards will save you a lot; visit www.clippercard.com. For ferry schedules and maps, visit www.sanfranciscobayferry.com or call 415-705-8291.

### NORTH BAY

The **Golden Gate Ferry Service** is the premier North Bay water link, with daily service connecting San Francisco with the Marin County cities of Larkspur and Sausalito. Ferries depart for San Francisco from the Larkspur Ferry Terminal and a Sausalito dock located just off of Bridgeway, the city's main street. There is plenty of free parking at the Larkspur facility, and metered parking close to the Sausalito launch point. Food and drinks are available. The trip across the Bay takes about 30 minutes, and cost depends on distance traveled. One-way fares to Sausalito are $11.25 for adults ($5.50 for seniors, disabled passengers, and youth under 19). To Larkspur, they are $10.50 for adults ($5.25 for seniors, disabled passengers, and youth under 19). As with most transit systems in the Bay Area, the Clipper Card is a major money saver (www.clippercard.com). Visit www.goldengateferry.org or call 415-455-2000.

### ADDITIONAL FERRY SERVICE

- **Angel Island–Tiburon Ferry**, 415-435-2131 and 415-435-1531, www.angelislandferry.com
- **Blue and Gold Fleet,** round-trip services and cruises throughout the Bay Area; departing from Pier 41 in San Francisco (415-705-8200, www.blueandgoldfleet.com)

# COMMUTER TRAINS

## CALTRAIN

For Peninsula and South Bay residents, the commuter rail option is **Caltrain** (800-660-4287, TTY 415-508-6448, www.caltrain.com). Service runs between Gilroy in the South Bay and San Francisco's 4th Street Station, with many stops in between. Once you arrive in San Francisco you'll need to hop a bus, light rail, taxi, or bike (or walk!) to the Financial District. Fares on Caltrain are based on distance traveled within zones. They range from $3.25 to $13.25 and are available for purchase at any Caltrain station. Deep discounts are available by using a Clipper Card (www.clippercard.com), and monthly passes are available. For bicycle allowances on Caltrain, visit www.caltrain.com/riderinfo/Bicycles/Bicycle_FAQs.html.

## SONOMA MARIN AREA RAIL TRANSIT (SMART)

A new commuter rail system, **SMART** is slated for completion in 2016, connecting cities throughout Sonoma and Marin counties for the first time. This voter-approved system is the biggest infrastructure project in the North Bay in generations. For route maps and construction updates, visit www.sonomamarintrain.org and www.facebook.com/sonomamarintrain.

## AMTRAK

**Amtrak** trains don't board in San Francisco; stations are in Emeryville, Oakland, and San Jose. From San Francisco, catch the Amtrak bus at 5 Embarcadero Center, Pier 39 (near Fisherman's Wharf), 835 Market St, 1139 Market St, 747 Howard St, 301 Townsend St, or the Transbay Terminal. The bus will take you over the Bay Bridge to the Amtrak stations. Or take BART to Oakland and transfer (visit www.bart.gov for details). In San Jose, Amtrak is located at 65 Cahill St, where you can connect with commuter trains and buses.

For more information, visit www.amtrak.com or call 800-USA-RAIL (872-7245), TTY 800-523-6590. Visit www.amtrakcalifornia.com for local specials and promotions. Current and recent students with a Student Advantage card can expect deep discounts at www.studentadvantage.com/amtrakcard.

## ALTAMONT CORRIDOR EXPRESS (ACE)

**Altamont Corridor Express** (call it ACE, pronounced "ace") is a commuter train service connecting Stockton and San Jose, with additional stops in Lathrop/Manteca, Tracy, Vasca Road, Livermore, Pleasanton, Fremont, and Santa Clara. Fares depend on distance traveled, and range from $4–13.50 for a one-way trip. Monthly passes are available. For more information, visit www.acerail.com or call 800-411-RAIL (7245).

## GREYHOUND

**Greyhound** has numerous stations throughout the Bay Area. For more information, visit www.greyhound.com or call 800-231-2222, TTY 800-345-3109.

## MEGABUS

At long last, budget-minded **Megabus** has found its way to the Bay Area, connecting San Francisco, Oakland, and San Jose to Sacramento, Los Angeles, and Reno. Ultra-cheap rides (as low as $1) are available if you plan ahead. For more information, visit www.megabus.com or call 877-462-6342.

# AIRPORTS & AIRLINES

### SAN FRANCISCO INTERNATIONAL AIRPORT (SFO)

About 15 miles south of downtown San Francisco sits **SFO**—the seventh busiest airport in the nation—off Highway 101 near the cities of Millbrae and San Bruno. SFO is generally welcoming and tidy, but one warning: fog can be a problem, causing delays.

The drive from downtown during rush hour is about 40 minutes (20 to 25 minutes at other times). There's no shortage of transportation options between the airport and San Francisco. One of the best is BART, which runs directly to SFO, where it connects with an air tram that shuttles you straight to your terminal. Be sure to check the schedule ahead of time, as service is less frequent outside rush hours and on weekends. A taxi will set you back about $60. Ridesharing services like Lyft, Uber, and Sidecar are allowed to pick up and drop off at SFO. Shuttle vans like SuperShuttle (800-258-3826, www.supershuttle.com) cost about $17 (additional passengers in your party are $10 each) but you may have to sit through several stops before you get to your destination (they claim no more than four stops per trip). If you've got time to spare and want to save cash, catch a SamTrans bus right outside the terminals for a ride to downtown San Francisco. (For more on SamTrans see above.)

For more information on SFO visit www.flysfo.com or call 800-435-9736. Some of the airlines serving SFO:

- **Aer Lingus,** 516-622-4222, www.aerlingus.com
- **AeroMexico,** 800-237-6639, www.aeromexico.com
- **Air Canada**, 888-247-2262, www.aircanada.com
- **Air China**, 800-882-8122, www.airchina.com
- **Air France**, 800-237-2747, www.airfrance.com
- **Air New Zealand**, 800-262-1234, www.airnewzealand.com
- **Alaska Airlines**, 800-252-7522, www.alaskaair.com
- **American Airlines**, 800-433-7300, www.aa.com
- **ANA**, 800-235-9262, www.ana.co.jp
- **Asiana Airlines,** 888-437-7718, www.flyasiana.com
- **British Airways**, 800-247-9297, www.britishairways.com
- **Cathay Pacific,** 800-233-2742, www.cathaypacific.com
- **China Airlines**, 800-277-5118, www.china-airlines.com
- **Continental**, 800-523-3273, www.continental.com

TRANSPORTATION

403

- **Delta**, 800-221-1212, www.delta.com
- **Hawaiian Airlines**, 800-367-5320, www.hawaiianair.com
- **Japan Airlines**, 800-525-3663, www.ar.jal.com
- **JetBlue**, 800-538-2583, www.jetblue.com
- **KLM**, 800-225-2525, www.klm.com
- **Korean Air**, 800-438-5000, www.koreanair.com
- **Lufthansa**, 800-645-3880, www.lufthansa.com
- **Philippine Airlines**, 800-435-9725, www.philippineairlines.com
- **Qantas**, 800-227-4500, www.qantas.com
- **Singapore Airlines**, 800-742-3333, www.singaporeair.com
- **Southwest Airlines**, 800-435-9792, www.southwest.com
- **United**, 800-864-8331, www.united.com
- **US Airways** (merged with American Airlines in 2015), 800-428-4322, www.usairways.com
- **Virgin America**, 877-359-8474, www.virginamerica.com
- **Virgin Atlantic**, 800-821-5438, www.virgin-atlantic.com

## OAKLAND INTERNATIONAL AIRPORT

This East Bay airport is easier to navigate than San Francisco's for one simple reason: it's much smaller. While SFO is serviced by more major American and international carriers, **Oakland Airport** still has almost everything you need. About nine miles south of downtown Oakland, the airport is easy to jump in and out of by car. But beware: taking BART requires switching to a shuttle bus at the Coliseum stop ($6 extra fee). The airport is located at the west end of Hegenberger Road, a clearly marked exit from Highway 880.

For more information on Oakland Airport, visit www.oaklandairport.com or call 510-563-3300. Airlines serving Oakland Airport:

- **Alaska**, 800-426-0333, www.alaskaair.com
- **Allegiant Air**, 702-505-8888, www.allegiantair.com
- **Delta**, 800-221-1212, www.delta.com
- **Hawaiian Airlines**, 800-367-5320, www.hawaiianair.com
- **JetBlue**, 800-538-2583, www.jetblue.com
- **Norwegian Air**, 800-357-4159, www.norwegian.com
- **Southwest**, 800-435-9792, www.southwest.com
- **Spirit**, 801-401-2222, www.spirit.com
- **US Airways** (merged with American Airlines in 2015), 800-428-4322, www.usairways.com

## SAN JOSE INTERNATIONAL AIRPORT

Just north of downtown San Jose, **San Jose International Airport** is relatively easy to navigate, but getting here by public buses and trains from San Francisco, Oakland, Berkeley, and other points in the Bay Area is a nightmare for many newcomers. Bus and train connections are seemingly designed to confuse you—best to stick to taxis, rideshares, or driving your own car. If you don't drive, plan ahead and pay careful attention to connection points. Still, despite these issues, this is a large international airport, and often offers cheaper flights than San Francisco and Oakland.

For more information, visit www.flysanjose.com or call 408-392-3600. Some of the airlines serving San Jose include:

- **Alaska Airlines**, 800-426-0333, www.alaskaair.com
- **ANA**, 800-235-9262, www.ana.co.jp
- **American Airlines**, 800-433-7300, www.aa.com
- **Delta**, 800-221-1212, www.delta.com
- **Hainan Airlines**, 888-688-8813, www.hainanairlines.com
- **Hawaiian Airlines**, 800-367-5320, www.hawaiianair.com
- **JetBlue**, 800-538-2583, www.jetblue.com
- **Southwest**, 800-435-9792, www.southwest.com
- **United**, 800-241-6522, www.united.com
- **US Airways** (merged with American Airlines in 2015), 800-428-4322, www.usairways.com
- **Volaris**, 866-988-3527, www.volaris.com

## ONLINE RESOURCES—AIR TRAVEL

To score the lowest airfare and most reward points redeemable for flights, newcomers should run comparisons at travel websites www.kayak.com, www.expedia.com, www.hotwire.com, www.orbitz.com, and www.priceline.com—take your pick. For most flexibility in pricing and schedules, go to the heavyweight champion of airfare search: ITA Software (www.itasoftware.com, recently acquired by Google), and click "airfare search."

For insider tips on points and miles, visit www.thepointsguy.com, an unbeatable source of daily insider deals. In addition to the Points Guy, take a glance at Flyer Talk (www.flyertalk.com), a points-and-miles chat board, where thousands of self-styled "point heads" post their tricks.

To register a complaint against an airline, contact the Department of Transportation (www.transportation.gov/airconsumer, 202-366-2220, Office of Aviation Enforcement and Proceedings, Aviation Consumer Protection Division, 1200 New Jersey Ave, SE, Washington, DC 20590).

**U**NLESS YOU PLAN TO STEP OFF THE PLANE OR TRAIN AND WALK INTO your new house or apartment, you'll need an interim place to hang your hat. You'll find no shortage of hotels, motels, and bed & breakfasts in the Bay Area—from elegant Victorian lodges overlooking the ocean and hills to serviceable motels at budget rates. Most San Francisco hotels are downtown or at Fisherman's Wharf, a popular destination on first arrival—but there are countless neighborhood hotels that'll give you a sense of what it could be like to live in a particular area. Budget-minded newcomers might want to consider one of the single-room occupancy hotels (SROs) that dot much of downtown. These often get slammed in online reviews, as they typically feature little more than a bed and dresser. Still, SROs are the least expensive options by the day, week, or month. Just be wary: low-rent buildings are clustered in the seedier parts of town—around 6th and Mission streets south of Market Street, and the Tenderloin, just north of Market.

The most popular lodging service is **Airbnb**, whose website and mobile app let private homeowners rent furnished homes directly to newcomers. Headquartered in San Francisco, Airbnb recently garnered a mountain of press when the city took to the ballot box over a proposal to cap the number of days Airbnb hosts could rent homes (the proposed cap was 75 nights per year). In San Francisco, the service has consumed a major portion of local housing, taking apartments off the market in a city that desperately needs available housing. An economic study commissioned by the city showed that every home converted to a short-term rental costs San Francisco up to $300,000 annually. But Airbnb disputes that claim, saying that short-term visitors boost San Francisco's economy by spending a total of $56 million locally—$12.7 million on renting and $43.1 million on local businesses annually. The disagreement has been heated.

In any case, Airbnb seems a win-win-win for private hosts, renters, and local merchants. You might consider booking through Airbnb upon your arrival (www. airbnb.com). Just be aware that that won't sit well with Airbnb's vocal critics,

405

including many housing activists and journalists, who argue that—unless regulated more closely—Airbnb not only exacerbates the city's housing crisis, but harms the Bay Area culturally, quickening the exodus of lower-income residents.

Rooms at bigger, more mainstream hotels can be found by searching www. kayak.com, www.expedia.com, www.hotels.com, www.hotwire.com, and the mobile app Hotels Tonight (headquartered in San Francisco, with deep last-minute discounts on hotels throughout the Bay Area and elsewhere). Always ask about the cancellation policy when booking through discount sites, as charges may apply. Some companies ask for full payment upon making the reservation.

For guest reviews of hotels, visit www.tripadvisor.com—and always, *always* research the hotel you're considering at www.bedbugregistry.com. This word of wisdom applies to all hotels, no matter the price range.

## RESIDENCE CLUBS & EXTENDED-STAY SUITES

Residence clubs and extended stays offer furnished suites—some with meals, community entertainment rooms, and message service. All the better if your employer is footing the bill for relocation. This isn't the cheapest form of housing (for budget stays, see the next section), but the pampering you receive while searching for something permanent may be worth the added expense. Most extended stays offer month-to-month or week-to-week suites, typically studios or one-bedroom apartments with kitchens. Higher-end spots come loaded with hotel-style amenities, including laundry service and fitness centers.

A select handful to get started:

- **BridgeStreet** has several corporate housing sites in the Bay Area; weekly, monthly and yearlong rentals are available. The company offers fully furnished units, fitness facilities, and parking. Families are welcome (800-278-7338, www.bridgestreet.com).
- **ExecuStay** is a nationwide Marriott–affiliated service offering furnished apartments, kitchens, and in-unit washers and dryers; some apartments accommodate pets (888-340-2565, www.execustay.com).
- **Gaylord Suites**, 620 Jones St, San Francisco, 415-673-8445, www.gaylordsuites.com
- **Key Housing Connections** offers furnished accommodation Bay Area–wide for a minimum of 30 days, depending on availability (800-989-0410, www.keyhousing.net).
- **Kenmore Residence Club**, 1570 Sutter St, San Francisco, 415-776-5815, www.kenmorehotelsf.com
- **Monroe Residence Club**, 1870 Sacramento St, San Francisco, 415-474-6200, www.monroeresidenceclub.com
- **Oakwood Corporate Apartments** features furnished apartments customized to suit your needs; minimum stay is 30 days, but some locations allow

shorter stays. There are locations throughout the Bay Area (877-902-0832, www.oakwood.com).

- **Suite America** provides short-term rentals throughout the Bay Area (800-784-8341, www.suiteamerica.com).
- **Trinity Management Services** rents studios and one-bedrooms, furnished or unfurnished, with leases available from one month to one year at numerous locations in San Francisco; pets not allowed (415-433-3333, www.trinitymanagement.com).
- **Vantaggio Suites** has three locations in San Francisco: 835 Turk St, 415-922-0111; 505 O'Farrell St, 415-771-0525; 246 McAllister St, 415-614-2400 (www.vantaggiosuites.com).

## LESS EXPENSIVE MOTELS & HOTELS

The Bay Area has hundreds of less expensive basic motels and hotels—most located near highways, bridges, and airports. While there are cheaper options out there than those listed below, what follows is a sample of better-rated budget options. If you're counting every dollar, your best bet is to search www.kayak.com and sort by price. "Budget motels" in the Bay Area are still more expensive than those in most parts of the country.

### SAN FRANCISCO

- **Capri Motel**, 2015 Greenwich St, 415-346-4667, www.sfmotelcapri.com
- **Comfort Inn**, 2775 Van Ness Ave, 415-928-5000, www.choicehotels.com
- **Hotel Beresford**, 635 Sutter St, close to Union Square (415-673-9900, www.beresford.com/beresford)
- **Royal Pacific Motor Inn**, free parking included (a San Francisco rarity!), 661 Broadway, close to Chinatown and North Beach (415-781-6661, www.royalpacificmotorinn.com)
- **San Remo** is a charming old hotel from 1906 (it has chain toilets) with odd-shaped rooms, shared bathrooms, a Victorian ambiance, a wine bar, and lots of European guests; located in North Beach, 2237 Mason St (415-776-8688, www.sanremohotel.com).
- **Seal Rock Inn** is located on the ocean, in the fog belt of the Richmond district. It's a good place to stay if you want to get a taste of the Richmond or Sunset districts; find it at 545 Point Lobos Ave (415-752-8000, www.sealrockinn.com).

### NORTH BAY

- **Days Inn**, 8141 Redwood Blvd, Novato, 415-897-7111, www.daysinn.com
- **Hotel Petaluma**, 106 Washington St, 707-559-3393, www.hotelpetaluma.com
- **Point Reyes Station Inn**, 11591 Highway 1, Point Reyes, 415-663-9372, www.pointreyesstationinn.com
- **Villa Inn**, 1600 Lincoln Ave, San Rafael, 415-456-4975, www.villainn.com

## EAST BAY

- **Days Inn**, various locations; suites with kitchenettes available, 800-225-3297, www.daysinn.com
- **Imperial Inn**, budget-friendly, a short walk to the BART station, 490 W. MacArthur Blvd, 510-653-4225, www.imperialinnoakland.com
- **Jack London Inn**, easy access to the ferry terminal and Amtrak station, 444 Embarcadero West, Oakland, 510-444-2032, www.jacklondoninnoakland.com

## PENINSULA & SOUTH BAY

- **Arena Hotel**, quick walk to the SAP Center indoor arena, 817 Alameda, San Jose, 408-294-6500, www.arenahotelsj.com
- **Cherry Orchard Inn**, outdoor pool and free breakfast, close to the convention center and Apple campus, 1071 E. El Camino Real, Sunnyvale, 408-244-9000, www.cherryorchardinn.com
- **Fontaine Inn**, low-key option within easy reach of Great America amusement park and San Jose airport, 2460 Fontaine Rd, San Jose, 408-270-7666, www.fontaineinn.com

## MEDIUM-PRICED HOTELS

The next step up in amenities and aesthetics:

## SAN FRANCISCO

- **The Buchanan** (formerly Hotel Tomo), sleekly designed with modernist Japanese aesthetics in the heart of Japantown, 1800 Sutter St (415-921-4000, www.thebuchananhotel.com)
- **Chancellor Hotel**, Union Square location, meeting facilities available, 433 Powell St, San Francisco (415-362-2004, www.chancellorhotel.com)
- **Courtyard by Marriott**, 299 2nd St, San Francisco (800-321-2211, www.marriott.com/courtyard)
- **Hotel Boheme**, an ode to the beatniks, 444 Columbus Ave in North Beach (415-433-9111, www.hotelboheme.com)
- **Hotel California (Best Western)**, 580 Geary St (800-227-4223, www.hotelcaliforniasf.com)
- **Hotel Vertigo**, located in Lower Nob Hill; the site of the Empire Hotel, made famous in Alfred Hitchcock's classic *Vertigo*, 940 Sutter St (415-885-6800, www.hotelvertigosf.com)
- **Hotel Rex**, cozy boutique in the heart of the theater district, 562 Sutter St (415-433-4434, www.thehotelrex.com)
- **King George Hotel**, located downtown, with a popular tea room, 334 Mason St (415-781-5050, www.kinggeorge.com)
- **The Phoenix Hotel**, a San Francisco legend, is an artistic hotel built around an enclosed courtyard pool, with a popular adjoining bar; it's a frequently used pit

stop for touring rock bands. It's also on the expensive side, but is more stylishly colorful than luxurious; 601 Eddy St (415-776-1380, www.jdvhotels.com).

## NORTH BAY
- **Hotel Sausalito**, 16 El Portal, Sausalito, 888-442-0700, www.hotelsausalito.com
- **Fairfax Inn Bed and Breakfast**, 15 Broadway Blvd, Fairfax, 415-455-8702, www.fairfaxinn.com
- **Hotel Sausalito**, 16 El Portal, Sausalito, 888-442-0700, www.hotelsausalito.com
- **Inn Marin**, 250 Entrada Dr, Novato, 415-883-5952, www.innmarin.com
- **San Anselmo Inn**, 339 San Anselmo Ave, San Anselmo, 415-455-5366, www.sananselmoinn.com

## EAST BAY
- **Berkeley City Club**, 2315 Durant Ave, Berkeley, 510-848-7800, www.berkeleycityclub.com
- **Berkeley Travelodge**, 1820 University Ave, Berkeley, 510-843-4262, www.travelodge.com
- **Oakland Marriott**, downtown with great views of Lake Merritt and the Bay, 1001 Broadway, Oakland (510-451-4000, www.marriott.com)
- **San Ramon Marriott**, 2600 Bishop Dr, San Ramon, 925-867-9200, www.marriott.com

## PENINSULA & SOUTH BAY
- **Cupertino Inn**, event services and business amenities, 10889 North De Anza Blvd, Cupertino (800-222-4828, www.cupertinoinn.com)
- **Hotel Strata**, geared for business travelers, offers a variety of extended stay options, 93 W El Camino Real, Mountain View (800-445-7774, www.hotelstrata.com)
- **Hyatt House Santa Clara**, suites geared for extended stay, 3915 Rivermark Plaza, Santa Clara (408-486-0800, www.santaclara.house.hyatt.com)
- **Cupertino Inn**, event services and business amenities, 10889 North De Anza Blvd, Cupertino, 800-222-4828, www.cupertinoinn.com
- **Hotel Strata**, geared for business travelers, offers a variety of extended stay options, 93 W El Camino Real, Mountain View, 800-445-7774, www.hotelstrata.com
- **Hotel Valley Park**, a short drive to the upscale shops of Santana Row and the Westfield Valley Fair mall, 2404 Stevens Creek Blvd, San Jose, 408-293-5287, www.thevalleyparkhotel.com
- **Hyatt House Santa Clara**, suites geared for extended stay, 3915 Rivermark Plaza, Santa Clara, 408-486-0800, www.santaclara.house.hyatt.com

## LUXURY HOTELS

The finest the Bay Area has to offer; if you can afford to splurge, you'll be well taken care of here:

### SAN FRANCISCO

- **The Clift** is one of the trendiest hotels in the city, with a chic party atmosphere that gets rowdy in the evenings; be prepared for a parade of downtown club-goers (495 Geary St, 415-775-4700, www.clifthotel.com).
- **The Fairmont**, atop Nob Hill, is one of the city's most opulent, old-world hotels (950 Mason St, 415-772-5000, www.fairmont.com).
- **The Ritz-Carlton** features modern elegance and luxury in Nob Hill (600 Stockton St, 415-296-7465, www.ritzcarlton.com/en/Properties/SanFrancisco).
- **The Westin St. Francis** is a luxurious grand hotel in the heart of Union Square (335 Powell St, 415-397-7000, www.westinstfrancis.com).

### NORTH BAY

- **Harvest Inn** by Charlie Palmer offers secluded elegance, modernist design, and impressive rustic charm framed by the tranquil vineyards in Napa County's St. Helena. Enjoy two cozy outdoor hot tubs, a floral garden, brand-new lofts, and a chic new restaurant; some rooms include your own wood-burning fireplace (1 Main St, St. Helena, 707-963-9463, www.harvestinn.com).
- **Hotel Les Mars** is a luxurious French-style hotel within a block of the elegant, historic downtown (27 North St, Healdsburg, 707-433-4211, www.hotellesmars.com).
- **Kenwood Inn & Spa**, 10400 Sonoma Highway, Kenwood, 800-353-6966, www.kenwoodinn.com
- **Solage Calistoga**, 755 Silverado Trail N, Calistoga, 707-266-7534, www.solagecalistoga.com

### EAST BAY

- **Claremont Hotel Club and Spa** is a sprawling Victorian spa (41 Tunnel Rd, Berkeley, 510-843-3000, www.claremontresort.com).
- **Hotel Shattuck Plaza**, 2086 Allston Way, Berkeley, 510-845-7300, www.hotelshattuckplaza.com
- **Waterfront Hotel**, 10 Washington St, Oakland, 510-836-3800, www.jdvhotels.com

### PENINSULA & SOUTH BAY

- **The Fairmont**, elegance in the heart of downtown, 170 South Market St, San Jose (408-998-1900, www.fairmont.com/san-jose)

- **Garden Court Hotel,** located downtown, convenient access to Silicon Valley and Stanford University; 520 Cowper St, Palo Alto (650-322-9000, www.gardencourt.com)
- **Hotel Los Gatos,** upscale Mediterranean-style building, convenient access to Silicon Valley, 210 E Main Street, Los Gatos (866-335-1700, www.hotellosgatos.com)
- **Ritz-Carlton Half Moon Bay** offers grand elegance and blissful indulgence right on the coast, with breathtaking resort amenities and golf courses above ocean waves. 261 of the guest rooms are newly upgraded, including irresistible fire-pit terraces and sweeping views of the water (1 Miramontes Point Rd, Half Moon Bay, 650-712-7000, www.ritzcarlton.com).
- **Stanford Park Hotel,** adjacent to Stanford University and Palo Alto, 100 El Camino Real, Menlo Park (866-241-2431, www.stanfordparkhotel.com)

## SUBLETS & HOME SHARING

As with all things housing, check **www.craigslist.org** (and particularly the "sublets/temporary" tab) for countless daily listings in the Bay Area. Craigslist was born and raised in San Francisco, where the website is headquartered. It is enormously popular with newcomers and locals. Another alternative, entirely free, is crashing on locals' couches by joining **www.couchsurfing.com**. Couchsurfing is a globally popular social network, also headquartered in San Francisco.

Newer to the Bay Area's home-sharing game—but wildly popular—are sites like **Airbnb** (www.airbnb.com), which lets private homeowners rent out furnished homes. From strong support to fierce local criticism, Airbnb's game-changing presence on the housing scene has garnered a ton of media attention because San Francisco housing is getting prohibitively expensive. Airbnb's supporters say that by generating income for private hosts, the service helps keep—rather than displace—thousands of locals. Whatever your perspective on the effects of Airbnb, the website and mobile app offer the widest range of sublets in size, price, quality, and location.

### BED & BREAKFASTS

There are hundreds of B&Bs in the Bay Area, ranging from opulent spots in historic, regal Victorians to self-contained carriage houses and private cottages; **www.bbonline.com** offers a network of B&Bs in the Bay Area, but **www.airbnb.com** and **www.vrbo.com** have a wider selection. The more official route brings you to the **California Association of Boutique & Breakfast Inns** (www.cabbi.com).

## HOSTELS/YMCAS

In addition to the hostels listed below, you can find out more about local youth hostels at www.hiusa.org.

- **Adelaide Hostel**, basic, funky, private, and dorm-style rooms; full of budget-minded Europeans; located in downtown San Francisco (5 Isadora Duncan Ln, 877-359-1915, www.adelaidehostel.com)
- **AYH City Center**, 685 Ellis St, San Francisco, 415-474-5721, www.sfhostels.com/city-center
- **AYH Hostel Union Square**, 312 Mason St, San Francisco, 415-788-5604, www.sfhostels.com/downtown
- **AYH Hostel Fisherman's Wharf**, Fort Mason, San Francisco, Bldg #240, 415-771-7277, www.sfhostels.com/fishermans-wharf
- **Globetrotters Inn**, 494 Broadway, San Francisco, 415-346-5786, www.globetrottersinn.com
- **Hidden Villa Hostel**, 26870 Moody Rd, Los Altos Hills, 650-949-8650, www.hiddenvilla.org/hostel.php
- **Sanborn Park Hostel**, 15808 Sanborn Rd, Saratoga, 408-741-0166, 408-741-9555, www.sanbornparkhostel.org
- **YMCA**, 631 Howard St, Suite 500, San Francisco, 415-777-9622, www.ymcasf.org (from this main website, check for locations throughout the city)

## ACCESSIBLE LODGING FOR THE DISABLED

The Bay Area is sensitive to the needs of those of all ability levels. Check with your hotel before booking, to ensure accessibility.

A couple of helpful websites:

- **www.sanfrancisco.travel** includes a thorough access guide to the Bay Area, featuring both hotels and major city attractions
- **www.accessnca.com** includes links to accessibility options for travel throughout Northern California

A S SCENIC AS THE CITY OF SAN FRANCISCO IS, QUICK GETAWAYS ARE part of the Bay Area's appeal, and you have limitless destinations within striking distance of all parts of the Bay Area. One of the most majestic trailhead sites is Tuolumne Meadows in Yosemite National Park, at an elevation of 8,600 feet. But there are closer promised lands. Below are just a few.

## NORTH OF SAN FRANCISCO

If you don't want to drive far from San Francisco, ditch the car and hop the ferry to **Angel Island**, the 740-acre state park in the middle of the Bay, for picnics, softball games, kayaking, and scenic trails framed by stunning views (www.angelisland. org). If you'd rather a road trip, drive up to Marin County to the cedar lodge at **Green Gulch Farm Zen Center** (1601 Shoreline Highway, Sausalito, 415-383-3134, www. sfzc.org), and join the tea ceremony, meditative sessions, and organic gardening.

On clear days head up the coastal curves of Highway 1, past the Zen Center, where you can descend to **Stinson Beach** for sunbathing, surfing, and exploring the shore. A more tranquil getaway is **Point Reyes National Seashore**, with 30 miles of coastline and 70,000 acres of pristine wilderness marked by rugged bluffs, wooded canyons, dense forests, and open meadows. To reserve camp sites at Point Reyes, contact the visitors' center (415-464-5100, www.nps.gov/por).

The Bay Area's most popular getaway is in **Napa** and **Sonoma counties,** home of taste-bud-seducing orchards, regal estates, and neatly landscaped wineries (more than 600 of them), as well as award-winning meals at pioneering organic kitchens (reservations required) like the **French Laundry** (6640 Washington St, Yountville, www.frenchlaundry.com); **Auberge du Soleil** (180 Rutherford Hill Rd, Rutherford, www.aubergedusoleil.com); **Tra Vigne** (1050 Charter Oak Ave, St. Helena, www.travignerestaurant.com); and the exceptionally inventive new restaurant **Archetype** (1429 Main St, St. Helena, www.archetypenapa.com). Yountville has more Michelin stars per capita than anywhere else in the United

States. Visitors can hop a wine train to eat, drink, and view the rolling landscape all the way from St. Helena to Napa, without having to designate a driver. (For information about the train visit www.winetrain.com or call 800-427-4124.)

Napa and Sonoma counties also host rustic spa resorts specializing in volcanic-ash mud baths, offering both glamorous indulgence and refined relaxation. Most spas are in the town of Calistoga. Below is a short list of highly rated destinations—many of them with indoor and outdoor pools, mineral baths, steam rooms, oh-so-cleansing mud baths, salt scrubs, massages, and more:

- **Calistoga Spa Hot Springs**, 1006 Washington St, Calistoga, 866-822-5772, 707-942-6269, www.calistogaspa.com
- **Dr. Wilkinson's Hot Springs**, 1507 Lincoln Ave, Calistoga, 707-942-4102, www.drwilkinson.com
- **Fairmont Sonoma Mission Inn**, 100 Boyes Blvd, 707-938-9000, www.fairmont.com/sonoma
- **Indian Springs**, 1712 Lincoln Ave, Calistoga, 707-942-4913, www.indianspringscalistoga.com

Beyond the iced cucumber water and chrysanthemum tea before and after your mineral-springs soak, there are plenty of places offering hot air balloon rides, sailing, and waterskiing at and near Lake Berryessa (just don't run a Google search for "Lake Berryessa" and "Zodiac"). For more information about the region, visit www.visitnapavalley.com and www.sonomacounty.com.

Another North Bay getaway is the old logging region of **Russian River**, a rustic retreat with pinot noir vineyards and apple orchards surrounding a stoic river that flows south and turns abruptly toward the Pacific in a beckoning gesture, guiding you to the tranquil coast. Russian River is an unfussy resort destination with forested lodging, cozy restaurants, camping, horseback riding, and canoeing. Begin in the town of Forestville and head downriver to Guerneville. The next day, take a trip down the Russian River Wine Road (www.wineroad.com) to sample award-winning wine, and make a pit stop at the lovingly restored Bank of Guerneville, which isn't a bank at all but rather a new art hub that sells pies and ice cream. The location reopened in 2015 after being meticulously restored to its 1921 glory (16290 Main St, Guerneville, 707-666-9411, www.guernevillebankclub.com). Not far away is the similarly idyllic town of Sebastopol, which in 2015 inaugurated a "hi-noon" ritual: every Friday at noon, the merchants and pedestrians on Main Street step outside and wave to one another. Yes, this merits headlines in slow-moving Sebastopol. The "hi-noon" initiative was approved unanimously by the Sebastopol Downtown Association.

Heading toward the coastline around **Mendocino**, three and half hours north of San Francisco, you'll find breathtaking scenery. Watch for whales, wade in tide pools, hike in Mendocino Headlands State Park, and camp under towering redwoods at Van Damme State Park. At the **Jug Handle State Reserve** you can spot tectonic uplifts and pygmy forests. If riding horses along the beach strikes a chord, contact Ricochet Ridge Ranch (707-964-7669, www.horse-vacation.com).

The community of **Sea Ranch**, 100 miles north of San Francisco via Highway 1, offers house rentals with ocean views and trails. Abalone diving, kayaking, horseback riding, and swimming are highlights (www.searanchgetaway.com).

## PENINSULA & SOUTH BAY

The coastline from San Francisco all the way south to Santa Cruz offers a scenic getaway with mesmerizing bluffs, beaches, and surfing spots—one of the most rewardingly beautiful coastlines in the world. Half Moon Bay is pumpkin paradise—the world championship of pumpkins shows up each October—where you can pick pumpkins at patches along the highway. Sixty miles south of San Francisco awaits **Año Nuevo State Reserve**, home to the largest mainland breeding colony of northern elephant seals, with memorable tours during breeding season from December to March (www.parks.ca.gov/anonue, 650-879-2025).

**Monterey/Carmel** is also known as John Steinbeck country, as he based many of his novels here, including *Cannery Row*, *Of Mice and Men*, and *The Grapes of Wrath*. Now the canneries are closed, and resorts and tourist sites stand in their stead. The Monterey Bay Aquarium brings you eye to eye with sharks, rays, barracuda, and elegant jellyfish. The aquarium also runs the renowned Seafood Watch program at www.seafoodwatch.org, with free consumer guides.

These days, Carmel skews toward tourists—the city is full of restaurants, art galleries, gift shops, and inns. It's an easy spot for children and elderly visitors to get around. The scenery is spectacular, with sea lions, coves, rocky beaches, windwhipped cypress trees, and well-maintained indigenous gardens. The legendary Pebble Beach Golf Course is here, where Tiger Woods etched his name into the record books, winning the 100th US Men's Open by 15 strokes. In the early 1900s, Carmel-by-the-Sea became a hub for artists and writers. Robert Louis Stevenson, Ansel Adams, Sinclair Lewis, Mary Austin, Edward Weston, and Upton Sinclair settled at one time in Carmel. Poet Robinson Jeffers' home has been made into a museum; contact Tor House (www.torhouse.org, 831-624-1813) for details. The Henry Miller Memorial Library, a landmark named in the author's honor, is located nearby in Big Sur (www.henrymiller.org, 831-667-2574). Residents gather to watch the sunset at Nepenthe restaurant along the cliffs of Big Sur (48510 Highway One, 831-667-2345, www.nepenthebigsur.com).

A more restful, restorative outing in **Big Sur** is famously on offer at the Esalen Institute's seaside hot springs (831-667-3000, www.esalen.org). Designed to foster personal and social transformation, the institute offers seminars, lodging, hot springs, a pool, massages, and unbeatable views of the California coastline. Esalen's popular outdoor bathing allows for soaking in healing waters from 1–3 a.m. (a.m., indeed) by calling 831-667-3047 between 9 a.m.–noon daily for same-day reservations ($30 each).

On the northern part of Monterey Bay sits **Santa Cruz**, the bohemian-hippie enclave of college students, surfers, and leftist activists of all ages—a striking contrast to the more conservative town of Carmel. With the sunniest beaches in the Bay Area, Santa Cruz is as lovely and lively as any beach town, and is highlighted by windswept trees, rolling hills, and ocean vistas—though most outsiders come for the Santa Cruz Beach Boardwalk (400 Beach Street, 831-423-5590, www.beachboardwalk.com). The main attraction is the rickety wooden rollercoaster in the old-style amusement park, down the hill from the University of California at Santa Cruz, whose laid-back students work hard and party hard, throwing one of California's largest 4/20 forest parties (look it up—better yet, if you need to look it up, don't). Visit the Santa Cruz Municipal Wharf for the Santa Cruz Surfing Museum at 701 W Cliff Drive (831-420-6289, www.santacruzsurfingmuseum.org). Thrift shopping is active along Capitola Avenue, and sunset strolls through fields of wild chamomile and lavender are idyllic near the beaches of New Brighton, Seacliff, Rio del Mar, and Manresa. For more information, visit www.santacruz.org.

Geologists flock to the epicenter of the 1989 Loma Prieta quake, found on what's known as the **Earthquake Trail** in **Nisene Marks State Park**. Located 80 miles south of San Francisco, just a few miles outside of Santa Cruz, the area is sheltered by pines and oaks, with gentle streams running through portions of its 10,000-acre forest (www.santacruzstateparks.org/parks/nisene).

## SIERRAS AND GOLD COUNTRY

Twenty-five miles north of Auburn, in the **Sierra Nevada foothills,** is **Gold Country**. See what the original gold rushers encountered when they flocked here in search of their fortunes. This old mining territory lets you pan for "gold," swim, and sunbathe on a rock while being sprayed by the cooling foam of the Yuba River. If you're a homesick Northeasterner, come in the autumn for the brilliantly colored maple and aspen leaves, and in summer and fall you can fish for trout or bass. Hiking is exceptional at Buttermilk Bend and Independence Trail—or, if you're in top shape, the steep Humbug Trail (www.nevadacitychamber.com, 800-655-6569).

Ambitious climbers set out for the highest peak in the contiguous United States, at Mount Whitney—an elevation of 14,505 feet. And some of the best whitewater rafting and kayaking in California waits along the American, Stanislaus, Tuolumne, and Merced rivers—all weaving through the Sierra foothills.

Although it doesn't snow in San Francisco, skiing is within reach in the Sierras, where dozens of downhill and cross-country choices make **Lake Tahoe** a renowned haven for skiers and snowboarders. The lake itself has loads of activities in the summer, including waterskiing, kayaking, rafting, and tubing the chilly Truckee River. Camping and rock climbing in the Sierras are both first rate (www.gotahoenorth.com).

If Las Vegas is a bit too far for you, **Reno** is nearby. It's a mini Vegas–style get-away with ample roulette wheels, card tables, "free" cocktails, and slot machines. But 24-hour casinos aren't the only entertainment; hearty buffets, big-name country and pop musicians, local lounge acts, and golf are all popular. Fans of the latter should know that Reno is home to PGA Tour host Montreux Golf and Country Club. For more details visit www.reno.com.

## NATIONAL PARKS

To make camping reservations at the national parks, visit www.nps.gov and www. recreation.gov or call 877-444-6777, TTY 877-833-6777. The National Park Service Office in the Bay Area is located at Fort Mason, Building 201, San Francisco (415-561-4700).

### YOSEMITE NATIONAL PARK

Beloved by Californians and out-of-state visitors for its sweeping trails and enor-mous scale, Yosemite is a monument to exploration and unbeatable adventure, though most Bay Area locals head here in the fall, after the summer crowds have gone. It doesn't take President Theodore Roosevelt's endorsement of Yosemite as "the most beautiful place on earth" to convince Californians of its appeal. Photog-rapher Ansel Adams and naturalist John Muir were so awestruck that they spent years documenting the area's incredible beauty, including Half Dome, El Capitan, and Nevada Falls. Yosemite's popular points get crowded, and the valley floor is often packed with tourists, so many try to avoid it by heading to the backcountry hiking trails. Intrepid visitors hike 17 steep miles to the top of Half Dome, while rock climbers finesse their way up El Capitan. There's a hut system for luxury camping, but permits are issued by lottery and can be difficult to obtain; wilderness permits are required for overnight travel into the park's backcountry (call 209-372-0740 for details). For general information about Yosemite, call 209-372-0200 or visit www. nps.gov/yose and www.yosemitepark.com.

### NATIONAL FOREST SERVICE

If you're planning a camping trip, call the National Forest Service's reserva-tion line at 877-444-6777, TDD, 877-833-6777—or make reservations online at www.recreation.gov.

EVERY DAY—EVERY MINUTE, IN FACT—THERE'S SOMETHING EDUCA-
tional and entertaining to see, taste, hear, or join in this culturally rich
region. Here's a snapshot of the annual celebrations and events that make
the Bay Area a cultural destination. Specific dates are not provided as they may
change depending on the year. Locations are provided when possible—but they
too sometimes jump around from year to year. Check websites for updates.

## JANUARY

- **Chinese New Year Celebration**, parades, lion dances, firecrackers, and street
  vendors bringing the party to the streets, beginning toward the end of the
  month and heading into February in Chinatown, San Francisco (415-982-3000,
  www.chineseparade.com)
- **Golden Gate Kennel Club Dog Show**, fashion on all fours, Cow Palace, Daly
  City (415-404-4100, www.goldengatekennelclub.com)
- **Martin Luther King, Jr., Birthday Celebration**, Bay Area freedom marches, art
  programs, community rallies, meals, and more; for information about events
  throughout the Bay Area, contact the Northern California Dr. Martin Luther
  King, Jr., Community Foundation (415-691-6212, www.sfmlkday.org)
- **Noir City: San Francisco Film Noir Festival**, Castro Theatre, San Francisco
  (www.noircity.com)
- **Peninsula Orchid Society Show & Sale**, Community Activities Building, 1400
  Roosevelt Ave, Redwood City (650-780-7250, www.penorchidsoc.org)
- **Silicon Valley International Auto Show**, McEnery Convention Center, San Jose
  (415-380-8390, www.svautoshow.com)
- **Tet Festival**, Vietnamese Lunar New Year (sometimes in February), in San
  Francisco's Civic Center and Tenderloin neighborhoods (415-351-1038,

www.vietccsf.org); sprawling celebration in the South Bay at the Santa Clara
County Fairgrounds, San Jose (408-494-3247, www.tetvietnamsj.com)
- **Whale Watching** (through March), Point Reyes National Seashore (415-464-5100, www.nps.gov/pore)

## FEBRUARY

- **Arts of Pacific Asia Show**, Fort Mason, San Francisco (415-345-7500, www.caskeylees.com)
- **Black History Month Celebration**, Oakland Museum of California, Oakland (510-318-8400, www.museumca.org); Oakland Public Libraries (Oakland, 510-238-3134, www.oaklandlibrary.org); Westlake Park, Daly City (650-991-8001); MLK Jr. Community Center, San Mateo (650-522-7470, www.cityofsanmateo.org/exploreourparks)
- **Chinese New Year Celebration,** Bay Area Discovery Museum, Sausalito (415-339-3900, www.baykidsmuseum.org)
- **Chinese New Year Parade**, Chinatown, San Francisco (415-982-3000, www.chineseparade.com)
- **The Marin Show: Art of the Americas**, acclaimed gathering of Native American art collections, Marin Civic Center, San Rafael (310-822-9145, www.marinshow.com)
- **Noise Pop**, independent rock, pop, art parties, various locations (415-375-3370, www.noisepop.com)
- **Pacific Orchid Exposition**, Fort Mason, San Francisco (415-345-7500, www.orchidsanfrancisco.org)
- **Russian Festival**, Sutter and Divisadero sts, San Francisco (415-921-7631, www.russiancentersf.com)
- **Tall Ships Exposition**, Jack London Square, Oakland (800-200-5239, www.jacklondonsquare.com)

## MARCH

- **CAAM Film Festival (Center for Asian American Media)**, various locations, San Francisco (415-863-0814, www.caamedia.org)
- **Chinatown Community Street Fair**, Chinatown (www.sanfranciscochinatown.com)
- **East Bay International Jewish Film Festival**, www.eastbayjewishfilm.org
- **International Women's Day Celebration**, throughout the Bay Area, www.internationalwomensday.com
- **Jewish Music Festival**, throughout San Francisco and Berkeley (510-848-0237, www.jewishmusicfestival.org)
- **Russian River Wine Barrel Tasting**, local wineries strut their stuff; locations in Sonoma County (www.wineroad.com)

- **Saint Patrick's Day Parade**, Market St, San Francisco (www.sfstpatricksdayparade.com)
- **San Francisco Women's Film Festival**, San Francisco (www.womensfilminstitute.com)
- **Sebastopol Documentary Film Festival**, various locations, Sebastopol (www.sebastopolfilmfestival.org)
- **Sonoma County Home and Garden Show**, Sonoma County Fairgrounds, Santa Rosa (700-655-0655, www.sonomacountyhomeshow.com)
- **White Elephant Sale**, presented by the Oakland Museum of California's Women's Board, Oakland (510-536-6800, www.whiteelephantsale.org)

## APRIL

- **Bodega Bay Fisherman's Festival**, benefit for Bodega Bay community services; Westside Park, Bodega Bay (707-875-3866, www.bbfishfest.org)
- **Cal Day**, open house at UC Berkeley (www.berkeley.edu/calday)
- **Cherry Blossom Festival**, Japantown (415-563-2313, www.nccbf.org)
- **Earth Day Events**, Civic Center Park, Berkeley, and multiple events and locations in Oakland and Marin (510-548-2220, www.ecologycenter.org)
- **How Weird Street Faire**, Howard and Second sts, San Francisco (www.howweird.org)
- **Opening Day on the Bay**, kicks off the local yachting season on the San Francisco Bay (www.picya.org)
- **San Francisco International Film Festival**, one of world's oldest film festivals, through May, various locations (415-561-5000, www.sffs.org)
- **Spring Garden Festival**, Marin Art & Garden Center, Ross (415-455-5260, www.magc.org)
- **Tiburon International Film Festival**, Tiburon (415-251-8433, www.tiburonfilmfestival.com)
- **Youth Arts Festival**, Berkeley Art Center, Berkeley (510-644-6893, www.berkeleyartcenter.org)

## MAY

- **Asian American and Pacific Islander Heritage Celebration**, events and locations throughout the Bay Area (www.apasf.org)
- **Arboretum Plant Sale**, the Bay Area's largest plant sale, including silent auctions, San Francisco Botanical Garden Nursery (www.sfbotanicalgarden.org)
- **Bay to Breakers**, a seven-mile cross-city run (most partiers walk), with oddball costumes and playful themes, San Francisco (415-359-2800, www.baytobreakers.com)
- **Carnaval**, street party in San Francisco, 24th and Mission sts (415-621-2255, www.carnavalsf.com)

- **Cinco de Mayo Celebration**, Stanford University, Palo Alto (650-723-2089); downtown San Jose (www.sanjose.com)
- **Cinco de Mayo Parade**, Dolores Park, San Francisco (415-206-7752, www.sfcincodemayo.com)
- **Healdsburg Jazz Festival**, acclaimed festival in idyllic setting surrounded by North Bay wine country, through June, Healdsburg (707-433-4633, www.healdsburgjazzfestival.org)
- **Hometown Days**, local arts and crafts, Burton Park, San Carlos (650-594-2700, www.sancarloshometowndays.com)
- **Maker Faire Bay Area**, San Mateo County Event Center, San Mateo (www.makerfaire.com)
- **Marin Motorcycle Film Festival**, a celebration of motorcycles with films from around the world, Larkspur (www.theharleymovie.com/filmfestival)
- **Nikkei Matsuri Japanese Festival**, Japantown, San Jose (www.nikkeimatsuri.org)
- **Oakland Greek Festival**, Greek Orthodox Cathedral, Oakland (510-531-3400, www.oaklandgreekfestival.com)
- **San Francisco International Beer Festival**, Fort Mason, Festival Pavilion, San Francisco (www.sfbeerfest.com)
- **San Francisco Green Film Festival**, through June, San Francisco (www.greenfilmfest.org)
- **San Francisco Silent Film Festival**, Castro Theatre, San Francisco (www.silentfilm.org)
- **San Francisco Sex Worker Film and Arts Festival**, San Francisco (www.sexworkerfest.com)
- **SFMade Week**, a weeklong celebration of local products and their makers (www.sfmade.org)
- **Stanford Powwow**, celebration and gathering of Native Americans, Stanford University, Palo Alto (powwow.stanford.edu)
- **Taiwanese American Cultural Festival**, Union Square, San Francisco (www.tafestival.org)
- **Tiburon Wine Festival**, Point Tiburon Plaza, Tiburon (415-435-5633, www.tiburonwinefestival.com)

## JUNE

- **Alameda County Fair**, through July, Alameda County Fairgrounds, Pleasanton (925-426-7610, www.alamedacountyfair.com)
- **Bicycle Music Festival**, Golden Gate Park and Potrero Hill (415-810-3696, www.bicyclemusicfestival.com)
- **Chamarita Festival**, Portuguese extravaganza, IDES Hall, Half Moon Bay (650-726-8380, www.coastsidelive.com)

- **Frameline International LGBT Film Festival**, the world's largest LGBT film festival, San Francisco (415-703-8650, www.frameline.org)
- **Haight-Ashbury Street Fair**, creative party at the Bay Area's free-love flash point, Haight between Masonic and Stanyon sts, San Francisco (www.haightashburystreetfair.org)
- The Jam at Neptune Beach, street festival with carnival rides, zip line, Ferris wheel, food trucks, and two stages of musicians along Webster Street, Alameda (www.alamedajam.com)
- **Juneteenth Celebration**, parade and celebration on Fillmore St, San Francisco (415-931-2729, www.sfjuneteenth.org); Richmond Juneteenth Parade & Festival, Richmond (www.richmondcajuneteenth.org)
- **Lesbian Gay Bisexual Transgender Celebration & Parade**, also known as the Gay Pride Parade, numerous Bay Area locations (415-864-0831, www.sfpride.org)
- **Mill Valley Wine, Beer & Gourmet Food Tasting**, Mill Valley (415-388-9700, www.millvalley.org)
- **Milpitas Summer Concert Series**, through August, various locations in Milpitas (408-586-3210, www.ci.milpitas.ca.gov)
- **Montclair Fine Arts Sidewalk Festival**, Montclair neighborhood of Oakland (www.pacificfinearts.com)
- National Queer Arts Festival, various Bay Area locations (www.qcc2.org)
- **North Beach Festival**, celebration of Italian and Italian American past and present, North Beach neighborhood of San Francisco (www.sresproductions.com/north_beach_festival.html)
- **Novato Art, Wine & Music Festival**, Old Town, Novato (415-897-1164, www.novatochamber.com)
- **Queer Women of Color Film Festival**, Brava Theater, San Francisco (www.qwocmap.org)
- **San Francisco Black Film Festival**, acclaimed festival in various San Francisco venues (www.sfbff.org)
- **San Francisco Documentary Film Festival (DocFest)**, Roxie Theater (415-820-3907, www.sfindie.com)
- **San Francisco Jewish Film Festival**, the first and largest Jewish film festival in the world, throughout the summer (San Francisco, www.sfjff.org)
- **SFJazz Festival**, various locations in San Francisco (www.sfjazz.org)
- **Silicon Valley Pride Parade & Festival**, various locations in San Jose (www.svpride.com)
- **Solano County Fair**, Solano County Fairgrounds (707-551-2000, www.scfair.com)
- **Sonoma-Marin Fair**, Petaluma Fairgrounds, Petaluma (707-283-3247, www.sonoma-marinfair.org)
- **Stanford Jazz Festival**, the Bay Area's best-rated and one of the world's most acclaimed festivals, through August, Palo Alto (www.stanfordjazz.org)

- **Stern Grove Festival**, San Francisco's oldest free outdoor music festival, in the Stern Grove amphitheater, 19th Ave and Sloat Blvd, San Francisco (415-252-6252, www.sterngrove.org)
- **Sunnyvale Art & Wine Festival**, downtown Sunnyvale (408-736-4971, www.sunnyvaledowntown.com)
- **Trips for Kids Bike Swap**, huge bicycle event serving at-risk youth, San Rafael (www.tripsforkids.org)
- **Union Street Festival**, music, art, fashion, and food, Union and Fillmore sts, San Francisco (800-310-6563, www.unionstreetfestival.com)

## JULY

- **Berkeley Kite Festival** and **West Coast Kite Flying Championships**, Cesar Chavez Park, Berkeley (510-235-5483, www.highlinekites.com)
- **Big Time Festival at Kule Loklo**, Native American trade festival, Bear Valley Visitor Center, Point Reyes National Seashore, south of Olema (415-464-5140, www.nps.gov/pore/planyourvisit/events_bigtime.htm)
- **Chinese Summer Festival**, Kelly Park, San Jose (www.chcp.org)
- **Festa Italiana**, plenty of pasta and pesto, San Mateo (650-349-9879, www.festafoundation.org)
- **Fillmore Jazz Festival**, biggest outdoor jazz festival in San Francisco, Fillmore between Jackson and Eddy sts (800-310-6563, www.fillmorestreetjazzfest.com)
- **Fourth of July Celebrations**, San Francisco, fireworks at Pier 39 (415-705-5500, www.pier39.com); Alameda (510 747-7400, www.cityofalameda.gov); Berkeley (510-981-7170, www.ci.berkeley.ca.us); San Jose (www.sanjoseca.gov); Oakland (www.jacklondonsquare.com)
- **Gilroy Garlic Festival**, a pungent party in the garlic capital of the world, Gilroy (408-842-1625, www.gilroygarlicfestival.com)
- **Los Altos Art & Wine Festival**, downtown Los Altos (650-949-5282, www.downtownlosaltos.org)
- **Marin County Fair**, billed as the greenest fair in the world, Marin County Fairgrounds, San Rafael (415-499-6800, www.marinfair.org)
- **Marin Shakespeare Festival**, July–September, Dominican College, San Rafael (415-499-4488, www.marinshakespeare.org)
- **Niles Essanay Silent Film Museum**, Fremont (510-494-1411, www.nilesfilmmuseum.org)
- **Obon Festival**, Buddhist Church, San Jose (408-293-9292, www.sjbetsuin.com)
- **Petaluma Music Festival**, Sonoma-Marin Fairgrounds & Event Center, Petaluma (www.petalumamusicfestival.org)
- **Puerto Rican Cultural Festival,** History Park, San Jose (www.wrprc.org)
- **Renegade Craft Fair**, Fort Mason, San Francisco (www.renegadecraft.com/san-francisco)
- **San Francisco Marathon,** www.thesfmarathon.com

- **San Jose Mexican Heritage and Mariachi Festival**, various locations in San Jose (www.vivafest.org)
- **Salsa Festival on the Fillmore**, Fillmore St, San Francisco (www.salsaonfillmore.com)
- **Scottish Highland Games**, Dunsmuir House, Oakland (510-562-0328, www.dunsmuir-hellman.com)
- **Shakespeare in the Park,** free performances, Pleasanton, Cupertino, and San Francisco (www.sfshakes.org)
- **Summer Festival & Chili Cook-off**, Mitchell Park, Palo Alto (www.cityofpaloalto.org)

## AUGUST

- **Burning Man**, massive festival of art and self-expression in Nevada's Black Rock Desert, drawing tens of thousands of revelers from the Bay Area (www.burningman.org)
- **Eat Drink SF**, food and wine festival, San Francisco (www.eatdrink-sf.com)
- **Goodguys Rod and Custom Classic Car Show**, Alameda County Fairgrounds, Pleasanton (925-838-9876, www.good-guys.com)
- **J-POP Summit Festival,** Fort Mason, San Francisco (www.j-pop.com)
- **Nihonmachi Street Fair**, a celebration of Japanese culture, Japantown, San Francisco (415-771-9861, www.nihonmachistreetfair.org)
- **Oakland Jazz Festival,** Pioneer Amphitheater, Hayward (www.oaklandjazzfestival.com)
- **Palo Alto Festival of the Arts**, Palo Alto (831-438-4751, www.mlaproductions.com)
- **Park Street Art & Wine Faire**, Alameda (510-523-1392, www.shopparkstreet.com)
- **Pistahan Parade & Festival**, part of Filipino American Arts Exposition, Yuerba Buena Gardens, San Francisco (www.pistahan.net)
- **San Francisco Aloha Festival**, Pacific Islander cultural celebration, San Francisco (415-240-7547, www.pica-org.org/alohafest)
- **San Francisco Outside Lands Music & Arts Festival**, Golden Gate Park (www.sfoutsidelands.com)
- **San Jose Jazz Festival**, Plaza de Cesar Chavez, San Jose (408-288-7557, www.sanjosejazz.org)
- **San Mateo County Fair**, San Mateo County Expo Center, San Mateo (www.sanmateocountyfair.com)
- **Santa Clara County Fair**, Santa Clara County Fairgrounds, San Jose (408-494-3247, www.thefair.org)
- **Strawberry Festival at Monterey Bay**, including a pie-eating contest, Watsonville (831-768-3240, www.cityofwatsonville.org/visitors/strawberry-festival)

## SEPTEMBER

- **Chocolate Festival**, Ghiradelli Square (415-775-5500, www.ghirardellisq.com)
- **Bay Area Blues Festival**, Martinez (www.bayareabluesfestival.com)
- **Fall Arts Festival**, Mill Valley (415-381-8090, www.mvfaf.org)
- **Folsom Street Fair**, the world's biggest leather parade, with fleshy fashion and public spankings, Folsom between 7th and 12th sts, San Francisco (www.folsomstreetfair.com)
- **Monterey Jazz Festival**, voted world's best jazz festival by several music magazines and fan polls, it's also one of the world's longest-running jazz events, Monterey County Fairgrounds, Monterey (www.montereyjazzfestival.org)
- **Opera in the Park**, free arias, Sharon Meadow, Golden Gate Park, San Francisco (www.sfopera.com)
- **Pacific Coast Fog Fest**, Palmetto & Salada Aves, Pacifica (650-355-8200, www.pacificcoastfogfest.com)
- **Renaissance Pleasure Faire**, journey back to Elizabethan England, Hollister (408-847-3247, www.norcalrenfaire.org)
- **San Francisco Dragon Boat Festival**, Treasure Island (www.sfdragonboat.com)
- **San Francisco Fringe Festival**, a celebration of the offbeat, various locations, San Francisco (415-931-1094, www.sffringe.org)
- **San Francisco Latino Film Festival**, various locations, San Francisco (www.sflatinofilmfestival.com)
- **Sausalito Art Festival**, Sausalito (415-332-3555, www.sausalitoartfestival.org)
- **Sausalito Floating Homes Tour**, Sausalito (415-332-1916, www.floatinghomes.org)
- **Santa Clara Art & Wine Festival**, Central Park, Santa Clara (www.santaclaraartandwinefestival.com)
- **Sir Francis Drake Kennel Club Dog Show**, Marin Civic Center, San Rafael (415-472-3500, www.sfdkc.og)
- **Solano Stroll**, massive street fair, Solano Ave, Albany and Berkeley (www.solanoavenueassn.org)

## OCTOBER

- **Castro Street Fair**, Castro St, San Francisco (www.castrostreetfair.org)
- **Fiesta on the Hill**, Cortland Ave between Bocana and Folsom sts, Bernal Heights neighborhood of San Francisco (www.bhnc.org)
- **Fleet Week**, celebrating San Francisco's long relationship with the US Navy, Marina wharf (415-599-5057, www.fleetsweeksf.org)
- **Grand National Rodeo**, Cow Palace, Daly City (415-404-4111, www.grandnationalrodeo.com)
- **Half Moon Bay Pumpkin Festival**, Main St, Half Moon Bay (www.pumpkinfest.miramarevents.com)

- **Halloween Celebration**, Jack London Square, Oakland (www.jacklondonsquare.com)
- **Halloween at the Winchester Mystery House**, a sprawling, haunted Victorian mansion, San Jose (408-247-2101, www.winchestermysteryhouse.com)
- **Hardly Strictly Bluegrass**, Hellman Hollow, Golden Gate Park, San Francisco (www.hardlystrictlybluegrass.com)
- **Harvest Festival**, various locations across the Bay Are (415-447-3205, www.harvestfestival.com)
- **Italian Heritage Day**, parade and festival in North Beach and Fisherman's Wharf, San Francisco (www.sfcolumbusday.org)
- **Litquake**, literary festival with celebrated author readings, guiding walking tours, and storytelling hours, San Francisco (www.litquake.org)
- **Mill Valley Film Festival**, Smith Rafael Film Center, San Rafael (415-383-5256, www.mvvf.com)
- **Pacific Fine Arts Festival**, Menlo Park (www.pacificfinearts.com)
- **Sandcastle Classic**, architects vs. amateurs in sandcastle building, Ocean Beach, San Francisco (www.leaparts.org)
- **Sonoma County Harvest Fair**, Santa Rosa (www.sonomacountyfair.com)
- **Treasure Island Music Festival**, Treasure Island, San Francisco (www.treasureislandfestival.com)

## NOVEMBER

- **American Indian Film Festival**, Palace of Fine Arts, San Francisco (415-554-0525, www.aifisf.com)
- **Celebration of Craftswomen**, Fort Mason (415-731-5539, www.celebrationofcraftswomen.org)
- **Dias de los Muertos (Day of the Dead)**, celebration and parade of spirits; altars in the park, great costumes and food, 24th and Bryant sts to Garfield Park, Mission District in San Francisco (www.dayofthedeadsf.org)
- **Harvest Festival**, various locations across the Bay Area (415-447-3205, www.harvestfestival.com)
- **Hip-Hop Dance Festival**, Palace of Fine Arts, San Francisco (www.sfhiphopdancefest.com)
- Napa Valley Film Festival, Calistoga, St. Helena, Yountville, Napa (www.napavalleyfilmfest.org)
- **San Francisco Green Festival**, Concourse Exhibition Center, San Francisco (www.greenfestivals.org)
- **San Francisco International Auto Show**, Moscone Center (415-331-4406, www.sfautoshow.com)

## DECEMBER

- **Arts & Crafts Faire**, Mill Valley Community Center, Mill Valley (415-383-1370, www.cityofmillvalley.org)
- **Berkeley Artisans Holiday Open Studios**, various locations in Berkeley (www.berkeleyartisans.com)
- **Christmas in the Park**, Plaza de Cesar Chavez, San Jose (www.christmasinthepark.com)
- **Hanukkah Family Celebration**, Osher Marin Jewish Community Center, San Rafael (415-444-8000, www.marinjcc.org); locate other Hanukkah events through the Jewish Community Federation at www.jewishfed.org
- **Lighted Yacht Parade**, Jack London Square, Oakland (www.lightedyachtparade.com)
- **Menorah Lighting**, Ghirardelli Square, San Francisco (415-775-5500, www.ghirardellisq.com)
- **San Jose Holiday Parade**, downtown San Jose (408-794-6200, www.holidayparade.com)
- **Trains for Tots**, South Bay, Peninsula, and San Francisco stops with Santa along the Caltrain corridor (800-660-4287, www.caltrain.com)

T HERE ARE LONG SHELVES OF BOOKS ABOUT THE BAY AREA, COVERING A wide range of topics: from the music of the first Chinese immigrants, to the free-speech and anti-war movements, to the geological treasures you'll enjoy when hiking the mountains. Below is a selection of guides, works of fiction, and historical collections that will help acclimate you to your new home.

## ART

- *Art in the San Francisco Bay Area: 1945–1980: An Illustrated History* by Thomas Albright
- *Artful Players: Artistic Life in Early San Francisco* by Brigitta Hjalmarson
- *Bay Area Graffiti* by Steve Rotman
- *Bay Area Wild: A Celebration of the Natural Heritage of the San Francisco Bay Area* by Galen Rowell

## FICTION

- *The Best of Adair Lara* by Adair Lara
- *China Boy* by Gus Lee
- *City Lights Pocket Poets Anthology* edited by Lawrence Ferlinghetti
- *Daughter of Fortune* by Isabel Allende
- *Eyes of a Child* by Richard North Patterson
- *The Flower Drum Song* by C.Y. Lee
- *The Golden Gate* by Vikram Seth
- *Homeboy* by Seth Morgan
- *Jack London: Stories of Adventure* by Jack London
- *The Joy Luck Club* by Amy Tan
- *Letters from the Earth* by Mark Twain
- *Lonesome Traveler* by Jack Kerouac

- *The Maltese Falcon* by Dashiell Hammett
- *McTeague* by Frank Norris
- *On the Road* by Jack Kerouac
- *Our Lady of Darkness* by Fritz Leiber
- *San Francisco Stories: Great Writers on the City* edited by John Miller
- *The Subterraneans* by Jack Kerouac
- *Tales of the City* by Armistead Maupin
- *Valencia* by Michelle Tea
- *The Woman Warrior* by Maxine Hong Kingston

## LOCAL LIT JOURNALS

- *Catamaran Literary Reader*, www.catamaranliteraryreader.com
- *Instant City: A Literary Exploration of San Francisco*, www.instantcity.org
- *McSweeney's*, www.mcsweeneys.net
- *Zoetrope: All-Story*, www.all-story.com
- *Zyzzyva*, www.zyzzyva.org

## FOOD

- *Bread and Chocolate: My Food Life in San Francisco* by Fran Gage
- *The Cheese Board: Collective Works: Bread, Pastry, Cheese, Pizza* by the Cheese Board Collective
- *Chez Panisse Cooking* by Paul Bertolli with Alice Waters
- *The Chowhound's Guide to the San Francisco Bay Area* by Chowhound
- *Farm City: The Education of an Urban Farmer* by Novella Carpenter
- *Flour + Water: Pasta* by Thomas McNaughton
- *How to Be Vegan: Tips, Tricks, and Strategies for Cruelty-Free Eating, Living, Dating, Travel, Decorating, and More* by Elizabeth Castoria
- *A New Napa Cuisine* by Christopher Kostow
- *Patricia Unterman's San Francisco Food Lover's Guide* by Patricia Unterman
- *The San Francisco Chronicle Cookbook Volumes I & II* by Michael Bauer
- *San Francisco in a Teacup* by Ulrica Hume
- *Zagat Survey, San Francisco Bay Area Restaurants*

## HISTORY

- *Baghdad by the Bay* by Herb Caen
- *The Barbary Coast: An Informal History of the San Francisco Underworld* by Herbert Asbury
- *Blues City: A Walk in Oakland* by Ishmael Reed
- *Chinese San Francisco* by Yong Chen
- *The Griots of Oakland: Voices from the African-American Oral History Project* edited by Angela Zusman

- *Harlem of the West: The San Francisco Fillmore Jazz Era* by Elizabeth Pepin and Lewis Watts
- *Historic San Francisco* by Rand Richards
- *Infinite City: A San Francisco Atlas* edited by Rebecca Solnit
- *Island: Poetry and History of Chinese Immigrants on Angel Island, 1910–1940,* edited by Mark Him Lai, Genny Lim, and Judy Yung
- *The Mayor of Castro Street: The Life and Times of Harvey Milk* by Randy Shilts
- *Reclaiming San Francisco History, Politics, Culture; a City Lights Anthology* edited by James Brook, Chris Carlsson, and Nancy J. Peters
- *San Francisco Chinatown* by Philip Choy
- *San Francisco: The Musical History Tour* by Joel Selvin
- *San Francisco Then & Now* by Bill Yenne
- *Speak it Louder: Asian Americans Making Music* by Deborah Wong
- *Tales of San Francisco* by Samuel Dickson
- *The World of Herb Caen* by Barnaby Conrad
- *The White Album* by Joan Didion
- *The Wild Parrots of Telegraph Hill* by Mark Bittner
- *Zodiac* by Robert Graysmith

## KIDS

- *The Cable Car and the Dragon* by Herb Caen
- *The City by the Bay: A Magical Journey Around San Francisco* by Tricia Brown and Elisa Kleven
- *Fun Places to go with Children in Northern California* by Elizabeth Pomada
- *Humphrey the Lost Whale: A True Story* by Wendy Tokuda, Richard Hall, and Hanako Wakiyama
- *Larry Loves San Francisco* by John Skewes
- *San Francisco: A Mini-History* by Phyllis Zauner

## OUTDOORS

- *Adventuring in the San Francisco Bay Area* by Peggy Wayburn
- *Backcountry Adventures: Northern California* by Peter Massey and Jeanne Wilson
- *Bay Area Backroads* by Doug McConnell
- *Bay Area Bike Rides* by Ray Hosler
- *Cruising Guide to San Francisco Bay* by Carolyn Mehaffy and Bob Mehaffy
- *East Bay Trails: Outdoor Adventures in Alameda and Contra Costa Counties* by David Weintraub
- *Foghorn Outdoors: 101 Great Hikes of the San Francisco Bay Area* by Ann Marie Brown
- *Foghorn Outdoors: Bay Area Biking—60 of the Best Road and Trail Rides* by Ann Marie Brown

- *Golden Gate Trailblazer: Where to Hike, Walk, and Bike in San Francisco and Marin* by Jerry Sprout and Janine Sprout
- *Inside/Out Northern California: Best Places Guide to the Outdoors* by Dennis J. Oliver
- *Roaming the Backroads of Northern California* by Peter Browning
- *Sailing the Bay* by Kimball Livingston
- *San Francisco Running Guide: The 45 Best Routes in the Bay Area* by Bob Cooper
- *Short Bike Rides: San Francisco* by Henry Kingman

## SAN FRANCISCO GUIDES

These offbeat and theme-oriented guides to San Francisco will get you exploring— away from the hordes of tourists.

- *Best Hikes Near San Francisco* by Linda Hamilton
- *Broke-Ass Stuart's Guide to Living Cheaply in San Francisco* by Stuart Schuffman
- *The Dog Lover's Companion to the Bay Area* by Maria Goodavage
- *Footsteps in the Fog: Alfred Hitchcock's San Francisco* by Jeff Kraft
- *Get Lost! The Cool Guide to San Francisco* by Claudia Lehan
- *Ghost Hunter's Guide to the Bay Area* by Jeff Dwyer
- *Romantic Days and Nights in San Francisco* by Donna Peck
- *Jazz on the Barbary Coast* by Tom Stoddard
- *San Francisco As You Like It: 23 Tailor-Made Tours for Culture Vultures, Shopaholics, Neo-Bohemians, Famished Foodies, Savvy Natives & Everyone Else* by Bonnie Wach
- *San Francisco Bizarro* by Jack Boulware
- *San Francisco Noir* by Nathaniel Rich
- *San Francisco Secrets* by John Snyder
- *The Underground Guide to San Francisco* by Jennifer Joseph

O NCE YOU ORDER PHONE SERVICE OR MOVE INTO YOUR NEW HOME, Valley Yellow Pages will deliver the White and Yellow Pages to your door—even in today's Bay Area, the center of the digital revolution. You can access the Yellow Pages at www.myyp.com and download the mobile app by searching your app market for "Valley Yellow Pages." Although not as extensive as the print Yellow Pages and websites like www.yelp.com, the list below includes some of the most useful contacts:

## AMBULANCE

- All areas, 911

## ANIMALS

- **Animal Bites**, 911
- **Animal Care & Control**, 415-554-6364, www.sfgov.org/acc
- **Homeless Cat Network**, 650-286-9013, www.homelesscatnetwork.com
- **Hopalong & Second Chance Rescue**, 415-267-1915, www.hopalong.org
- **Humane Society of Contra Costa County**, 925-279-2247, www.cchumane.org
- **Humane Society of Berkeley–East Bay**, 510-845-3633, www.berkeleyhumane.org
- **Humane Society of Marin County**, 415-883-4621, www.marinhumanesociety.org
- **Humane Society of Peninsula**, 650-340-8200, www.peninsulahumanesociety.org
- **Humane Society of Silicon Valley**, 408-262-2133, www.hssv.org
- **Humane Society of Sonoma County**, 707-542-0882, www.sonomahumane.org
- **San Francisco Lost Pet Services**, 415-567-8738, www.sfgov.org/acc
- **Silicon Valley Friends of Ferals**, www.svff.org

- **Society for the Prevention of Cruelty to Animals (SPCA)**, 415-554-3000, www.sfspca.org

## AUTOMOBILES

- **American Automobile Association (AAA)**, 800-922-8228, www.csaa.com
- **Better Business Bureau Auto Line**, 800-955-5100, www.bbb.org
- **California Department of Motor Vehicles**, 800-777-0133, TTY 800-368-4327, www.dmv.ca.gov

## PARKING, TOWING, AND TRAFFIC

### SAN FRANCISCO

- **AutoReturn**, if you suspect your vehicle has been towed, 415-865-8200, www.autoreturn.com
- **Citation Division**, 415-701-3000; pay traffic/parking citations with credit card, 415-701-3099, www.sfgov.org/onlineservices
- **DMV**, 800-777-0133, TTY 800-368-4327, www.dmv.ca.gov
- **Information**, 415-701-2311
- **Parking Permits**, 415-701-3000, www.sfmta.com
- **San Francisco Municipal Transportation Agency**, 415-701-2311, www.sfmta.com

### NORTH BAY

- **DMV**, 800-777-0133, TTY 800-368-4327, www.dmv.ca.gov
- **Marin County Parking Authority**, 800-281-7275; in San Rafael 415-458-5333; in Sausalito 415-289-4149

### EAST BAY

- **DMV**, 800-777-0133, TTY 800-368-4327, www.dmv.ca.gov
- **Oakland Parking Bureau**, 800-500-6484
- **Traffic Division of the Superior Court, Alameda County,** 510-627-4701

### PENINSULA & SOUTH BAY

- **DMV**, 800-777-0133, TTY 800-368-4327, www.dmv.ca.gov
- **San Mateo, Parking Permits, Residential & City Parking Facilities,** 650-522-7326

## BIRTH & DEATH CERTIFICATES

- **Alameda County**, 510-272-6362, www.acgov.org/auditor/clerk
- **Contra Costa County**, 925-335-7900, www.ccclerkrec.us
- **Marin County**, 415-499-7215, www.marincounty.org
- **Napa County**, 707-253-4247, www.countyofnapa.org

- **San Francisco County**, 415-554-2700, www.sfdph.org
- **San Mateo County**, 650-363-4500, www.smcare.org
- **Santa Clara County**, 408-299-5669, www.sccgov.org
- **Solano County**, 707-784-6294, www.co.solano.ca.us
- **Sonoma County**, 707-565-3800, www.sonoma-county.org

## CITY & COUNTY GOVERNMENT

### SAN FRANCISCO

- **Assessor-Recorder**, 415-554-5596, www.sfassessor.org
- **Board of Supervisors**, 415-554-5184, www.sfbos.org
- **California Governor**, 916-445-2841, www.gov.ca.gov
- **California Public Utilities Commission**, Public Advisor's Office in San Francisco, 866-849-8390, www.cpuc.ca.gov
- **California Registrar of Voters**, 916-657-2166, TTY 800-833-8683, www.sos.ca.gov/elections
- **City Attorney**, 415-554-4700, www.sfcityattorney.org
- **City Hall**, 415-554-4000, www.sfgsa.org
- **County Clerk**, 415-554-4950, www.sfgov.org
- **District Attorney**, 415-553-1752, www.sfdistrictattorney.org
- **Health Department**, 415-554-2500, www.sfdph.org
- **Marriage Licenses**, 415-554-4950, www.sfgov.org
- **Mayor's Office**, 415-554-6141, www.sfmayor.org
- **Parks and Recreation**, 415-831-2750, www.sfrecpark.org
- **Recycling Program**, 415-355-3700, www.sfenvironment.org
- **Rent Stabilization Board**, 415-252-4600, www.sfrb.org
- **Residential Parking Permits**, 415-701-3000, www.sfmta.com
- **San Francisco Public Utilities Commission**, 415-554-3155, www.sfwater.org
- **San Francisco Unified School District**, 415-241-6000, www.sfusd.edu

### NORTH BAY—ONLINE

- **Corte Madera**, www.ci.corte-madera.ca.us
- **Fairfax**, www.town-of-fairfax.org
- **Marin County**, www.marincounty.org
- **Mill Valley**, www.cityofmillvalley.org
- **Napa County**, www.countyofnapa.org
- **Novato**, www.novato.org
- **Petaluma,** www.cityofpetaluma.net
- **San Rafael**, www.cityofsanrafael.org
- **Santa Rosa**, www.ci.santa-rosa.ca.us
- **Sausalito**, www.ci.sausalito.ca.us
- **Sonoma County**, www.sonomacounty.ca.gov
- **Tiburon**, www.townoftiburon.org

## EAST BAY—ONLINE
- **Alameda City**, www.alamedaca.gov
- **Alameda County**, www.acgov.org
- **Albany**, www.albanyca.org
- **Antioch**, www.ci.antioch.ca.us
- **Berkeley**, www.ci.berkeley.ca.us
- **Concord**, www.ci.concord.ca.us
- **Contra Costa County**, www.co.contra-costa.ca.us
- **Danville**, www.ci.danville.ca.us
- **El Cerrito**, www.el-cerrito.org
- **Emeryville**, www.ci.emeryville.ca.us
- **Fremont**, www.fremont.gov
- **Hayward**, www.ci.hayward.ca.us
- **Hercules**, www.ci.hercules.ca.us
- **Lafayette**, www.ci.lafayette.ca.us
- **Livermore**, www.cityoflivermore.net
- **Martinez**, www.cityofmartinez.org
- **Moraga**, www.moraga.ca.us
- **Newark**, www.ci.newark.ca.us
- **Oakland**, www.oaklandnet.com
- **Oakley**, www.ci.oakley.ca.us
- **Orinda**, www.cityoforinda.org
- **Piedmont**, www.ci.piedmont.ca.us
- **Pinole**, www.ci.pinole.ca.us
- **Pittsburg**, www.ci.pittsburg.ca.us
- **Pleasant Hill**, www.ci.pleasant-hill.ca.us
- **Pleasanton**, www.cityofpleasantonca.gov
- **Richmond**, www.ci.richmond.ca.us
- **San Leandro**, www.sanleandro.org
- **San Pablo**, www.ci.san-pablo.ca.us
- **San Ramon**, www.ci.san-ramon.ca.us
- **Union City**, www.ci.union-city.ca.us
- **Walnut Creek**, www.walnut-creek.org

## PENINSULA & SOUTH BAY—ONLINE
- **Atherton**, www.ci.atherton.ca.us
- **Belmont**, www.ci.belmont.ca.us
- **Brisbane**, www.ci.brisbane.ca.us
- **Burlingame**, www.burlingame.org
- **Campbell**, www.ci.campbell.ca.us
- **Cupertino**, www.cupertino.org
- **Daly City**, www.dalycity.org
- **Foster City**, www.fostercity.org

- **Half Moon Bay**, www.half-moon-bay.ca.us
- **Hillsborough**, www.hillsborough.net
- **Los Gatos**, www.town.los-gatos.ca.us
- **Menlo Park**, www.menlopark.org
- **Millbrae**, www.ci.millbrae.ca.us
- **Mountain View**, www.ci.mtnview.ca.us
- **Pacifica**, www.cityofpacifica.org
- **Palo Alto**, www.cityofpaloalto.org
- **Redwood City**, www.redwoodcity.org
- **San Bruno**, www.sanbruno.ca.gov
- **San Carlos**, www.cityofsancarlos.org
- **San Jose**, www.sanjose.org
- **San Mateo City**, www.cityofsanmateo.org
- **San Mateo County**, www.smcgov.org
- **Santa Clara City**, www.santaclaraca.gov
- **Santa Clara County**, www.sccgov.org
- **Saratoga**, www.saratoga.ca.us
- **South San Francisco**, www.ssf.net
- **Sunnyvale**, www.sunnyvale.ca.gov
- **Woodside**, www.woodsidetown.org

## COMMUNITY EVENTS & ENTERTAINMENT

For a more comprehensive list of Bay Area newspapers, magazines, websites, and mobile apps, see the **Media Landscape** section earlier in this book. For event tickets, see the **Tickets** section. A few highlights:

- *Bay City Guide*, www.baycityguide.com
- **City of San Francisco**, www.sfgov.org
- *East Bay Express*, www.eastbayexpress.com
- *48 Hills*, www.48hills.org
- **KQED**, www.kqed.org
- **KTVU Channel 2**, www.ktvu.com
- **KRON Channel 4**, www.kron4.com
- *Oakland Tribune*, www.oaklandtribune.com
- *San Francisco Chronicle*, www.sfgate.com
- *San Francisco Examiner*, www.sfexaminer.com
- *San Francisco.com*, www.sanfrancisco.com
- *San Francisco Magazine*, www.modernluxury.com/san-francisco
- *San Jose Mercury News*, www.mercurynews.com
- *SF Station.com*, www.sfstation.com
- *SF Weekly,* www.sfweekly.com
- *SFist,* www.sfist.com

## CONSUMER AGENCIES

- **Alameda County Bar Association,** 510-302-2222, www.acbanet.org
- **Better Business Bureau, Oakland Branch,** 510-844-2000, www.bbb.org/greater-san-francisco
- **California Attorney General,** 800-952-5225, TTY 800-735-2929, www.oag.ca.gov
- **California Department of Consumer Affairs,** 800-952-5210, www.dca.ca.gov
- **California Public Utilities Commission,** 415-703-2782, www.cpuc.ca.gov/puc
- **California State Directory Information Service,** 800-807-6755, TTY 916-464-1580, www.cold.ca.gov
- **Federal Citizen Information Center (and Consumer Action Handbook),** 888-878-3256, www.pueblo.gsa.gov, www.consumeraction.gov
- **Federal Communications Commission,** 888-225-5322, TTY 888-835-5322, www.fcc.gov
- **Federal Trade Commission,** 877-382-4357, www.ftc.gov
- **Financial Consumer Information,** 800-333-4636, www.mymoney.gov
- **San Francisco Bar Association Lawyer Referral Service,** 415-989-1616, www.sfbar.org/lawyerreferrals
- **San Francisco District Attorney,** 415-553-1752, www.sfdistrictattorney.org
- **San Francisco Public Utilities Commission,** 415-554-3155, www.sfwater.org
- **San Mateo County Bar Association,** 650-298-4030, www.smcba.org
- **Santa Clara County Bar Association,** 408-287-2557, www.sccba.com
- **State Bar of California,** 800-843-9053, www.calbar.ca.gov
- **Telecommunications Research and Action Center (TRAC),** www.trac.org
- **The Utility Reform Network (TURN),** 415-929-8876, www.turn.org

## CRISIS RESOURCES

- **Asian Women's Shelter,** 877-751-0880, www.sfaws.org
- **California Youth Crises Line,** 800-843-5200, www.youthcrisisline.org
- **Community United Against Violence,** 415-333-HELP, www.cuav.org
- **Dimensions Clinic,** 415-934-7789, www.dimensionsclinic.org
- **Gay Youth Talk Line,** 800-246-7743, www.glbtnationalhelpcenter.org
- **Larkin Street Youth Services,** 415-673-0911, www.larkinstreetyouth.org
- **LYRIC,** 127 Collingwood St, 415-701-6150, www.lyric.org
- **National Suicide Prevention Lifeline,** 800-273-8255, www.suicidepreventionlifeline.org
- **Suicide Prevention,** Marin, 415-499-1100, www.fsamarin.org/suicide-prevention-crisis-hotline
- **Suicide Prevention,** San Francisco, 415-781-0500, www.sfsuicide.org
- **Westside Crisis Services,** 415-355-0311, www.westside-health.org
- **Youthline,** 888-977-3399, www.youthlinesf.org

## ALCOHOL AND DRUG DEPENDENCY

- **Behavioral Health Services Community Access**, 888-750-2727, www.sfdph.org/dph
- **Cocaine Anonymous**, 415-226-1300, www.norcalca.com
- **Contra Costa County Alcoholics Anonymous**, 925-939-4155, www.contracostaaa.org
- **East Bay Alcoholics Anonymous**, 510-839-8900, www.eastbayaa.org
- **Marin County Alcoholics Anonymous**, 415-499-0400, www.aasf.org
- **Napa County Alcoholics Anonymous**, 707-255-4900, www.aanapa.org
- **Narcotics Anonymous**, 415-621-8600, www.sfna.org
- **San Francisco Alcoholics Anonymous**, 415-674-1821, www.aasf.org
- **San Mateo County Alcoholics Anonymous**, 650-577-1310, www.aa-san-mateo.org
- **Santa Clara County Alcoholics Anonymous**, 408-374-8511, www.aasanjose.org
- **Smokers' Helpline**, 800-662-8887, www.nobutts.org

## CHILD ABUSE/PROTECTION

- **Alameda County Child Protective Services**, 510-259-1800, www.alamedasocialservices.org
- **Child Abuse Council of Santa Clara County**, 408-299-2071, www.sccgov.org
- **Child Abuse Prevention Council of Contra Costa County,** 925-798-0546
- **Domestic Violence Hotline**, 800-799-7233, for emergencies dial 911; www.thehotline.org
- **Marin Child Abuse Prevention Council**, 415-507-9016, www.marinadvocates.org
- **Marin Child Protective Services**, 415-473-7153, www.marinhhs.org
- **San Francisco Child Abuse Prevention Center**, 415-668-0494, www.sfcapc.org
- **Talk Line Family Support Center**, 415-441-5437, www.talklineforparents.org

## RAPE/DOMESTIC VIOLENCE

- **Bay Area Women Against Rape (Crisis Line)**, 415-647-7273, 510-845-7273, www.sfwar.org
- **Casa de Las Madres**, 877-503-1850, www.lacasa.org (offers shelter and advocacy to battered women and children)
- **Domestic Violence Hotline**, 800-799-7233, for emergencies dial 911; www.thehotline.org
- **Marin Rape Crisis Center and Community Violence Solutions**, 800-670-7273, www.cvsolutions.org
- **Rape Treatment Center** (24 hours), 415-437-3000, www.traumarecoverycenter.org
- **YWCA Rape Crisis Center**, 408-287-3000, 650-493-7273, www.ywca-sv.org

## EARTHQUAKE INFORMATION

- **American Red Cross, Bay Area Chapter,** 415-427-8000, www.redcross.org/ca/san-francisco
- **Bay Area Earthquake Information**, resilience.abag.ca.gov
- **California Earthquake Authority**, 916-325-3800, www.earthquakeauthority.com
- **California Seismic Safety Commission**, 916-263-5506, www.seismic.ca.gov
- **Federal Emergency Management Agency (FEMA)**, 800-621-3362, TTY 800-462-7585, www.fema.gov
- **US Geological Survey**, 888-275-8747, www.usgs.gov

## ELECTED OFFICIALS

### STATE OF CALIFORNIA

- **Governor's Office**, 916-445-2841, www.gov.ca.gov
- **State Assembly**, 916-319-2856, www.assembly.ca.gov
- **State Senate**, 916-319-2856, www.sen.ca.gov

### UNITED STATES

- **US Senate**, 202-224-3121, www.senate.gov
- **US House of Representatives**, 202-224-3121, TTY 202-225-1904, www.house.gov
- **White House**, 202-456-1111, TTY 202-456-6213, www.whitehouse.gov

## EMERGENCY NUMBERS

- **Disaster Assistance Information (FEMA)**, 800-621-3362, TTY 800-462-7585, www.fema.gov
- **Division of Emergency Communications**, 415-558-3800, www.sfdem.org
- **Fire, Police, Medical Emergency,** 911
- **Poison Control**, 800-222-1222, www.poison.org
- **Rape Treatment Center**, 415-437-3000, www.traumarecoverycenter.org
- **Rape Crisis Line**, free and confidential, 415-647-7273, www.sfwar.org

## HEALTH AND MEDICAL CARE

- **Alameda County Public Health Department**, 510-267-8000, www.acphd.org
- **American Board of Medical Specialties**, 866-275-2267, www.abms.org
- **Berkeley Drop-In Center**, 510-653-3808, www.alameda.networkofcare.org
- **Berkeley Free Clinic**, 800-625-4642, www.berkeleyfreeclinic.org
- **Cancer Care**, 800-813-4673, www.cancercare.org
- **Lead Poisoning Prevention Program**, 510-567-8280, www.achhd.org
- **Marin Department of Health and Human Services**, 415-499-3696, www.marinhhs.org

- **Medical Board of California**, 800-633-2322, www.mbc.ca.gov
- **Poison Control**, 800-222-1222, www.poison.org
- **San Francisco General Hospital**, 415-206-8000
- **San Francisco Department of Public Health**, 415-554-2500, www.sfdph.org
- **Santa Clara County Department of Public Health**, 408-792-5050, www.sccgov.org/sites/sccphd
- **Sexually Transmitted Diseases (San Francisco City Clinic)**, 415-487-5500, www.sfcityclinic.org
- **Suicide Prevention**, 415-781-0500, www.sfsuicide.org
- **Women's Daytime Drop-In Center,** 510-548-2884, www.womensdropin.org

## HIV TESTING

- **AIDS Legal Referral Panel**, 415-701-1100, 510-451-5353, www.alrp.org
- **HIV/AIDS Nightline**, San Francisco, 415-434-2437, www.sfsuicide.org/our-programs/hiv-nightlines
- **HIV/AIDS Testing**, Marin, 415-473-4400, www.marinhhs.org/hivaids-services-program
- **San Francisco City Clinic**, 415-487-5500, www.sfcityclinic.org

## HOUSING

- **A Home Away From Homelessness,** 415-561-5533, www.homeaway.org
- **Bay Area Legal Aid,** 415-982-1300, 408-283-3700, www.baylegal.org
- **Berkeley Rent Stabilization Program**, 510-981-7368, TTY 510-981-6903, www.ci.berkeley.ca.us/rent
- **California Department of Fair Employment and Housing**, 800-884-1684, TTY 800-700-2320, www.dfeh.ca.gov
- **Community Boards**, specializes in landlord-tenant disputes in San Francisco, 415-920-3820, www.communityboards.org
- **Contractors State License Board**, 800-321-2752, www.cslb.ca.gov
- **East Palo Alto Rent Stabilization Program**, 650-853-3109, www.ci.east-palo-alto.ca.us/rentprogram
- **Eviction Defense Center**, 510-452-4541, www.evictiondefense.org
- **Homeless Action Center,** 510-540-0878, www.homelessactioncenter.org
- **Homeless Children's Network,** 415-437-3990, www.hcnkids.org
- **Homeless Prenatal Program**, 415-546-6756, www.homelessprenatal.org
- **Homeless Youth Alliance**, 415-565-1941, www.homelessyouthalliance.org
- **Housing and Homeless Services,** 415-557-5000, www.sfhsa.org
- **National Health Care for the Homeless Council**, www.nhchc.org
- **Project Homeless Connect**, 855-588-7968, www.projecthomelessconnect.org
- **Project Sentinel**, specializes in landlord-tenant disputes in the South Bay, 408-720-9888, www.housing.org

- **Ruby's Place** (formerly Emergency Shelter Program of Hayward), shelter for up to 40 women and children per day, 888-339-SAFE, www.rubysplace.org
- **San Francisco Rent Board**, 415-252-4600, www.sfrb.org
- **San Francisco Tenants Union**, 415-282-6622, www.sftu.org
- **San Jose Rental Rights and Referrals**, 408-975-4480, www.sanjoseca.gov
- **St. Peter's Housing Committee**, 415-487-9203, www.sfhomeless.wikia.com

## LEGAL MEDIATION OR REFERRAL

- **AIDS Legal Referral Panel**, 415-701-1100, 510-451-5353, www.alrp.org
- **Alameda County Bar Association**, 510-302-2222, www.acbanet.org
- **American Civil Liberties Union of Northern California**, 415-621-2488, www.aclunc.org
- **California Courts**, www.courts.ca.gov
- **Legal Aid of Santa Clara County**, 408-998-5200, www.legalaidsociety.org
- **Legal Aid of Marin County**, 415-492-0230, www.legalaidmarin.org
- **Legal Aid of Napa County**, 707-259-0579, www.legalaidnapa.org
- **Legal Aid of San Mateo County**, 650-558-0915, www.legalaidsmc.org
- **Legal Aid of Sonoma County**, 707-542-1290, www.legalaidsc.org
- **San Francisco Bar Association Lawyer Referral Service**, 415-989-1616, www.sfbar.org/lawyerreferrals
- **San Mateo County Bar Association**, 650-298-4030, www.smcba.org
- **Santa Clara County Bar Association**, 408-287-2557, www.sccba.com
- **SEEDS Community Resolution Center**, 510-548-2377, www.seedscrc.org
- **State Bar of California**, 415-538-2000, www.calbar.ca.gov

## SMALL CLAIMS COURTS

See **Consumer Protection** section in the **Helpful Services** chapter.

## MARRIAGE LICENSES

- **Alameda County**, 510-272-6363, www.acgov.org/auditor/clerk
- **Contra Costa County**, 925-335-7900, www.ccclerkrec.us/clerk/marriage
- **Marin County**, 415-499-3003, www.marincounty.org
- **Napa County**, 707-253-4247, www.countyofnapa.org
- **San Francisco**, 415-554-4950, www.sfgov.org
- **San Mateo County**, 650-363-4712, www.smcare.org/clerk/marriage
- **Santa Clara County**, 408-299-5669, www.sccgov.org
- **Solano County,** 707-784-7510, www.solanocounty.com
- **Sonoma County,** 707-565-3800, www.sonoma-county.org/clerk/marriage

## PARKS AND RECREATION DEPARTMENTS

- **Contra Costa County**, 925-313-1180, www.co.contra-costa.ca.us

- **East Bay Regional Park District**, 888-327-2757, www.ebparks.org
- **Golden Gate National Recreation Area**, 415-561-4700, www.nps.gov/goga
- **Marin County Parks and Recreation**, 415-499-6387, www.marincountyparks.org
- **Napa County Parks and Recreation**, 707-257-9529, www.cityofnapa.org
- **San Francisco Parks and Recreation**, 415-831-2700, www.parks.sfgov.org
- **San Mateo County Parks and Recreation**, 650-363-4020, www.co.sanmateo.ca.us
- **Santa Clara County Parks and Recreation**, 408-355-2200, www.parkhere.org
- **Solano County Parks and Recreation**, 707-784-6765, www.solanocounty.com
- **Sonoma County Regional Parks**, 707-565-2041, parks.sonomacounty.ca.gov

## POLICE

- **Bay Area Rapid Transit (BART) Police**, emergency: 911 or 510-464-7000; non-emergency: 877-679-7000; www.bart.gov
- **California Highway Patrol**, emergency: 911; non-emergency: 800-835-5247, TTY 707-648-5363, www.chp.ca.gov
- **Domestic Violence Response Unit**, 415-553-9225, 415-553-1071, www.sf-police.org
- **Emergency**, 911
- **Road Conditions**, 511
- **San Francisco Police Chief**, 415-553-1551
- **San Francisco Police**, non-emergency: 415-553-0123; TTY 415-626-4357

## POST OFFICE

- 800-275-8777, www.usps.com

## PUBLIC LIBRARIES

- **Berkeley Central Branch**, 510-981-6100, www.berkeleypubliclibrary.org
- **Marin County Library**, 415-499-6051, www.marinlibrary.org
- **Oakland Library**, 510-238-3134, www.oaklandlibrary.org
- **Peninsula Library**, 650-780-7018, www.plsinfo.org
- **San Francisco Main Branch**, 415-557-4400, www.sfpl.org
- **San Jose Library**, 408-808-2000, www.sjlibrary.org
- **Santa Clara County Library**, 408-293-2326, www.library.santaclaraca.gov

See the listings following each neighborhood and town for additional libraries.

## SANITATION—GARBAGE & RECYCLING

### CALIFORNIA
- **California Department of Conservation**, 916-445-0732, www.conservation.ca.gov
- **Earth 911**, 800-253-2687, www.earth911.org

## SAN FRANCISCO

- **Disposal and Recycling Company (Recology)**, 415-626-4000, www.goldengatedisposal.com
- **Recycling Hotline**, 415-355-3700, www.sfenvironment.com
- **San Francisco League of Urban Gardeners (SLUG)**, 415-519-2006
- **Waste Management**, 510-613-8740, wmcabay.wm.com

## NORTH BAY

- **Marin Recycling Center and Sanitary Service**, 415-453-1404, 415-456-2601, www.marinsanitaryservice.com

## EAST BAY

- **Pleasant Hill Bayshore Disposal**, serves most of Contra Costa County, 925-685-4711, www.pleasanthillbayshoredisposal.com
- **Republic Services**, 510-657-3500, www.republicservices.com
- **StopWaste.org (Alameda County Waste Management Authority)**, 510-891-6500, www.stopwaste.org
- **Waste Management**, 510-624-5900, wmcabay.wm.com

## PENINSULA & SOUTH BAY

- **Allied Waste Daly City** (serving Daly City, Colma, and Broadmoor), 650-756-1130, www.alliedwastedalycity.com
- **Allied Waste San Mateo County**, 650-592-2411, www.bfisanmateocounty.com
- **RecycleWorks** San Mateo County, www.recycleworks.org
- **Santa Clara County Recycling Hotline**, 408-924-5453, www.recyclestuff.org
- **Republic Services**, 408-432-1234, www.republicservices.com
- **South San Francisco Scavenger**, 650-589-4020, www.ssfscavenger.com
- **Zero Waste Palo Alto (Recycling Program)**, 650-496-5910, www.cityofpaloalto.org/gov/depts/pwd/zerowaste

## SENIORS

- **AARP California**, 888-687-2277, www.aarp.org
- **Elder Care Locator**, 800-677-1116, www.eldercare.gov
- **Institute on Aging**, 415-750-4180, www.ioaging.org
- **Legal Assistance for Seniors and HiCap**, 800-434-0222, www.lashicap.org
- **Legal Assistance to the Elderly**, 415-538-3333, www.laesf.org
- **Marin Adult Protection Services**, 415-499-7118, www.marinhhs.org
- **Meals on Wheels**, 415-920-1111, www.mowsf.org
- **Mission Hospice of San Mateo County**, 650-554-1000, www.missionhospice.org
- **United Way of the Bay Area**, 415-808-4300, www.uwba.org

## SHIPPING SERVICES

- **DHL Worldwide Express**, 800-225-5345, www.dhl-usa.com
- **FedEx**, 800-463-3339, www.fedex.com
- **United Parcel Service (UPS)**, 800-742-5877, TTY 800-833-0056, www.ups.com
- **US Postal Service**, 800-275-8777, www.usps.com

## SPORTS

- **Golden State Warriors**, 510-986-2222, www.nba.com/warriors
- **Oakland Athletics**, 510-638-0500, oakland.athletics.mlb.com
- **Oakland Raiders**, 510-864-5000, www.raiders.com
- **San Francisco 49ers**, www.49ers.com
- **San Francisco Giants**, 415-972-2000, www.sanfrancisco.giants.mlb.com
- **San Jose Earthquakes**, 877-782-5301, www.sjearthquakes.com
- **San Jose Sharks**, 408-999-5757, sharks.nhl.com

## STREET MAINTENANCE

- **Report an Overflowing Litter Receptacle**, 415-282-5326
- **Report Illegal Dumping**, 415-282-5326
- **San Francisco Department of Public Works**, 415-554-6920, TTY 415-554-6900, www.sfdpw.org
- **Street Cleaning**, 415-554-6920
- **Street Construction Coordination Center**, 415-554-5810
- **Street Use Permits**, 415-554-5810
- **Tree Planting, San Francisco Friends of the Urban Forest (FUF)**, 415-561-6890, www.fuf.net
- **Tree Removal and Pruning**, 415-282-5326

## TAXES

- **California Department of Finance**, 916-445-3878, www.dof.ca.gov
- **Internal Revenue Service**, 800-829-1040, www.irs.ustreas.gov
- **San Francisco Tax Collector**, 415-554-4400
- **State Franchise Tax Board**, 800-852-5711, www.ftb.ca.gov

## TELEPHONE

- **Astound**, 800-427-8686, www.astound.net
- **AT&T**, 800-222-0300, www.att.com
- **Credo Mobile**, 800-555-7774, www.credomobile.com; this company donates a portion of monthly fees to nonprofits
- **MetroPCS**, 888-863-8768, www.metropcs.com
- **Sprint**, 866-866-7509, www.sprint.com
- **T-Mobile**, 800-866-2453, www.t-mobile.com
- **Verizon**, 800-837-4966, www.verizon.com

## TICKETS

- **Eventbrite,** www.eventbrite.com
- **StubHub**, 866-788-2482, www.stubhub.com
- **Theatre Bay Area** (discount tickets), 415-430-1140, www.theatrebayarea.org
- **Ticketmaster**, 800-653-8000, www.ticketmaster.com
- **Tickets.com**, 800-352-0212, www.tickets.com
- **Tix Bay Area**, 415-433-7827, www.tixbayarea.org

## TRANSPORTATION

- **Bay Area Public Transportation**, 511, www.511.org
- **Carpool and Vanpool Services**, www.rideshare.511.org
- **Real-Time Traffic Updates**, www.chp.ca.gov

## TRAVEL AND TOURISM

- **International Association for Medical Assistance to Travellers**, 716-754-4883, www.iamat.org
- **National Park Service**, www.nps.gov
- **National Passport Information Center**, 877-487-2778, TTY 888-874-7793, www.travel.state.gov
- **San Francisco Travel Visitor Information Center**, 415-391-2000, www.onlyinsanfrancisco.com
- **US Department of State, Bureau of Consular Affairs, www.**travel.state.gov

## TRAINS AND BUSES

- **AC Transit**, 510-891-4700, TTY 800-448-9790, www.actransit.org
- **Altamont Corridor Express**, 800-411-7245, www.acerail.com
- **Amtrak**, 800-872-7245, www.amtrakcalifornia.com
- **Bay Area Rapid Transit (BART)**, 510-465-2278, 415-989-2278, 650-992-2278, TTY 510-839-2278, www.bart.gov
- **Caltrain**, 800-660-4287; TTY 415-508-6448, www.caltrain.com
- **Contra Costa County Connection**, 925-676-7500, TTY 800-735-2929, www.countyconnection.com
- **Golden Gate Transit**, 415-455-2000, TTY 711, www.goldengatetransit.org
- **Greyhound**, 800-231-2222, www.greyhound.com
- **MUNI (San Francisco Municipal Rail)**, 415-701-2311, TTY 415-701-2323, www.sfmta.com
- **SamTrans**, 800-660-4287; TTY 650-508-6448, www.samtrans.com
- **Santa Clara County Transit** (Valley Transportation Authority), 800-894-9908, TTY 408-321-2330, www.vta.org
- **Sonoma County Transit**, 707-576-7433, TTY 707-585-9817, www.sctransit.com
- **SuperShuttle**, 800-258-3826, www.supershuttle.com

## AIRPORTS

- **Oakland International Airport**, 510-563-3300; parking, 510-563-3200, www.flyoakland.com
- **San Francisco International Airport**, 800-435-9736, www.flysfo.com
- **San Jose International Airport**, 408-277-4759, www.flysanjose.com

## FERRIES

- **Angel Island–Tiburon Ferry**, 415-435-2131, www.angelislandferry.com
- **Blue and Gold Fleet**, 415-705-8200, www.blueandgoldfleet.com
- **Golden Gate Ferry Service** (Marin-San Francisco), 415-455-2000, www.goldengateferry.org
- **San Francisco Bay Ferry**, 415-705-8291, www.sanfranciscobayferry.com

## TAXIS

- See **Transportation** chapter

## UTILITIES

- **City of Palo Alto Utilities (CPAU)**, 650-329-2161, www.cityofpaloalto.org/utilities
- **Pacific Gas and Electric (PG&E)**, 800-743-5000, TTY 800-652-4712, www.pge.com
- **Santa Clara Green Power**, 408-244-SAVE
- **Silicon Valley Power**, 408-615-2300, www.siliconvalleypower.com

See **Water** in the **Getting Settled** chapter for water district numbers and websites.

## WEATHER

- **Regional Weather Reports**, www.wrh.noaa.gov/mtr

## ZIP CODE REQUEST

- 800-275-8777, www.usps.com

**D**ANIEL KING IS A SAN FRANCISCO–BASED WRITER SEARCHING FOR THE spiciest Szechuan noodles and subtlest soup dumplings in the Bay Area. He has been a staff writer at the *San Francisco Chronicle*, the *San Francisco Bay Guardian*, the *Village Voice*, and *JazzTimes*. He has also served as an editor at the Asian Art Museum in San Francisco, producing books and gallery shows about China, Japan, Korea, South and Southeast Asia, West Asia, and the Himalayas. When he isn't reporting on arts and culture, he is playing chess in the parks and struggling to improve a Neapolitan pizza-dough recipe. To learn more about his work, visit www.danielkingsf.com.

# INDEX

## C

# READER RESPONSE

We would appreciate your comments regarding this fifth edition of the *Newcomer's Handbook® for Moving to and Living in the San Francisco Bay Area.* If you've found any mistakes or omissions or if you would just like to express your opinion about the guide, please let us know. We will consider any suggestions for possible inclusion in our next edition, and if we use your comments, we'll send you a free copy of our next edition. Please email us at readerresponse@firstbooks.com, or mail or fax this response form to:

**Reader Response Department**
**First Books**
**6750 SW Franklin, Suite A**
**Portland, OR 97223-2542**
**Fax: 503.968.6779**

Comments: _____

_____

_____

_____

_____

_____

_____

_____

_____

_____

Name: _____

Address: _____

_____

Telephone: ( ) _____

Email: _____

**6750 SW Franklin, Suite A**
**Portland, OR 97223-2542**
**USA**
**P: 503.968.6777**
**www.firstbooks.com**

# RELOCATION RESOURCES

Utilizing an innovative grid and "static" reusable adhesive sticker format, *Furniture Placement and Room Planning Guide...Moving Made Easy* provides a functional and practical solution to all your space planning and furniture placement needs.

## MOVING WITH KIDS?

Look into *The Moving Book: A Kids' Survival Guide*. Divided into three sections (before, during, and after the move), it's a handbook, a journal, and a scrapbook all in one. Includes address book, colorful change-of-address cards, and a useful section for parents.

Children's Book of the Month Club "Featured Selection"; American Bookseller's "Pick of the List"; Winner of the Family Channel's "Seal of Quality" Award

And for your younger children, ease their transition with our brand-new title just for them, *Max's Moving Adventure: A Coloring Book for Kids on the Move*. A complete story book featuring activities as well as pictures that children can color; designed to help children cope with the stresses of small or large moves.

## NEWCOMER'S HANDBOOKS®

Regularly revised and updated, these popular guides are now available for Atlanta, Boston, Chicago, China, Dallas–Ft. Worth, Houston, London, Los Angeles, Minneapolis–St. Paul, New York City, Portland, San Francisco Bay Area, Seattle, and Washington DC.

"Invaluable ...highly recommended" – *Library Journal*

If you're coming from another country, don't miss the *Newcomer's Handbook® for Moving to and Living in the USA* by Mike Livingston, termed "a fascinating book for newcomers and residents alike" by the *Chicago Tribune*.

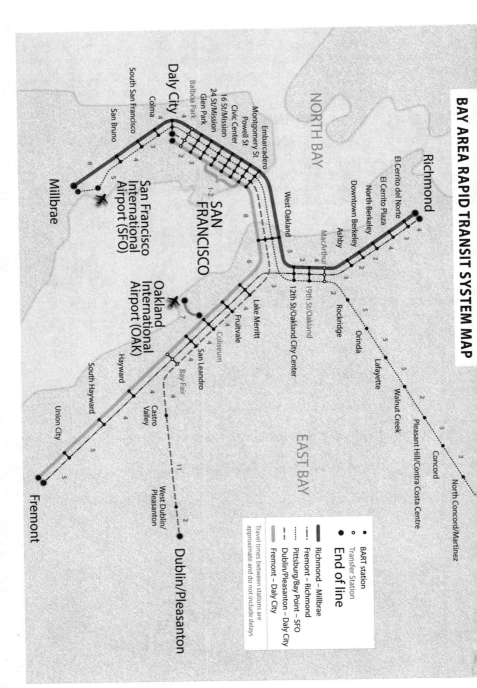